RECCHIONI - MAMMUCARI

ORPHANS

VOLUME TWO
LIES

ORPHANS series created by Roberto Recchioni and Emiliano Mammucari

Original lettering by Marina Sanfelice
Original logo created by Paolo Campana
Original book design by Officine Bolzoni with Cosimo Torsoli

English translation by Elena Cecchini and Valeria Gobbato
Localization, layout, and editing by Mike Kennedy

ISBN: 978-1-942367-52-9
Library of Congress Control Number: 2018931325

Orphans, Volume 2 published 2018 by The Lion Forge, LLC. © 2018 Sergio Bonelli Editore. First published in Italy in 2014 by Sergio Bonelli Editore S.p.A under the title *Orfani Issue Nos. 4-6* © 2014 Sergio Bonelli Editore. www.sergiobonellieditore.it. All rights reserved. MAGNETIC COLLECTION™, LION FORGE™, and their associated distinctive designs are trademarks of The Lion Forge, LLC. No similarity between any of the names, characters, persons, and/or institutions in this book with those of any living or dead person or institution is intended and any such similarity which may exist is purely coincidental.

Printed in China.

10 9 8 7 6 5 4 3 2 1

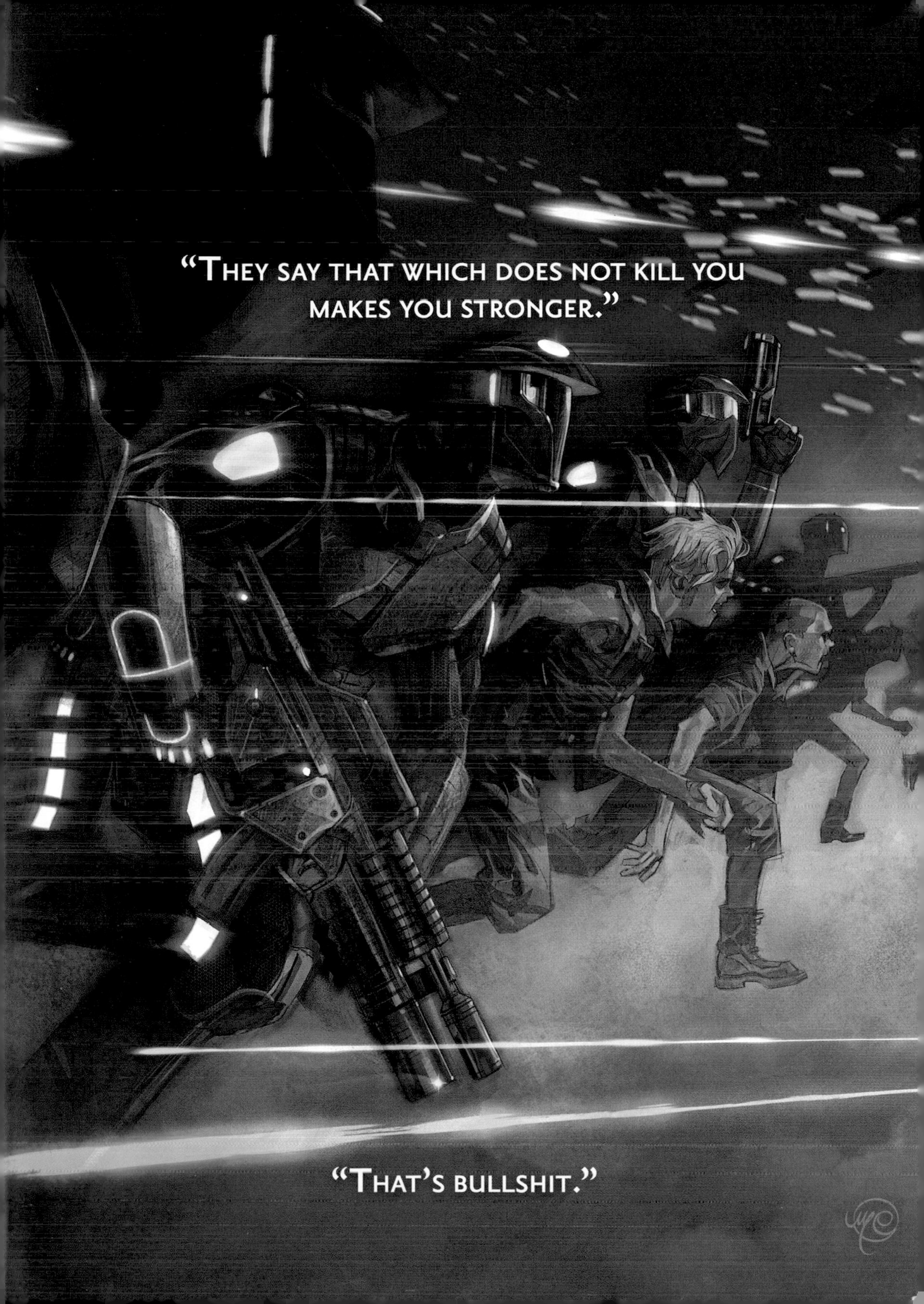
"They say that which does not kill you makes you stronger."
"That's bullshit."

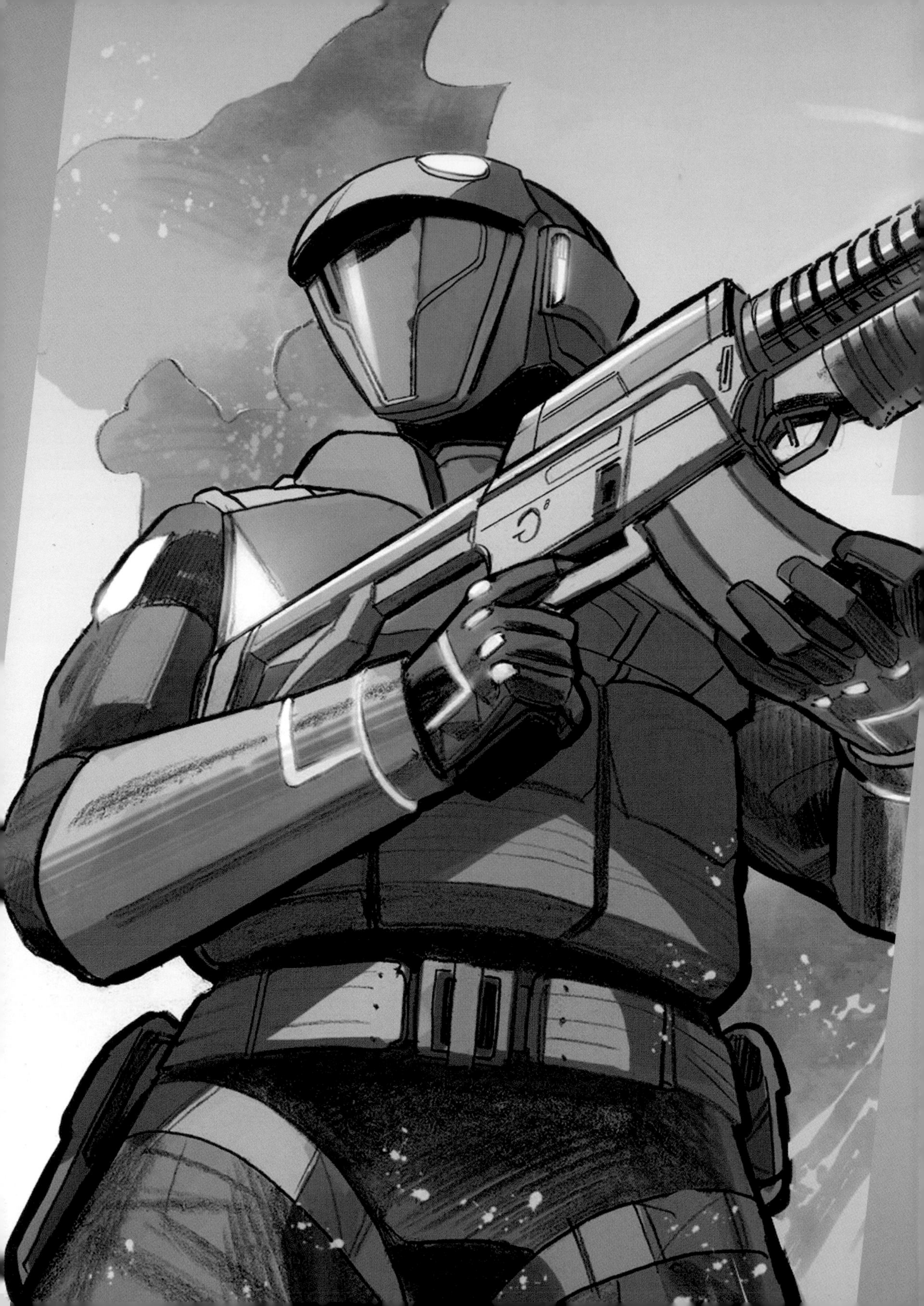

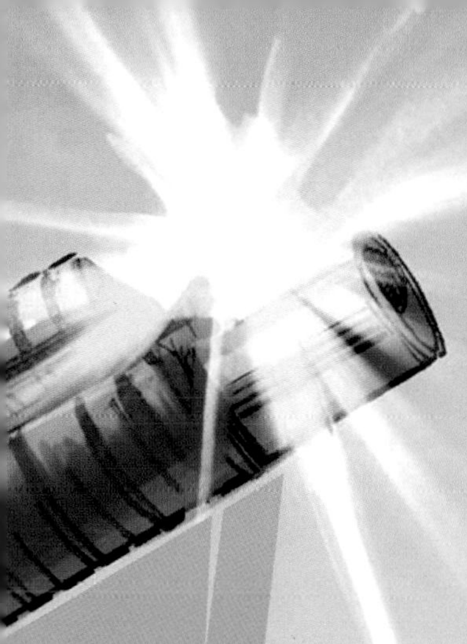

START

The blue skies of Volume One are turning an ominous red as the comforting daylight of what we've been introduced to fades slowly into darkness. The children of Roberto Recchioni's complex saga, orphaned by a disaster of unimaginable scale and conscripted into a life of military service and violence, march dutifully to war against an enemy they know nothing about: aliens with the ability to appear and disappear seemingly without a trace. But the real ghosts they are about to face are those from their past, wreaking more havoc on their lives than any million-megaton particle beam could.

This second volume will crack open the safety seal of reality and gently lead the noble members of Orphan Squad into a labyrinth of truth and lies so expertly crafted it's almost impossible to tell one from the other.

Darkness is falling. The monsters are waiting. And not all of them are from beyond the stars...

Previous page: illustration by Emiliano Mammucari

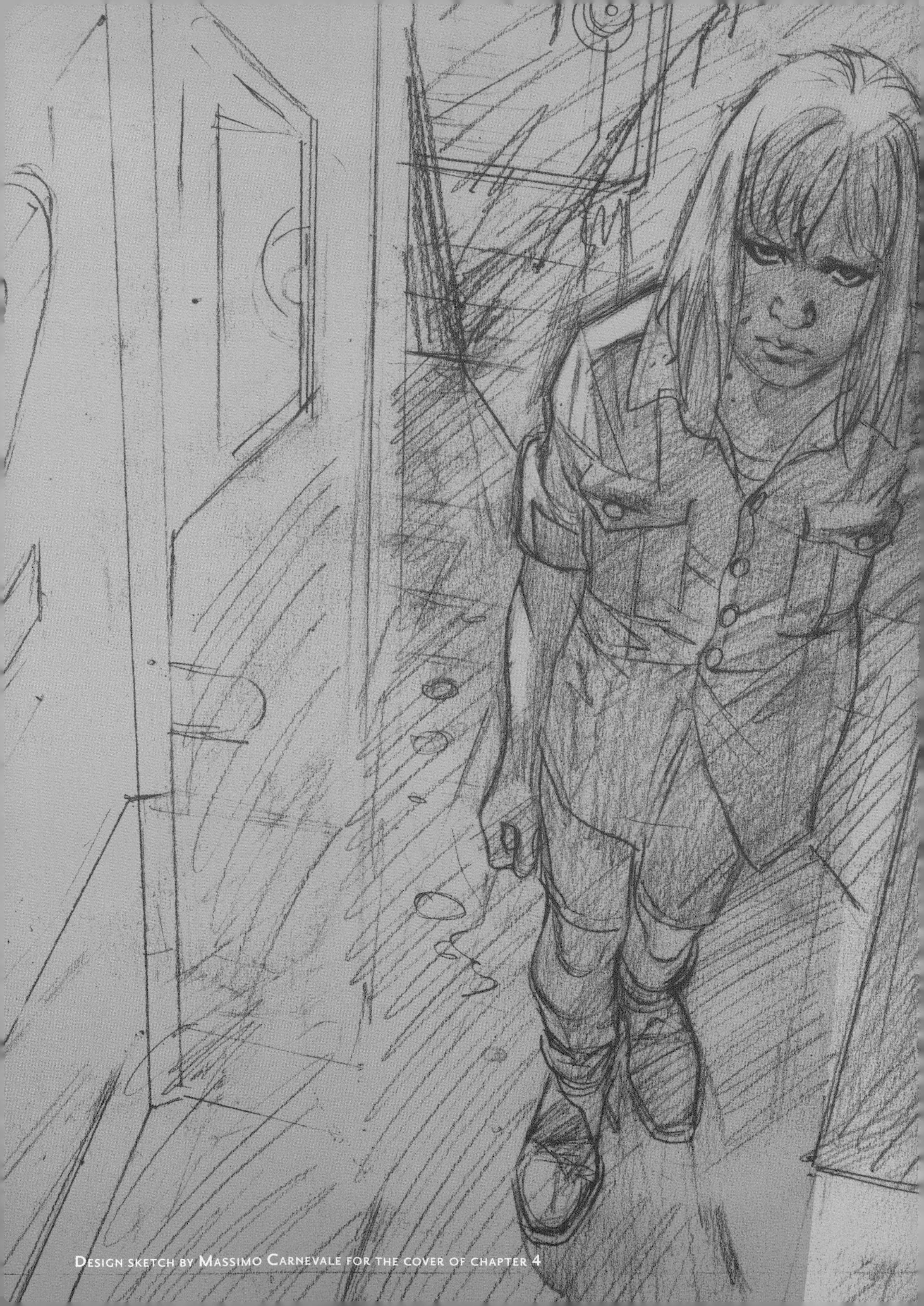

Design sketch by Massimo Carnevale for the cover of chapter 4

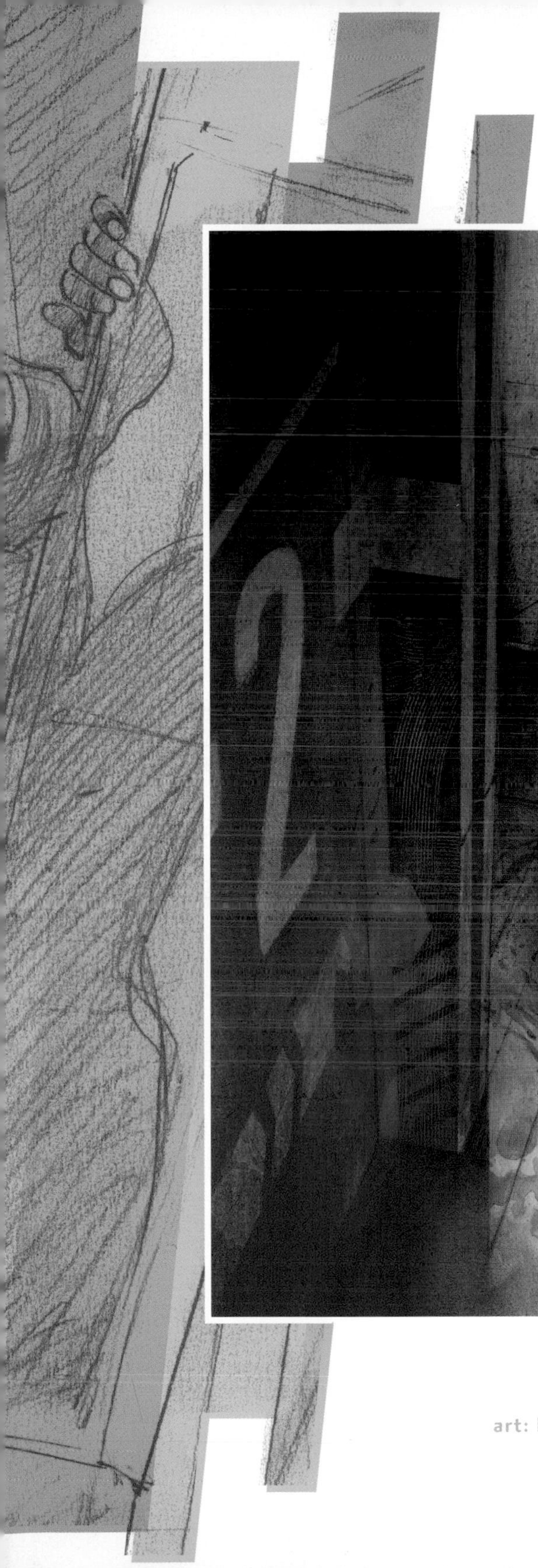

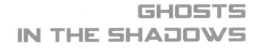

GHOSTS IN THE SHADOWS

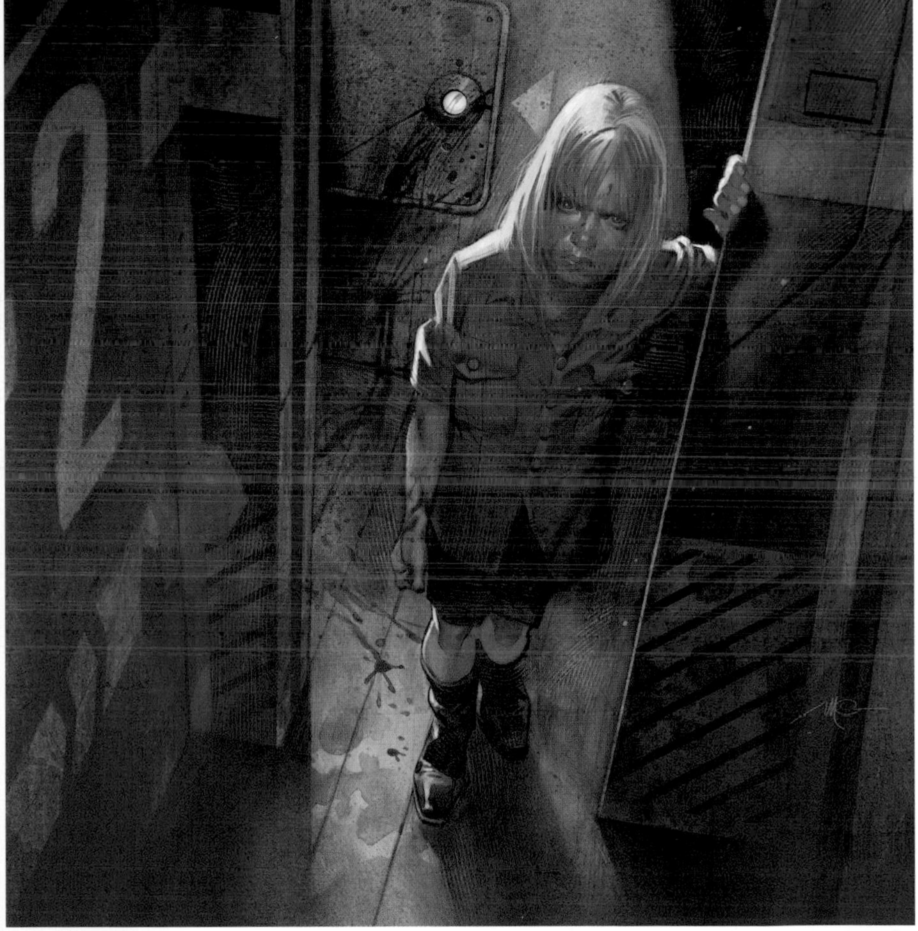

ORPHANS: CHAPTER 4

story: ROBERTO RECCHIONI
art: MASSIMO DALL'OGLIO and GIGI CAVENAGO
colors: LORENZO DE FELICI
cover: MASSIMO CARNEVALE

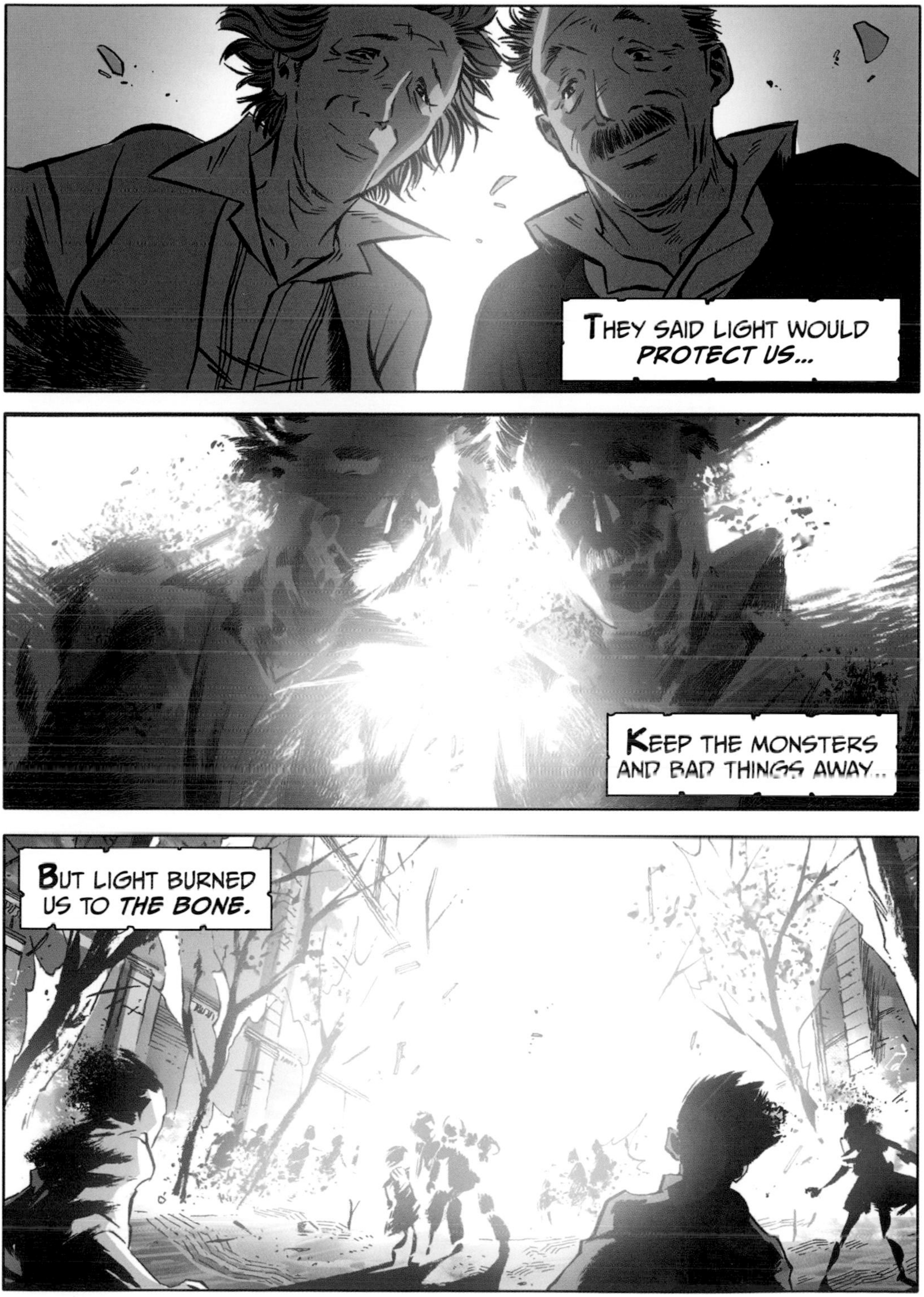
THEY SAID LIGHT WOULD PROTECT US...
KEEP THE MONSTERS AND BAD THINGS AWAY...
BUT LIGHT BURNED US TO THE BONE.

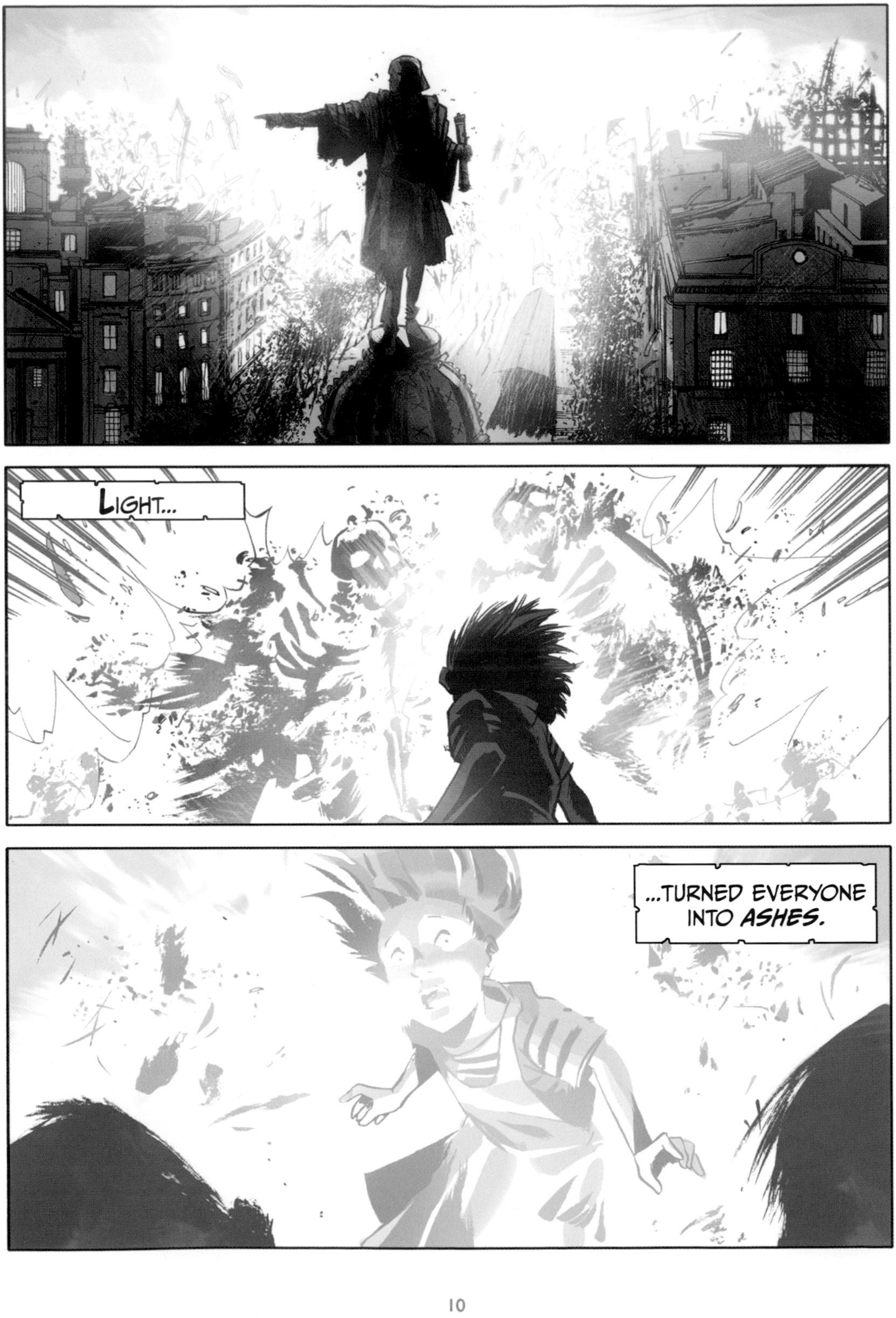
LIGHT...
...TURNED EVERYONE INTO ASHES.

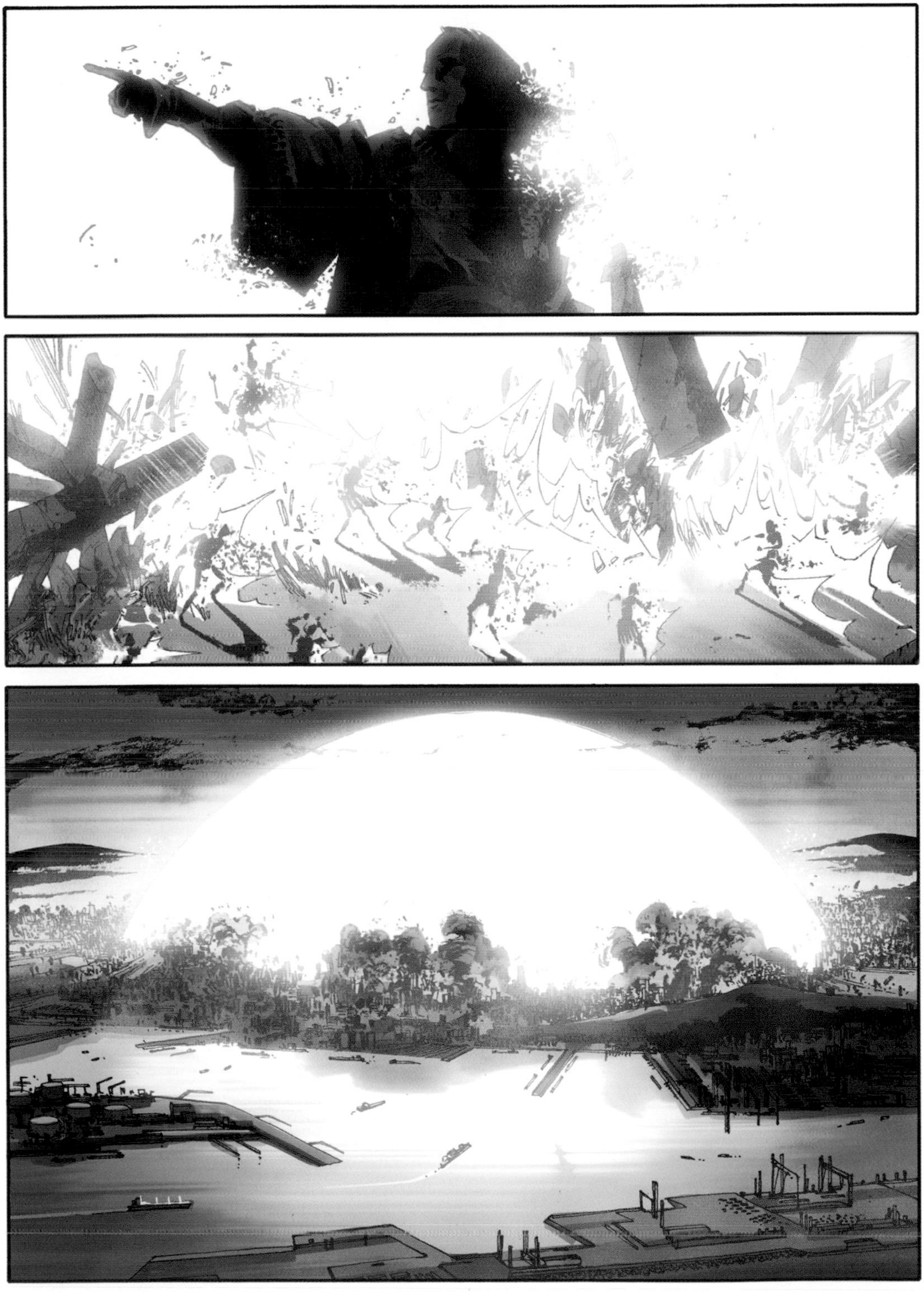

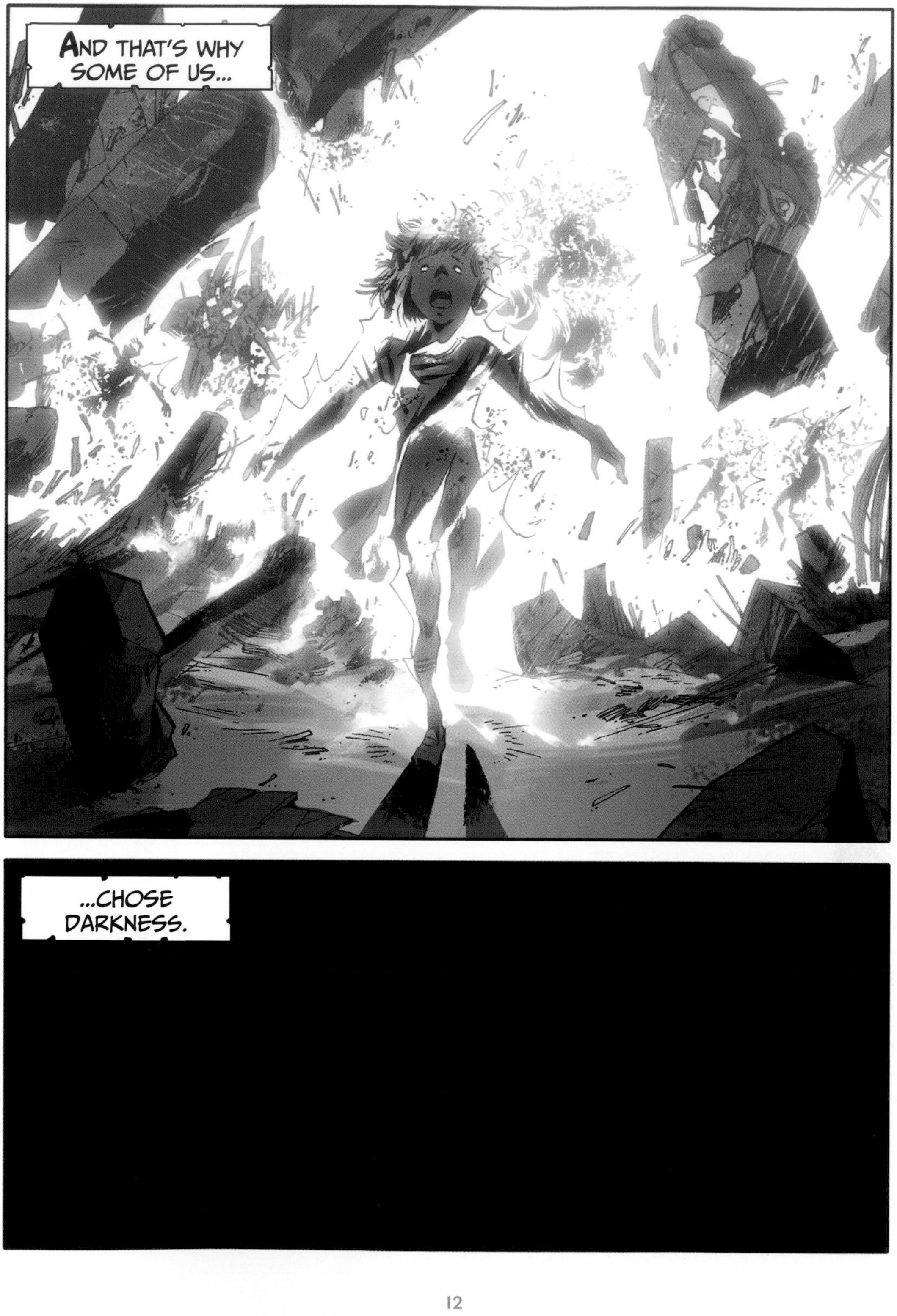
AND THAT'S WHY SOME OF US...
...CHOSE DARKNESS.

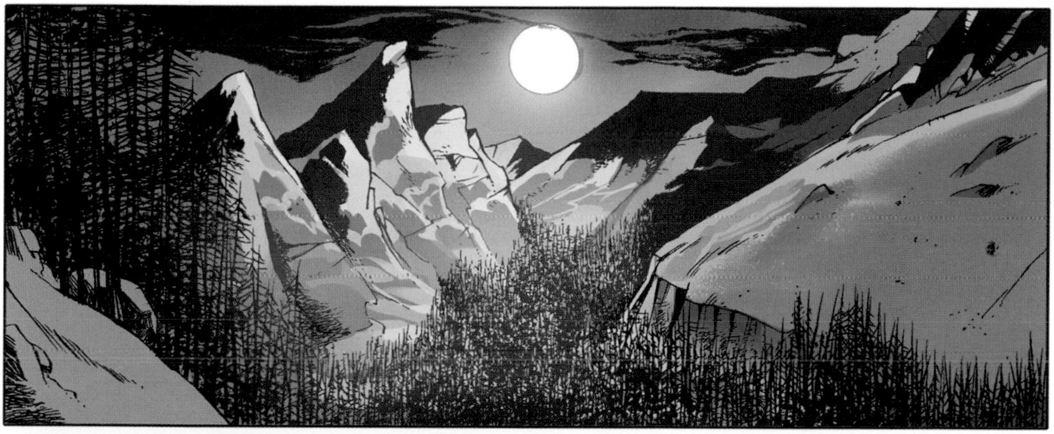

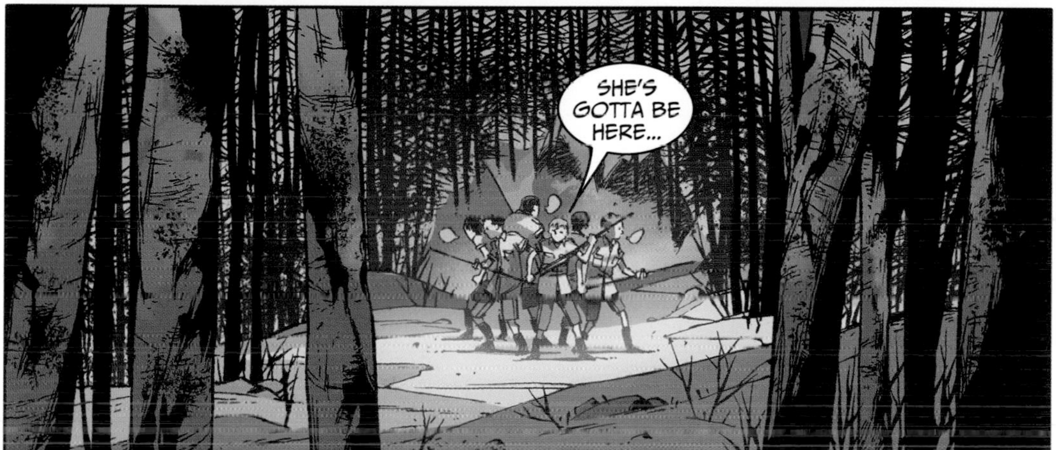
SHE'S GOTTA BE HERE...

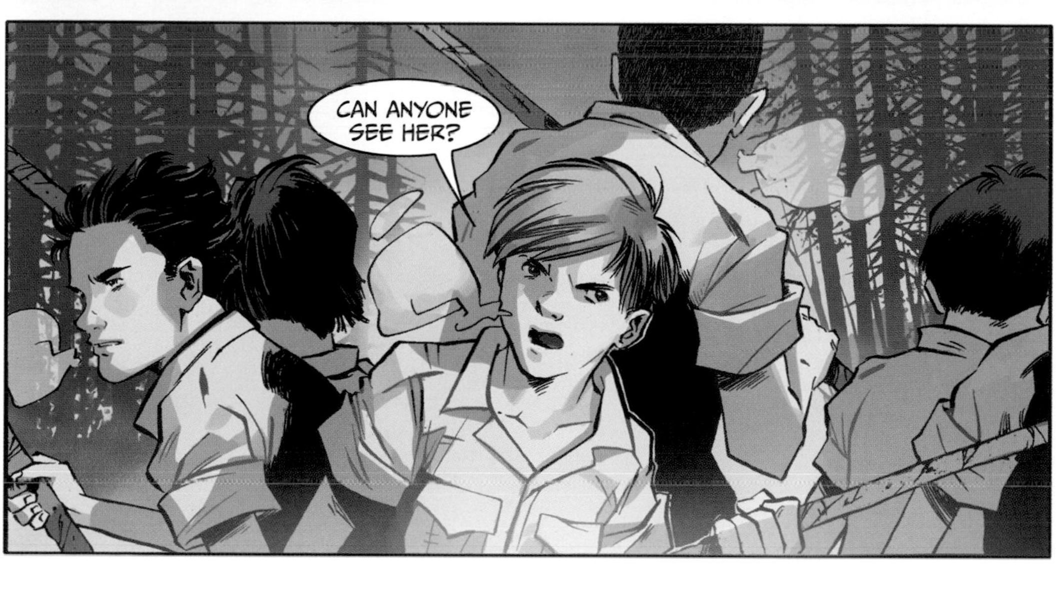
CAN ANYONE SEE HER?

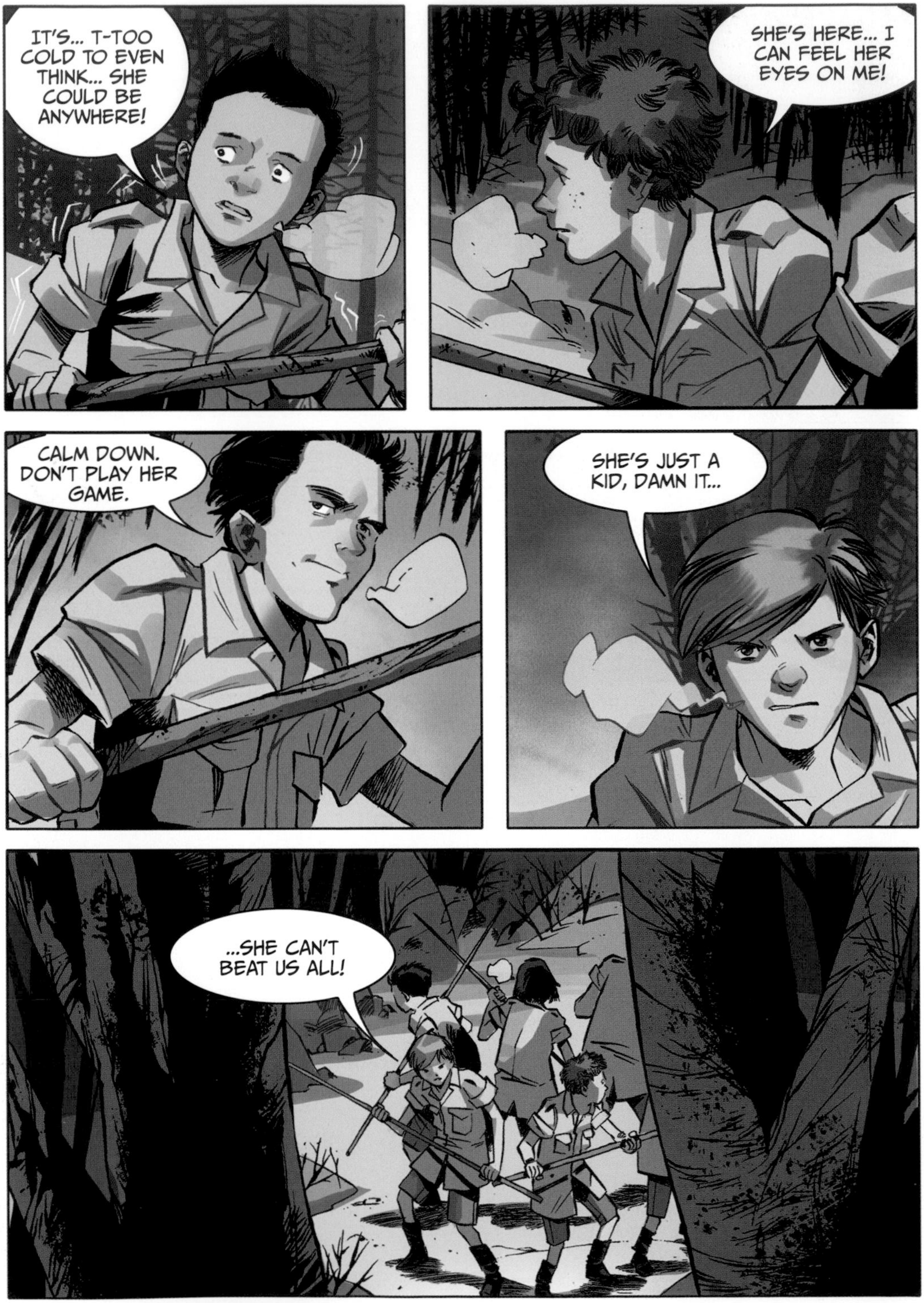
IT'S... T-TOO COLD TO EVEN THINK... SHE COULD BE ANYWHERE!
SHE'S HERE... I CAN FEEL HER EYES ON ME!
CALM DOWN. DON'T PLAY HER GAME.
SHE'S JUST A KID, DAMN IT...
...SHE CAN'T BEAT US ALL!

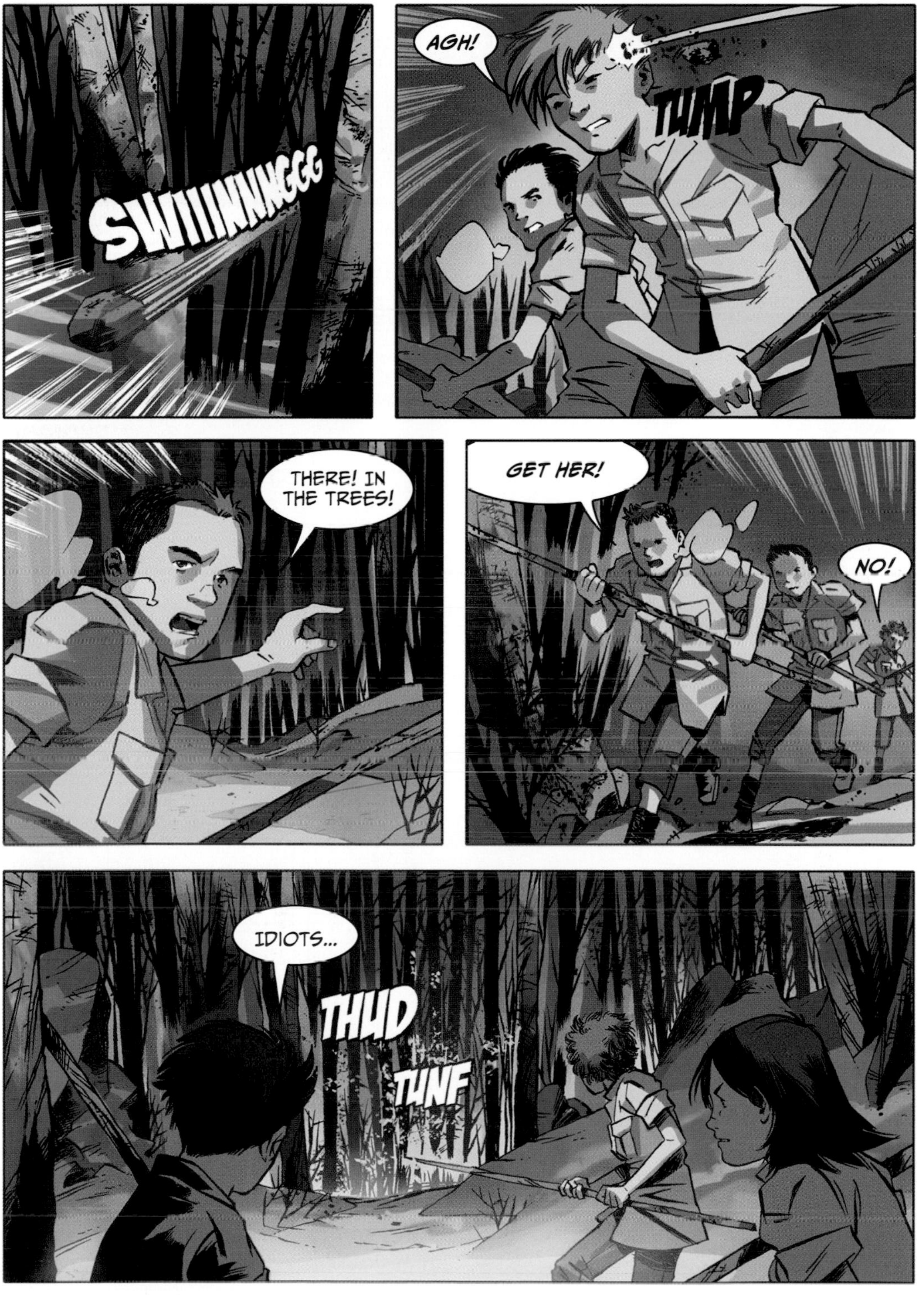
SWIIIINNNGGG
AGH!
TUMP
THERE! IN THE TREES!
GET HER!
NO!
IDIOTS...
THUD
TUNF

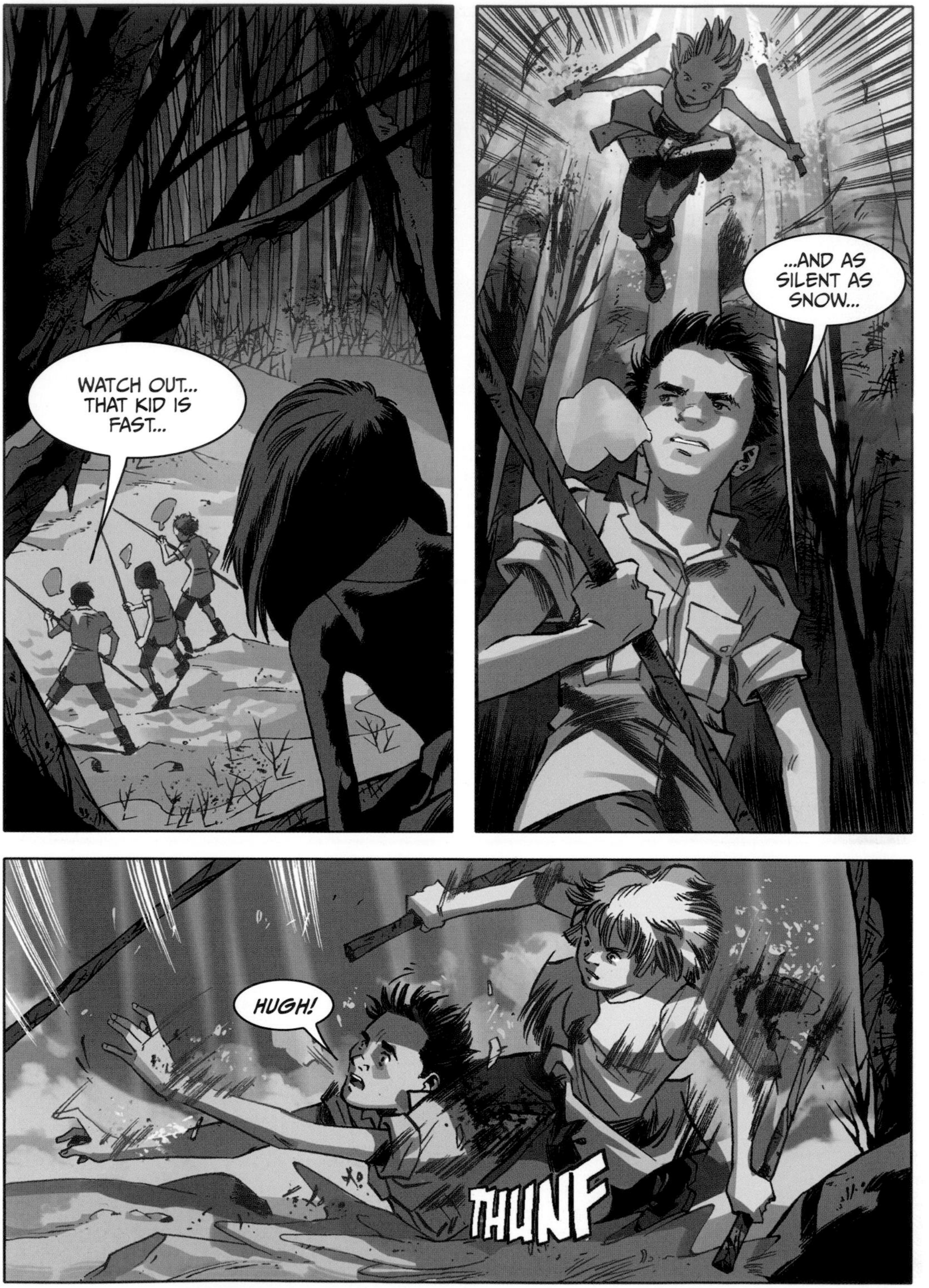
WATCH OUT... THAT KID IS FAST...
...AND AS SILENT AS SNOW...
HUGH!
THUNF

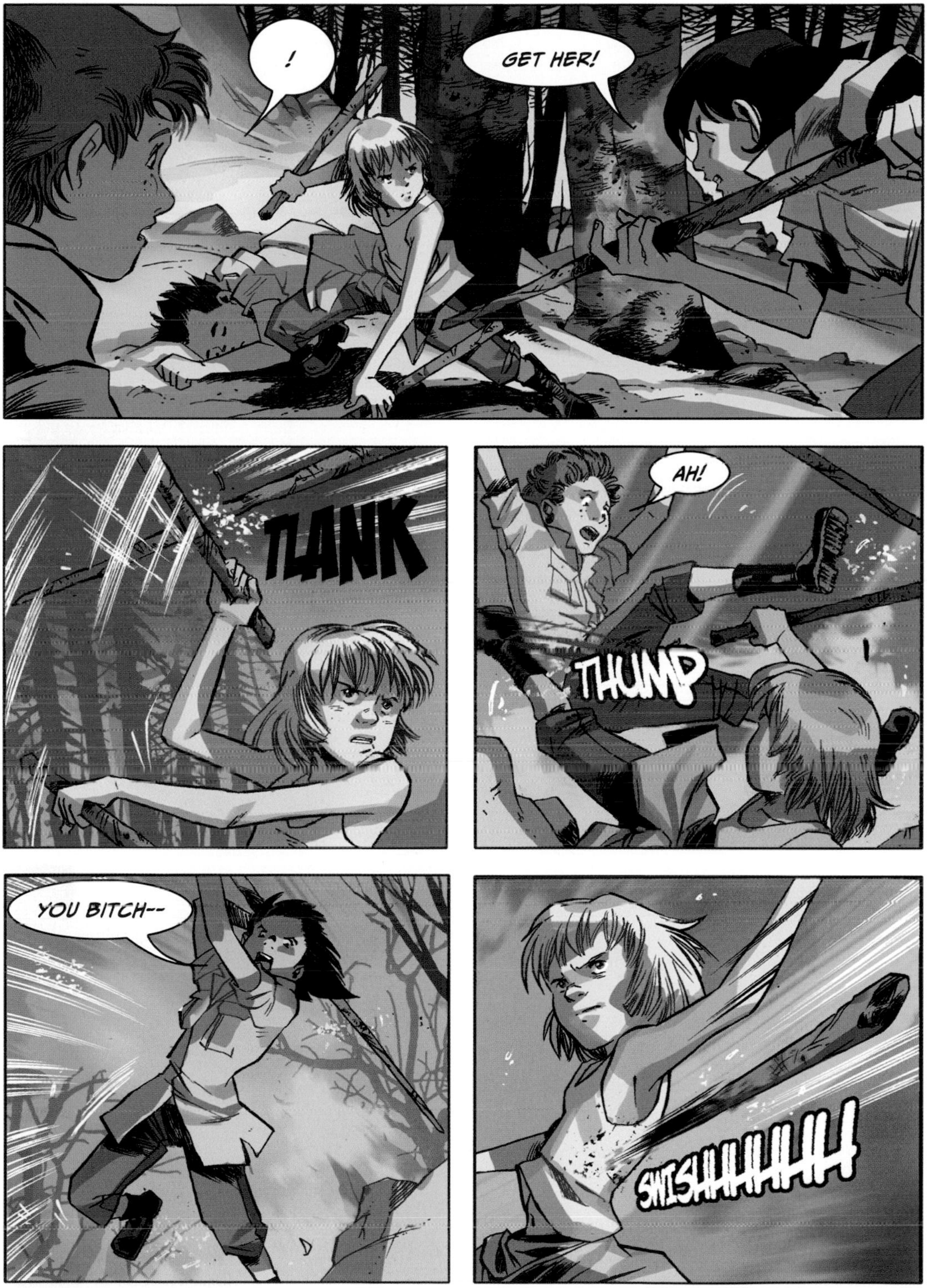
!
GET HER!
TLANK
AH!
THUMP
YOU BITCH--
SWISHHHHHH

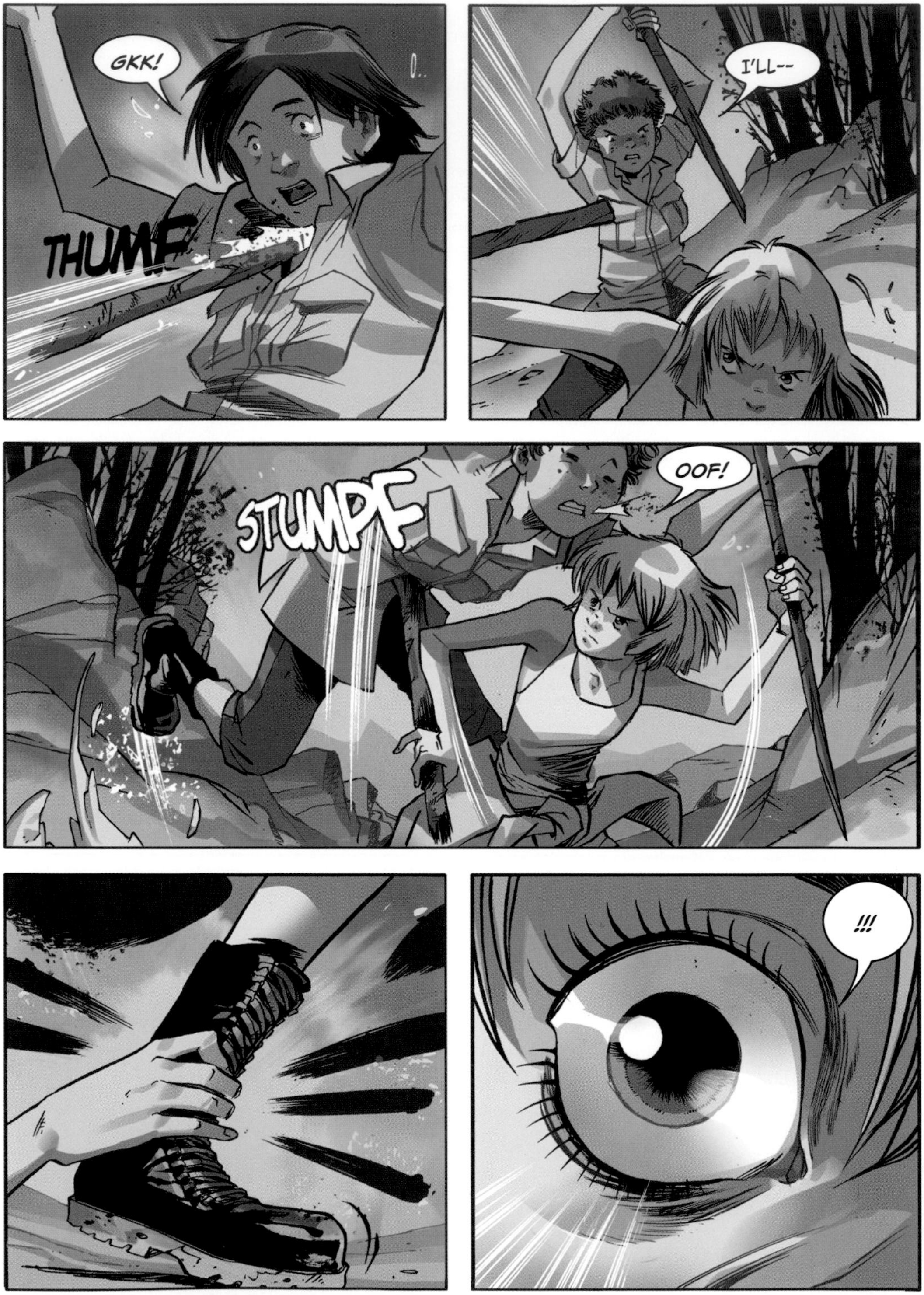
GKK!
THUMF
I'LL--
STUMPF
OOF!
!!!

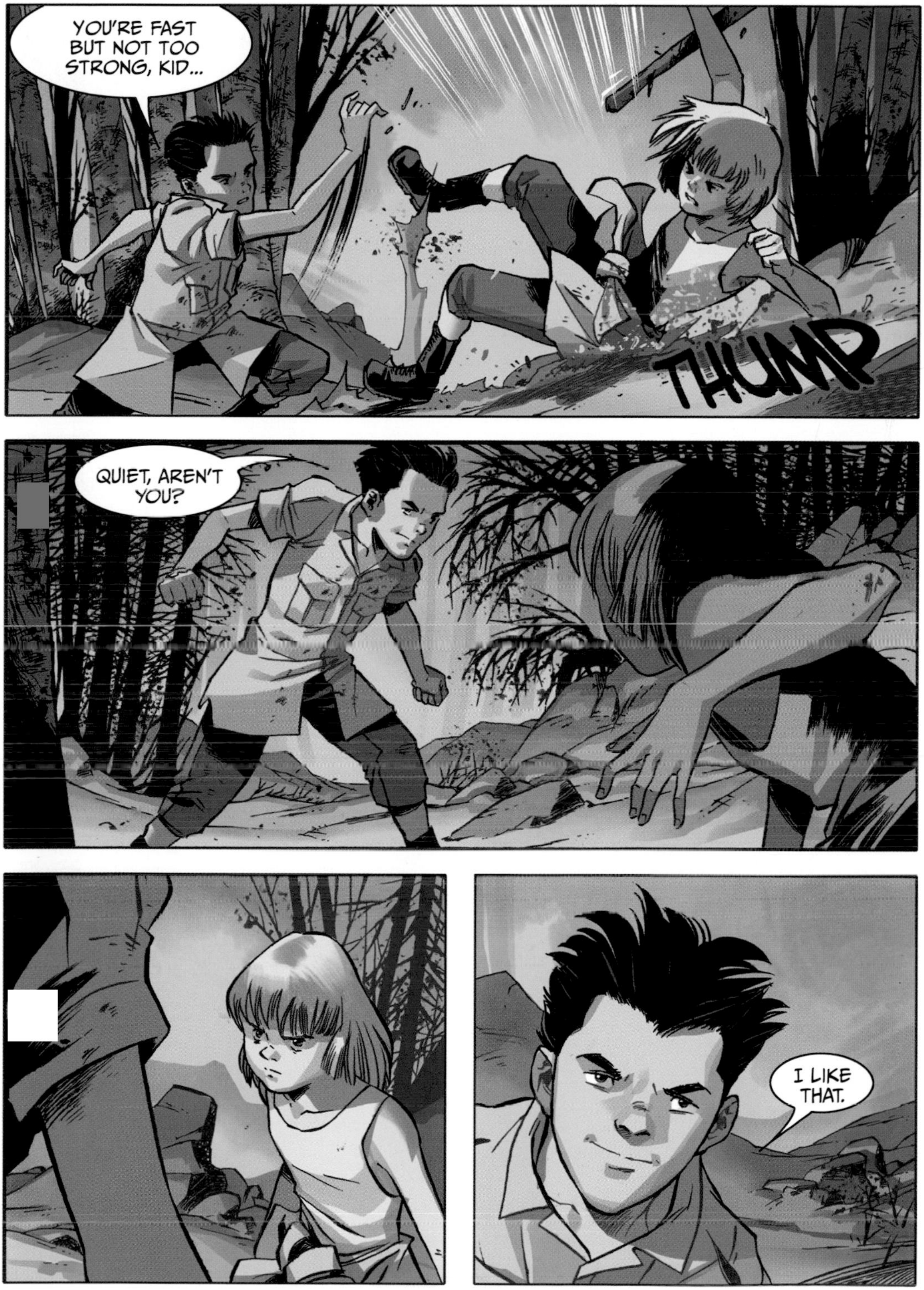
YOU'RE FAST
BUT NOT TOO
STRONG, KID...
THUMP
QUIET, AREN'T
YOU?
I LIKE
THAT.

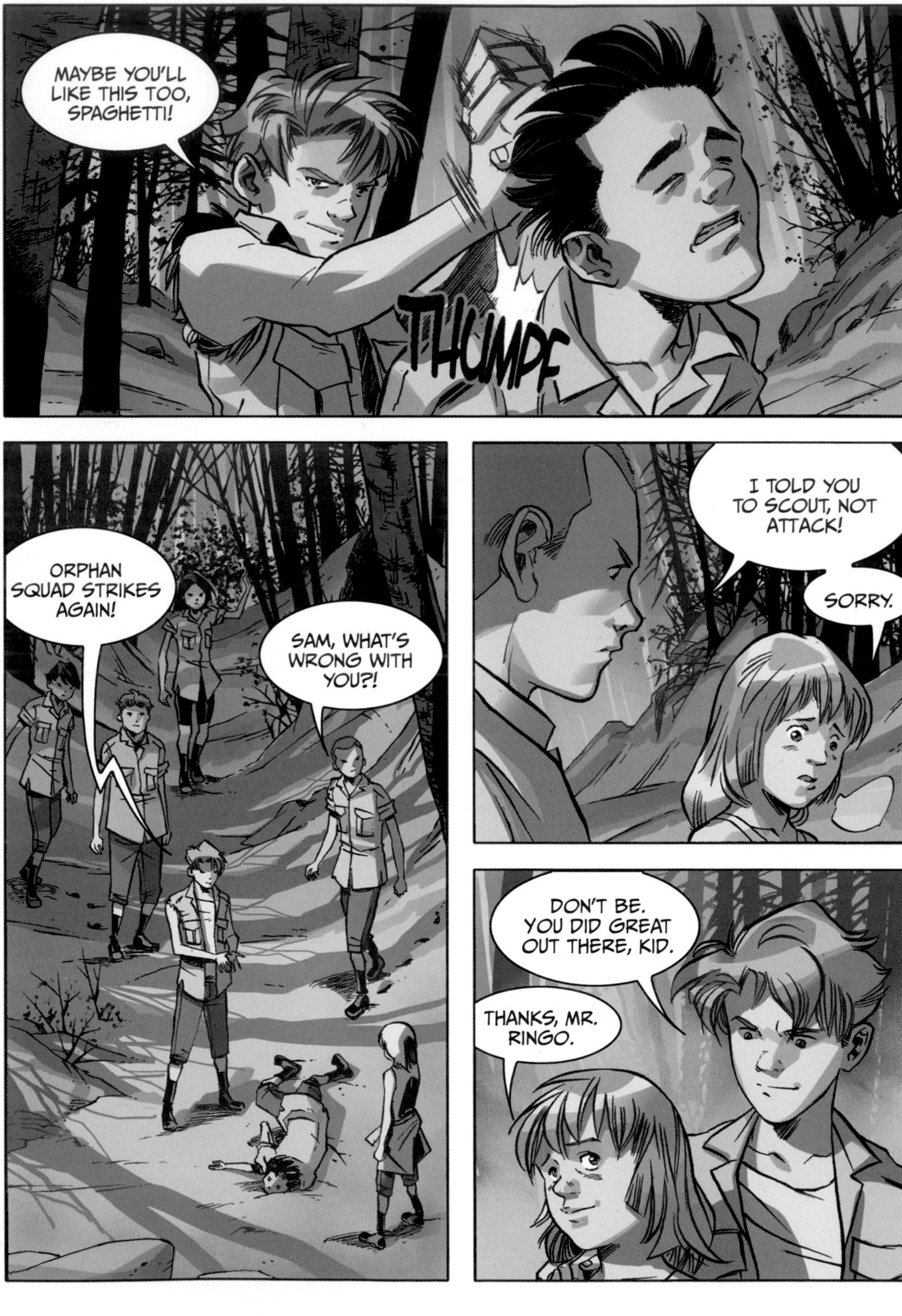
MAYBE YOU'LL LIKE THIS TOO, SPAGHETTI!
THUMPF
ORPHAN SQUAD STRIKES AGAIN!
SAM, WHAT'S WRONG WITH YOU?!
I TOLD YOU TO SCOUT, NOT ATTACK!
SORRY.
DON'T BE. YOU DID GREAT OUT THERE, KID.
THANKS, MR. RINGO.

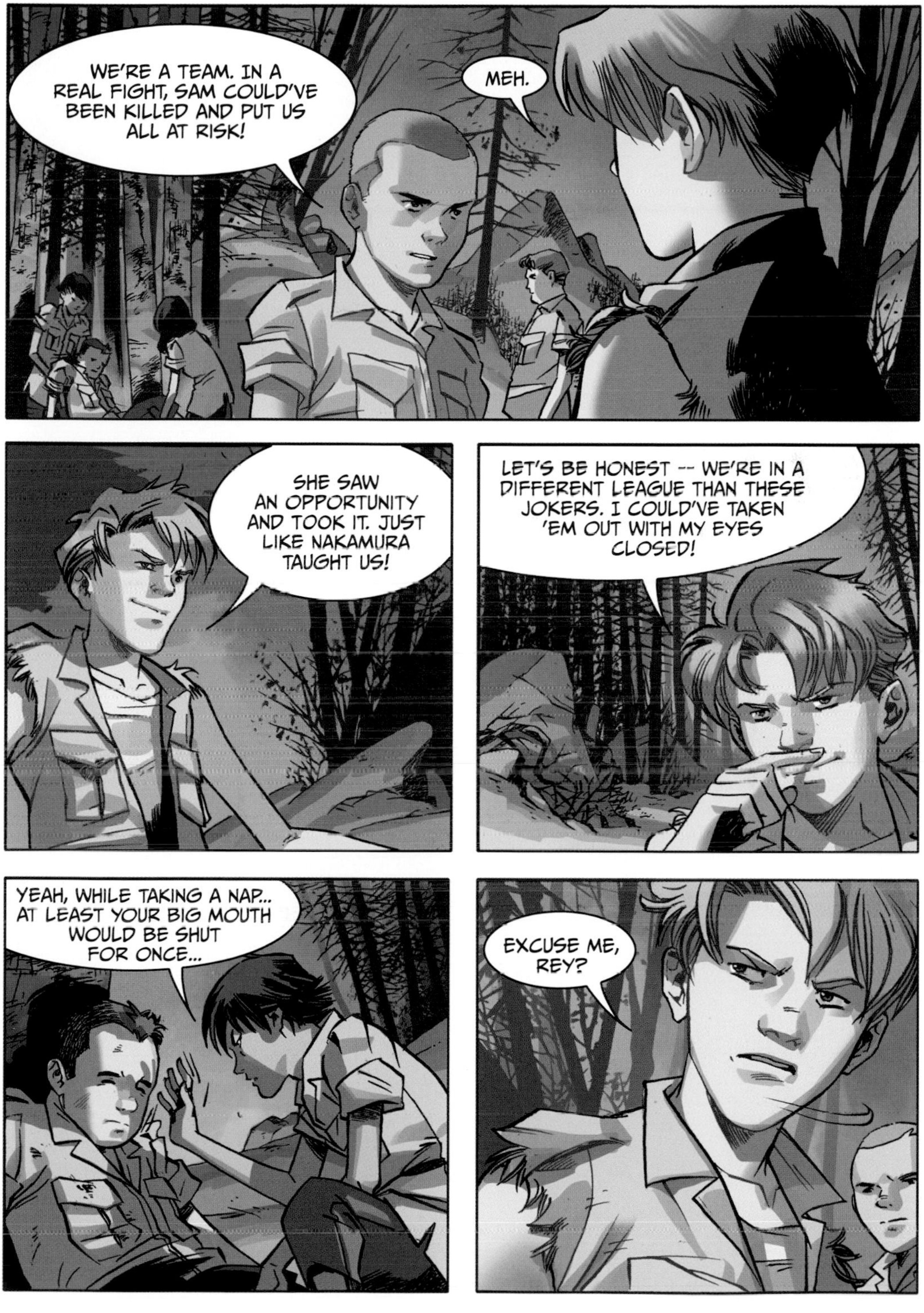
WE'RE A TEAM. IN A REAL FIGHT, SAM COULD'VE BEEN KILLED AND PUT US ALL AT RISK!
MEH.
SHE SAW AN OPPORTUNITY AND TOOK IT. JUST LIKE NAKAMURA TAUGHT US!
LET'S BE HONEST -- WE'RE IN A DIFFERENT LEAGUE THAN THESE JOKERS. I COULD'VE TAKEN 'EM OUT WITH MY EYES CLOSED!
YEAH, WHILE TAKING A NAP... AT LEAST YOUR BIG MOUTH WOULD BE SHUT FOR ONCE...
EXCUSE ME, REY?

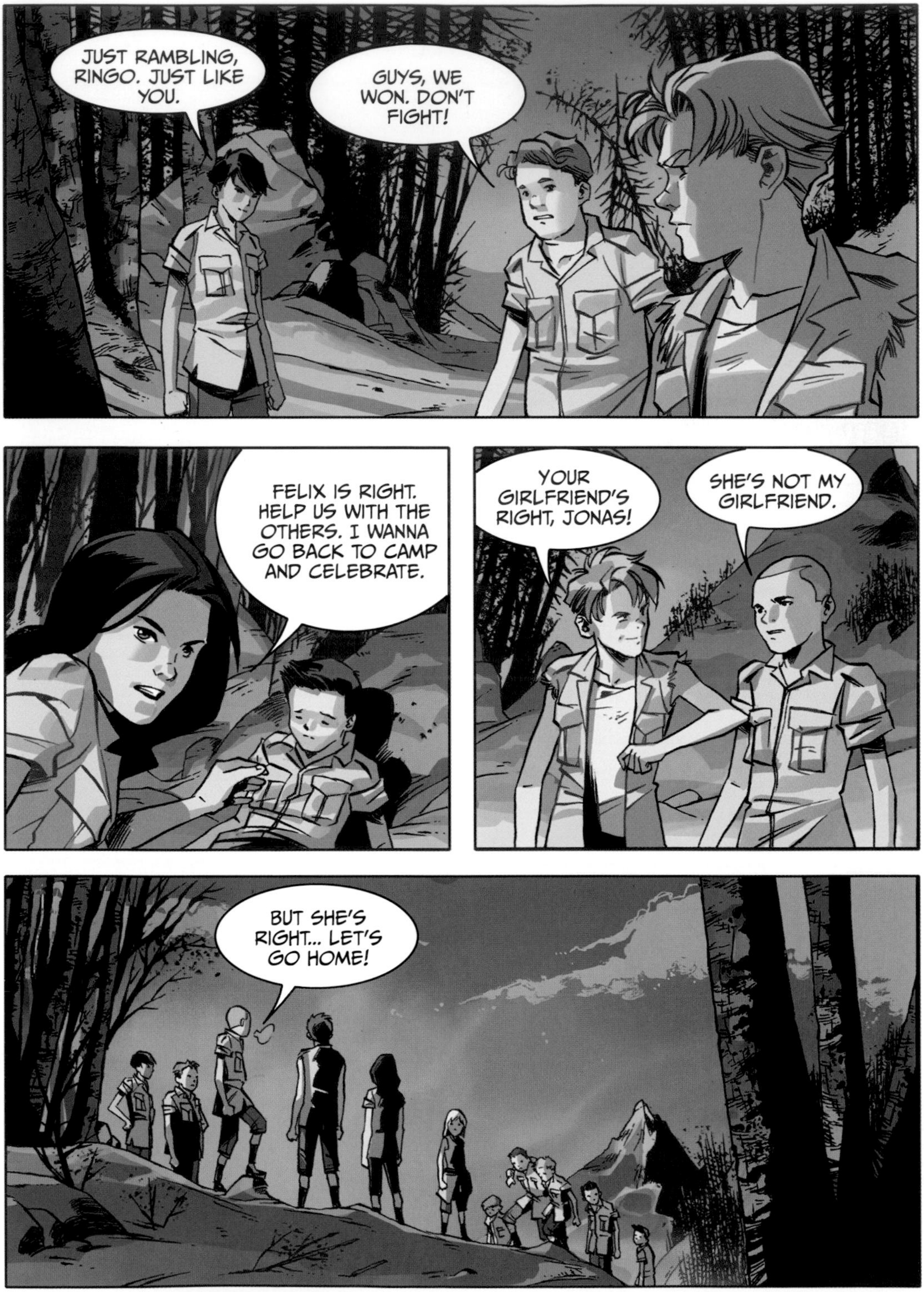
JUST RAMBLING, RINGO. JUST LIKE YOU.
GUYS, WE WON. DON'T FIGHT!
FELIX IS RIGHT. HELP US WITH THE OTHERS. I WANNA GO BACK TO CAMP AND CELEBRATE.
YOUR GIRLFRIEND'S RIGHT, JONAS!
SHE'S NOT MY GIRLFRIEND.
BUT SHE'S RIGHT... LET'S GO HOME!

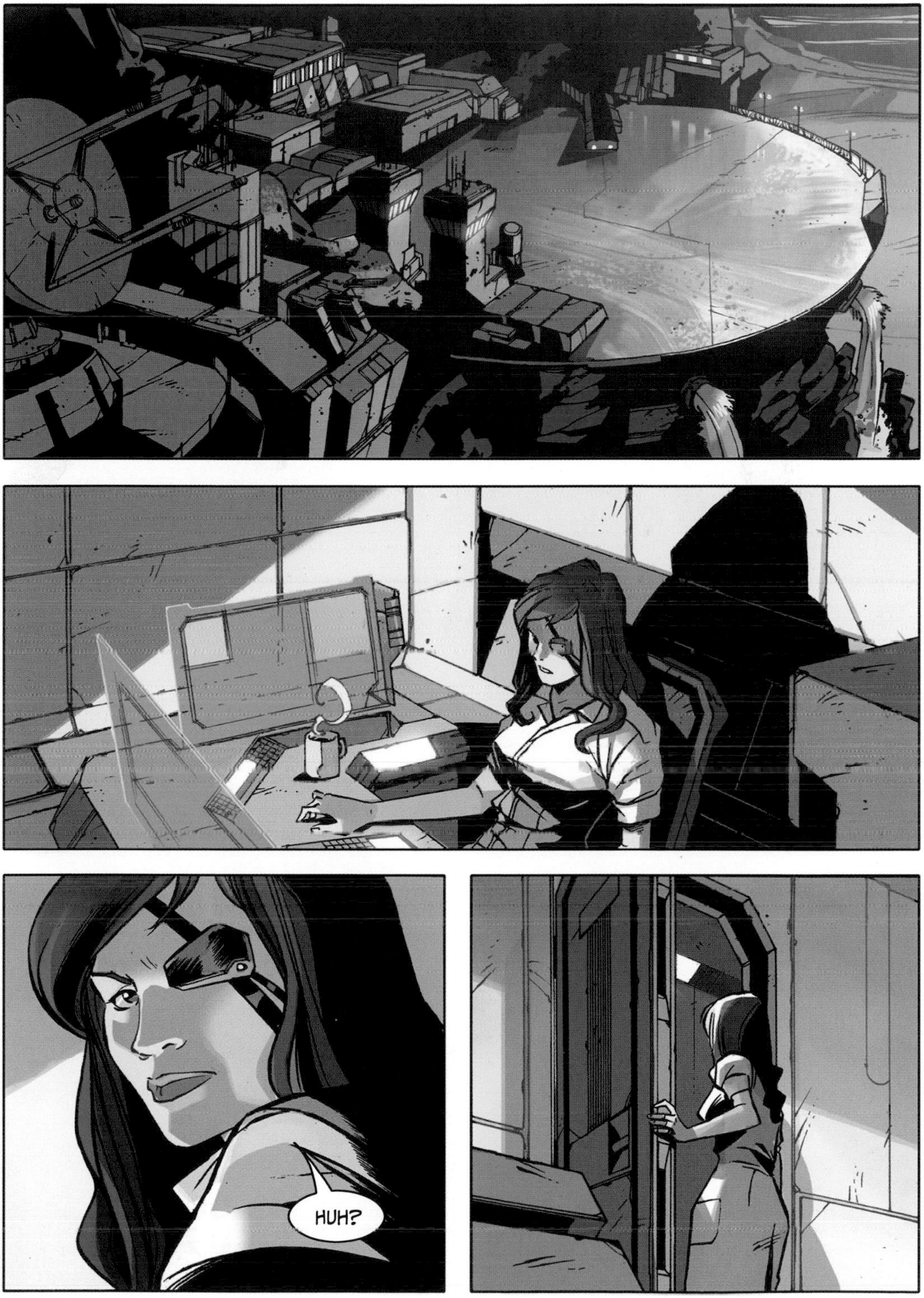
HUH?

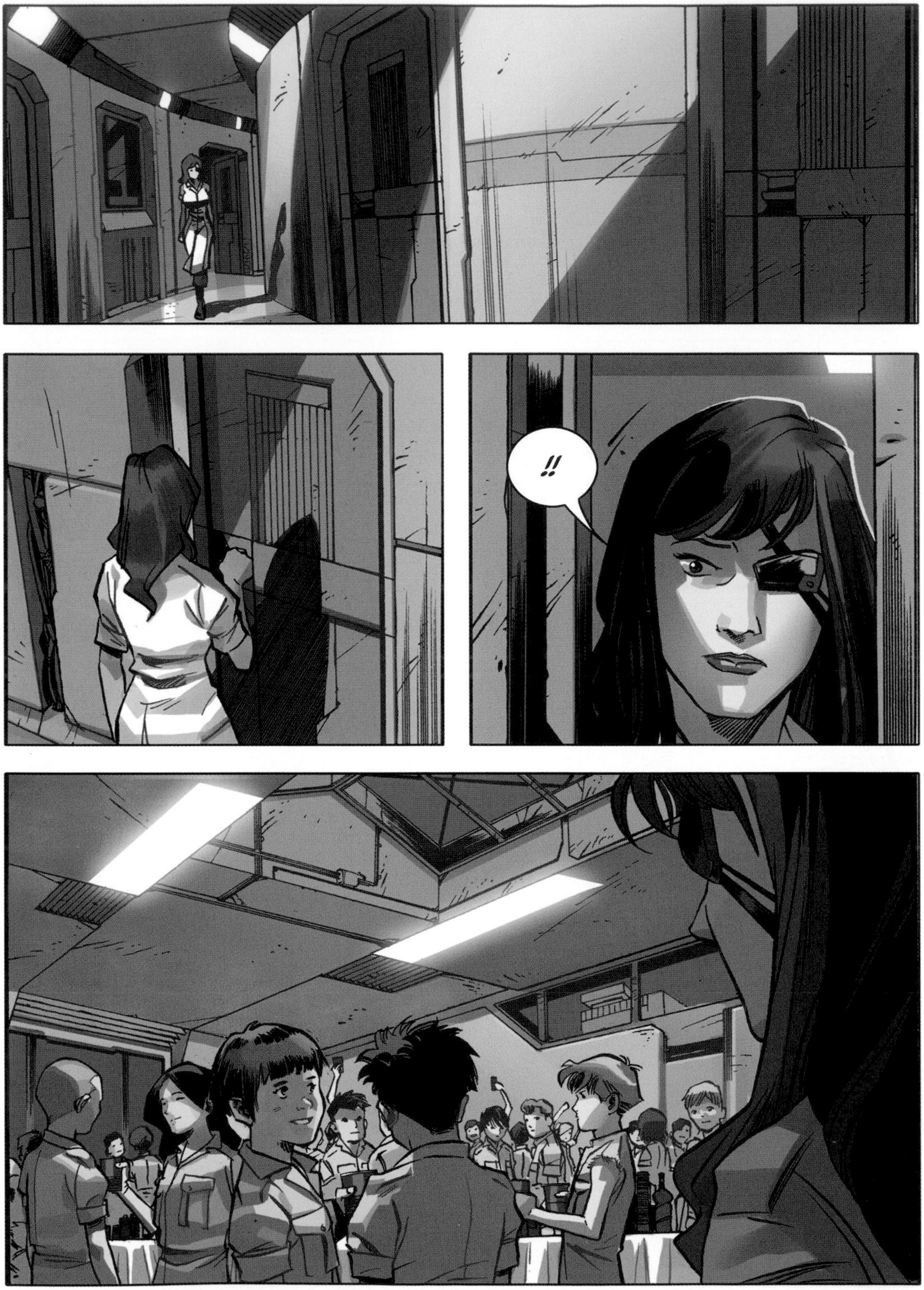
!!

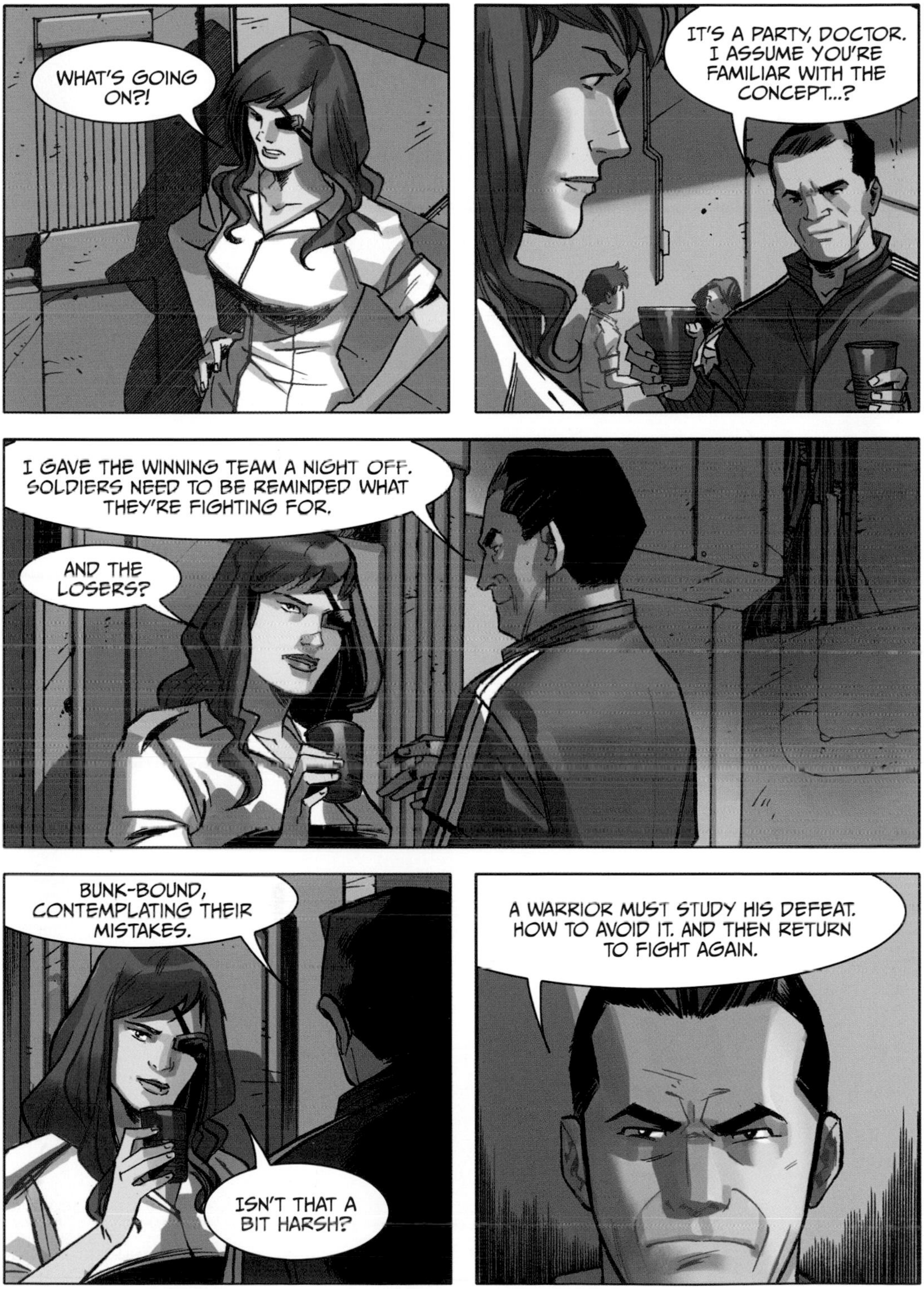
WHAT'S GOING ON?!
IT'S A PARTY, DOCTOR. I ASSUME YOU'RE FAMILIAR WITH THE CONCEPT...?
I GAVE THE WINNING TEAM A NIGHT OFF. SOLDIERS NEED TO BE REMINDED WHAT THEY'RE FIGHTING FOR.
AND THE LOSERS?
BUNK-BOUND, CONTEMPLATING THEIR MISTAKES.
ISN'T THAT A BIT HARSH?
A WARRIOR MUST STUDY HIS DEFEAT. HOW TO AVOID IT. AND THEN RETURN TO FIGHT AGAIN.

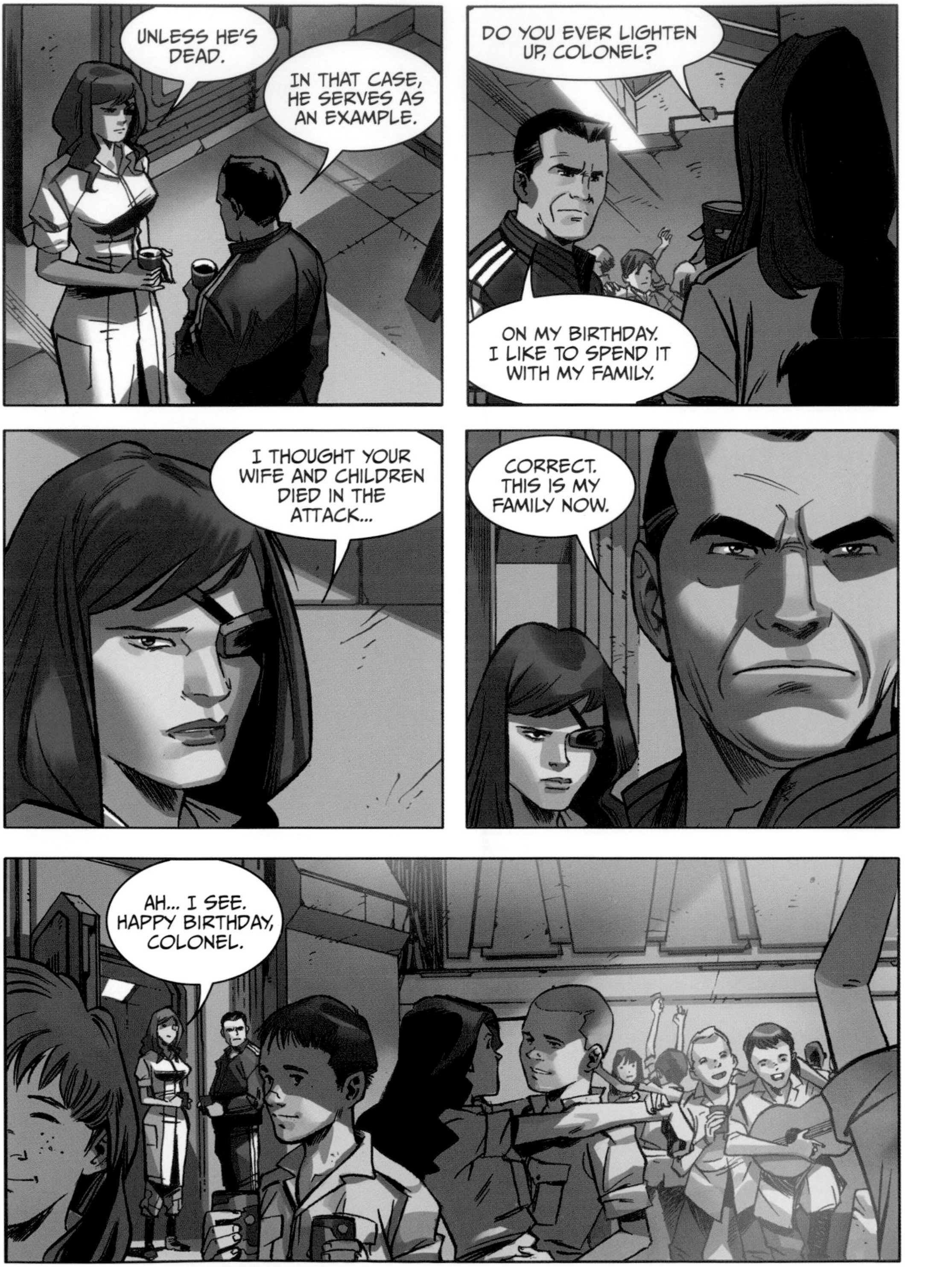
UNLESS HE'S DEAD.
IN THAT CASE, HE SERVES AS AN EXAMPLE.
DO YOU EVER LIGHTEN UP, COLONEL?
ON MY BIRTHDAY. I LIKE TO SPEND IT WITH MY FAMILY.
I THOUGHT YOUR WIFE AND CHILDREN DIED IN THE ATTACK...
CORRECT. THIS IS MY FAMILY NOW.
AH... I SEE. HAPPY BIRTHDAY, COLONEL.

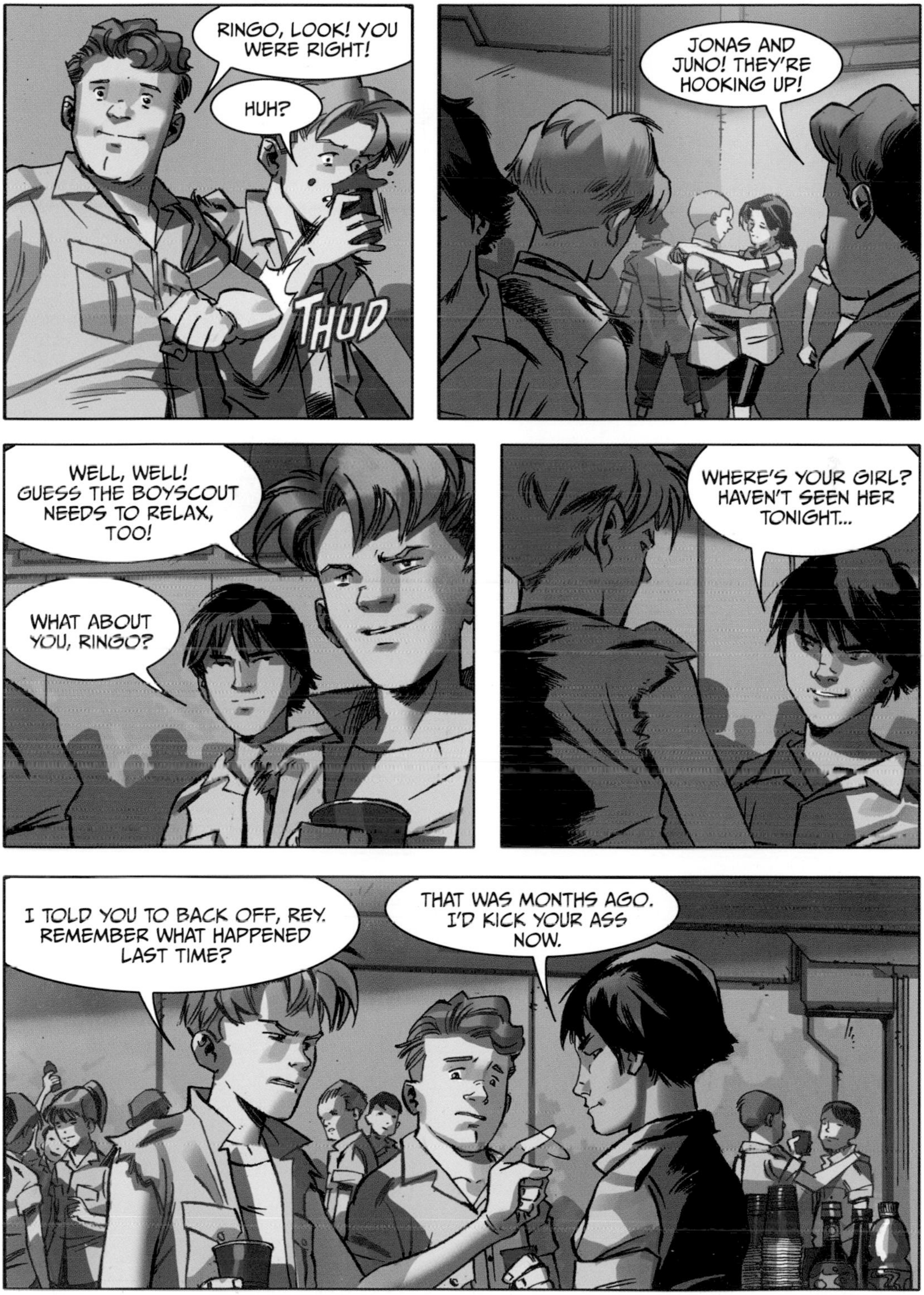
RINGO, LOOK! YOU WERE RIGHT!
HUH?
THUD
JONAS AND JUNO! THEY'RE HOOKING UP!
WELL, WELL! GUESS THE BOYSCOUT NEEDS TO RELAX, TOO!
WHAT ABOUT YOU, RINGO?
WHERE'S YOUR GIRL? HAVEN'T SEEN HER TONIGHT...
I TOLD YOU TO BACK OFF, REY. REMEMBER WHAT HAPPENED LAST TIME?
THAT WAS MONTHS AGO. I'D KICK YOUR ASS NOW.

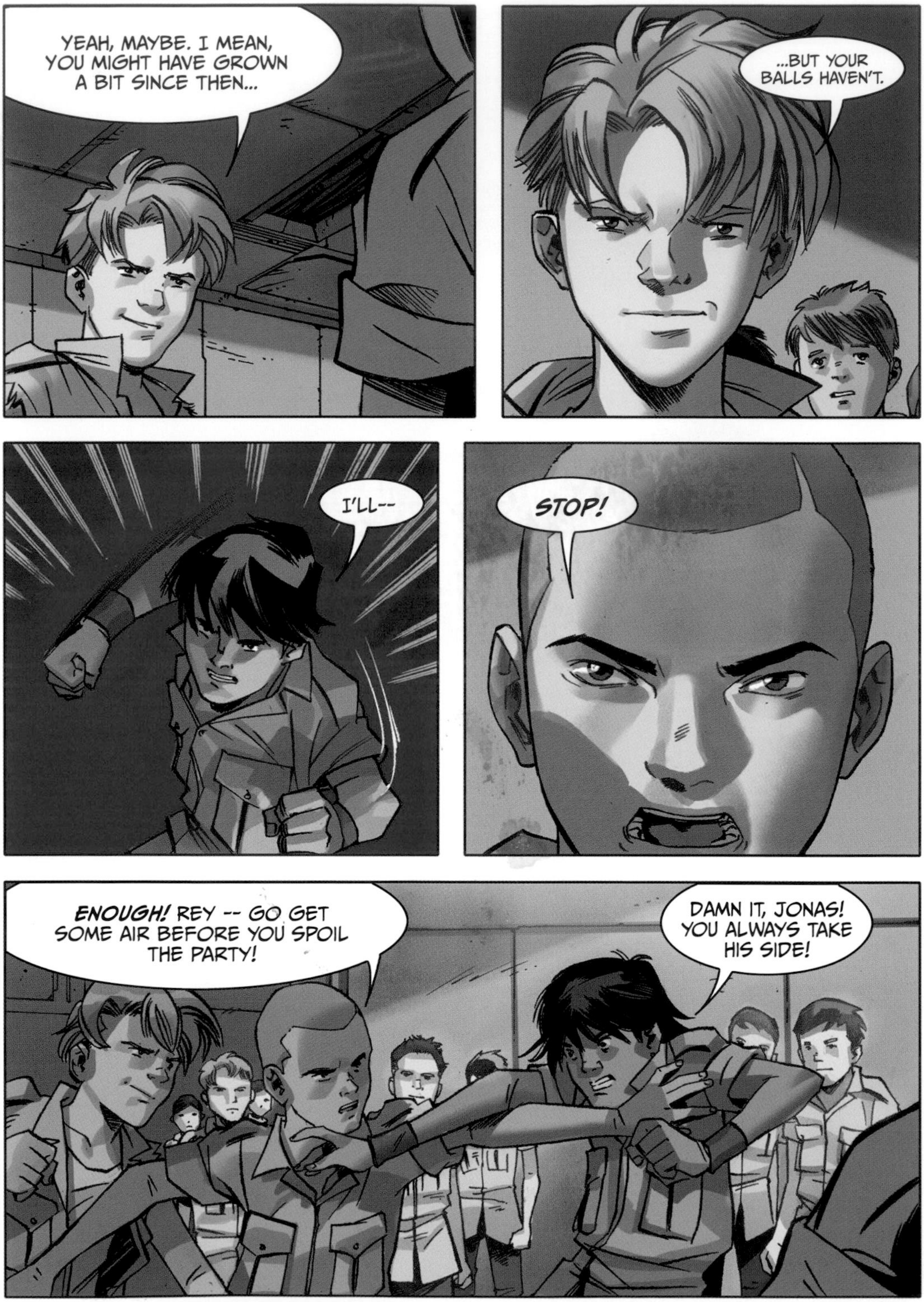
YEAH, MAYBE. I MEAN, YOU MIGHT HAVE GROWN A BIT SINCE THEN...
...BUT YOUR BALLS HAVEN'T.
I'LL--
STOP!
ENOUGH! REY -- GO GET SOME AIR BEFORE YOU SPOIL THE PARTY!
DAMN IT, JONAS! YOU ALWAYS TAKE HIS SIDE!

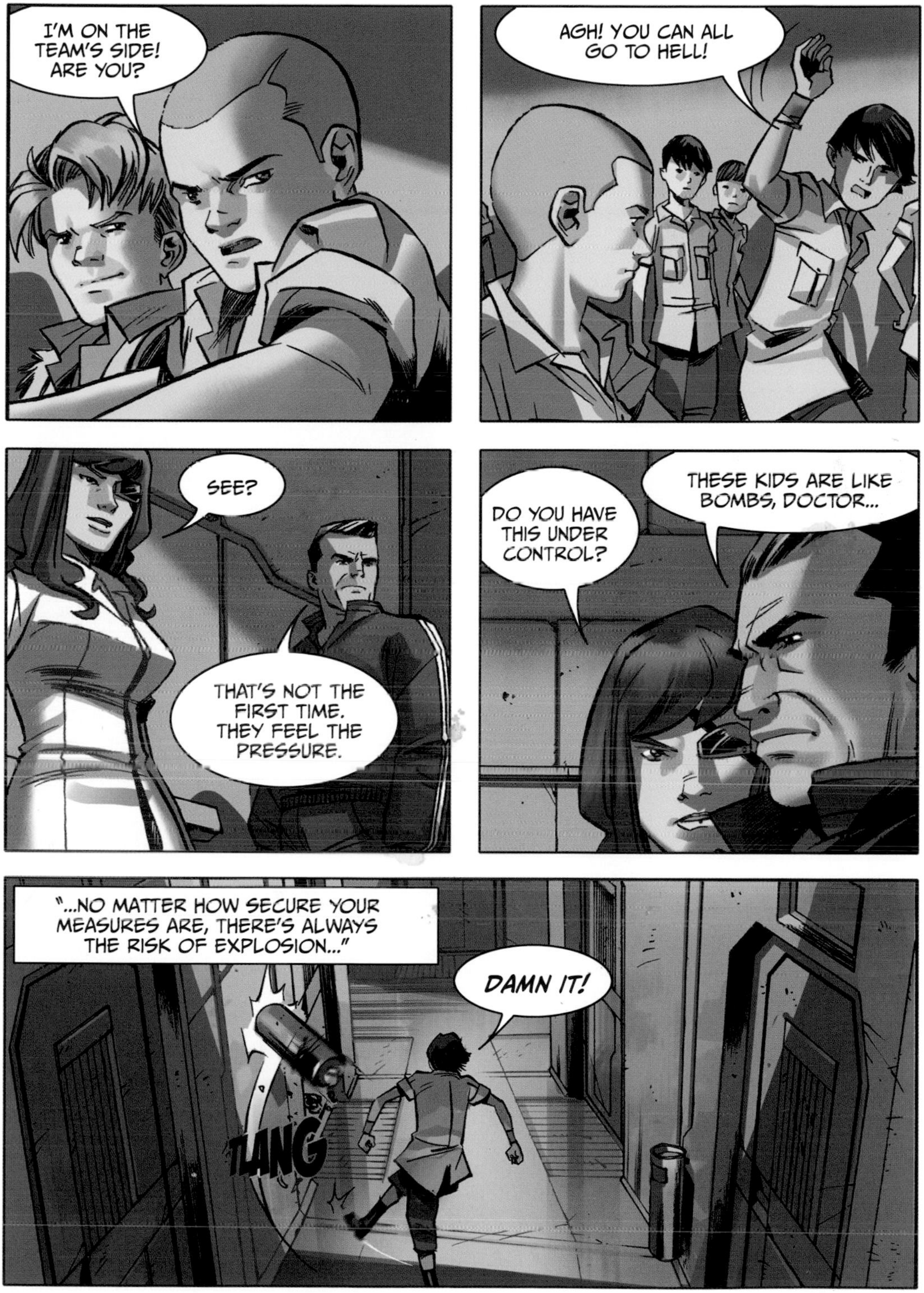
I'M ON THE TEAM'S SIDE! ARE YOU?
AGH! YOU CAN ALL GO TO HELL!
SEE?
THAT'S NOT THE FIRST TIME. THEY FEEL THE PRESSURE.
DO YOU HAVE THIS UNDER CONTROL?
THESE KIDS ARE LIKE BOMBS, DOCTOR...
"...NO MATTER HOW SECURE YOUR MEASURES ARE, THERE'S ALWAYS THE RISK OF EXPLOSION..."
DAMN IT!
TLANG

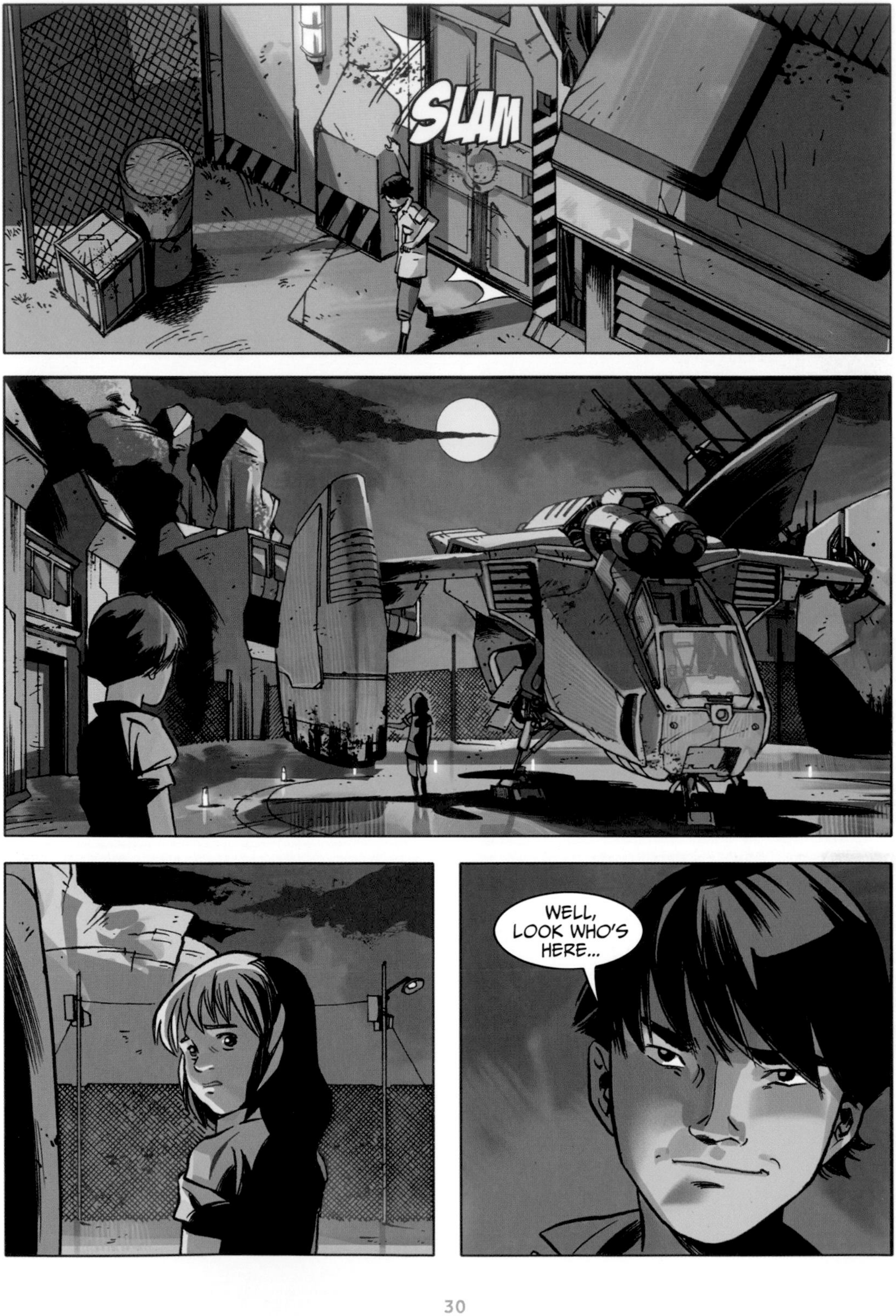
SLAM
WELL, LOOK WHO'S HERE...

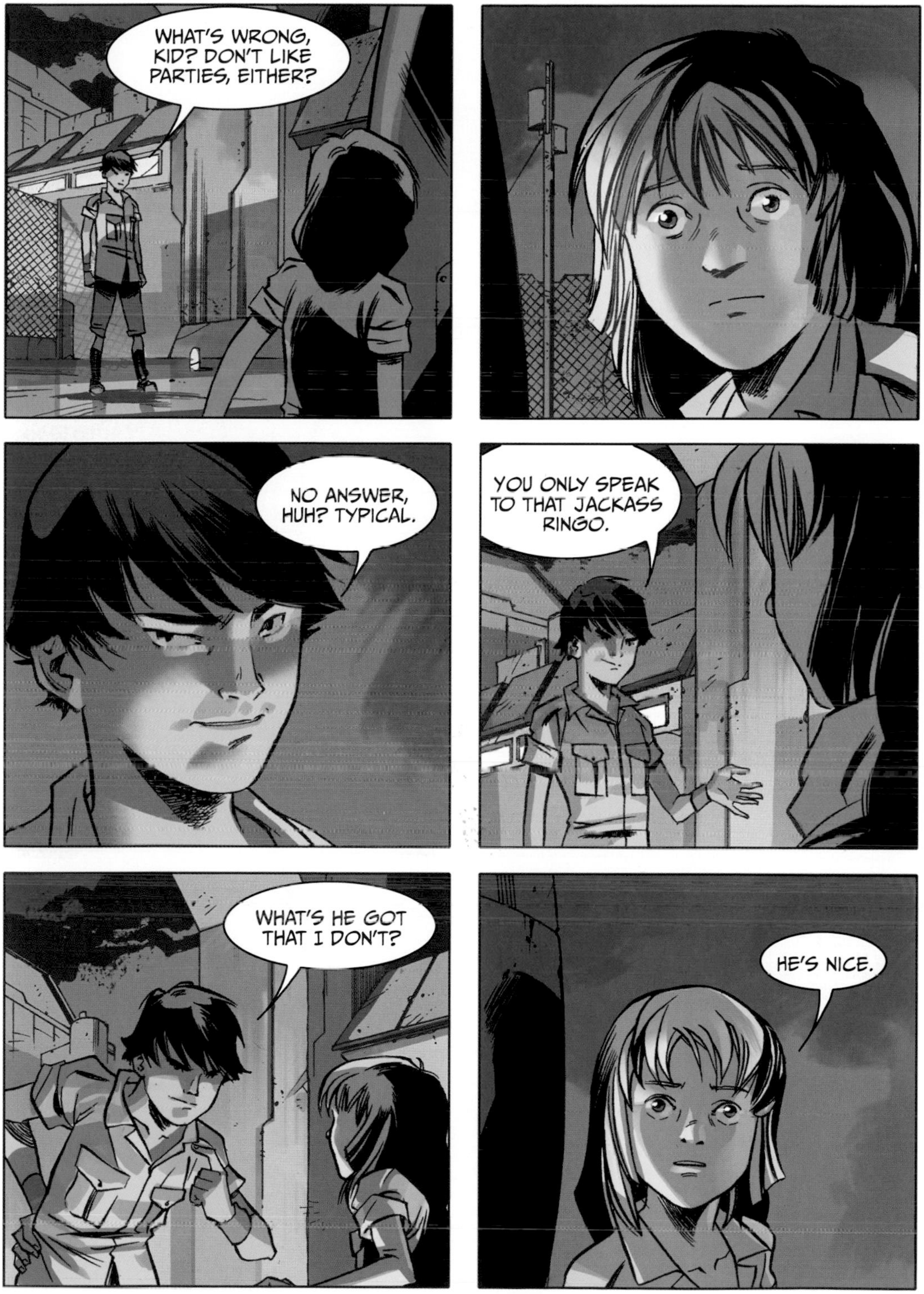
WHAT'S WRONG, KID? DON'T LIKE PARTIES, EITHER?
NO ANSWER, HUH? TYPICAL.
YOU ONLY SPEAK TO THAT JACKASS RINGO.
WHAT'S HE GOT THAT I DON'T?
HE'S NICE.

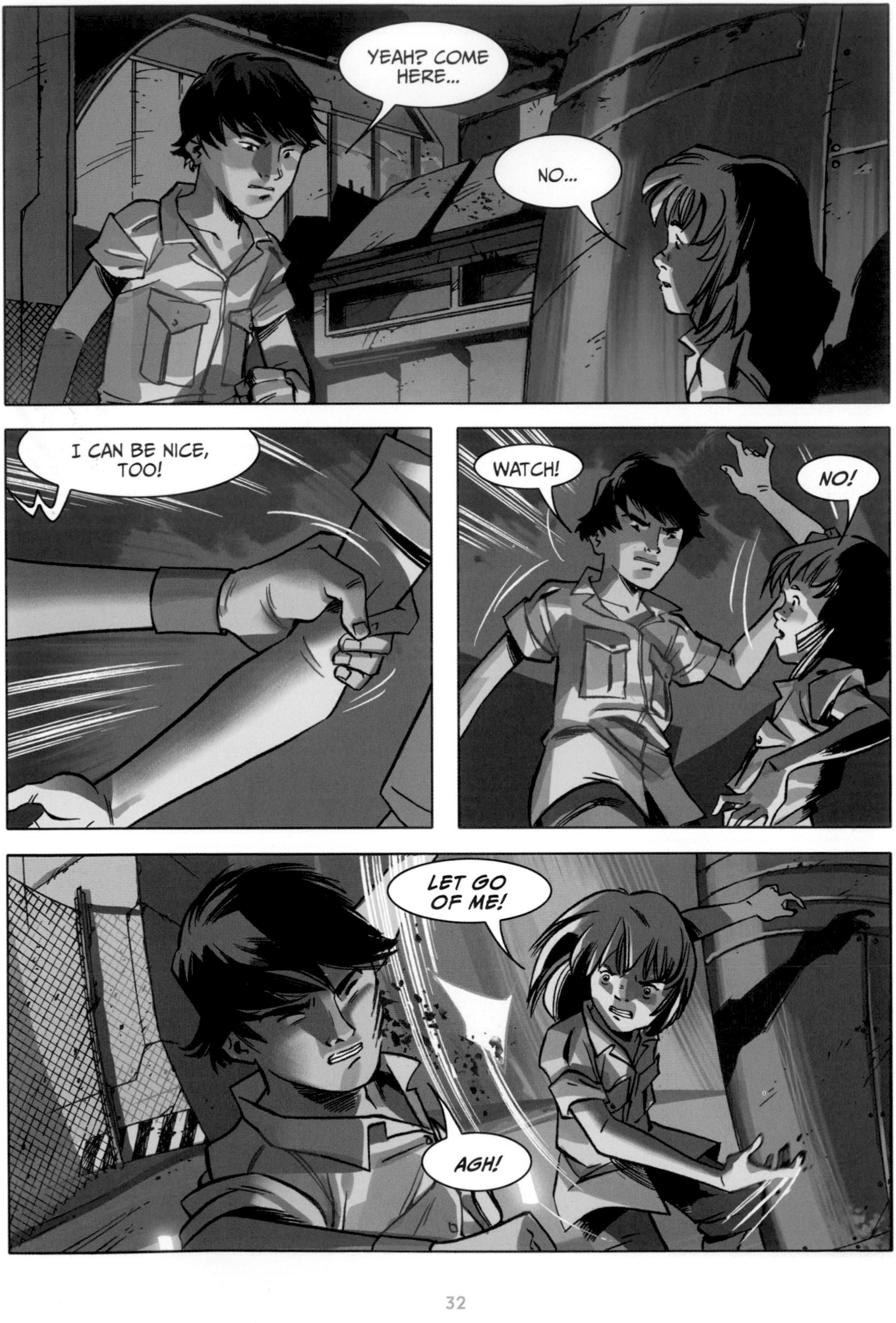
YEAH? COME HERE...
NO...
I CAN BE NICE, TOO!
WATCH!
NO!
LET GO OF ME!
AGH!

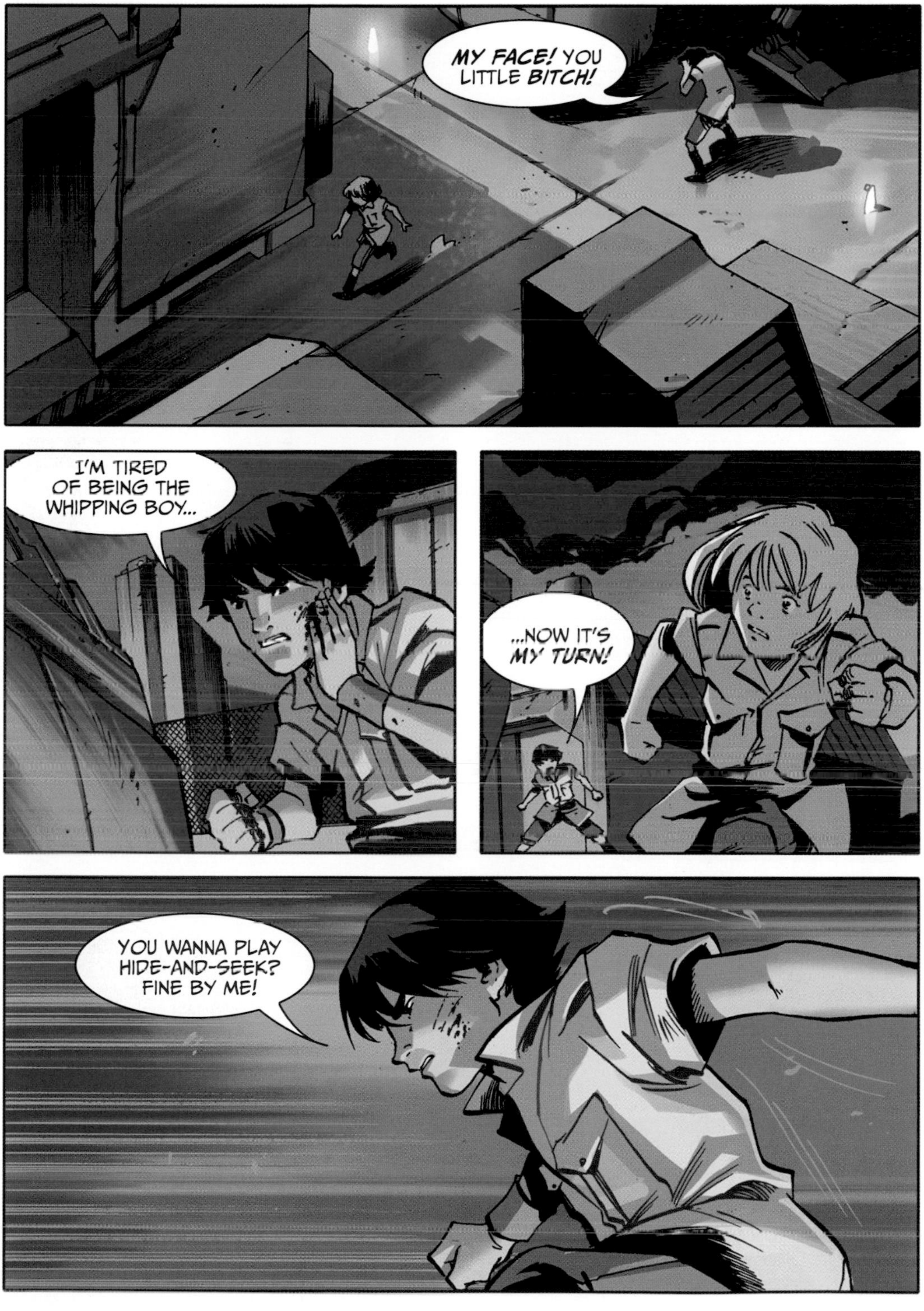
MY FACE! YOU LITTLE BITCH!
I'M TIRED OF BEING THE WHIPPING BOY...
...NOW IT'S MY TURN!
YOU WANNA PLAY HIDE-AND-SEEK? FINE BY ME!

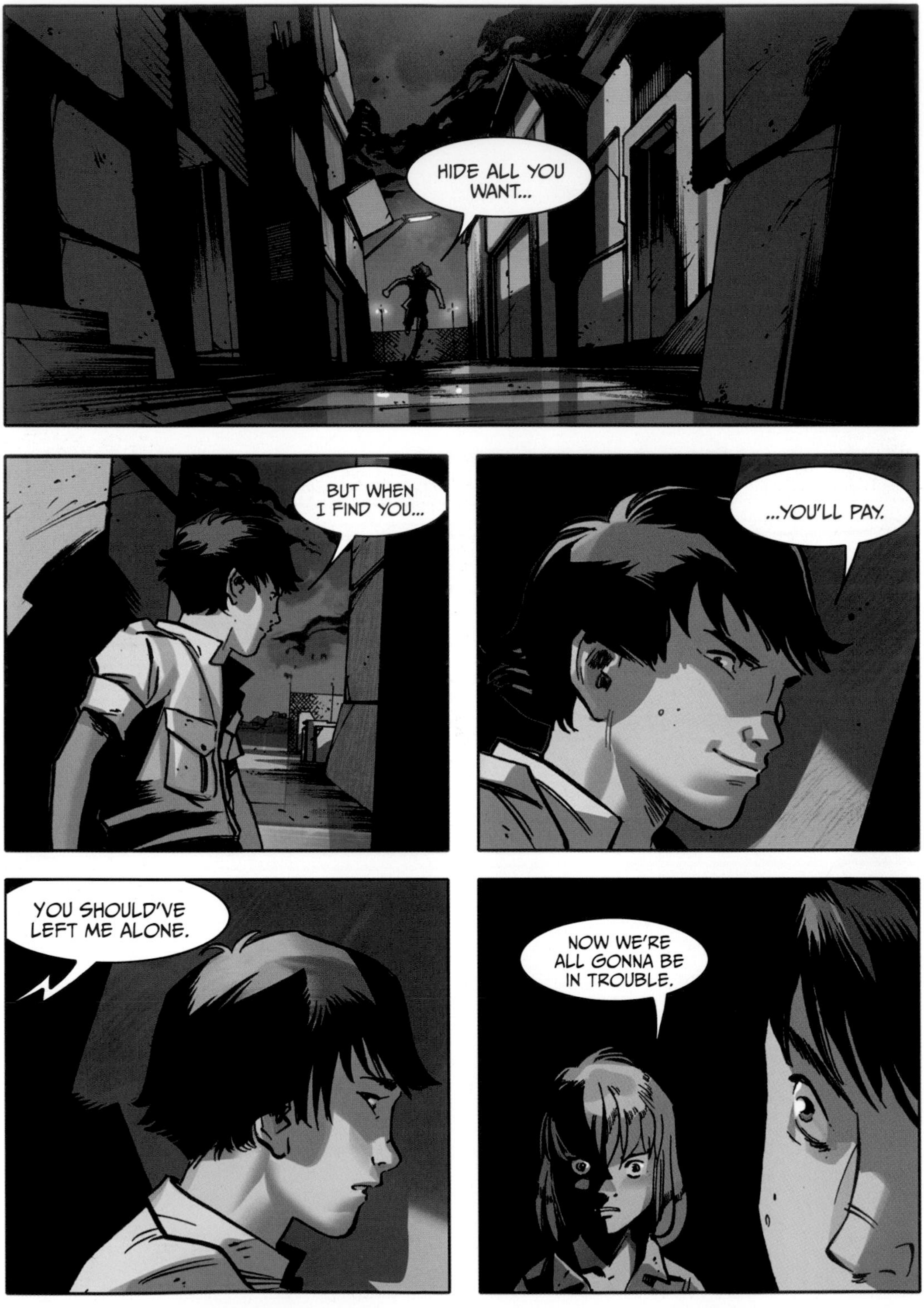
HIDE ALL YOU WANT...
BUT WHEN I FIND YOU...
...YOU'LL PAY.
YOU SHOULD'VE LEFT ME ALONE.
NOW WE'RE ALL GONNA BE IN TROUBLE.

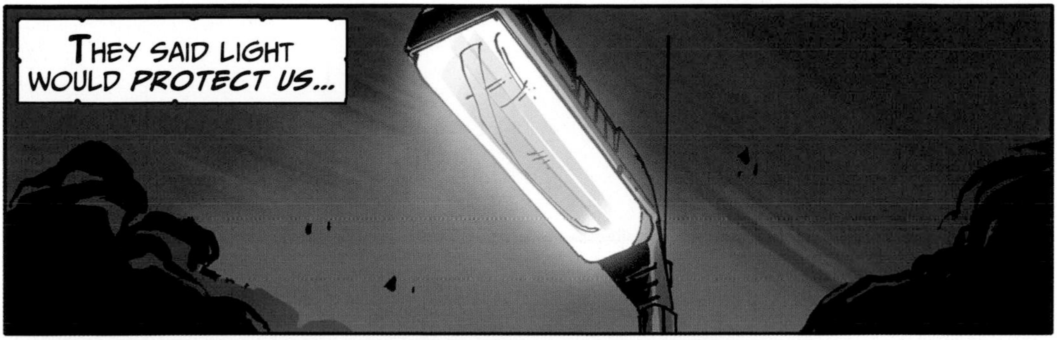
THEY SAID LIGHT WOULD PROTECT US...

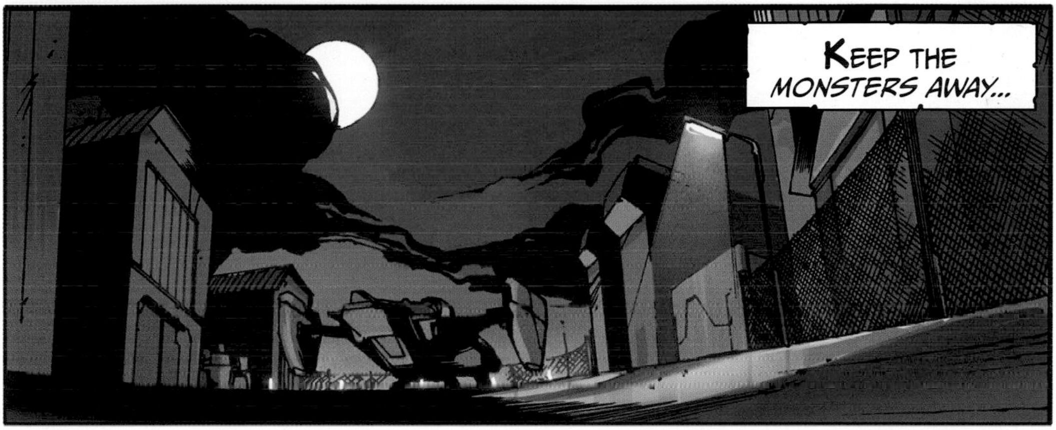
KEEP THE MONSTERS AWAY...

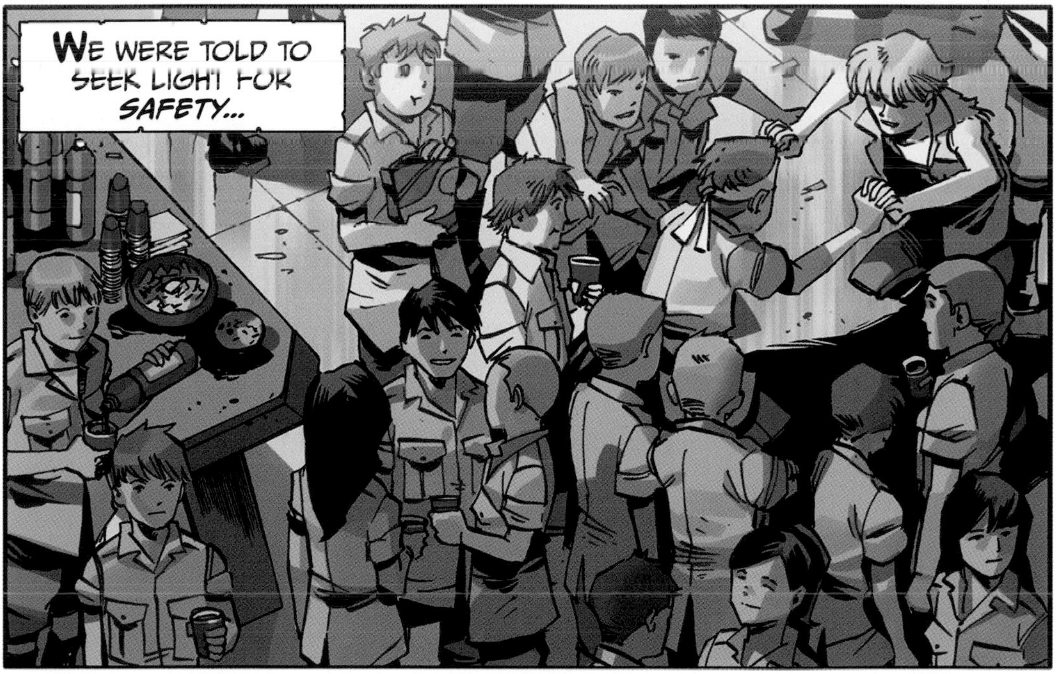
WE WERE TOLD TO SEEK LIGHT FOR SAFETY...

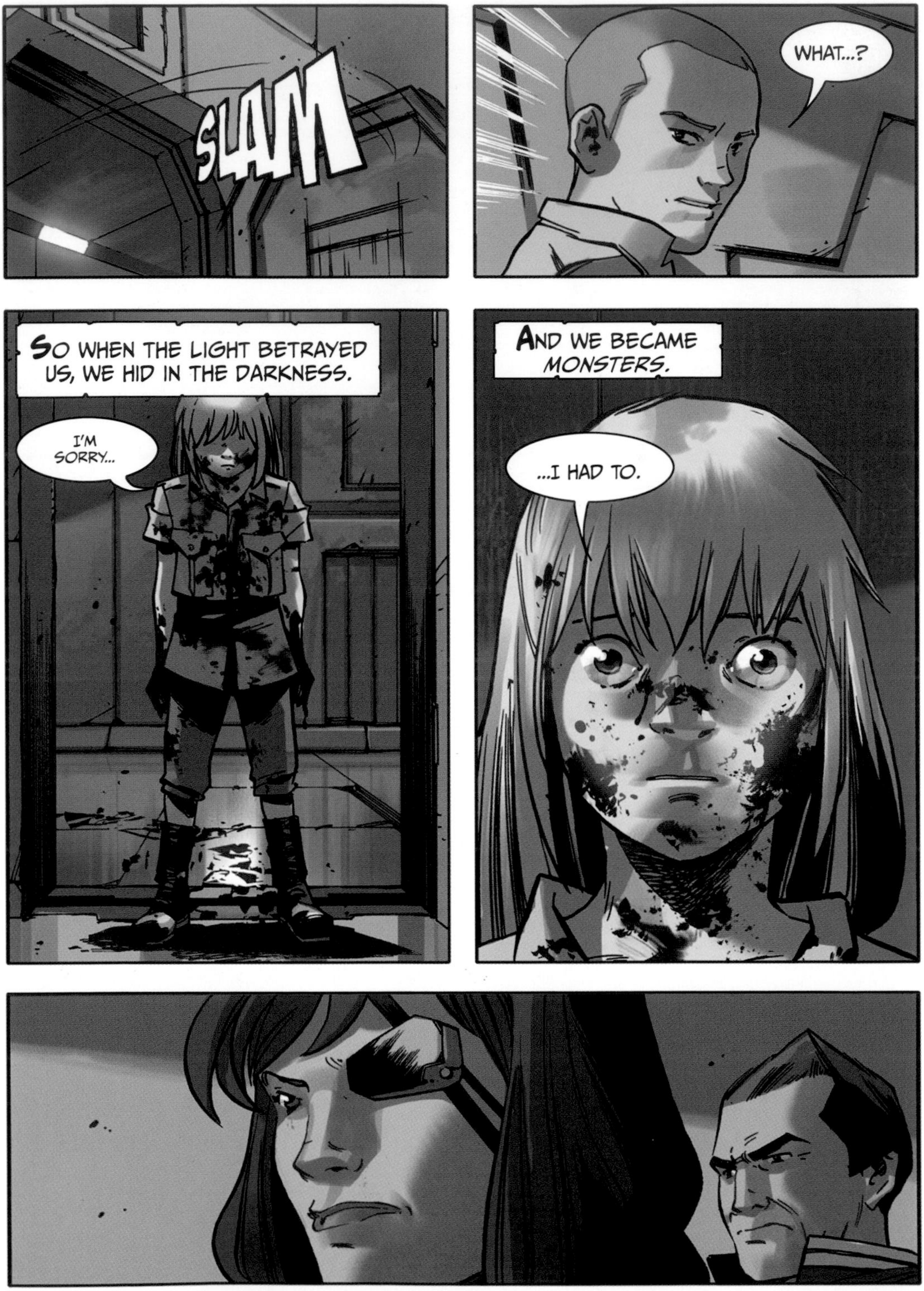
SLAM
WHAT...?
SO WHEN THE LIGHT BETRAYED US, WE HID IN THE DARKNESS.
I'M SORRY...
AND WE BECAME *MONSTERS*.
...I HAD TO.

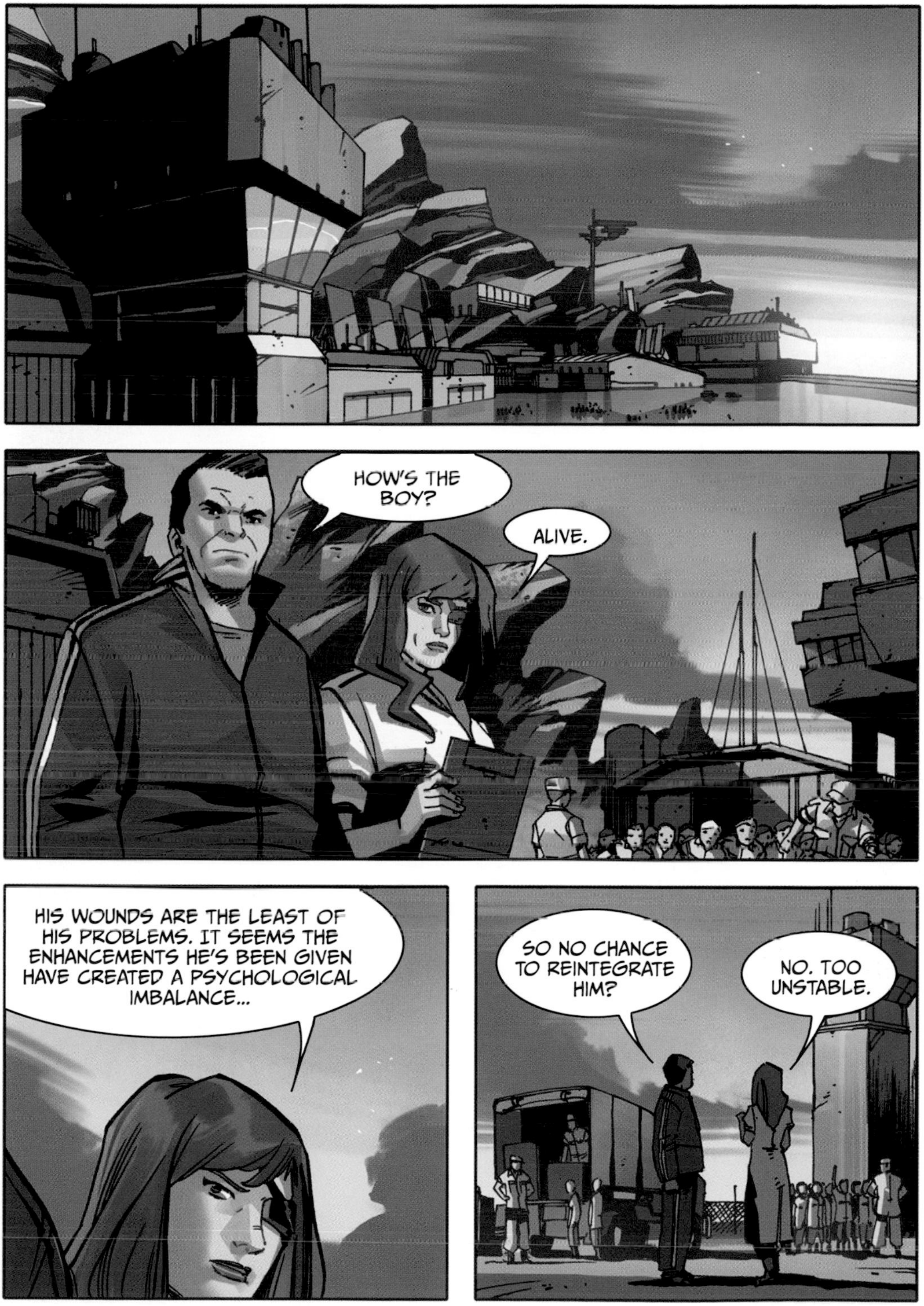
HOW'S THE BOY?
ALIVE.
HIS WOUNDS ARE THE LEAST OF HIS PROBLEMS. IT SEEMS THE ENHANCEMENTS HE'S BEEN GIVEN HAVE CREATED A PSYCHOLOGICAL IMBALANCE...
SO NO CHANCE TO REINTEGRATE HIM?
NO. TOO UNSTABLE.

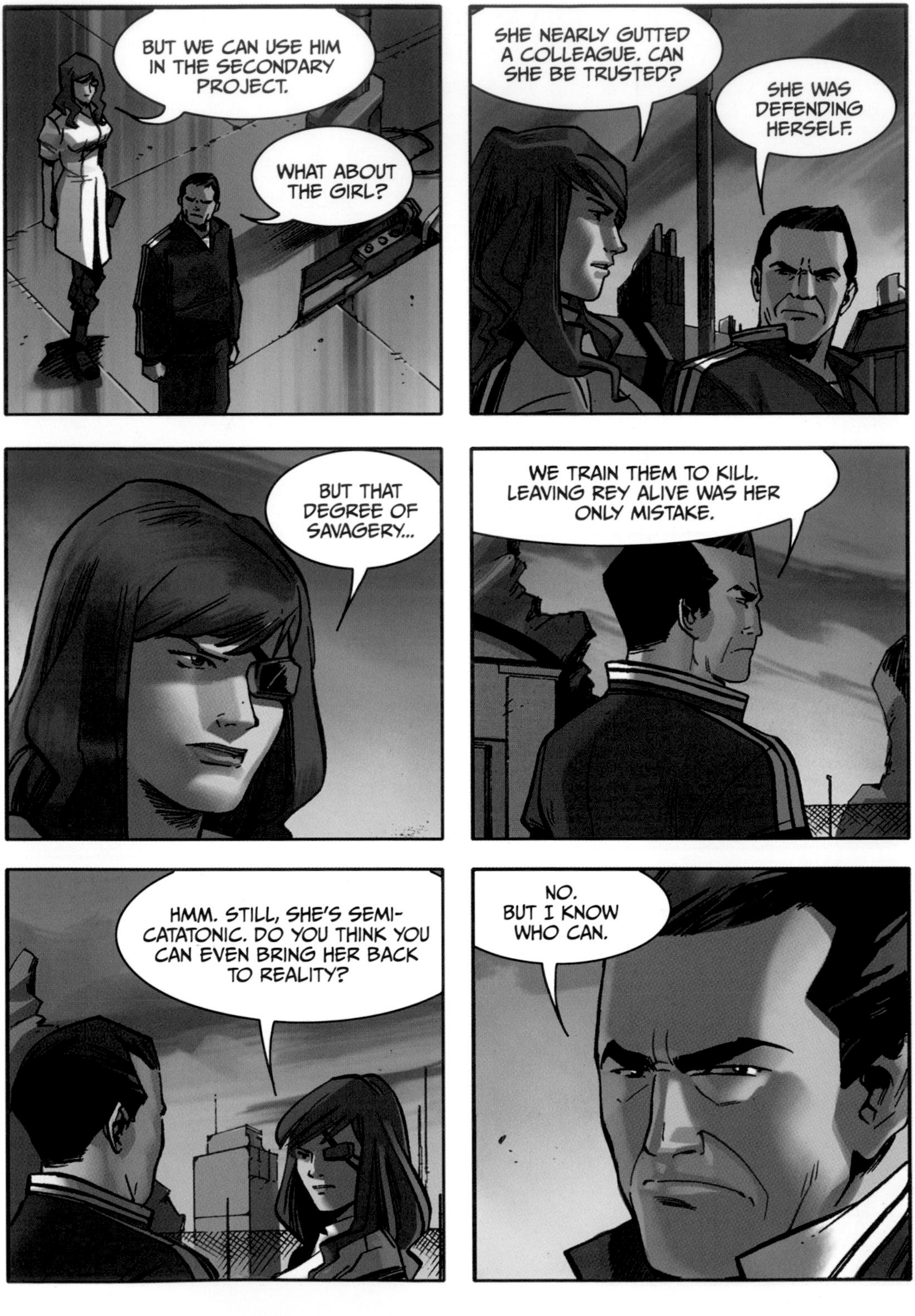
BUT WE CAN USE HIM IN THE SECONDARY PROJECT.
WHAT ABOUT THE GIRL?
SHE NEARLY GUTTED A COLLEAGUE. CAN SHE BE TRUSTED?
SHE WAS DEFENDING HERSELF.
BUT THAT DEGREE OF SAVAGERY...
WE TRAIN THEM TO KILL. LEAVING REY ALIVE WAS HER ONLY MISTAKE.
HMM. STILL, SHE'S SEMI-CATATONIC. DO YOU THINK YOU CAN EVEN BRING HER BACK TO REALITY?
NO. BUT I KNOW WHO CAN.

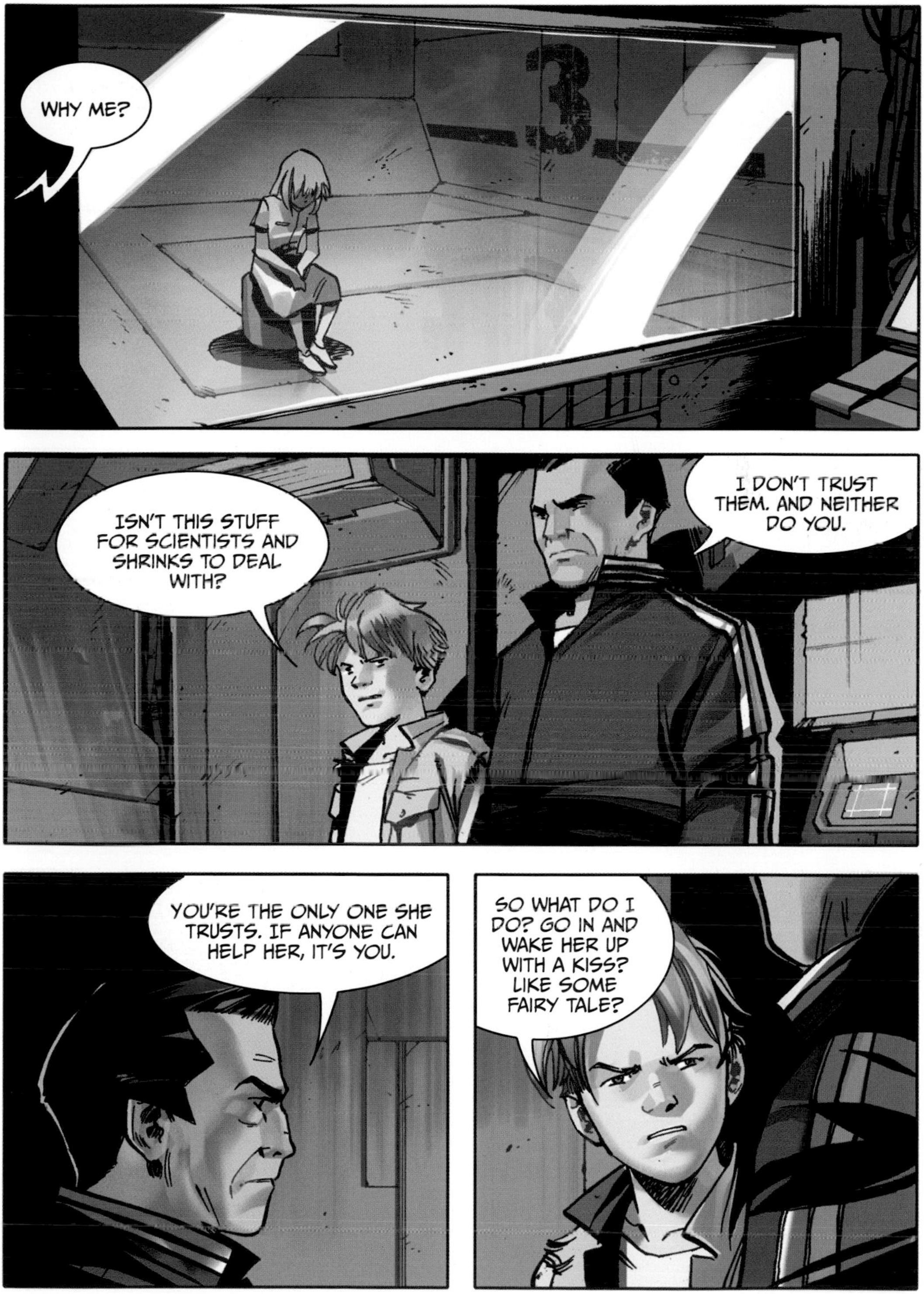
WHY ME?
ISN'T THIS STUFF FOR SCIENTISTS AND SHRINKS TO DEAL WITH?
I DON'T TRUST THEM. AND NEITHER DO YOU.
YOU'RE THE ONLY ONE SHE TRUSTS. IF ANYONE CAN HELP HER, IT'S YOU.
SO WHAT DO I DO? GO IN AND WAKE HER UP WITH A KISS? LIKE SOME FAIRY TALE?

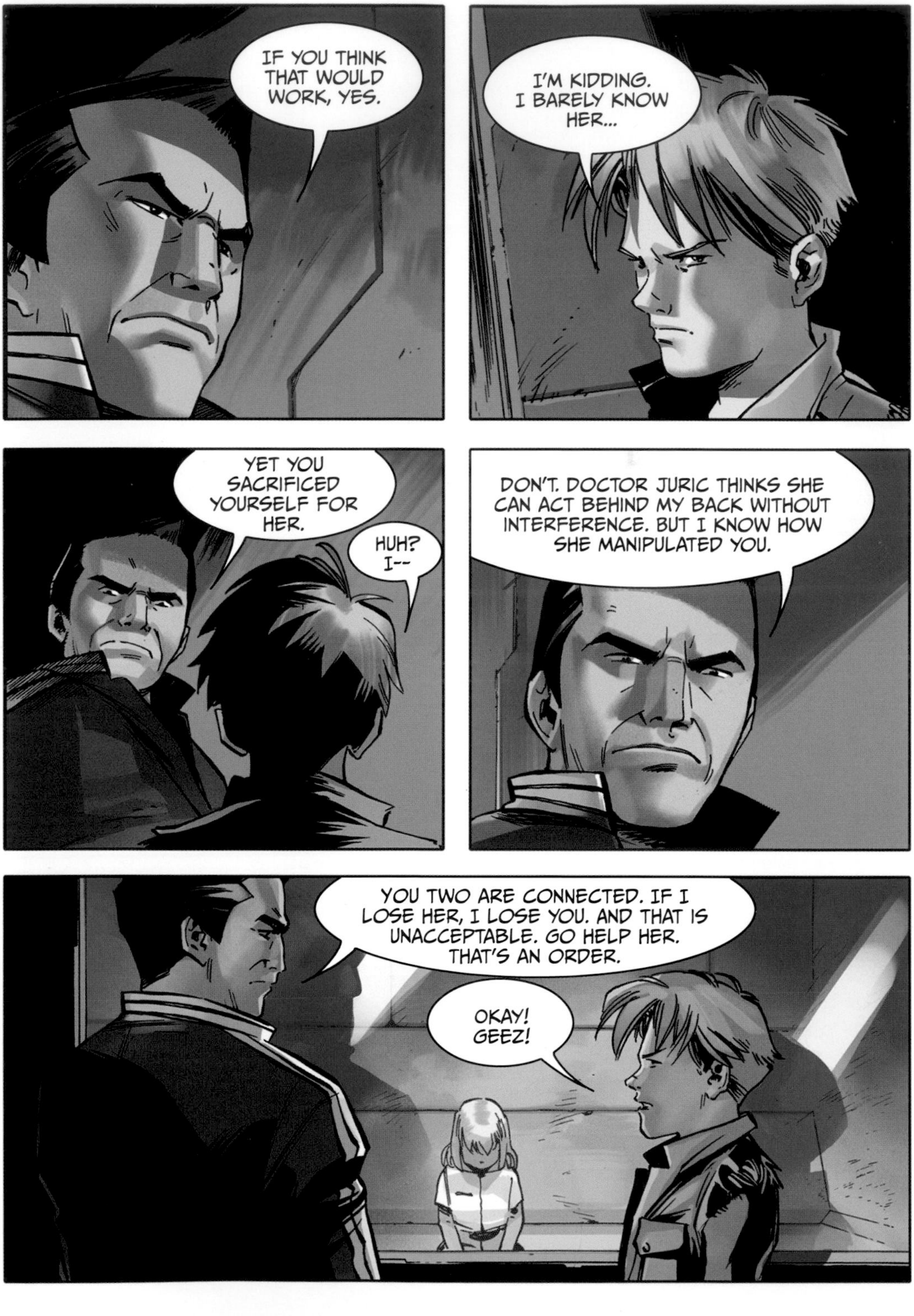
IF YOU THINK THAT WOULD WORK, YES.
I'M KIDDING. I BARELY KNOW HER...
YET YOU SACRIFICED YOURSELF FOR HER.
HUH? I--
DON'T. DOCTOR JURIC THINKS SHE CAN ACT BEHIND MY BACK WITHOUT INTERFERENCE. BUT I KNOW HOW SHE MANIPULATED YOU.
YOU TWO ARE CONNECTED. IF I LOSE HER, I LOSE YOU. AND THAT IS UNACCEPTABLE. GO HELP HER. THAT'S AN ORDER.
OKAY! GEEZ!

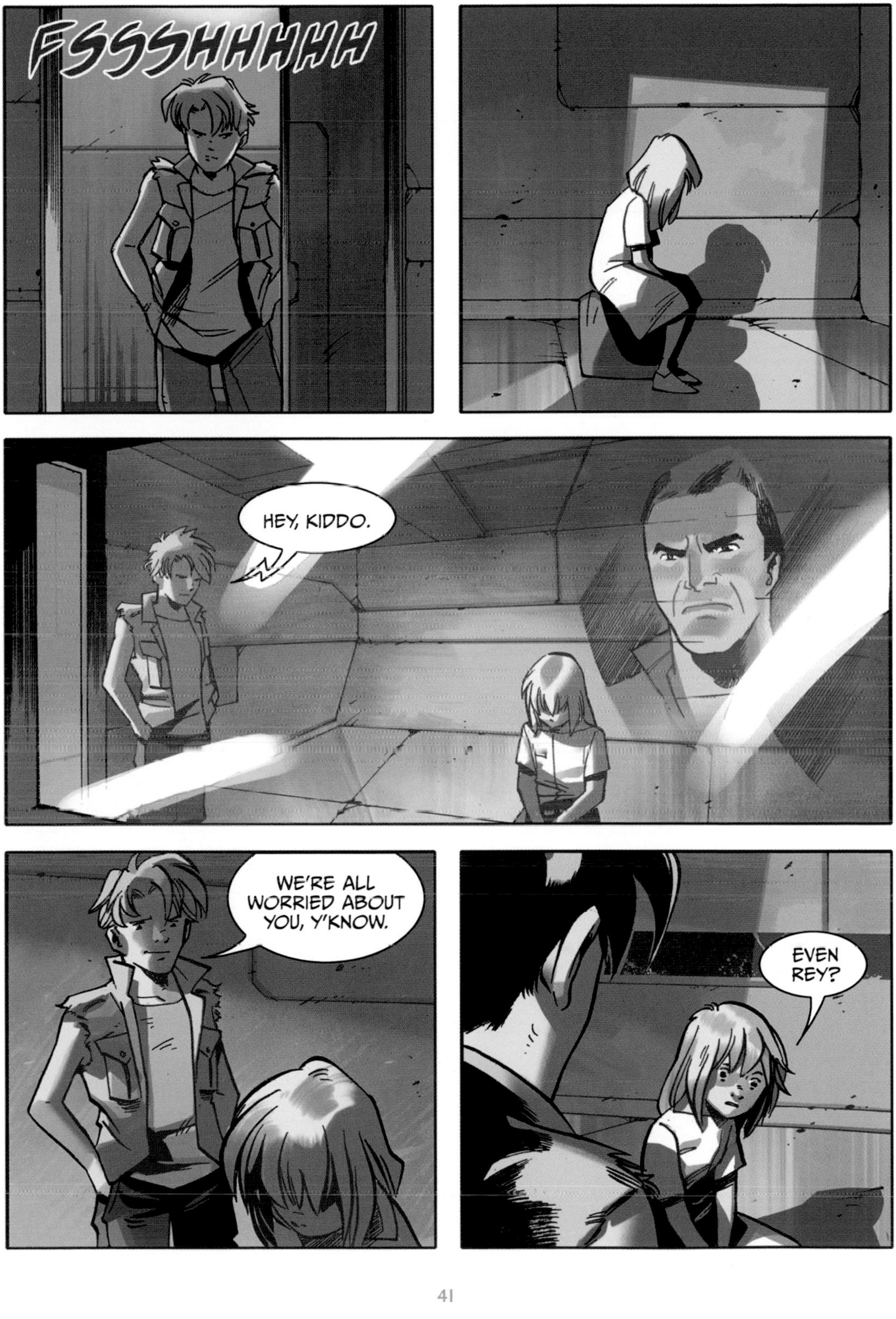
FSSSHHHHH
HEY, KIDDO.
WE'RE ALL WORRIED ABOUT YOU, Y'KNOW.
EVEN REY?

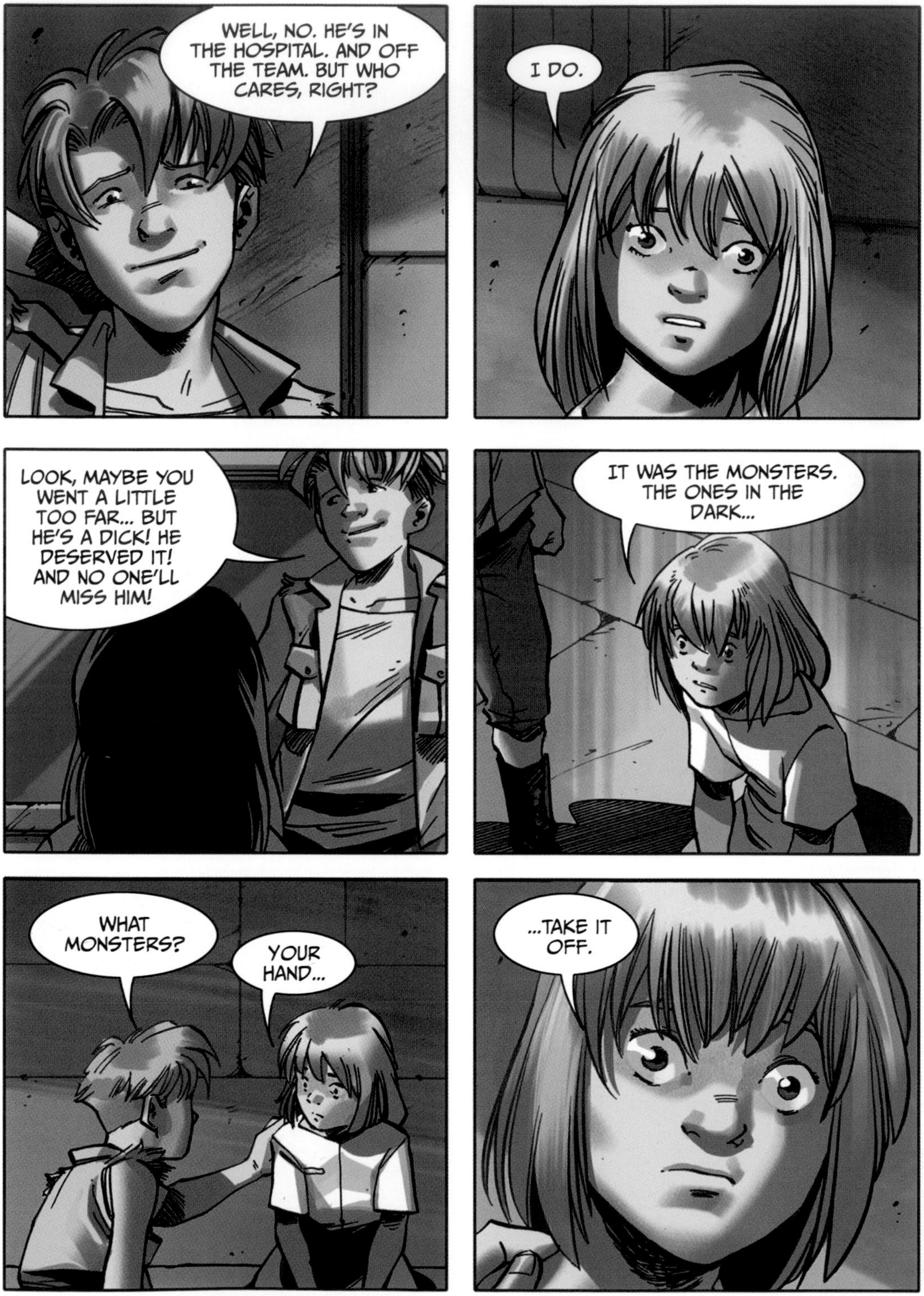
WELL, NO. HE'S IN THE HOSPITAL. AND OFF THE TEAM. BUT WHO CARES, RIGHT?
I DO.
LOOK, MAYBE YOU WENT A LITTLE TOO FAR... BUT HE'S A DICK! HE DESERVED IT! AND NO ONE'LL MISS HIM!
IT WAS THE MONSTERS. THE ONES IN THE DARK...
WHAT MONSTERS?
YOUR HAND...
...TAKE IT OFF.

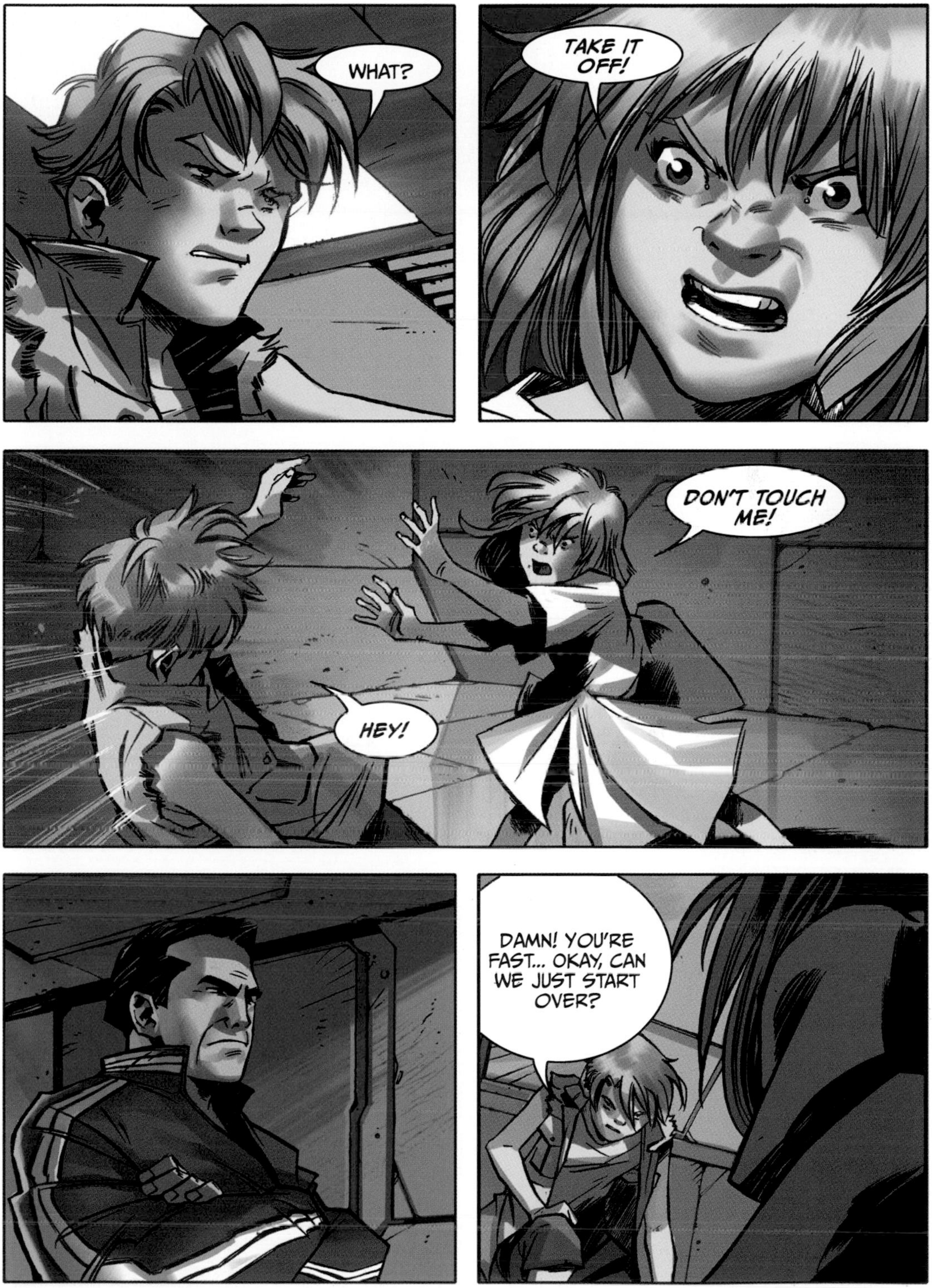
WHAT?
TAKE IT OFF!
DON'T TOUCH ME!
HEY!
DAMN! YOU'RE FAST... OKAY, CAN WE JUST START OVER?

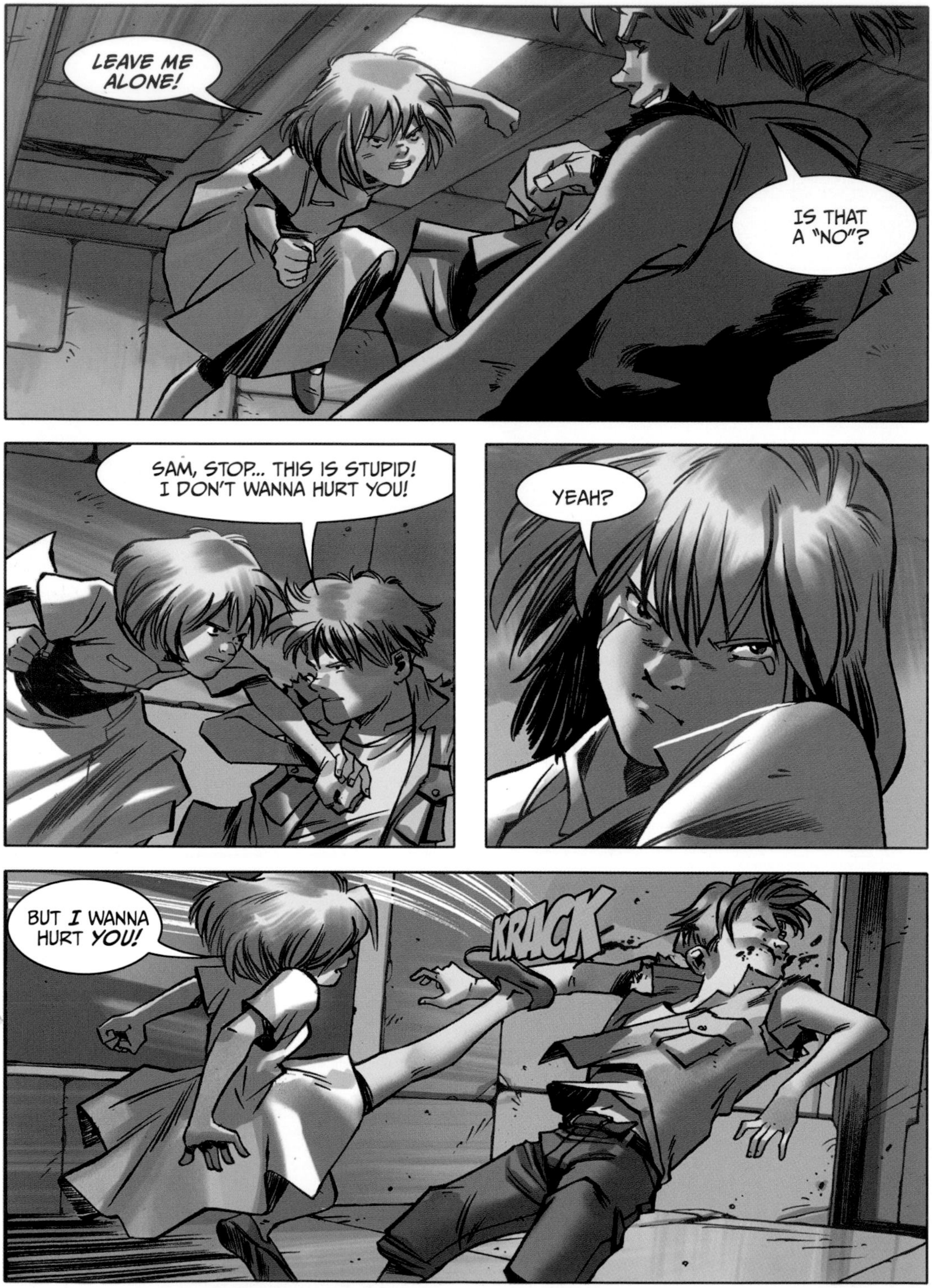
LEAVE ME ALONE!
IS THAT A "NO"?
SAM, STOP... THIS IS STUPID! I DON'T WANNA HURT YOU!
YEAH?
BUT I WANNA HURT YOU!
KRACK

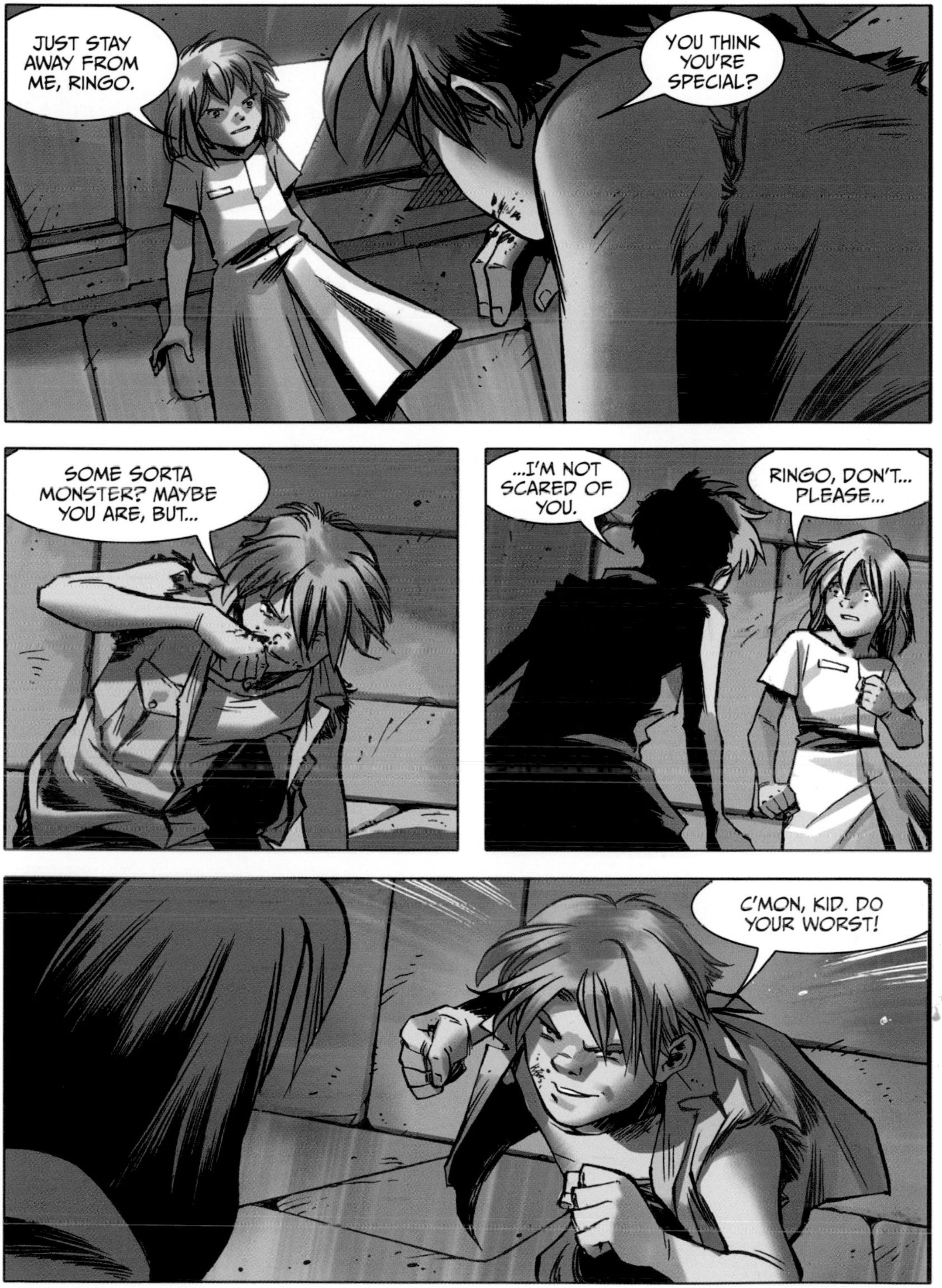
JUST STAY AWAY FROM ME, RINGO.
YOU THINK YOU'RE SPECIAL?
SOME SORTA MONSTER? MAYBE YOU ARE, BUT...
...I'M NOT SCARED OF YOU.
RINGO, DON'T... PLEASE...
C'MON, KID. DO YOUR WORST!

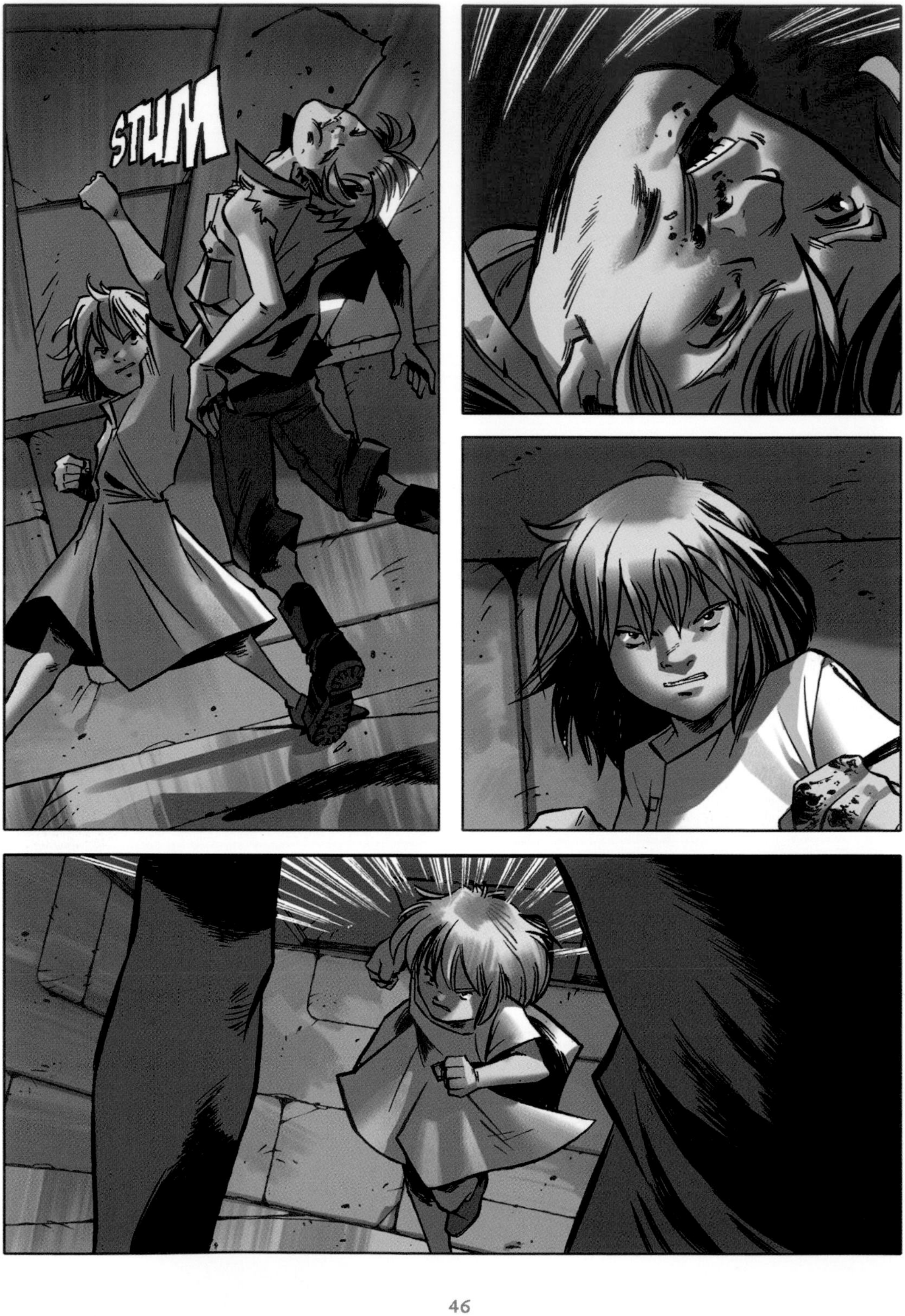
STUM

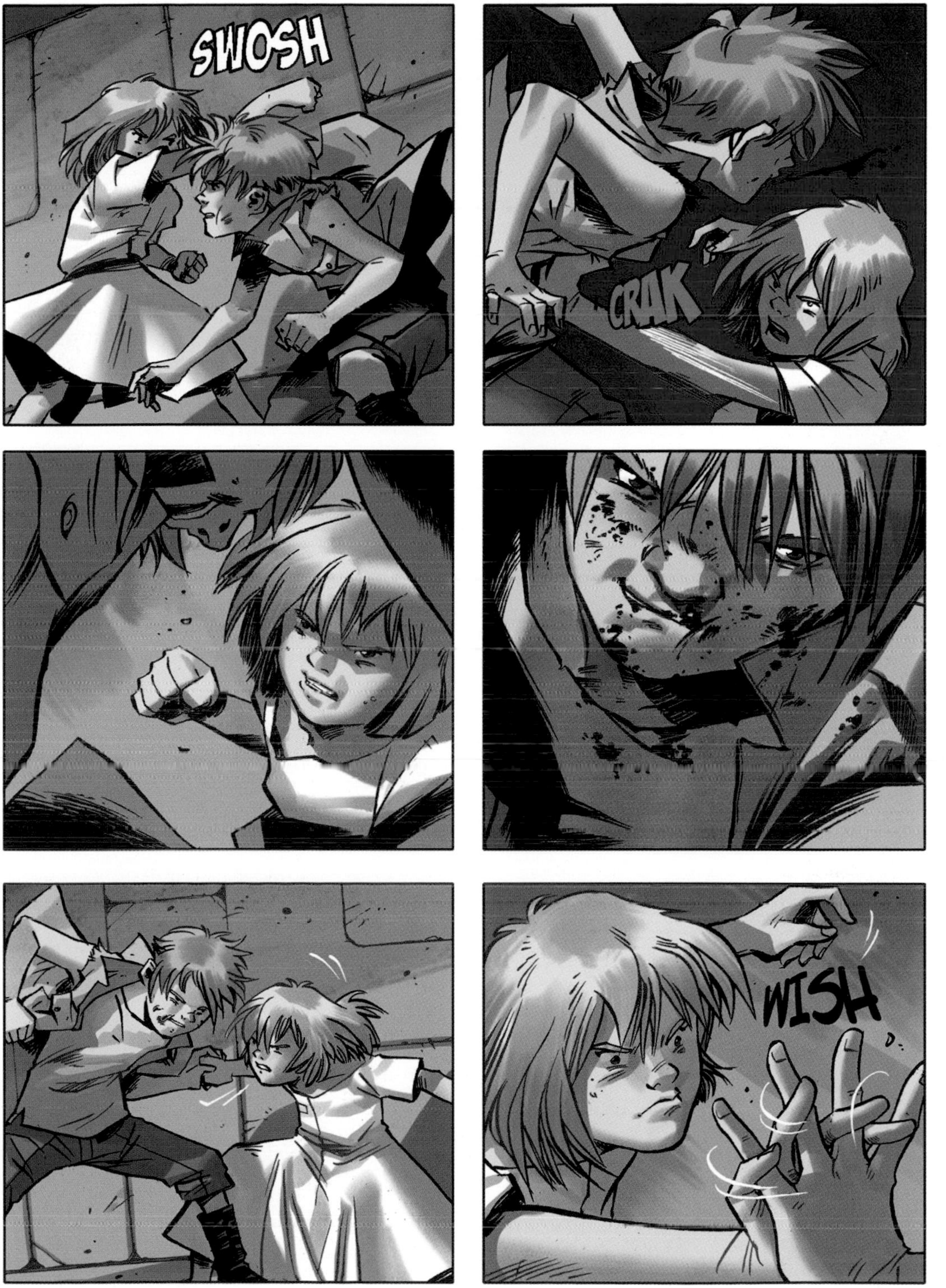
SWOSH
CRAK
WISH

CRAK
STUM

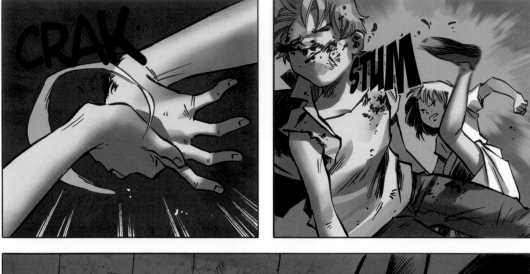

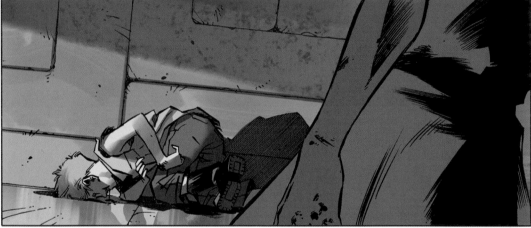

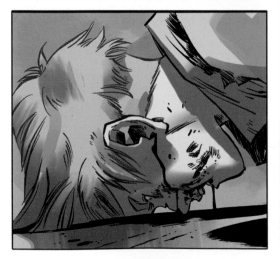

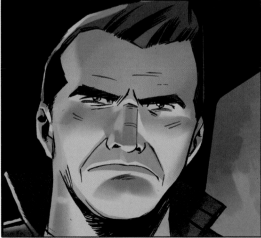

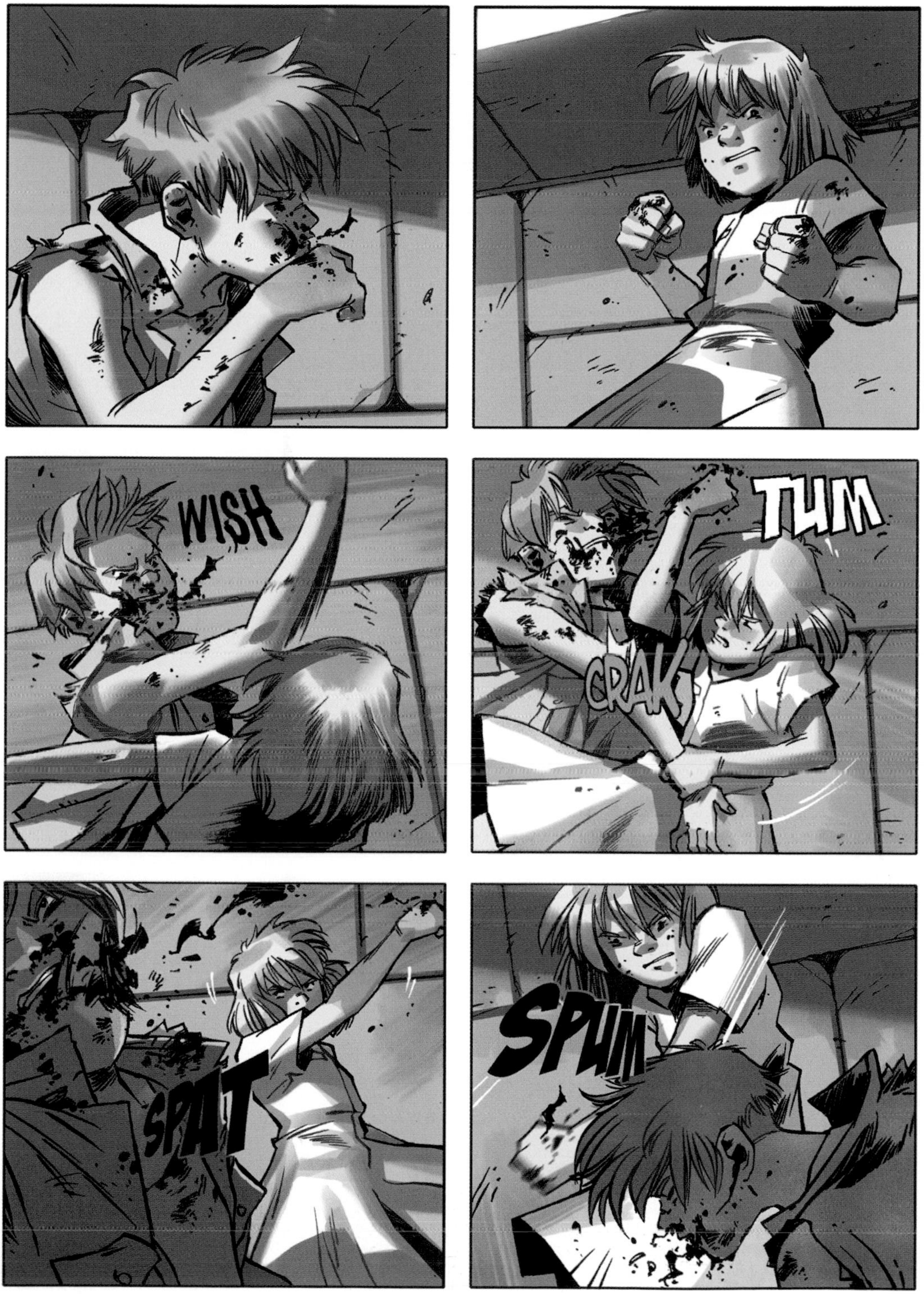
WISH
TUM
CRAK
SPAT
SPUM

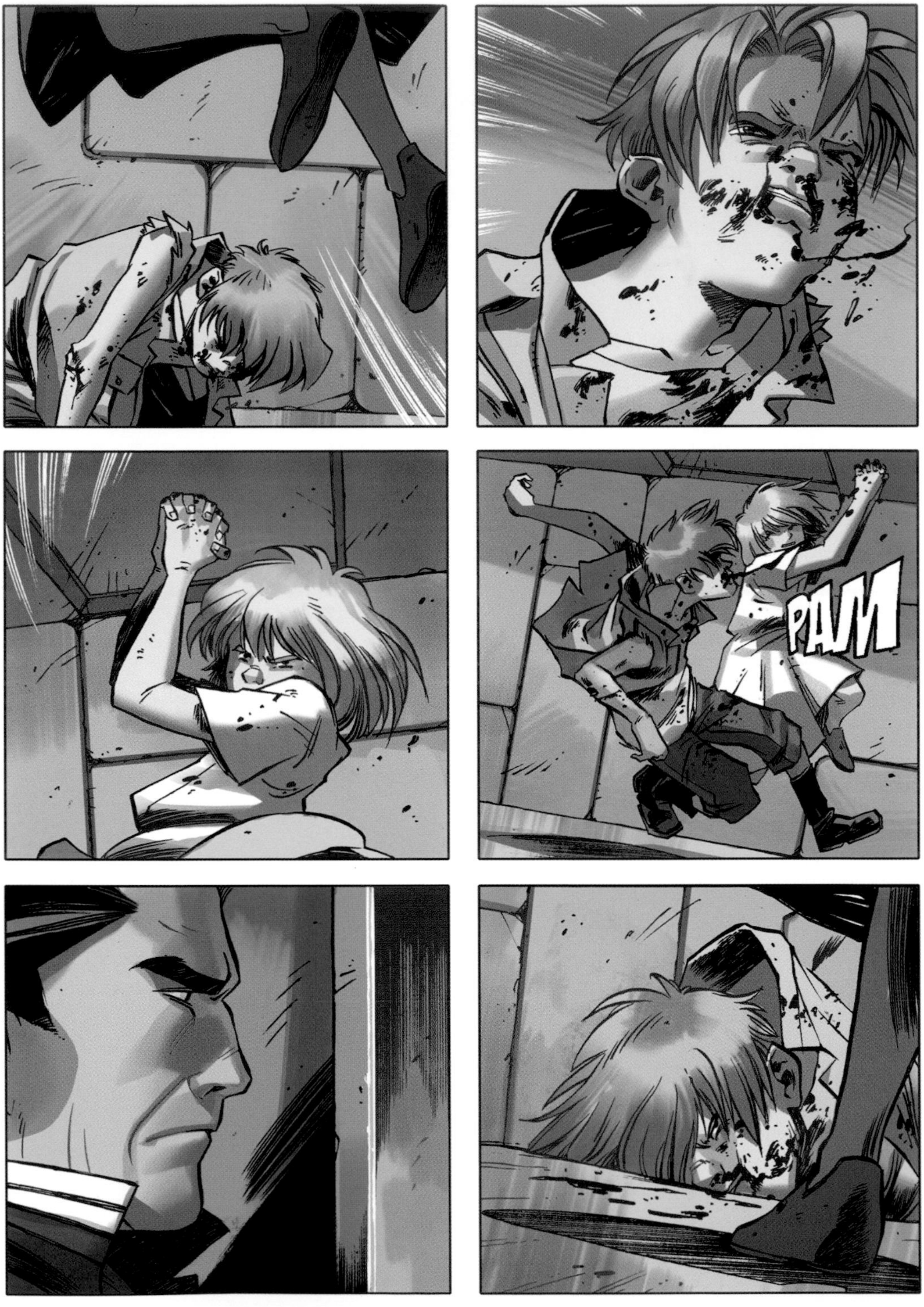
PAM

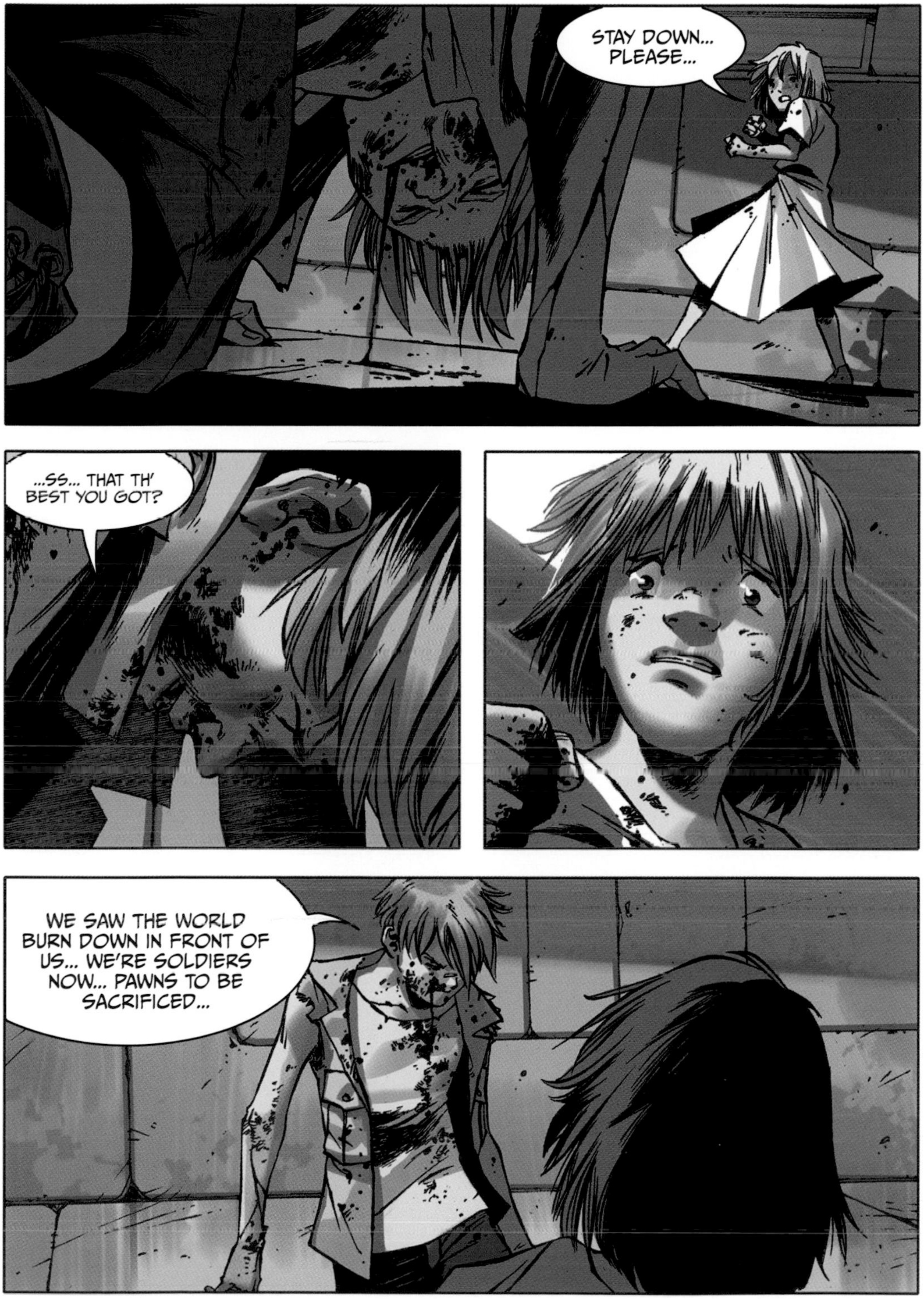
STAY DOWN... PLEASE...
...SS... THAT TH' BEST YOU GOT?
WE SAW THE WORLD BURN DOWN IN FRONT OF US... WE'RE SOLDIERS NOW... PAWNS TO BE SACRIFICED...

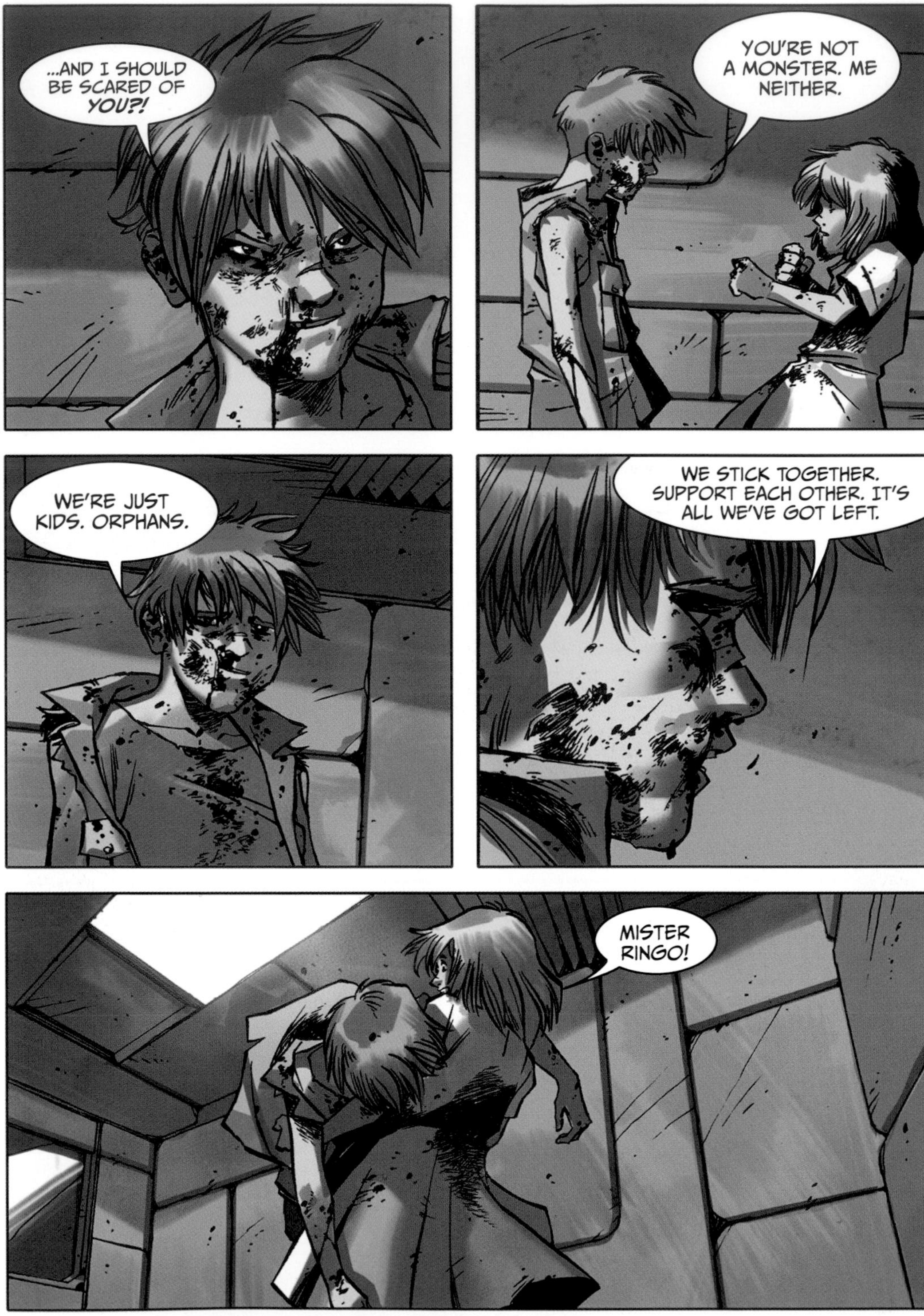
...AND I SHOULD BE SCARED OF *YOU?!*
YOU'RE NOT A MONSTER. ME NEITHER.
WE'RE JUST KIDS. ORPHANS.
WE STICK TOGETHER. SUPPORT EACH OTHER. IT'S ALL WE'VE GOT LEFT.
MISTER RINGO!

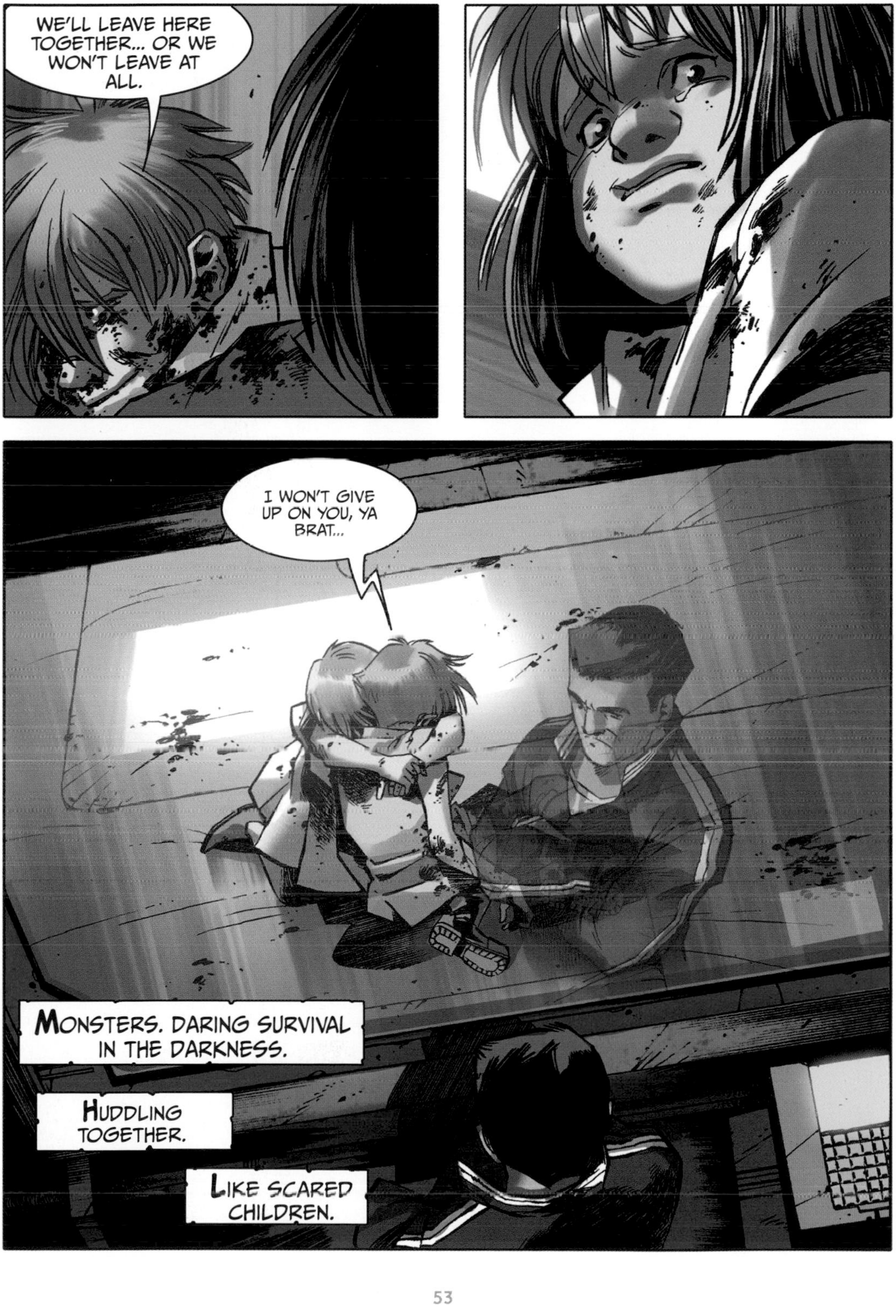
WE'LL LEAVE HERE TOGETHER... OR WE WON'T LEAVE AT ALL.
I WON'T GIVE UP ON YOU, YA BRAT...
MONSTERS. DARING SURVIVAL IN THE DARKNESS.
HUDDLING TOGETHER.
LIKE SCARED CHILDREN.

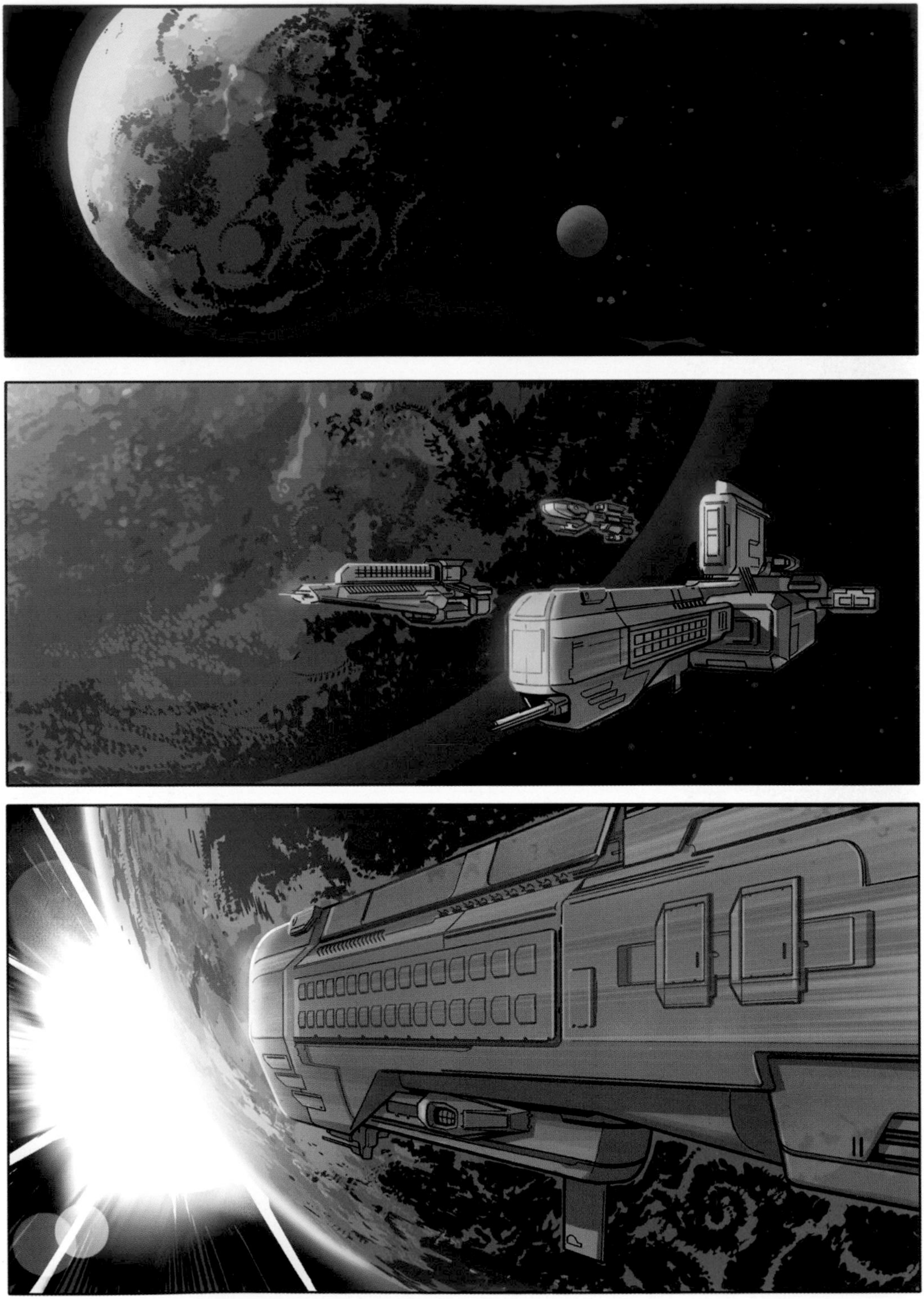

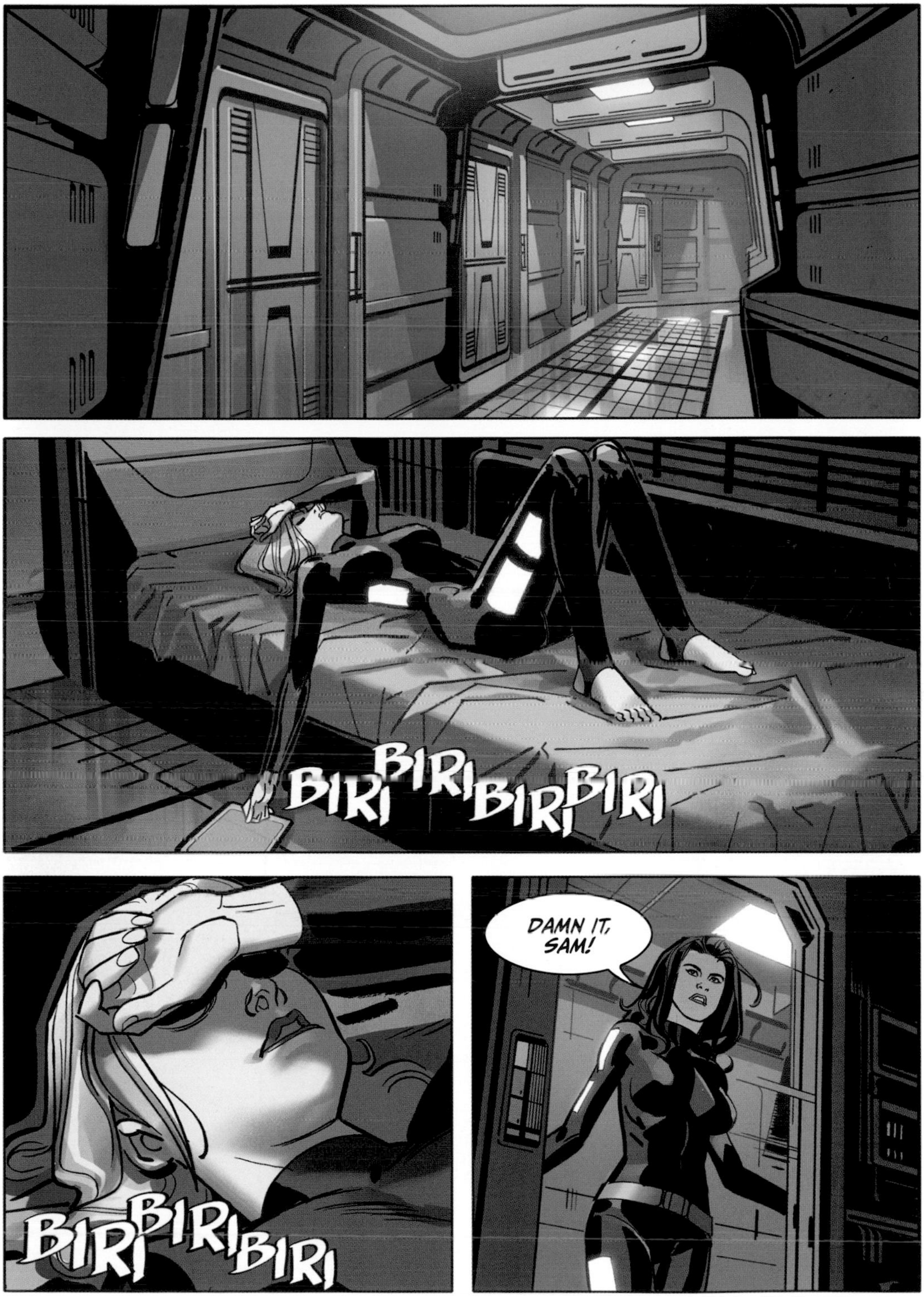
BIRI BIRI BIRI BIRI BIRI
BIRI BIRI BIRI BIRI
DAMN IT, SAM!

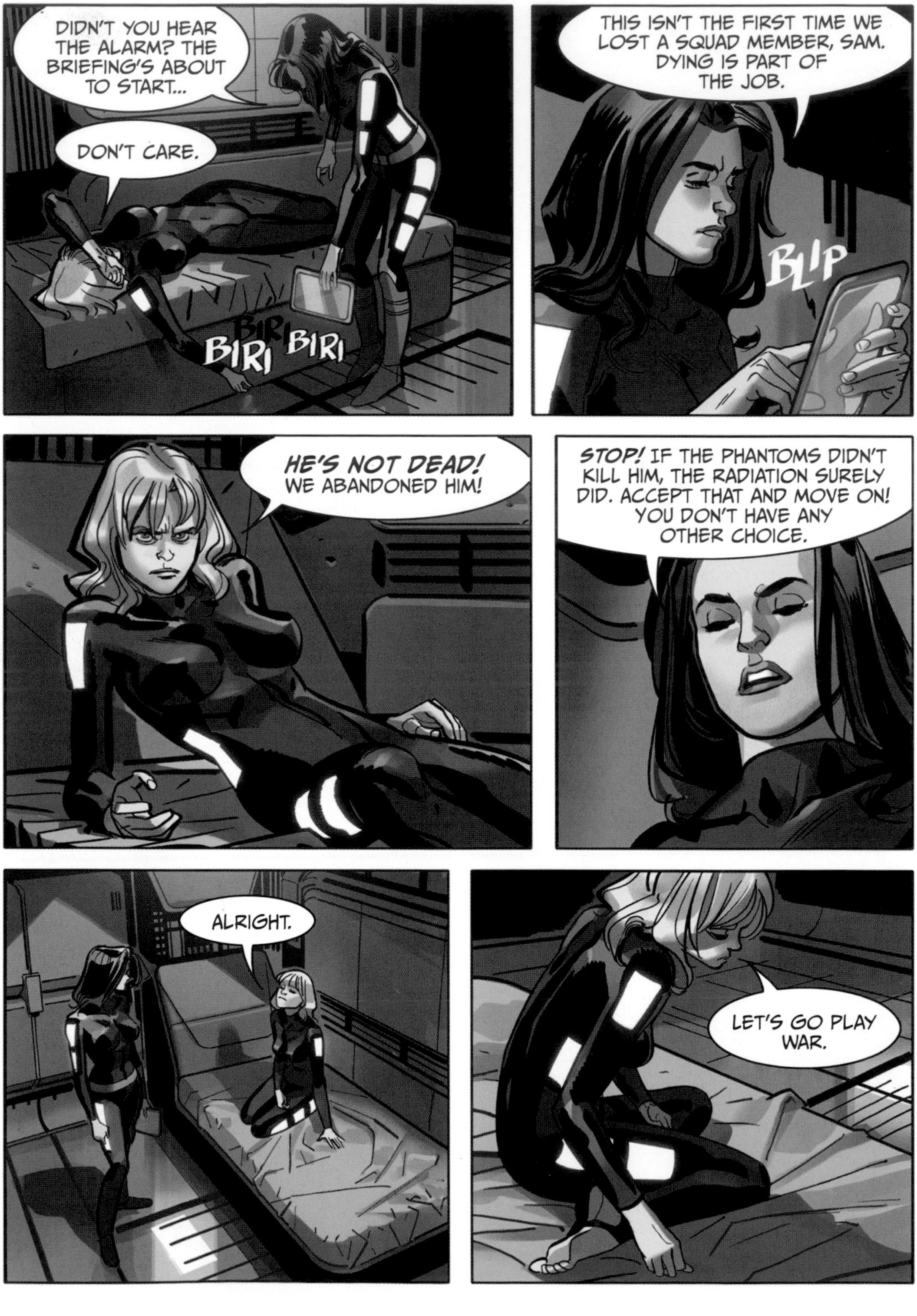
DIDN'T YOU HEAR THE ALARM? THE BRIEFING'S ABOUT TO START...
DON'T CARE.
BIRI BIRI BIRI
THIS ISN'T THE FIRST TIME WE LOST A SQUAD MEMBER, SAM. DYING IS PART OF THE JOB.
BLIP
HE'S NOT DEAD! WE ABANDONED HIM!
STOP! IF THE PHANTOMS DIDN'T KILL HIM, THE RADIATION SURELY DID. ACCEPT THAT AND MOVE ON! YOU DON'T HAVE ANY OTHER CHOICE.
ALRIGHT.
LET'S GO PLAY WAR.

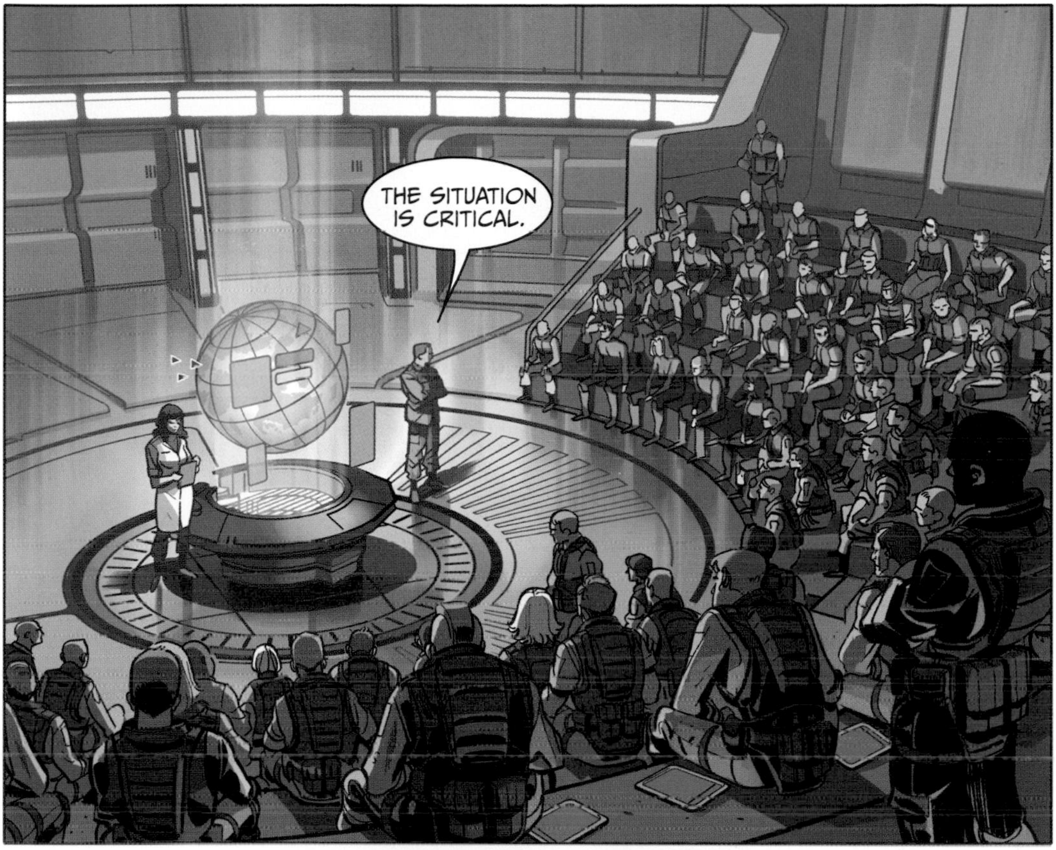
THE SITUATION IS CRITICAL.

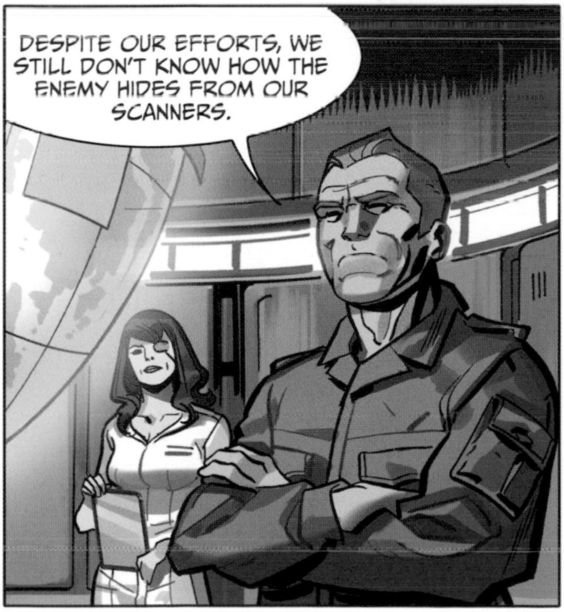
DESPITE OUR EFFORTS, WE STILL DON'T KNOW HOW THE ENEMY HIDES FROM OUR SCANNERS.

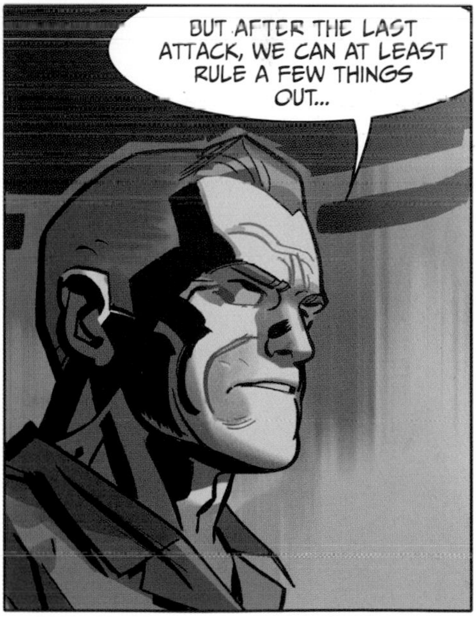
BUT AFTER THE LAST ATTACK, WE CAN AT LEAST RULE A FEW THINGS OUT...

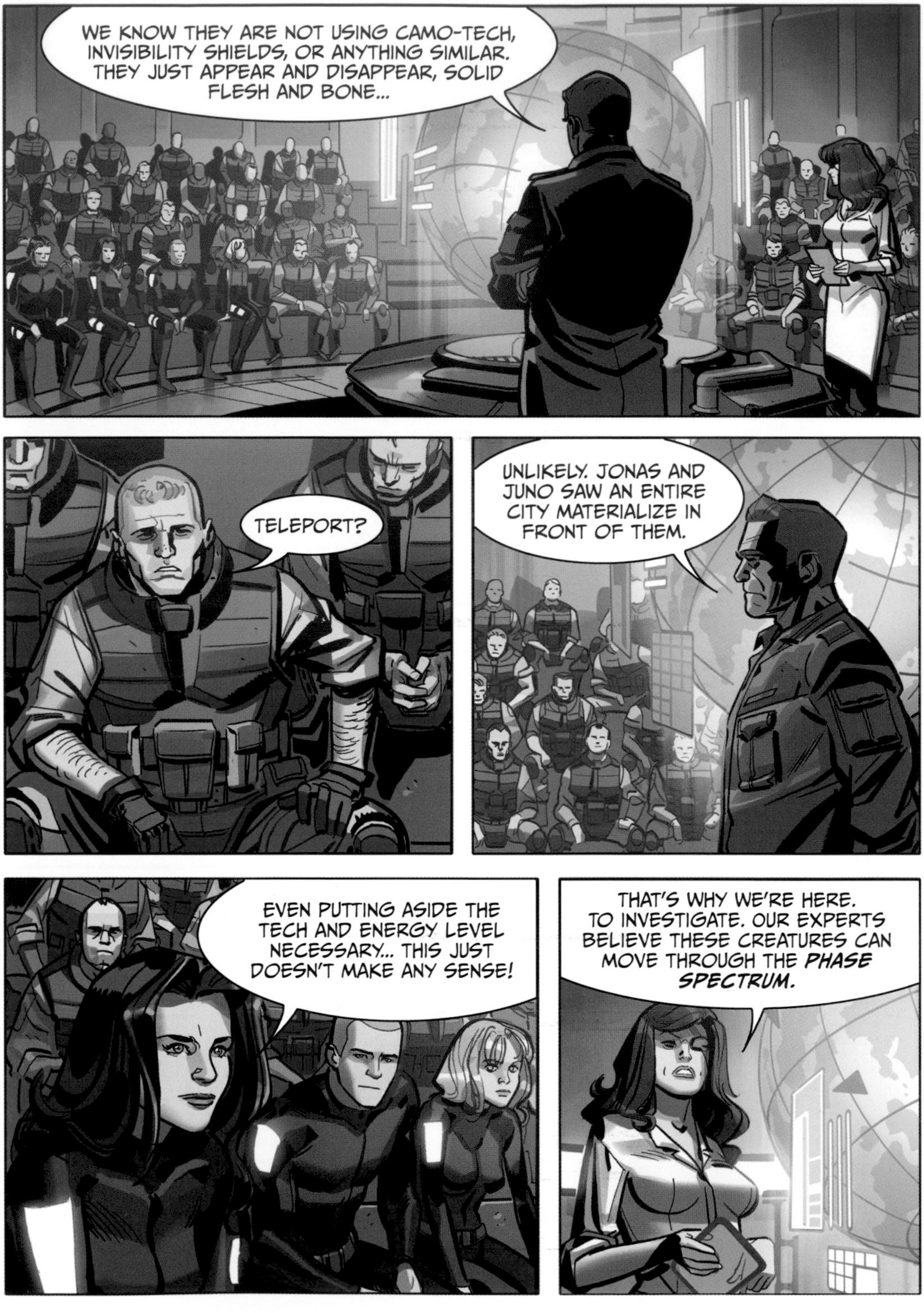
WE KNOW THEY ARE NOT USING CAMO-TECH, INVISIBILITY SHIELDS, OR ANYTHING SIMILAR. THEY JUST APPEAR AND DISAPPEAR, SOLID FLESH AND BONE...
TELEPORT?
UNLIKELY. JONAS AND JUNO SAW AN ENTIRE CITY MATERIALIZE IN FRONT OF THEM.
EVEN PUTTING ASIDE THE TECH AND ENERGY LEVEL NECESSARY... THIS JUST DOESN'T MAKE ANY SENSE!
THAT'S WHY WE'RE HERE. TO INVESTIGATE. OUR EXPERTS BELIEVE THESE CREATURES CAN MOVE THROUGH THE *PHASE SPECTRUM.*

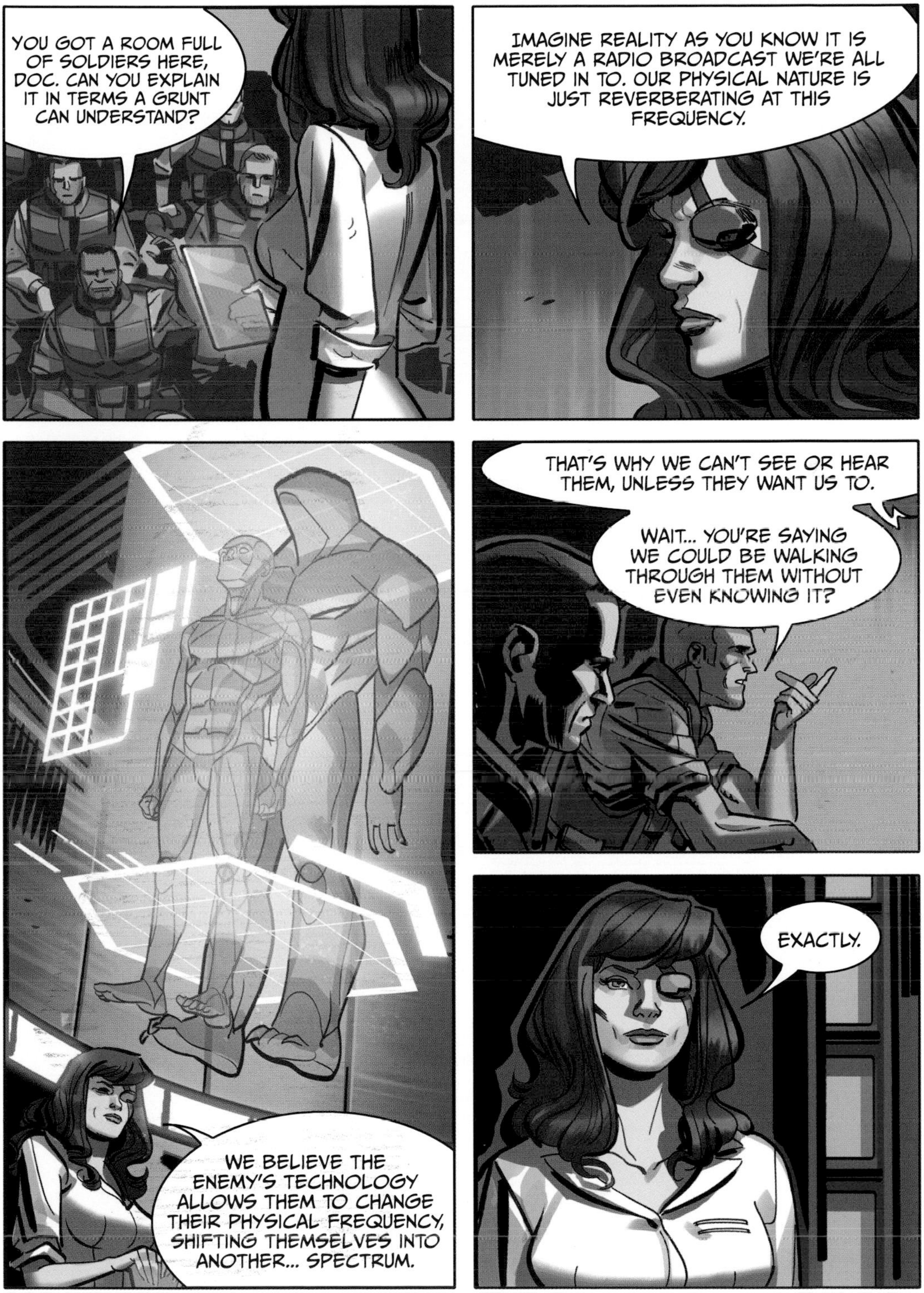
YOU GOT A ROOM FULL OF SOLDIERS HERE, DOC. CAN YOU EXPLAIN IT IN TERMS A GRUNT CAN UNDERSTAND?
IMAGINE REALITY AS YOU KNOW IT IS MERELY A RADIO BROADCAST WE'RE ALL TUNED IN TO. OUR PHYSICAL NATURE IS JUST REVERBERATING AT THIS FREQUENCY.
WE BELIEVE THE ENEMY'S TECHNOLOGY ALLOWS THEM TO CHANGE THEIR PHYSICAL FREQUENCY, SHIFTING THEMSELVES INTO ANOTHER... SPECTRUM.
THAT'S WHY WE CAN'T SEE OR HEAR THEM, UNLESS THEY WANT US TO.
WAIT... YOU'RE SAYING WE COULD BE WALKING THROUGH THEM WITHOUT EVEN KNOWING IT?
EXACTLY.

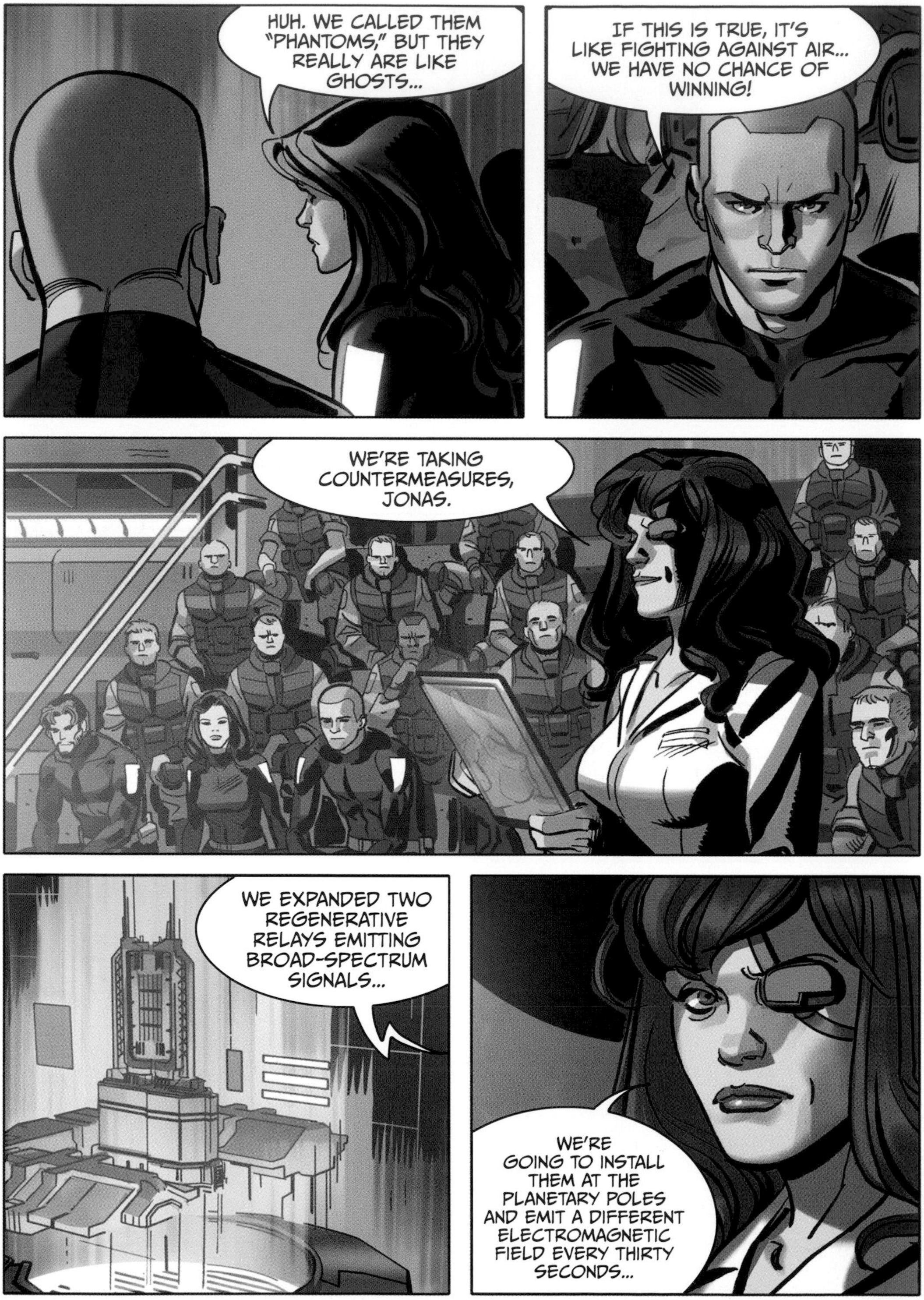
HUH. WE CALLED THEM "PHANTOMS," BUT THEY REALLY ARE LIKE GHOSTS...
IF THIS IS TRUE, IT'S LIKE FIGHTING AGAINST AIR... WE HAVE NO CHANCE OF WINNING!
WE'RE TAKING COUNTERMEASURES, JONAS.
WE EXPANDED TWO REGENERATIVE RELAYS EMITTING BROAD-SPECTRUM SIGNALS...
WE'RE GOING TO INSTALL THEM AT THE PLANETARY POLES AND EMIT A DIFFERENT ELECTROMAGNETIC FIELD EVERY THIRTY SECONDS...

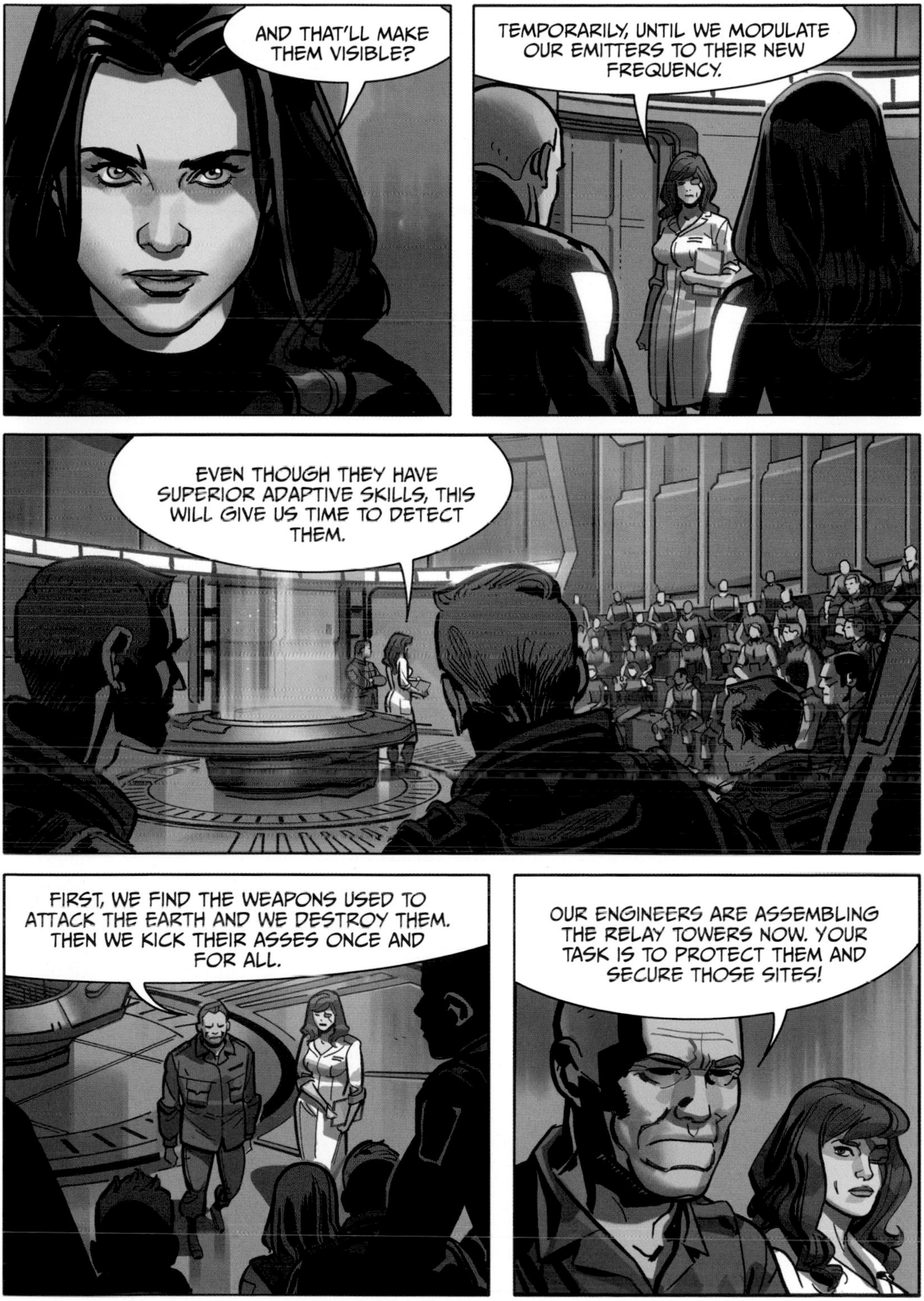
AND THAT'LL MAKE THEM VISIBLE?
TEMPORARILY, UNTIL WE MODULATE OUR EMITTERS TO THEIR NEW FREQUENCY.
EVEN THOUGH THEY HAVE SUPERIOR ADAPTIVE SKILLS, THIS WILL GIVE US TIME TO DETECT THEM.
FIRST, WE FIND THE WEAPONS USED TO ATTACK THE EARTH AND WE DESTROY THEM. THEN WE KICK THEIR ASSES ONCE AND FOR ALL.
OUR ENGINEERS ARE ASSEMBLING THE RELAY TOWERS NOW. YOUR TASK IS TO PROTECT THEM AND SECURE THOSE SITES!

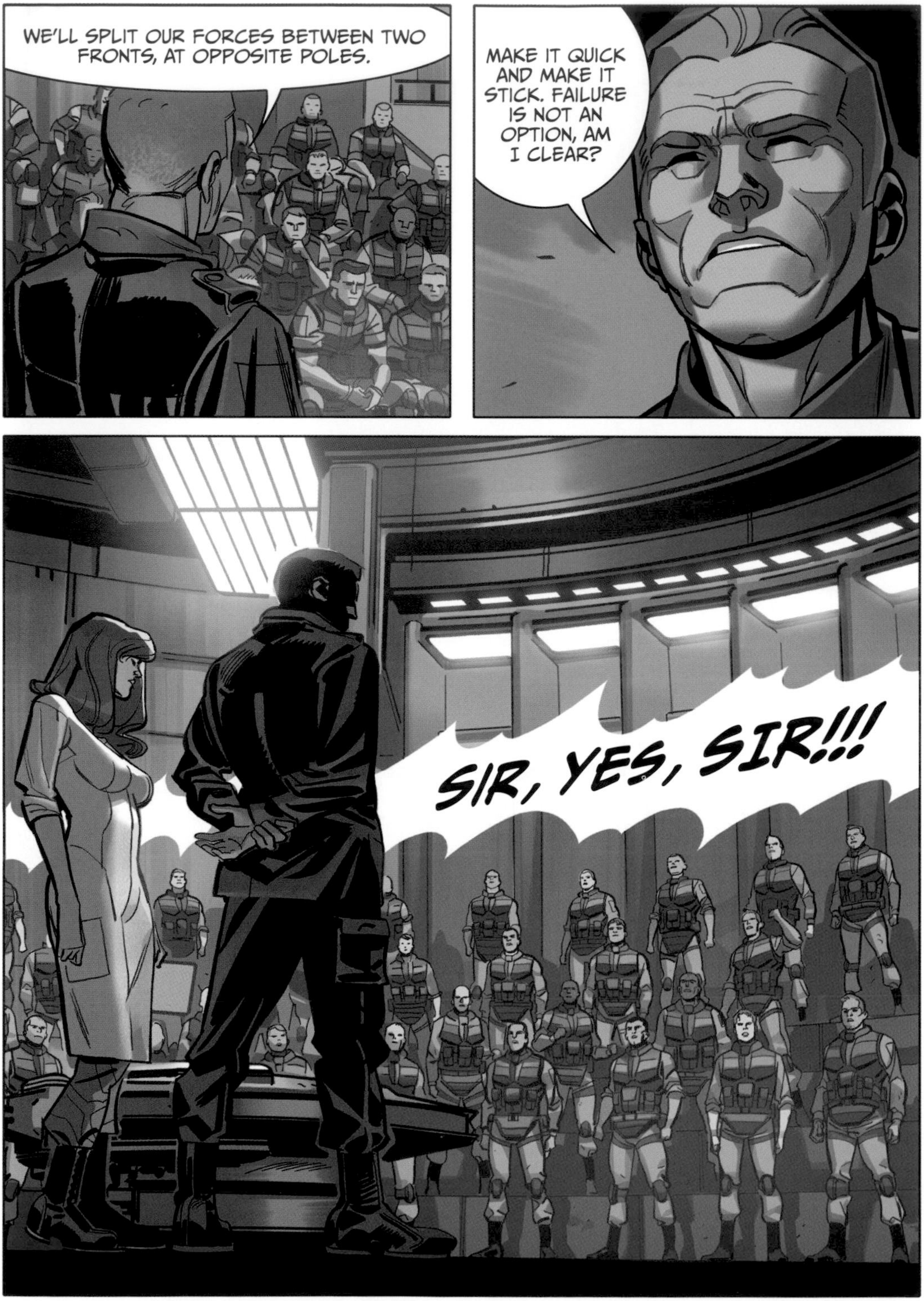
WE'LL SPLIT OUR FORCES BETWEEN TWO FRONTS, AT OPPOSITE POLES.
MAKE IT QUICK AND MAKE IT STICK. FAILURE IS NOT AN OPTION, AM I CLEAR?
SIR, YES, SIR!!!

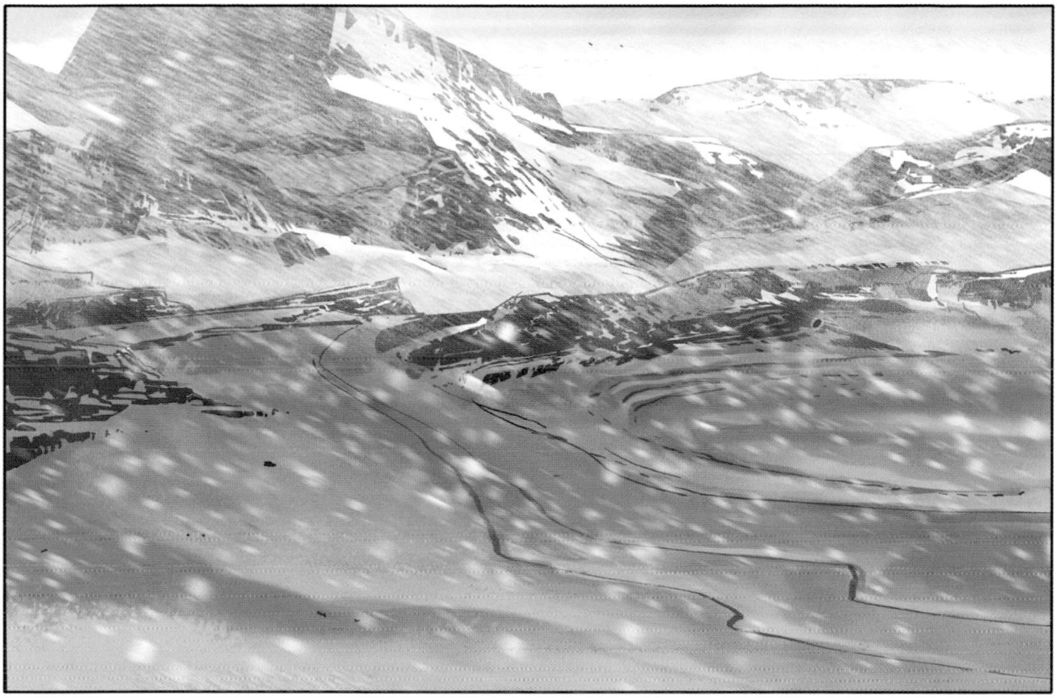

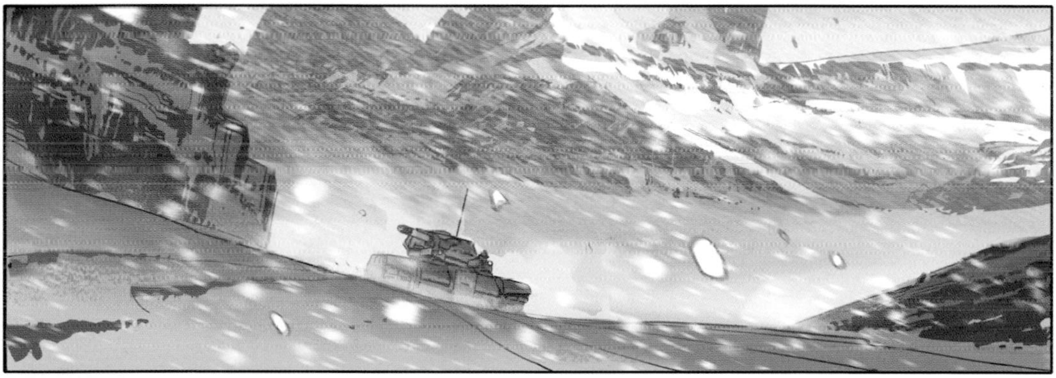

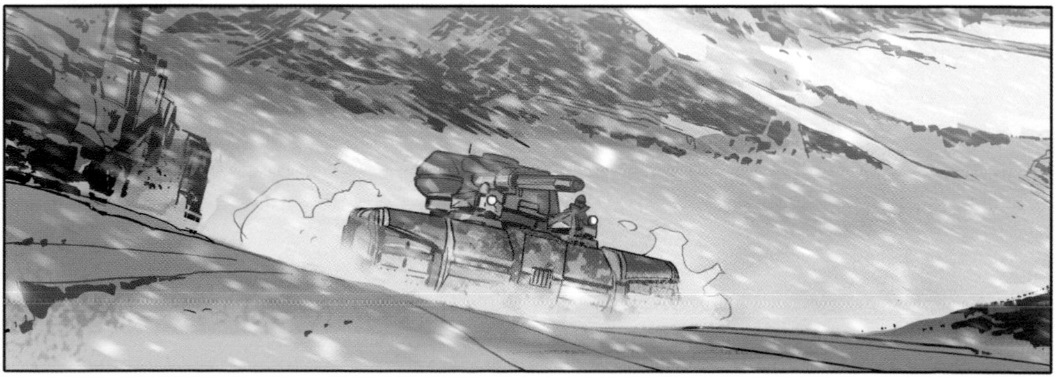

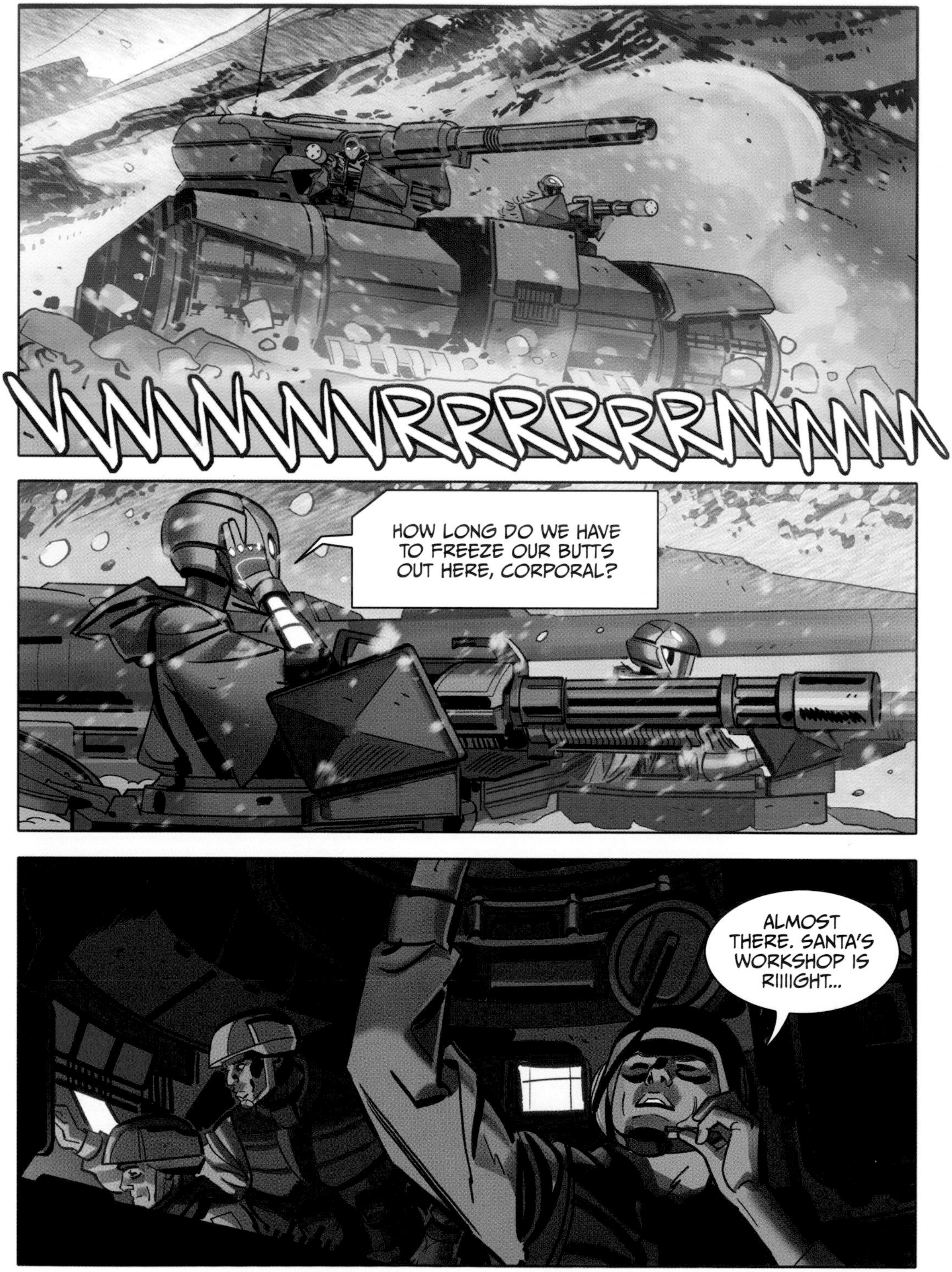
VVVVVVVVRRRRRRRMMMMM
HOW LONG DO WE HAVE TO FREEZE OUR BUTTS OUT HERE, CORPORAL?
ALMOST THERE. SANTA'S WORKSHOP IS RIIIIGHT...

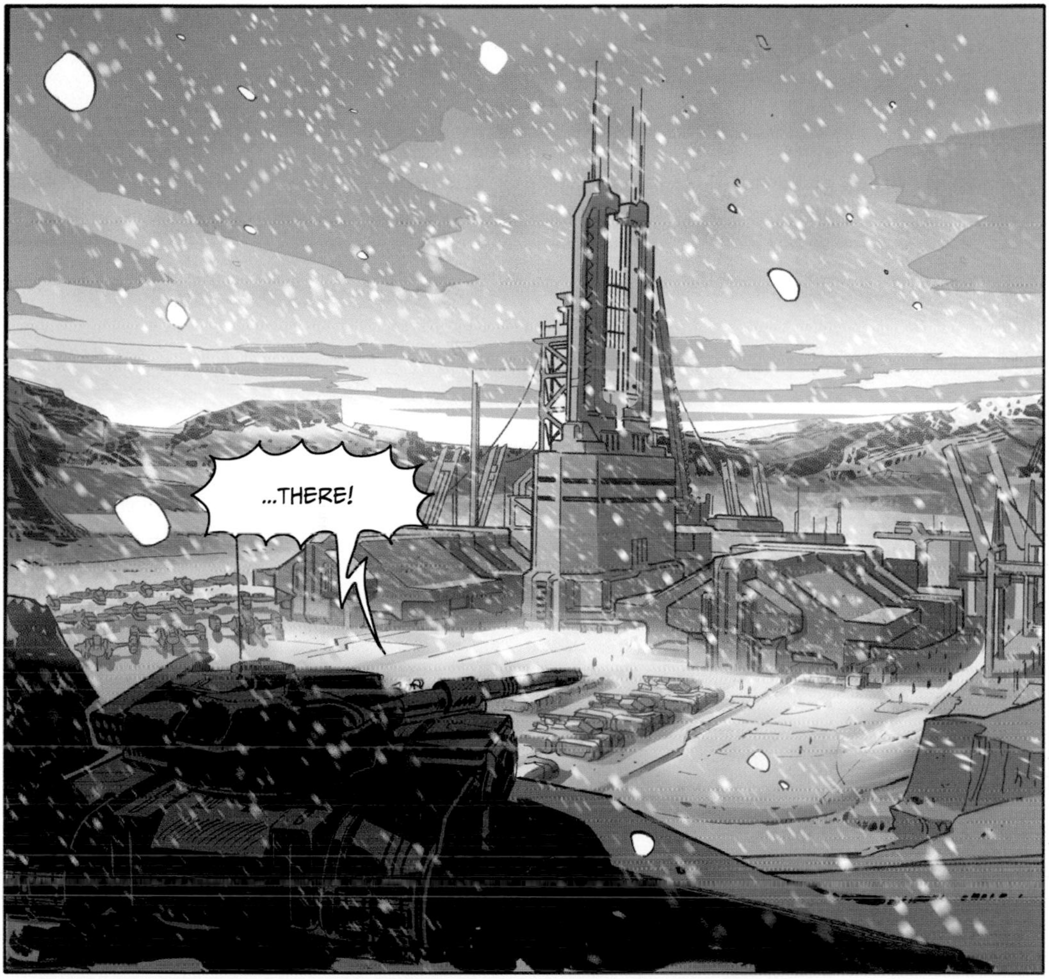
...THERE!

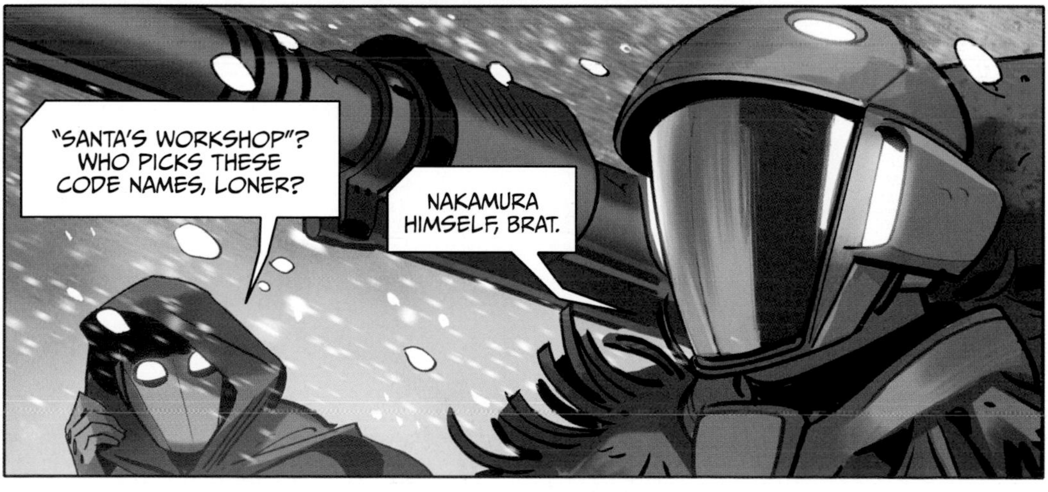
"SANTA'S WORKSHOP"? WHO PICKS THESE CODE NAMES, LONER?
NAKAMURA HIMSELF, BRAT.

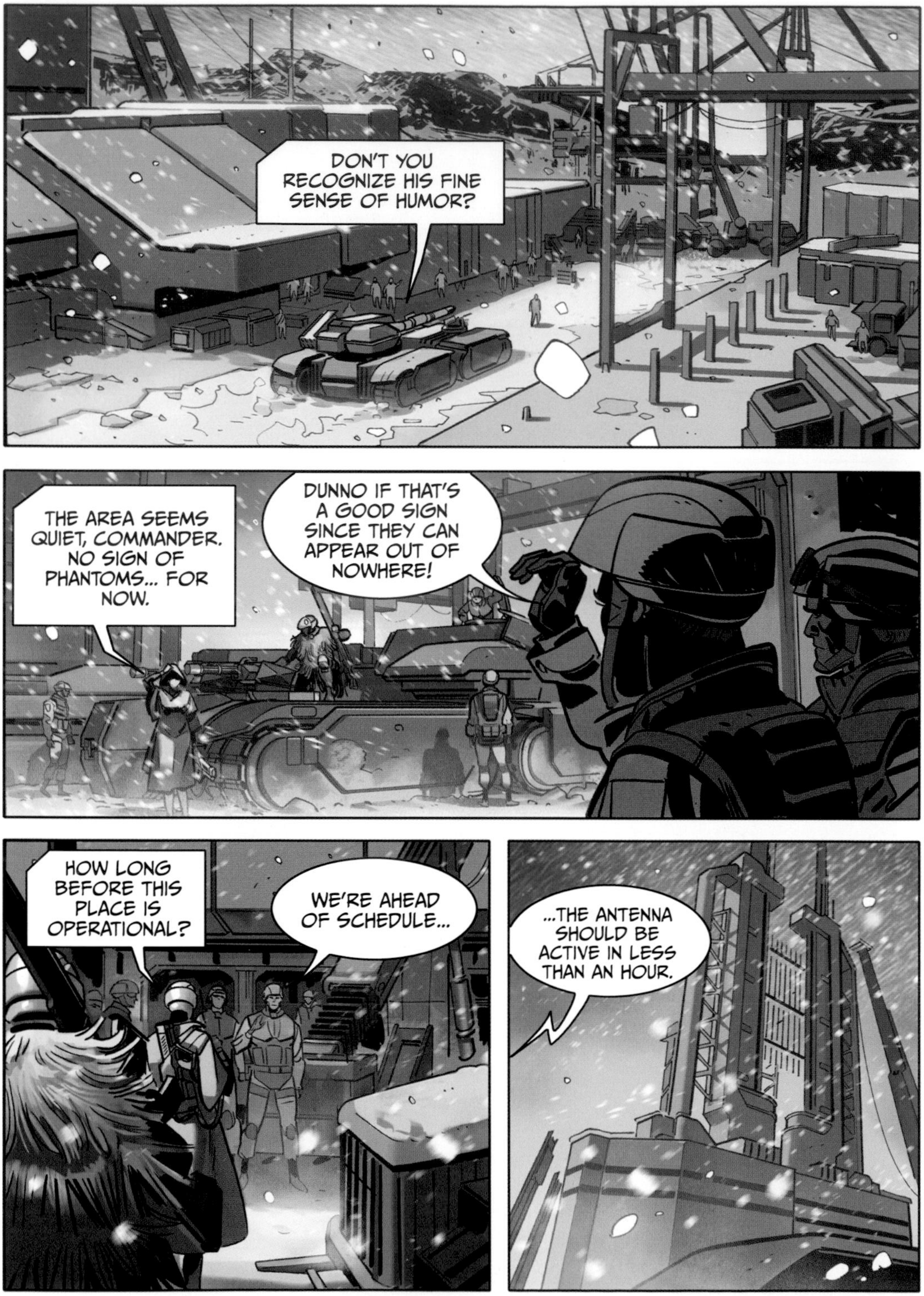
DON'T YOU RECOGNIZE HIS FINE SENSE OF HUMOR?
THE AREA SEEMS QUIET, COMMANDER. NO SIGN OF PHANTOMS... FOR NOW.
DUNNO IF THAT'S A GOOD SIGN SINCE THEY CAN APPEAR OUT OF NOWHERE!
HOW LONG BEFORE THIS PLACE IS OPERATIONAL?
WE'RE AHEAD OF SCHEDULE...
...THE ANTENNA SHOULD BE ACTIVE IN LESS THAN AN HOUR.

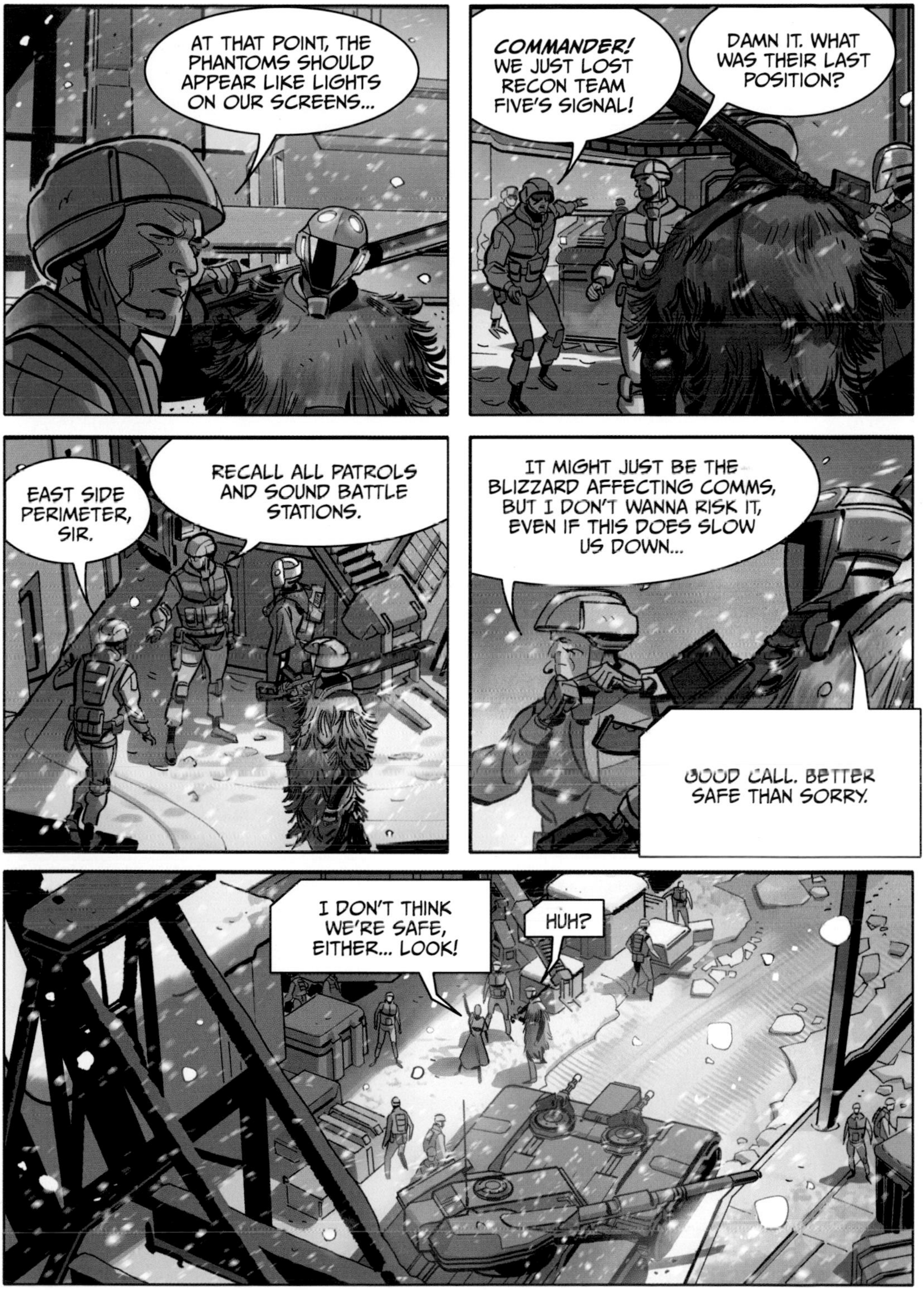
AT THAT POINT, THE PHANTOMS SHOULD APPEAR LIKE LIGHTS ON OUR SCREENS...
COMMANDER! WE JUST LOST RECON TEAM FIVE'S SIGNAL!
DAMN IT. WHAT WAS THEIR LAST POSITION?
EAST SIDE PERIMETER, SIR.
RECALL ALL PATROLS AND SOUND BATTLE STATIONS.
IT MIGHT JUST BE THE BLIZZARD AFFECTING COMMS, BUT I DON'T WANNA RISK IT, EVEN IF THIS DOES SLOW US DOWN...
GOOD CALL. BETTER SAFE THAN SORRY.
I DON'T THINK WE'RE SAFE, EITHER... LOOK!
HUH?

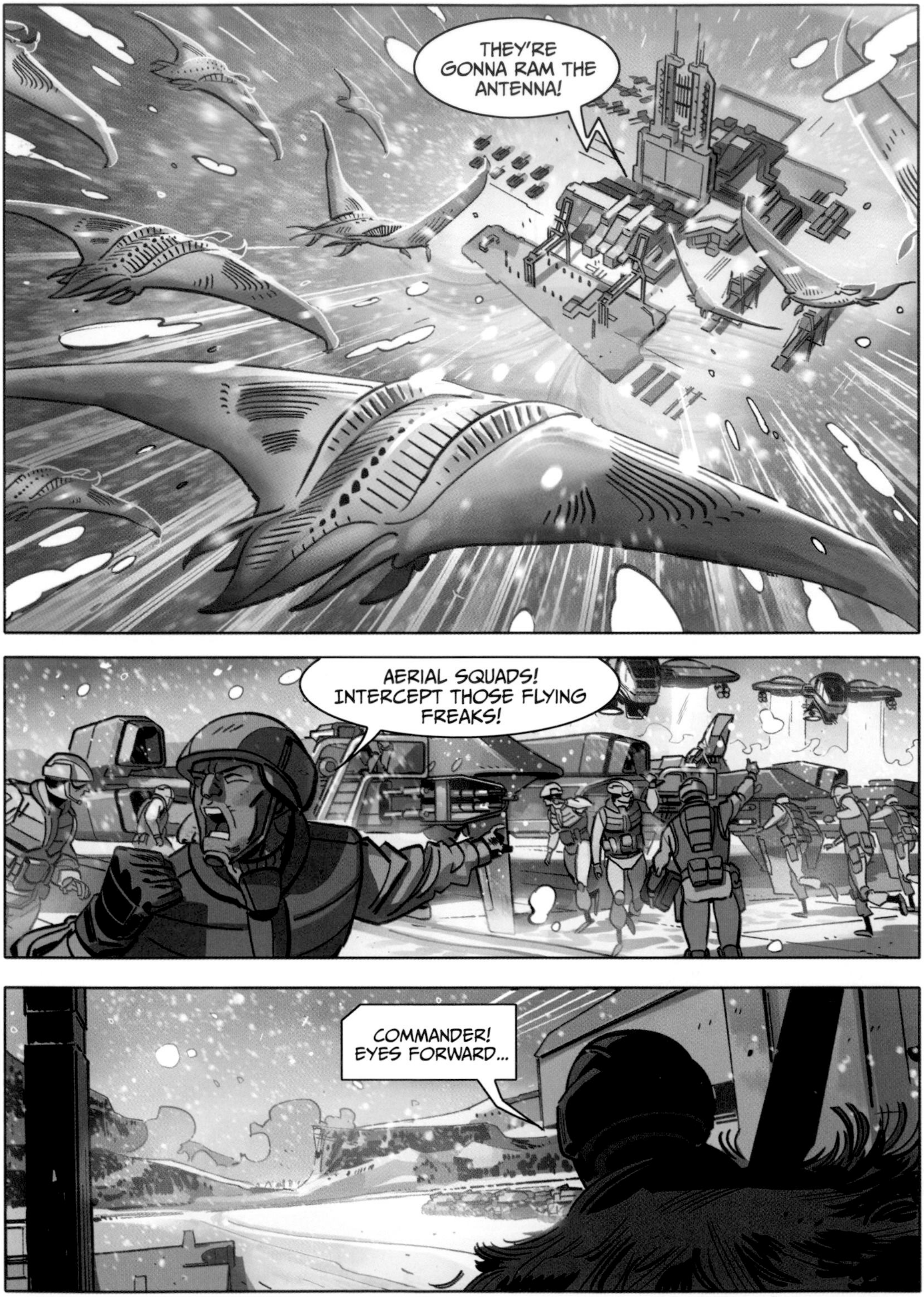
THEY'RE GONNA RAM THE ANTENNA!
AERIAL SQUADS! INTERCEPT THOSE FLYING FREAKS!
COMMANDER! EYES FORWARD...

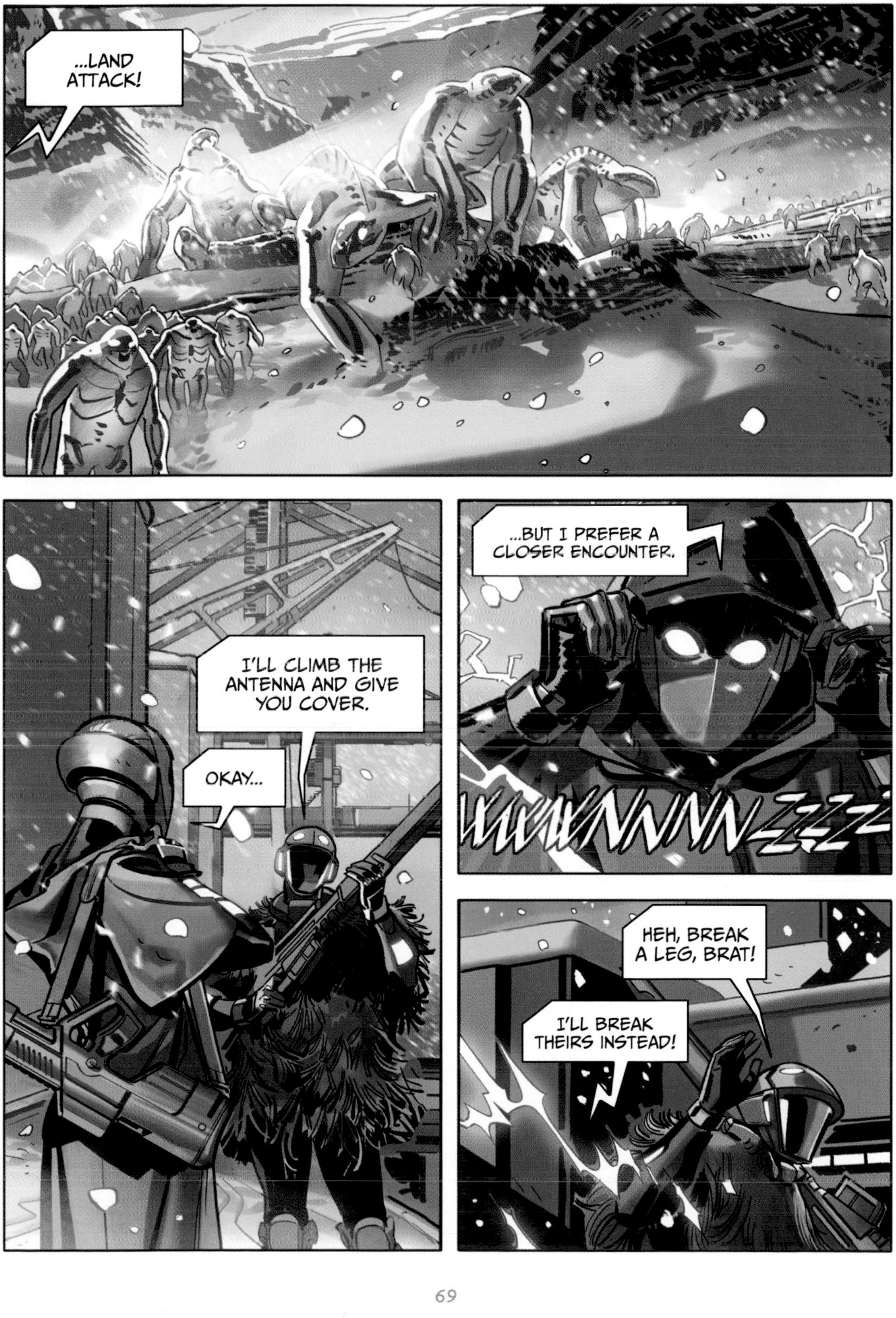
...LAND ATTACK!
I'LL CLIMB THE ANTENNA AND GIVE YOU COVER.
OKAY...
...BUT I PREFER A CLOSER ENCOUNTER.
WWWWNNNNNZZZZ
HEH, BREAK A LEG, BRAT!
I'LL BREAK THEIRS INSTEAD!

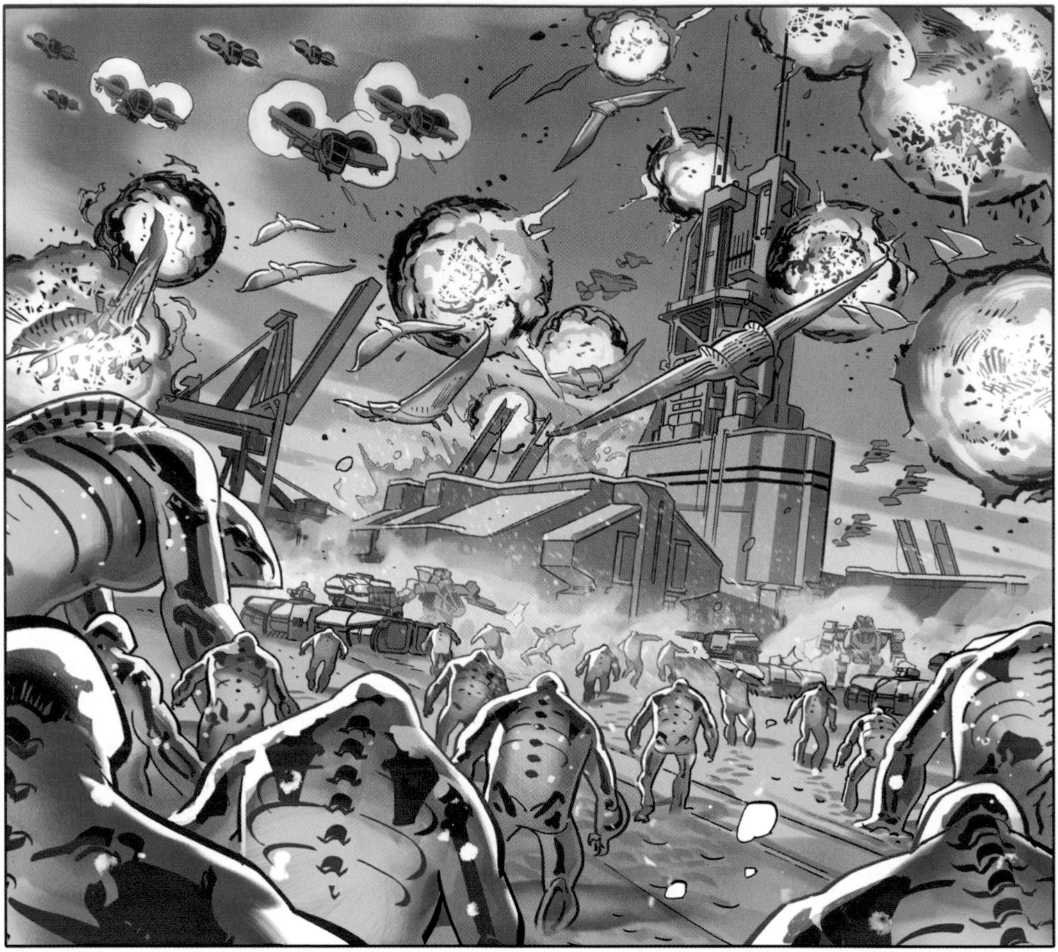

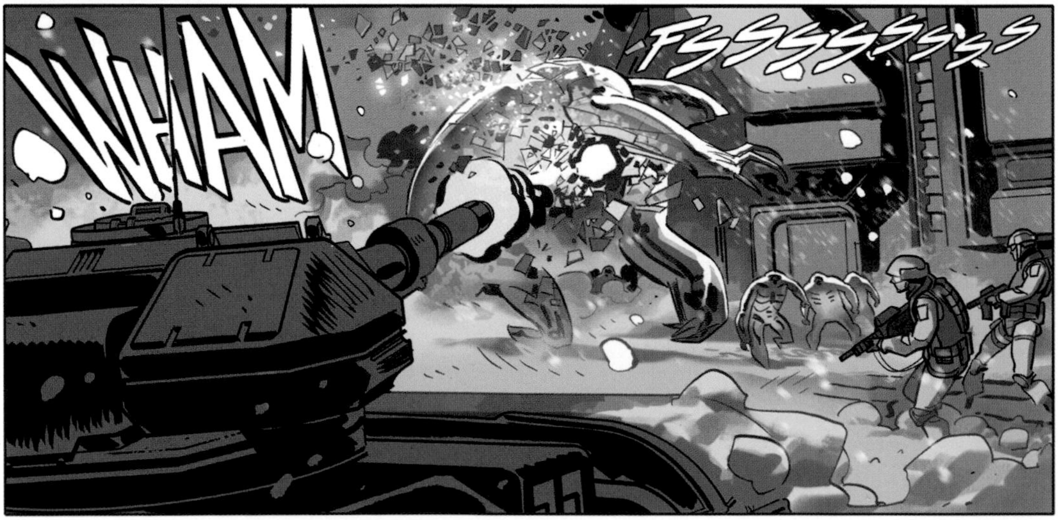
WHAM
FSSSSSSSSS

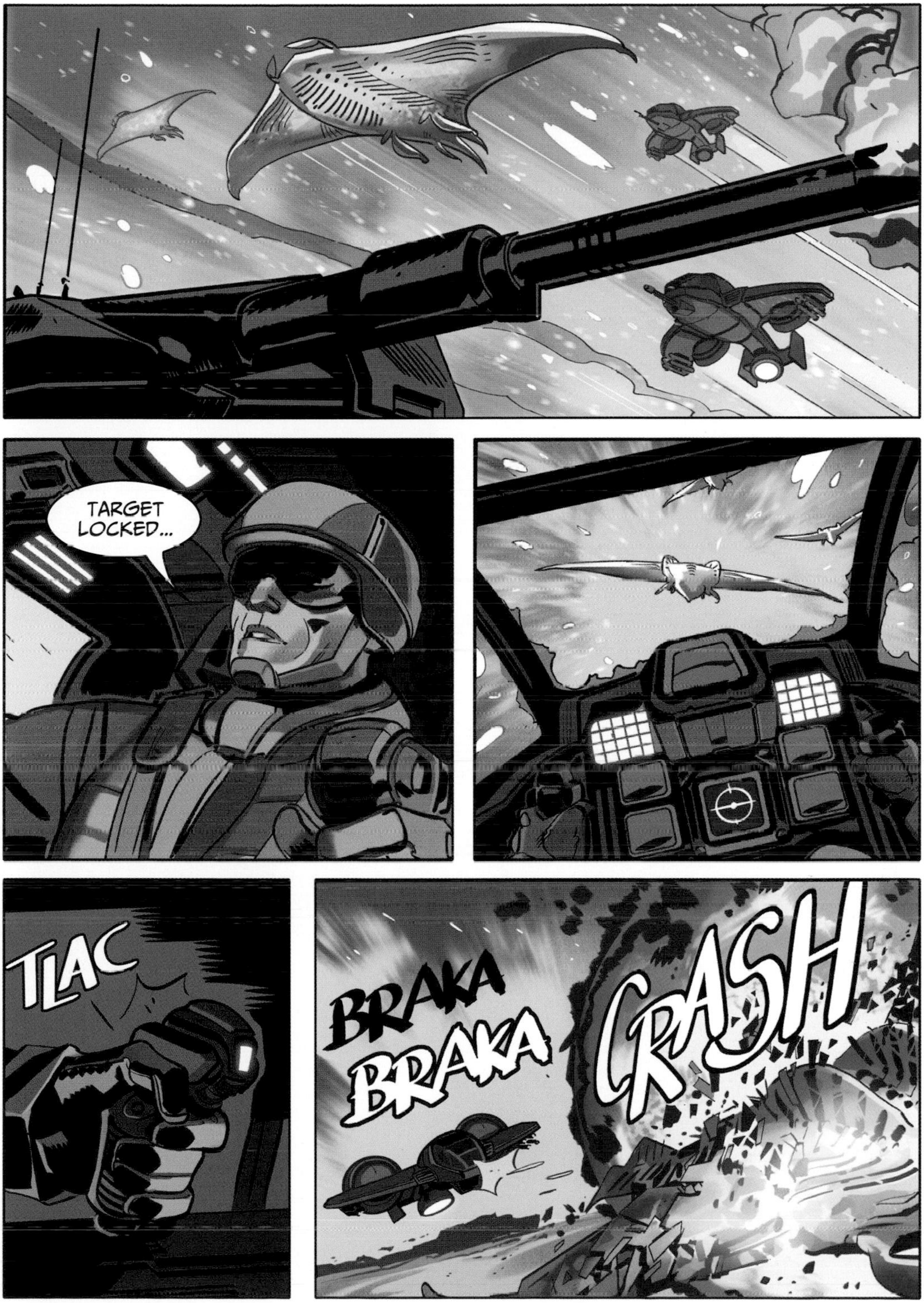
TARGET LOCKED...
TLAC
BRAKA
BRAKA
CRASH

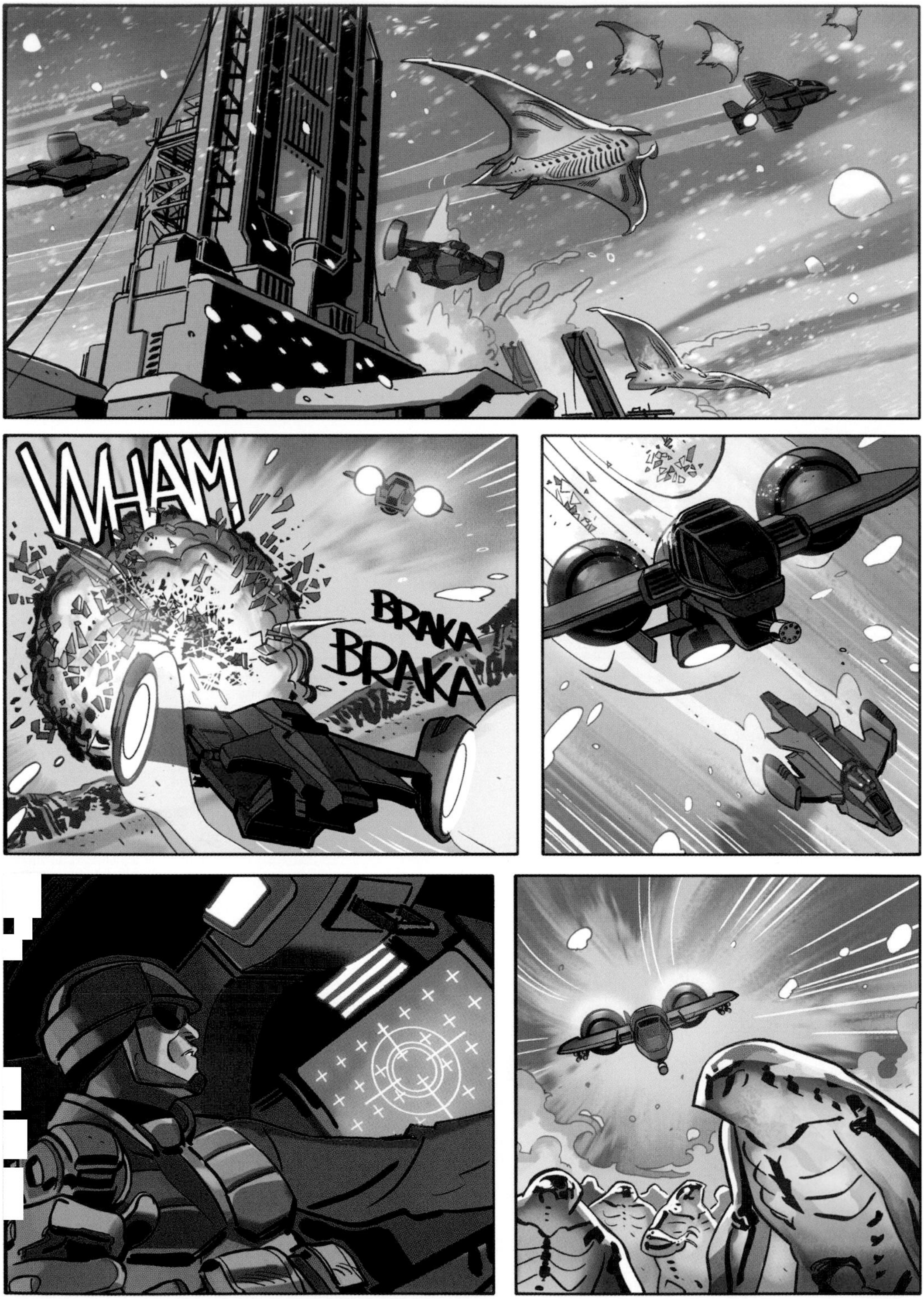
WHAM
BRAKA
BRAKA

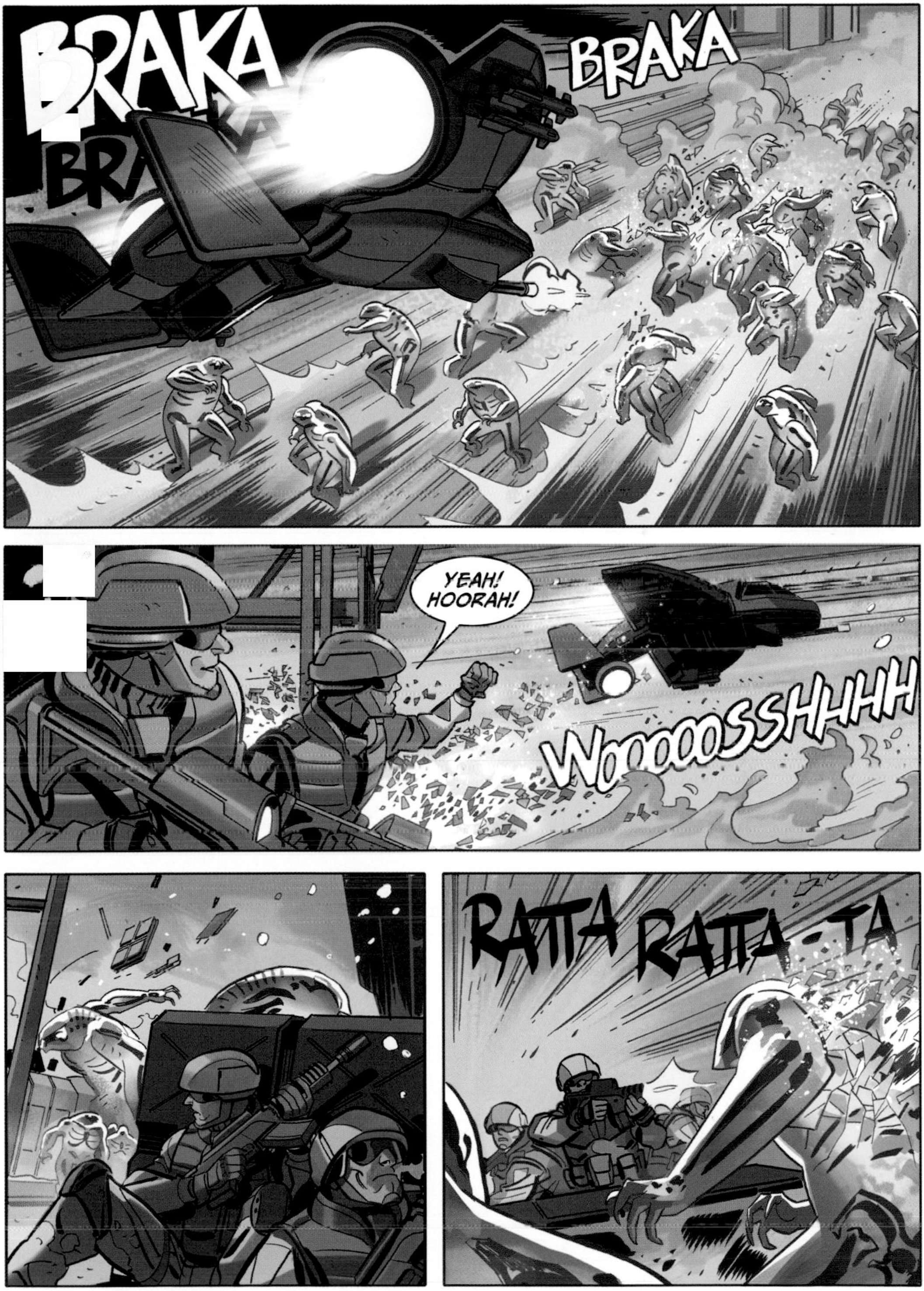
BRAKA
BRAKA
YEAH! HOORAH!
WOOOOOSSHHHH
RATTA RATTA-TA

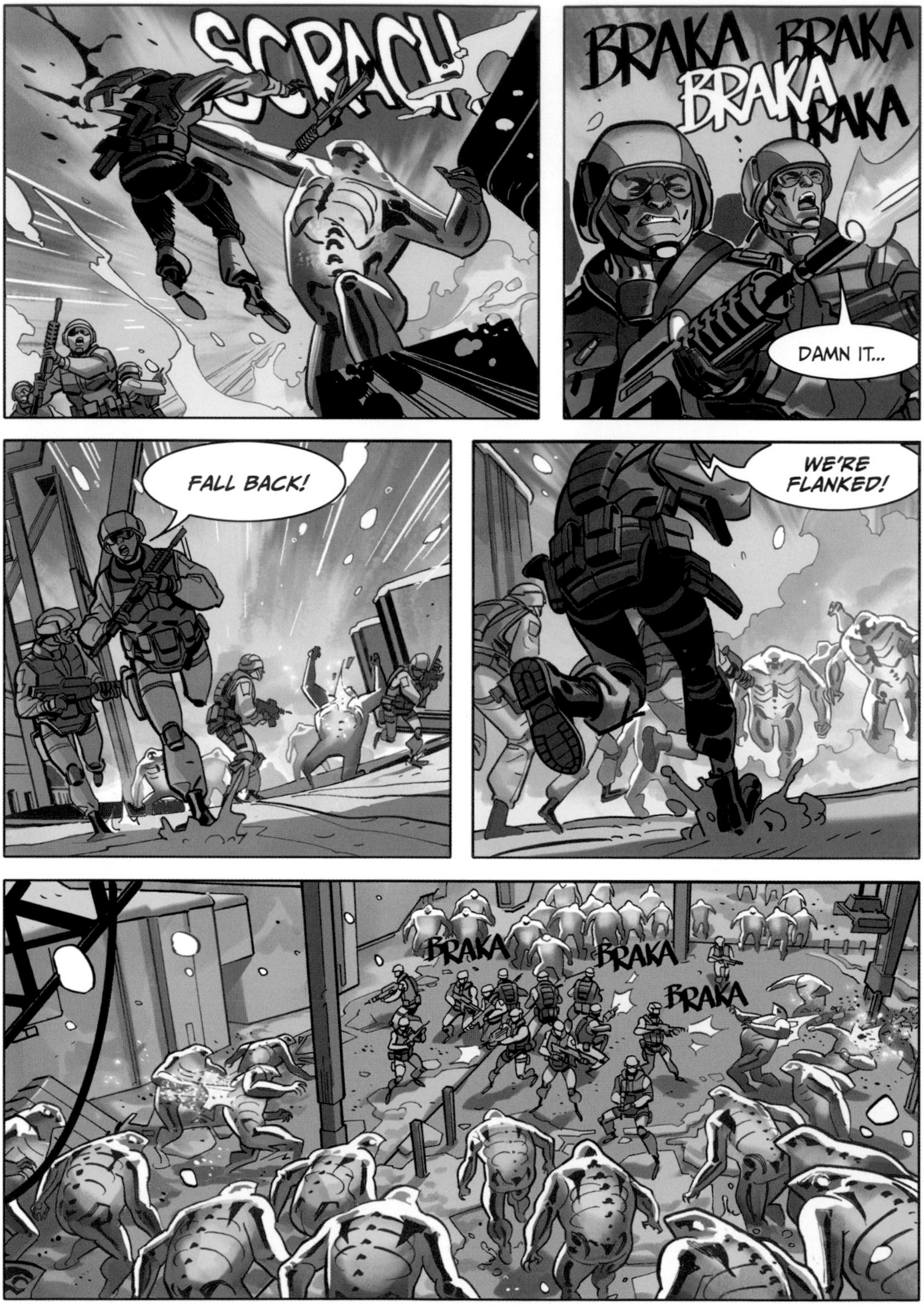
SCRACK!
BRAKA BRAKA
BRAKA
BRAKA
DAMN IT...
FALL BACK!
WE'RE FLANKED!
BRAKA
BRAKA
BRAKA

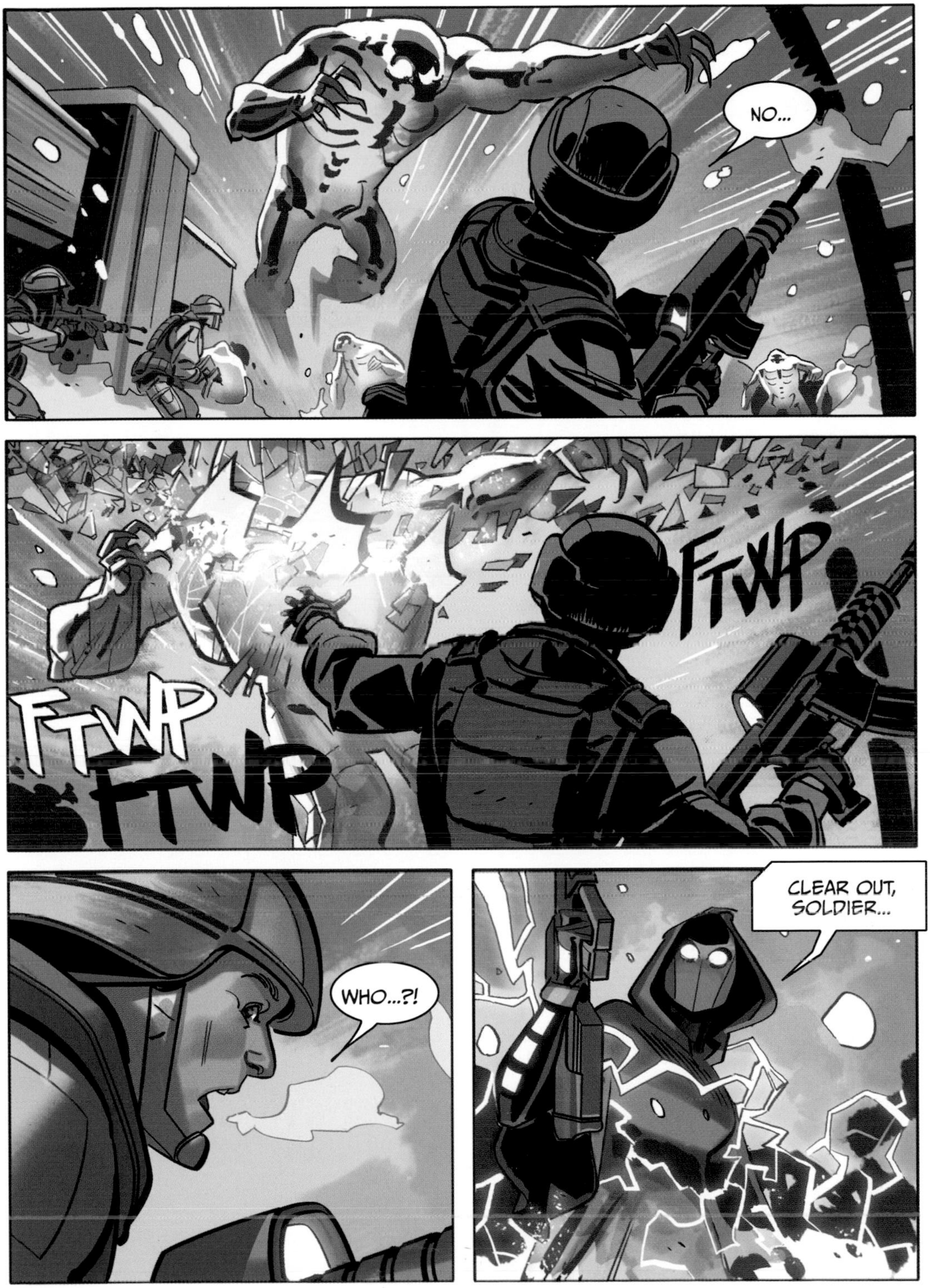
NO...
FTWP
FTWP
FTWP
WHO...?!
CLEAR OUT, SOLDIER...

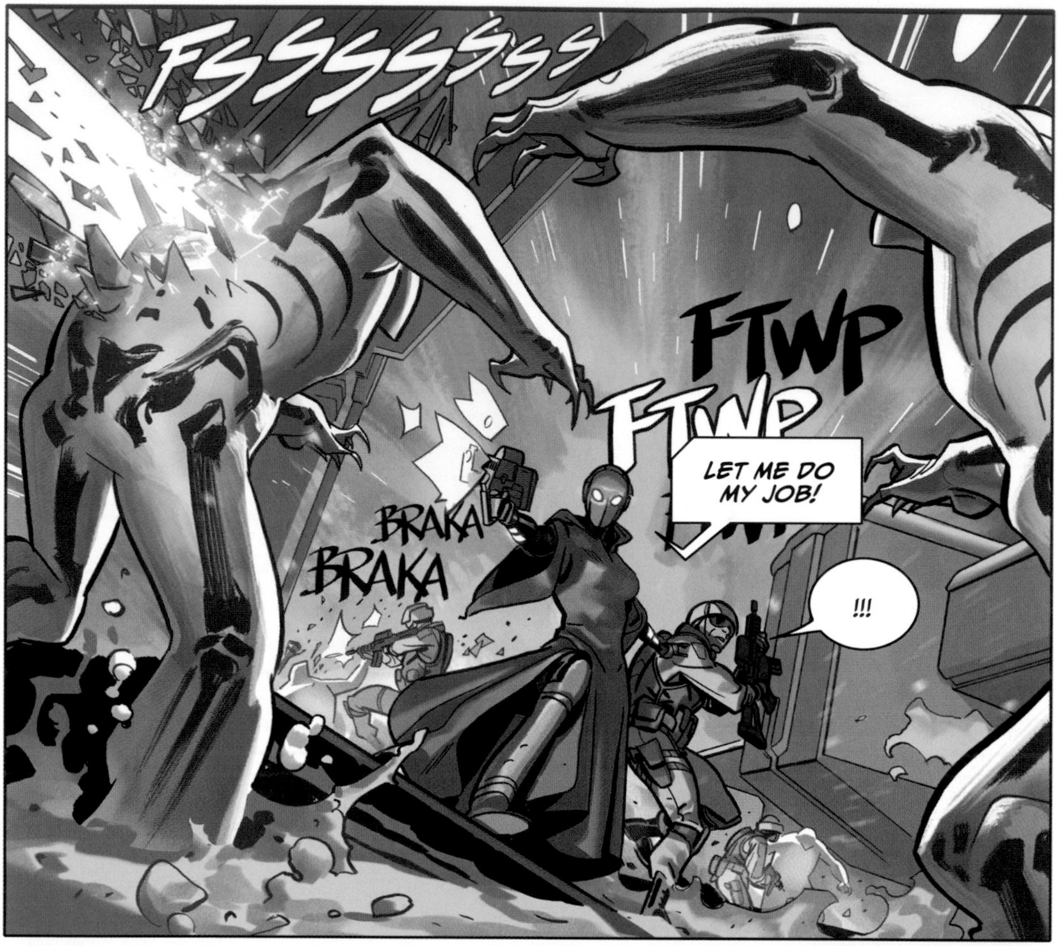
FSSSSSSSS
FTWP
FTWP
BRAKA
BRAKA
LET ME DO MY JOB!
!!!

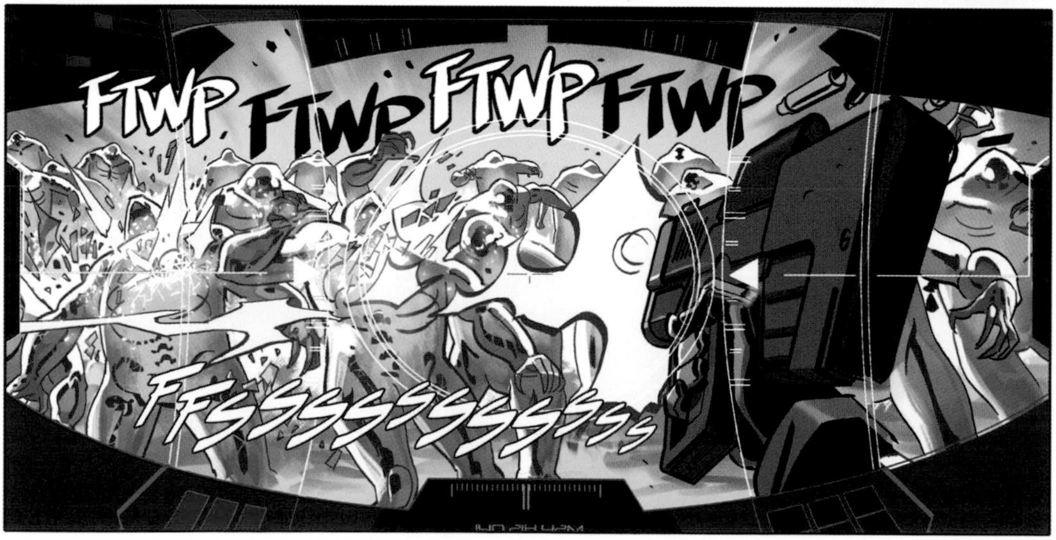
FTWP FTWP FTWP FTWP
FFSSSSSSSSSSSS

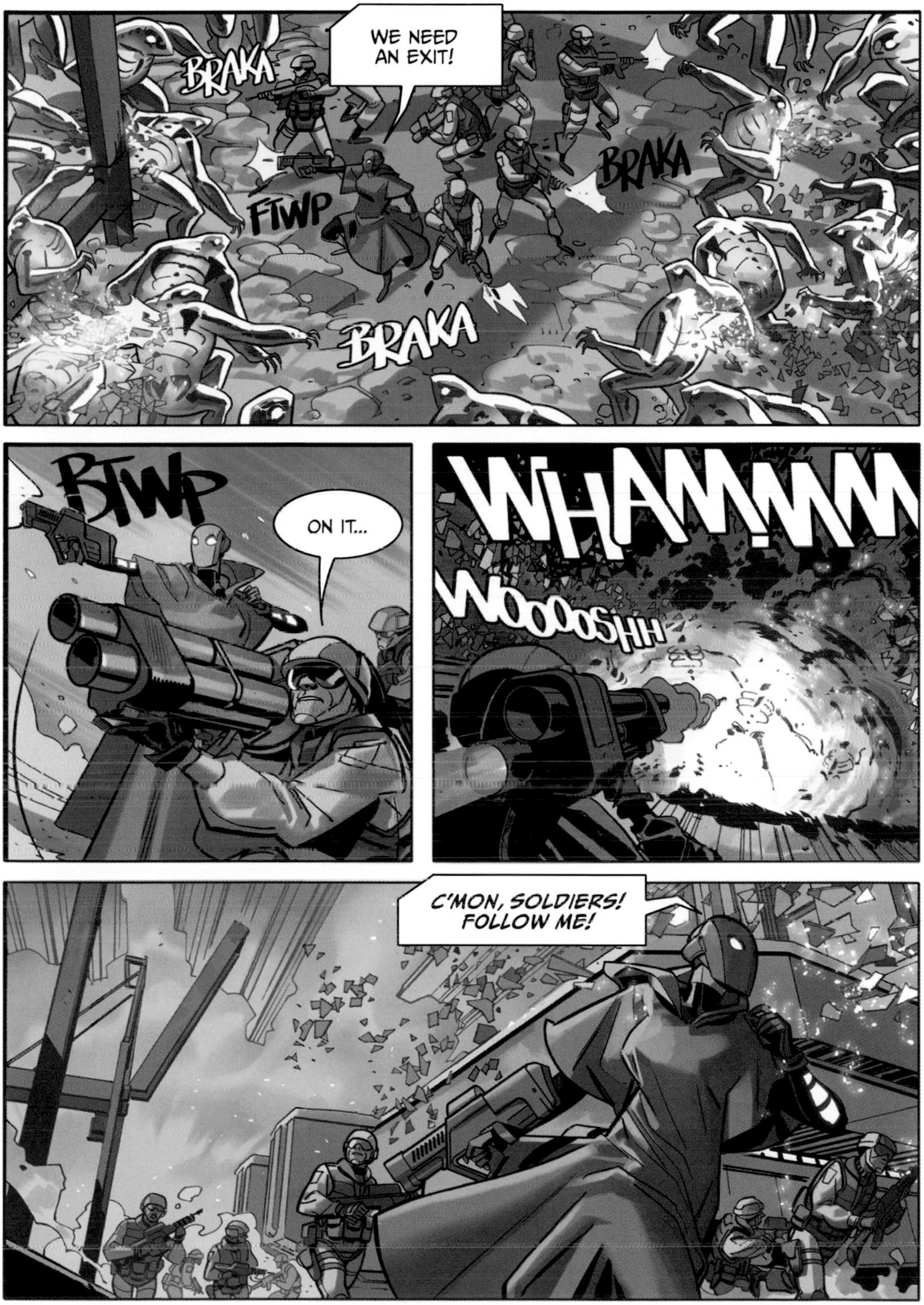
WE NEED AN EXIT!
BRAKA
FTWP
BRAKA
BRAKA
BTWP
ON IT...
WHAMMM
WOOOOSHH
C'MON, SOLDIERS! FOLLOW ME!

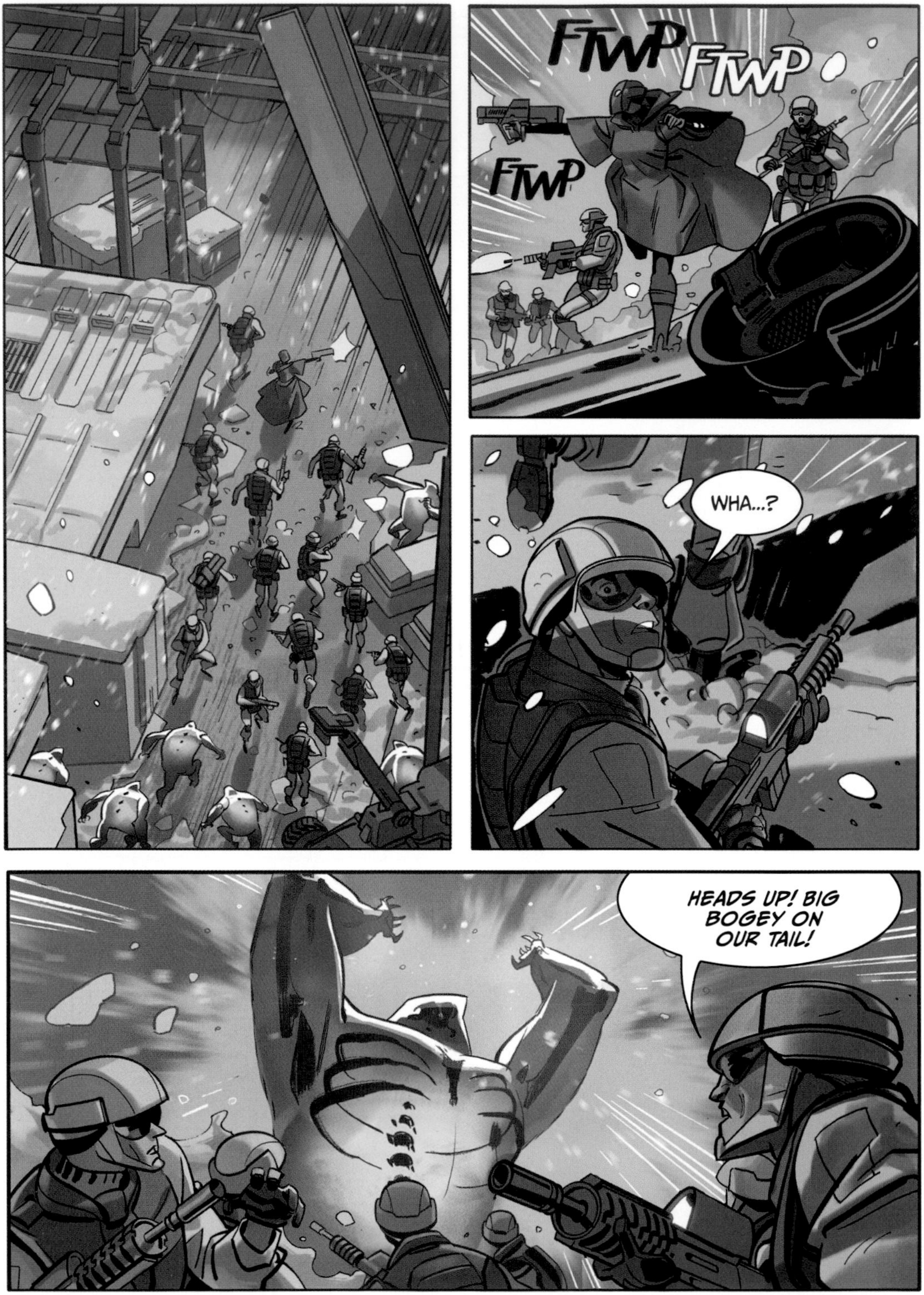
FTWP
FTWP
FTWP
WHA...?
HEADS UP! BIG BOGEY ON OUR TAIL!

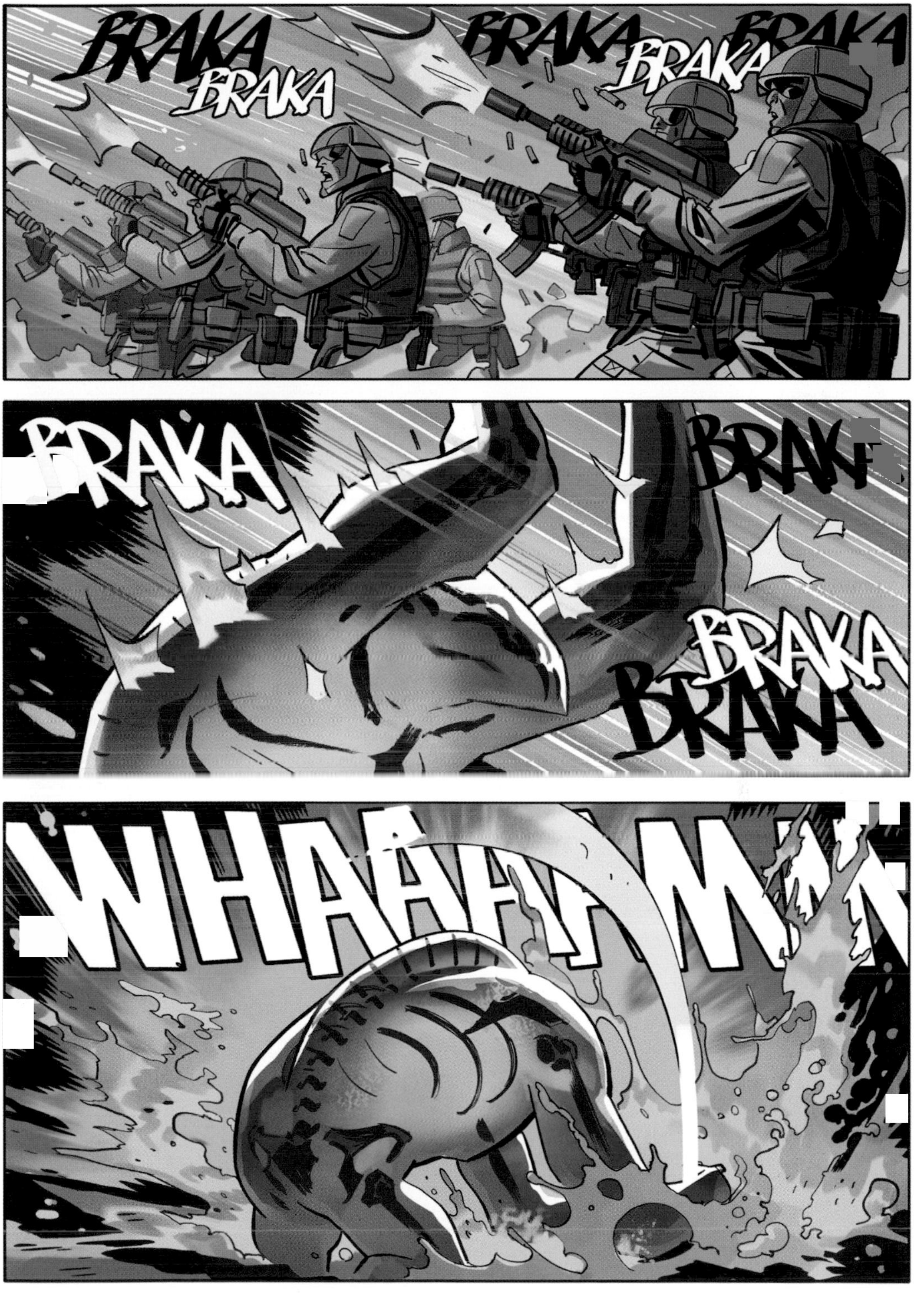
BRAKA
BRAKA
BRAKA
BRAKA
BRAKA
BRAKA
BRAKA
BRAKA
WHAAAAAM

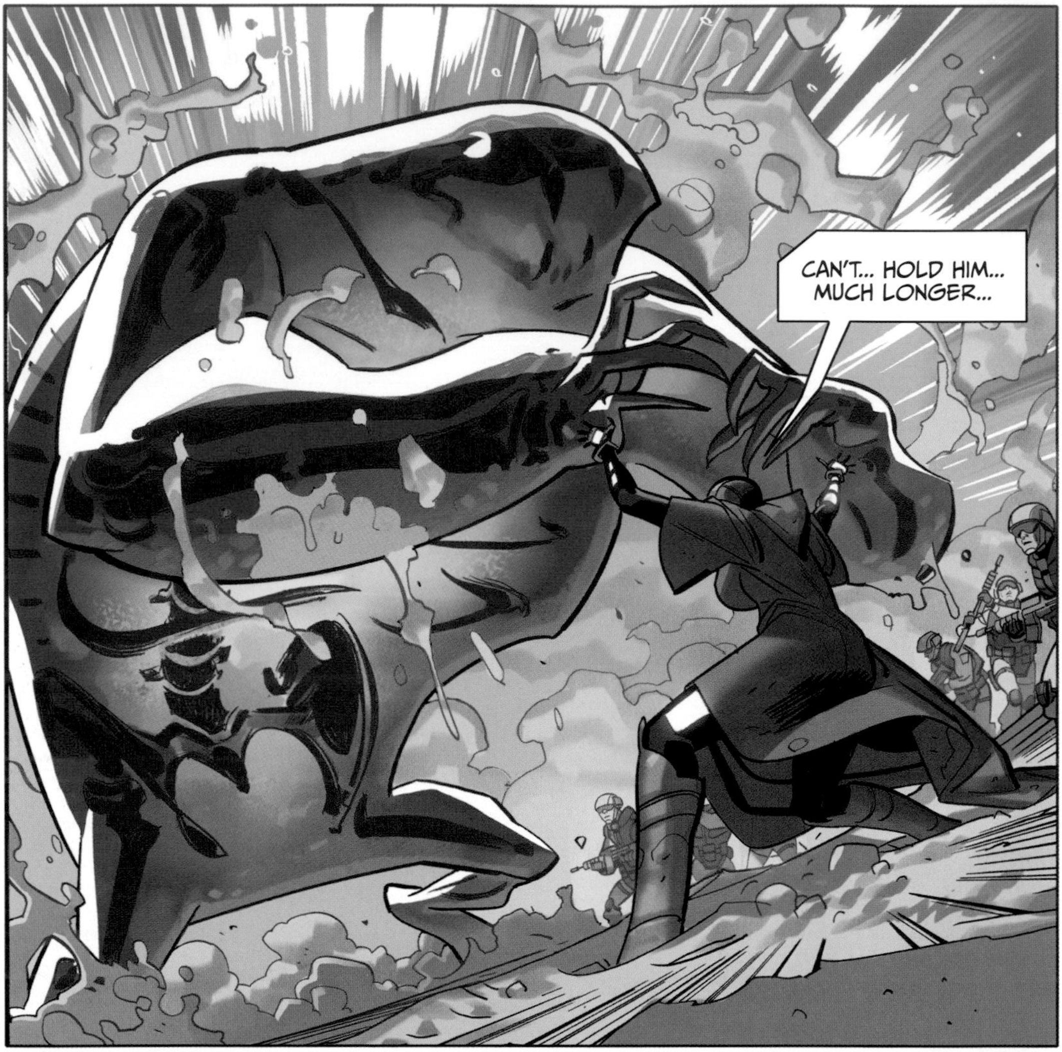
CAN'T... HOLD HIM... MUCH LONGER...

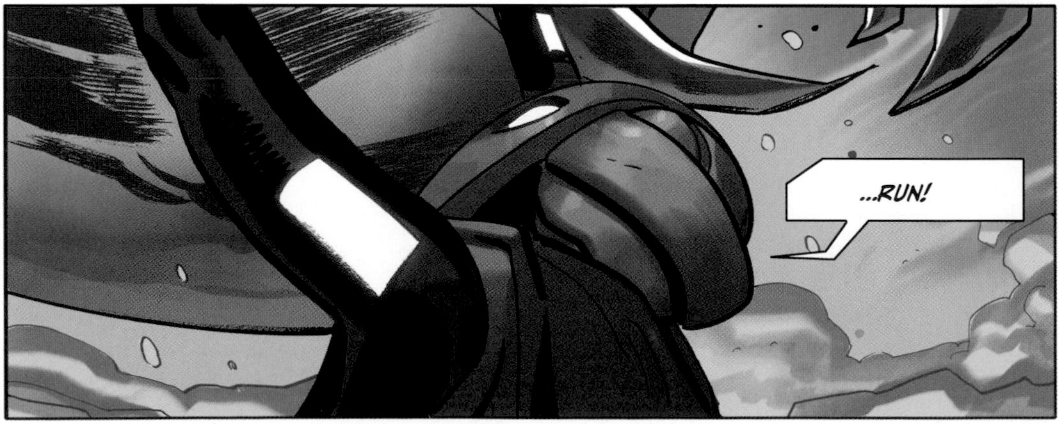
...RUN!

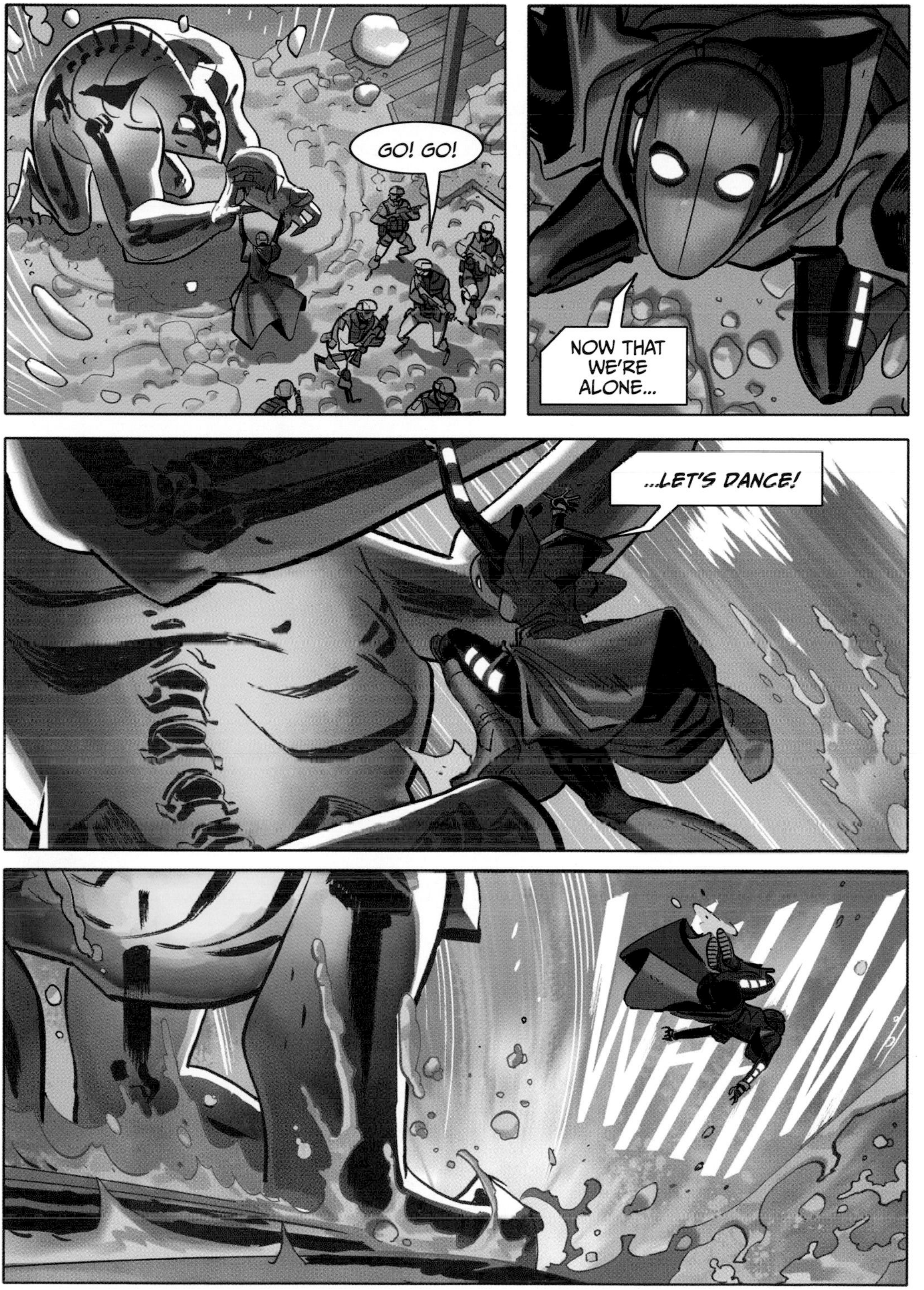
GO! GO!
NOW THAT WE'RE ALONE...
...LET'S DANCE!

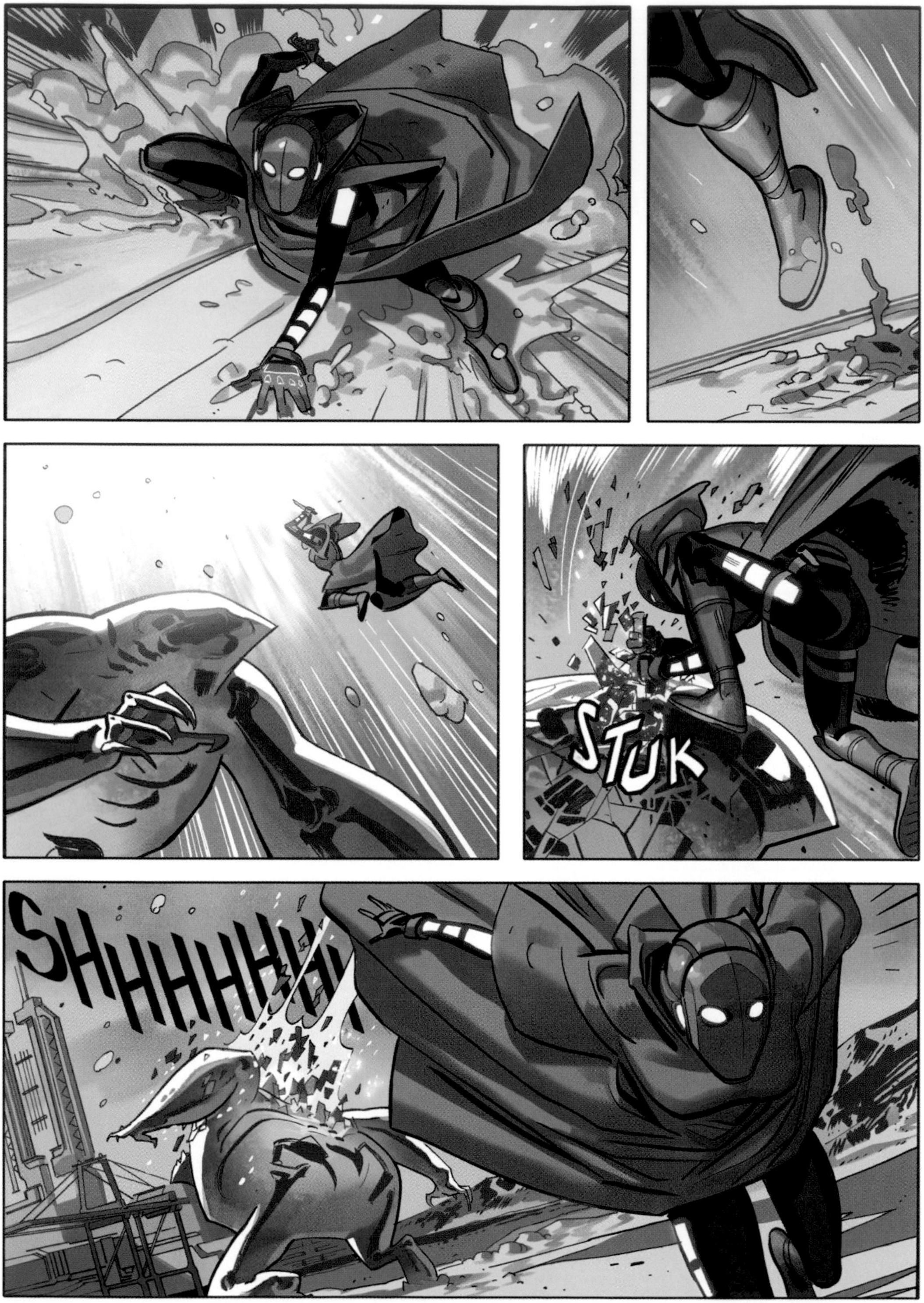
STUK
SHHHHHHH

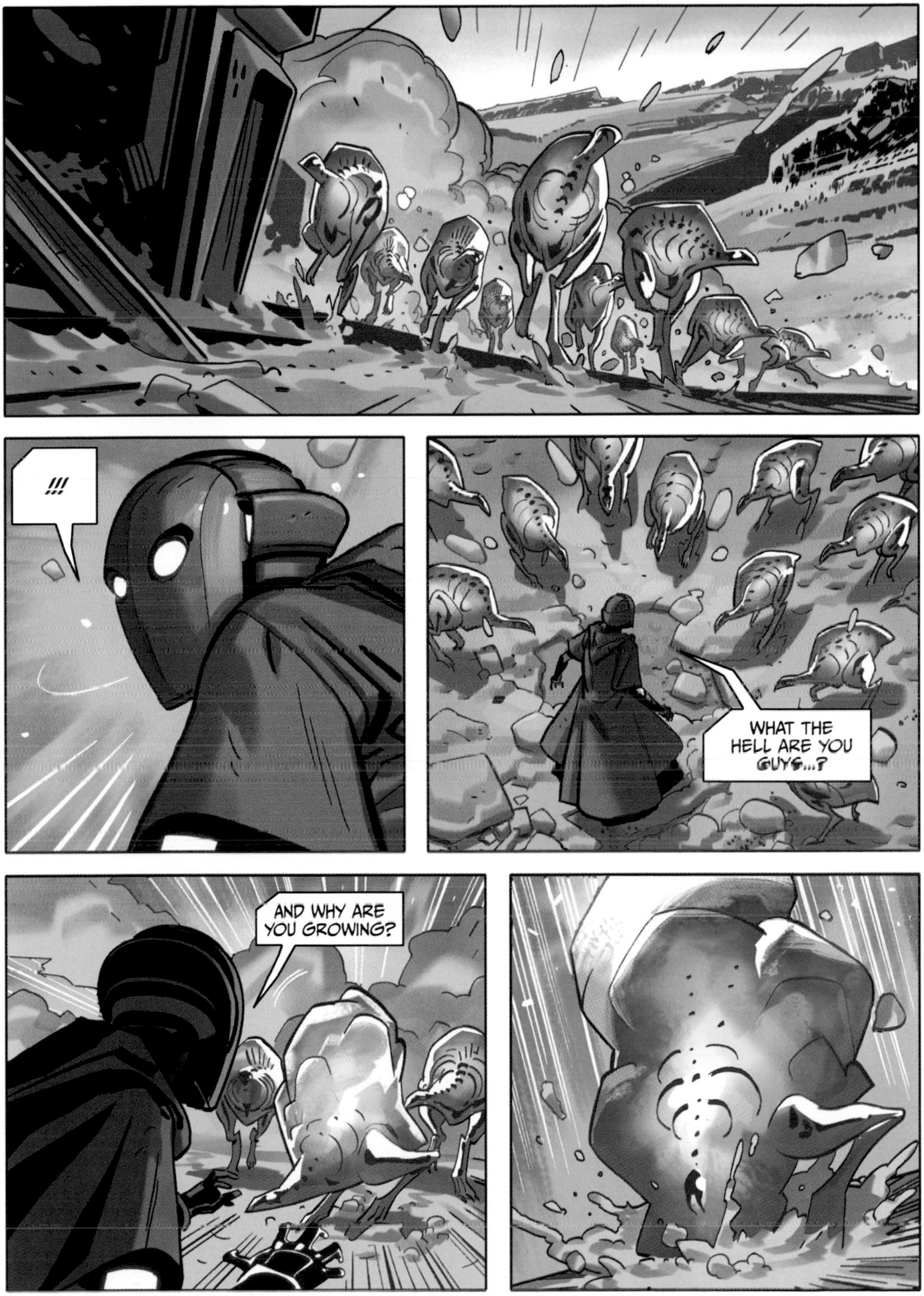
!!!
WHAT THE HELL ARE YOU GUYS...?
AND WHY ARE YOU GROWING?

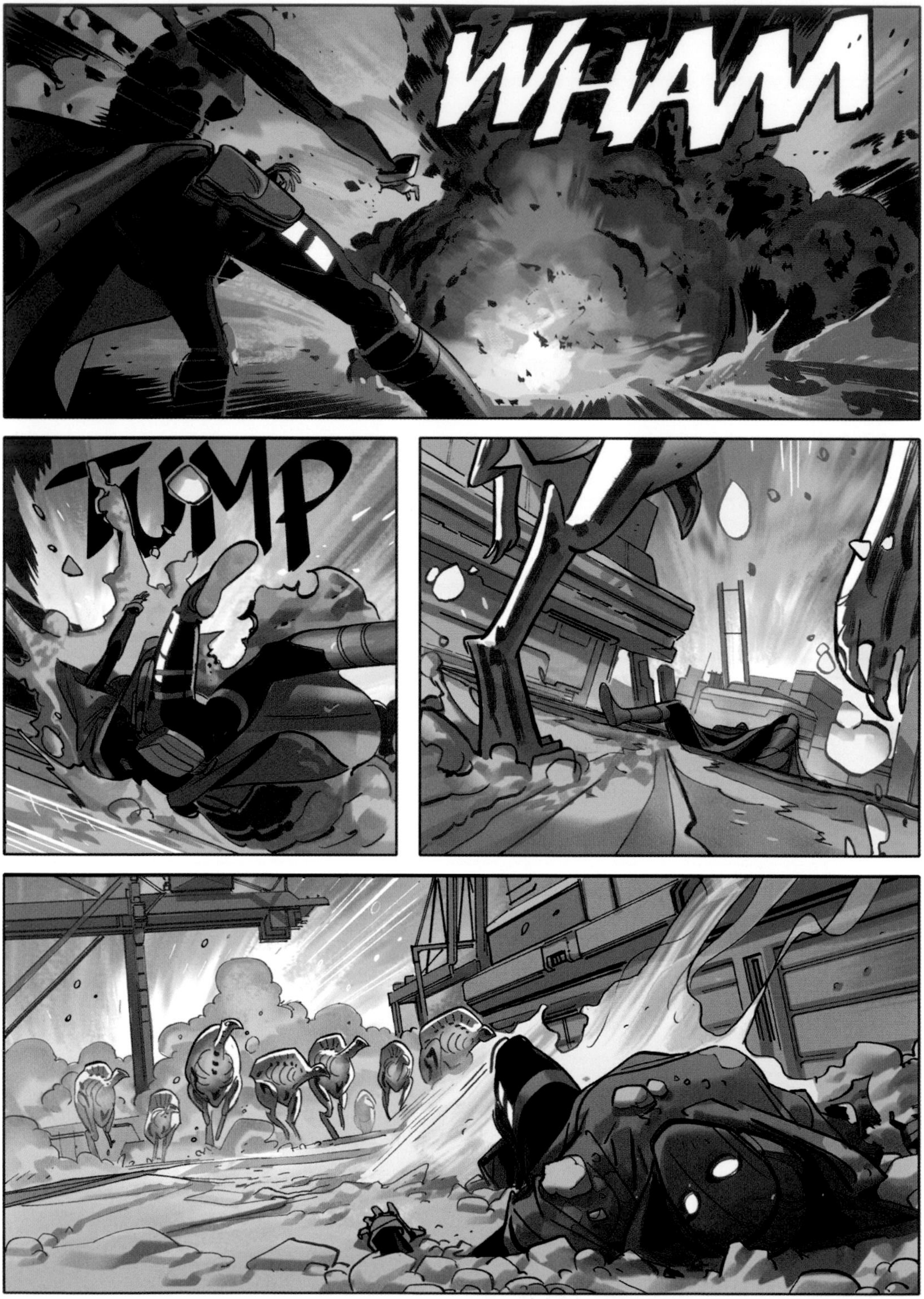
WHAM
TUMP

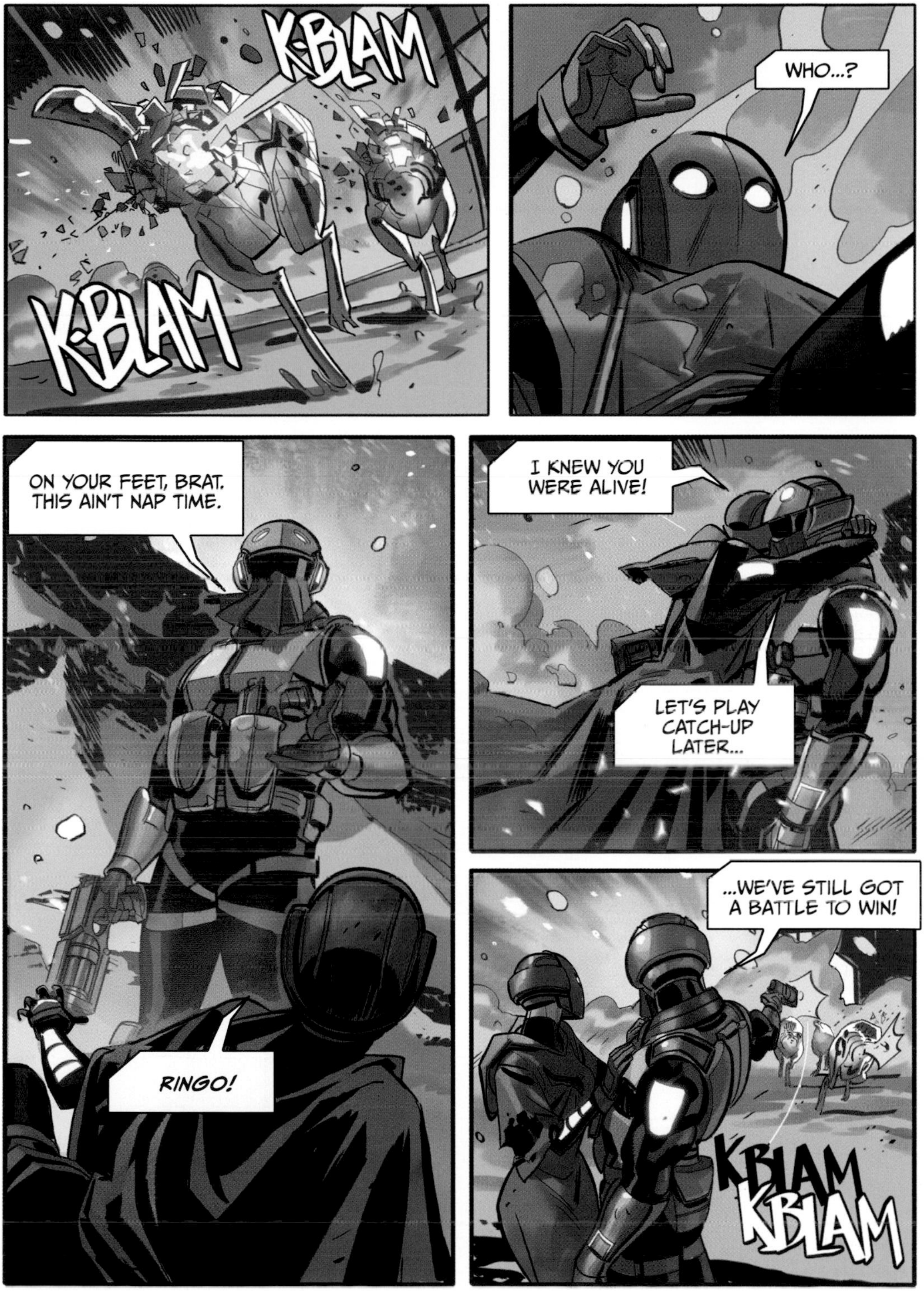
K-BLAM
K-BLAM
WHO...?
ON YOUR FEET, BRAT. THIS AIN'T NAP TIME.
RINGO!
I KNEW YOU WERE ALIVE!
LET'S PLAY CATCH-UP LATER...
...WE'VE STILL GOT A BATTLE TO WIN!
KBLAM
KBLAM

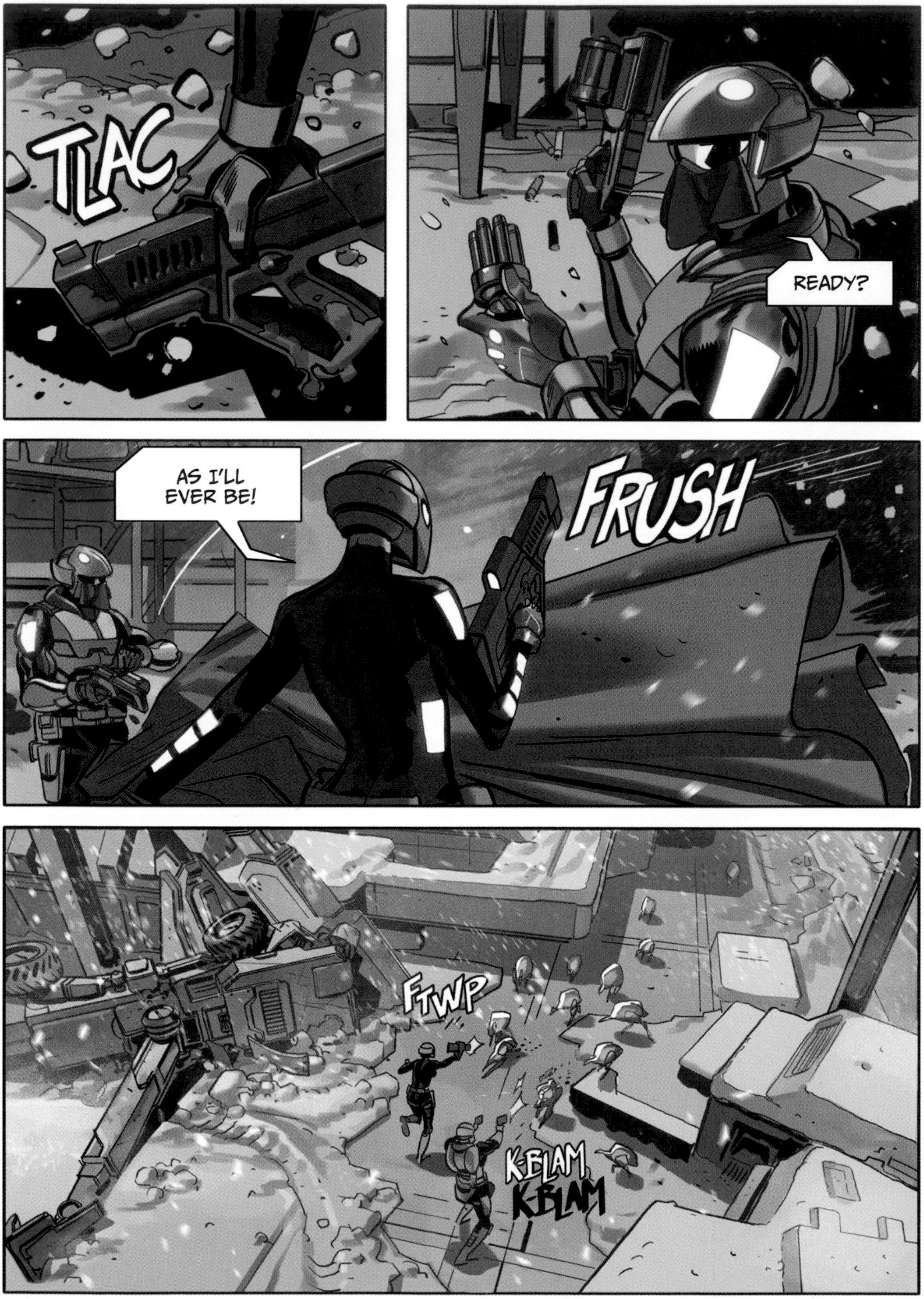
TLAC
READY?
AS I'LL EVER BE!
FRUSH
FTWP
K-BLAM
K-BLAM

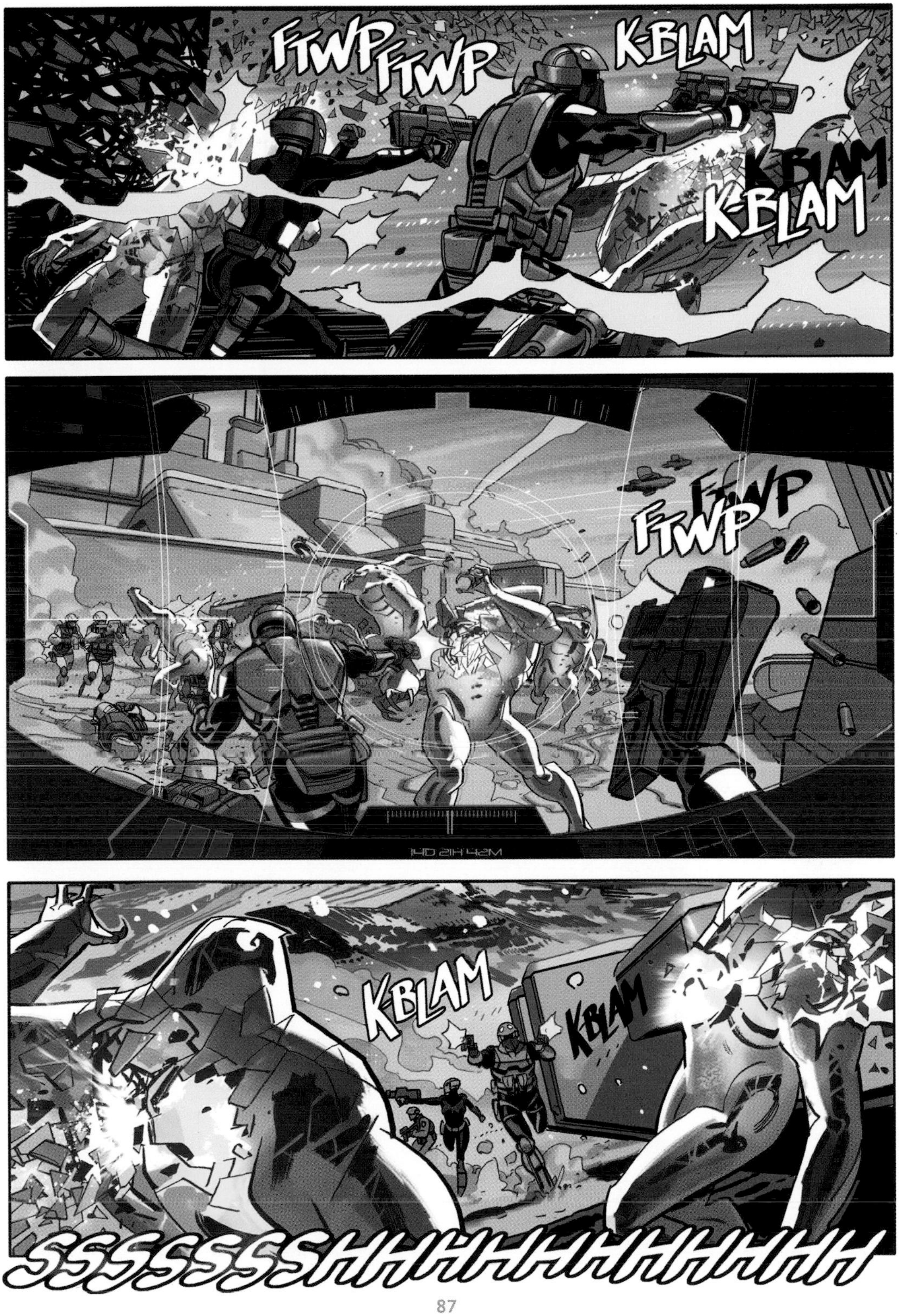
FTWP FTWP
K-BLAM
K-BLAM
K-BLAM
FTWP FTWP
14D 21H 42M
K-BLAM
K-BLAM
SSSSSSSHHHHHHHHHHHHH

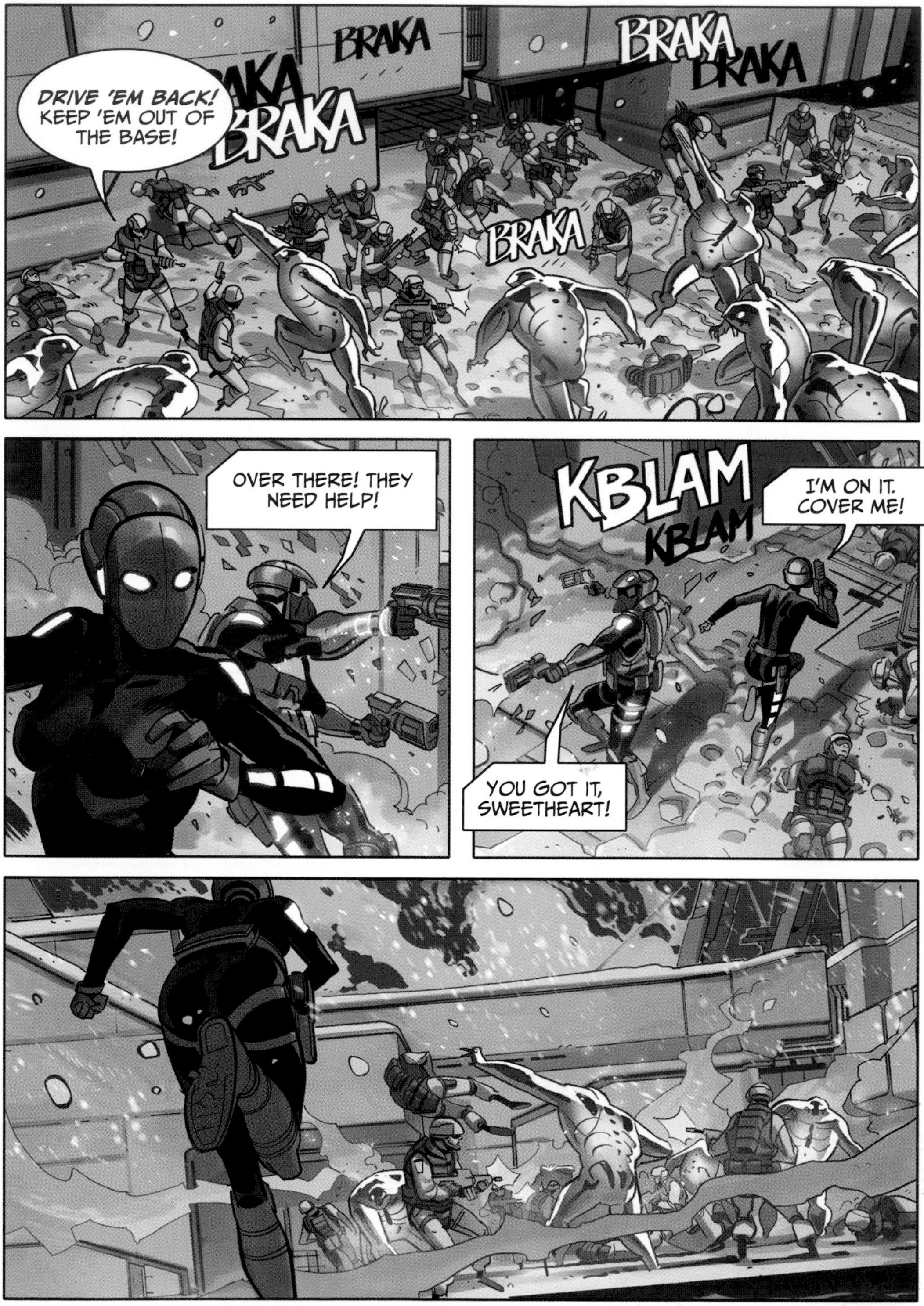
BRAKA
BRAKA
BRAKA
DRIVE 'EM BACK! KEEP 'EM OUT OF THE BASE!
BRAKA
BRAKA
BRAKA
OVER THERE! THEY NEED HELP!
KBLAM
KBLAM
I'M ON IT. COVER ME!
YOU GOT IT, SWEETHEART!

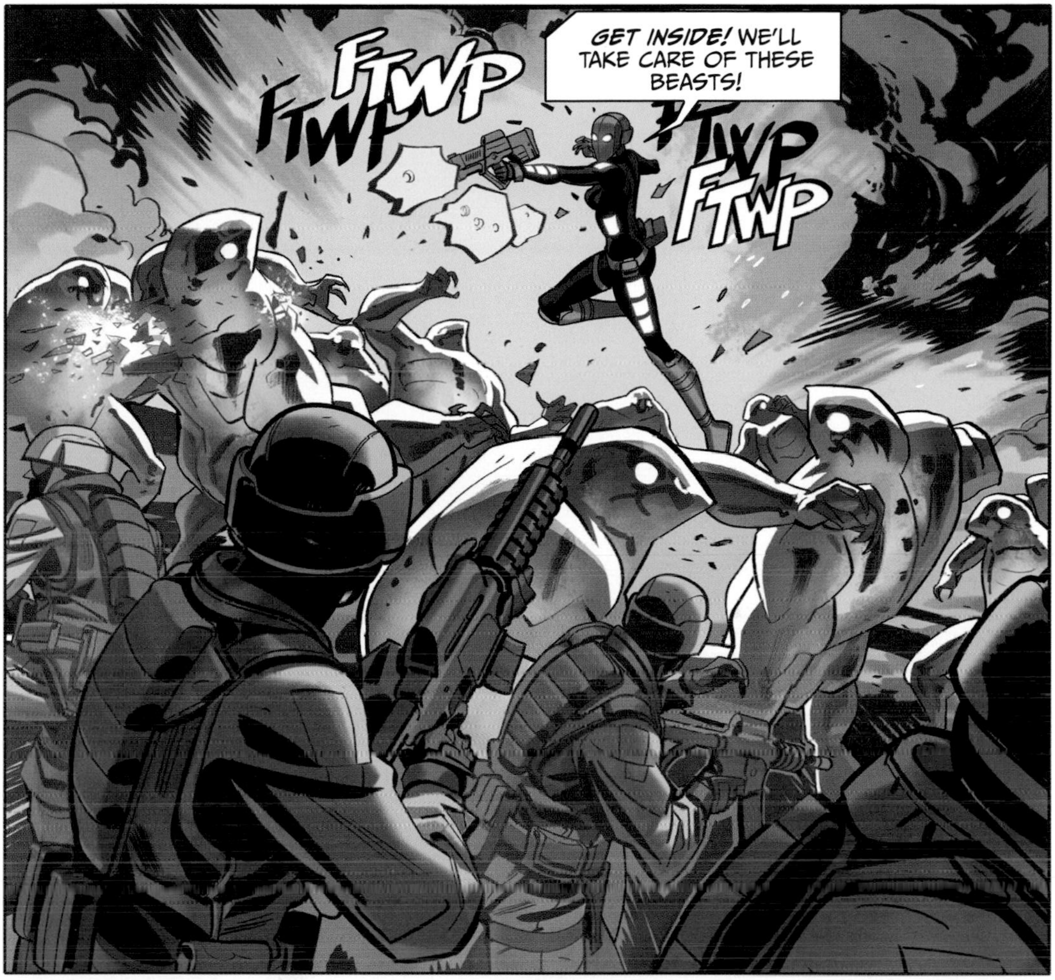
FTWP
FTWP
GET INSIDE! WE'LL TAKE CARE OF THESE BEASTS!
FTWP
FTWP

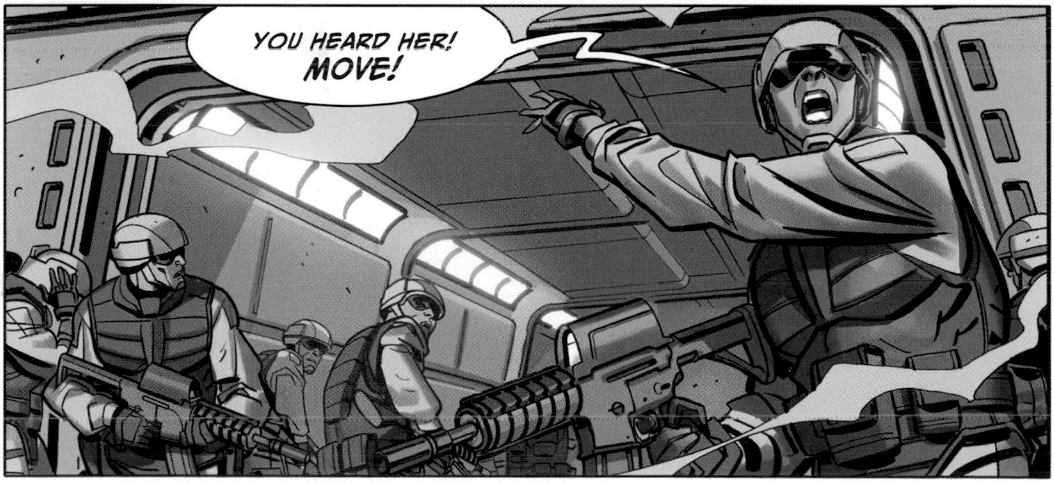
YOU HEARD HER! MOVE!

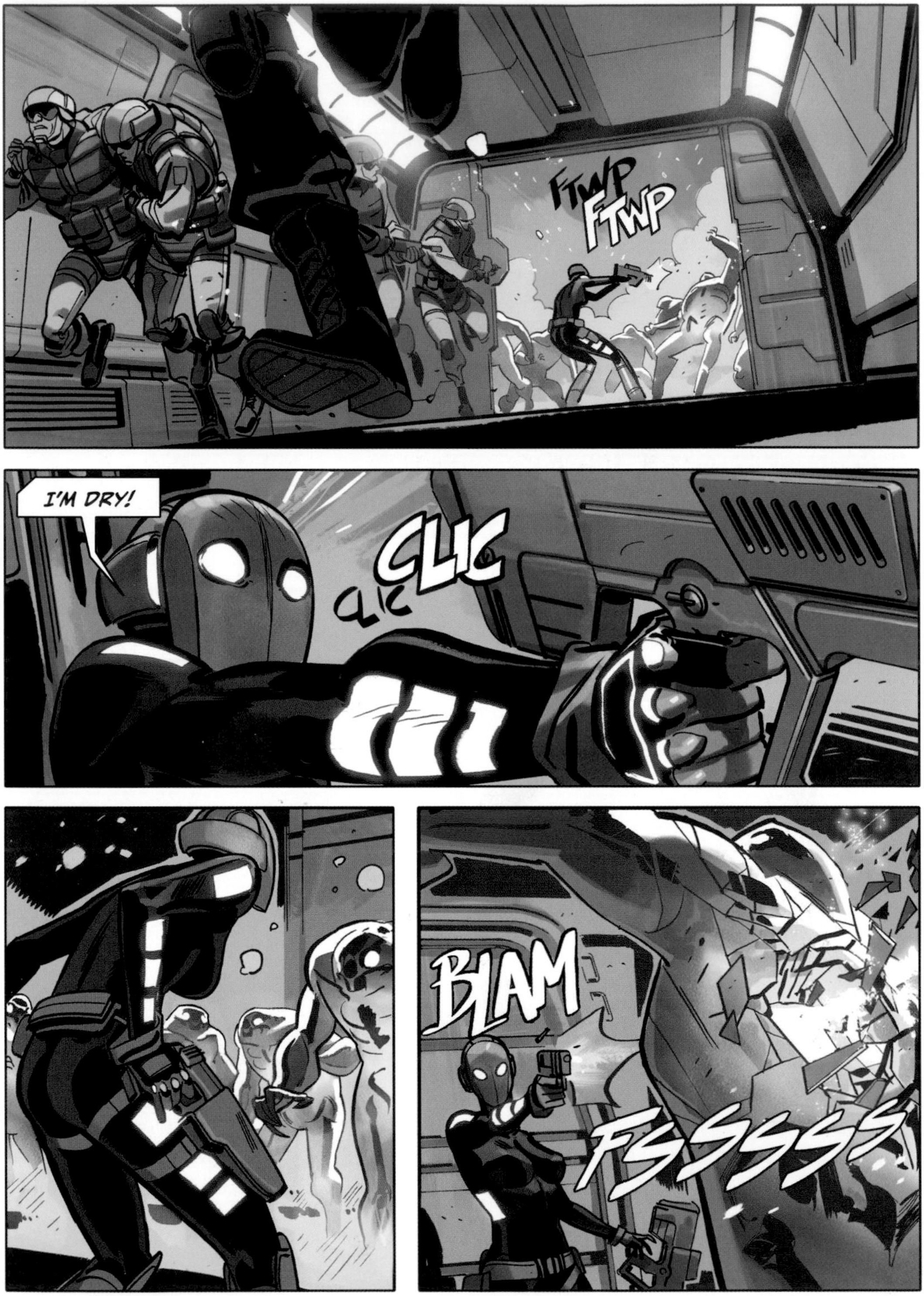
FTWP
FTWP
I'M DRY!
CLIC
CLIC
BLAM
FSSSSS

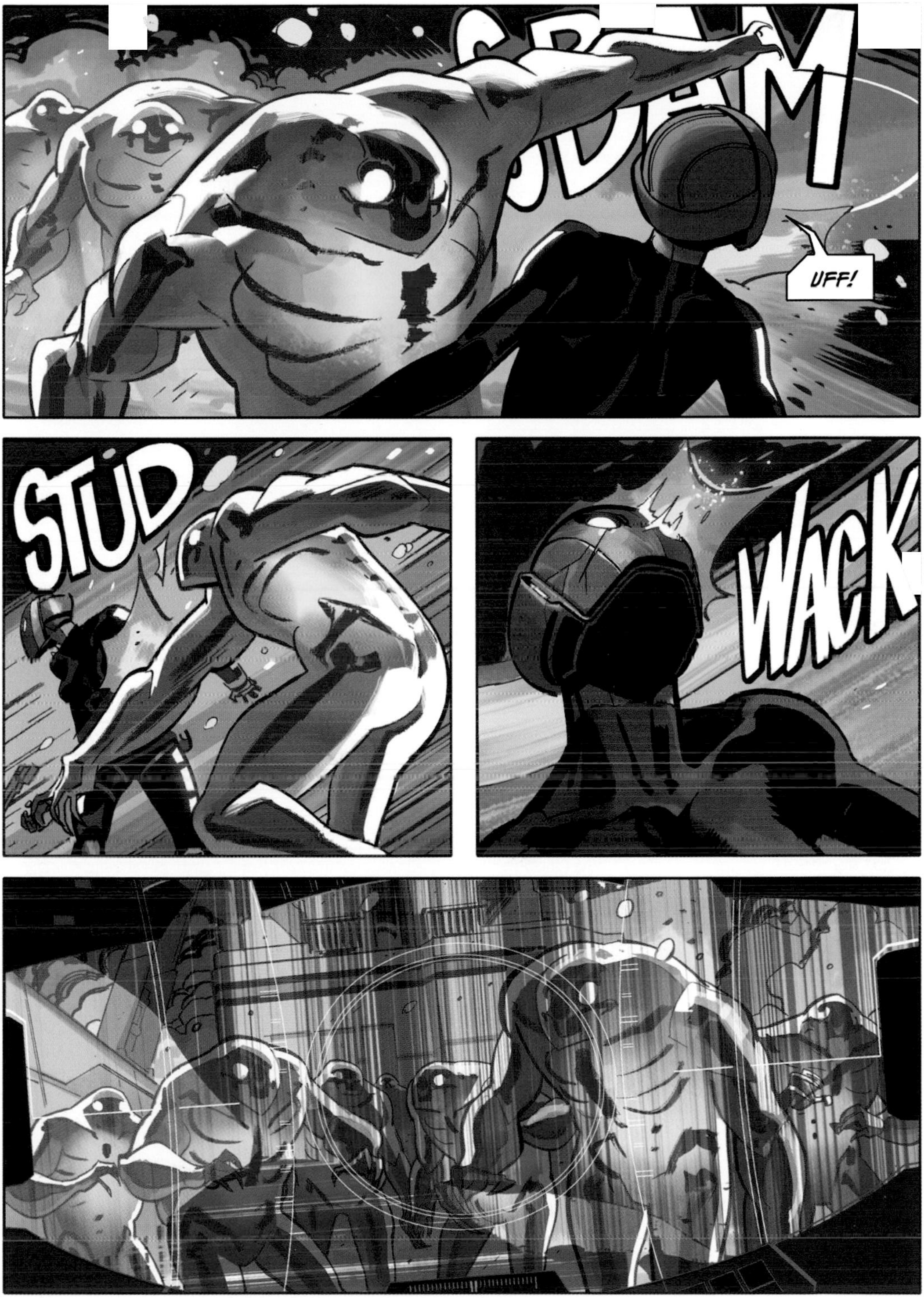
UFF!
STUD
WACK

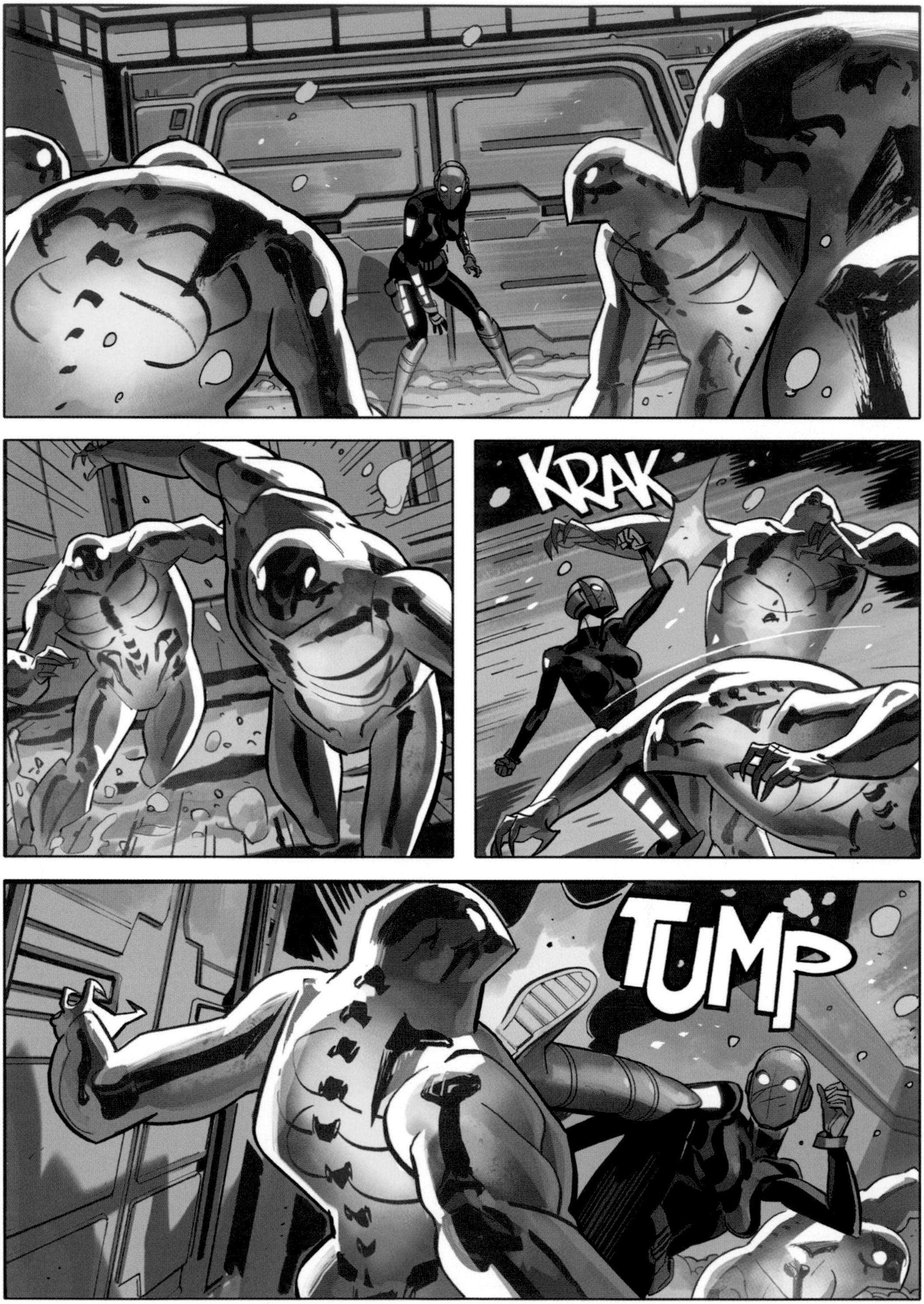
KRAK
TUMP

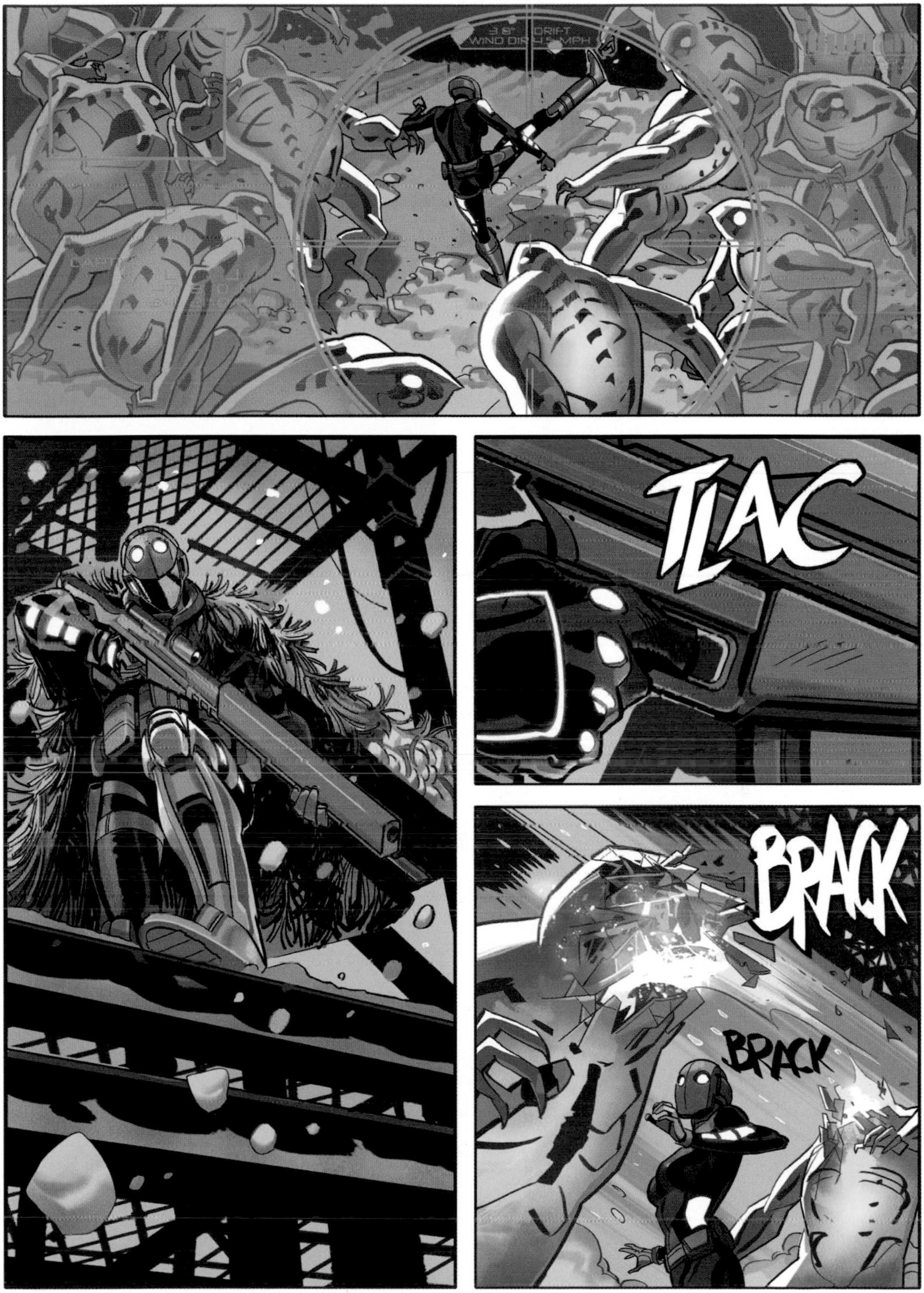
3.8" DRIFT
TLAC
BRACK
BRACK

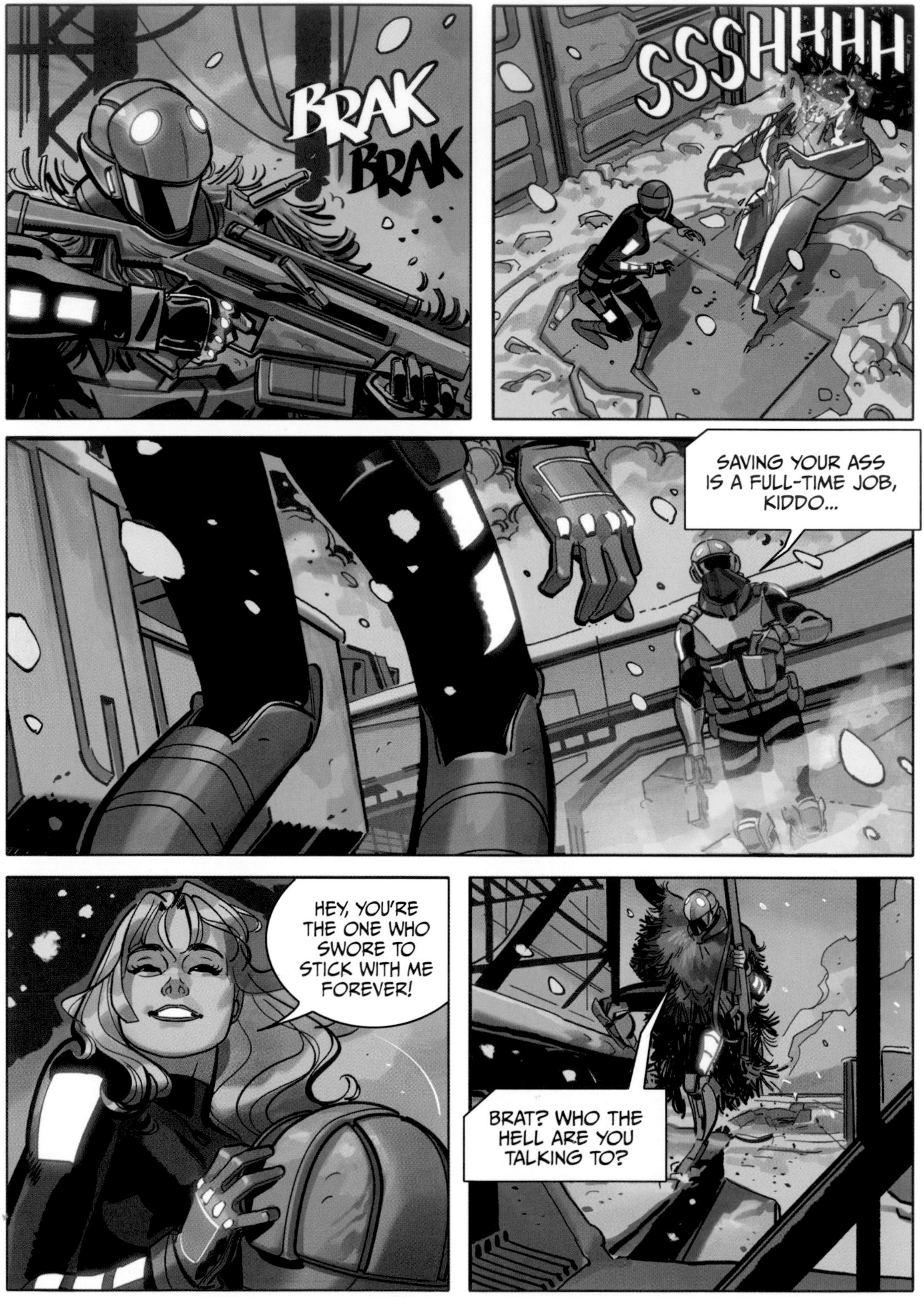
BRAK
BRAK
SSSHHHH
SAVING YOUR ASS IS A FULL-TIME JOB, KIDDO...
HEY, YOU'RE THE ONE WHO SWORE TO STICK WITH ME FOREVER!
BRAT? WHO THE HELL ARE YOU TALKING TO?

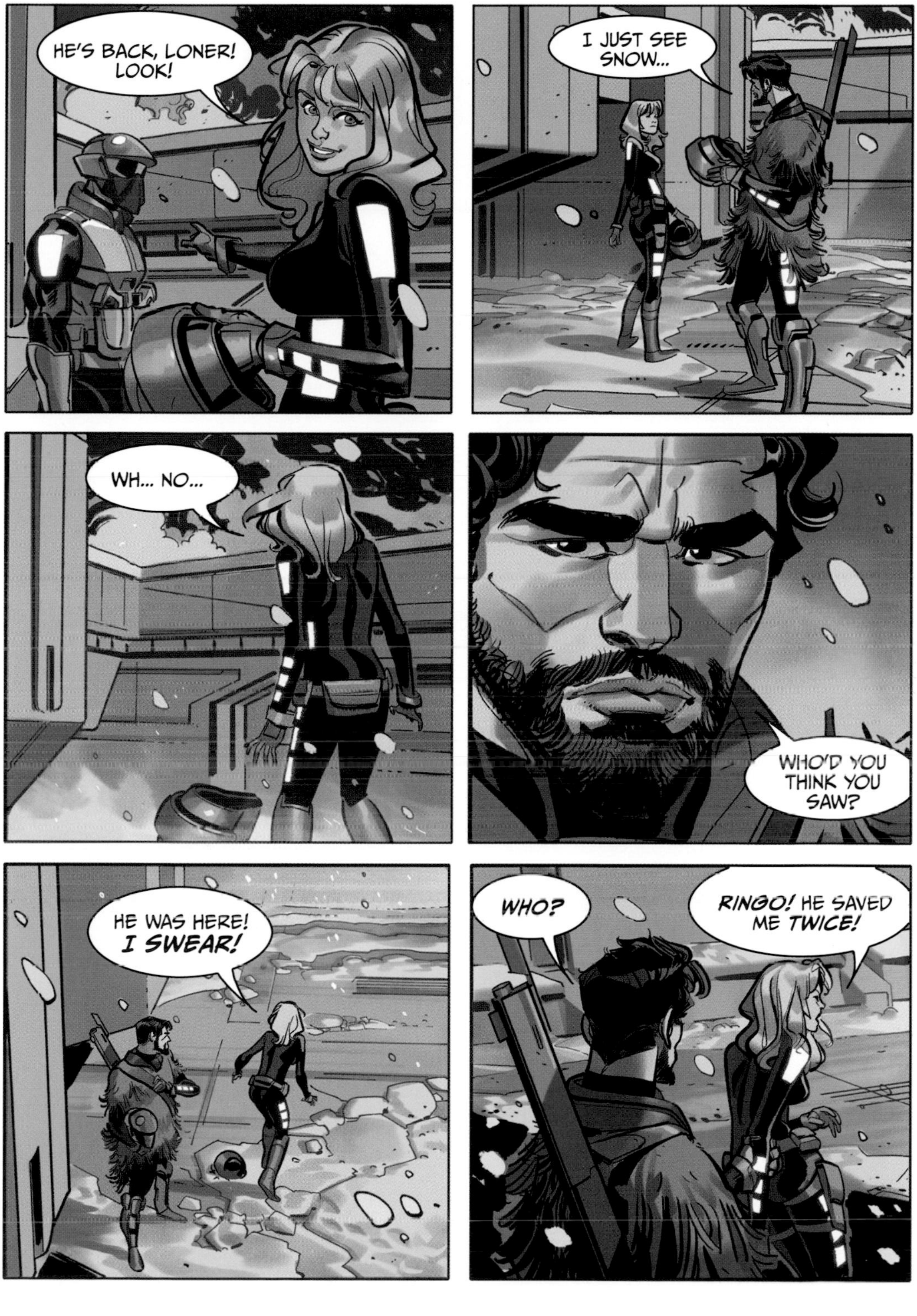
HE'S BACK, LONER! LOOK!
I JUST SEE SNOW...
WH... NO...
WHO'D YOU THINK YOU SAW?
HE WAS HERE! I SWEAR!
WHO?
RINGO! HE SAVED ME TWICE!

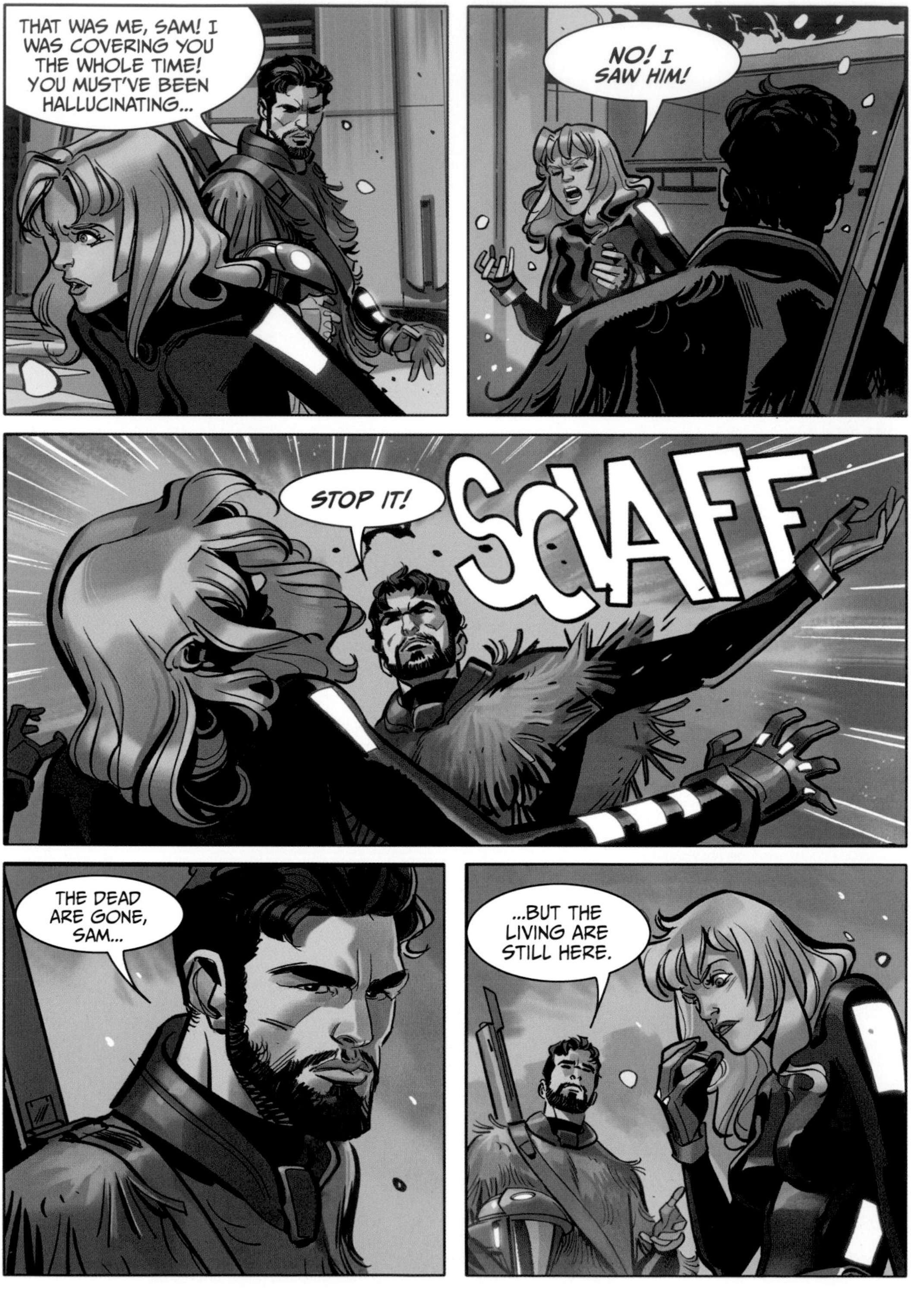
THAT WAS ME, SAM! I WAS COVERING YOU THE WHOLE TIME! YOU MUST'VE BEEN HALLUCINATING...
NO! I SAW HIM!
STOP IT!
SCIAFF
THE DEAD ARE GONE, SAM...
...BUT THE LIVING ARE STILL HERE.

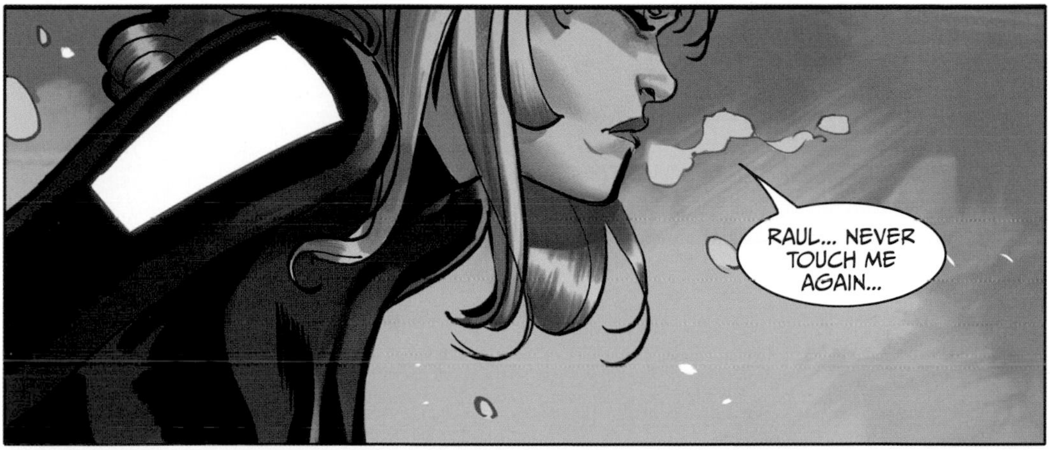
RAUL... NEVER TOUCH ME AGAIN...

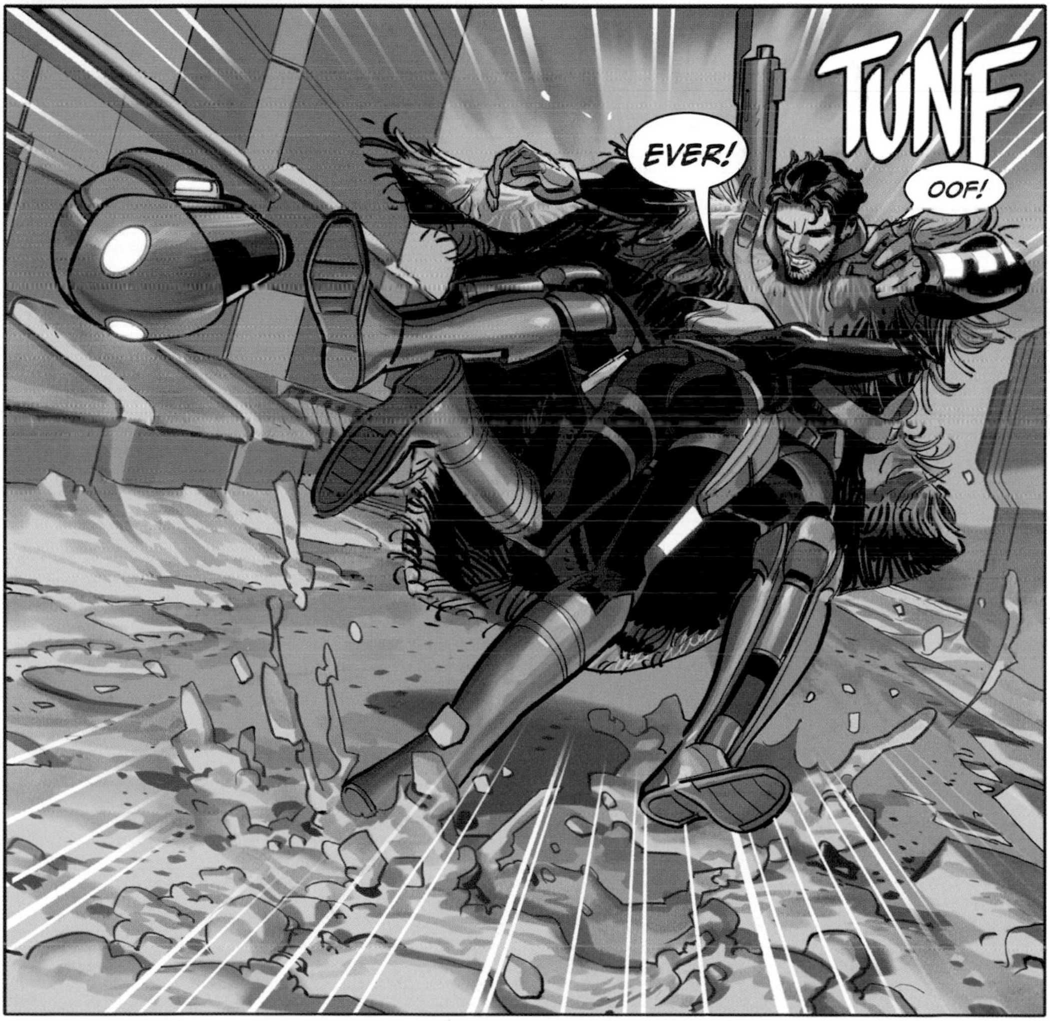
TUNF
EVER!
OOF!

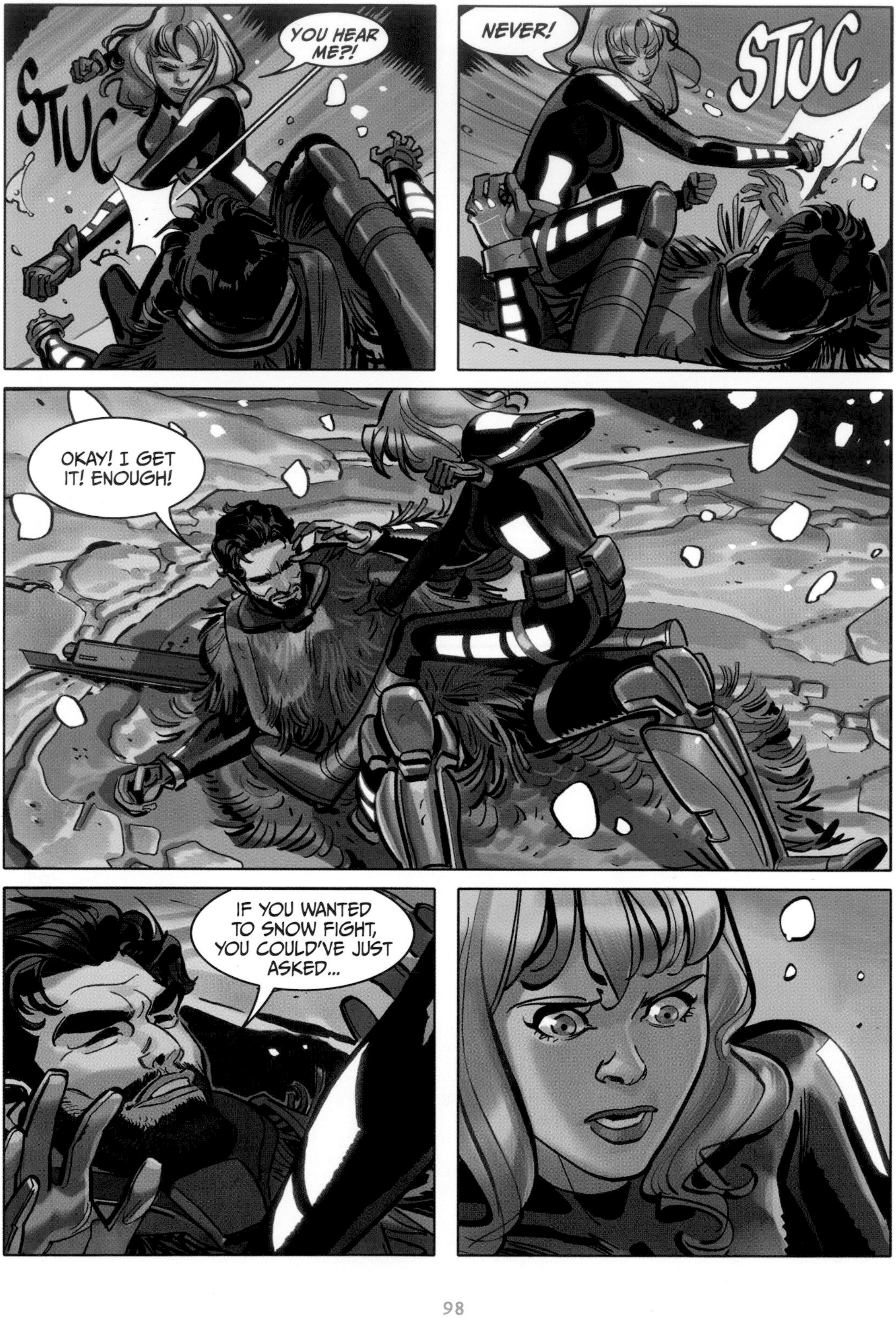
STUC
YOU HEAR ME?!
NEVER!
STUC
OKAY! I GET IT! ENOUGH!
IF YOU WANTED TO SNOW FIGHT, YOU COULD'VE JUST ASKED...

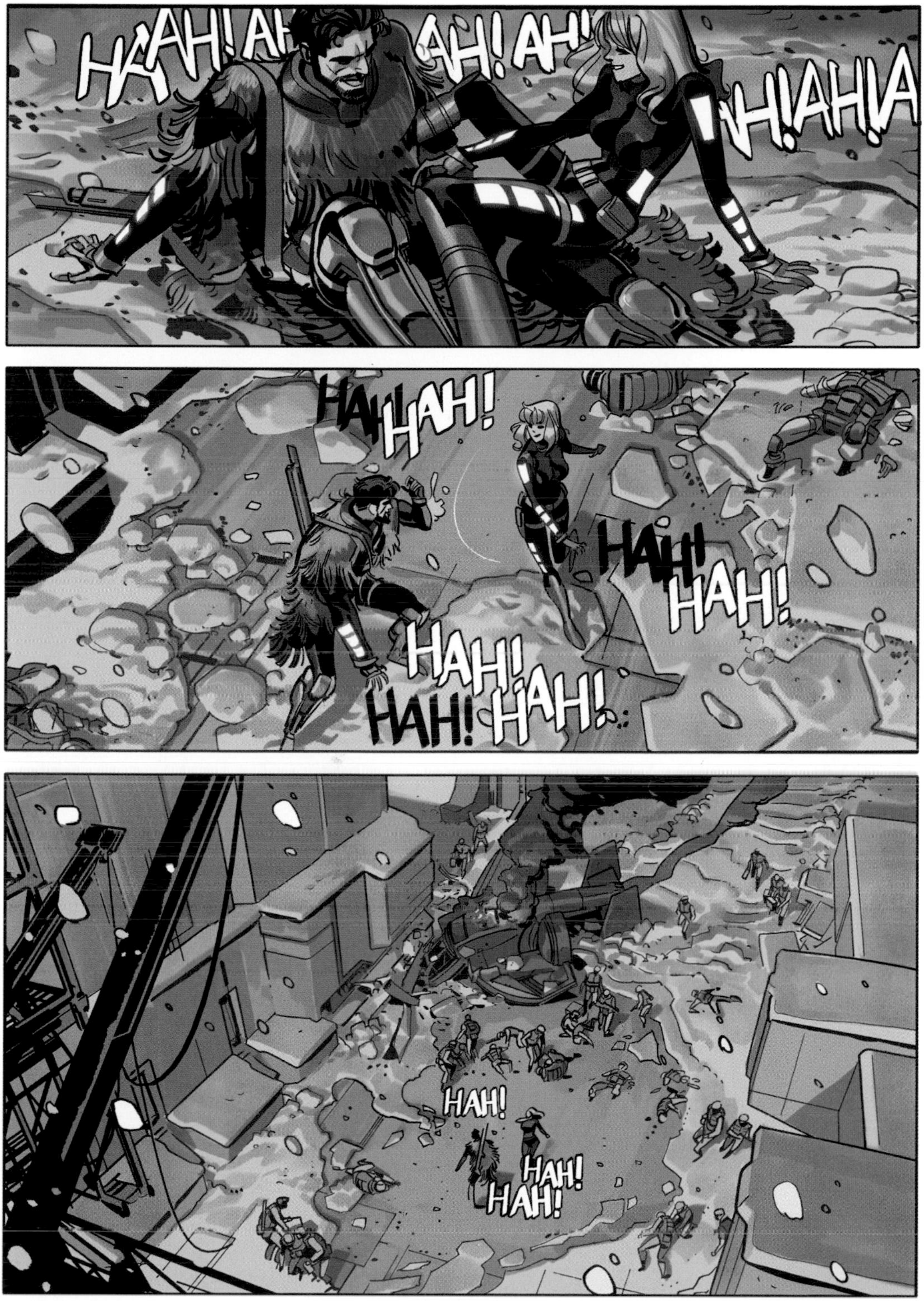
HAAH! AH
AH! AH!
H!AH!A
HAH HAH!
HAH! HAH!
HAH! HAH!
HAH! HAH!
HAH!
HAH!
HAH!

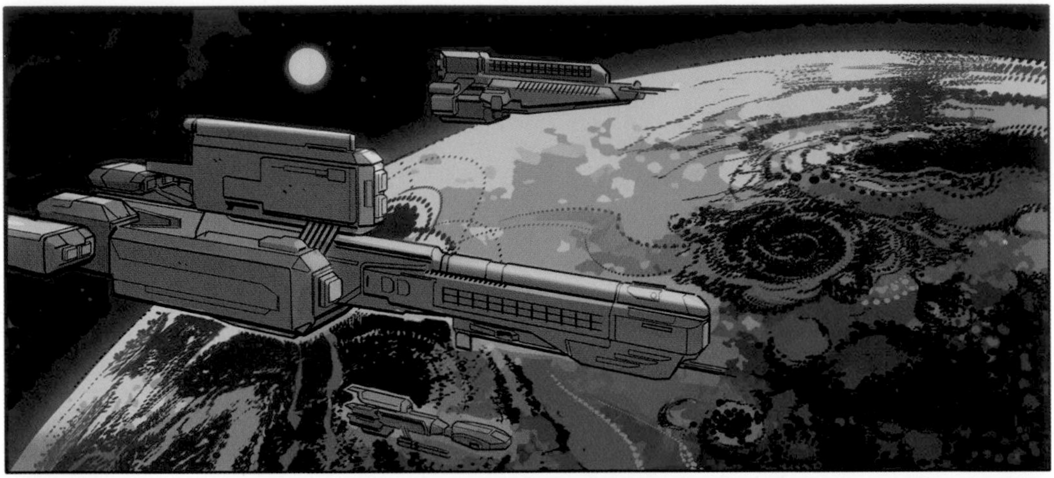

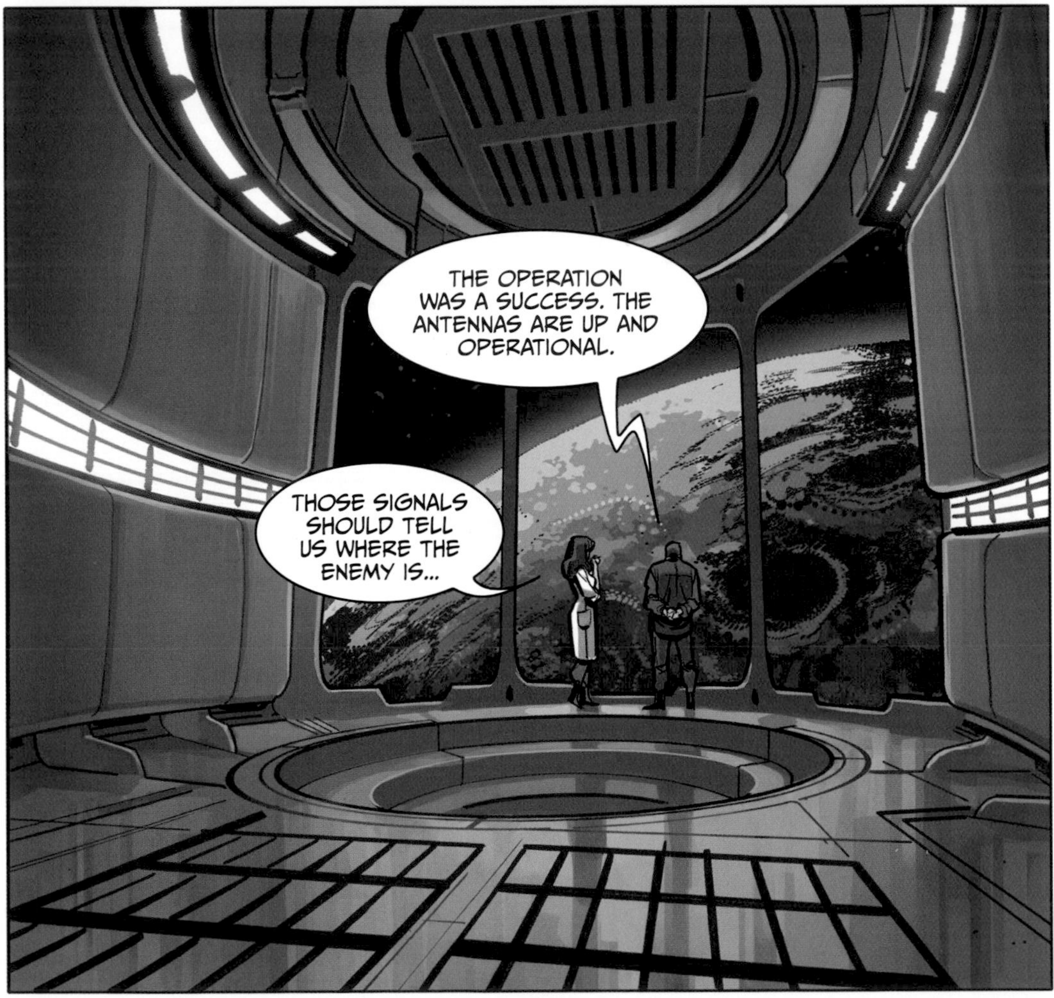
THE OPERATION WAS A SUCCESS. THE ANTENNAS ARE UP AND OPERATIONAL.
THOSE SIGNALS SHOULD TELL US WHERE THE ENEMY IS...

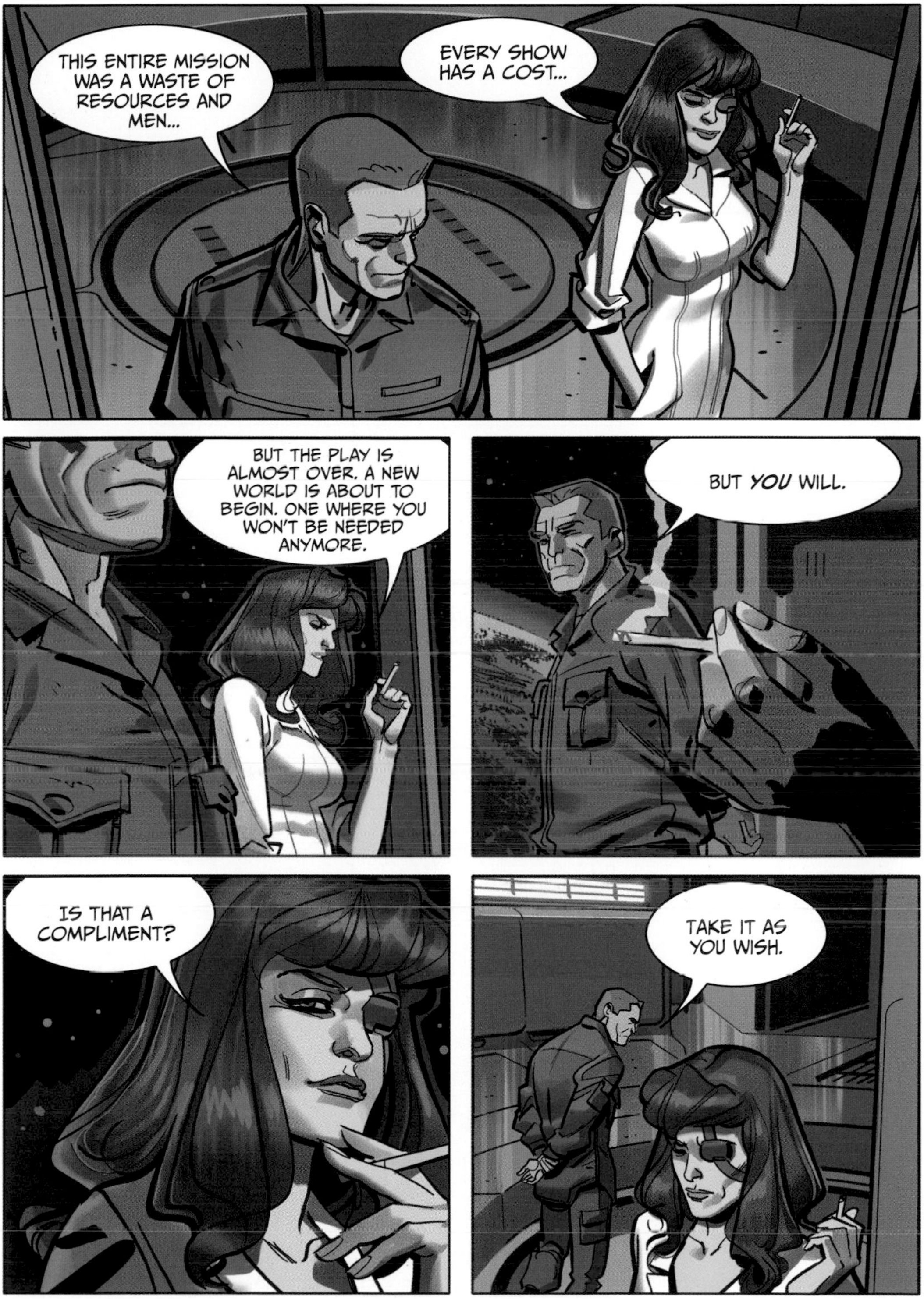
THIS ENTIRE MISSION WAS A WASTE OF RESOURCES AND MEN...
EVERY SHOW HAS A COST...
BUT THE PLAY IS ALMOST OVER. A NEW WORLD IS ABOUT TO BEGIN. ONE WHERE YOU WON'T BE NEEDED ANYMORE.
BUT *YOU* WILL.
IS THAT A COMPLIMENT?
TAKE IT AS YOU WISH.

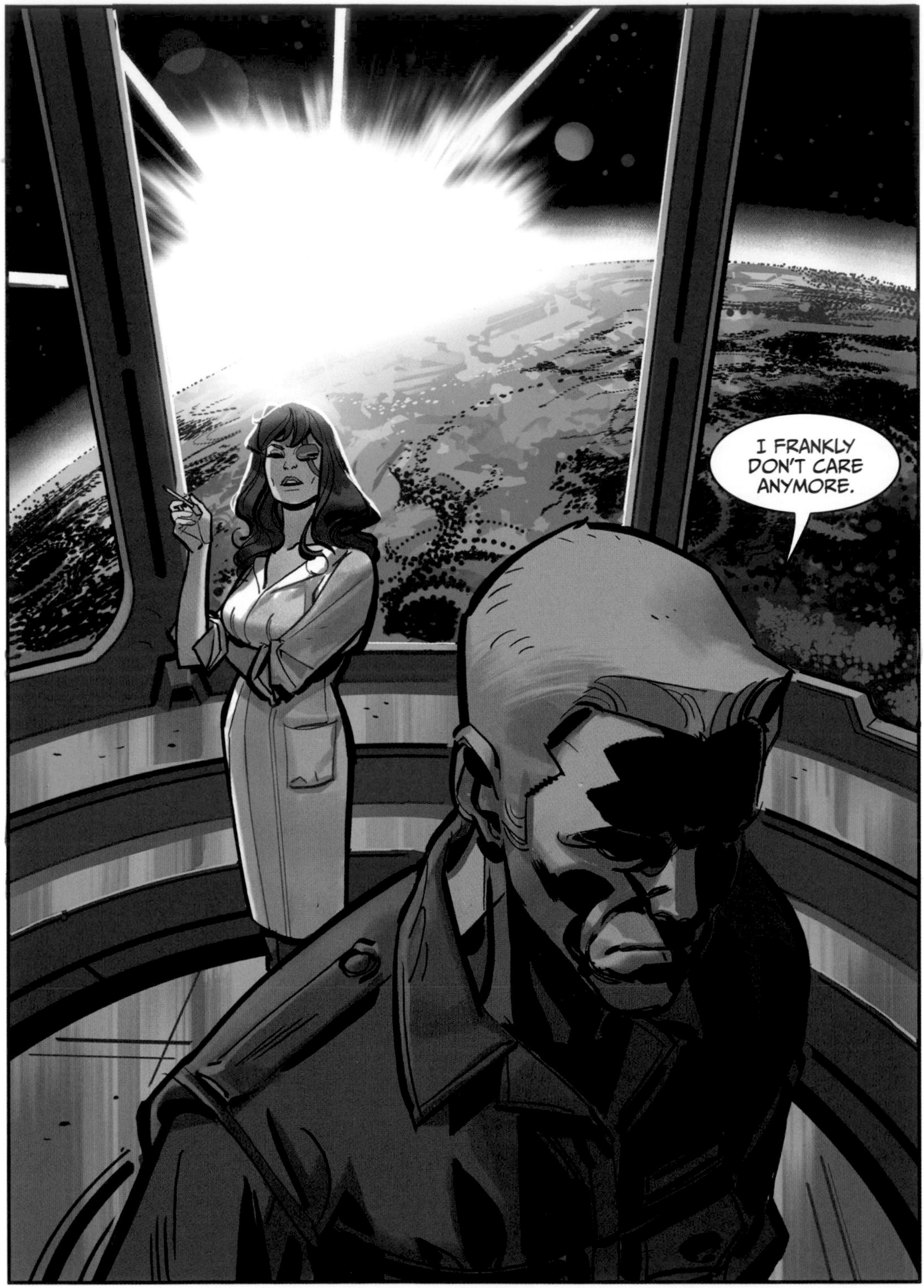
I FRANKLY DON'T CARE ANYMORE.

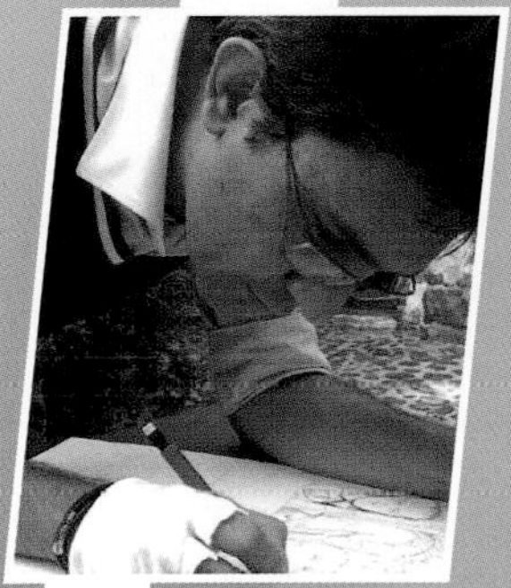

MASSIMO DALL'OGLIO
ARTIST

When and where were you born? Where do you live now?

I was born in San Gavino Monreale, Sardinia, and now I live in Cagliari.

What sort of artistic education did you have?

I'm a completely self-taught artist; I don't like drawing as an end, I only like to draw to make comics.

Tell us about your previous works, before *Orphans*.

I've worked with many publishers and writers in Italy and abroad, but the works that marked a turning point in my career are *Underskin* (my first work as a professional artist) written by Andrea Iovinelli and published in France by Les Humanoïdes Associés, *Jonathan Steele* (my first Italian publication for newsstand readers) written by Federico Memola and published by Star Comics, and *Lost Planet: First Colony* (my first international work) written by Izu and published by Glénat in collaboration with the prestigious video game company CAPCOM.

When did you start working on *Orphans*, and when did you finish drawing your chapter?

I started in summer 2011 and finished the first forty-five pages about a year later.

What tools did you use?

Traditional ones: pencil and ink nib.

What was the most difficult scene and which one did you have to redraw more times?

The first ten pages were the most complex ones, mainly due to managing the layout of the page and the rendering of the characters. It wasn't easy to be true to my own style while also staying faithful and coherent with the visual language of Bonelli comics.

If you could go back in time, what would you change about this chapter?

One of the things that distinguishes me most as an artist is that I don't look back. When I finish a task, I turn to the next one and I try to solve any shortcomings I faced with the previous work. So, to answer the question, I wouldn't change anything. These are the best pages I could draw at that period and in the situation I found myself at that time.

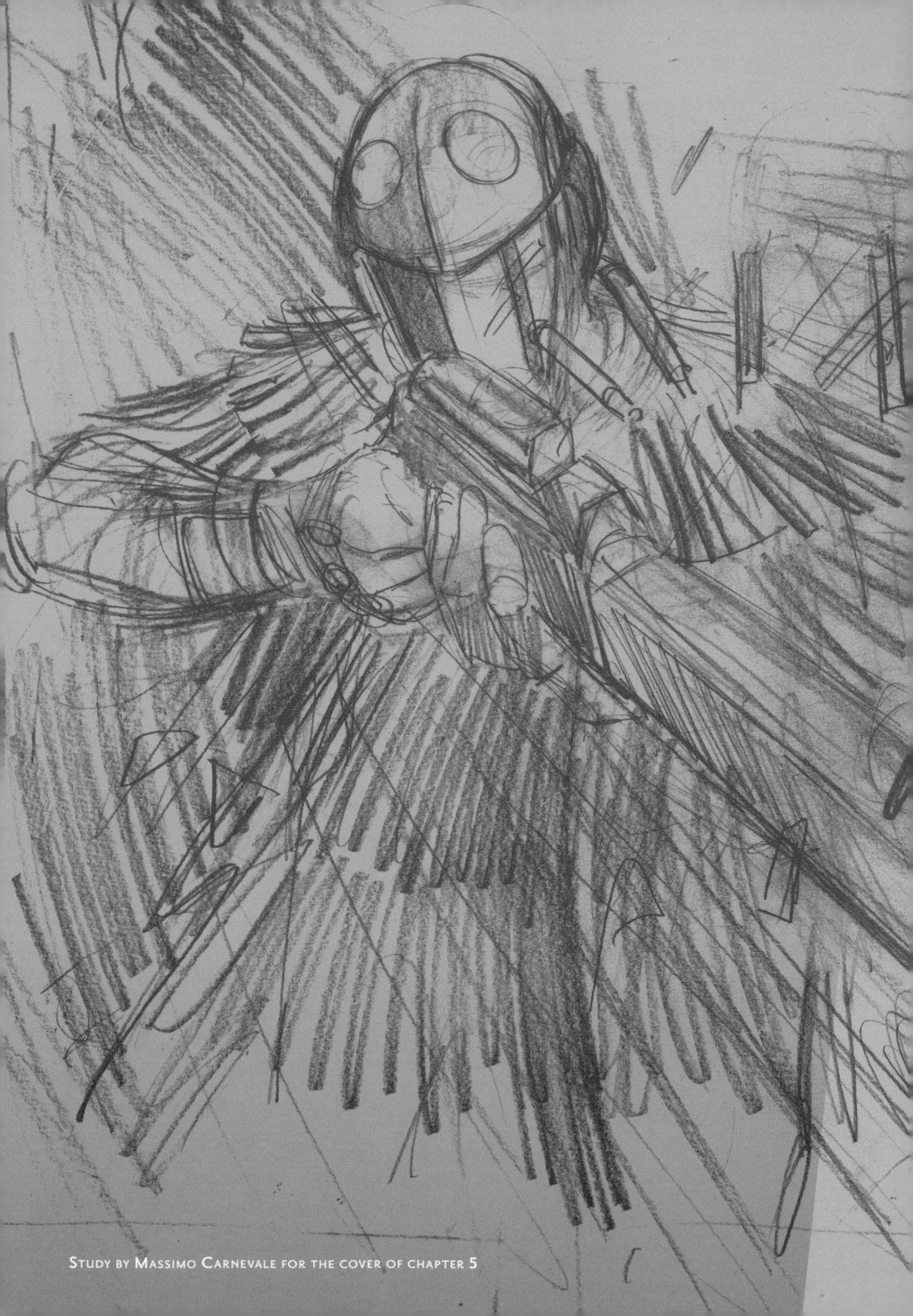

Study by Massimo Carnevale for the cover of chapter 5

THE RIFLEMAN

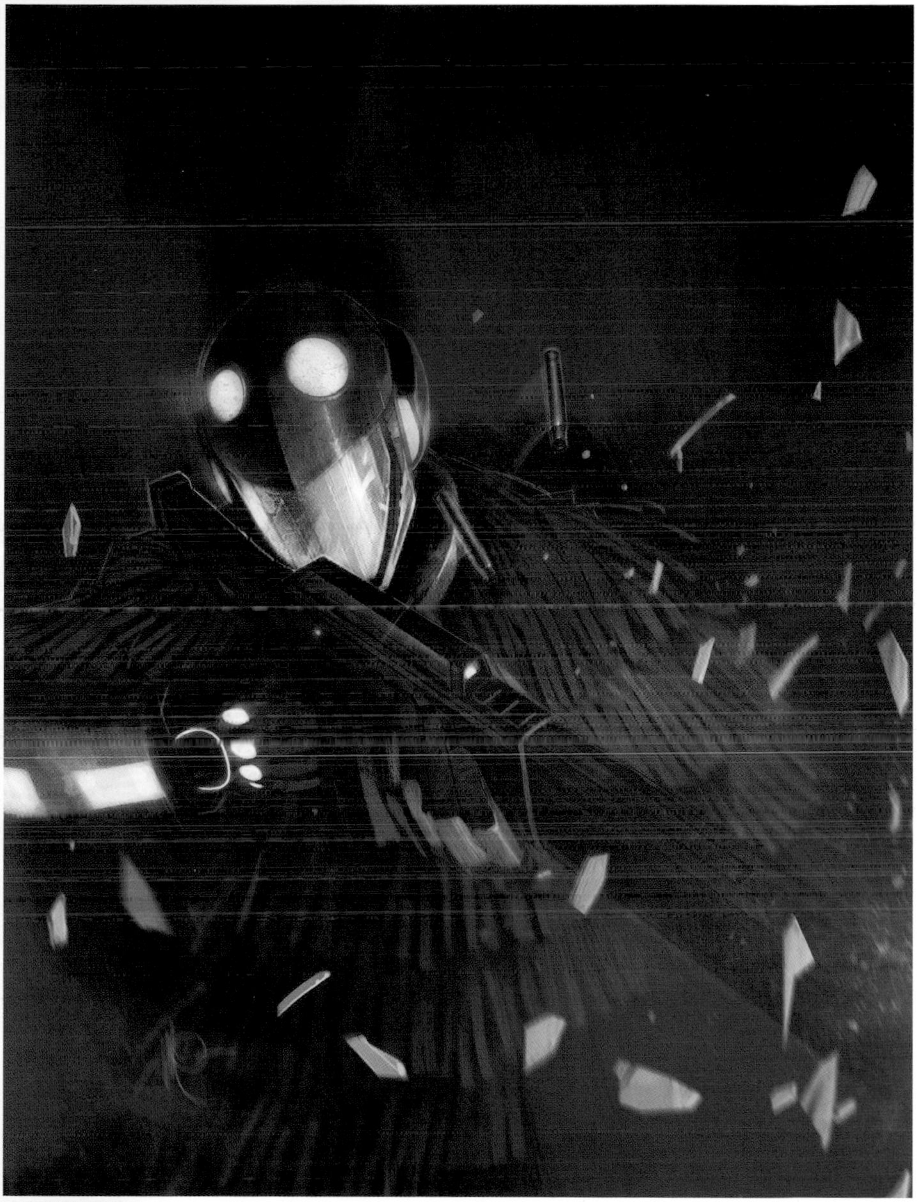

ORPHANS: CHAPTER 5

story: ROBERTO RECCHIONI
art: LUCA MARESCA
colors: ALESSIA PASTORELLO
cover: MASSIMO CARNEVALE

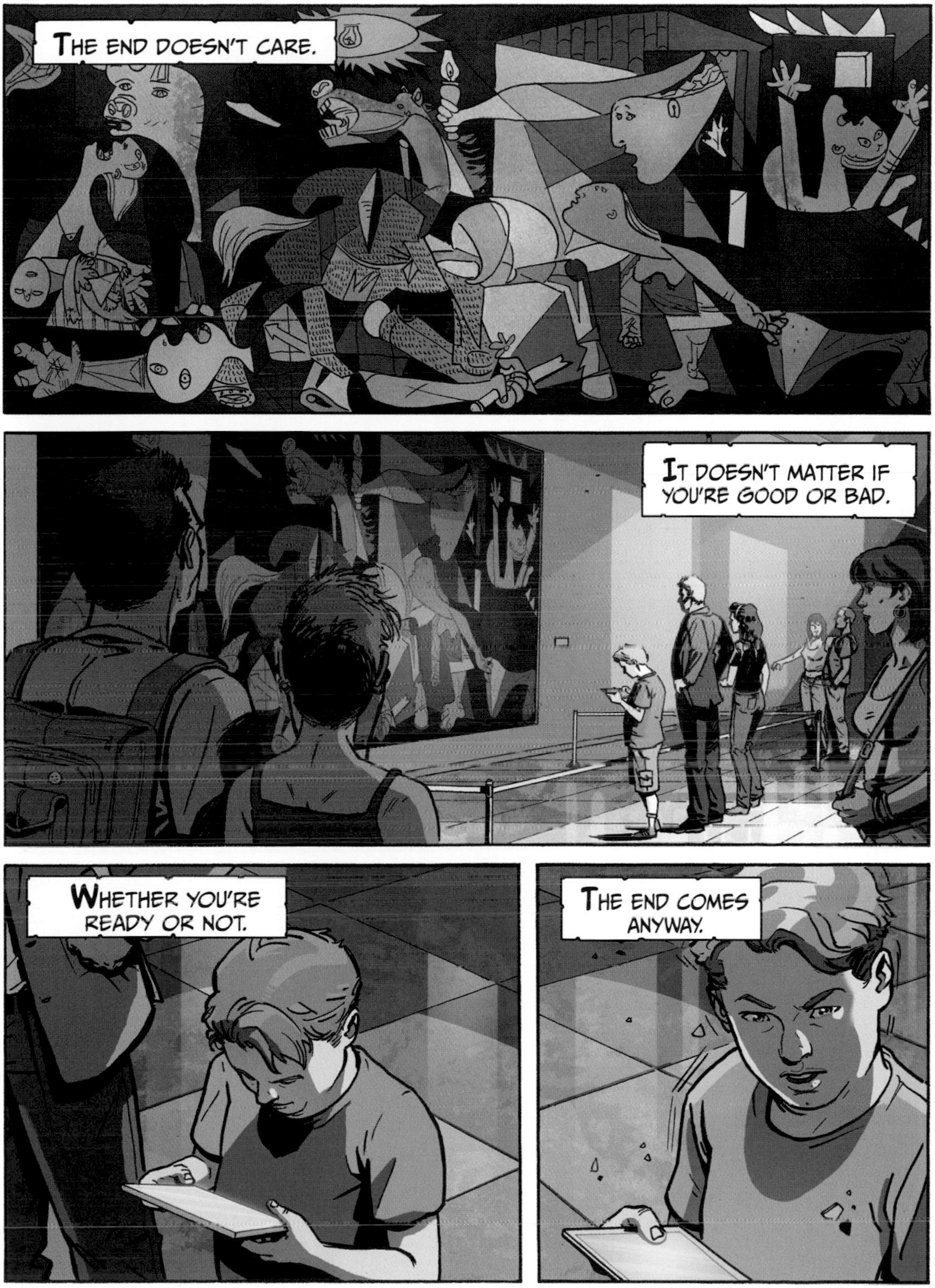
THE END DOESN'T CARE.
IT DOESN'T MATTER IF YOU'RE GOOD OR BAD.
WHETHER YOU'RE READY OR NOT.
THE END COMES ANYWAY.

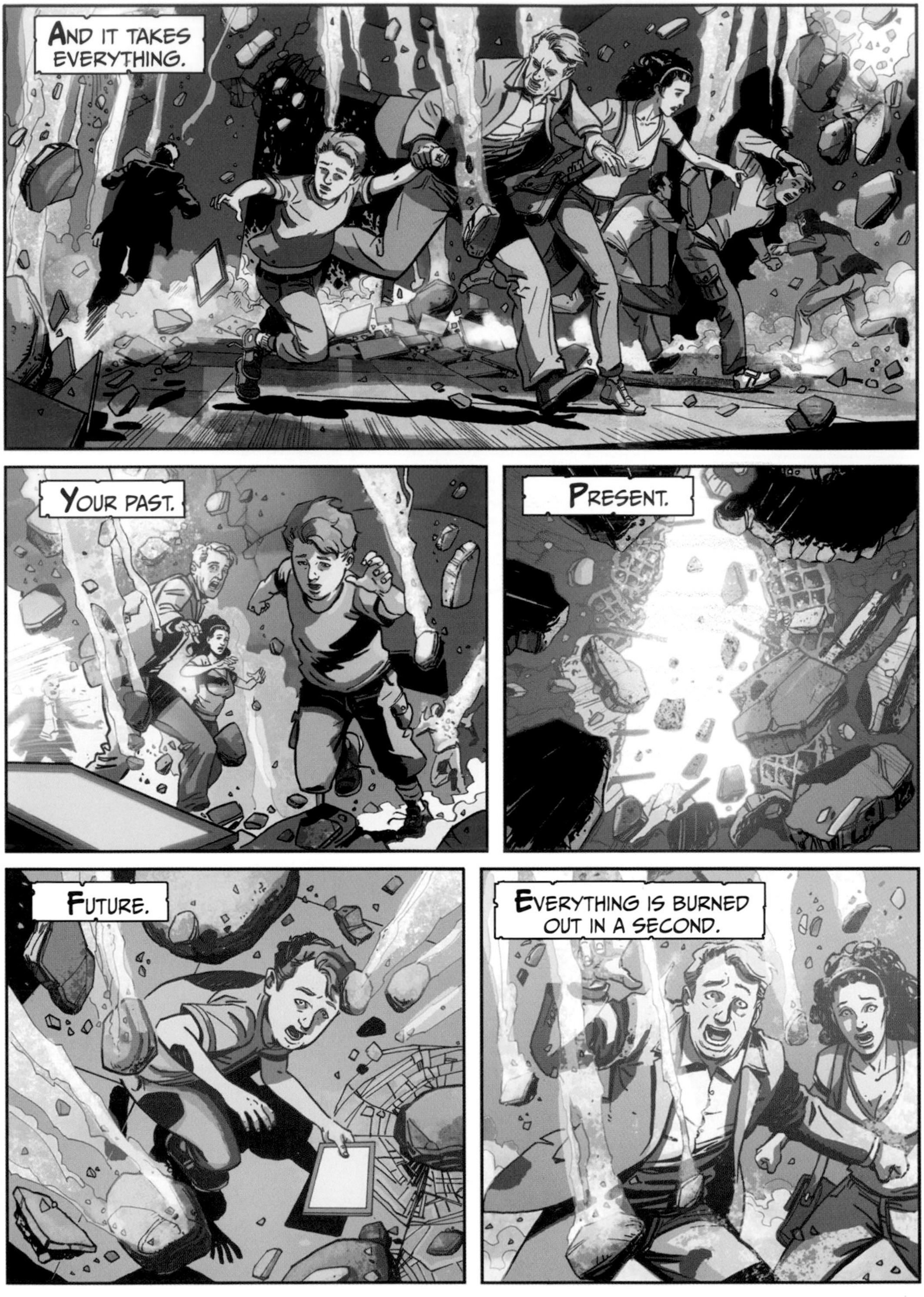
AND IT TAKES EVERYTHING.
YOUR PAST.
PRESENT.
FUTURE.
EVERYTHING IS BURNED OUT IN A SECOND.

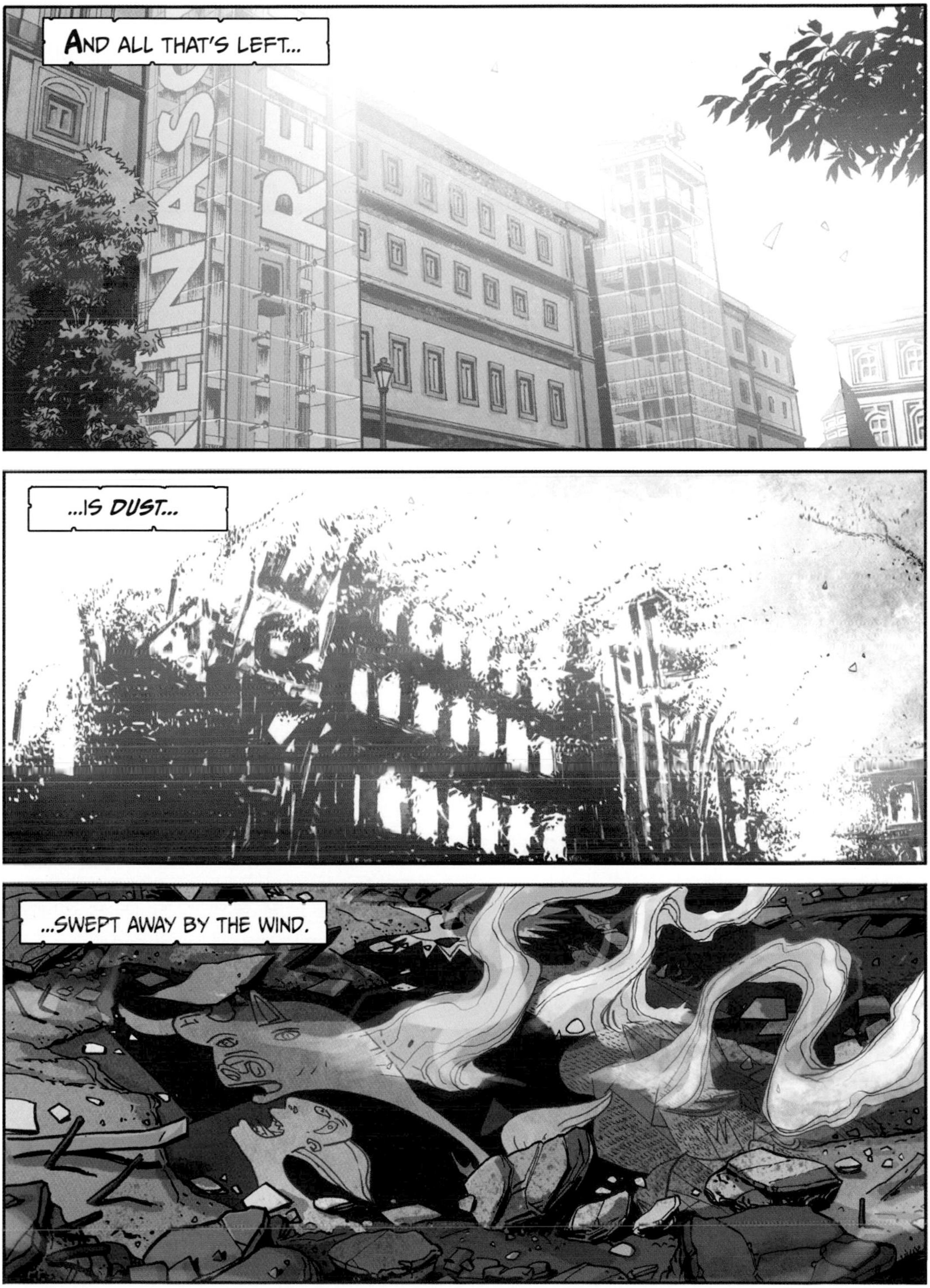
AND ALL THAT'S LEFT...
...IS DUST...
...SWEPT AWAY BY THE WIND.

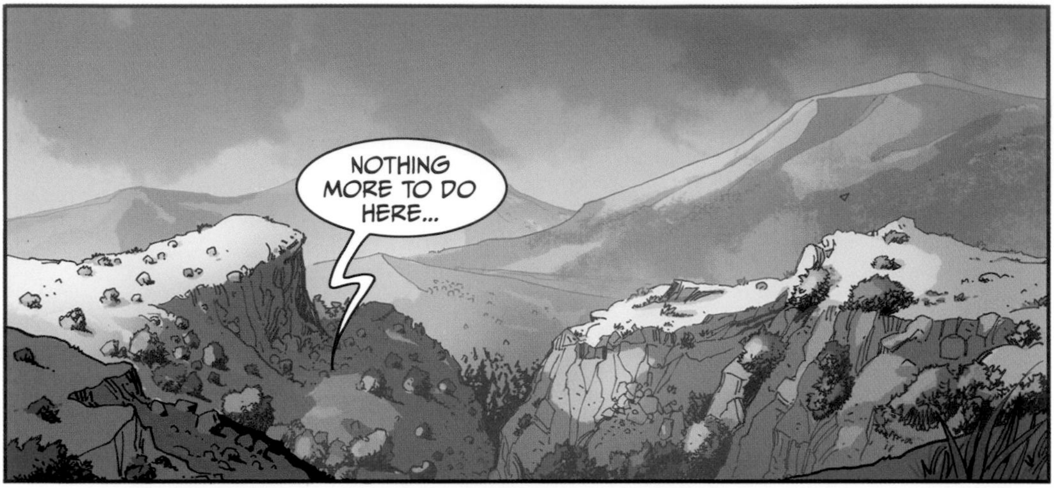
NOTHING MORE TO DO HERE...

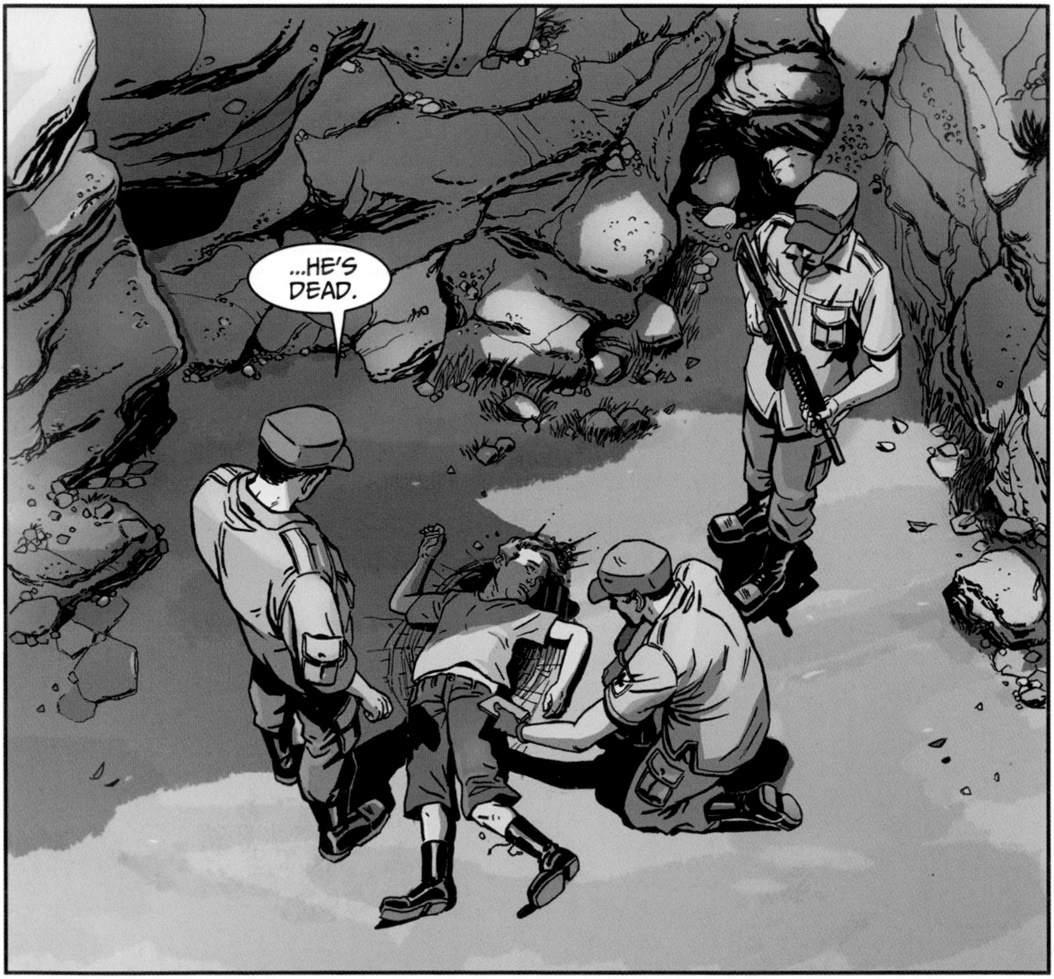
...HE'S DEAD.

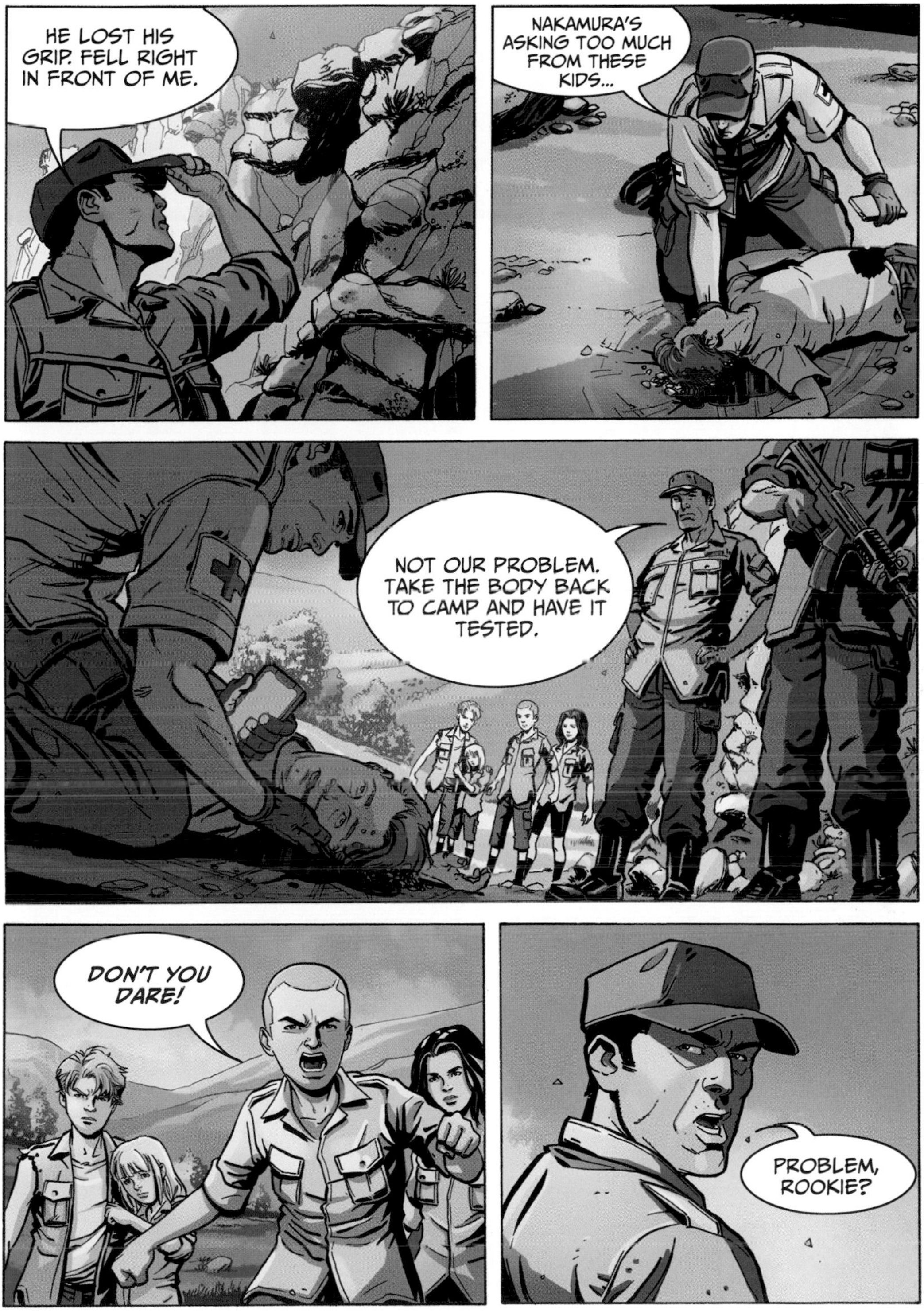
HE LOST HIS GRIP. FELL RIGHT IN FRONT OF ME.
NAKAMURA'S ASKING TOO MUCH FROM THESE KIDS...
NOT OUR PROBLEM. TAKE THE BODY BACK TO CAMP AND HAVE IT TESTED.
DON'T YOU DARE!
PROBLEM, ROOKIE?

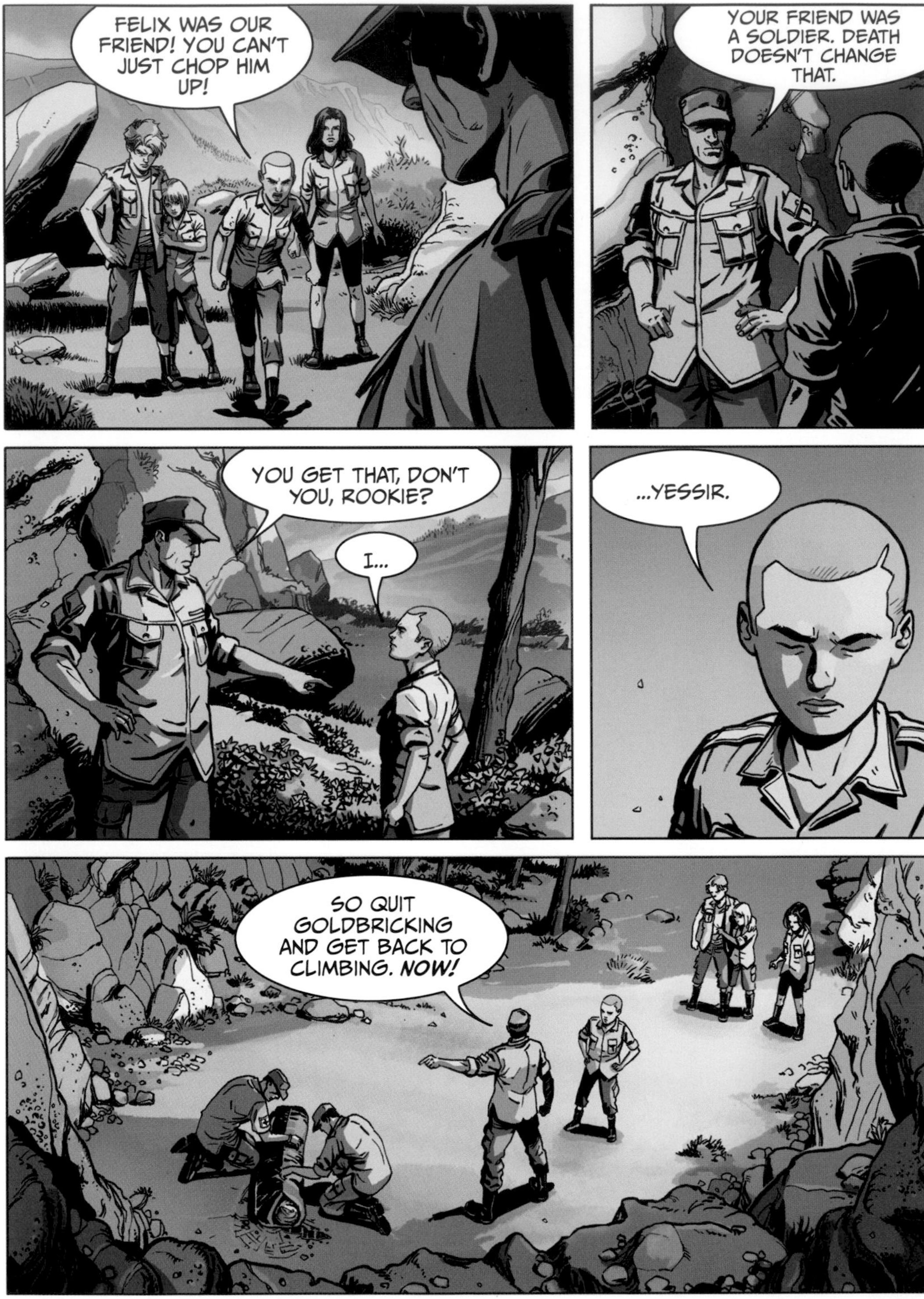
FELIX WAS OUR FRIEND! YOU CAN'T JUST CHOP HIM UP!
YOUR FRIEND WAS A SOLDIER. DEATH DOESN'T CHANGE THAT.
YOU GET THAT, DON'T YOU, ROOKIE?
I...
...YESSIR.
SO QUIT GOLDBRICKING AND GET BACK TO CLIMBING. *NOW!*

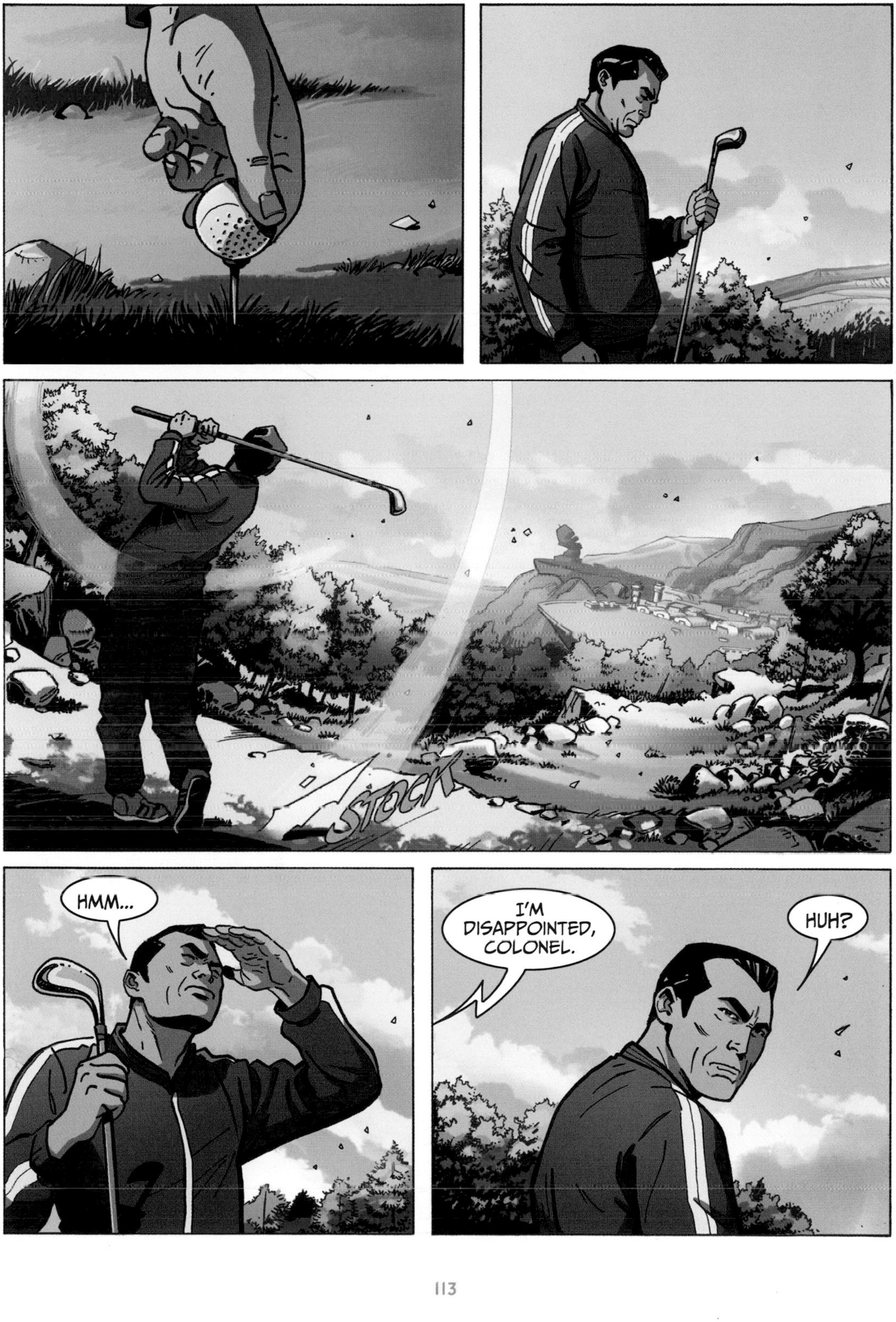
STOCK
HMM...
I'M DISAPPOINTED, COLONEL.
HUH?

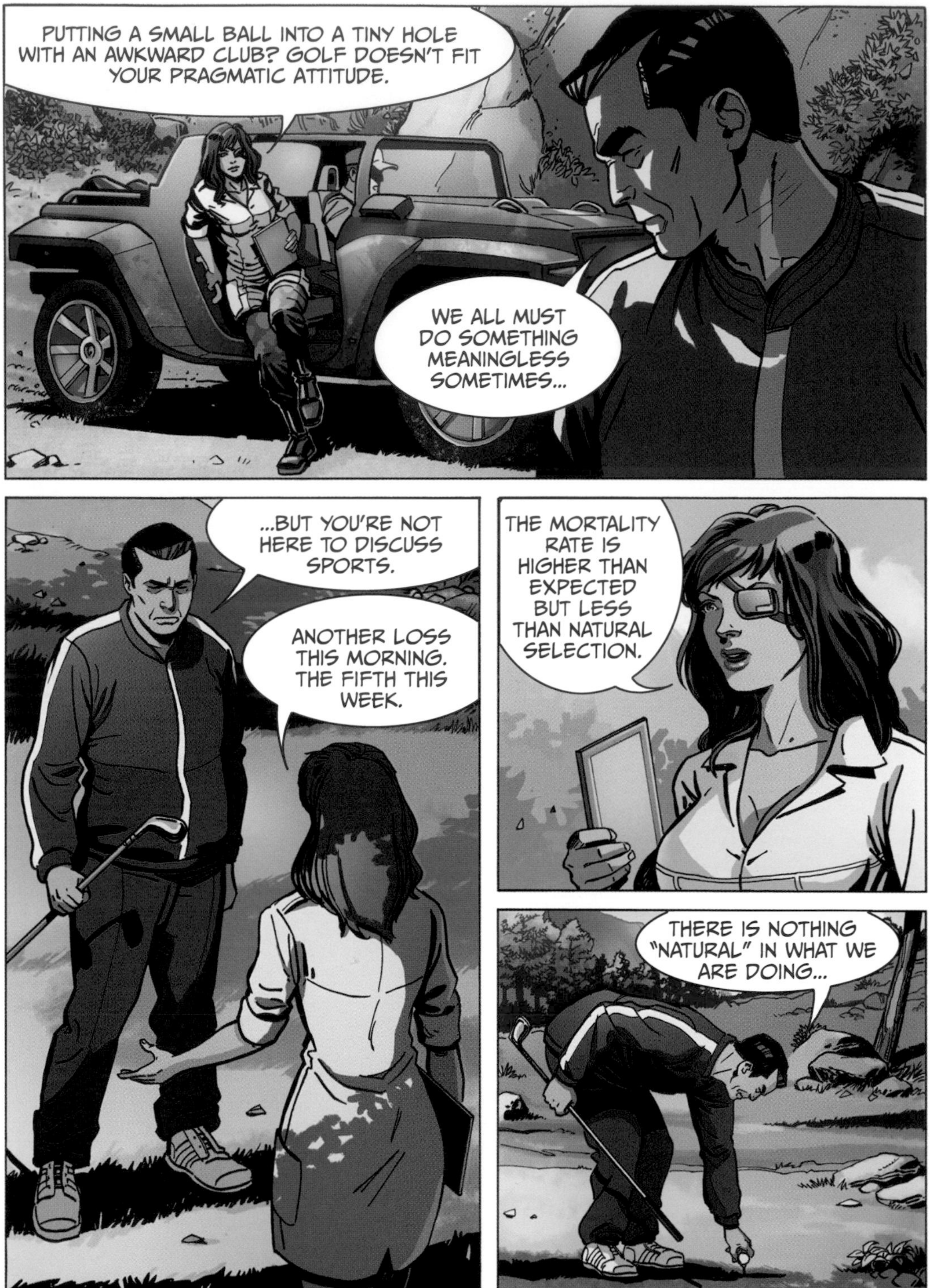
PUTTING A SMALL BALL INTO A TINY HOLE WITH AN AWKWARD CLUB? GOLF DOESN'T FIT YOUR PRAGMATIC ATTITUDE.
WE ALL MUST DO SOMETHING MEANINGLESS SOMETIMES...
...BUT YOU'RE NOT HERE TO DISCUSS SPORTS.
ANOTHER LOSS THIS MORNING. THE FIFTH THIS WEEK.
THE MORTALITY RATE IS HIGHER THAN EXPECTED BUT LESS THAN NATURAL SELECTION.
THERE IS NOTHING "NATURAL" IN WHAT WE ARE DOING...

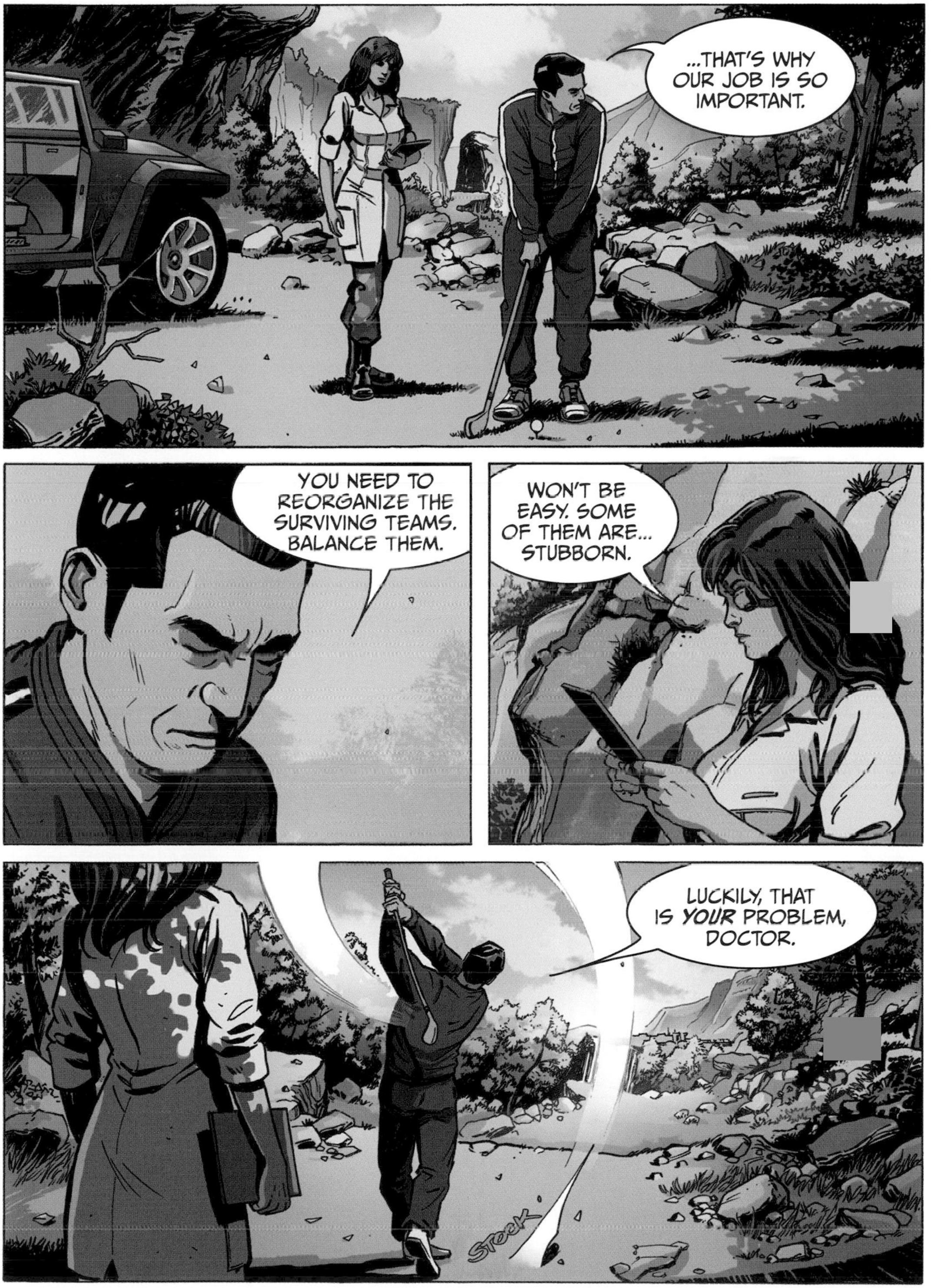
...THAT'S WHY OUR JOB IS SO IMPORTANT.
YOU NEED TO REORGANIZE THE SURVIVING TEAMS. BALANCE THEM.
WON'T BE EASY. SOME OF THEM ARE... STUBBORN.
LUCKILY, THAT IS *YOUR* PROBLEM, DOCTOR.
STOCK

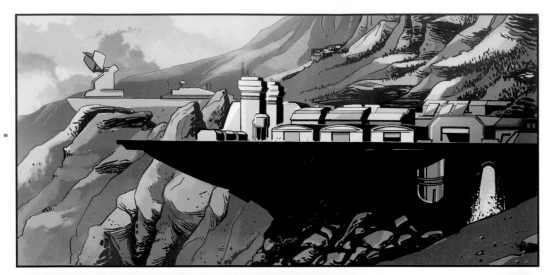

FIRST HECTOR, THEN REY. NOW FELIX... I PROMISED YOUR BROTHER I'D PROTECT YOU ALL...

...I FAILED.

IT'S NOT YOUR FAULT, JONAS.

THEN WHY DO I FEEL SO BAD?

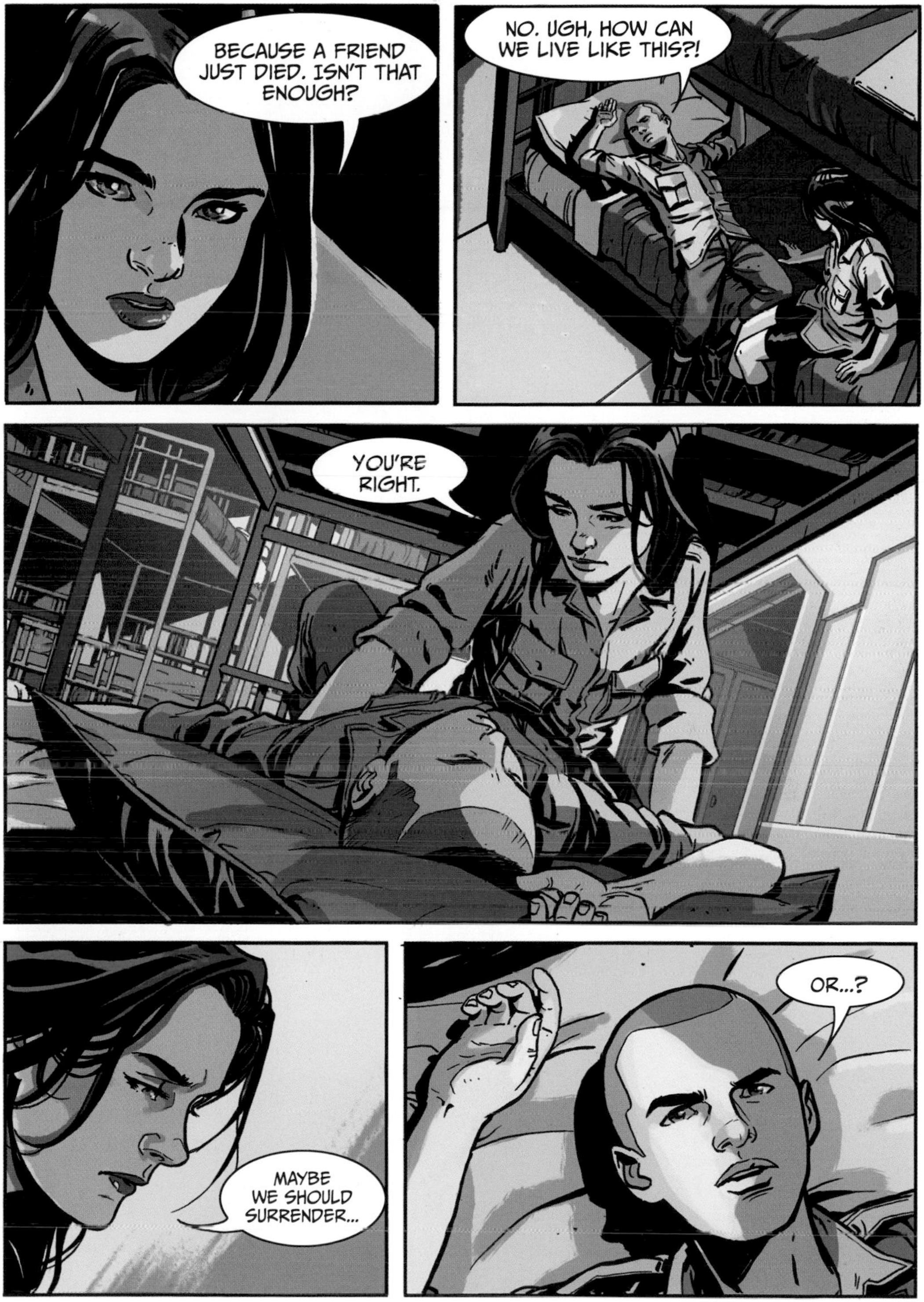
BECAUSE A FRIEND JUST DIED. ISN'T THAT ENOUGH?
NO. UGH, HOW CAN WE LIVE LIKE THIS?!
YOU'RE RIGHT.
MAYBE WE SHOULD SURRENDER...
OR...?

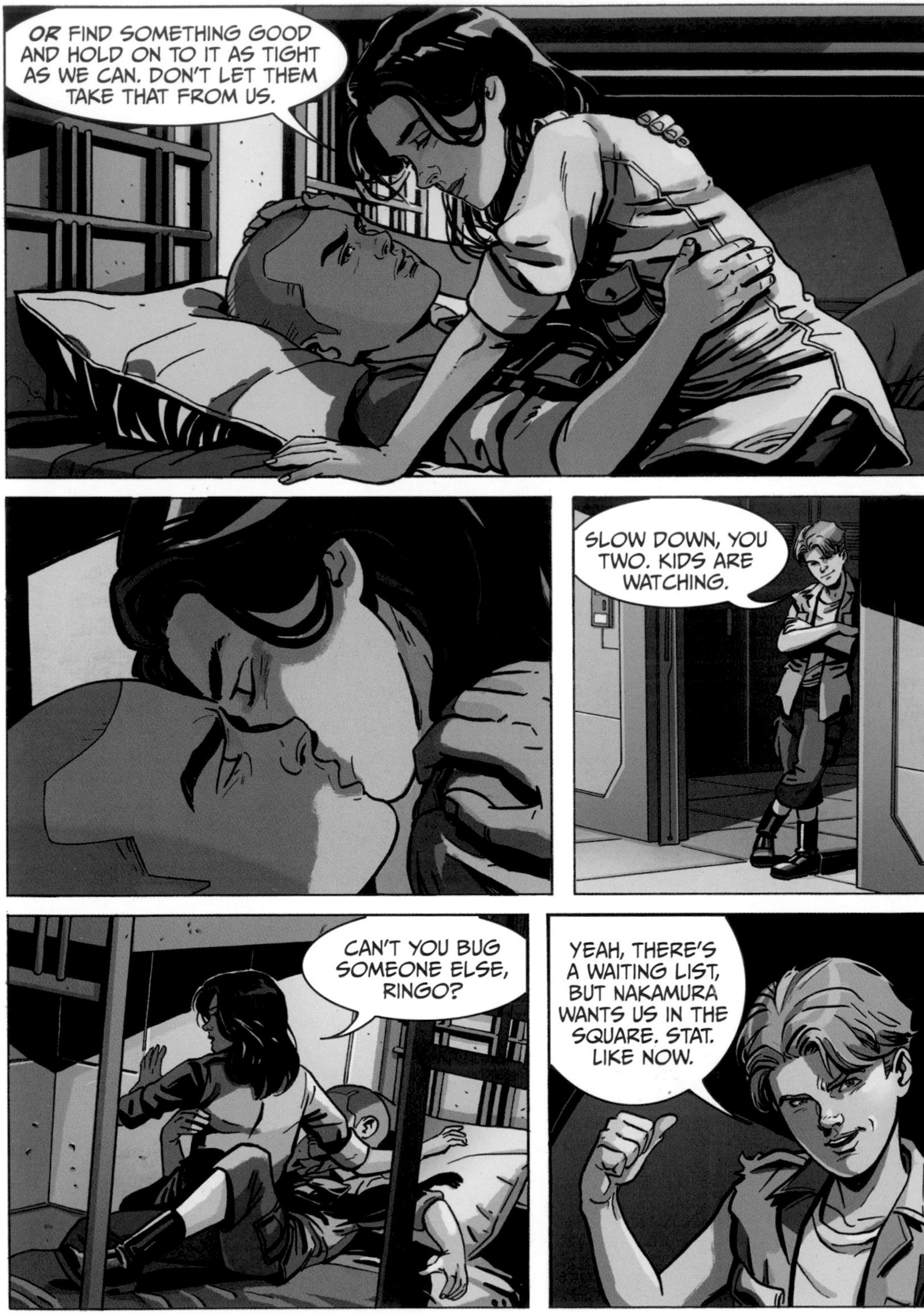
OR FIND SOMETHING GOOD AND HOLD ON TO IT AS TIGHT AS WE CAN. DON'T LET THEM TAKE THAT FROM US.
SLOW DOWN, YOU TWO. KIDS ARE WATCHING.
CAN'T YOU BUG SOMEONE ELSE, RINGO?
YEAH, THERE'S A WAITING LIST, BUT NAKAMURA WANTS US IN THE SQUARE. STAT. LIKE NOW.

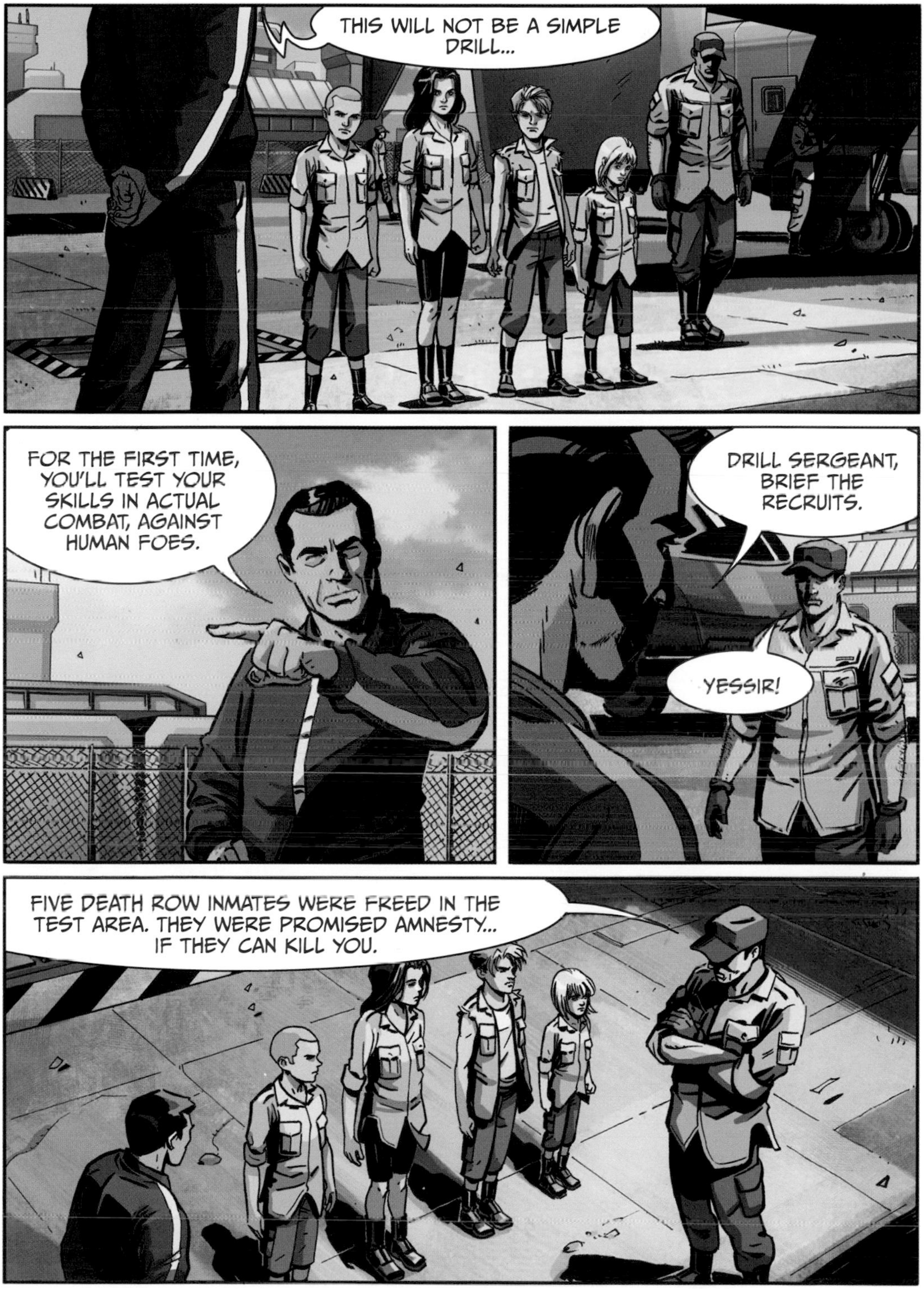
THIS WILL NOT BE A SIMPLE DRILL...
FOR THE FIRST TIME, YOU'LL TEST YOUR SKILLS IN ACTUAL COMBAT, AGAINST HUMAN FOES.
DRILL SERGEANT, BRIEF THE RECRUITS.
YESSIR!
FIVE DEATH ROW INMATES WERE FREED IN THE TEST AREA. THEY WERE PROMISED AMNESTY... IF THEY CAN KILL YOU.

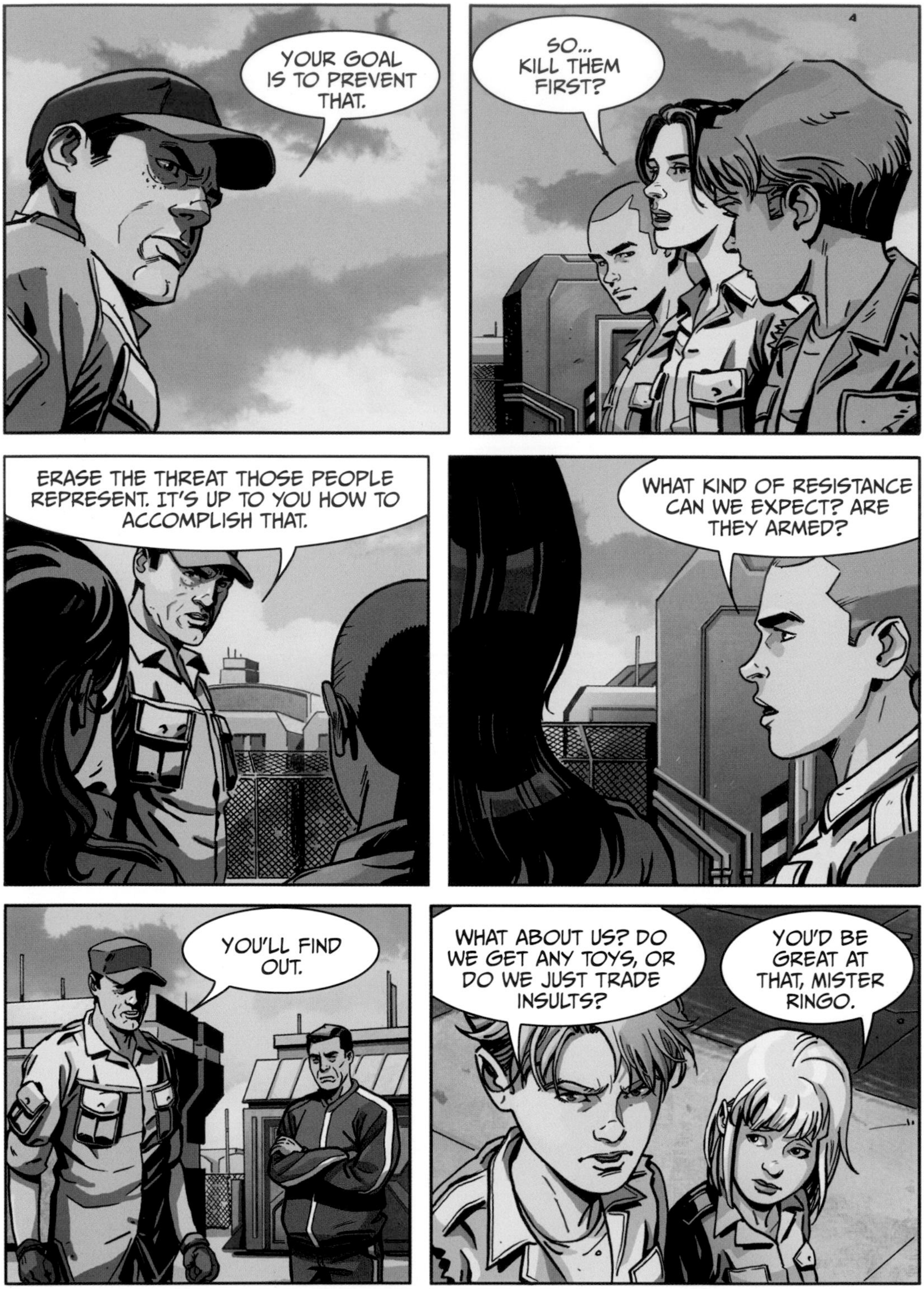
YOUR GOAL IS TO PREVENT THAT.
SO... KILL THEM FIRST?
ERASE THE THREAT THOSE PEOPLE REPRESENT. IT'S UP TO YOU HOW TO ACCOMPLISH THAT.
WHAT KIND OF RESISTANCE CAN WE EXPECT? ARE THEY ARMED?
YOU'LL FIND OUT.
WHAT ABOUT US? DO WE GET ANY TOYS, OR DO WE JUST TRADE INSULTS?
YOU'D BE GREAT AT THAT, MISTER RINGO.

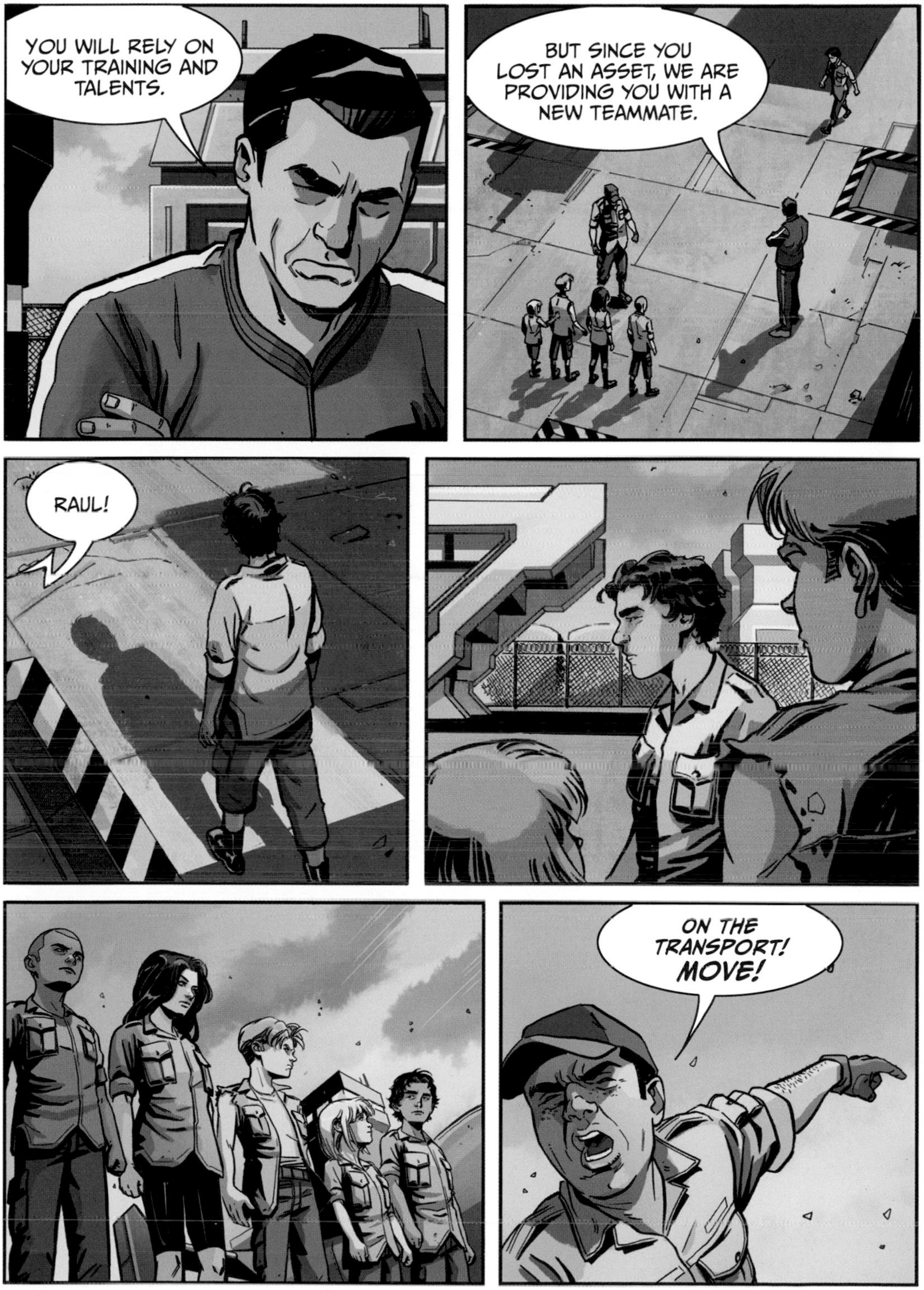
YOU WILL RELY ON YOUR TRAINING AND TALENTS.
BUT SINCE YOU LOST AN ASSET, WE ARE PROVIDING YOU WITH A NEW TEAMMATE.
RAUL!
ON THE TRANSPORT! MOVE!

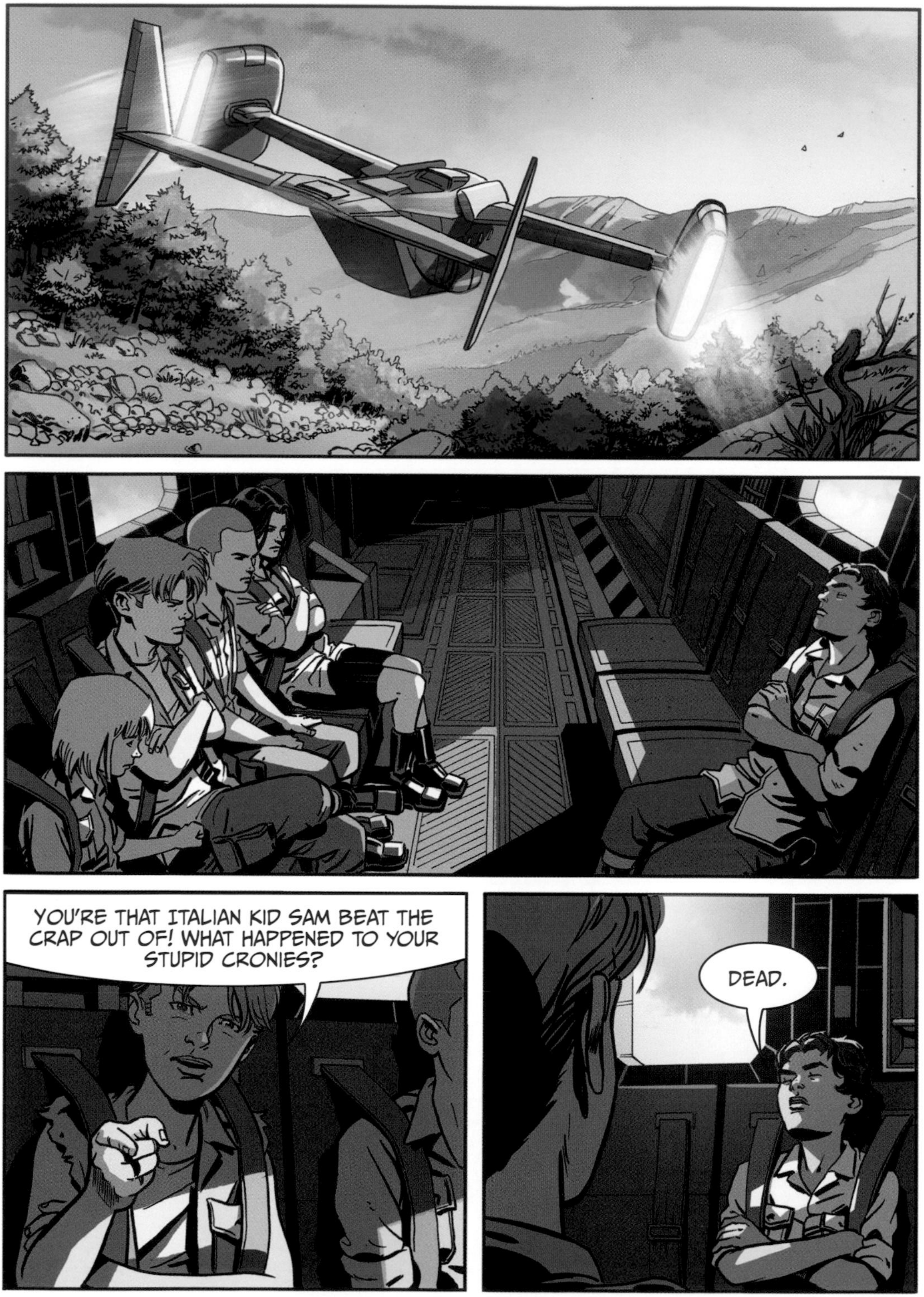
YOU'RE THAT ITALIAN KID SAM BEAT THE CRAP OUT OF! WHAT HAPPENED TO YOUR STUPID CRONIES?
DEAD.

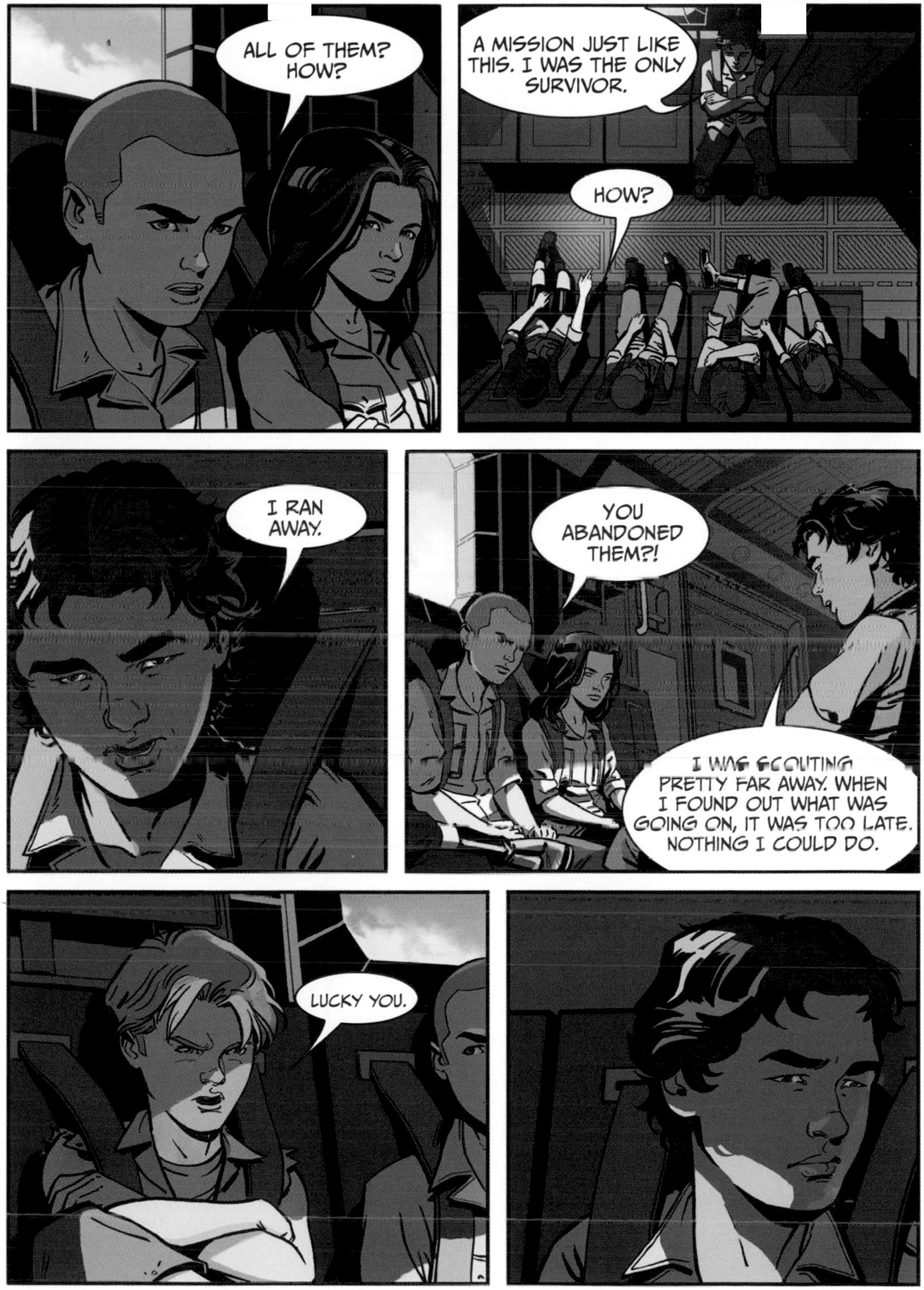
ALL OF THEM? HOW?
A MISSION JUST LIKE THIS. I WAS THE ONLY SURVIVOR.
HOW?
I RAN AWAY.
YOU ABANDONED THEM?!
I WAS SCOUTING PRETTY FAR AWAY. WHEN I FOUND OUT WHAT WAS GOING ON, IT WAS TOO LATE. NOTHING I COULD DO.
LUCKY YOU.

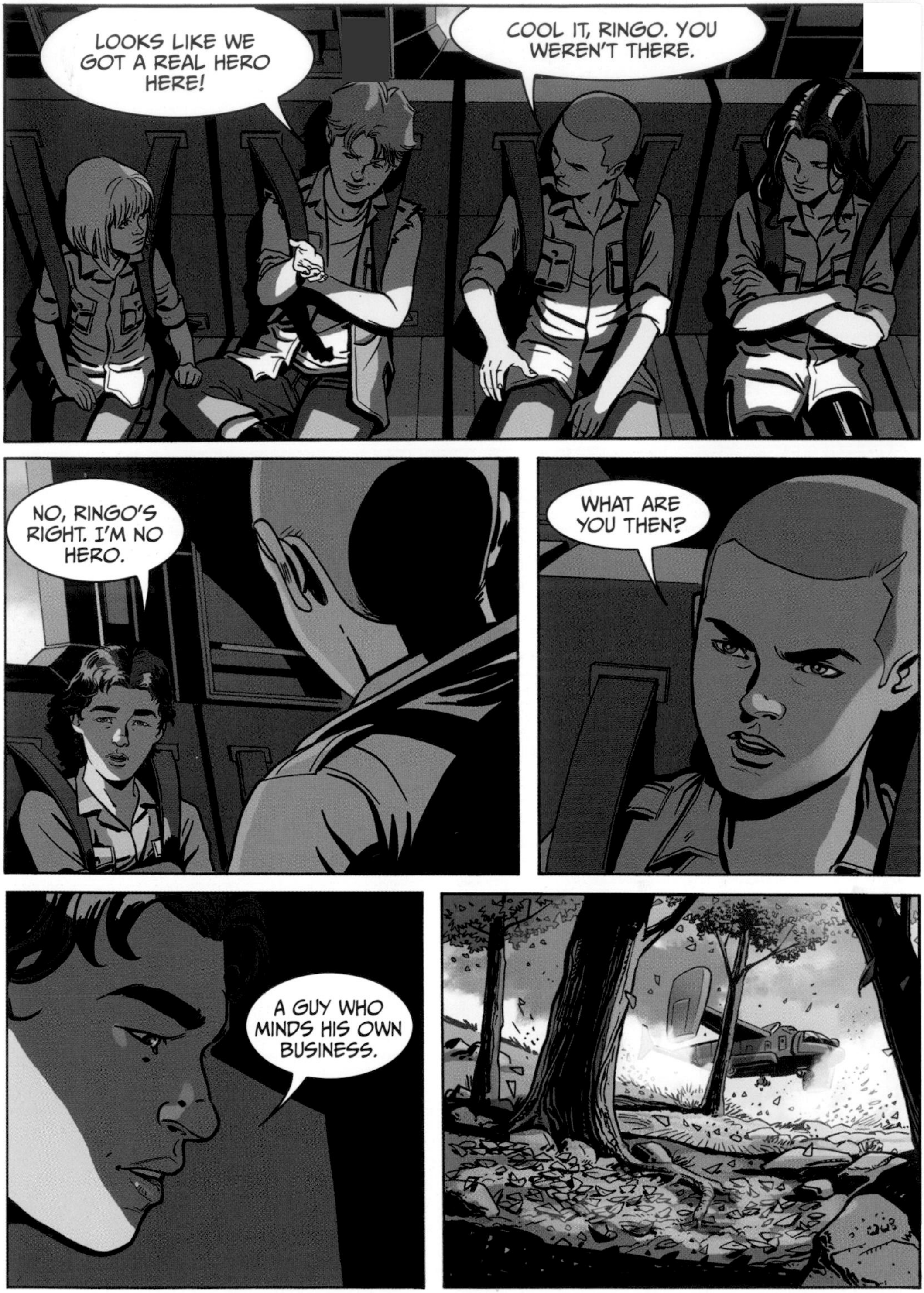
LOOKS LIKE WE GOT A REAL HERO HERE!
COOL IT, RINGO. YOU WEREN'T THERE.
NO, RINGO'S RIGHT. I'M NO HERO.
WHAT ARE YOU THEN?
A GUY WHO MINDS HIS OWN BUSINESS.

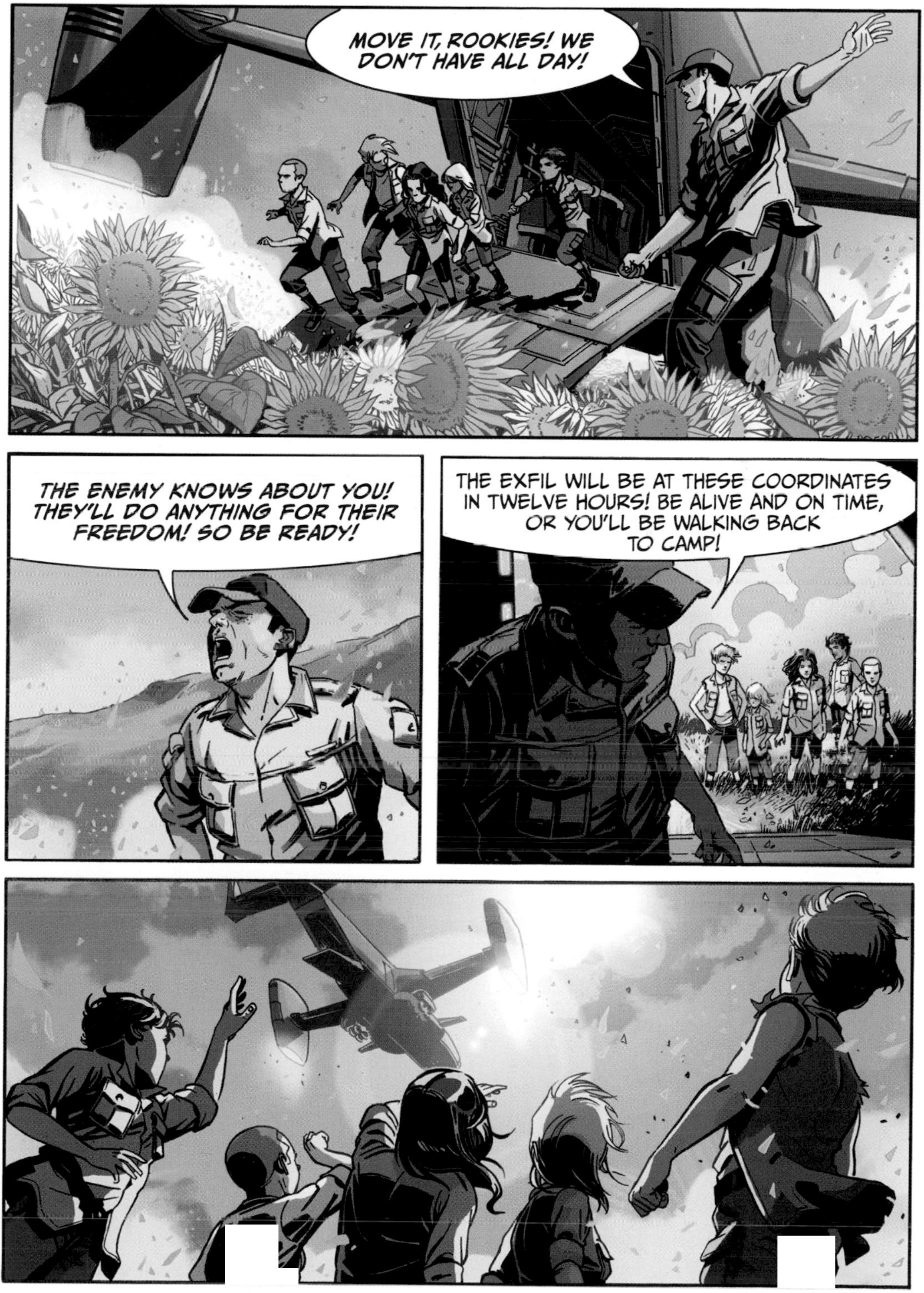
MOVE IT, ROOKIES! WE DON'T HAVE ALL DAY!
THE ENEMY KNOWS ABOUT YOU! THEY'LL DO ANYTHING FOR THEIR FREEDOM! SO BE READY!
THE EXFIL WILL BE AT THESE COORDINATES IN TWELVE HOURS! BE ALIVE AND ON TIME, OR YOU'LL BE WALKING BACK TO CAMP!

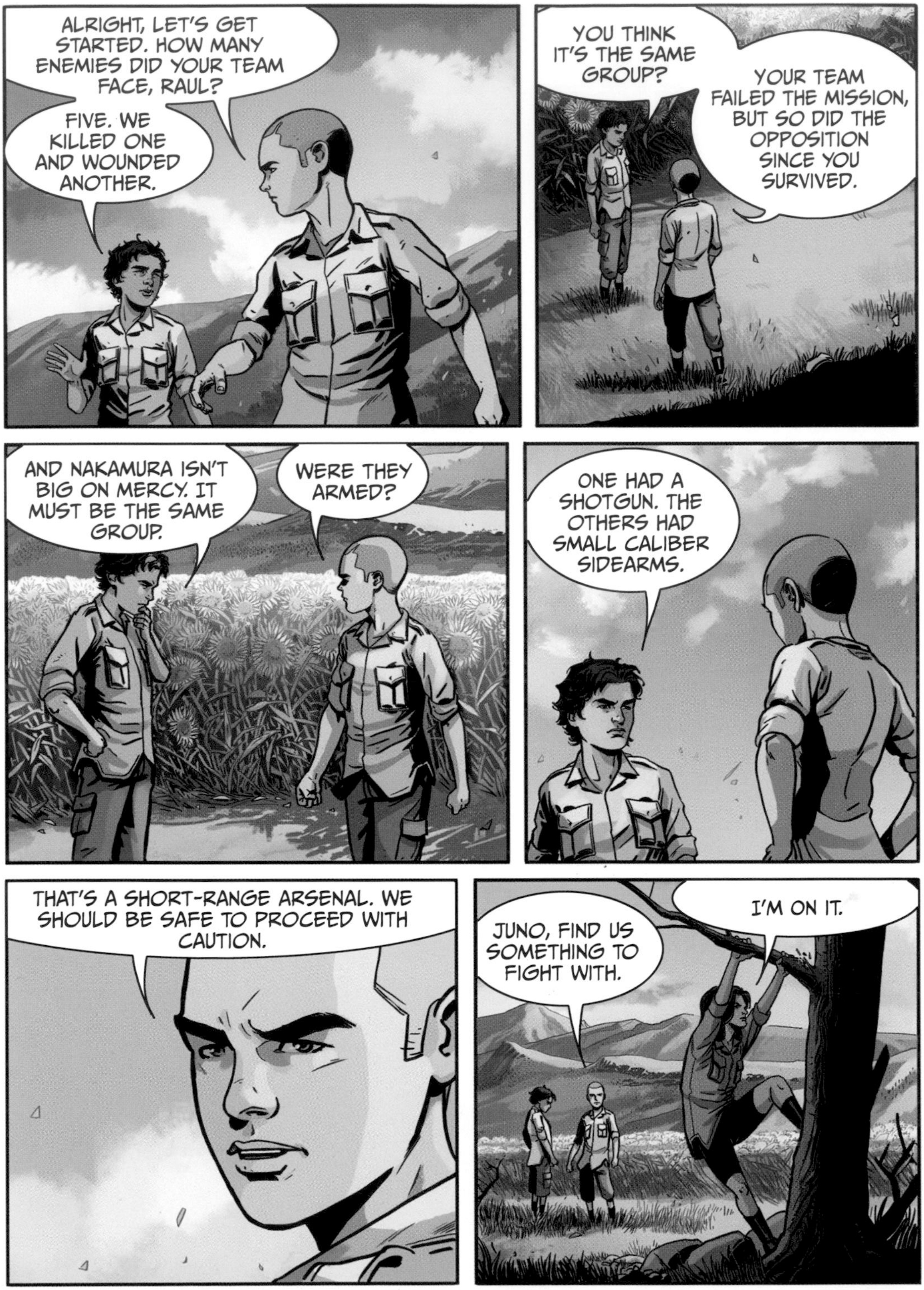
ALRIGHT, LET'S GET STARTED. HOW MANY ENEMIES DID YOUR TEAM FACE, RAUL?
FIVE. WE KILLED ONE AND WOUNDED ANOTHER.
YOU THINK IT'S THE SAME GROUP?
YOUR TEAM FAILED THE MISSION, BUT SO DID THE OPPOSITION SINCE YOU SURVIVED.
AND NAKAMURA ISN'T BIG ON MERCY. IT MUST BE THE SAME GROUP.
WERE THEY ARMED?
ONE HAD A SHOTGUN. THE OTHERS HAD SMALL CALIBER SIDEARMS.
THAT'S A SHORT-RANGE ARSENAL. WE SHOULD BE SAFE TO PROCEED WITH CAUTION.
JUNO, FIND US SOMETHING TO FIGHT WITH.
I'M ON IT.

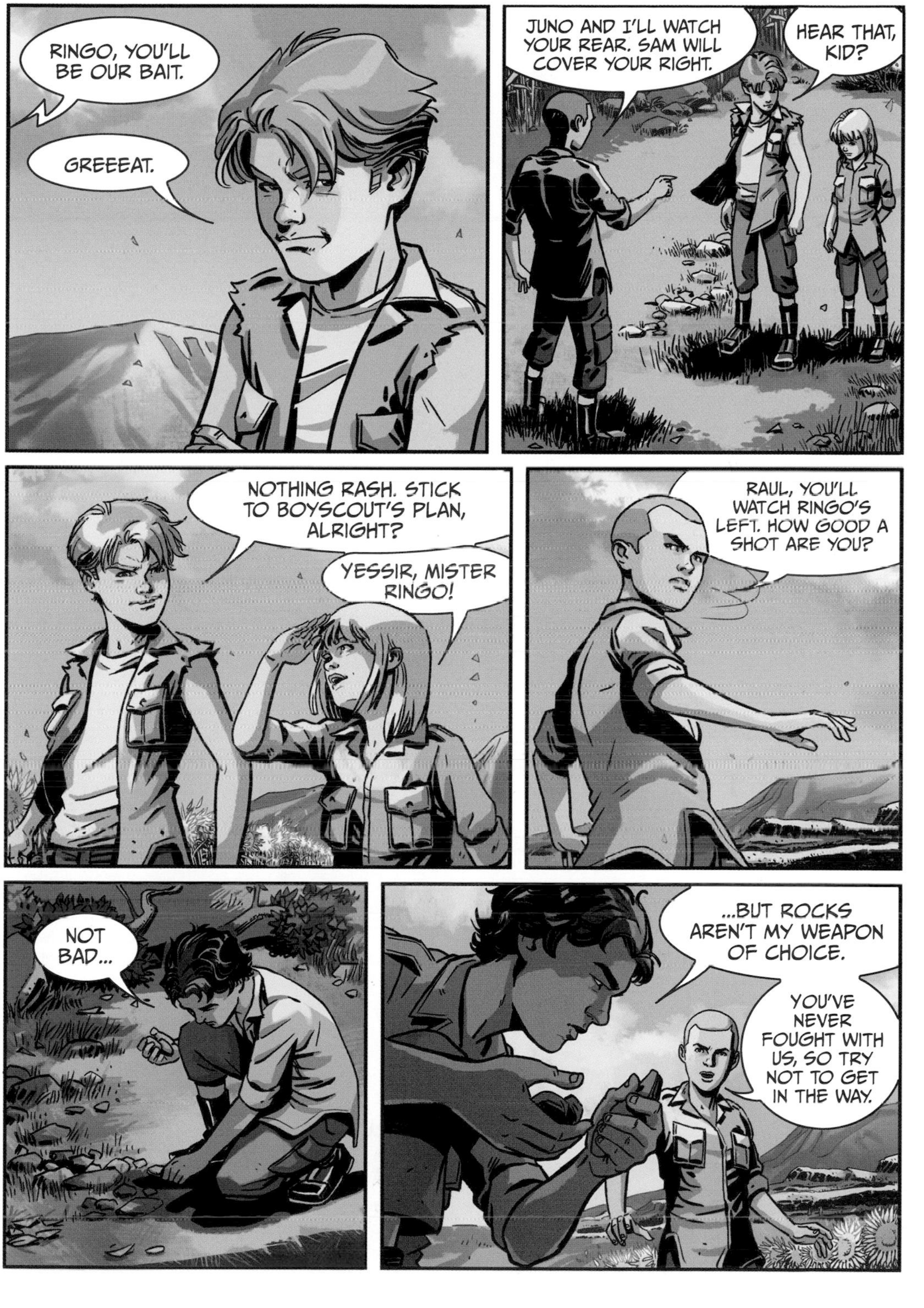
RINGO, YOU'LL BE OUR BAIT.
GREEEAT.
JUNO AND I'LL WATCH YOUR REAR. SAM WILL COVER YOUR RIGHT.
HEAR THAT, KID?
NOTHING RASH. STICK TO BOYSCOUT'S PLAN, ALRIGHT?
YESSIR, MISTER RINGO!
RAUL, YOU'LL WATCH RINGO'S LEFT. HOW GOOD A SHOT ARE YOU?
NOT BAD...
...BUT ROCKS AREN'T MY WEAPON OF CHOICE.
YOU'VE NEVER FOUGHT WITH US, SO TRY NOT TO GET IN THE WAY.

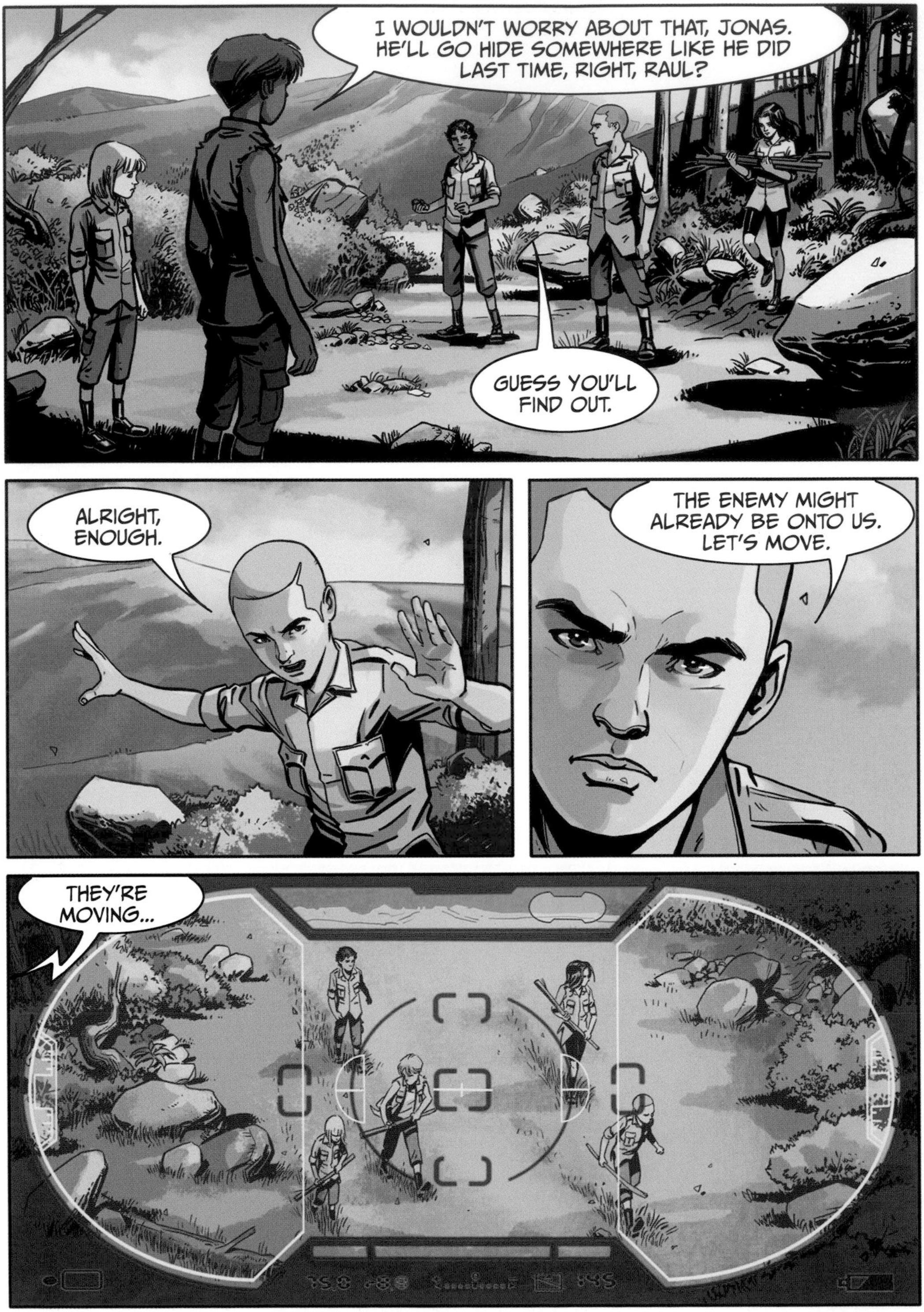
I WOULDN'T WORRY ABOUT THAT, JONAS. HE'LL GO HIDE SOMEWHERE LIKE HE DID LAST TIME, RIGHT, RAUL?
GUESS YOU'LL FIND OUT.
ALRIGHT, ENOUGH.
THE ENEMY MIGHT ALREADY BE ONTO US. LET'S MOVE.
THEY'RE MOVING...

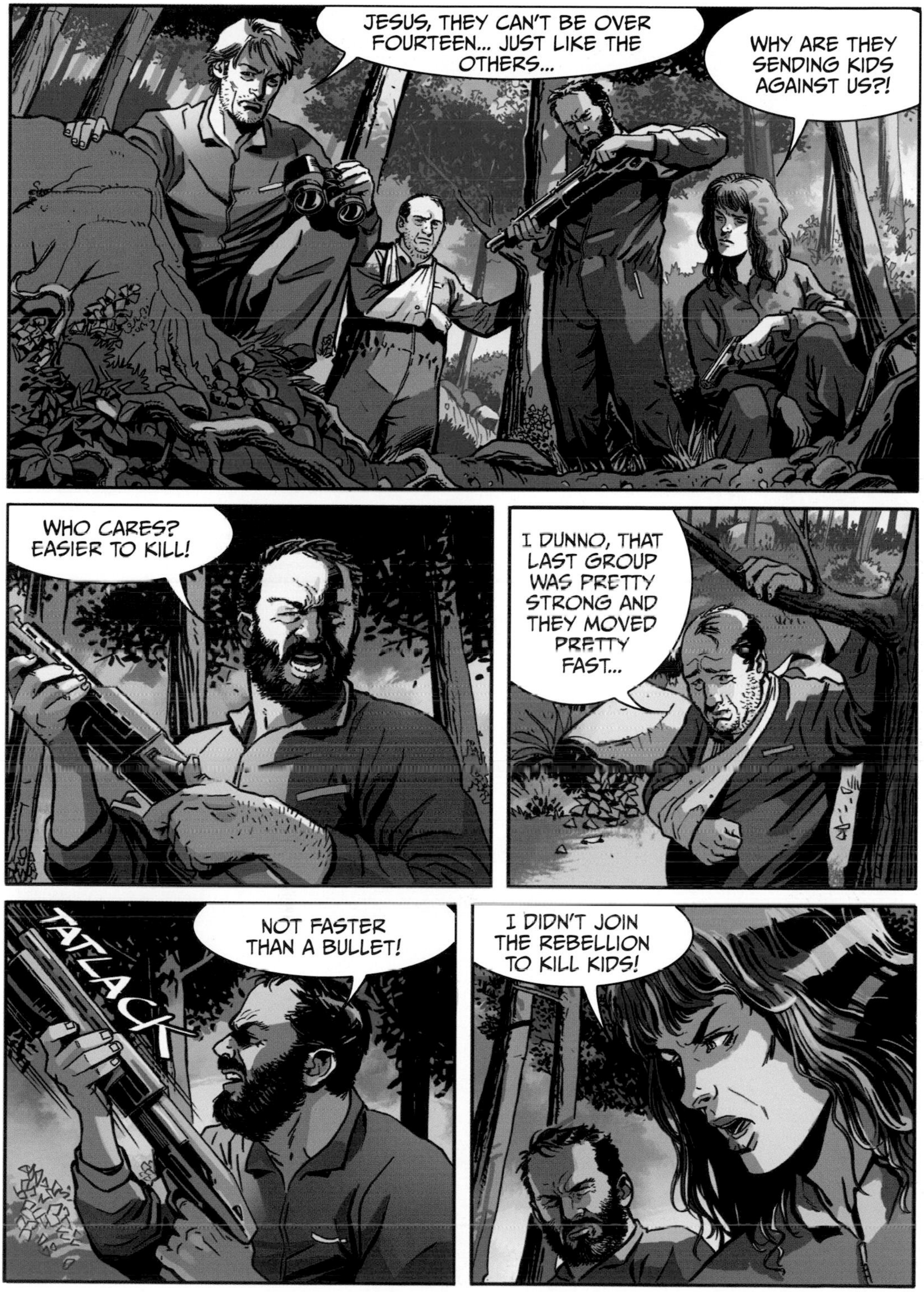
JESUS, THEY CAN'T BE OVER FOURTEEN... JUST LIKE THE OTHERS...
WHY ARE THEY SENDING KIDS AGAINST US?!
WHO CARES? EASIER TO KILL!
I DUNNO, THAT LAST GROUP WAS PRETTY STRONG AND THEY MOVED PRETTY FAST...
TATLACK
NOT FASTER THAN A BULLET!
I DIDN'T JOIN THE REBELLION TO KILL KIDS!

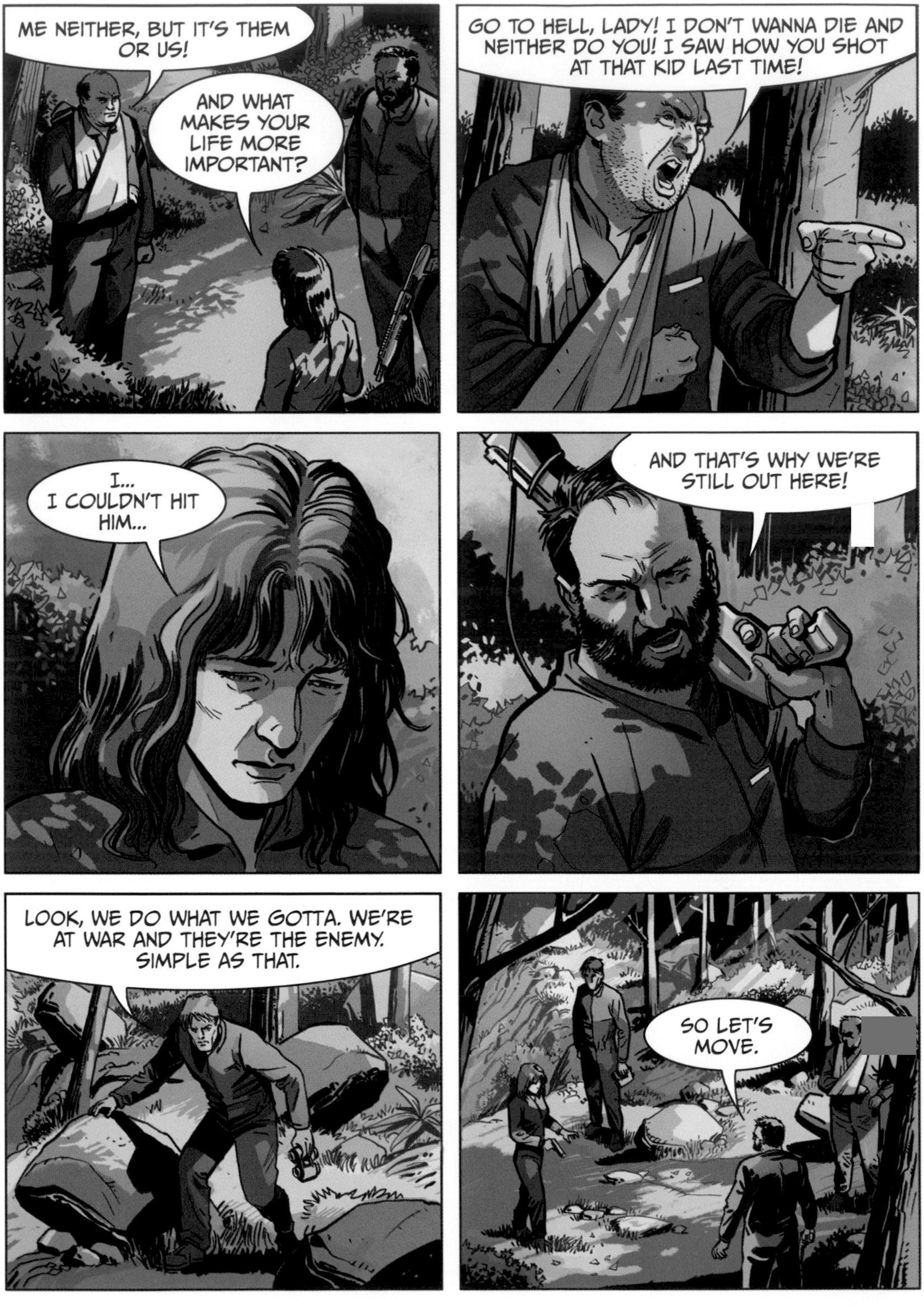
ME NEITHER, BUT IT'S THEM OR US!
AND WHAT MAKES YOUR LIFE MORE IMPORTANT?
GO TO HELL, LADY! I DON'T WANNA DIE AND NEITHER DO YOU! I SAW HOW YOU SHOT AT THAT KID LAST TIME!
I... I COULDN'T HIT HIM...
AND THAT'S WHY WE'RE STILL OUT HERE!
LOOK, WE DO WHAT WE GOTTA. WE'RE AT WAR AND THEY'RE THE ENEMY. SIMPLE AS THAT.
SO LET'S MOVE.

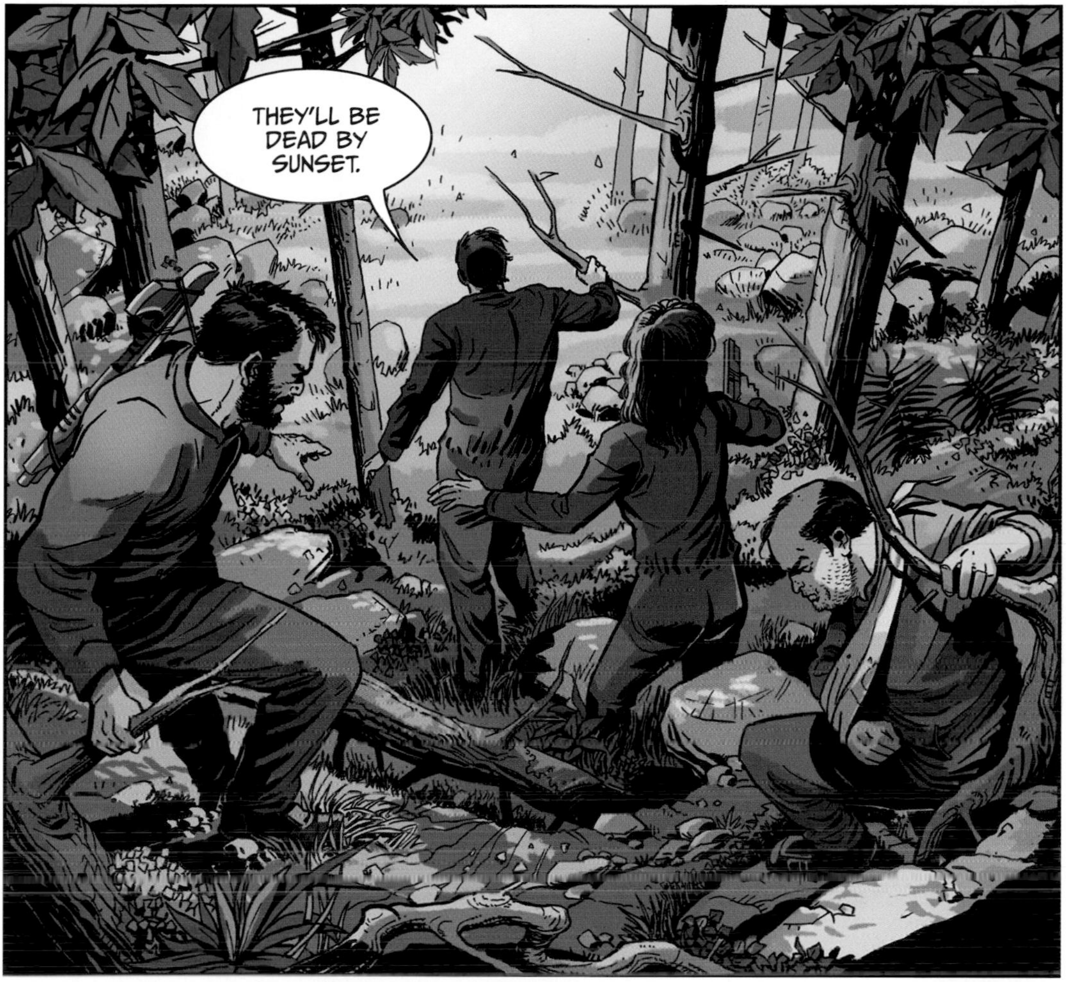
THEY'LL BE DEAD BY SUNSET.

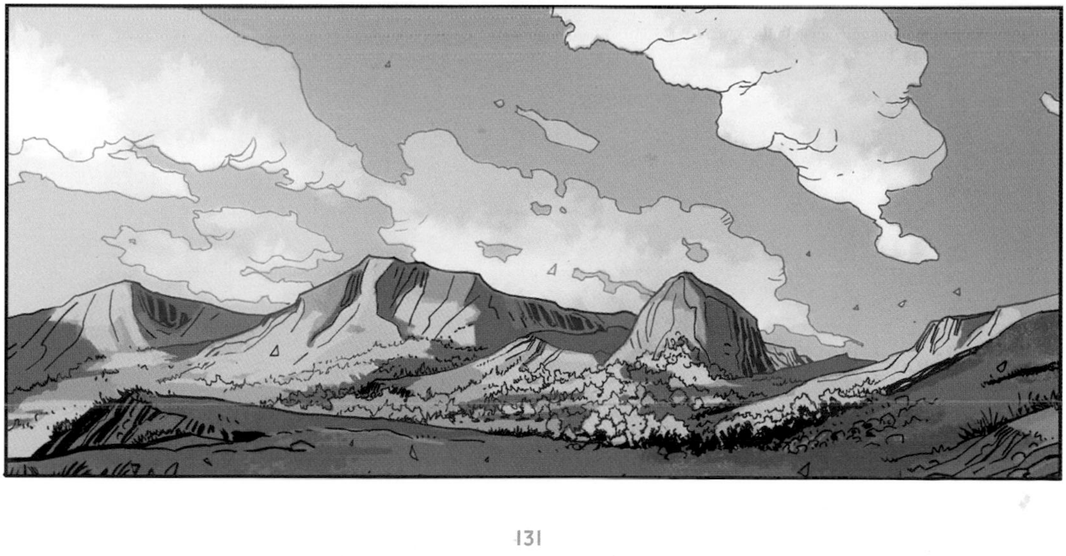

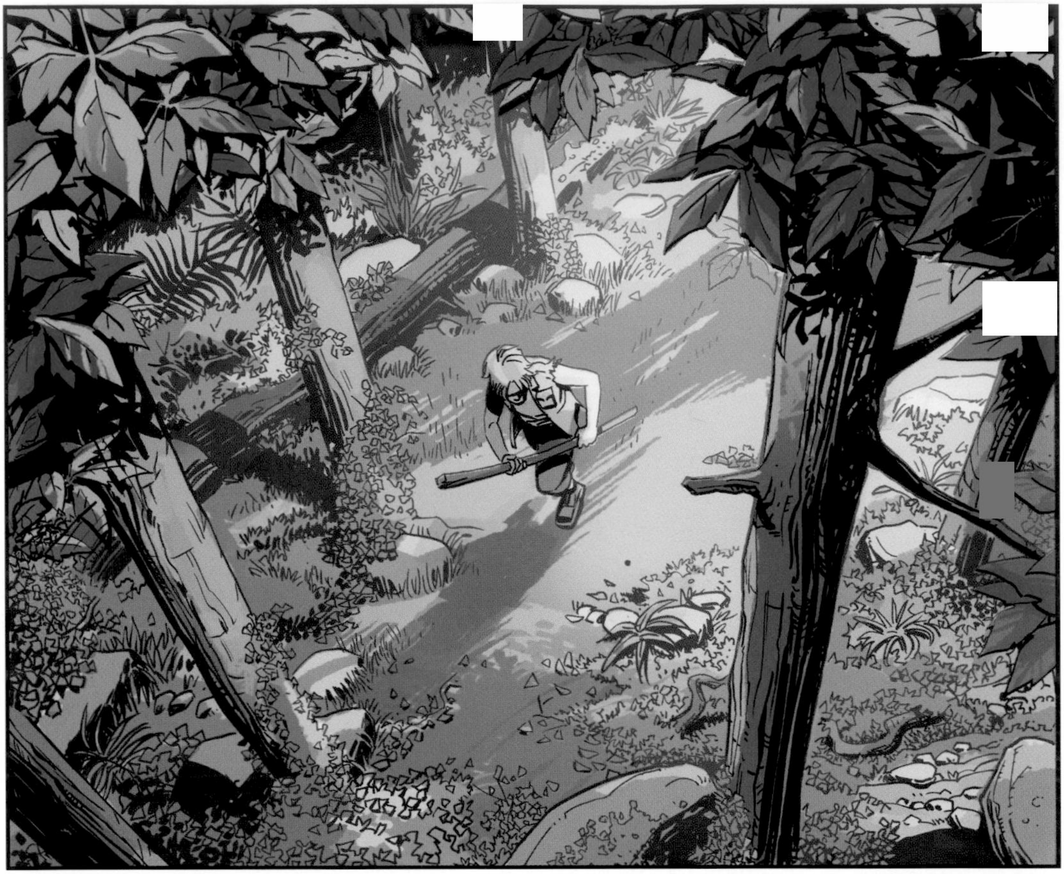

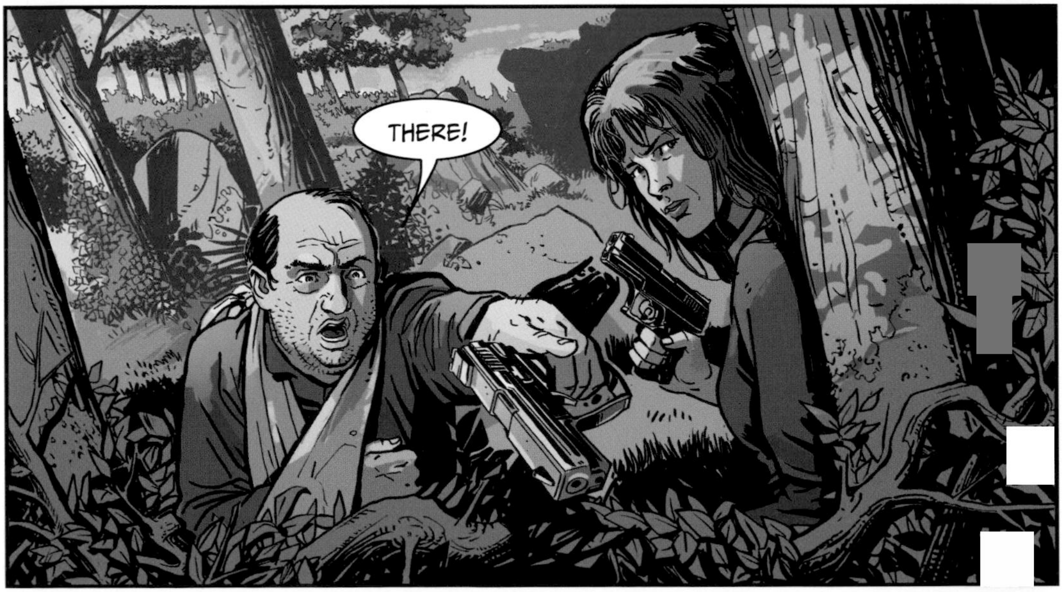
THERE!

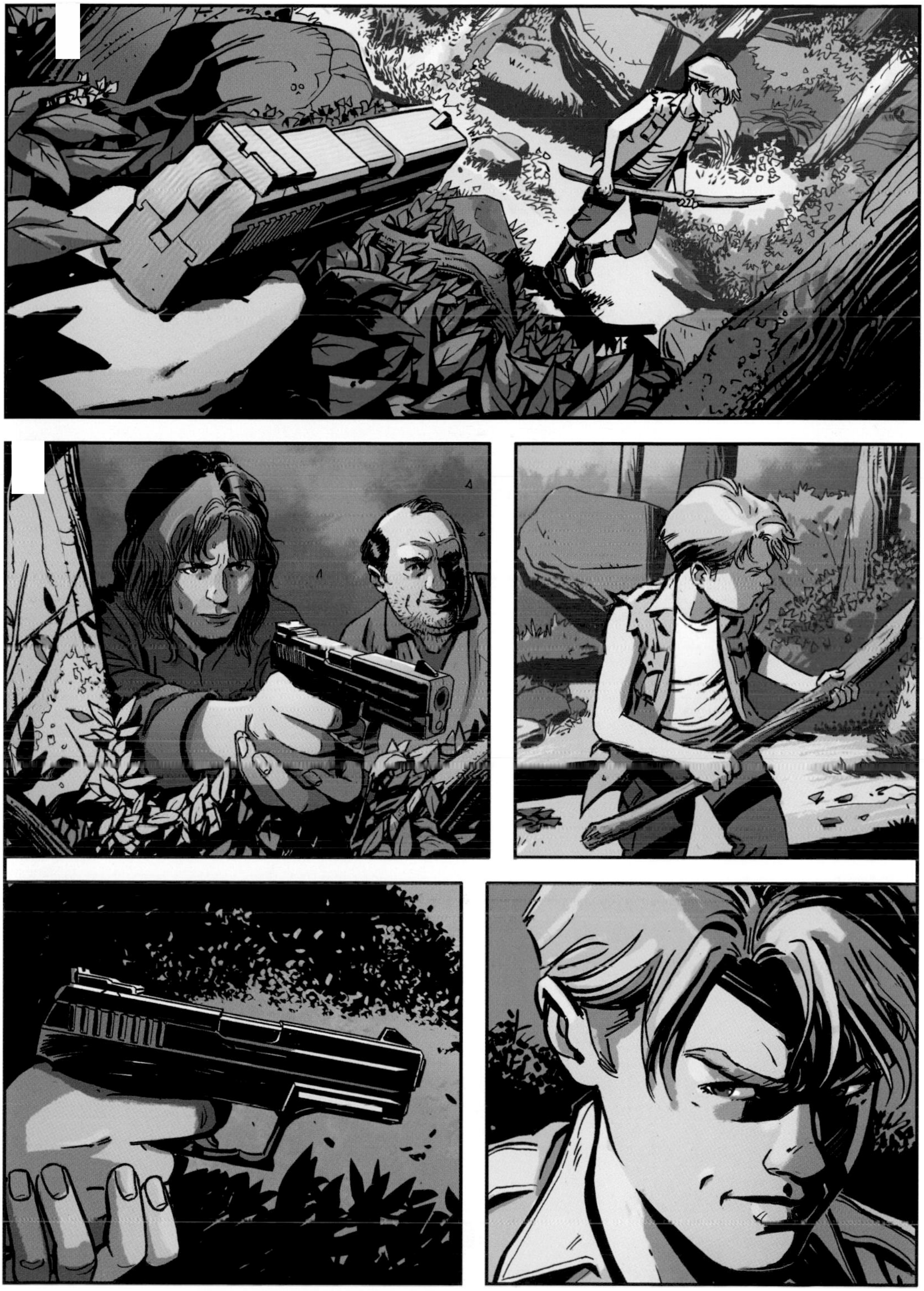

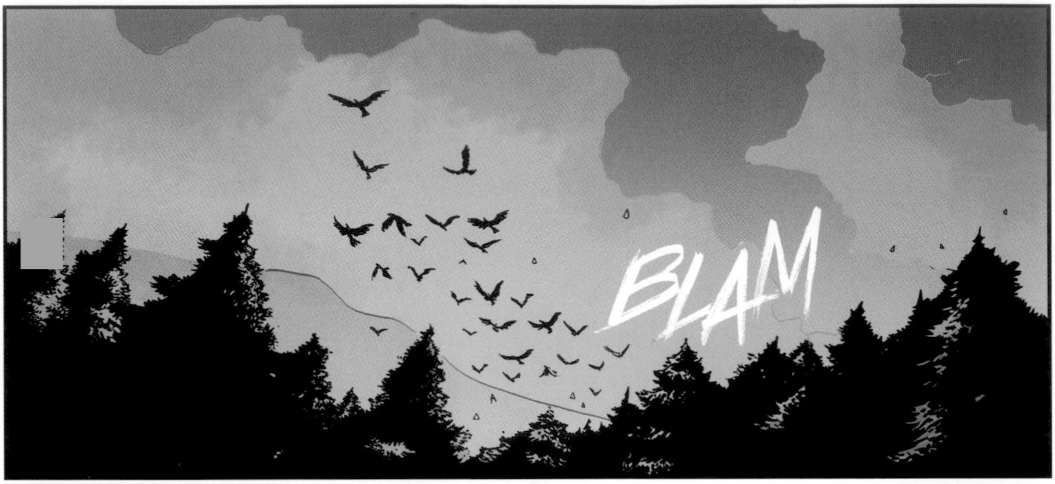
BLAM

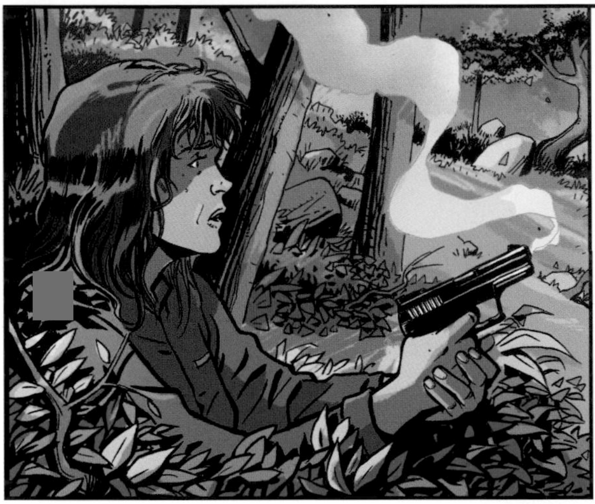

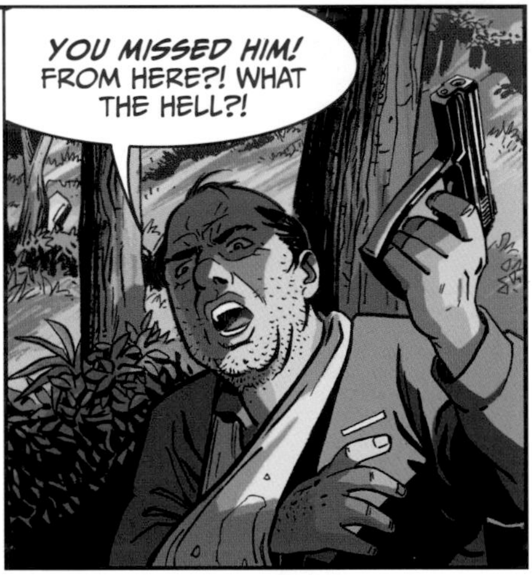
YOU MISSED HIM! FROM HERE?! WHAT THE HELL?!

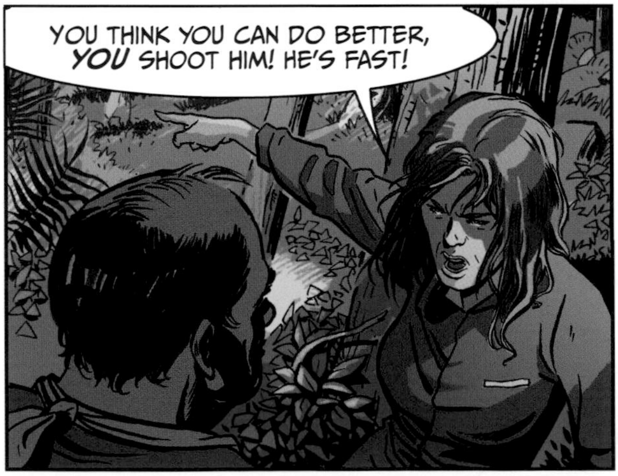
YOU THINK YOU CAN DO BETTER, *YOU* SHOOT HIM! HE'S FAST!

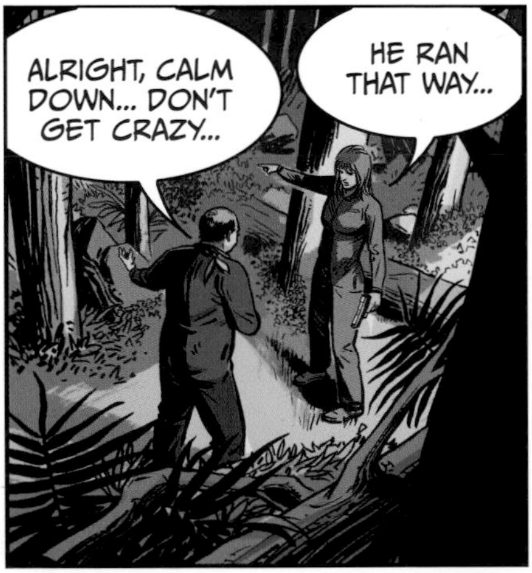
ALRIGHT, CALM DOWN... DON'T GET CRAZY...
HE RAN THAT WAY...

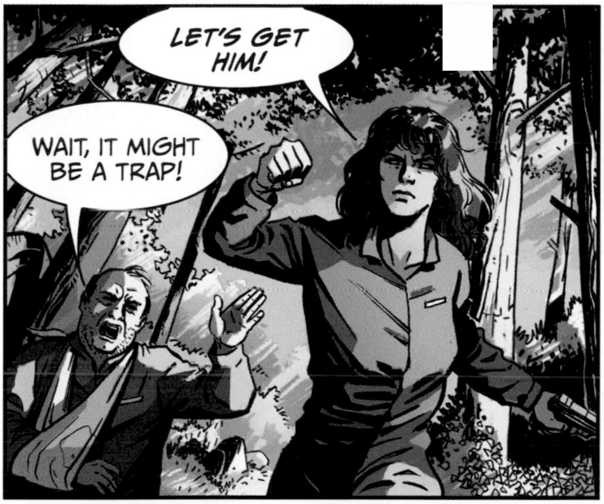
LET'S GET HIM!
WAIT, IT MIGHT BE A TRAP!

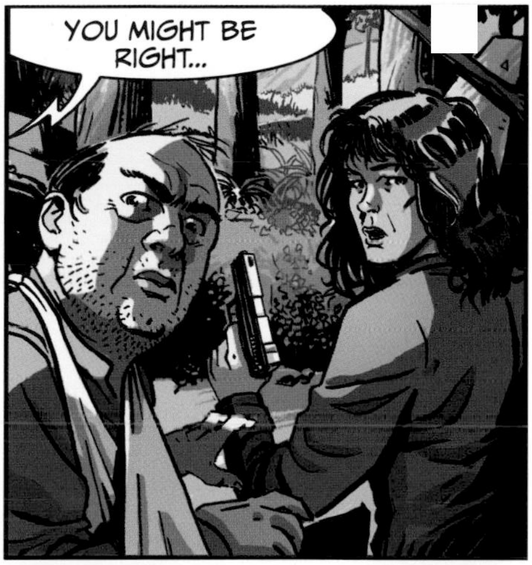
YOU MIGHT BE RIGHT...

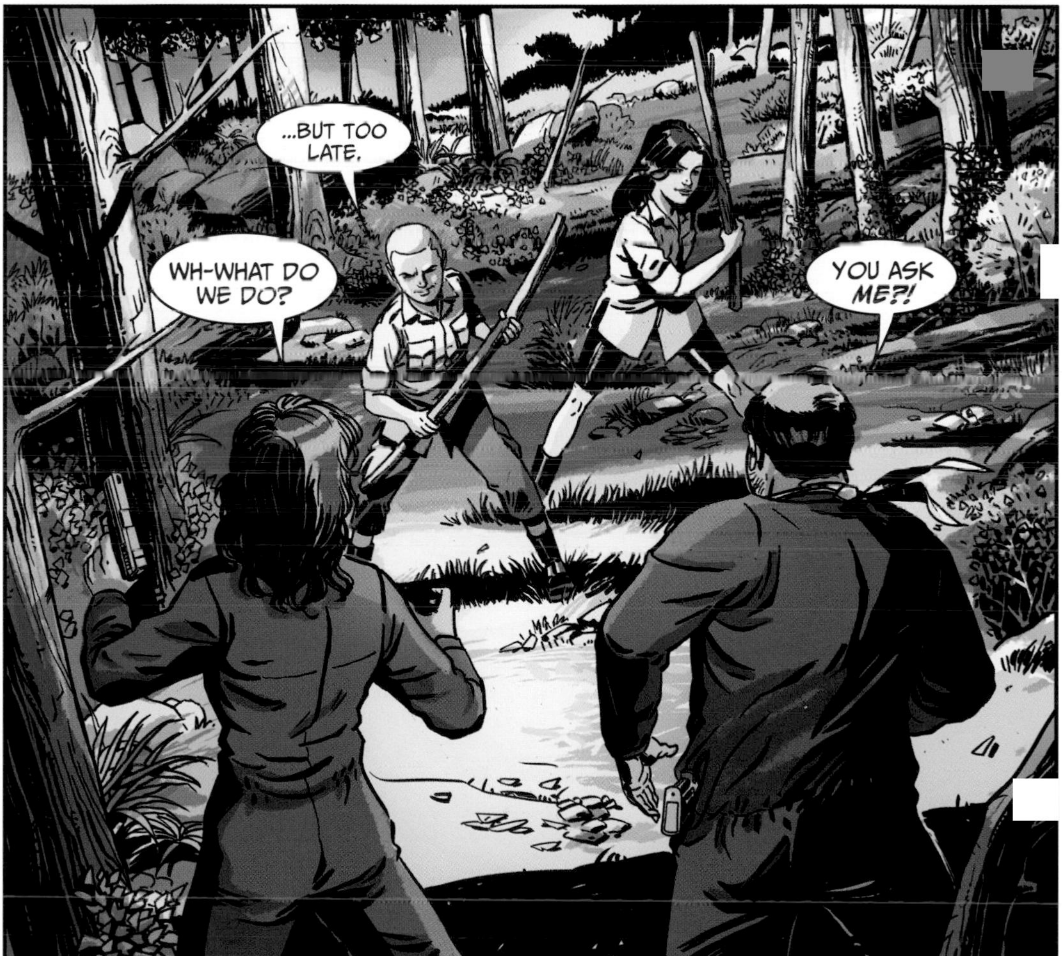
...BUT TOO LATE.
WH-WHAT DO WE DO?
YOU ASK ME?!

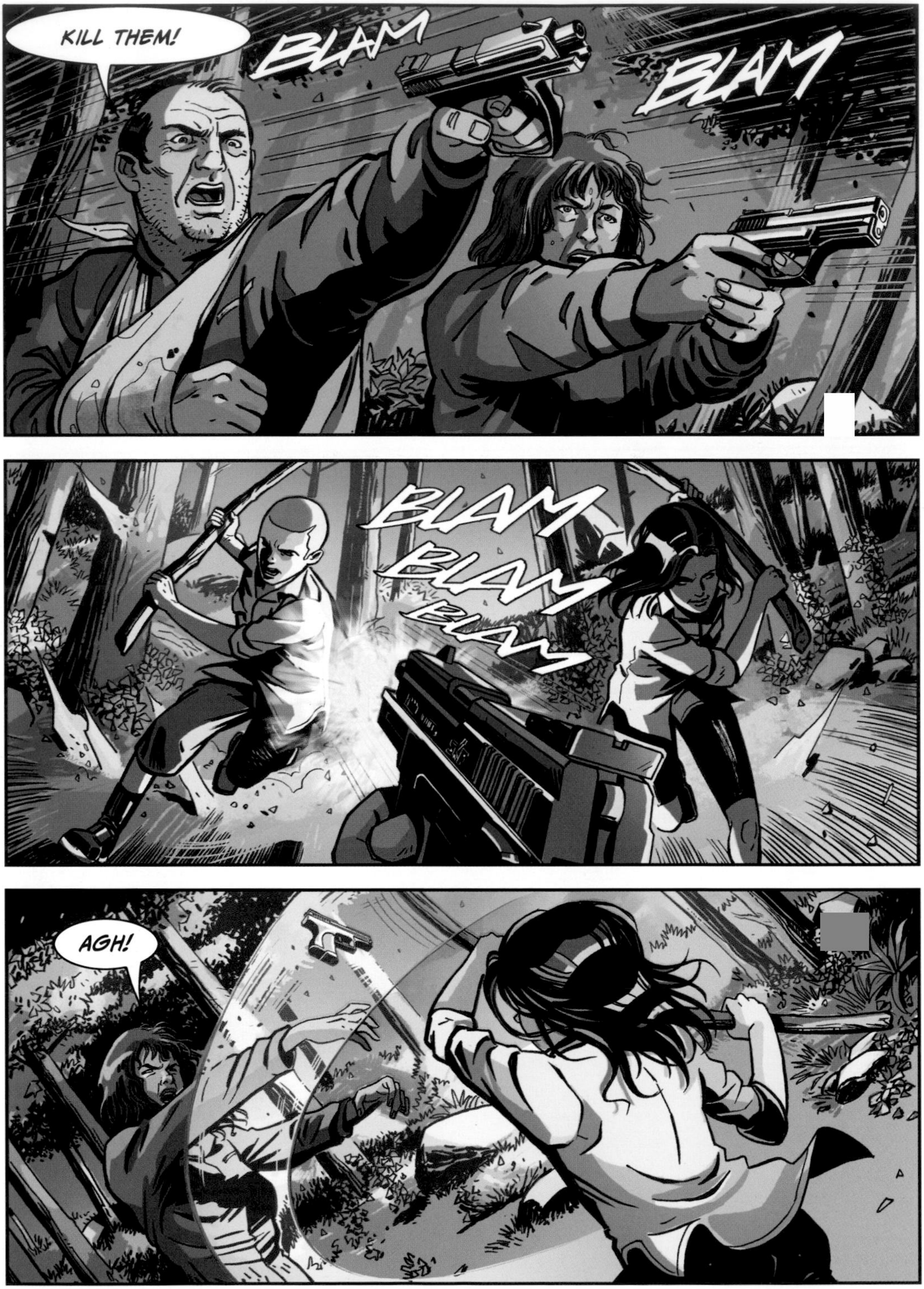
KILL THEM!
BLAM
BLAM
BLAM
BLAM
BLAM
AGH!

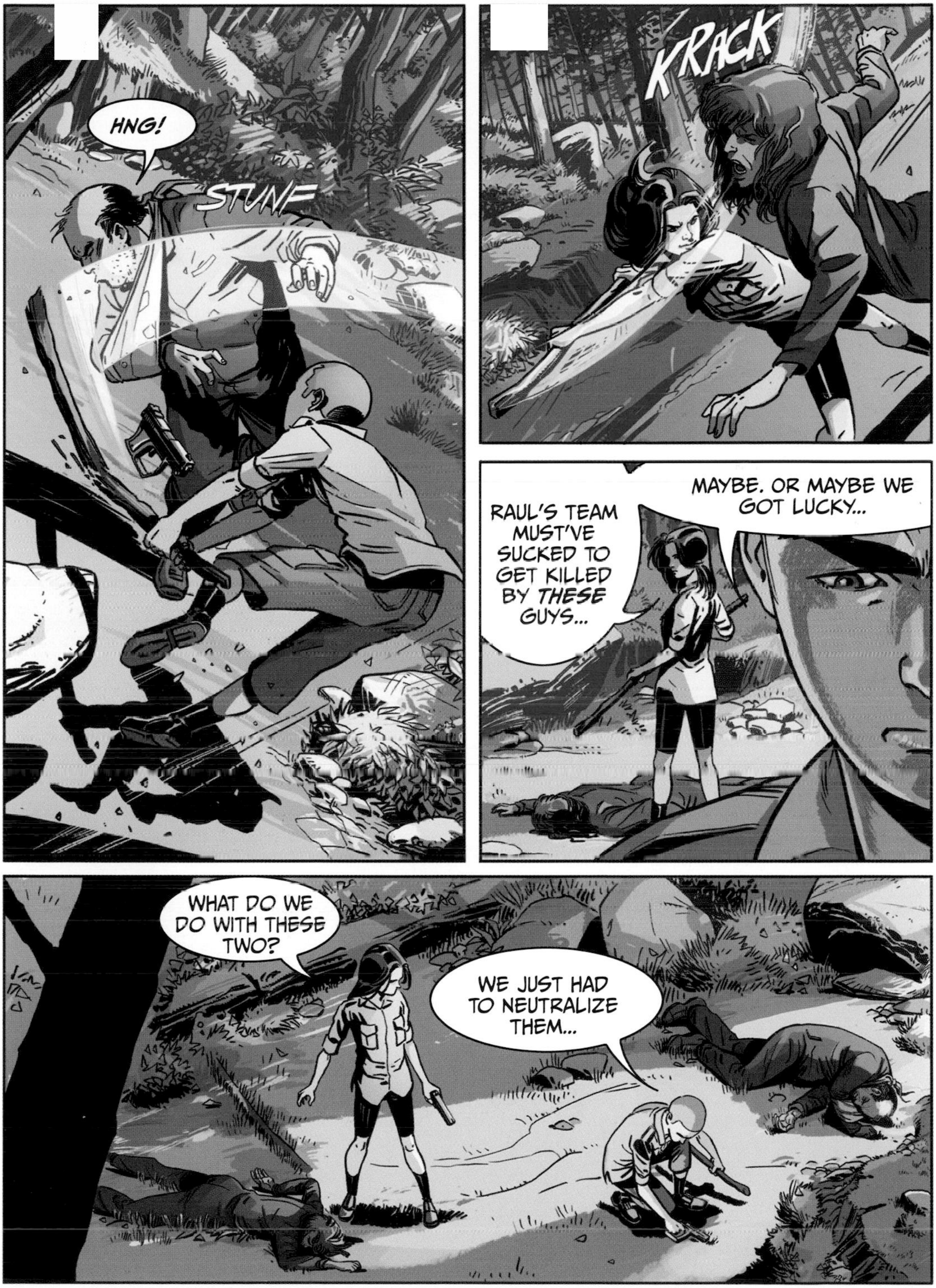
HNG!
STUNF
KRACK
RAUL'S TEAM MUST'VE SUCKED TO GET KILLED BY *THESE* GUYS...
MAYBE. OR MAYBE WE GOT LUCKY...
WHAT DO WE DO WITH THESE TWO?
WE JUST HAD TO NEUTRALIZE THEM...

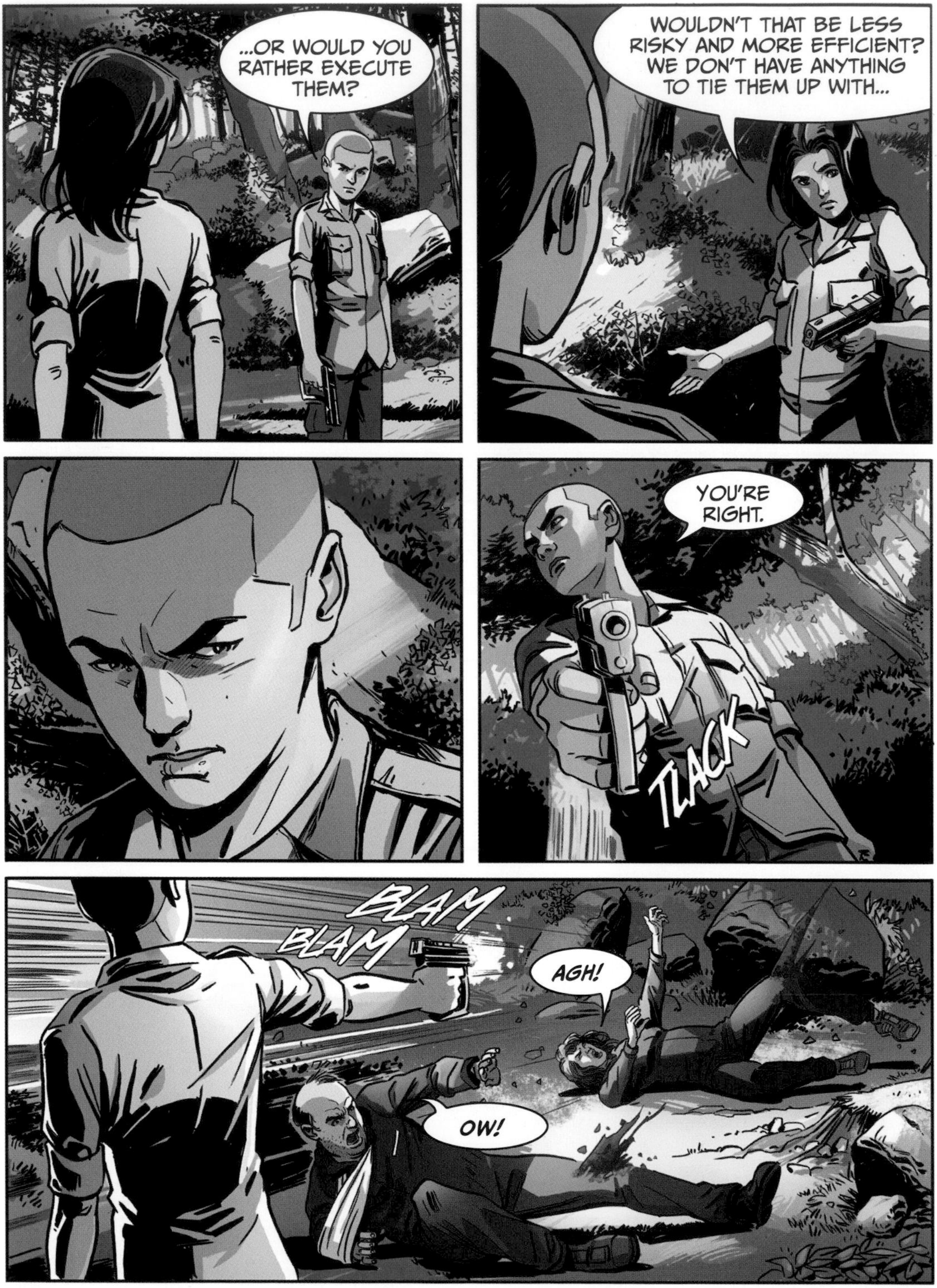
...OR WOULD YOU RATHER EXECUTE THEM?
WOULDN'T THAT BE LESS RISKY AND MORE EFFICIENT? WE DON'T HAVE ANYTHING TO TIE THEM UP WITH...
YOU'RE RIGHT.
TLACK
BLAM
BLAM
AGH!
OW!

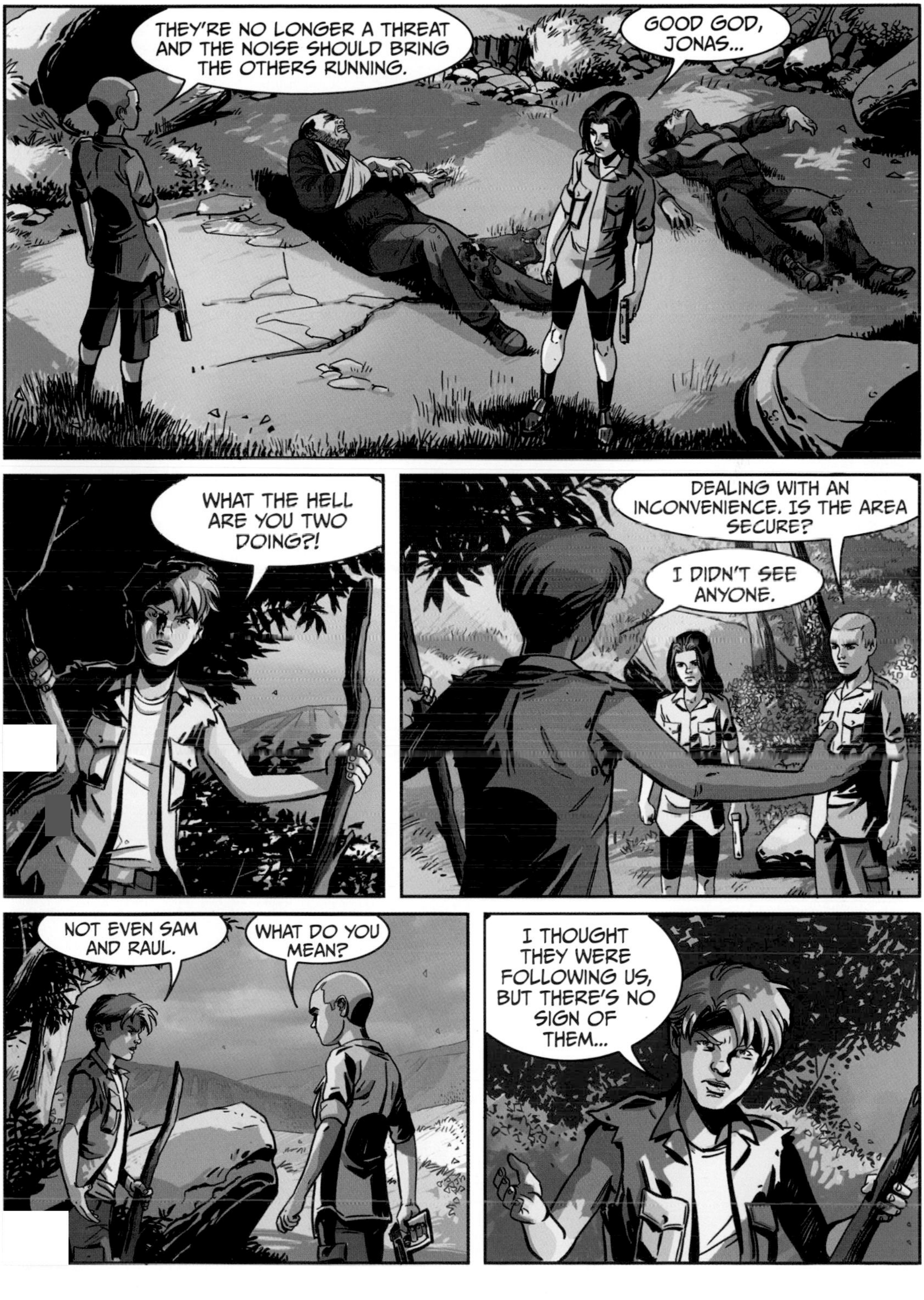
THEY'RE NO LONGER A THREAT AND THE NOISE SHOULD BRING THE OTHERS RUNNING.
GOOD GOD, JONAS...
WHAT THE HELL ARE YOU TWO DOING?!
DEALING WITH AN INCONVENIENCE. IS THE AREA SECURE?
I DIDN'T SEE ANYONE.
NOT EVEN SAM AND RAUL.
WHAT DO YOU MEAN?
I THOUGHT THEY WERE FOLLOWING US, BUT THERE'S NO SIGN OF THEM...

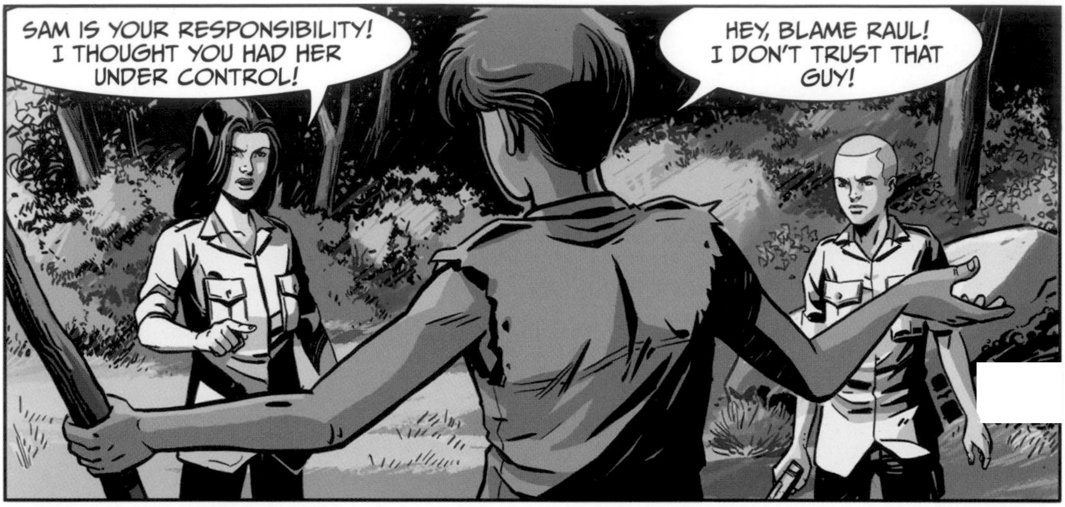
SAM IS YOUR RESPONSIBILITY! I THOUGHT YOU HAD HER UNDER CONTROL!
HEY, BLAME RAUL! I DON'T TRUST THAT GUY!

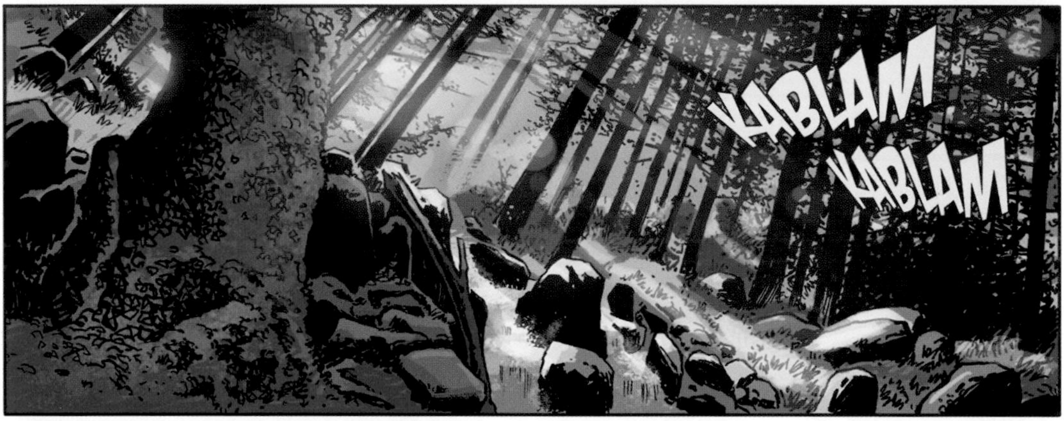
KABLAM
KABLAM

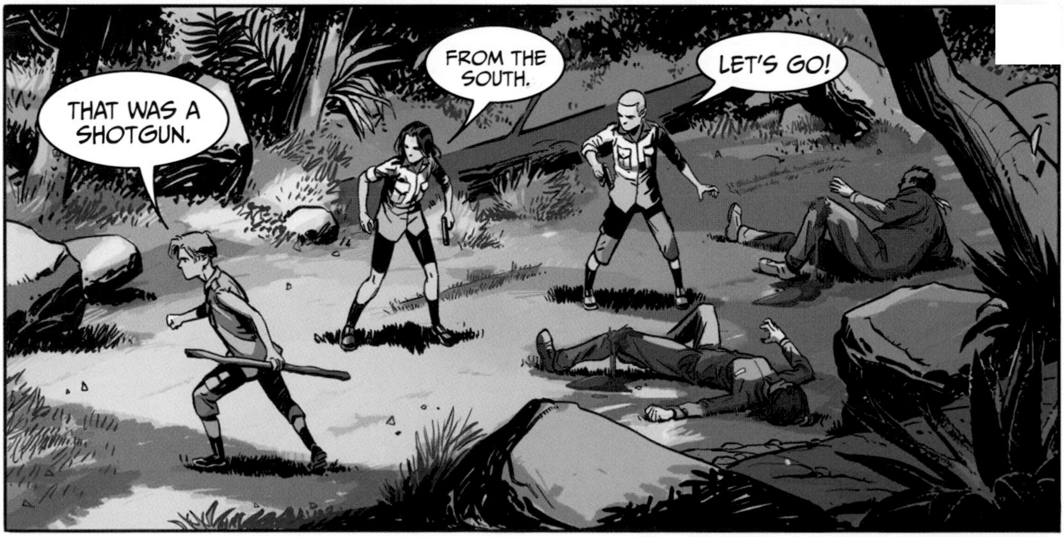
THAT WAS A SHOTGUN.
FROM THE SOUTH.
LET'S GO!

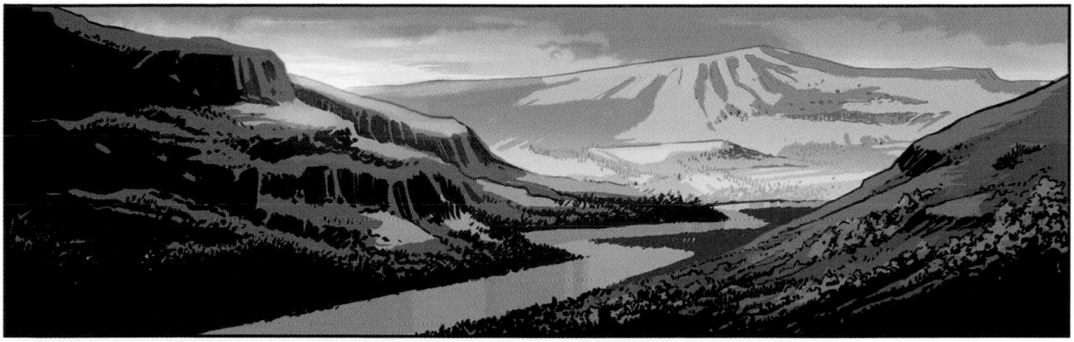

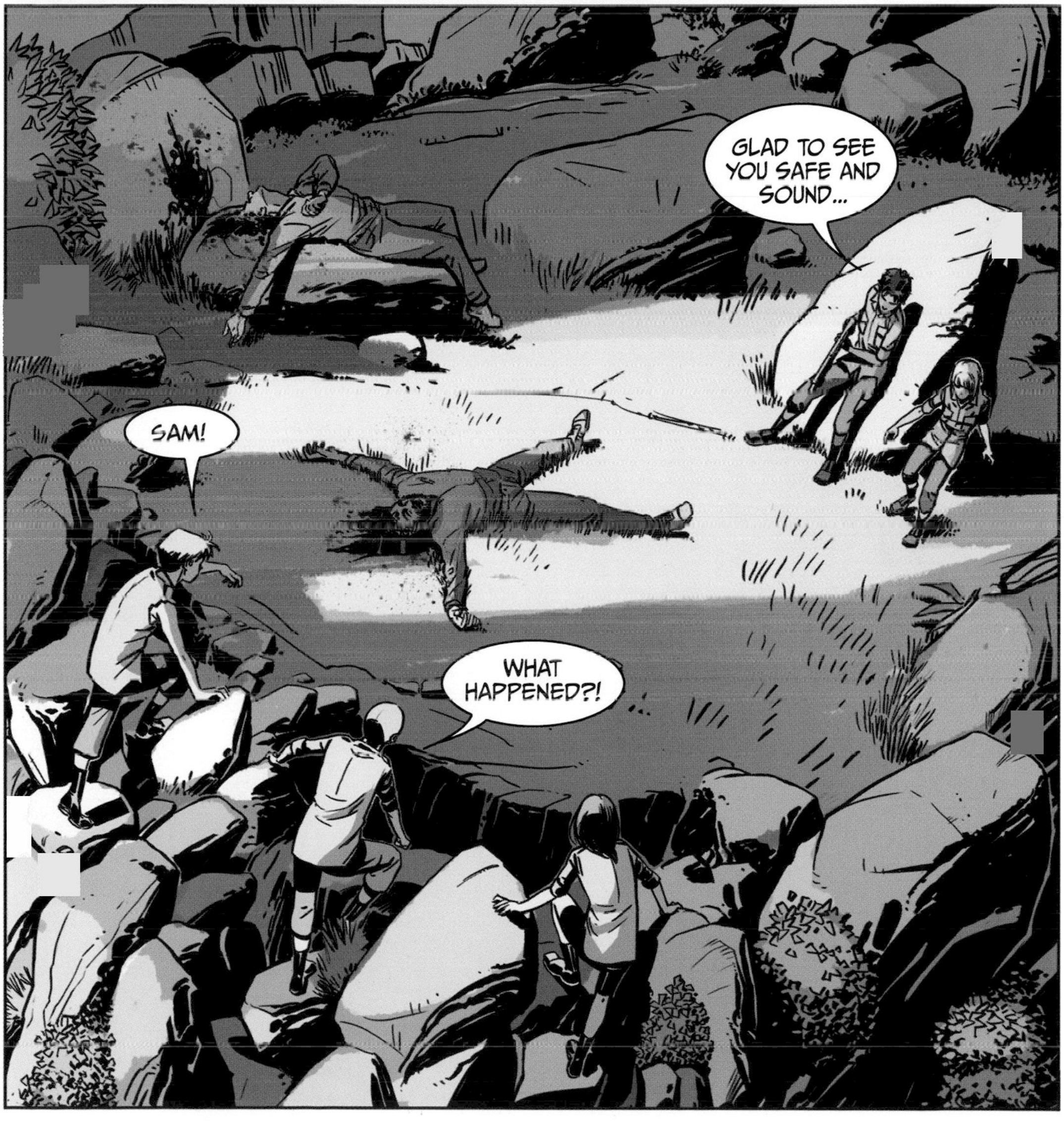
GLAD TO SEE YOU SAFE AND SOUND...
SAM!
WHAT HAPPENED?!

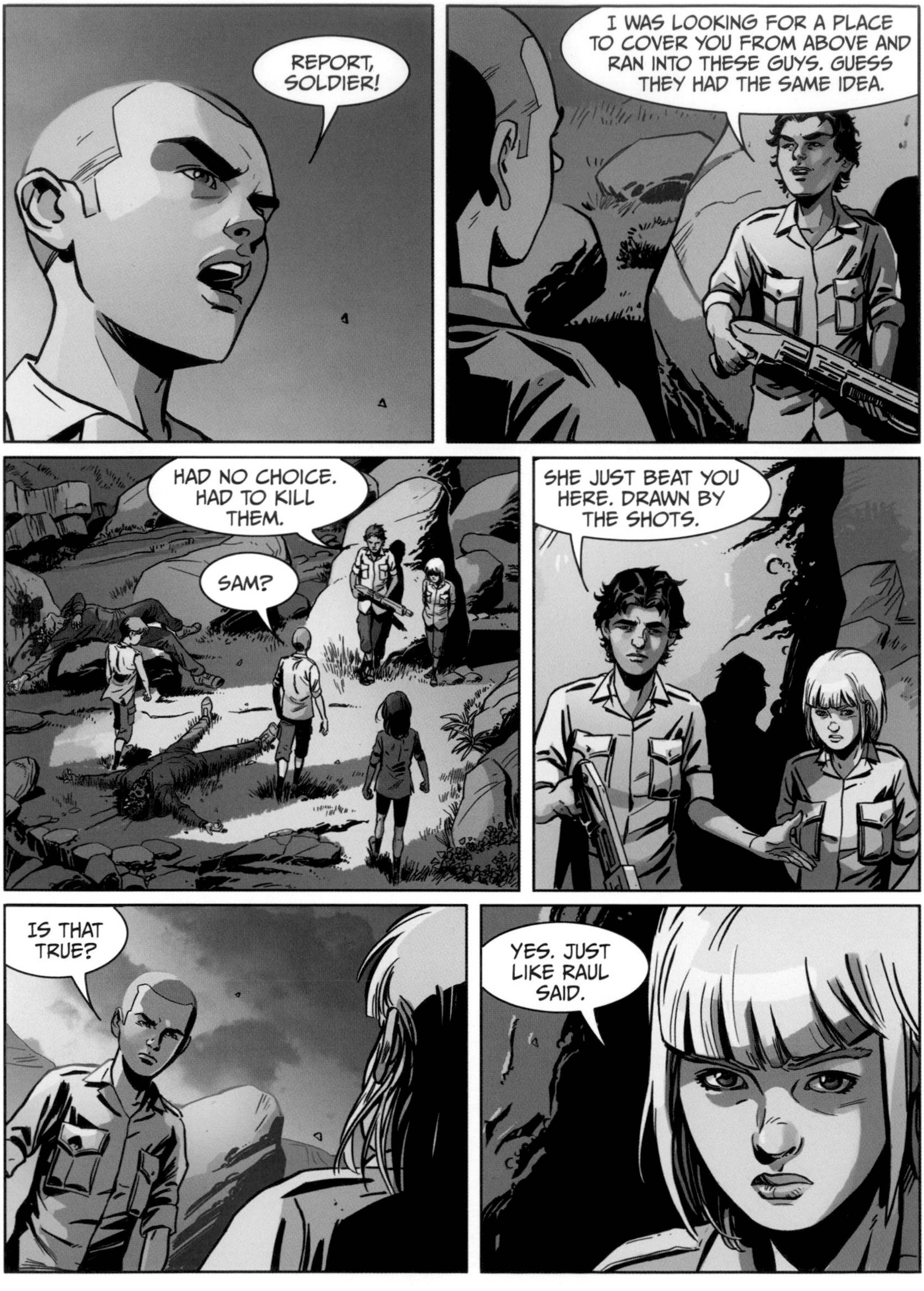
REPORT, SOLDIER!
I WAS LOOKING FOR A PLACE TO COVER YOU FROM ABOVE AND RAN INTO THESE GUYS. GUESS THEY HAD THE SAME IDEA.
HAD NO CHOICE. HAD TO KILL THEM.
SAM?
SHE JUST BEAT YOU HERE. DRAWN BY THE SHOTS.
IS THAT TRUE?
YES. JUST LIKE RAUL SAID.

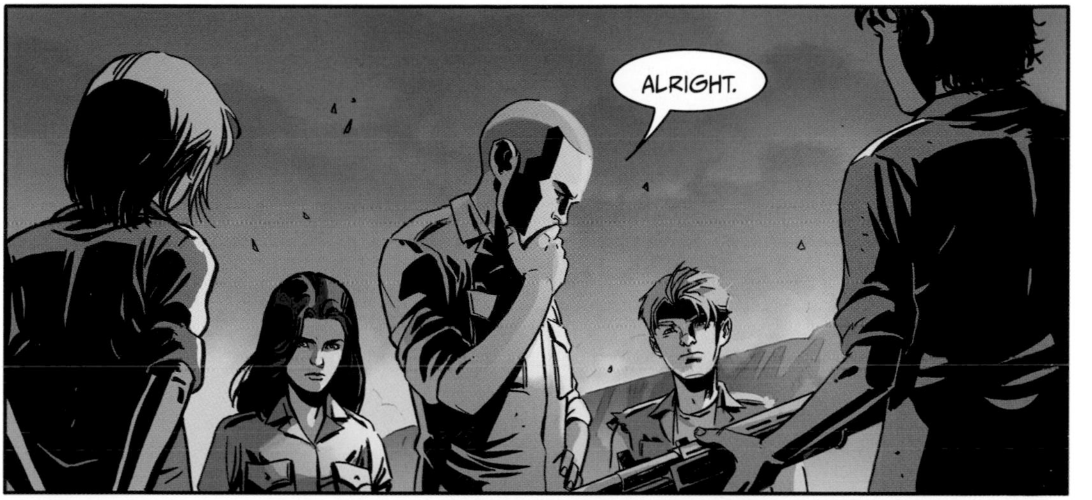
ALRIGHT.

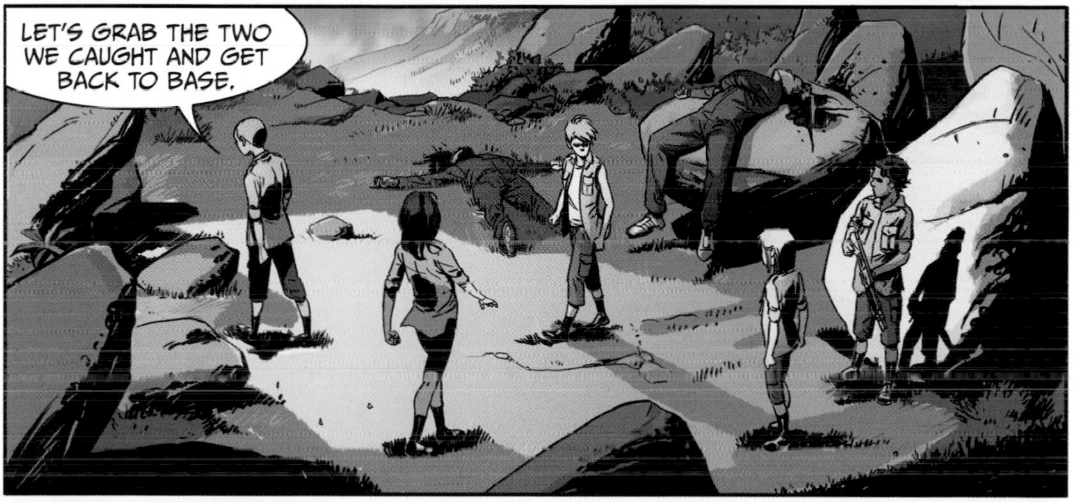
LET'S GRAB THE TWO WE CAUGHT AND GET BACK TO BASE.

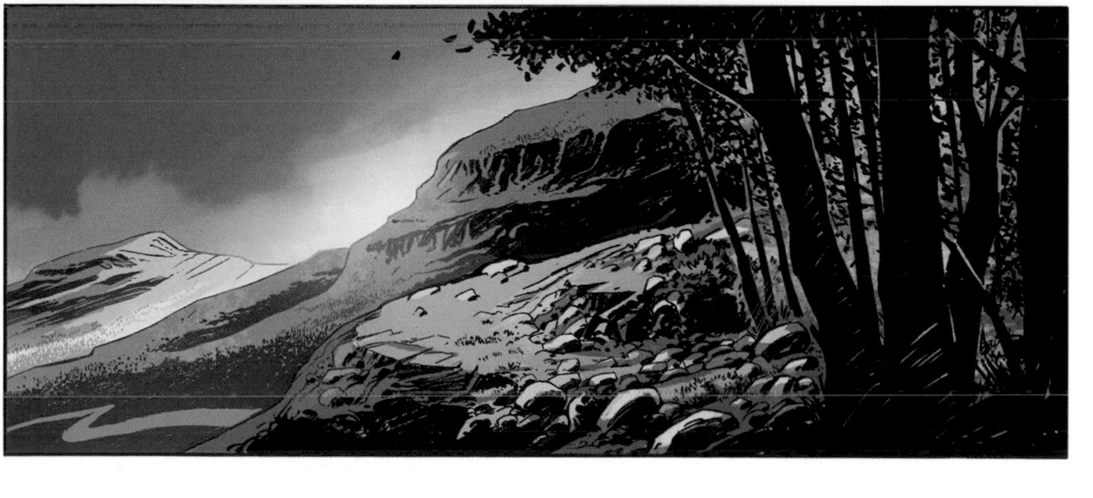

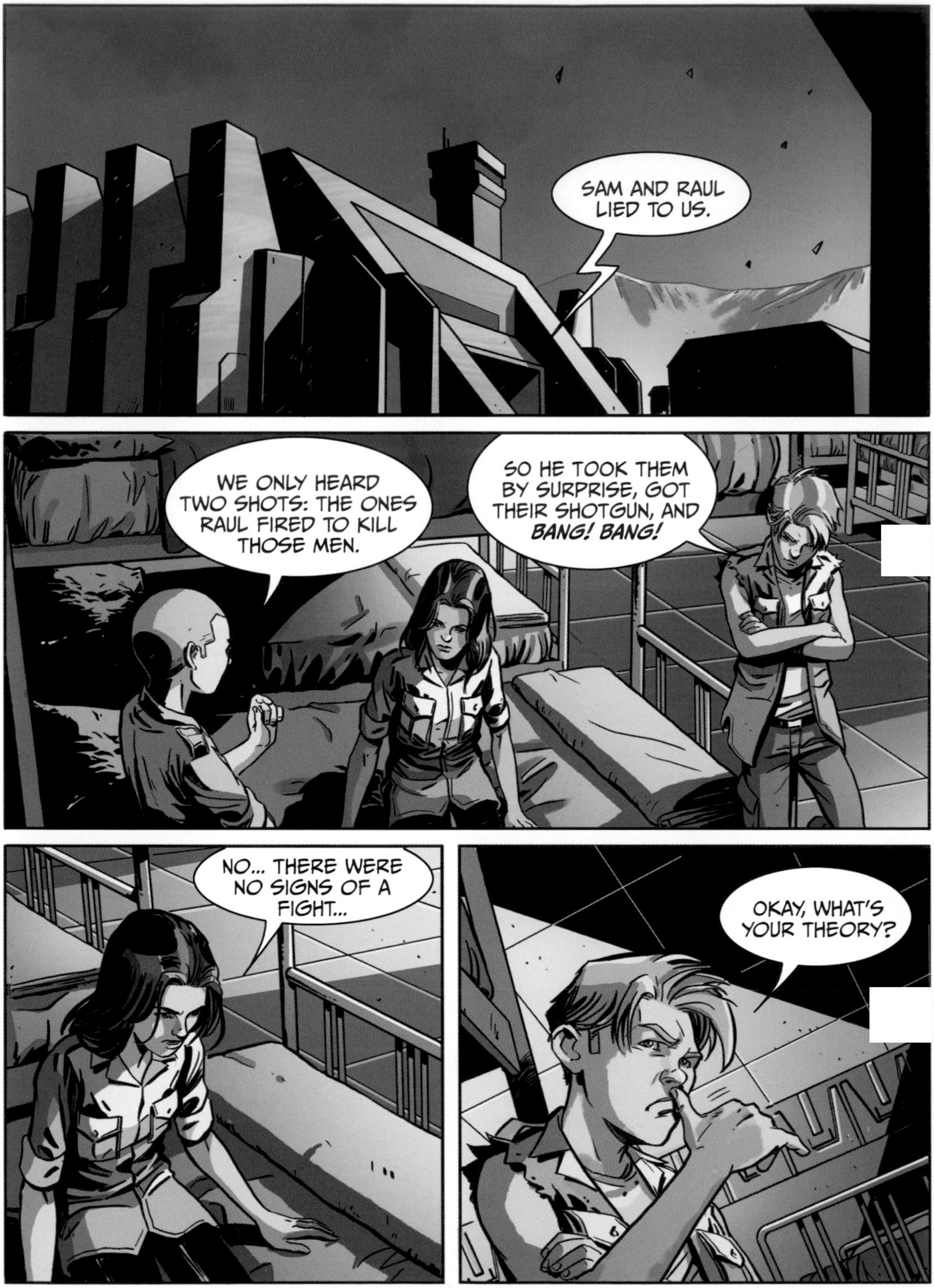
SAM AND RAUL LIED TO US.
WE ONLY HEARD TWO SHOTS: THE ONES RAUL FIRED TO KILL THOSE MEN.
SO HE TOOK THEM BY SURPRISE, GOT THEIR SHOTGUN, AND *BANG! BANG!*
NO... THERE WERE NO SIGNS OF A FIGHT...
OKAY, WHAT'S YOUR THEORY?

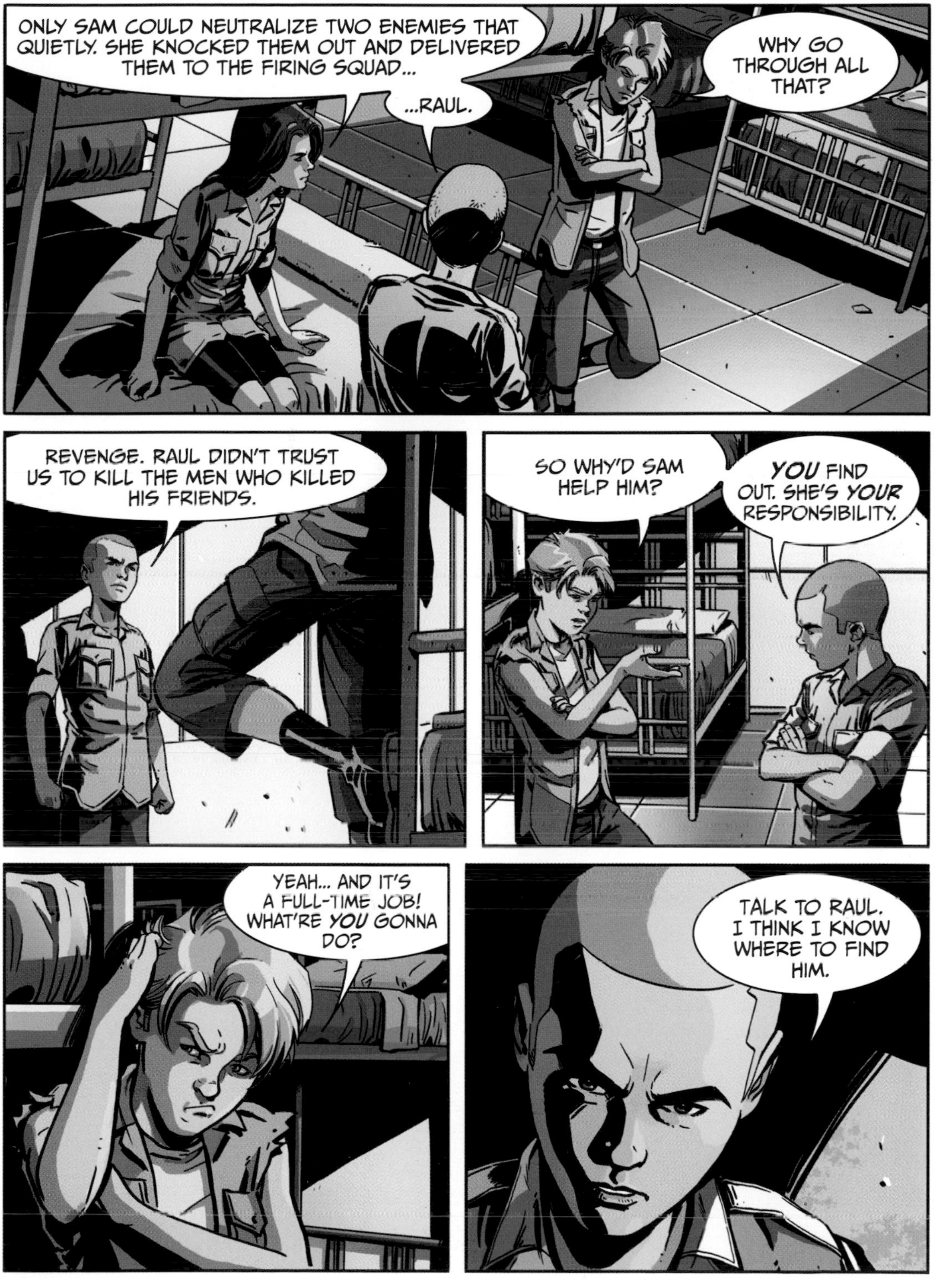
ONLY SAM COULD NEUTRALIZE TWO ENEMIES THAT QUIETLY. SHE KNOCKED THEM OUT AND DELIVERED THEM TO THE FIRING SQUAD...
...RAUL.
WHY GO THROUGH ALL THAT?
REVENGE. RAUL DIDN'T TRUST US TO KILL THE MEN WHO KILLED HIS FRIENDS.
SO WHY'D SAM HELP HIM?
YOU FIND OUT. SHE'S *YOUR* RESPONSIBILITY.
YEAH... AND IT'S A FULL-TIME JOB! WHAT'RE *YOU* GONNA DO?
TALK TO RAUL. I THINK I KNOW WHERE TO FIND HIM.

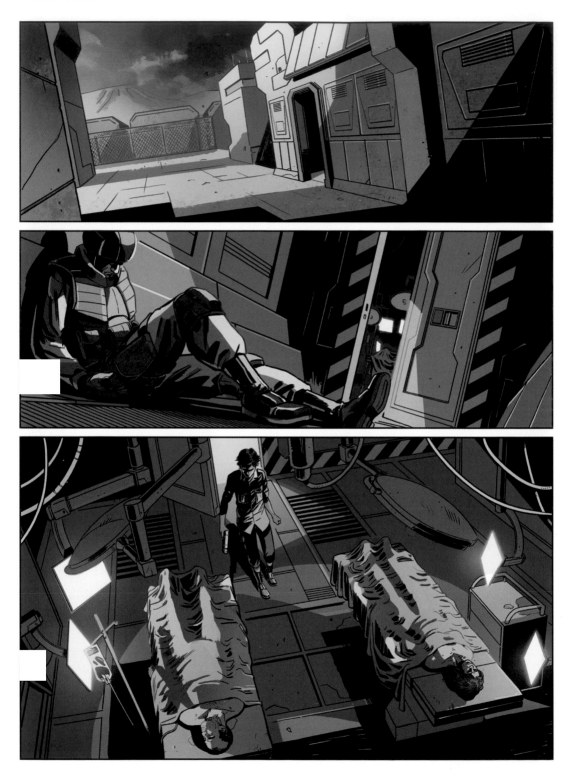

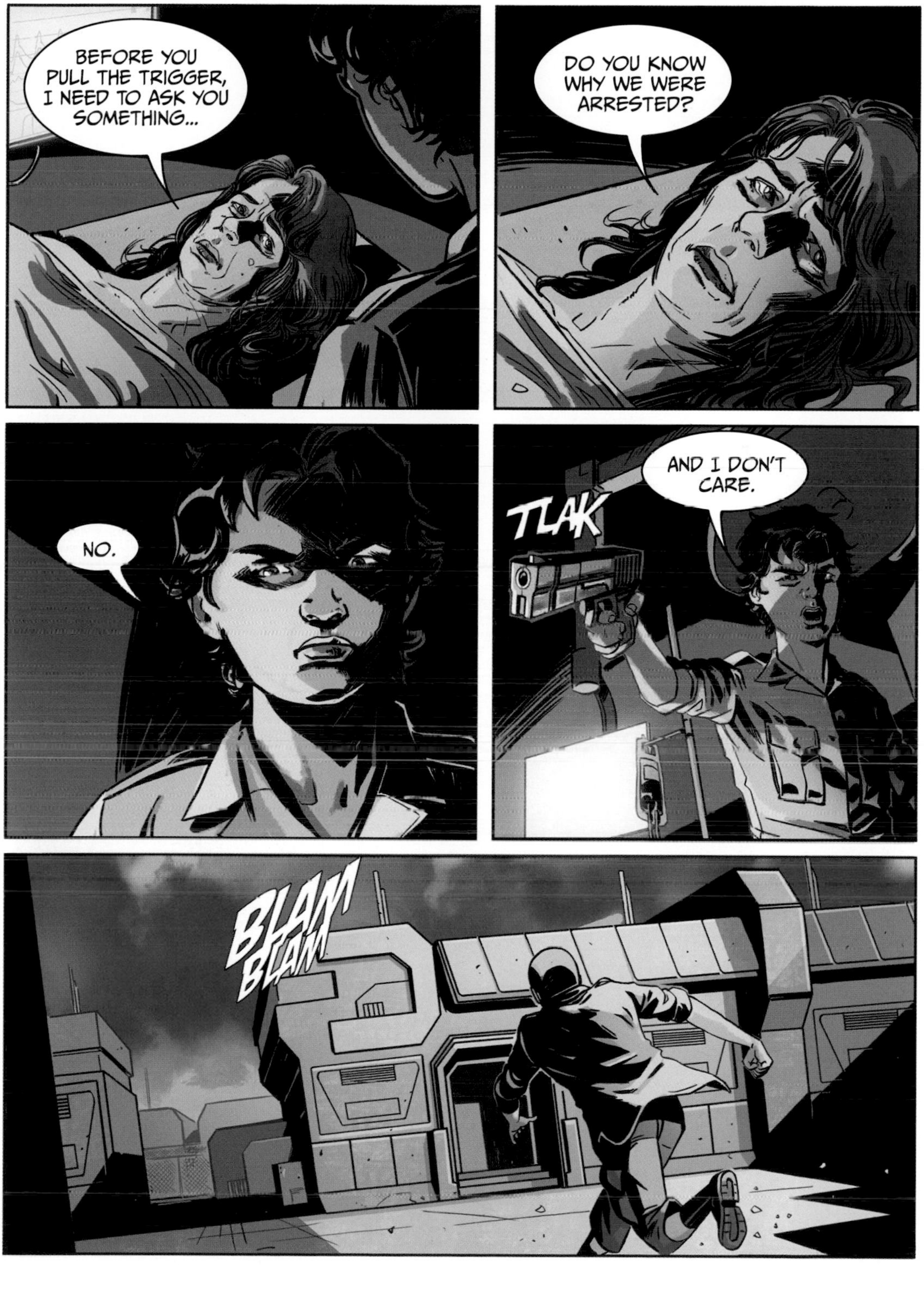
BEFORE YOU PULL THE TRIGGER, I NEED TO ASK YOU SOMETHING...
DO YOU KNOW WHY WE WERE ARRESTED?
NO.
TLAK
AND I DON'T CARE.
BLAM
BLAM

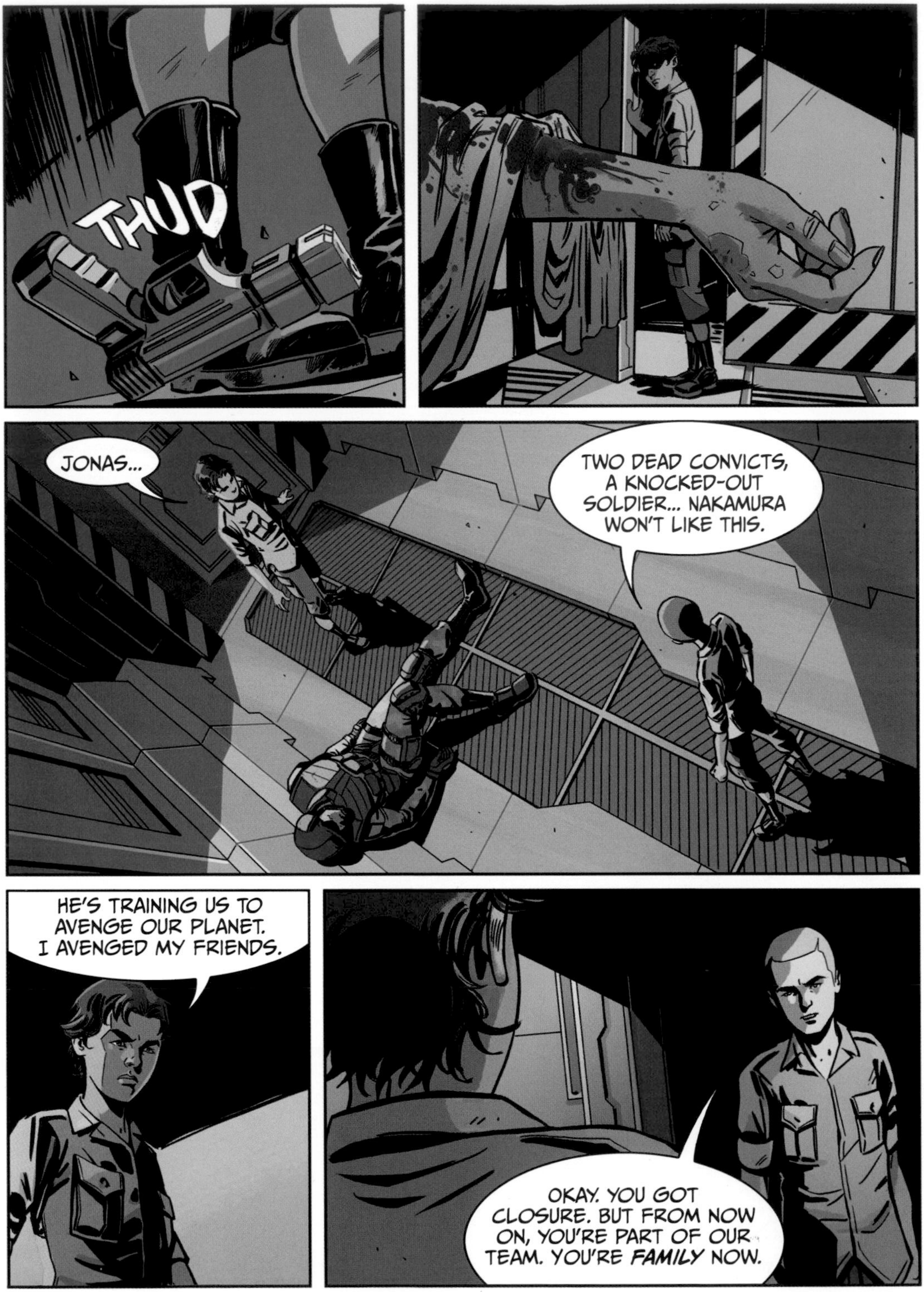
THUD
JONAS...
TWO DEAD CONVICTS, A KNOCKED-OUT SOLDIER... NAKAMURA WON'T LIKE THIS.
HE'S TRAINING US TO AVENGE OUR PLANET. I AVENGED MY FRIENDS.
OKAY. YOU GOT CLOSURE. BUT FROM NOW ON, YOU'RE PART OF OUR TEAM. YOU'RE *FAMILY* NOW.

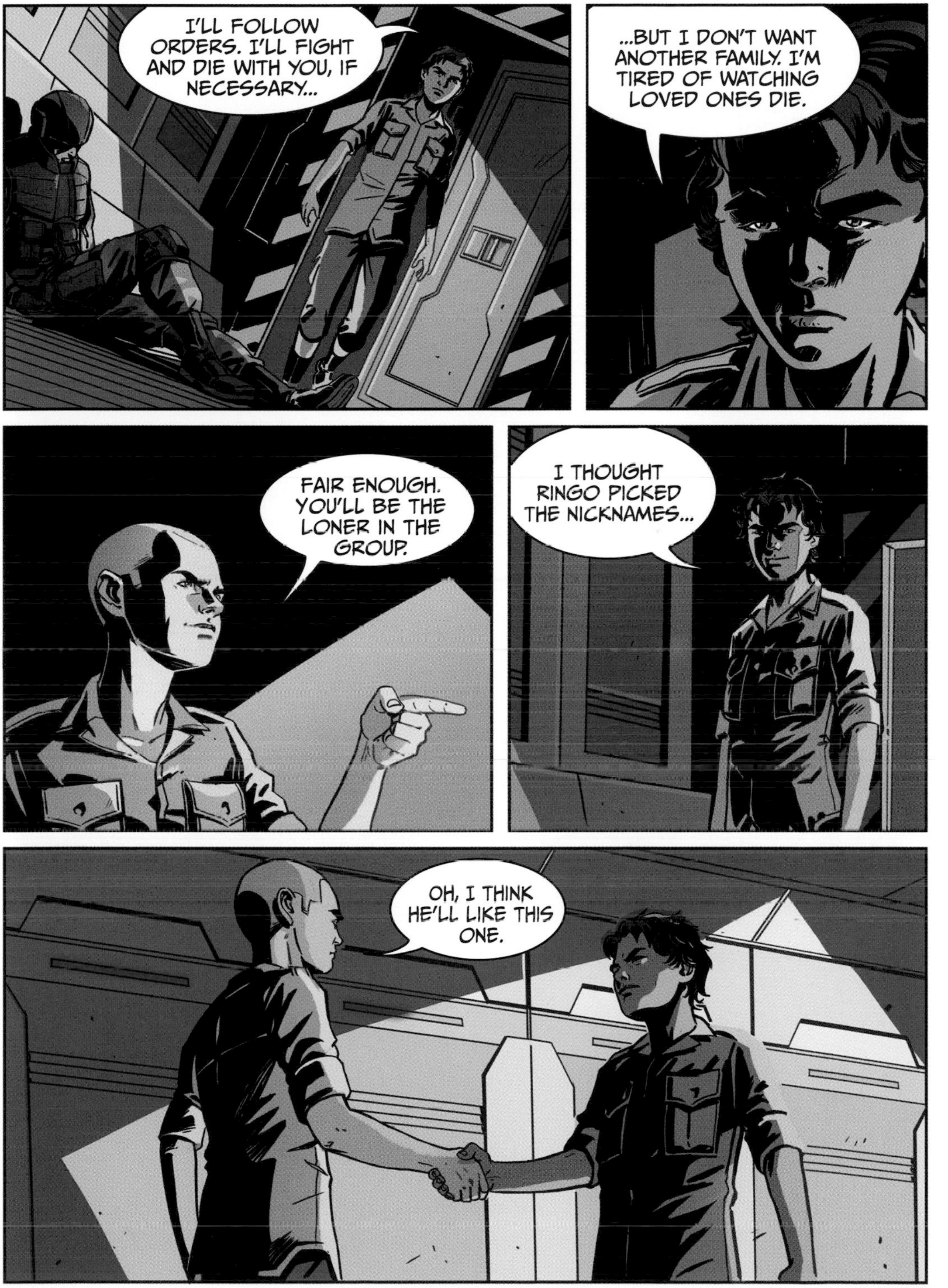
I'LL FOLLOW ORDERS. I'LL FIGHT AND DIE WITH YOU, IF NECESSARY...
...BUT I DON'T WANT ANOTHER FAMILY. I'M TIRED OF WATCHING LOVED ONES DIE.
FAIR ENOUGH. YOU'LL BE THE LONER IN THE GROUP.
I THOUGHT RINGO PICKED THE NICKNAMES...
OH, I THINK HE'LL LIKE THIS ONE.

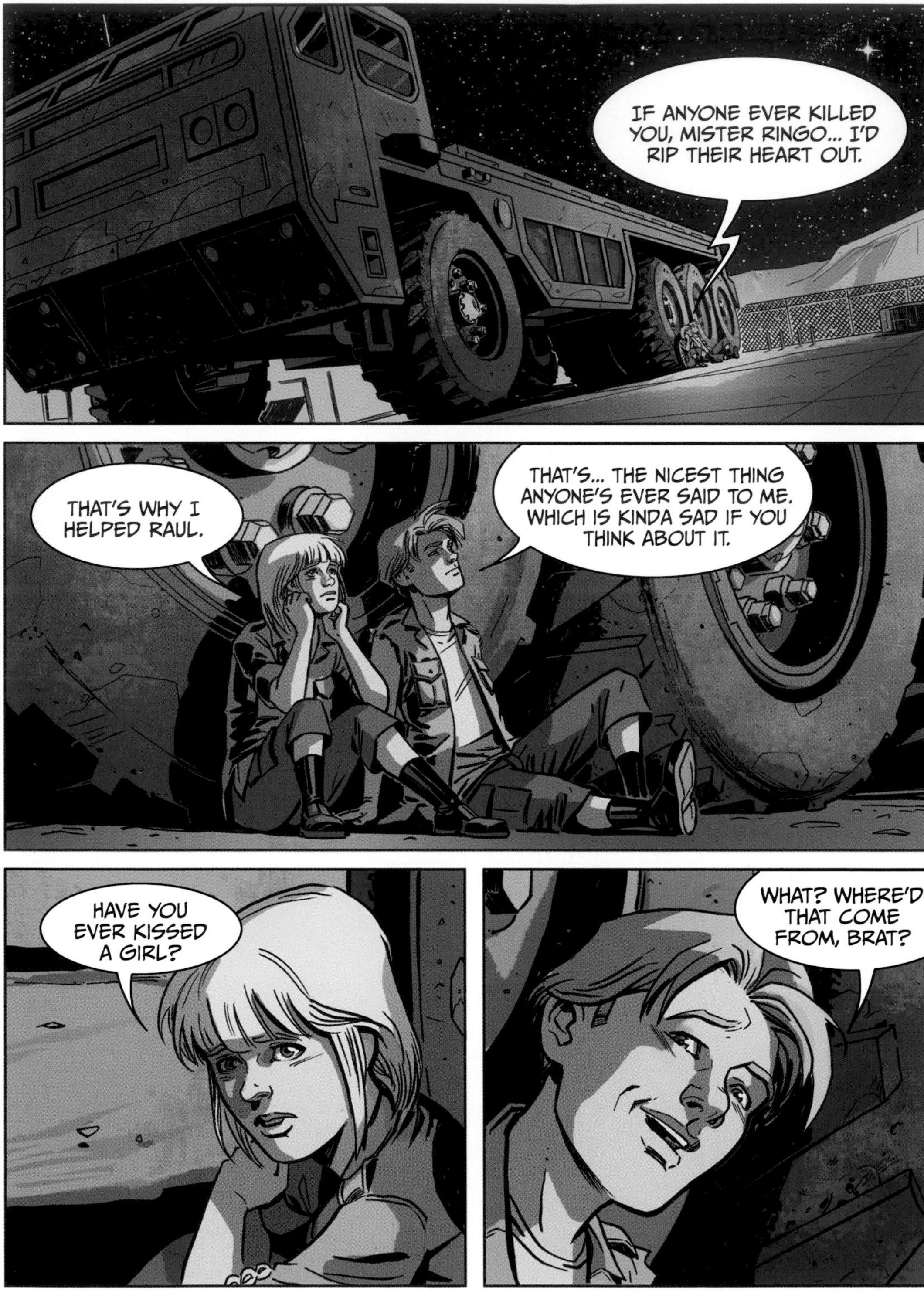
IF ANYONE EVER KILLED YOU, MISTER RINGO... I'D RIP THEIR HEART OUT.
THAT'S WHY I HELPED RAUL.
THAT'S... THE NICEST THING ANYONE'S EVER SAID TO ME. WHICH IS KINDA SAD IF YOU THINK ABOUT IT.
HAVE YOU EVER KISSED A GIRL?
WHAT? WHERE'D THAT COME FROM, BRAT?

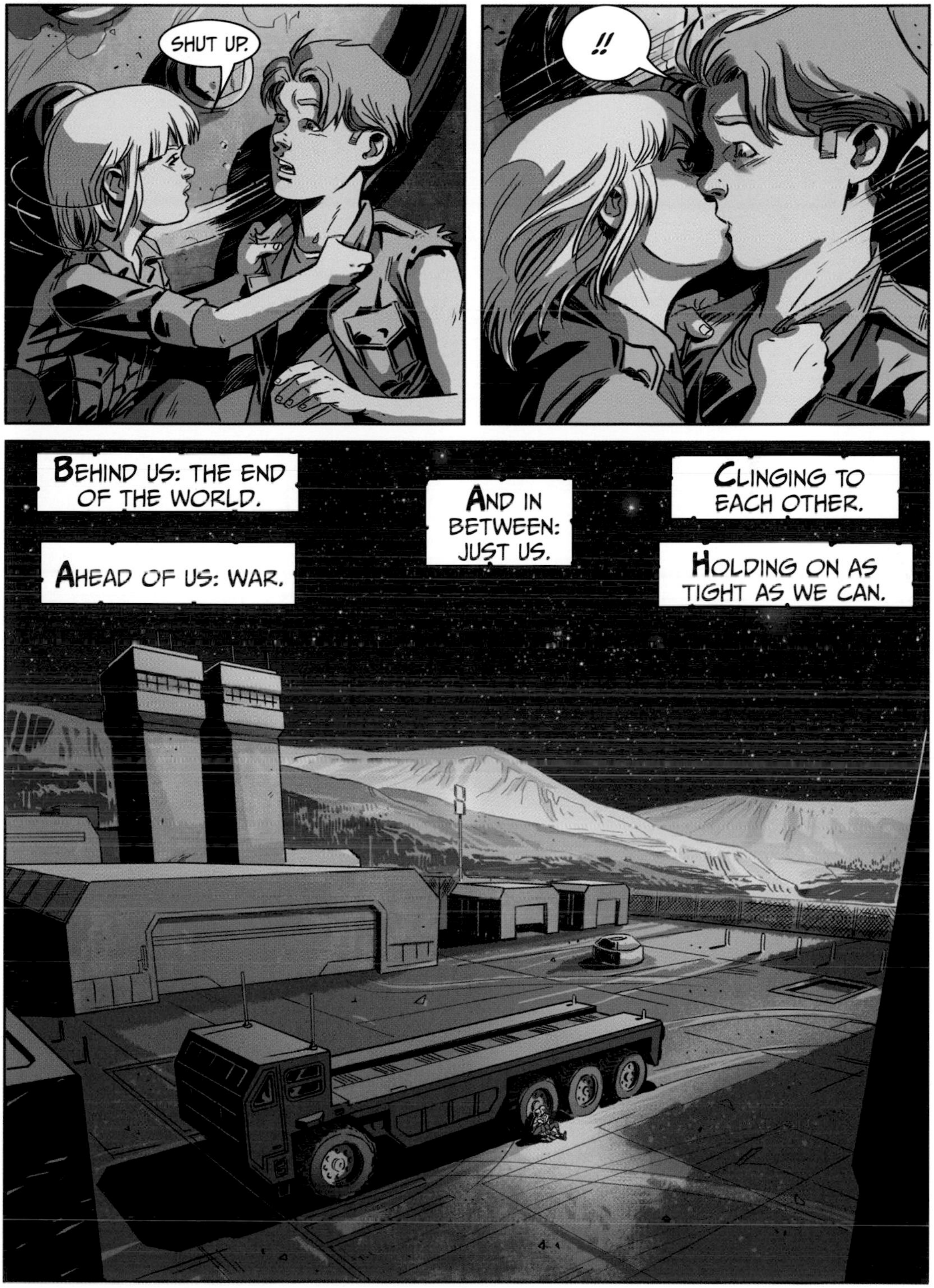
SHUT UP.
!!
BEHIND US: THE END OF THE WORLD.
AHEAD OF US: WAR.
AND IN BETWEEN: JUST US.
CLINGING TO EACH OTHER.
HOLDING ON AS TIGHT AS WE CAN.

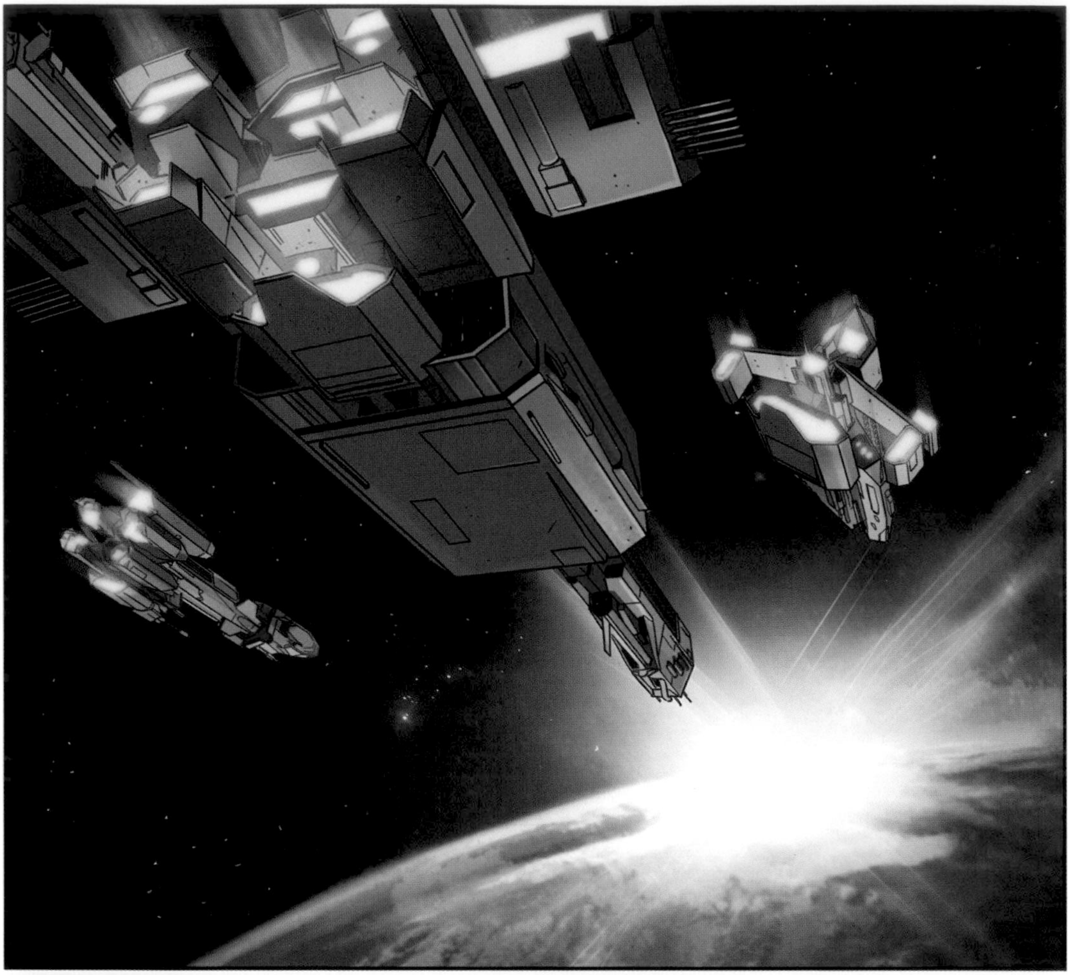

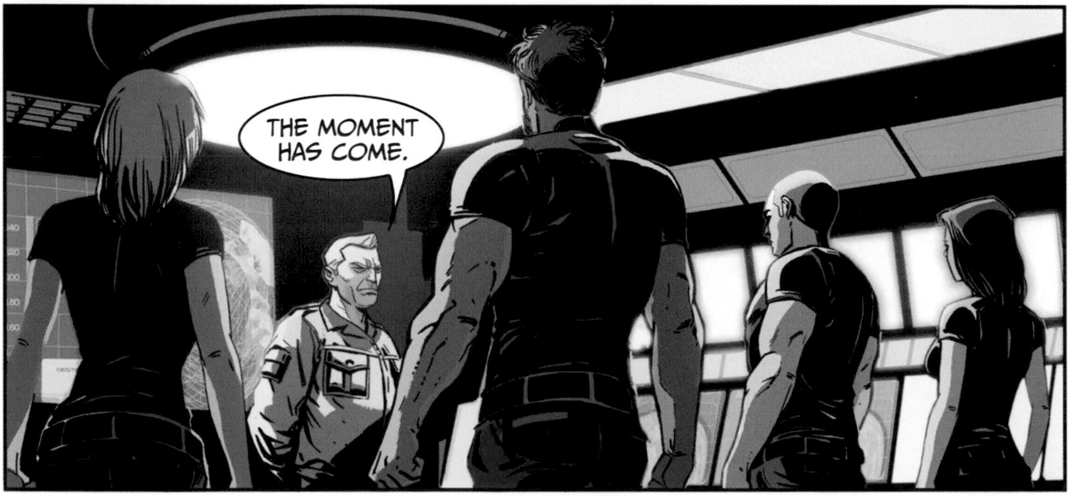
THE MOMENT HAS COME.

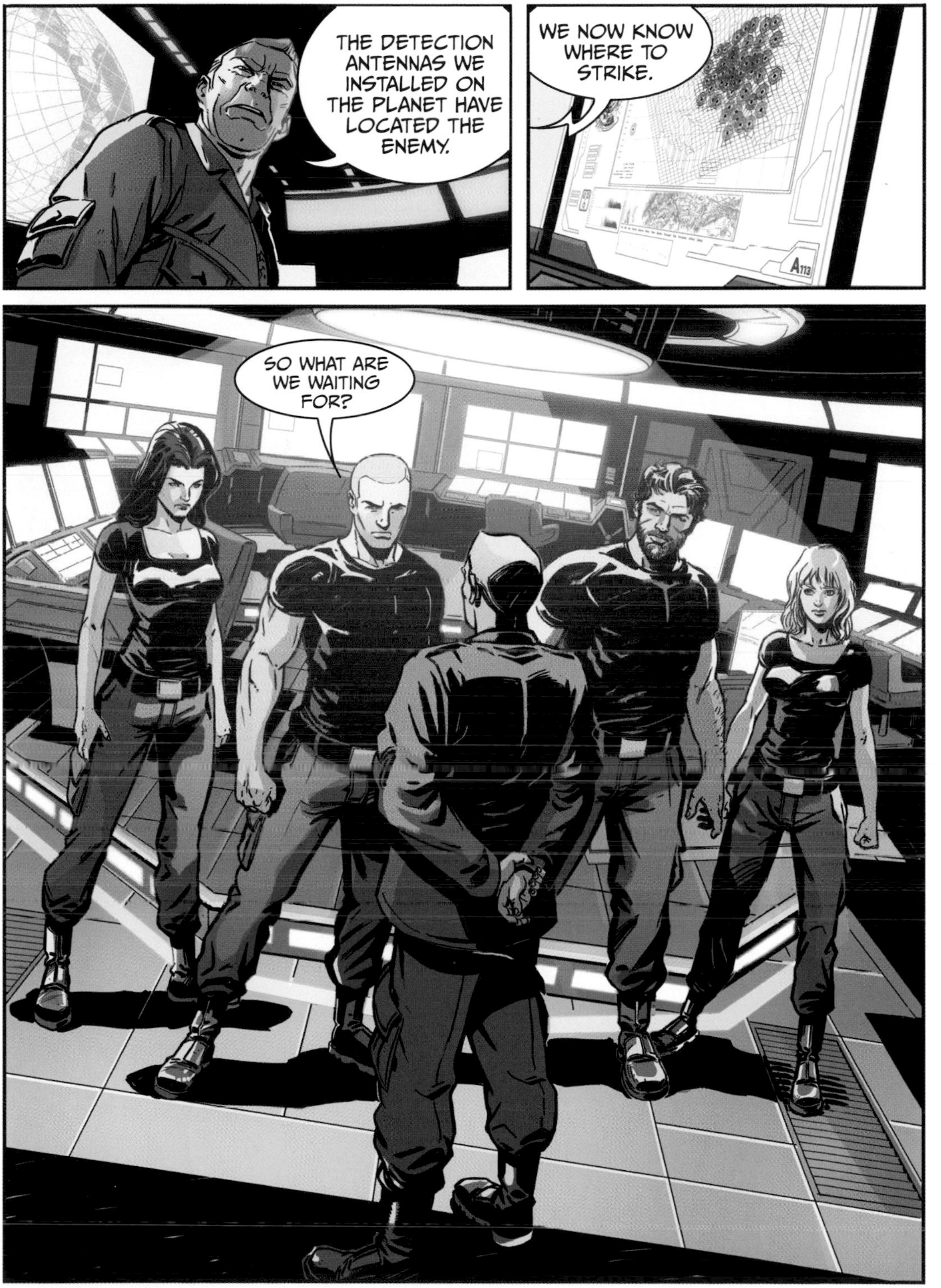
THE DETECTION ANTENNAS WE INSTALLED ON THE PLANET HAVE LOCATED THE ENEMY.
WE NOW KNOW WHERE TO STRIKE.
SO WHAT ARE WE WAITING FOR?

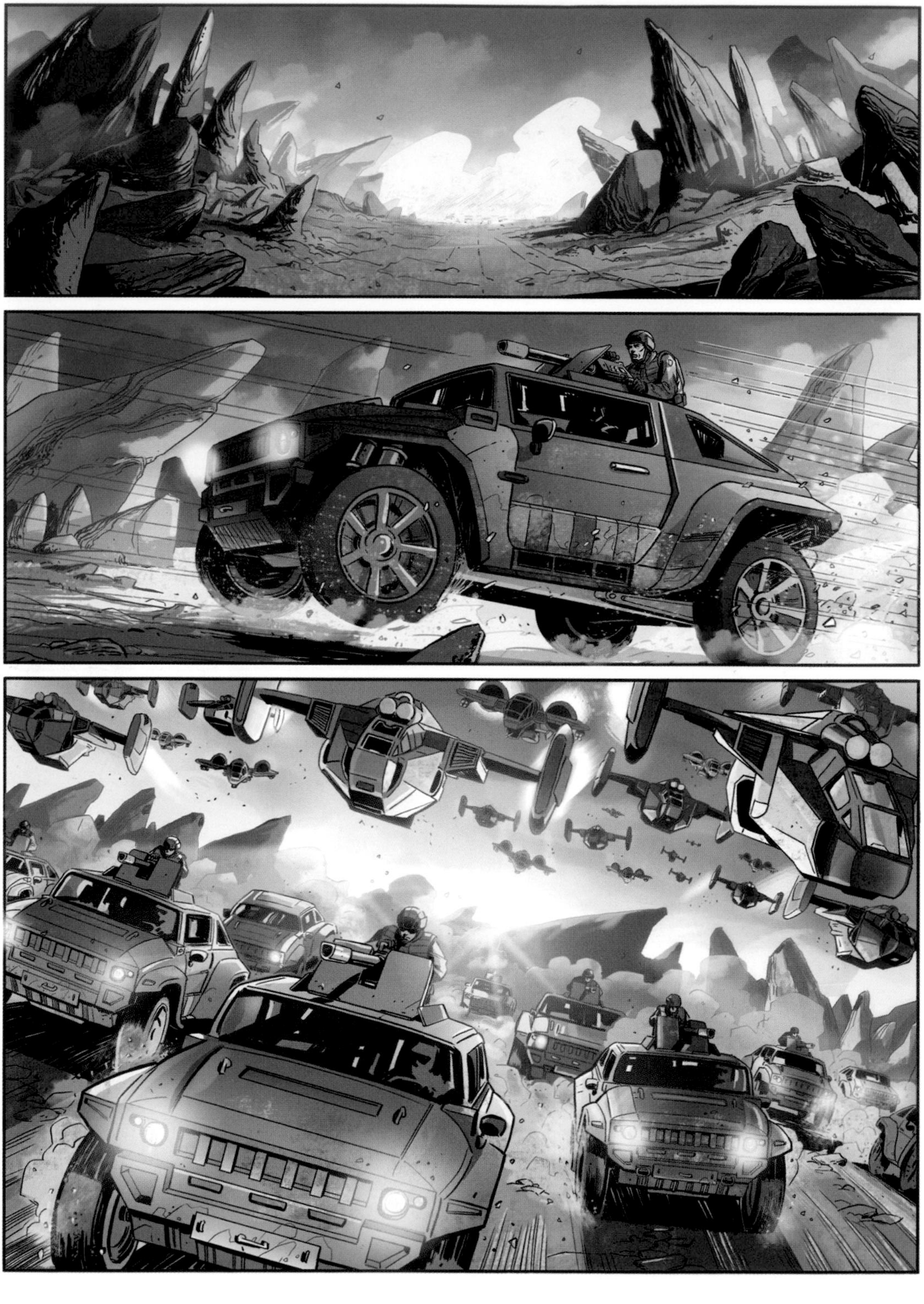

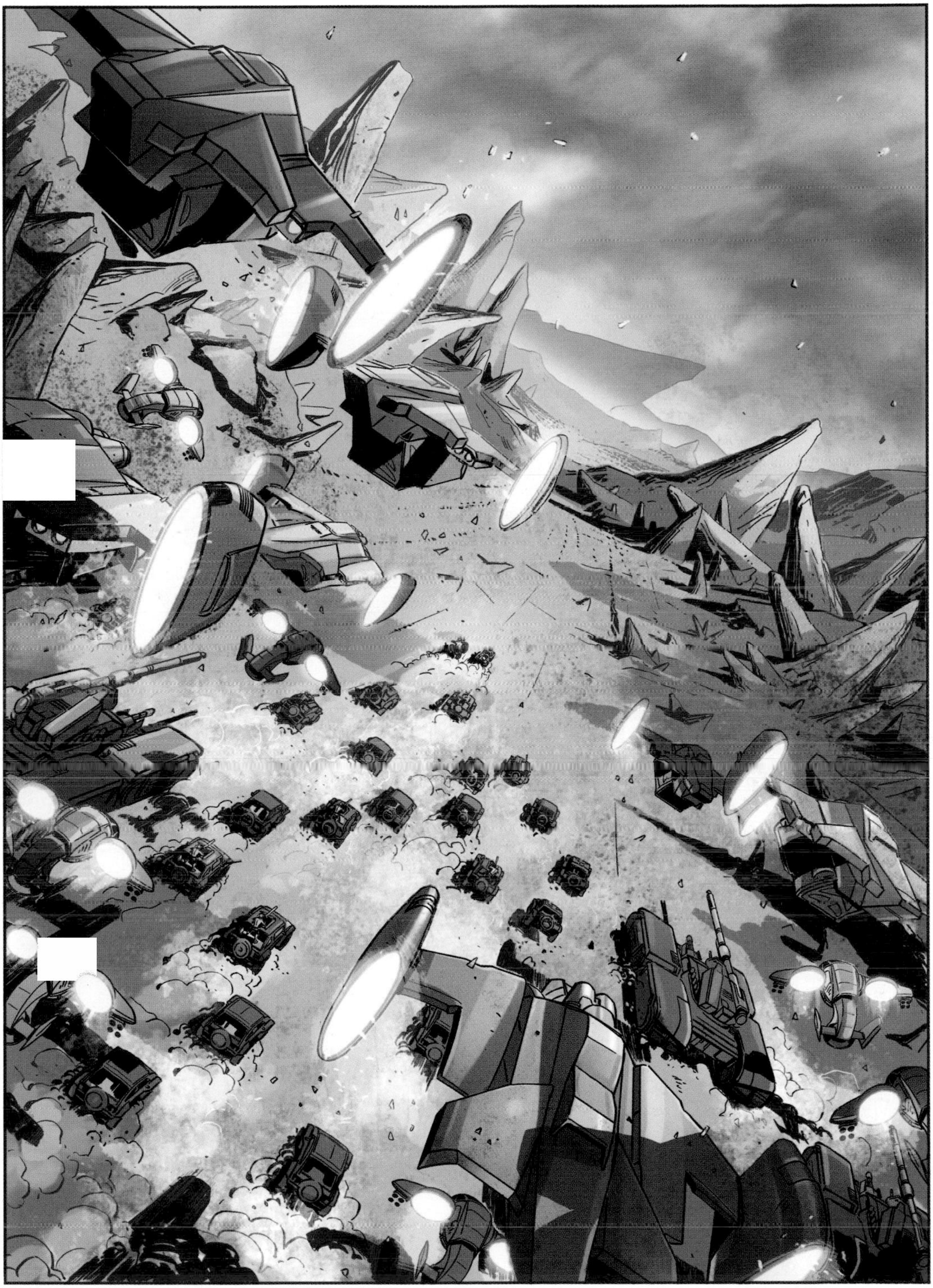

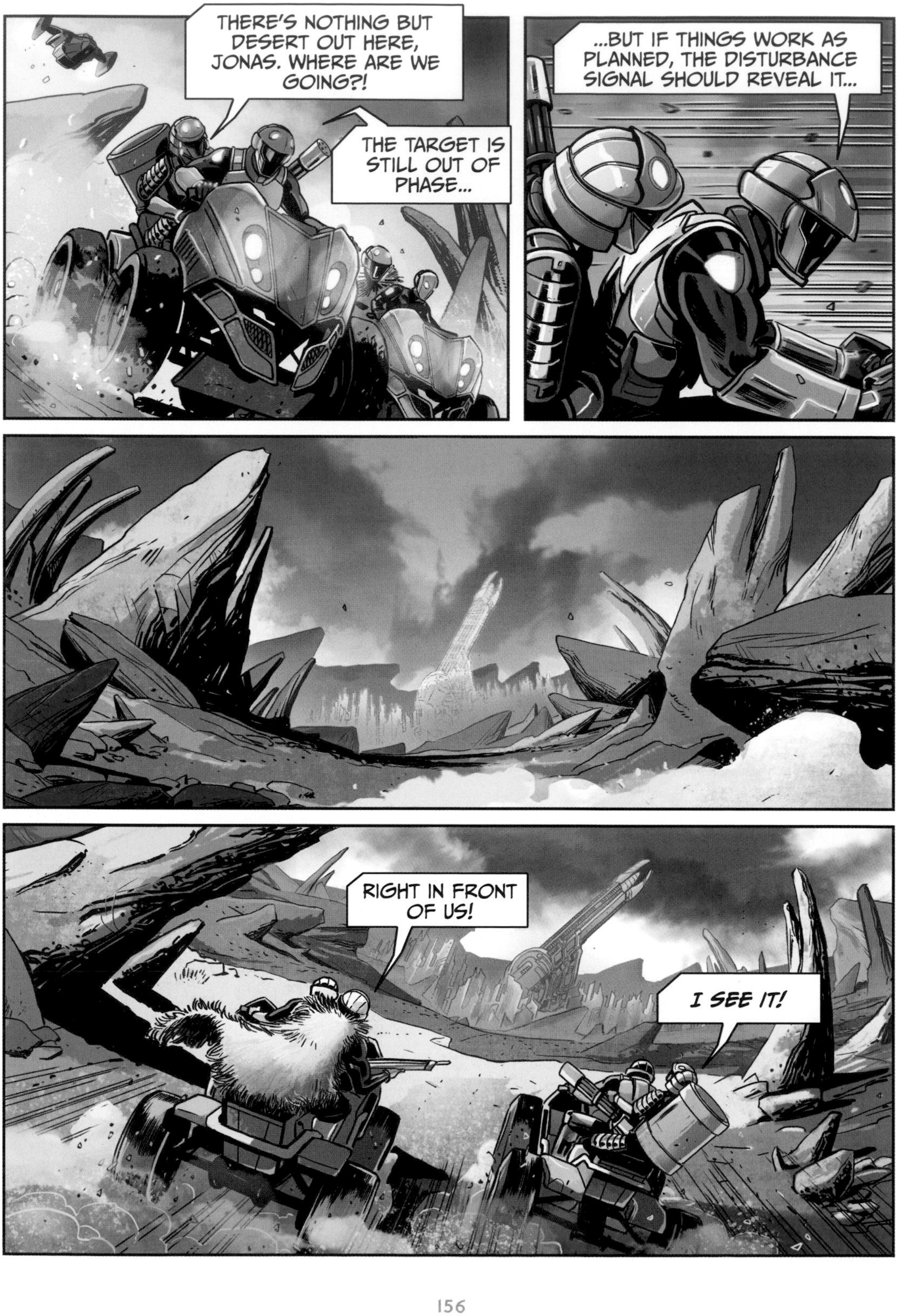
THERE'S NOTHING BUT DESERT OUT HERE, JONAS. WHERE ARE WE GOING?!
THE TARGET IS STILL OUT OF PHASE...
...BUT IF THINGS WORK AS PLANNED, THE DISTURBANCE SIGNAL SHOULD REVEAL IT...
RIGHT IN FRONT OF US!
I SEE IT!

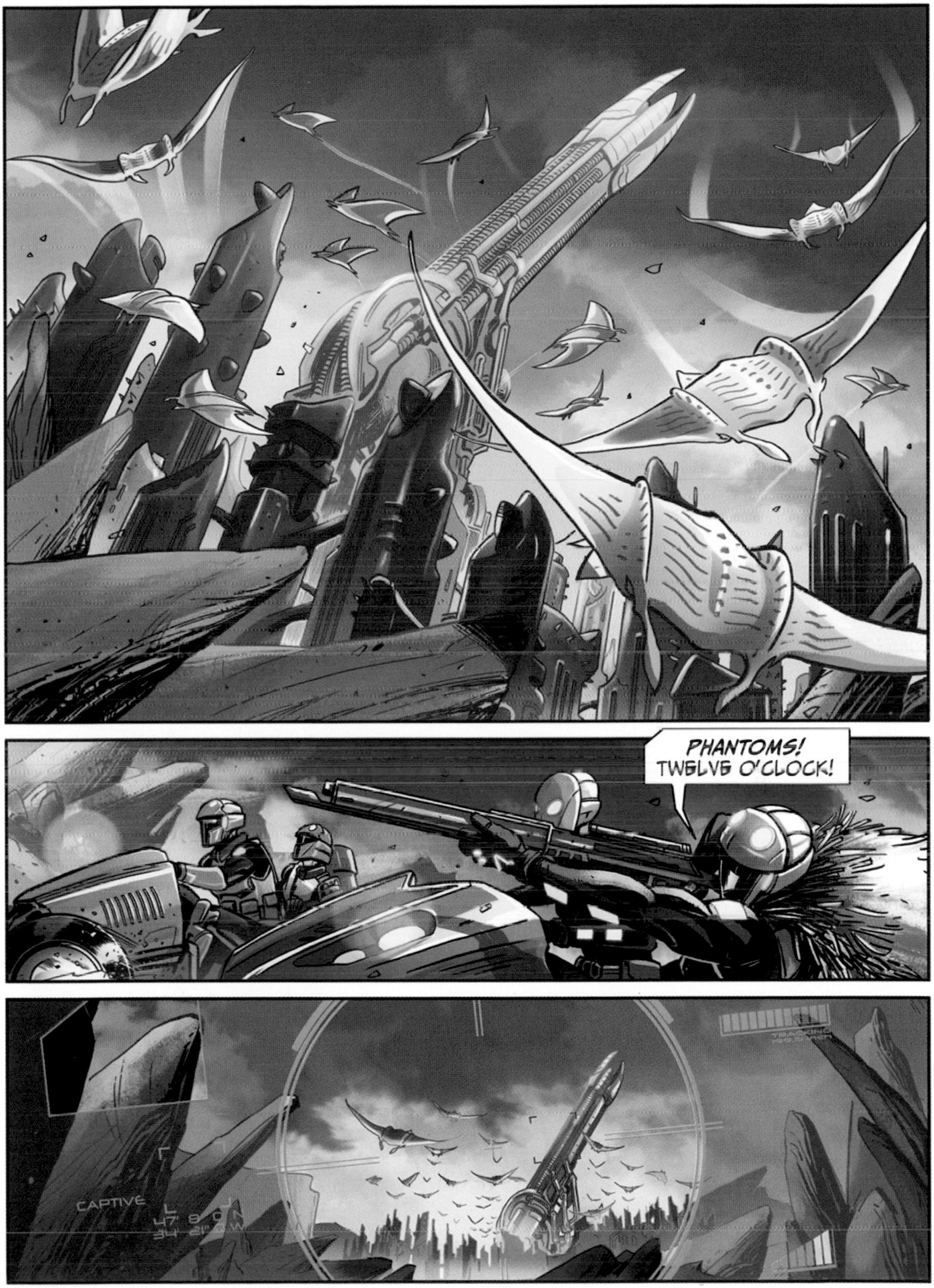
PHANTOMS!
TWELVE O'CLOCK!
CAPTIVE

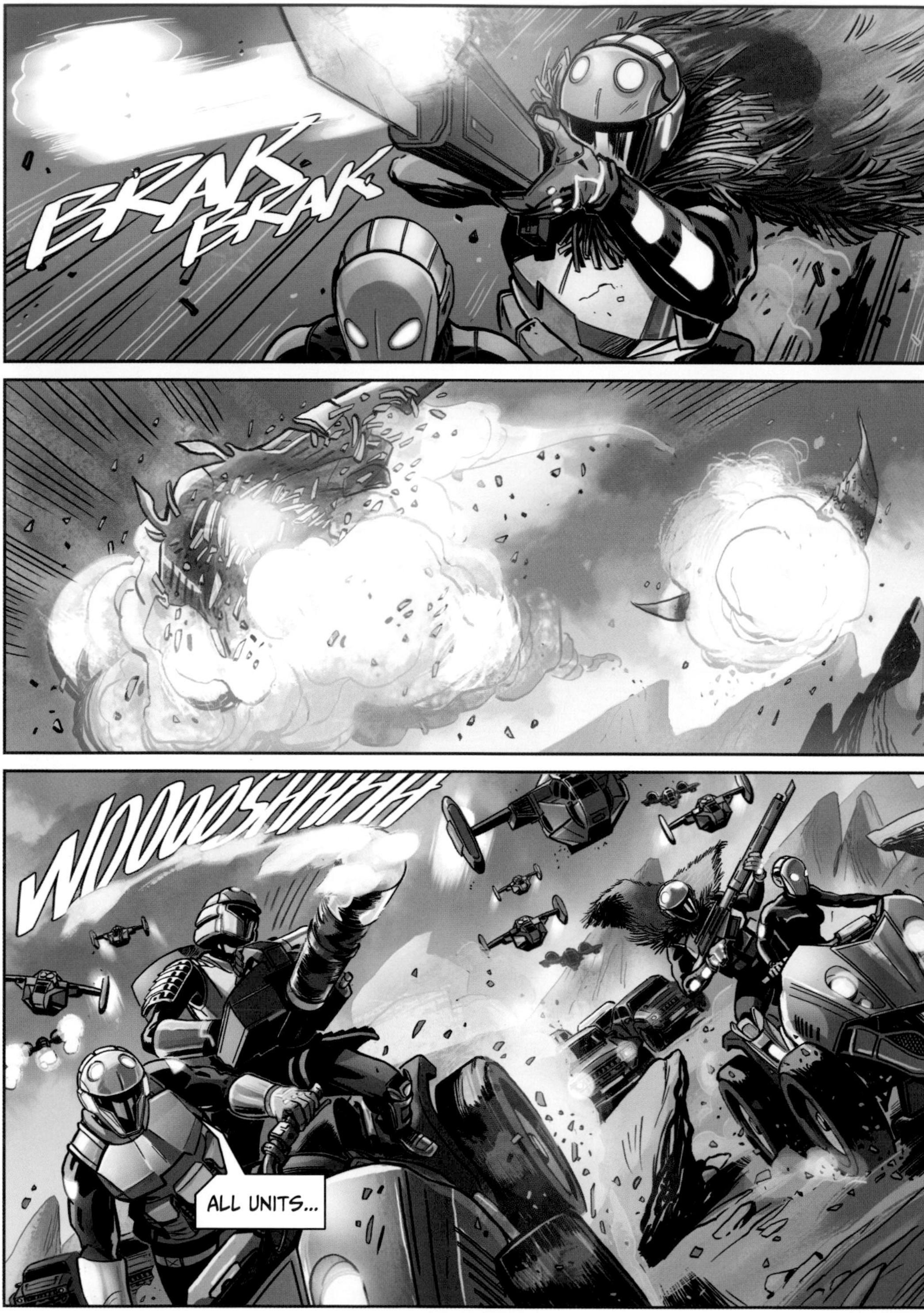
BRAK
BRAK
WOOOOSHHHH
ALL UNITS...

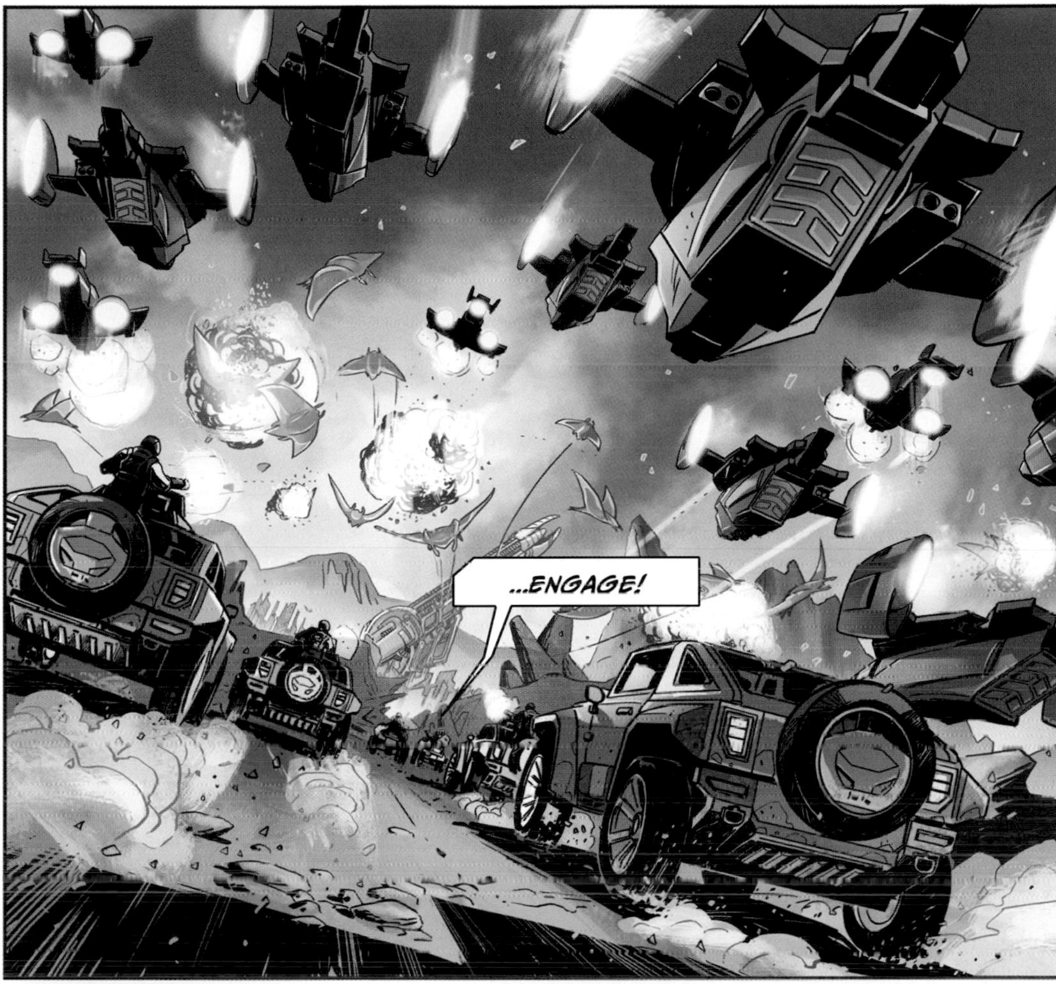
...ENGAGE!

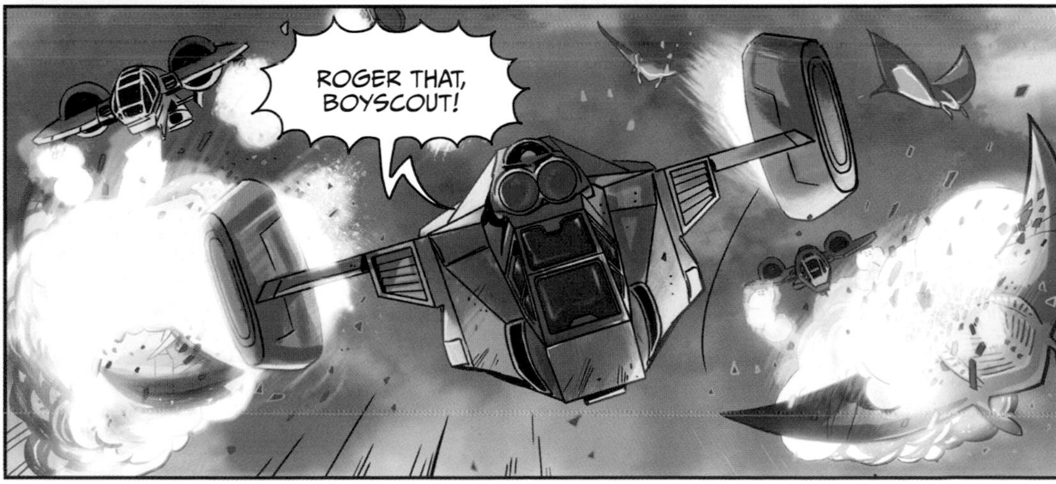
ROGER THAT, BOYSCOUT!

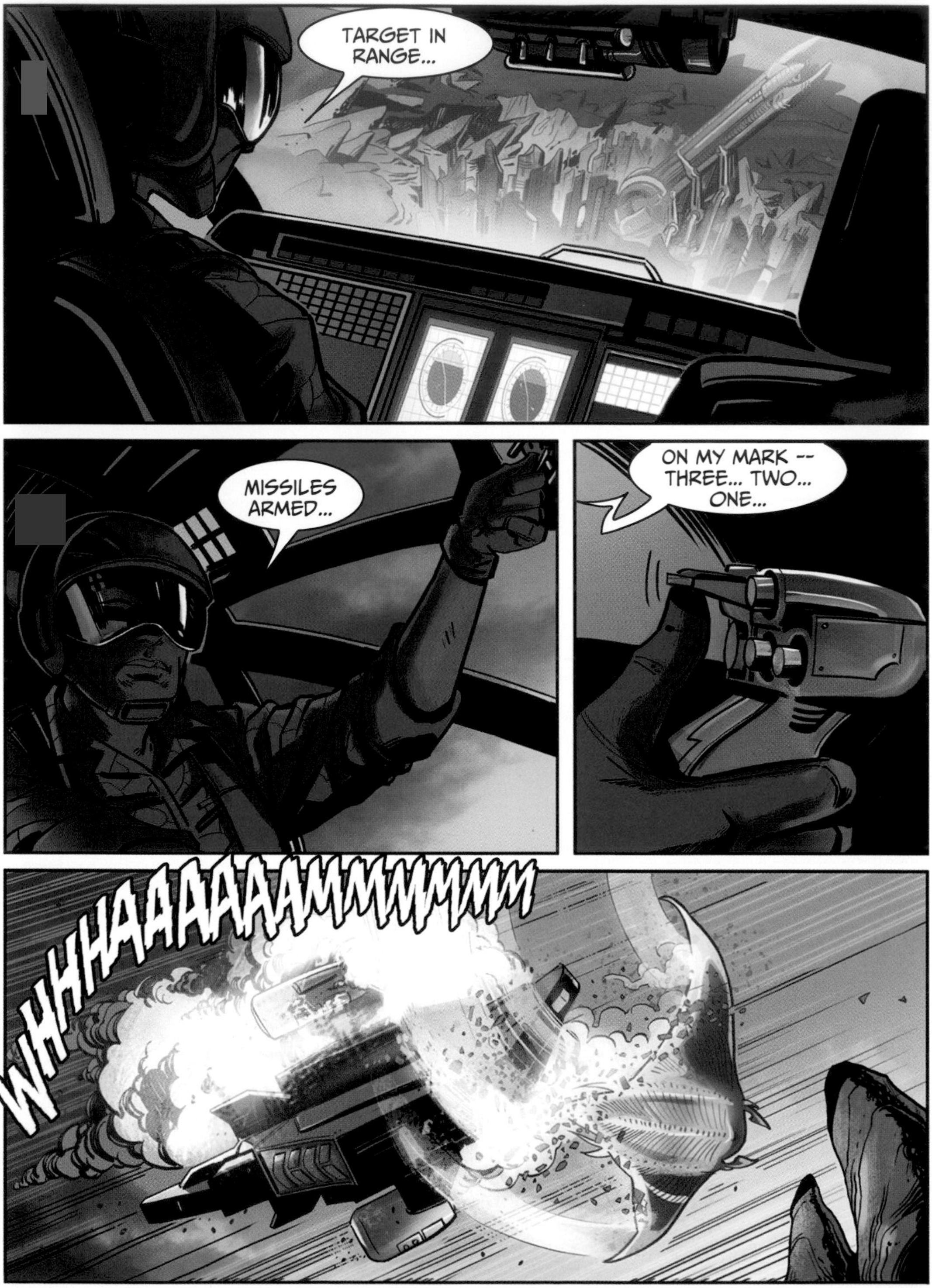
TARGET IN RANGE...
MISSILES ARMED...
ON MY MARK -- THREE... TWO... ONE...
WHHAAAAAMMMMMM

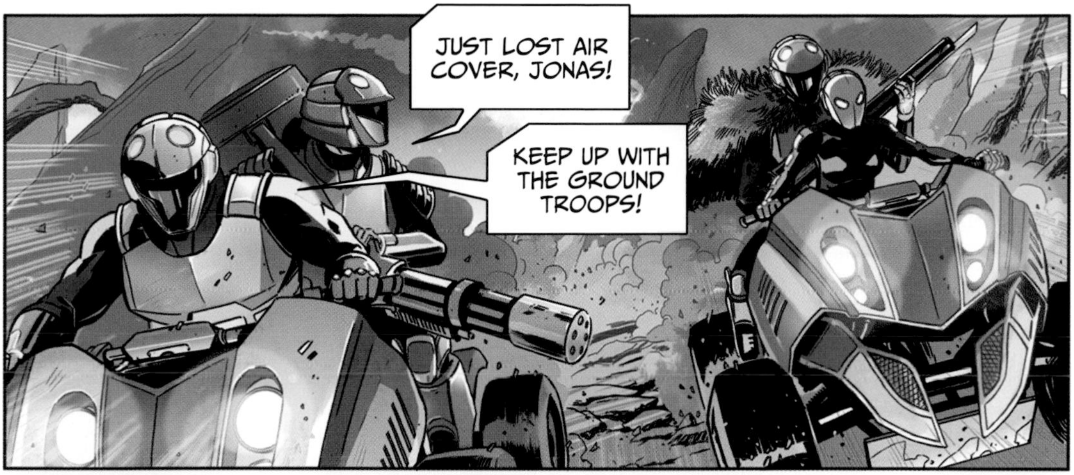
JUST LOST AIR COVER, JONAS!
KEEP UP WITH THE GROUND TROOPS!

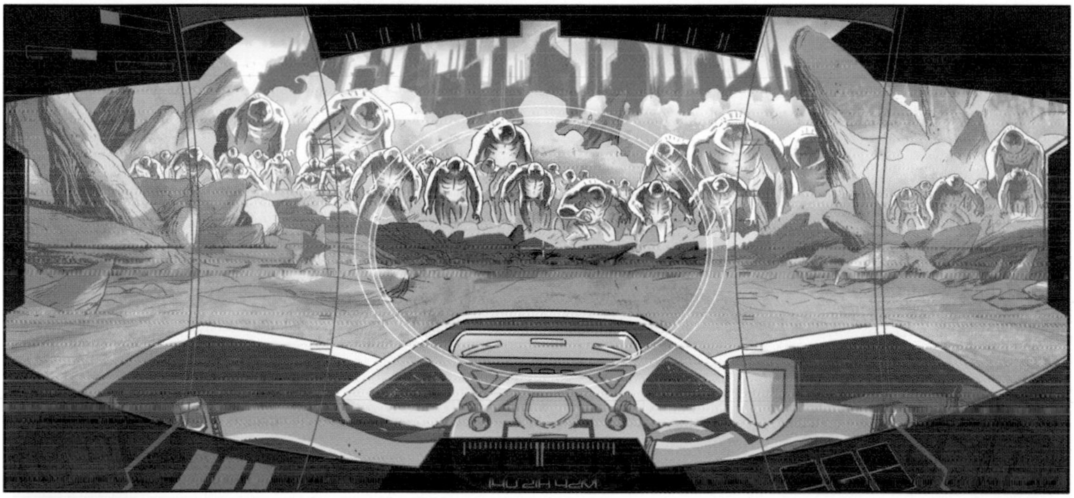

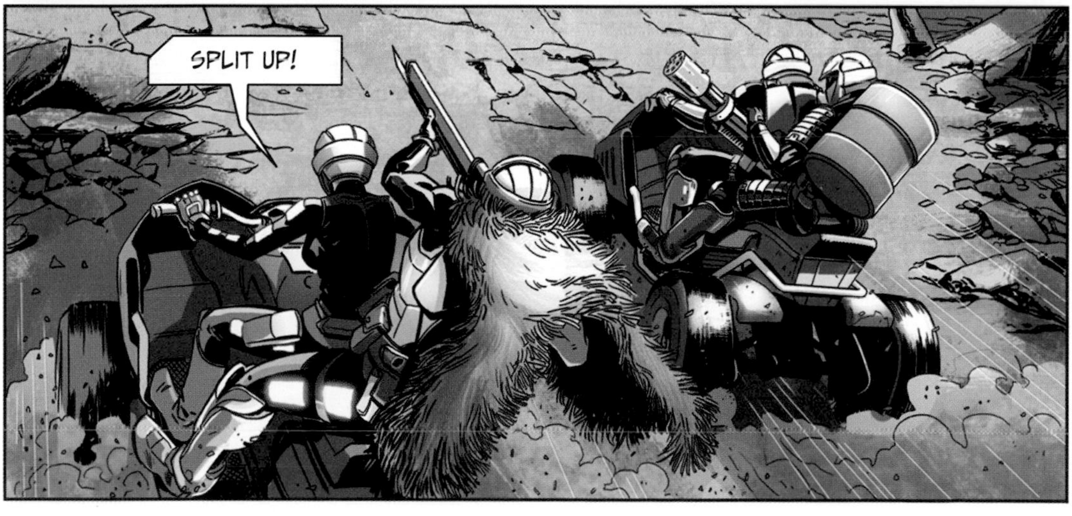
SPLIT UP!

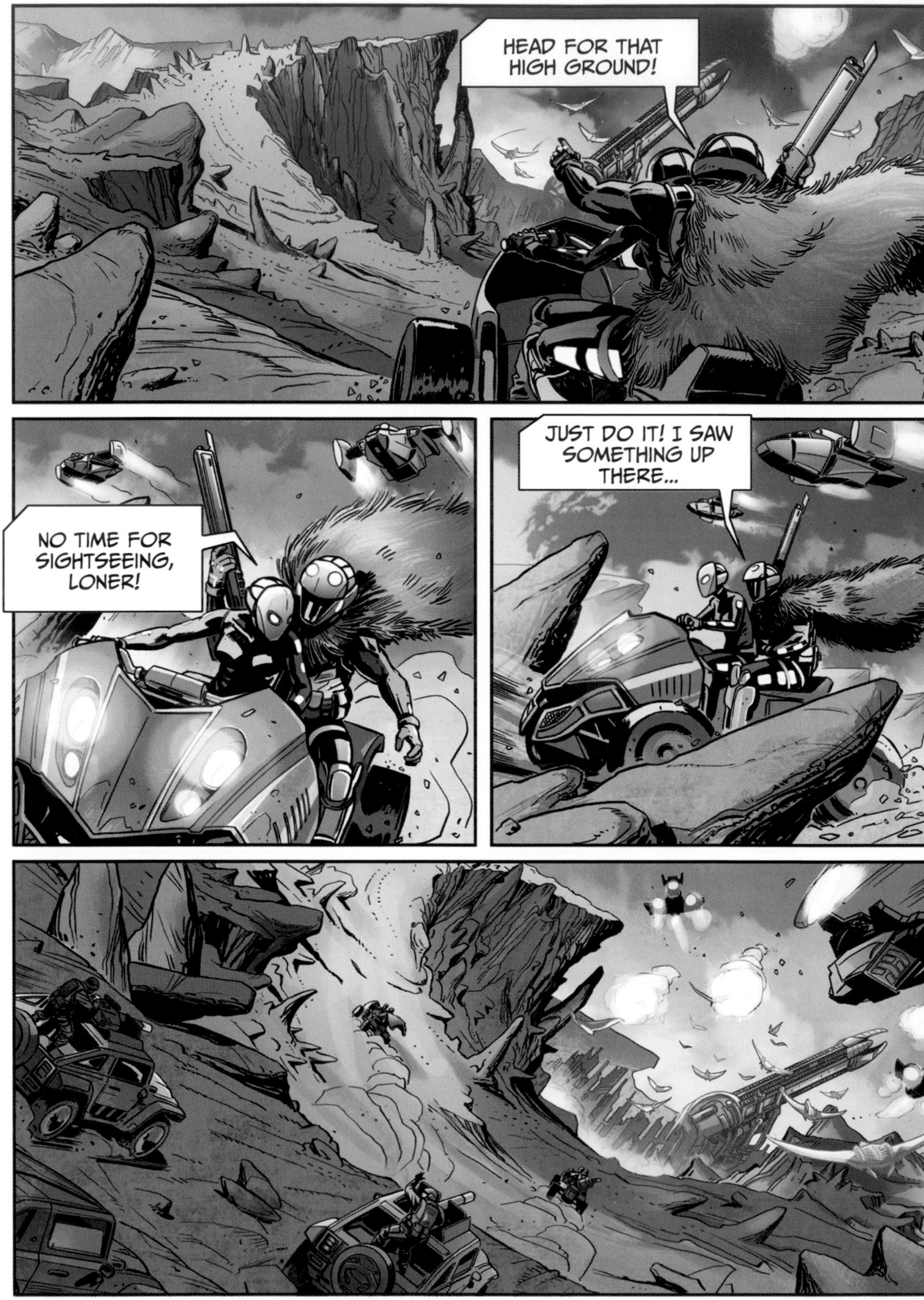
HEAD FOR THAT HIGH GROUND!
NO TIME FOR SIGHTSEEING, LONER!
JUST DO IT! I SAW SOMETHING UP THERE...

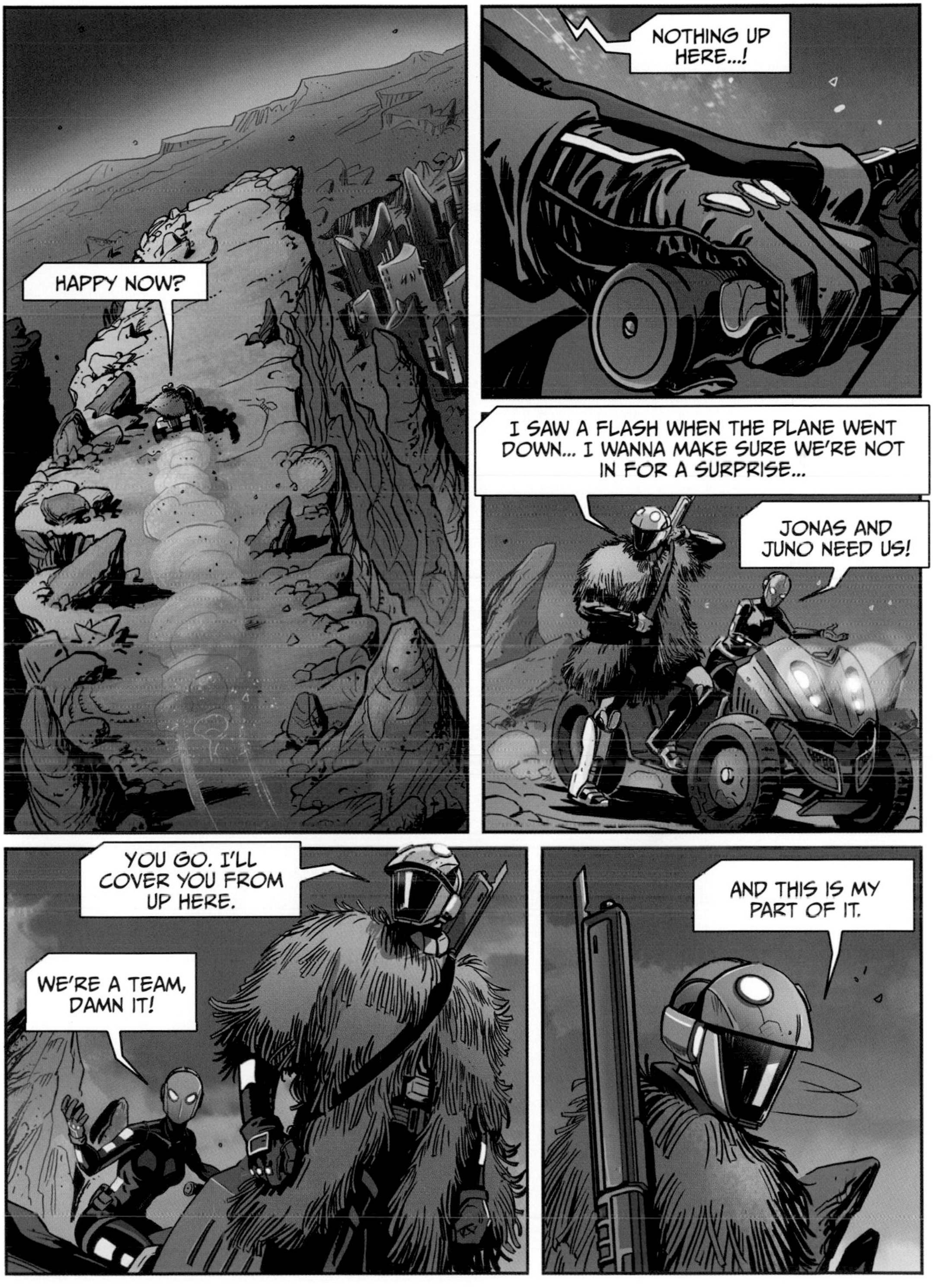
HAPPY NOW?
NOTHING UP HERE...!
I SAW A FLASH WHEN THE PLANE WENT DOWN... I WANNA MAKE SURE WE'RE NOT IN FOR A SURPRISE...
JONAS AND JUNO NEED US!
YOU GO. I'LL COVER YOU FROM UP HERE.
WE'RE A TEAM, DAMN IT!
AND THIS IS MY PART OF IT.

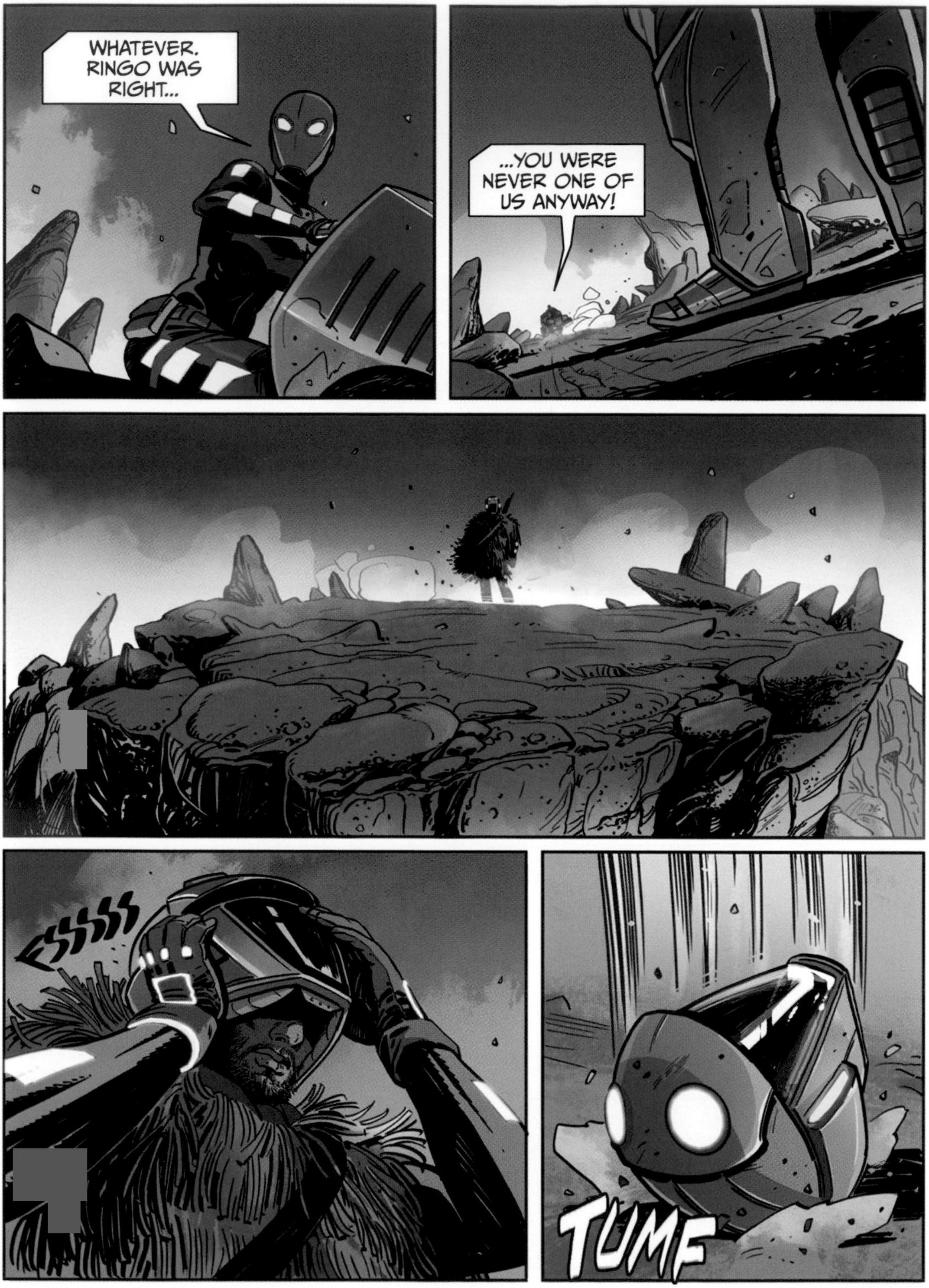
WHATEVER. RINGO WAS RIGHT...
...YOU WERE NEVER ONE OF US ANYWAY!
FSSSSSS
TUMF

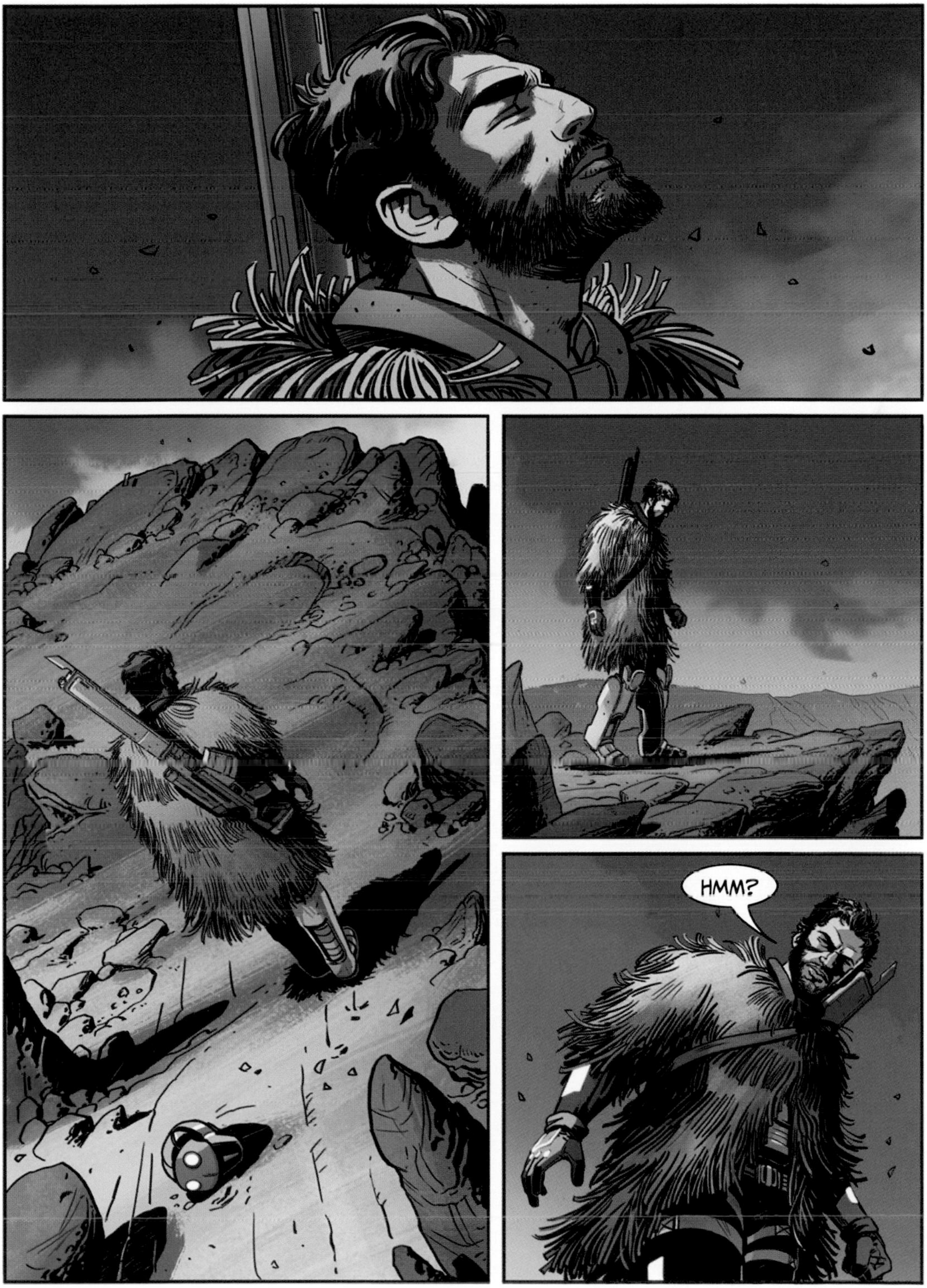
HMM?

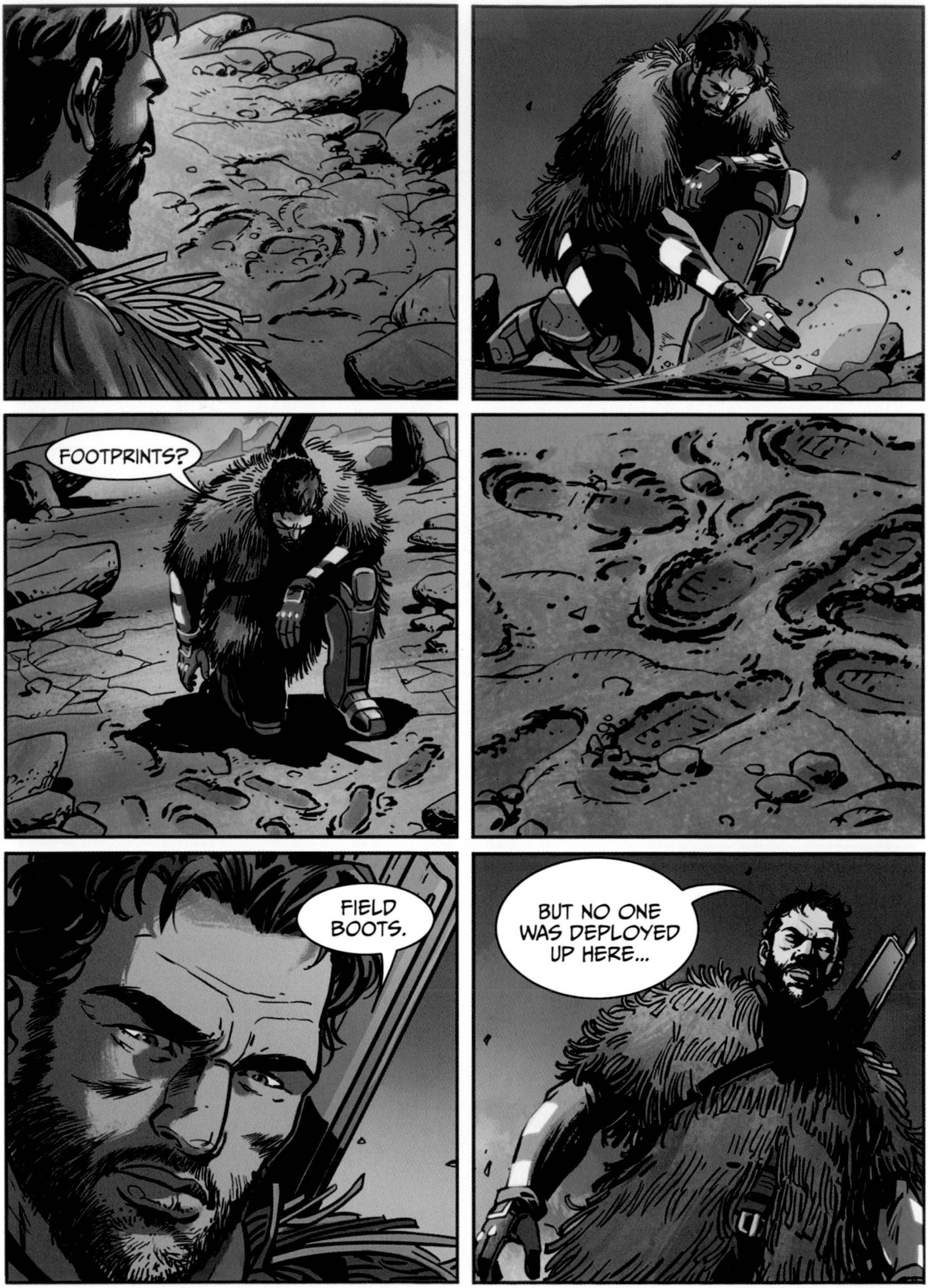
FOOTPRINTS?
FIELD BOOTS.
BUT NO ONE WAS DEPLOYED UP HERE...

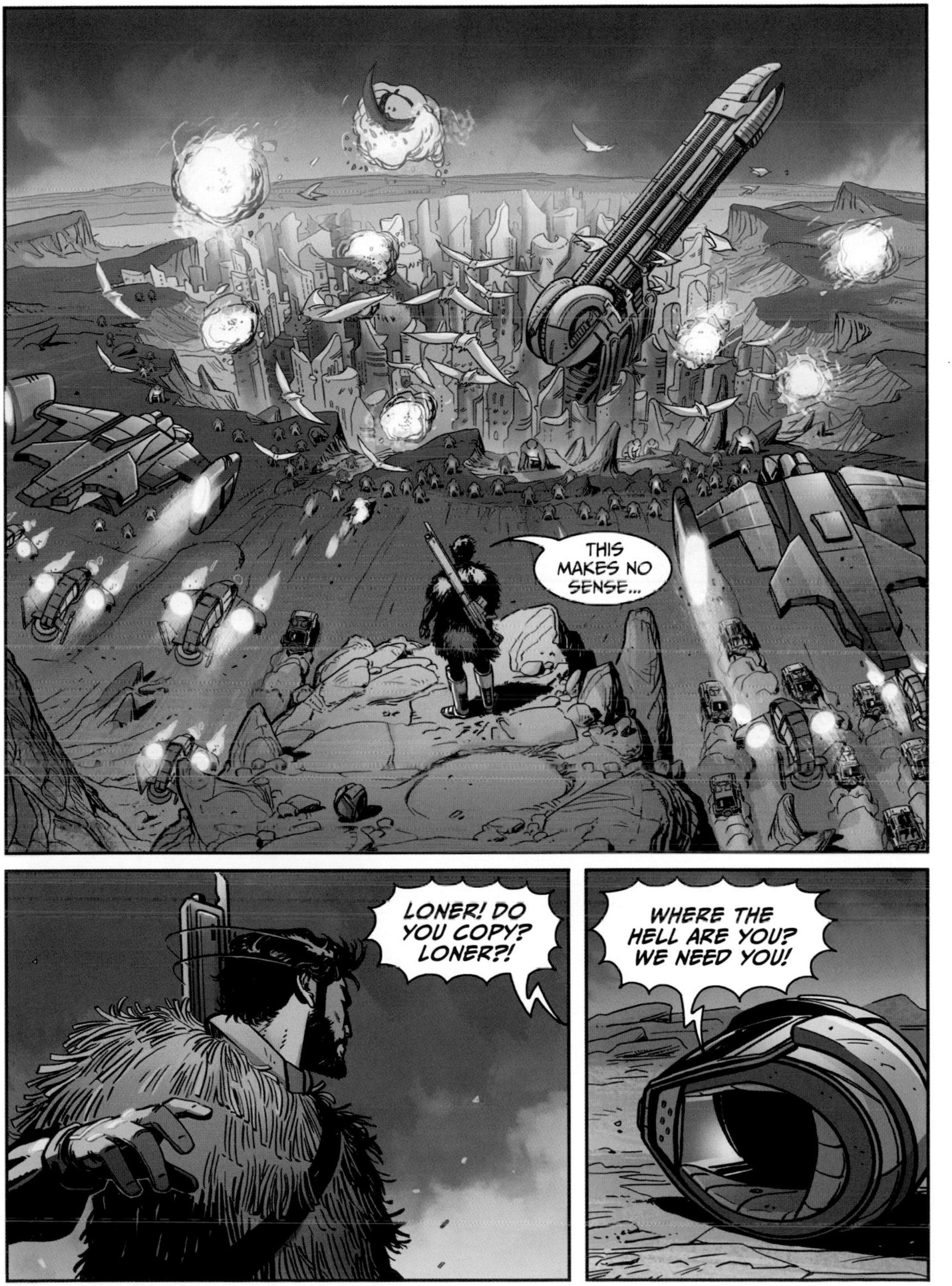
THIS MAKES NO SENSE...
LONER! DO YOU COPY? LONER?!
WHERE THE HELL ARE YOU? WE NEED YOU!

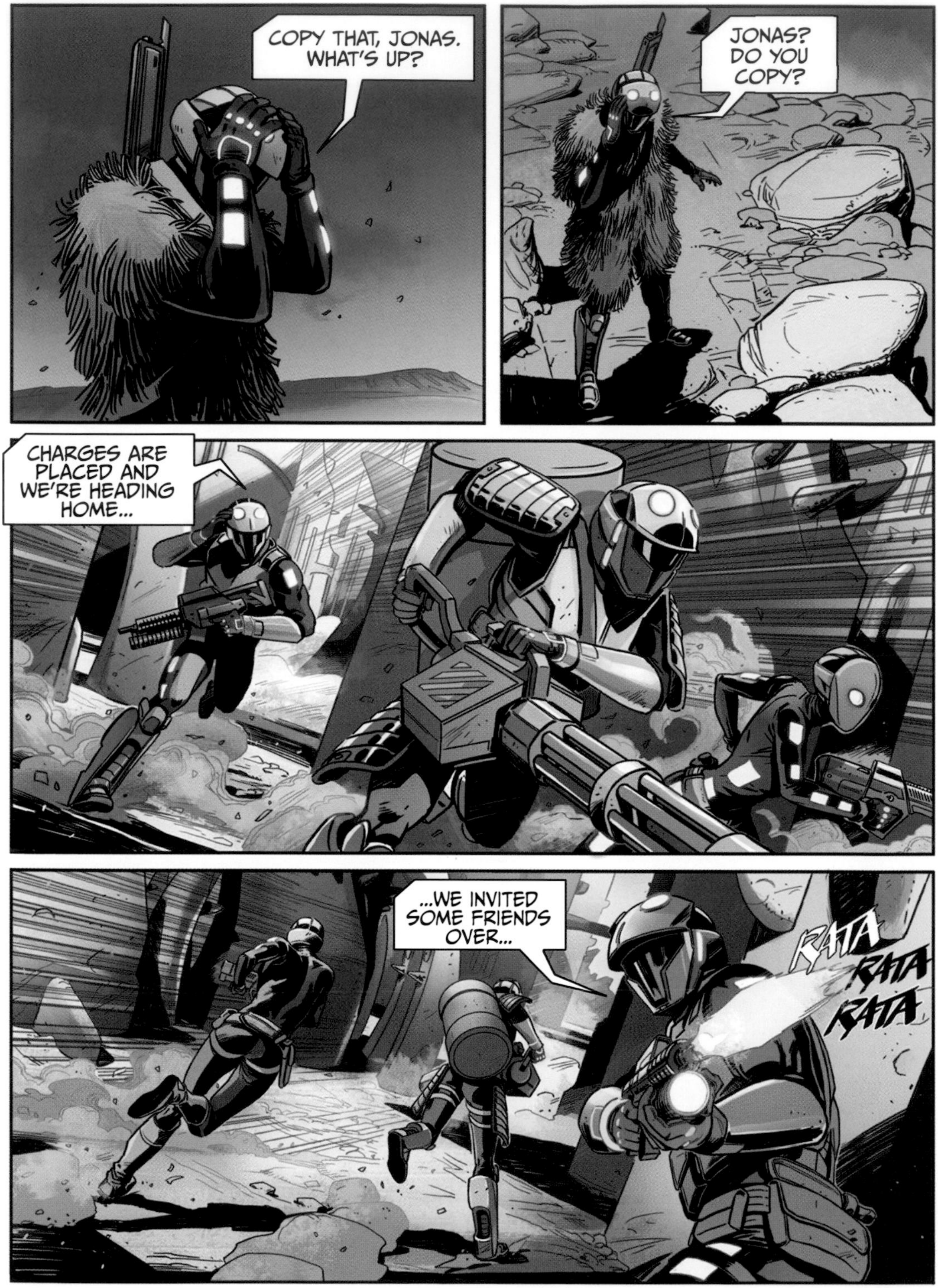
COPY THAT, JONAS. WHAT'S UP?
JONAS? DO YOU COPY?
CHARGES ARE PLACED AND WE'RE HEADING HOME...
...WE INVITED SOME FRIENDS OVER...
RATA RATA RATA

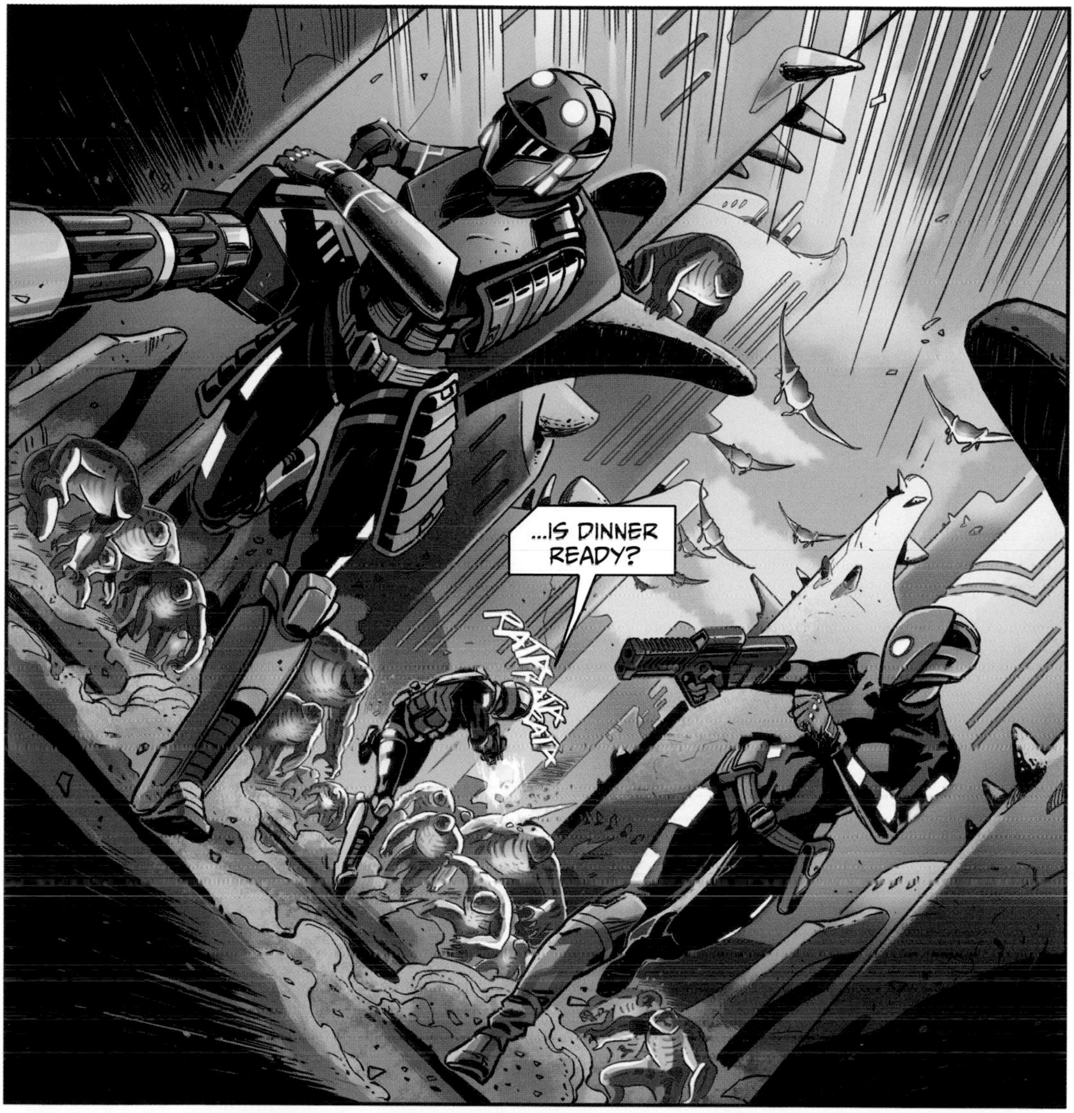
...IS DINNER READY?
RATATATATATA

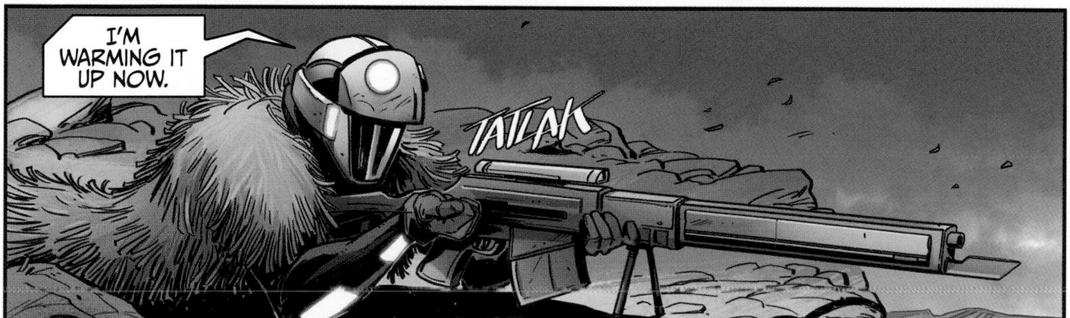
I'M WARMING IT UP NOW.
TATLAK

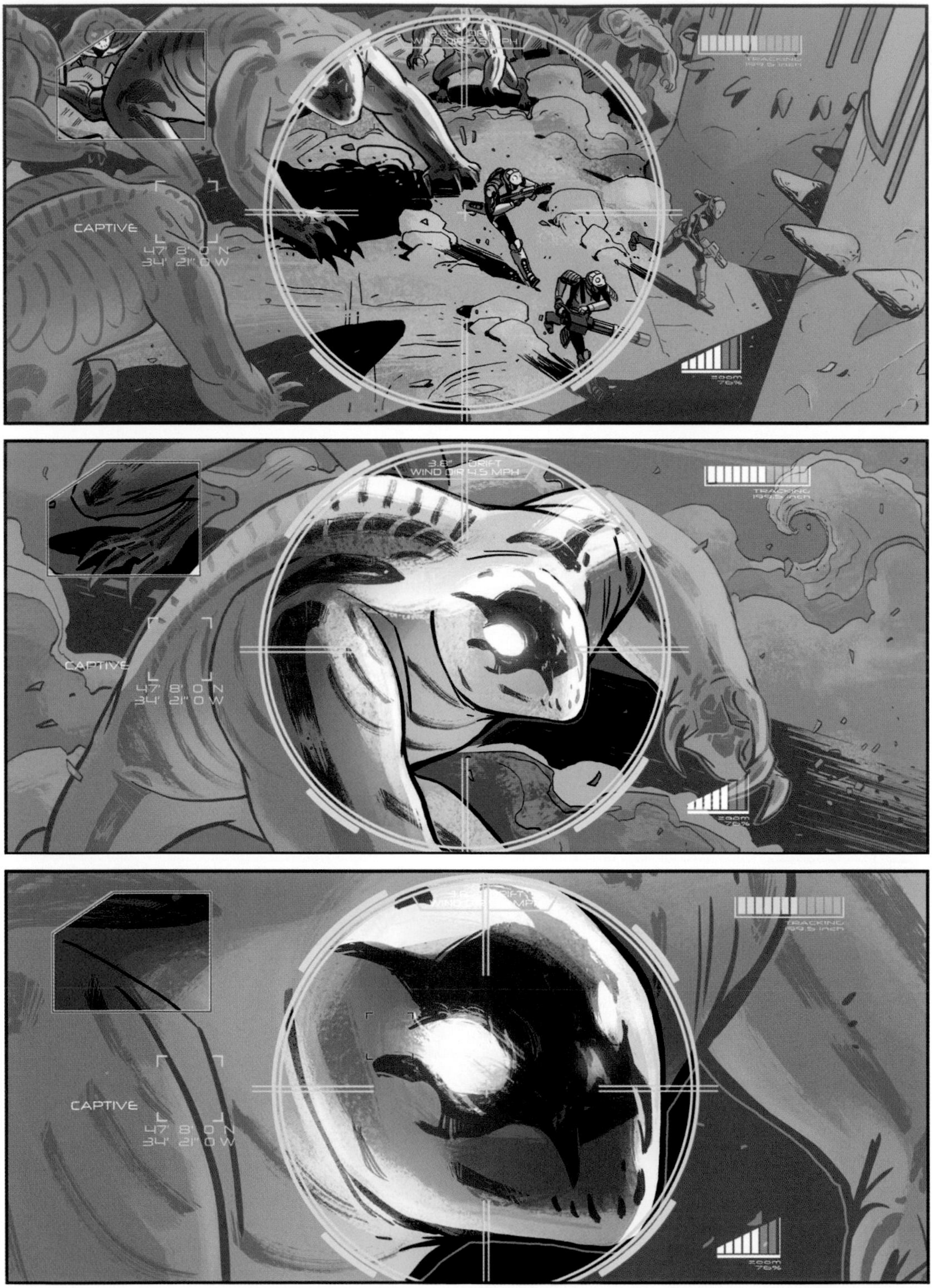
CAPTIVE
47' 8' 0 N
34' 21" 0 W
3.6" DRIFT
WIND DIR 4.5 MPH
TRACKING
CAPTIVE
47' 8' 0 N
34' 21" 0 W
CAPTIVE
47' 8' 0 N
34' 21" 0 W

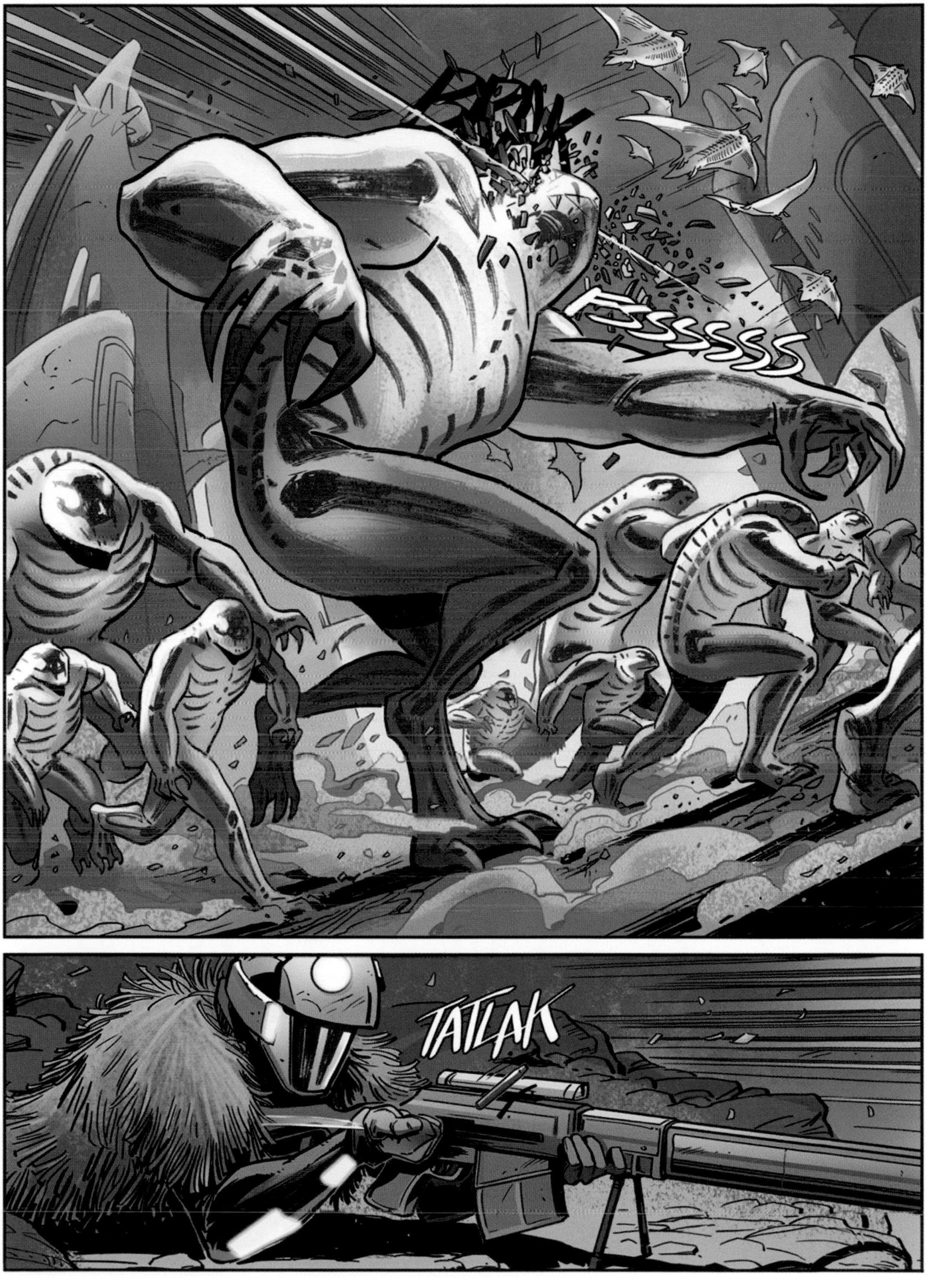
BRAK
FSSSSSS
TATLAK

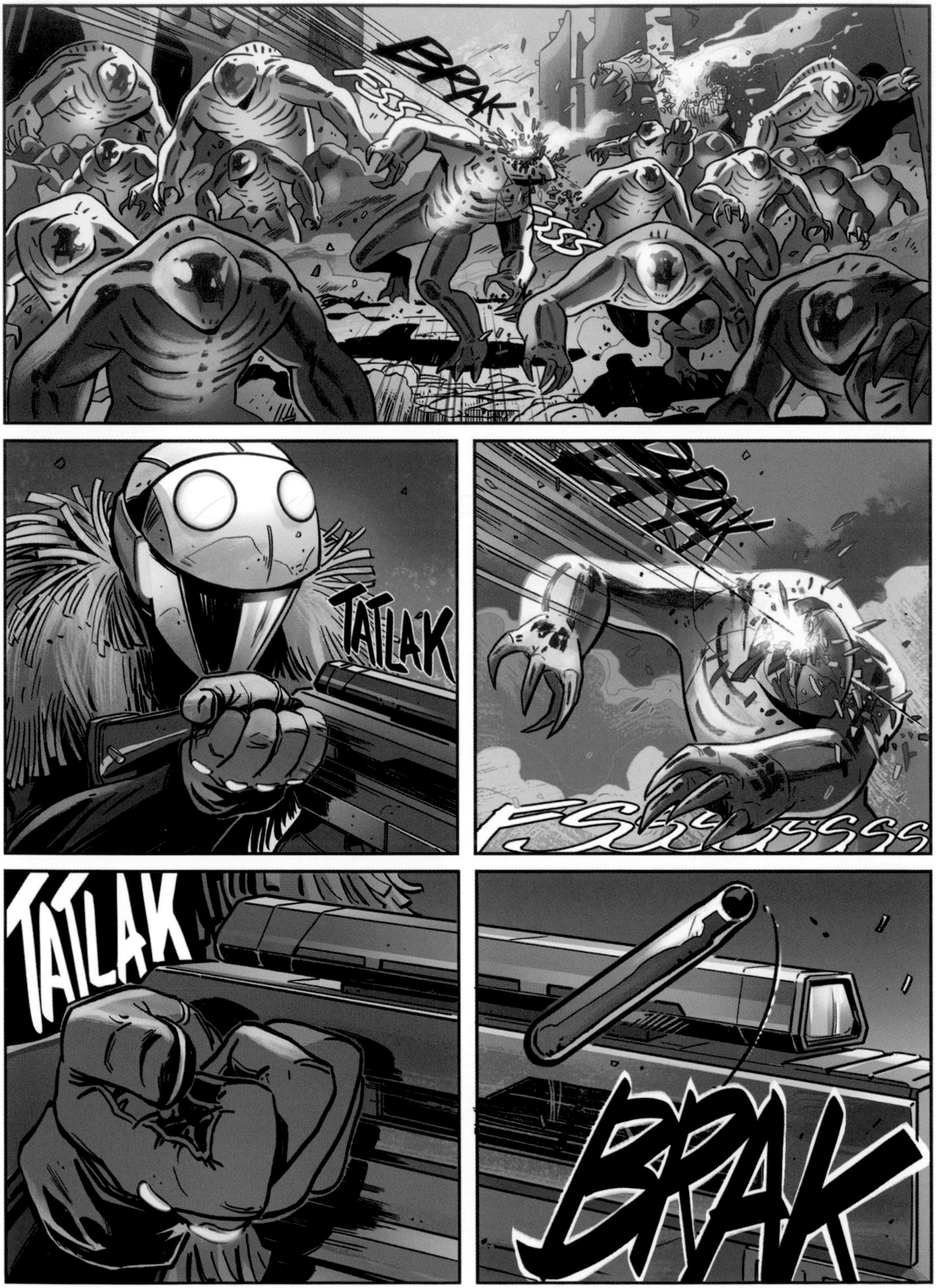
BRAK
TATLAK
TATLAK
BRAK

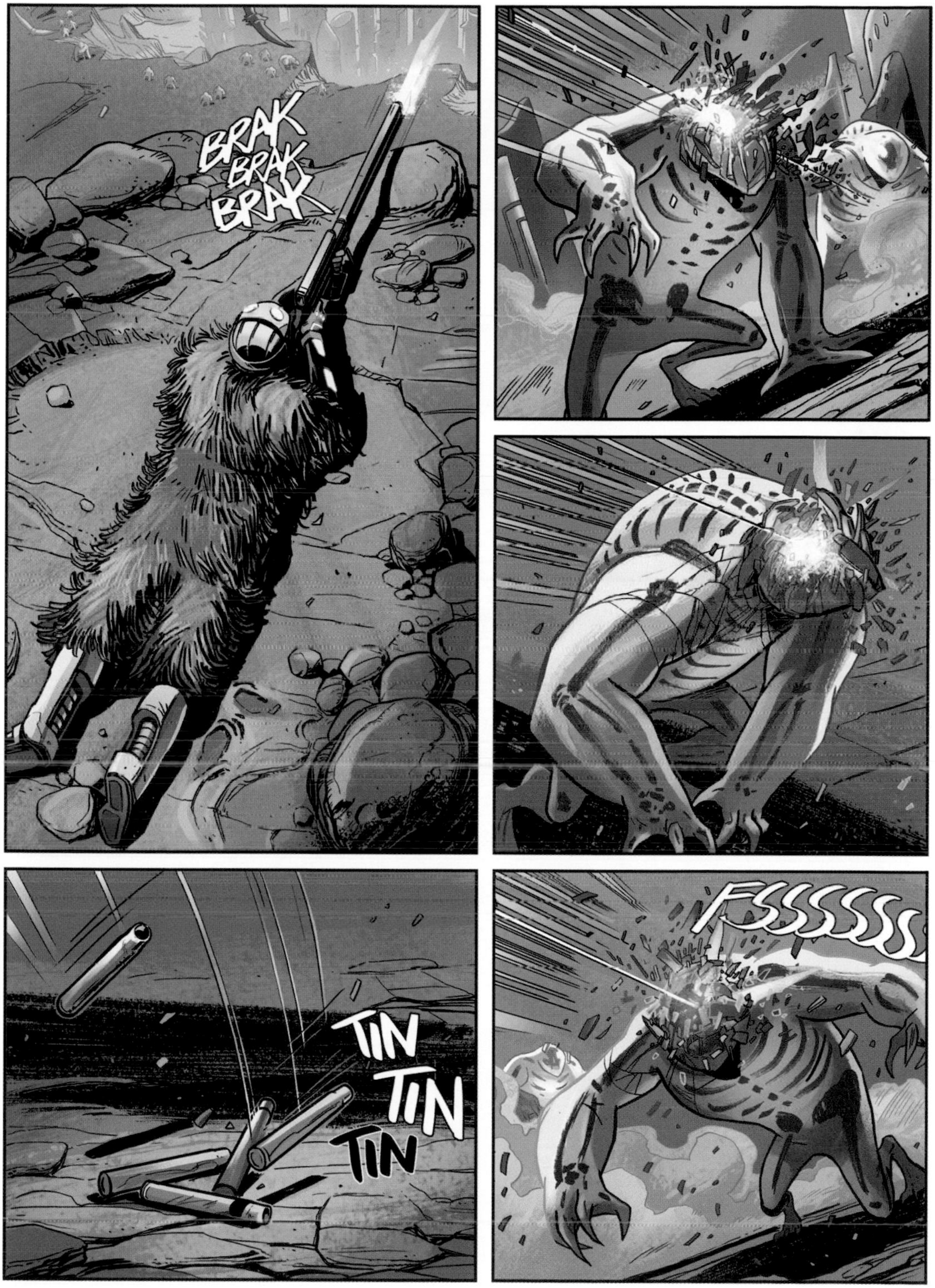
BRAK
BRAK
BRAK
TIN
TIN
TIN
FSSSSS

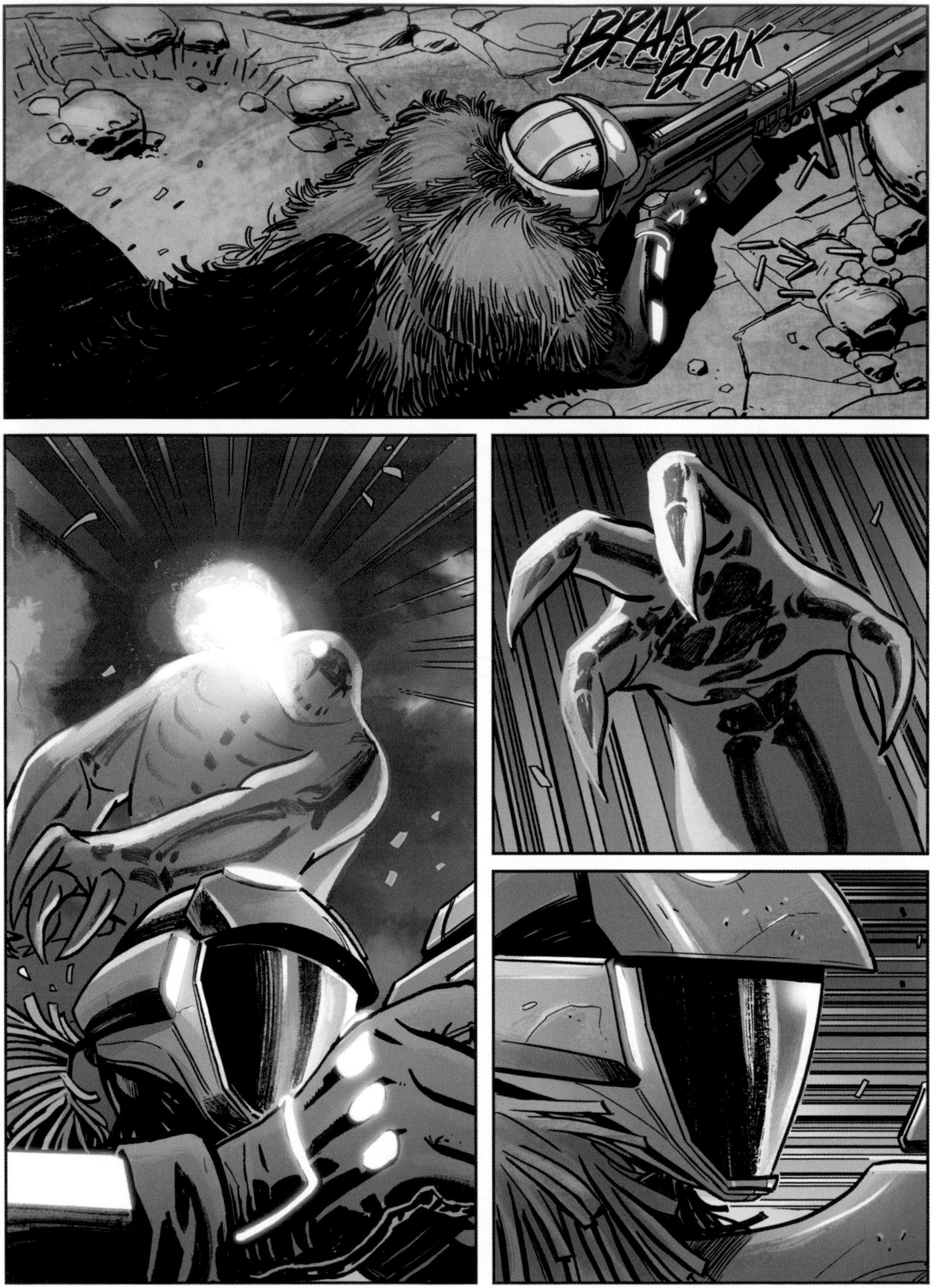
BRAK BRAK

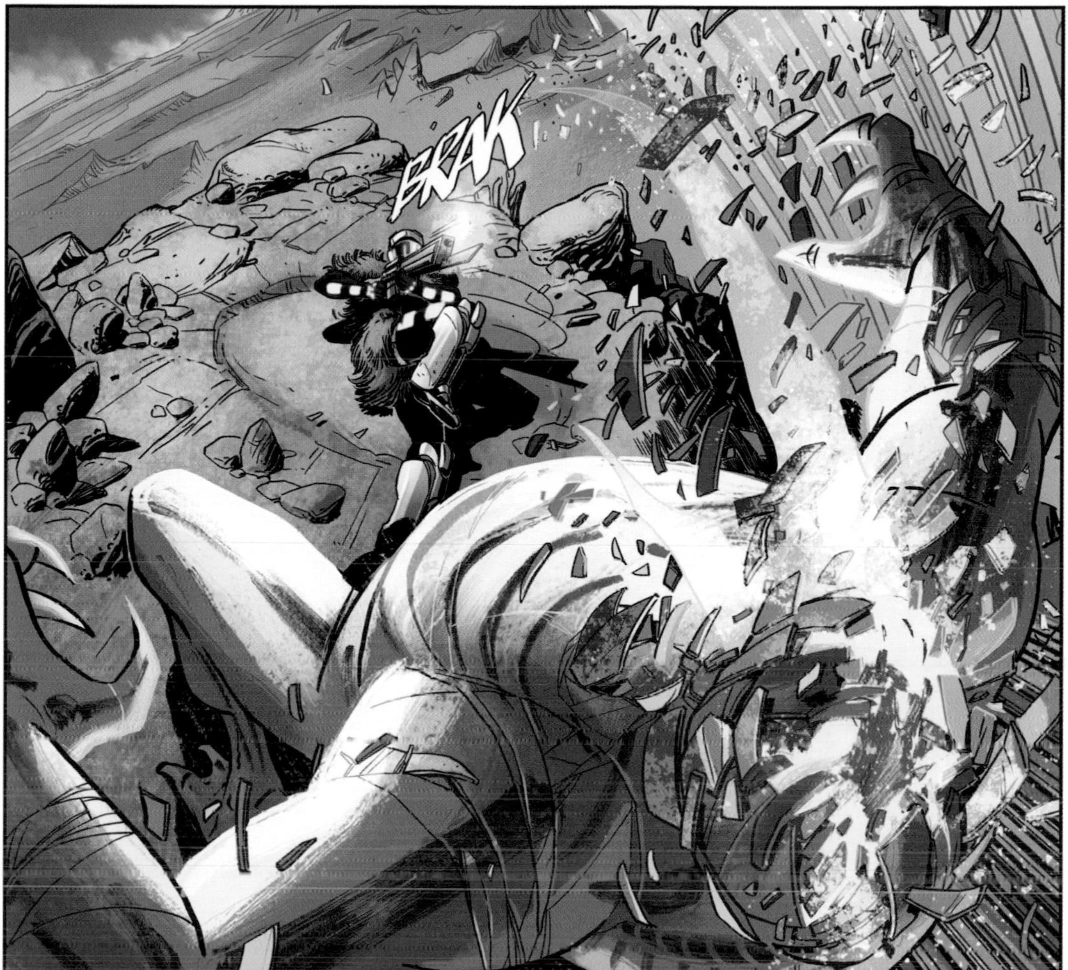
BRAK

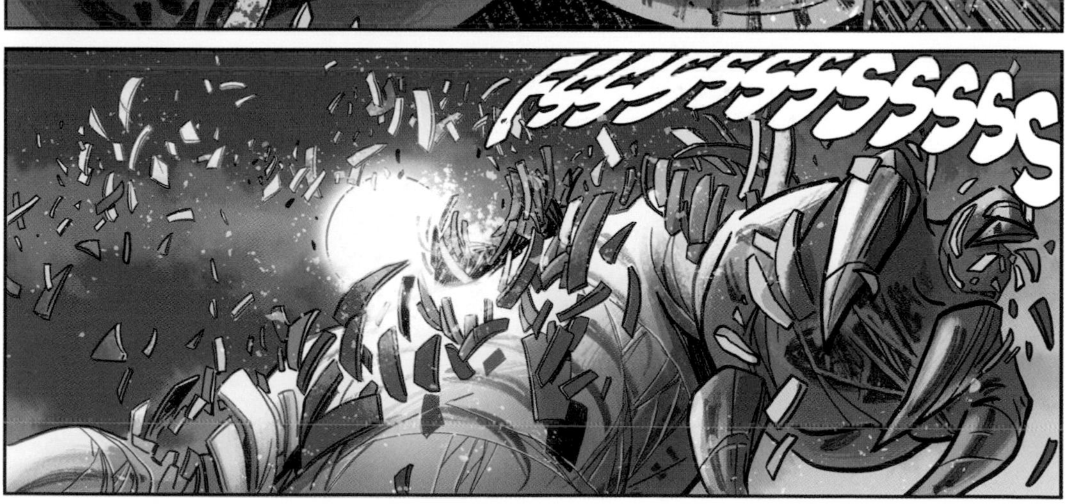
FSSSSSSSSSSSS

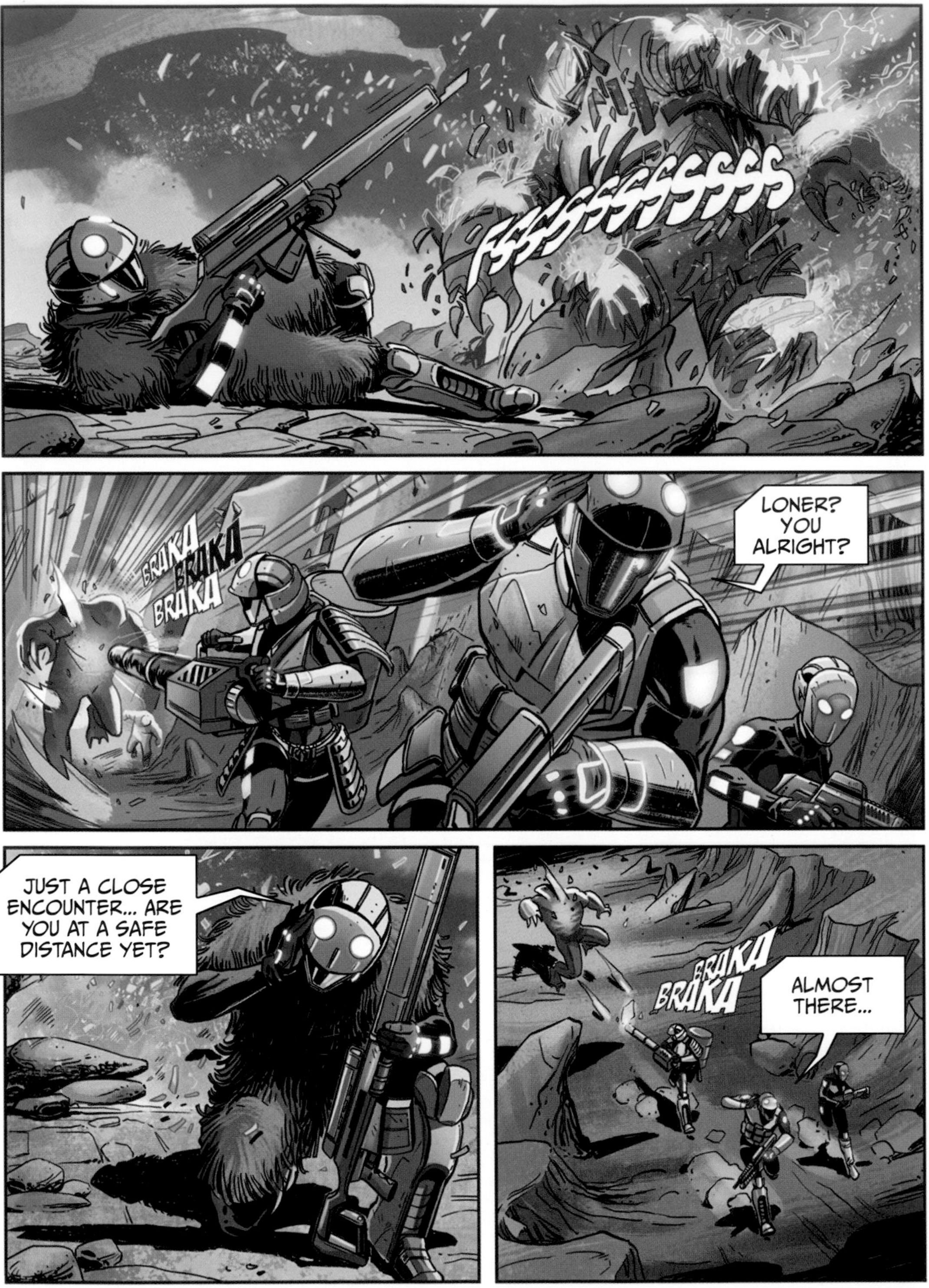
FSSSSSSSSSSS
BRAKA BRAKA BRAKA
LONER? YOU ALRIGHT?
JUST A CLOSE ENCOUNTER... ARE YOU AT A SAFE DISTANCE YET?
BRAKA BRAKA
ALMOST THERE...

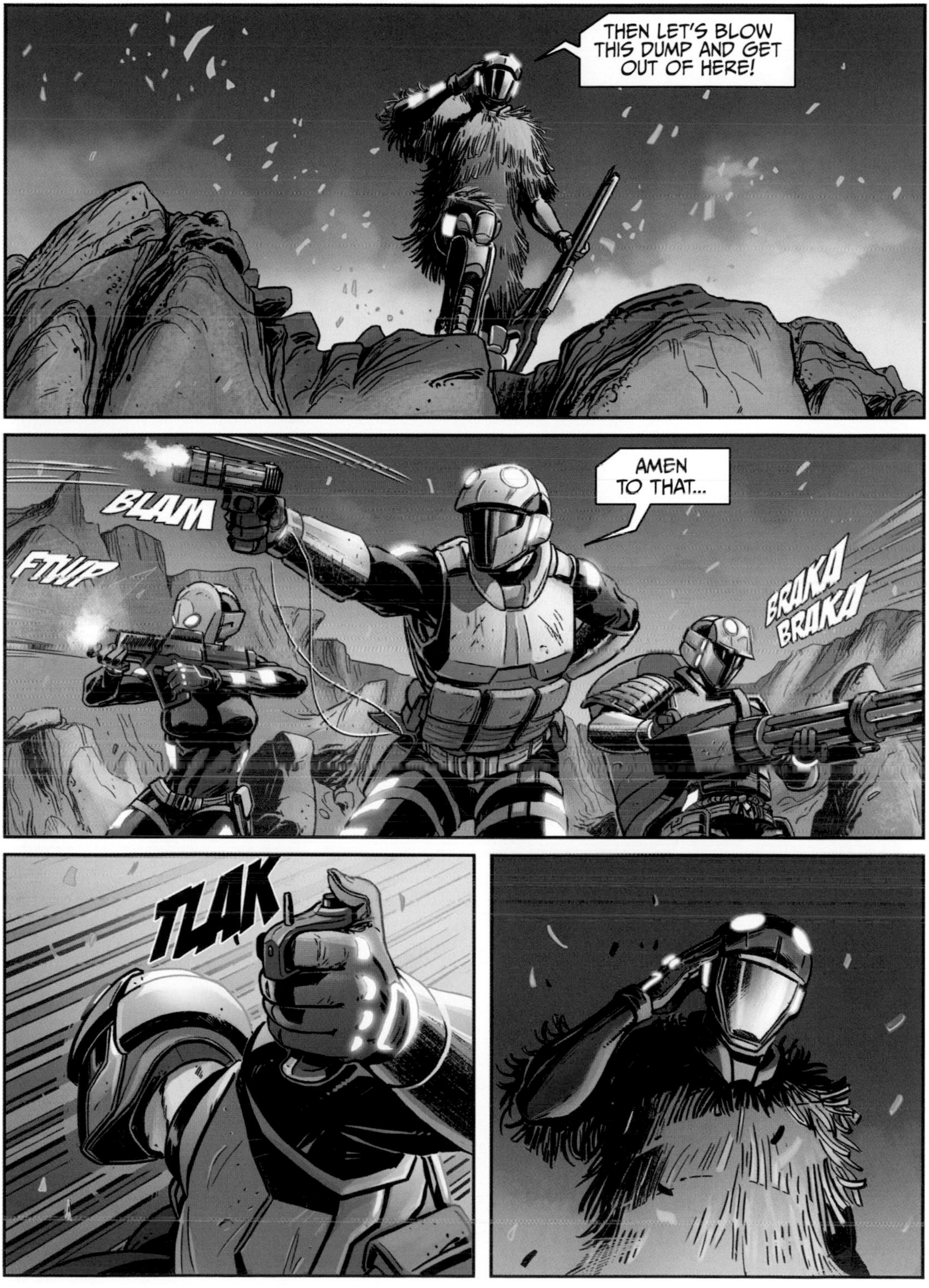
THEN LET'S BLOW THIS DUMP AND GET OUT OF HERE!
BLAM
FTWP
AMEN TO THAT...
BRAKA BRAKA
TLAK

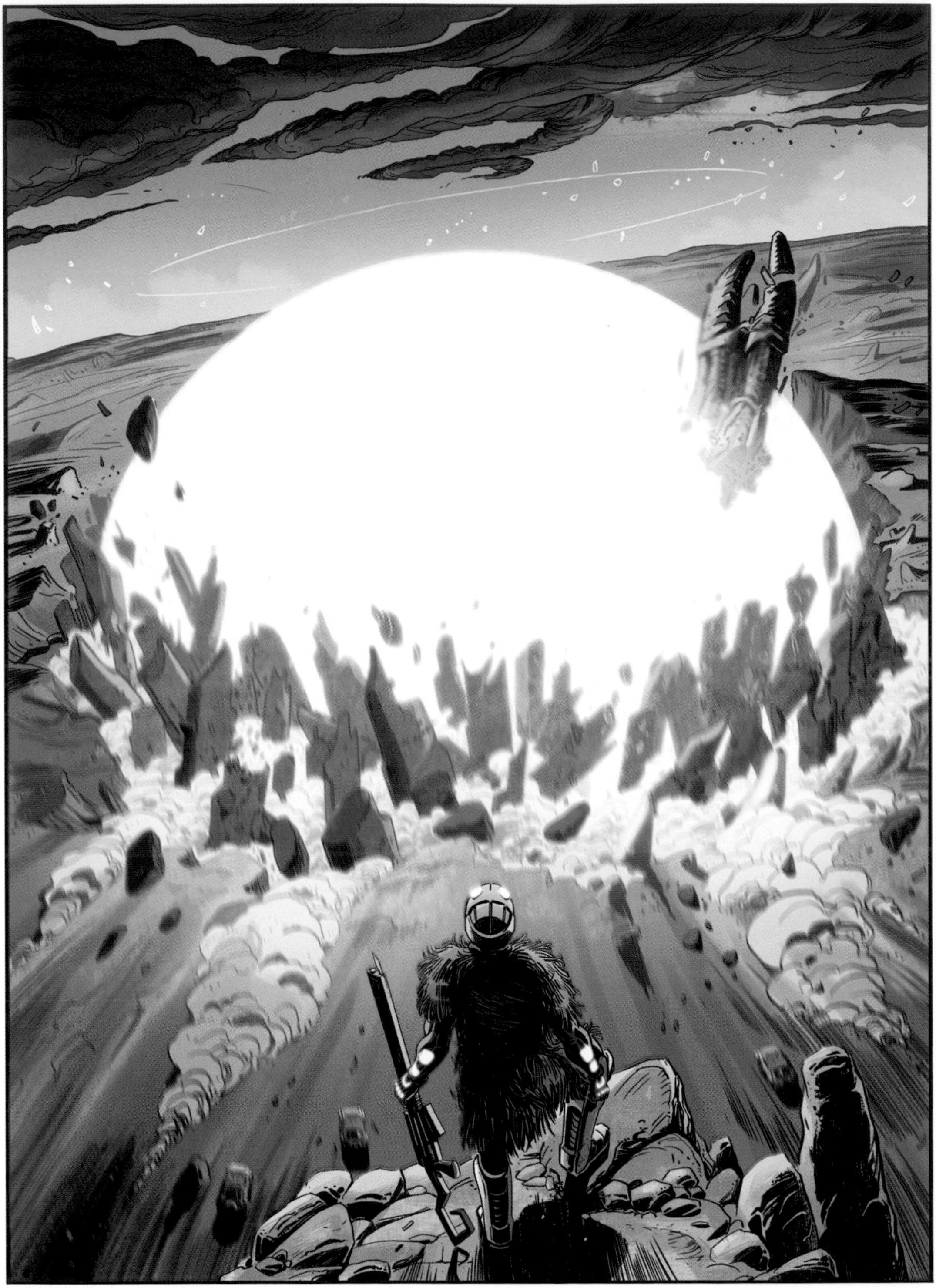

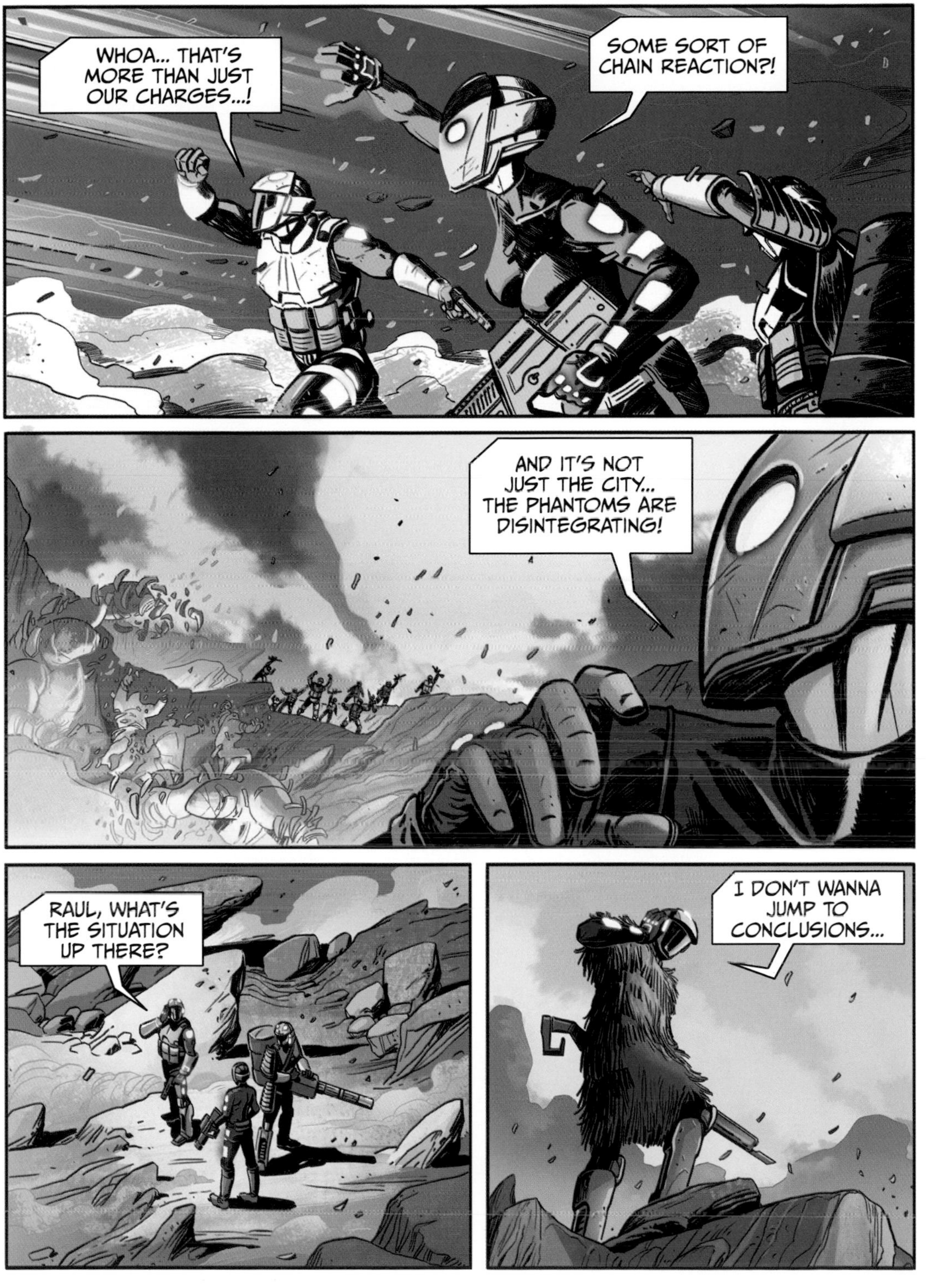
WHOA... THAT'S MORE THAN JUST OUR CHARGES...!
SOME SORT OF CHAIN REACTION?!
AND IT'S NOT JUST THE CITY... THE PHANTOMS ARE DISINTEGRATING!
RAUL, WHAT'S THE SITUATION UP THERE?
I DON'T WANNA JUMP TO CONCLUSIONS...

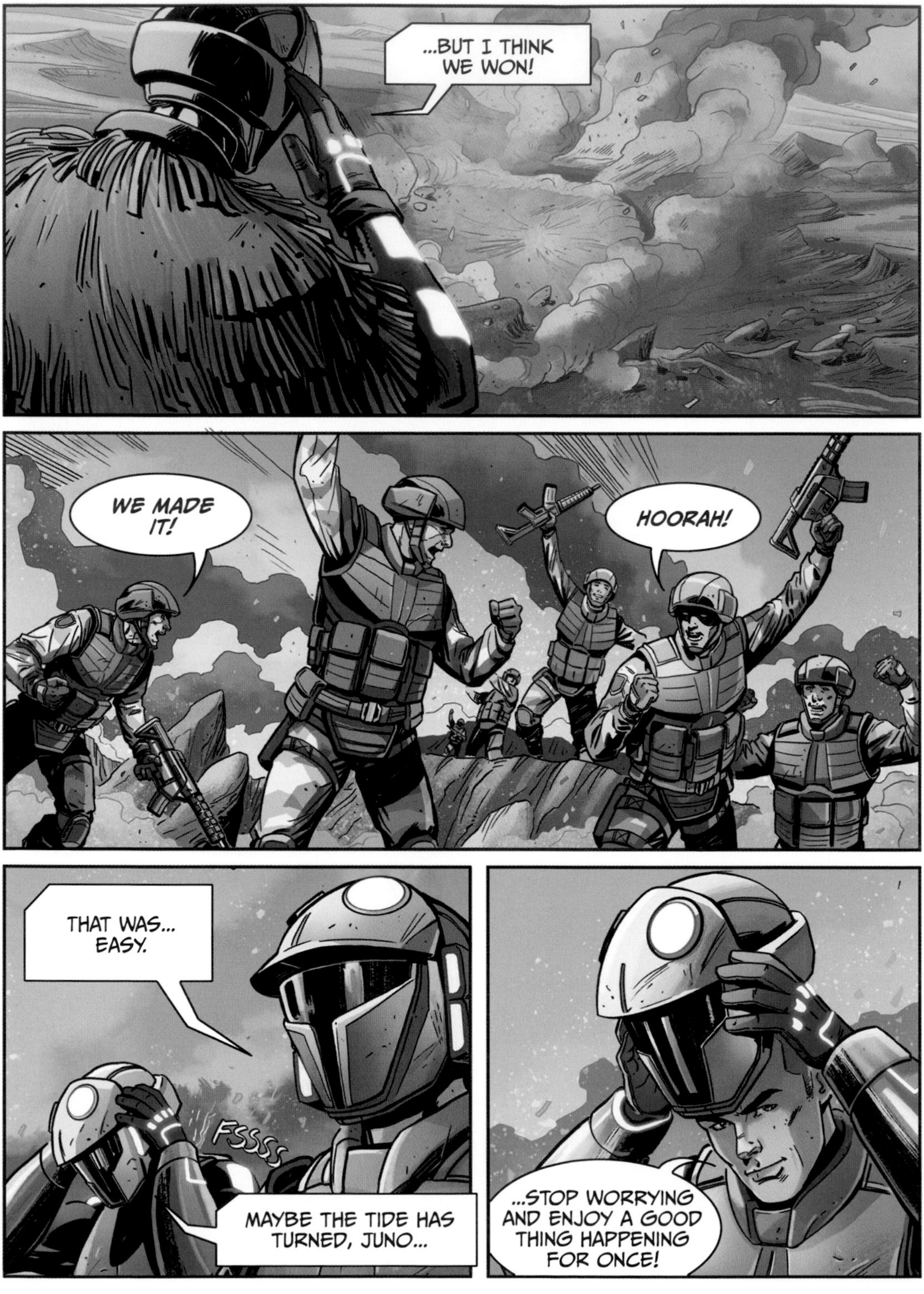
...BUT I THINK WE WON!
WE MADE IT!
HOORAH!
THAT WAS... EASY.
FSSSS
MAYBE THE TIDE HAS TURNED, JUNO...
...STOP WORRYING AND ENJOY A GOOD THING HAPPENING FOR ONCE!

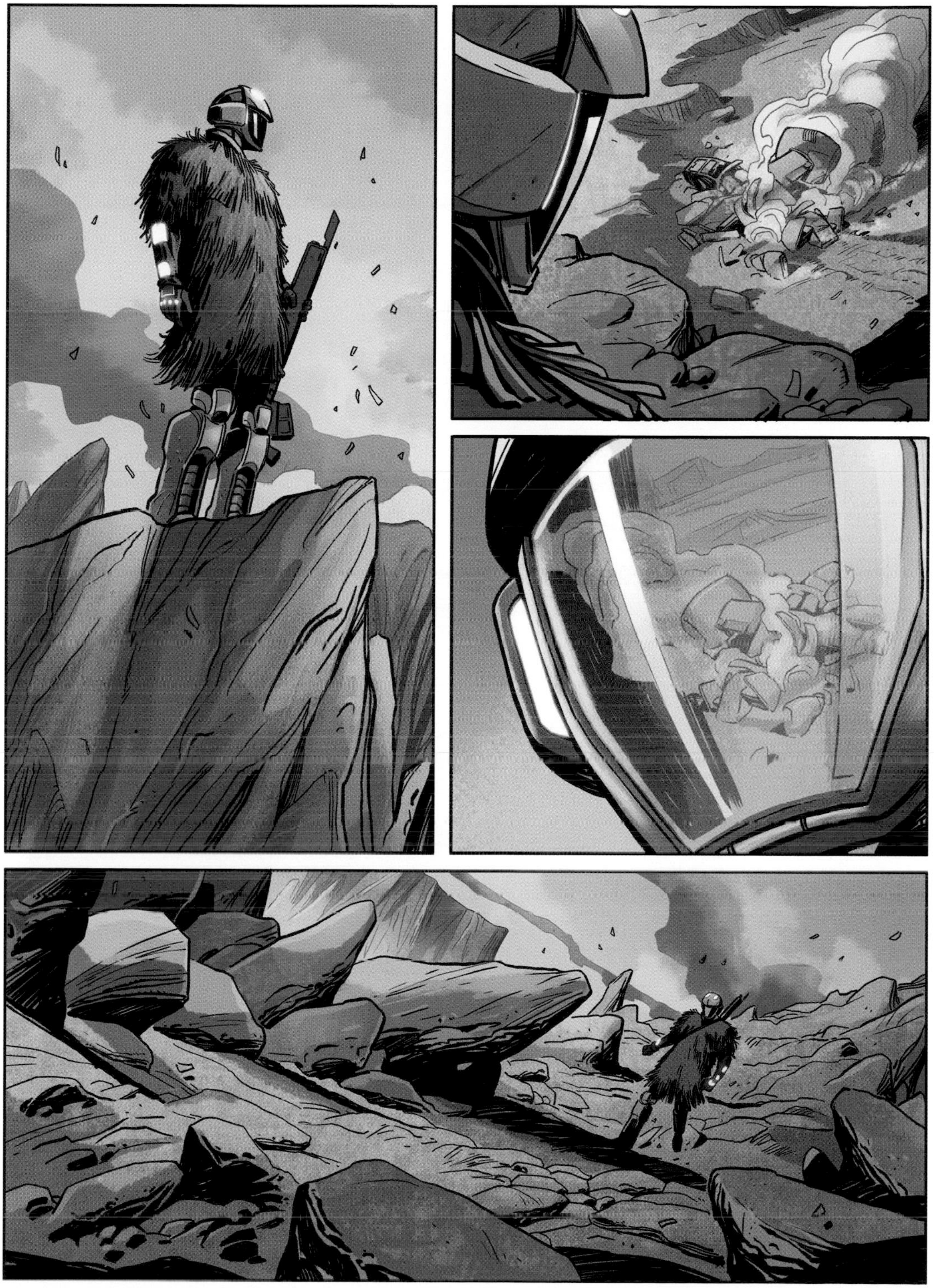

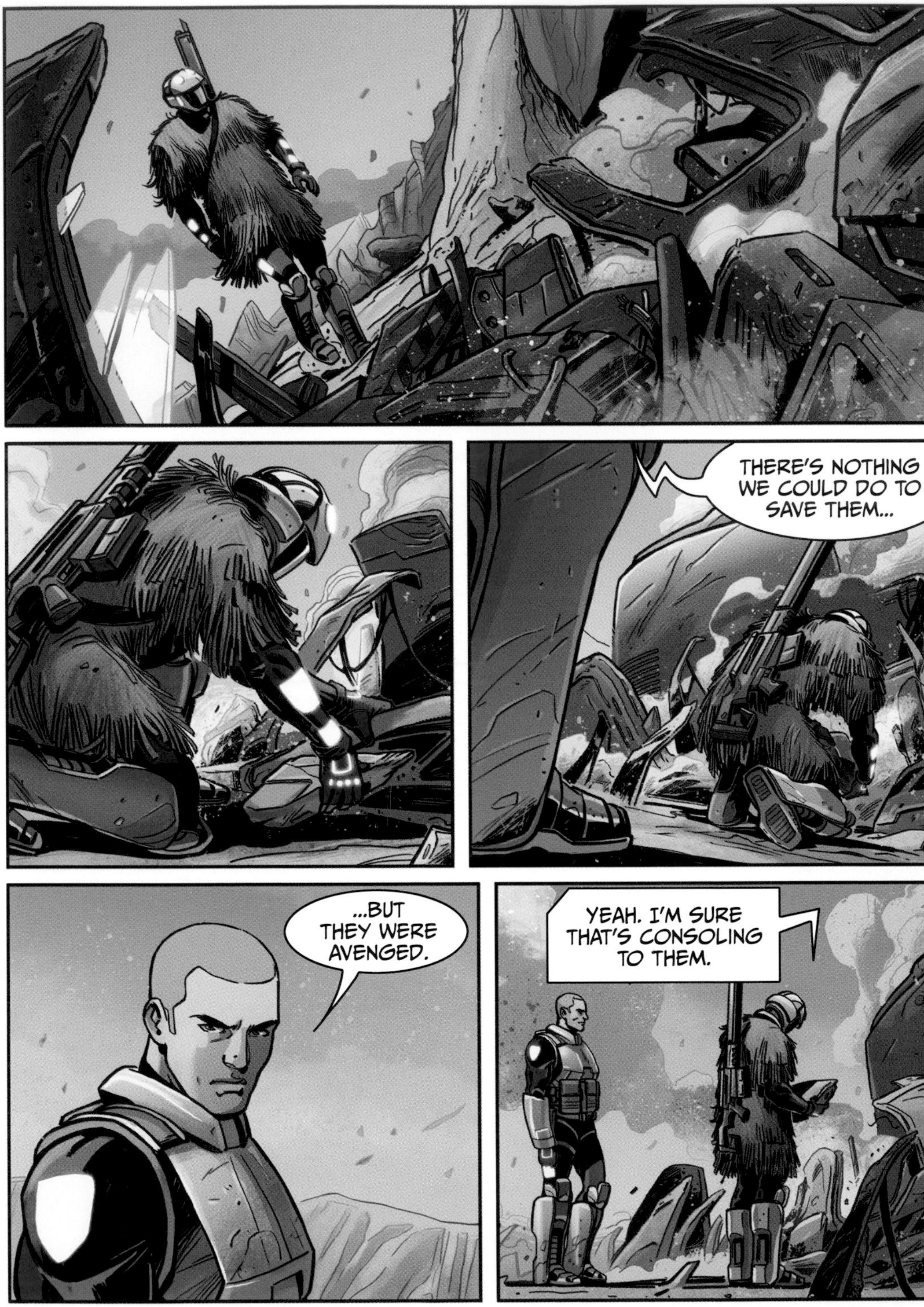
THERE'S NOTHING WE COULD DO TO SAVE THEM...
...BUT THEY WERE AVENGED.
YEAH. I'M SURE THAT'S CONSOLING TO THEM.

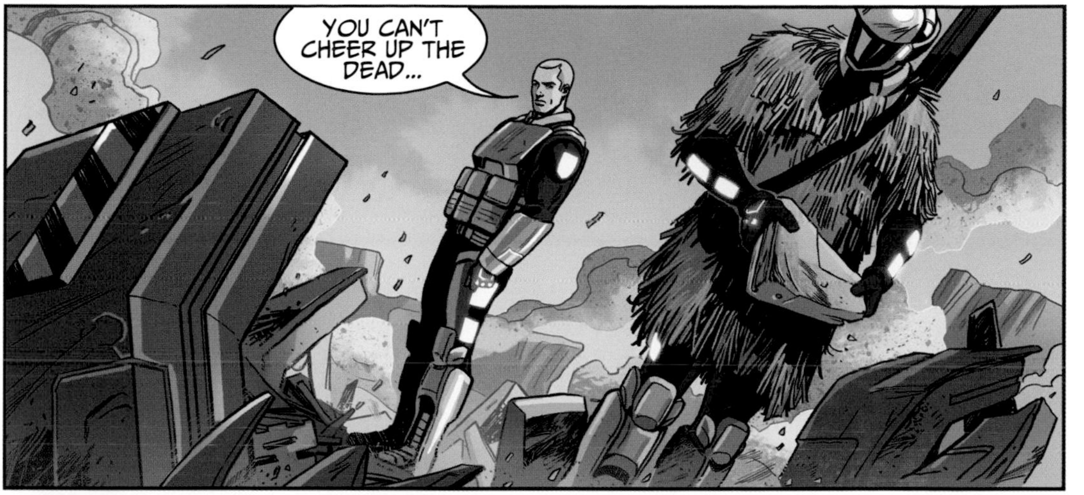
YOU CAN'T CHEER UP THE DEAD...

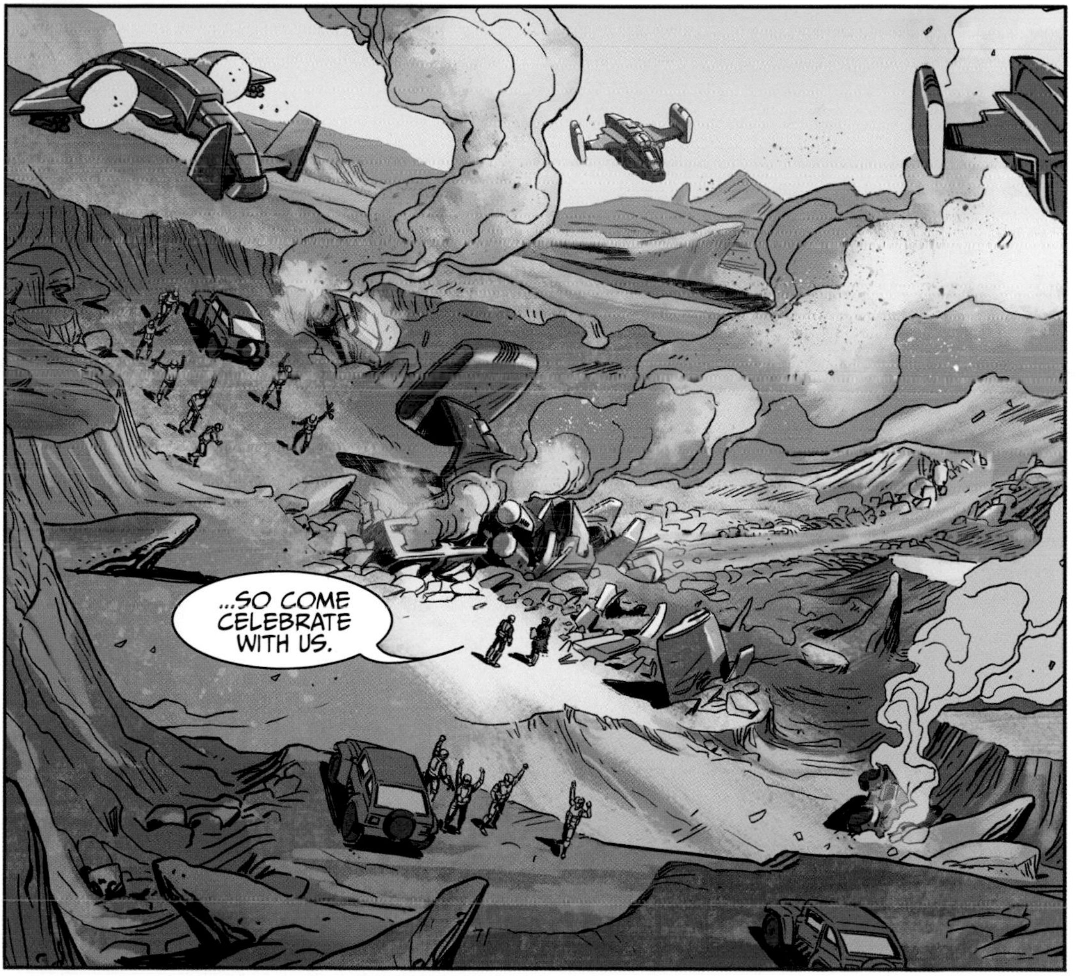
...SO COME CELEBRATE WITH US.

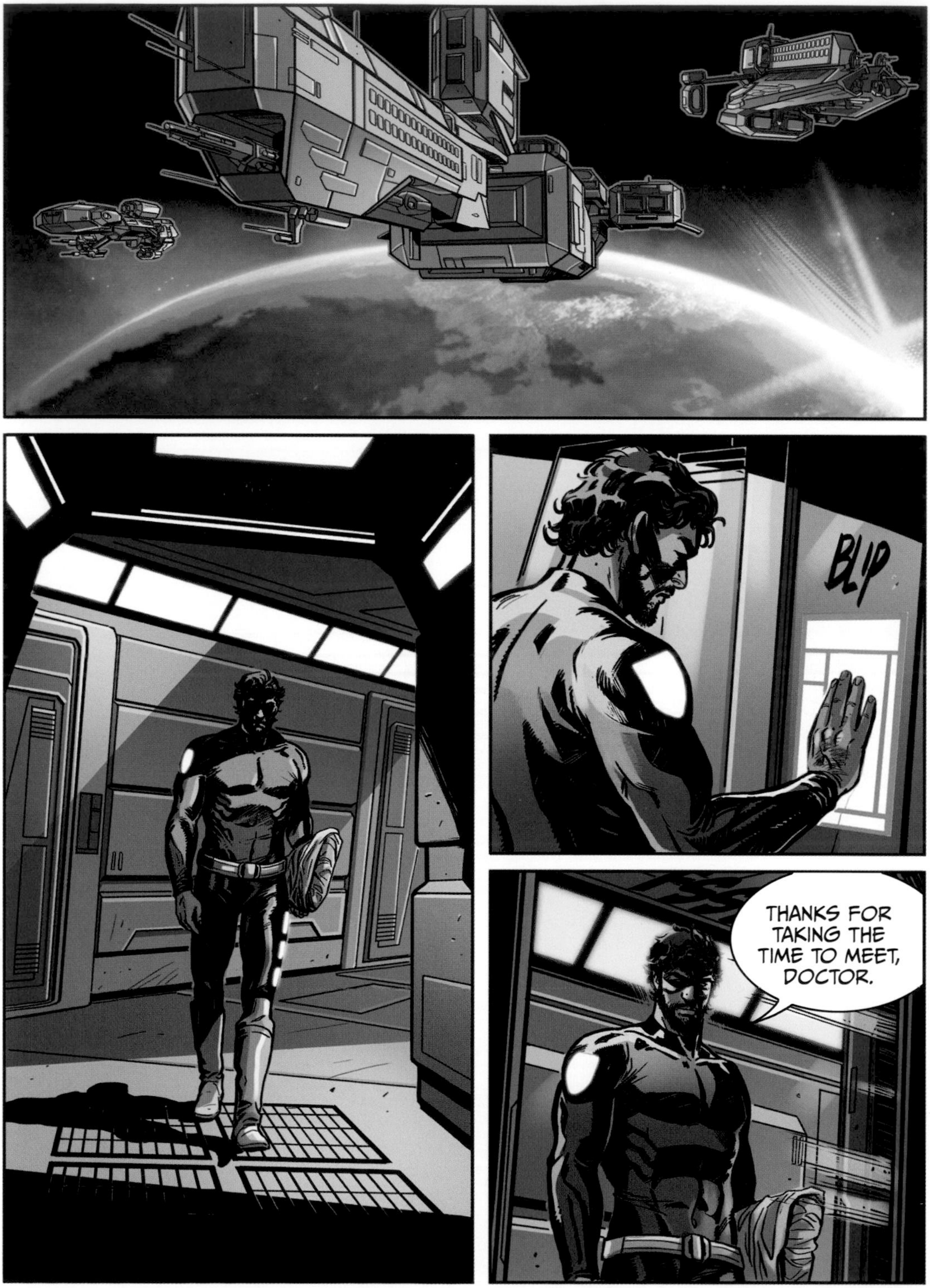
BLIP
THANKS FOR TAKING THE TIME TO MEET, DOCTOR.

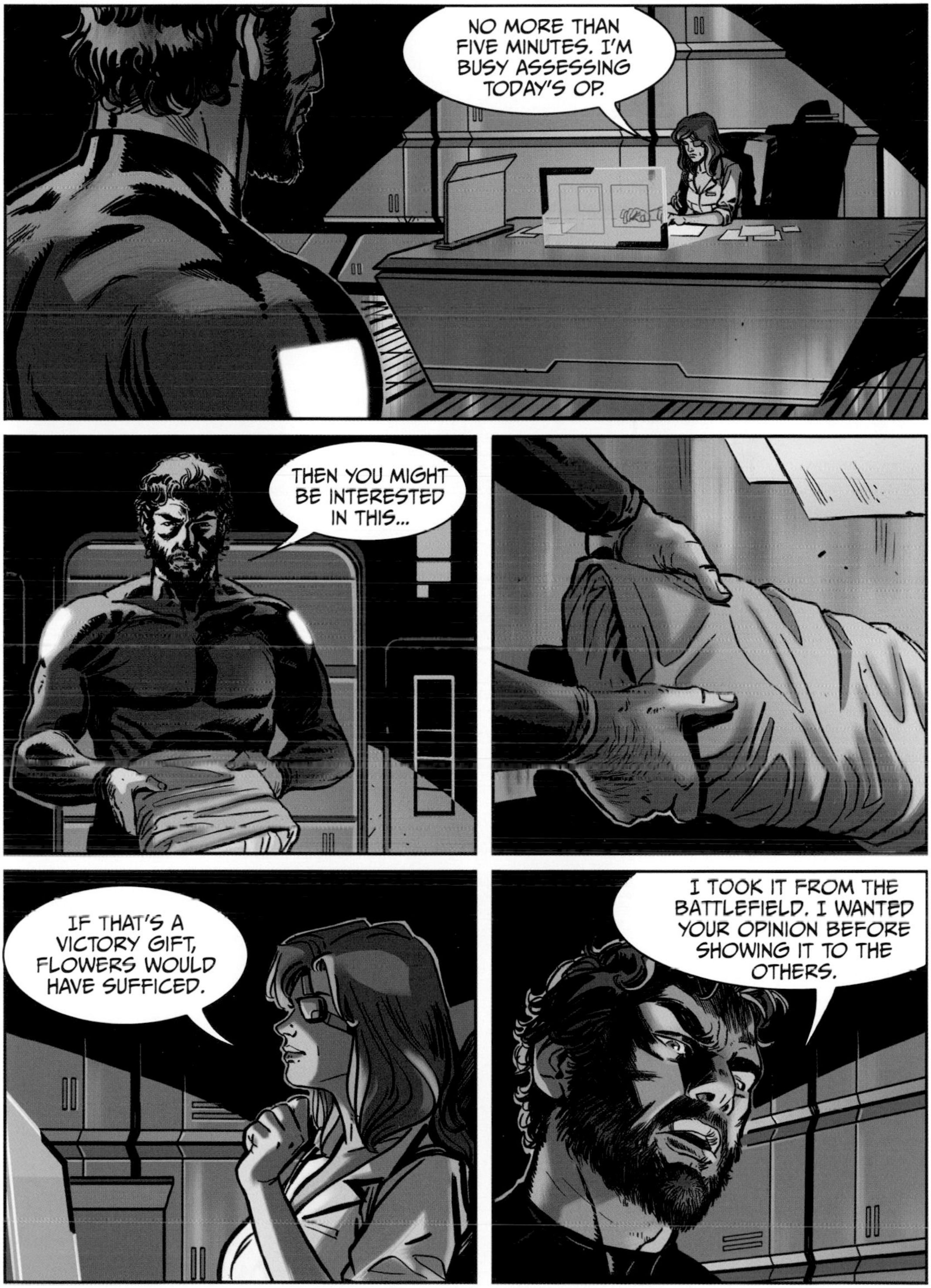
NO MORE THAN FIVE MINUTES. I'M BUSY ASSESSING TODAY'S OP.
THEN YOU MIGHT BE INTERESTED IN THIS...
IF THAT'S A VICTORY GIFT, FLOWERS WOULD HAVE SUFFICED.
I TOOK IT FROM THE BATTLEFIELD. I WANTED YOUR OPINION BEFORE SHOWING IT TO THE OTHERS.

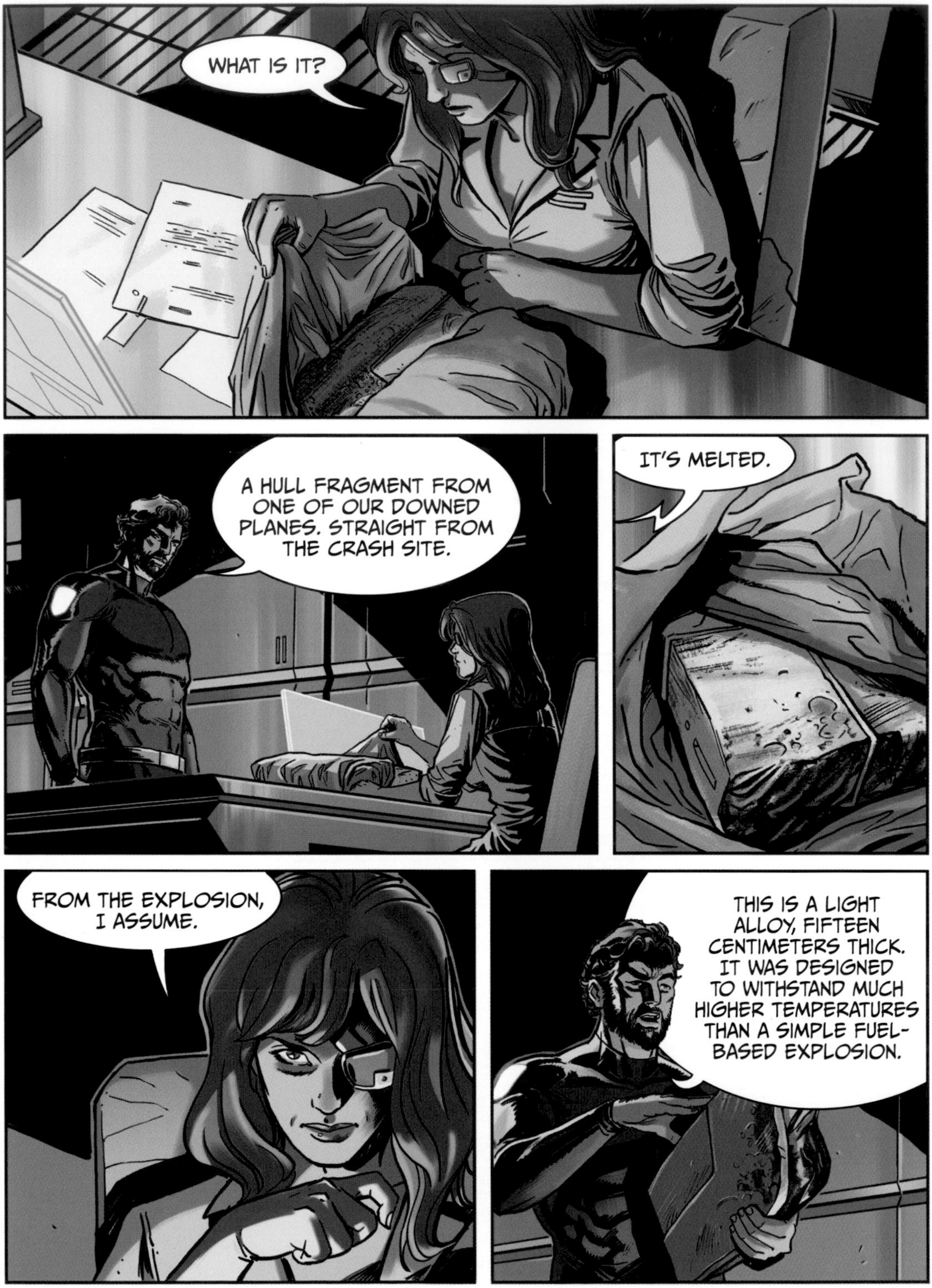
WHAT IS IT?
A HULL FRAGMENT FROM ONE OF OUR DOWNED PLANES. STRAIGHT FROM THE CRASH SITE.
IT'S MELTED.
FROM THE EXPLOSION, I ASSUME.
THIS IS A LIGHT ALLOY, FIFTEEN CENTIMETERS THICK. IT WAS DESIGNED TO WITHSTAND MUCH HIGHER TEMPERATURES THAN A SIMPLE FUEL-BASED EXPLOSION.

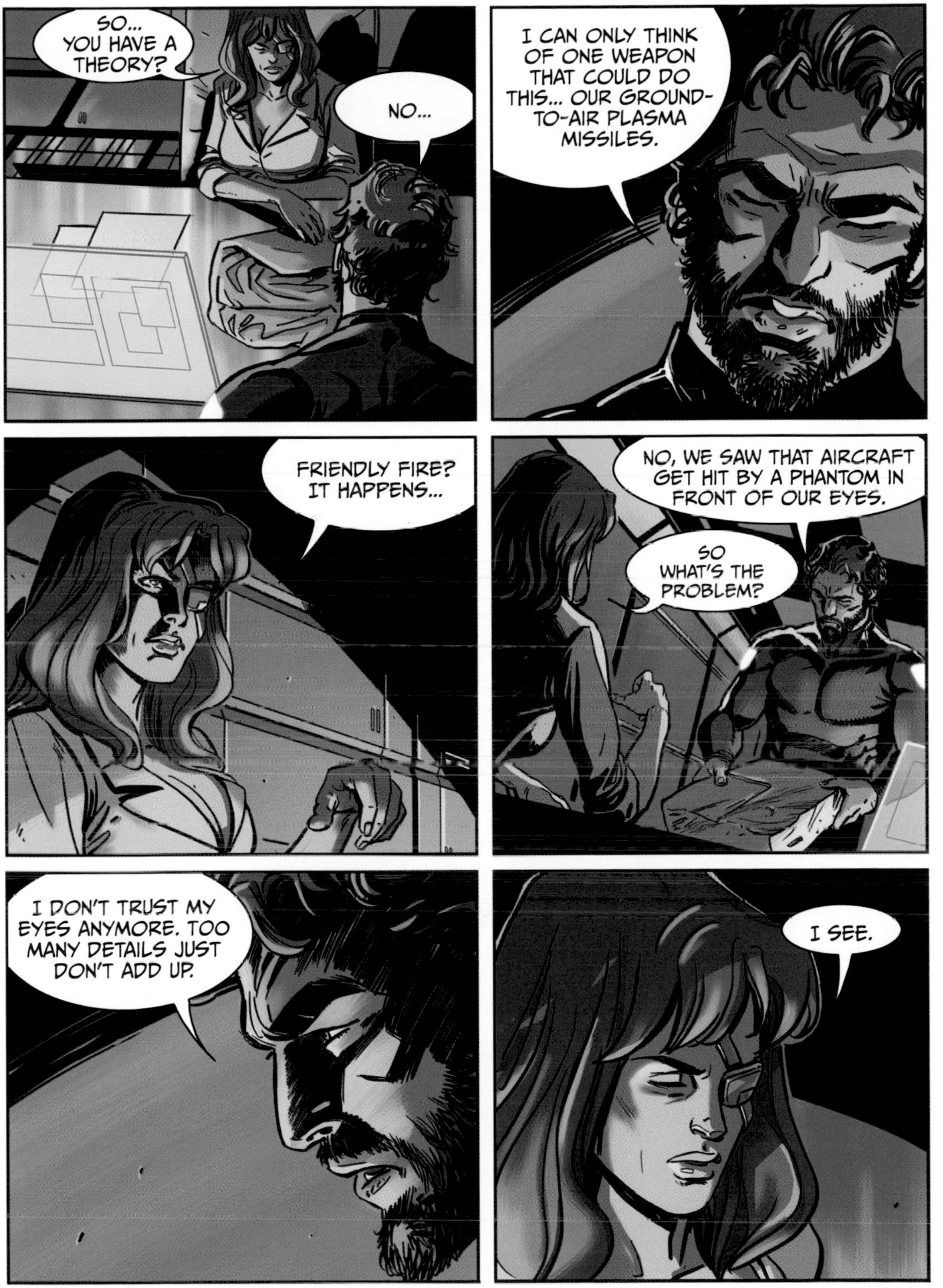
SO... YOU HAVE A THEORY?
NO...
I CAN ONLY THINK OF ONE WEAPON THAT COULD DO THIS... OUR GROUND-TO-AIR PLASMA MISSILES.
FRIENDLY FIRE? IT HAPPENS...
NO, WE SAW THAT AIRCRAFT GET HIT BY A PHANTOM IN FRONT OF OUR EYES.
SO WHAT'S THE PROBLEM?
I DON'T TRUST MY EYES ANYMORE. TOO MANY DETAILS JUST DON'T ADD UP.
I SEE.

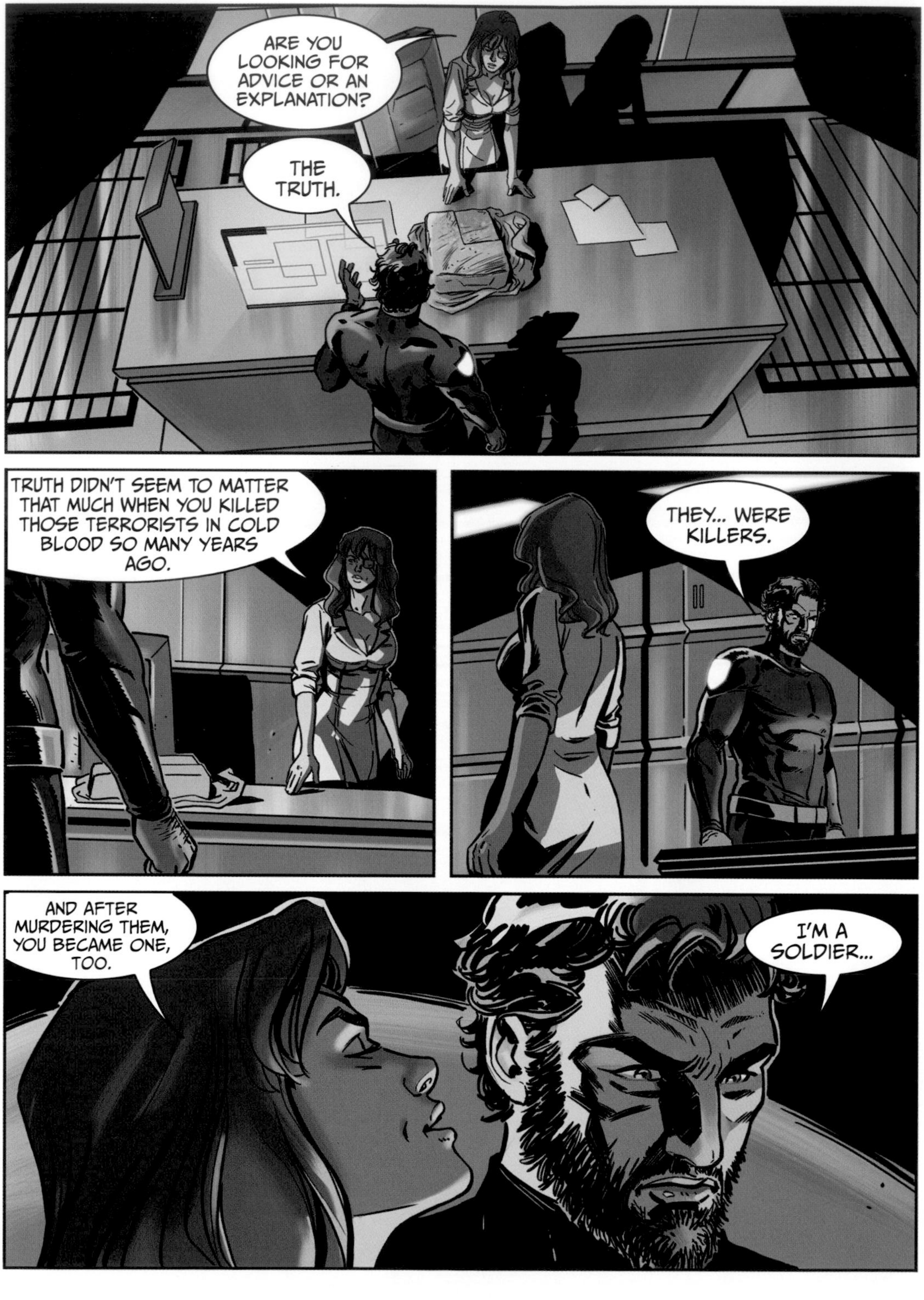
ARE YOU LOOKING FOR ADVICE OR AN EXPLANATION?
THE TRUTH.
TRUTH DIDN'T SEEM TO MATTER THAT MUCH WHEN YOU KILLED THOSE TERRORISTS IN COLD BLOOD SO MANY YEARS AGO.
THEY... WERE KILLERS.
AND AFTER MURDERING THEM, YOU BECAME ONE, TOO.
I'M A SOLDIER...

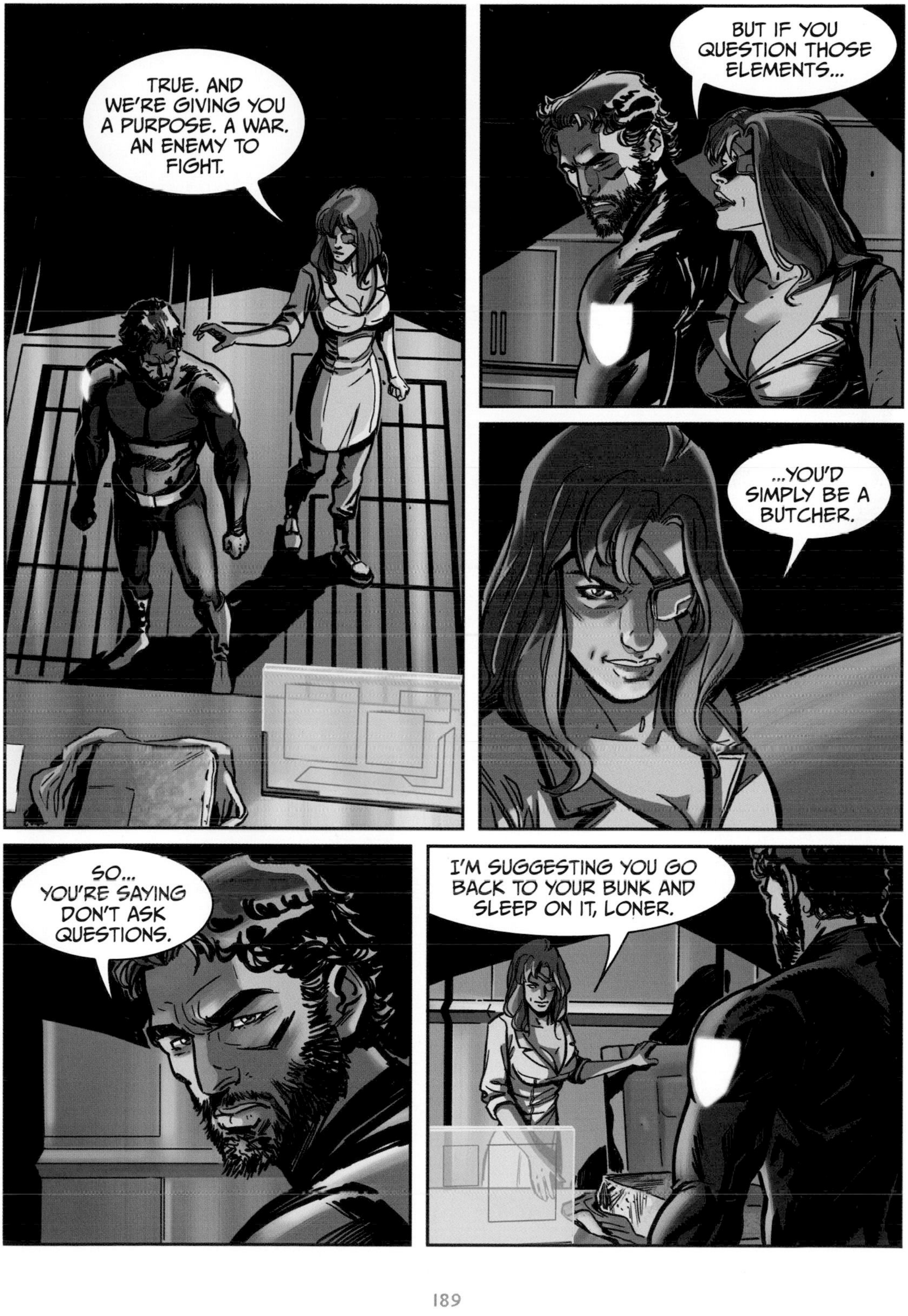
TRUE. AND WE'RE GIVING YOU A PURPOSE. A WAR. AN ENEMY TO FIGHT.
BUT IF YOU QUESTION THOSE ELEMENTS...
...YOU'D SIMPLY BE A BUTCHER.
SO... YOU'RE SAYING DON'T ASK QUESTIONS.
I'M SUGGESTING YOU GO BACK TO YOUR BUNK AND SLEEP ON IT, LONER.

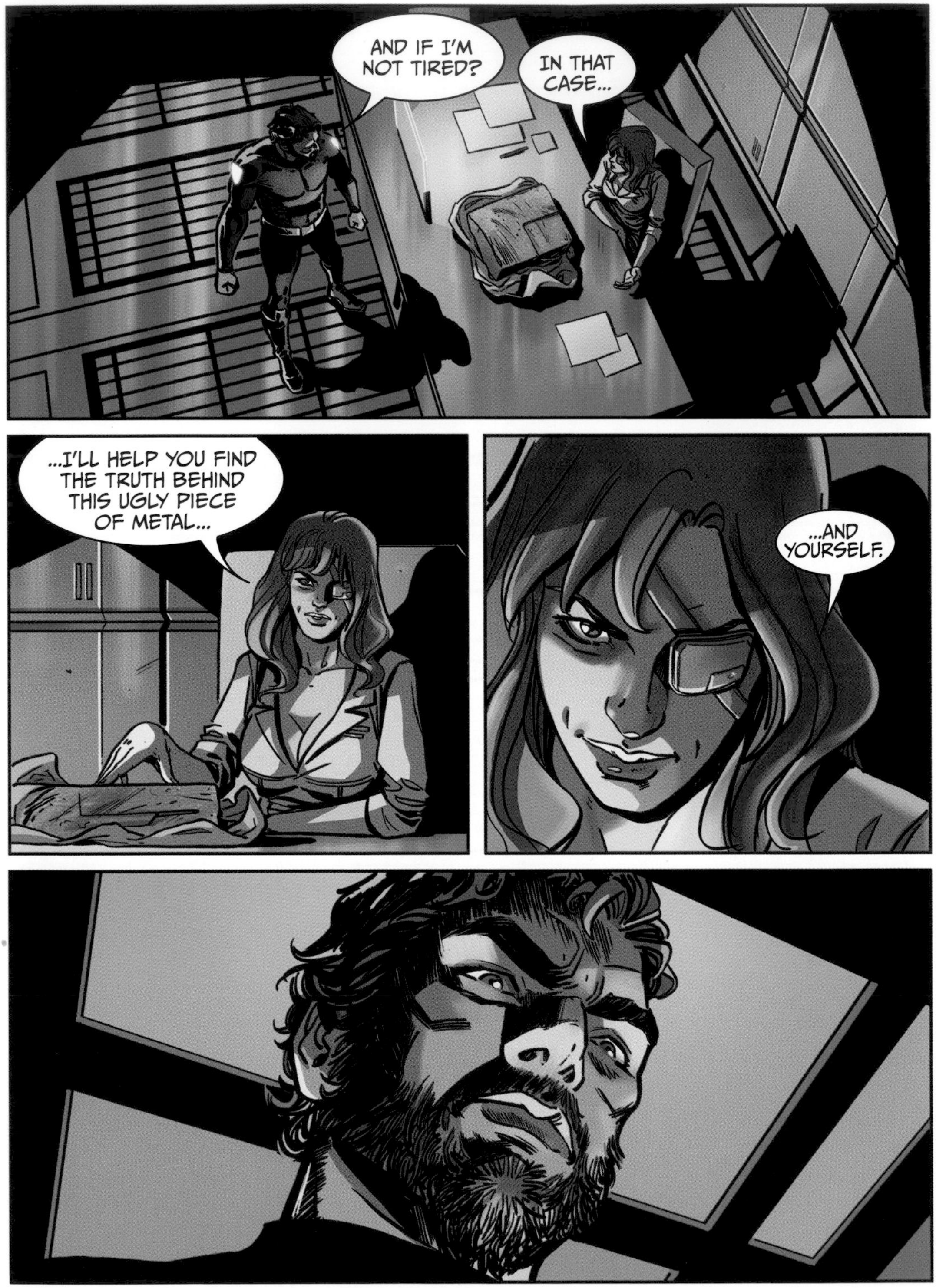
AND IF I'M NOT TIRED?
IN THAT CASE...
...I'LL HELP YOU FIND THE TRUTH BEHIND THIS UGLY PIECE OF METAL...
...AND YOURSELF.

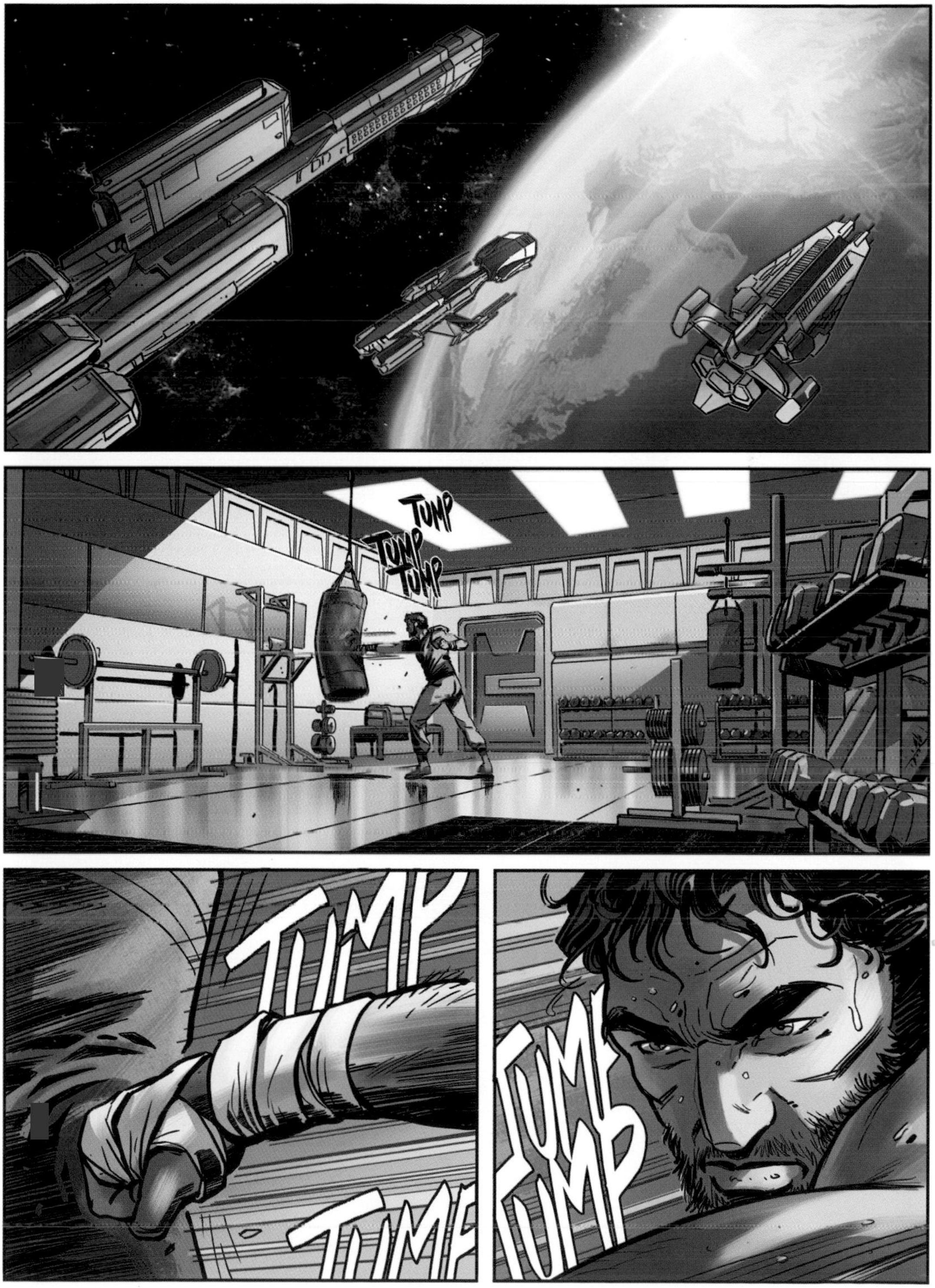
TUMP
TUMP
TUMP
TUMP
TUMP
TUMP
TUMP

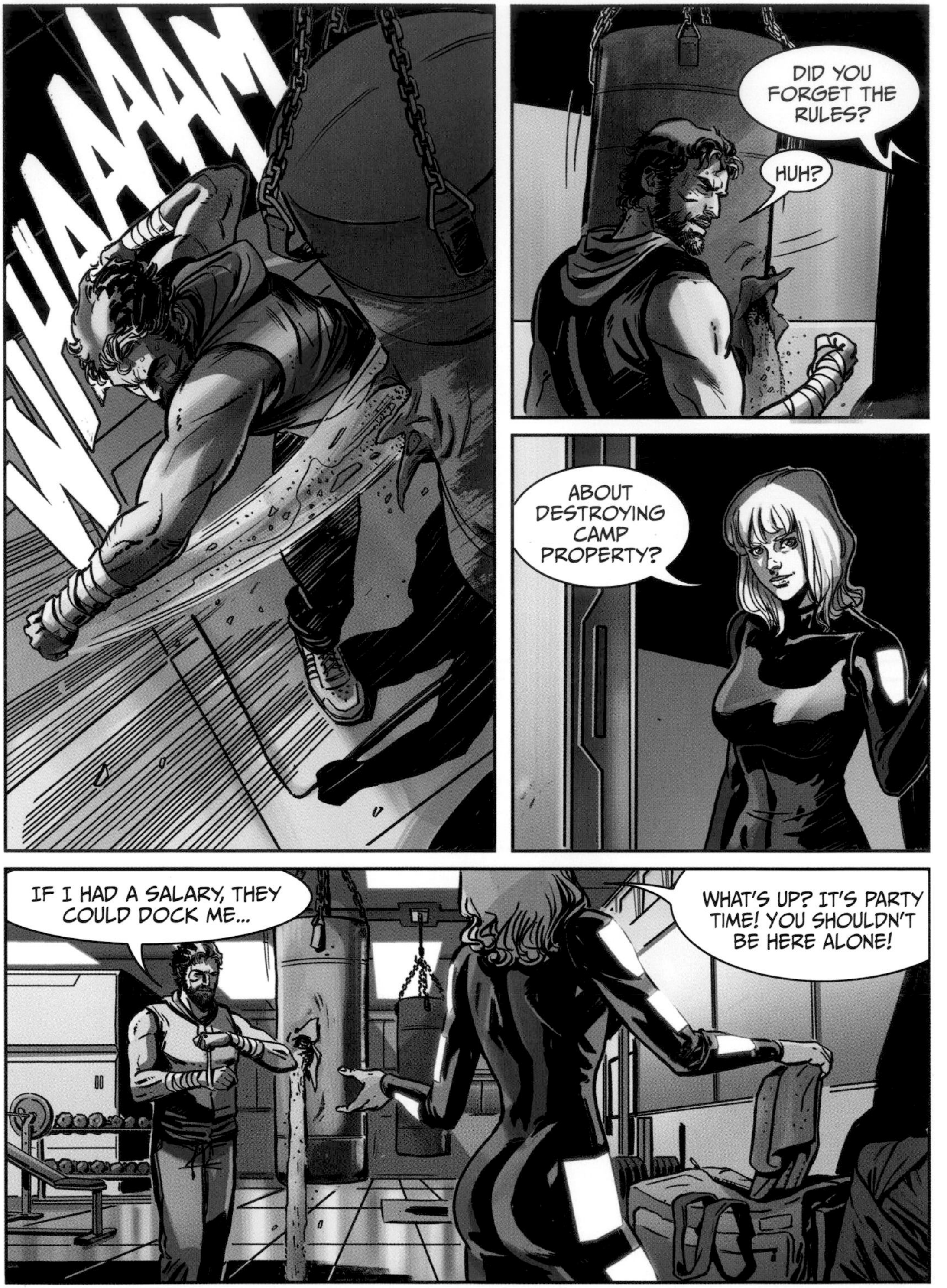
WHAAAAM
DID YOU FORGET THE RULES?
HUH?
ABOUT DESTROYING CAMP PROPERTY?
IF I HAD A SALARY, THEY COULD DOCK ME...
WHAT'S UP? IT'S PARTY TIME! YOU SHOULDN'T BE HERE ALONE!

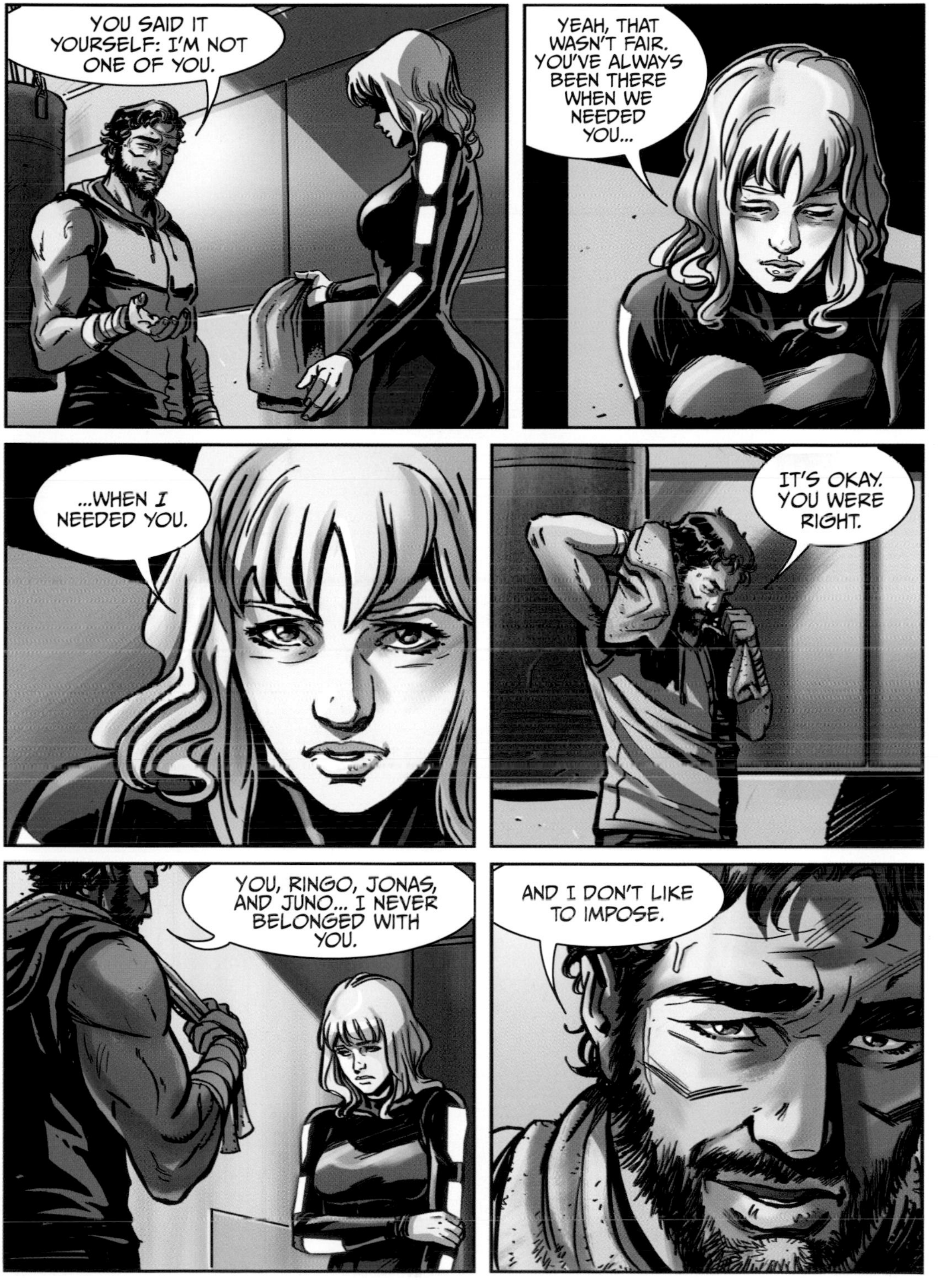
YOU SAID IT YOURSELF: I'M NOT ONE OF YOU.
YEAH, THAT WASN'T FAIR. YOU'VE ALWAYS BEEN THERE WHEN WE NEEDED YOU...
...WHEN I NEEDED YOU.
IT'S OKAY. YOU WERE RIGHT.
YOU, RINGO, JONAS, AND JUNO... I NEVER BELONGED WITH YOU.
AND I DON'T LIKE TO IMPOSE.

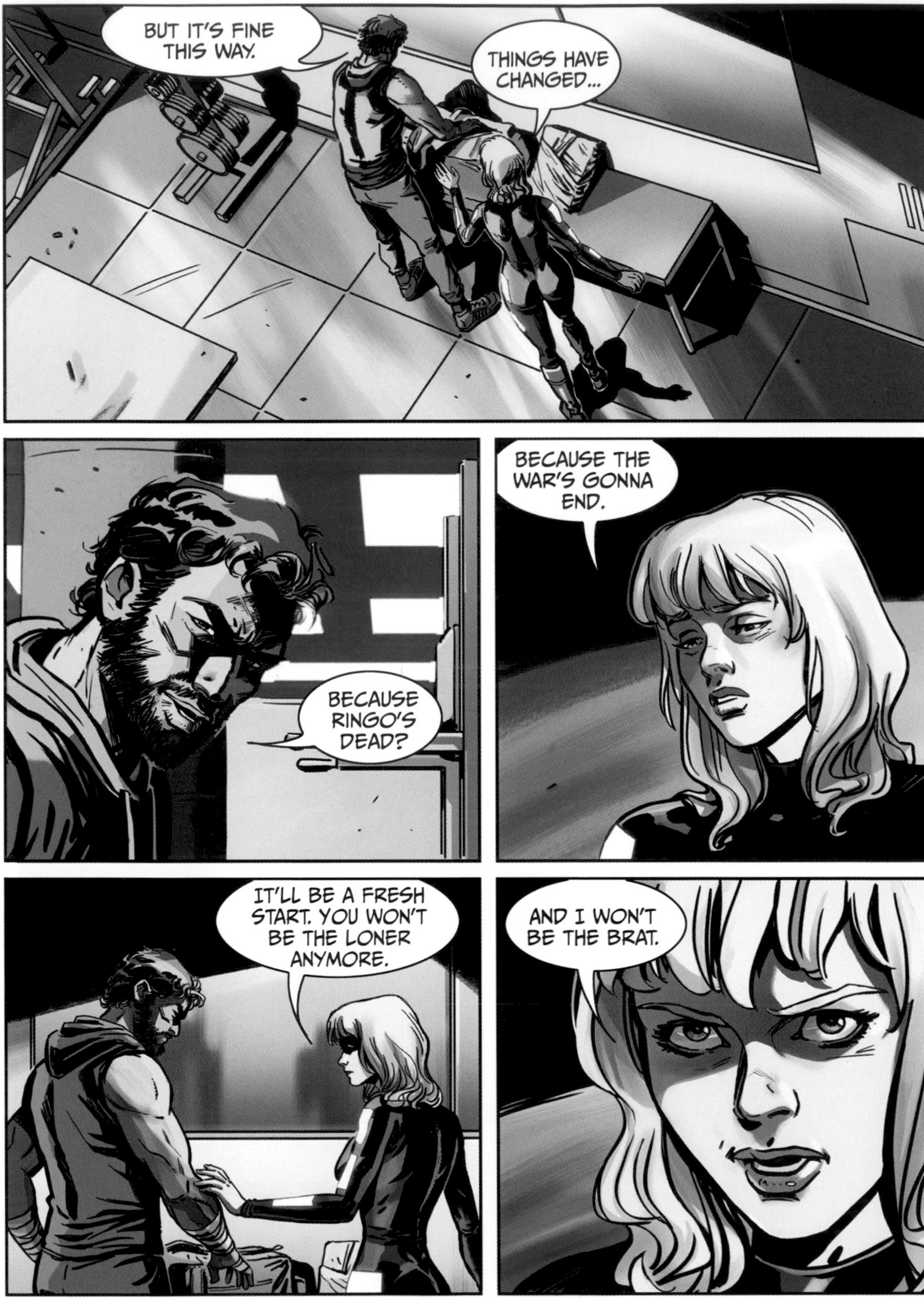
BUT IT'S FINE THIS WAY.
THINGS HAVE CHANGED...
BECAUSE RINGO'S DEAD?
BECAUSE THE WAR'S GONNA END.
IT'LL BE A FRESH START. YOU WON'T BE THE LONER ANYMORE.
AND I WON'T BE THE BRAT.

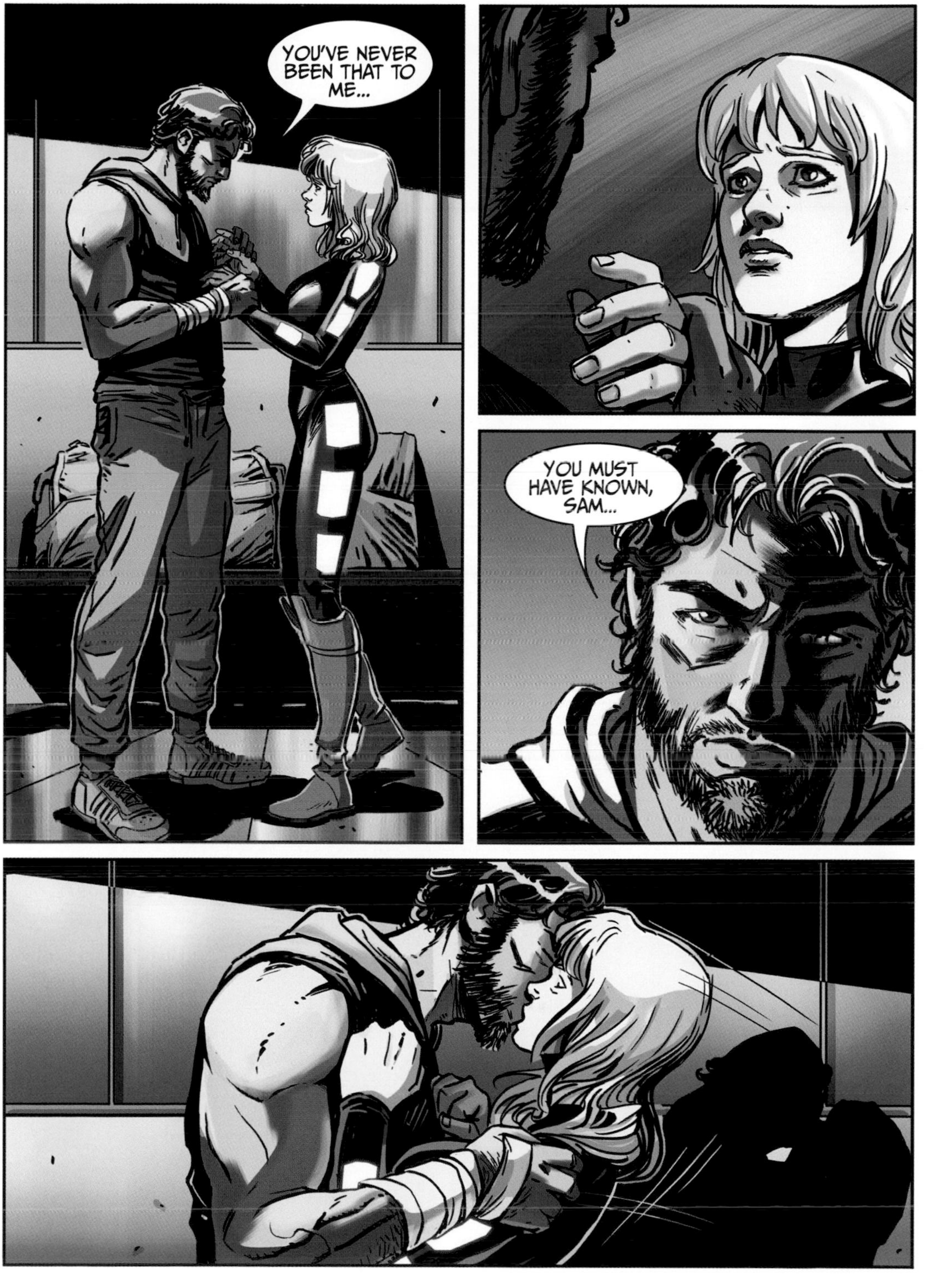
YOU'VE NEVER BEEN THAT TO ME...
YOU MUST HAVE KNOWN, SAM...

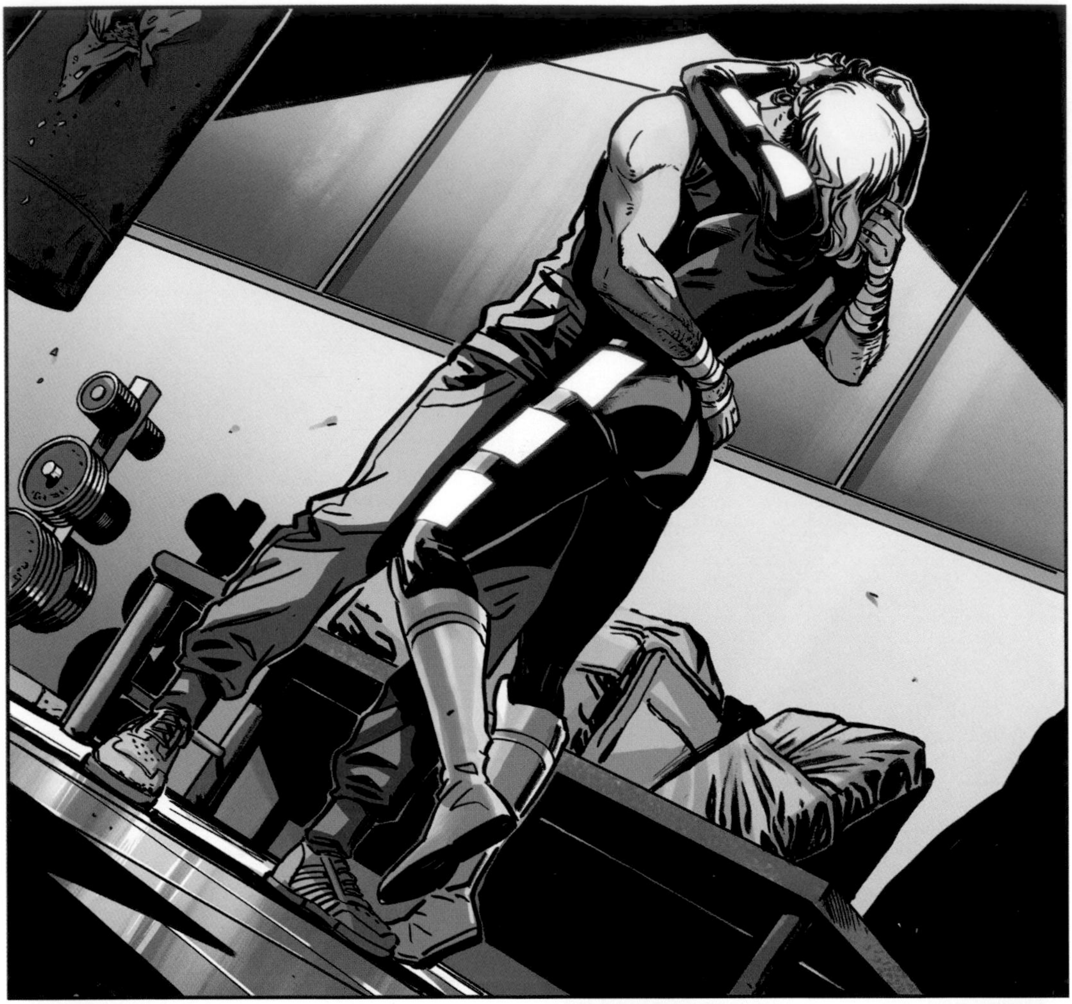

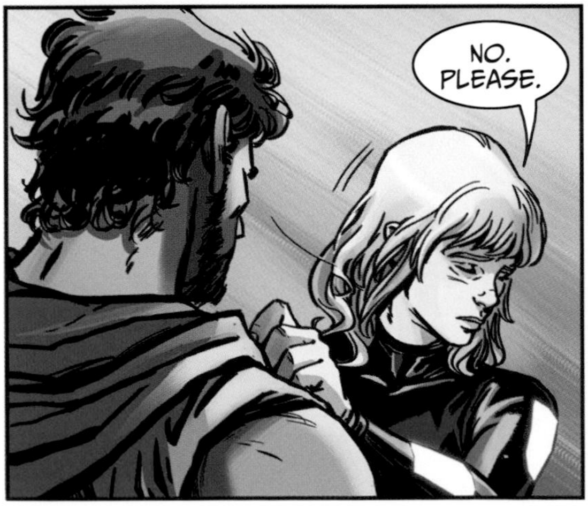
NO.
PLEASE.

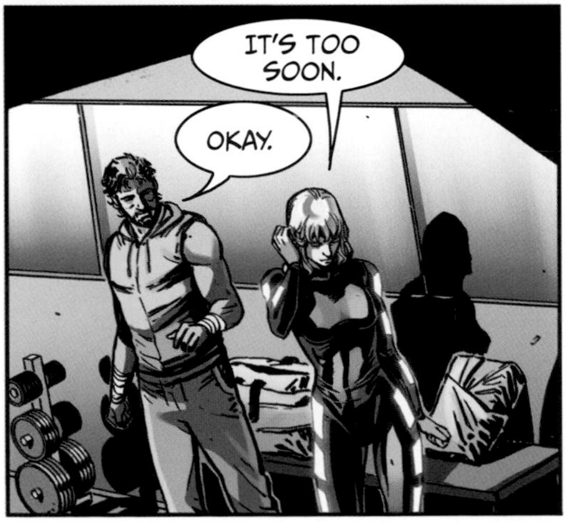
IT'S TOO
SOON.
OKAY.

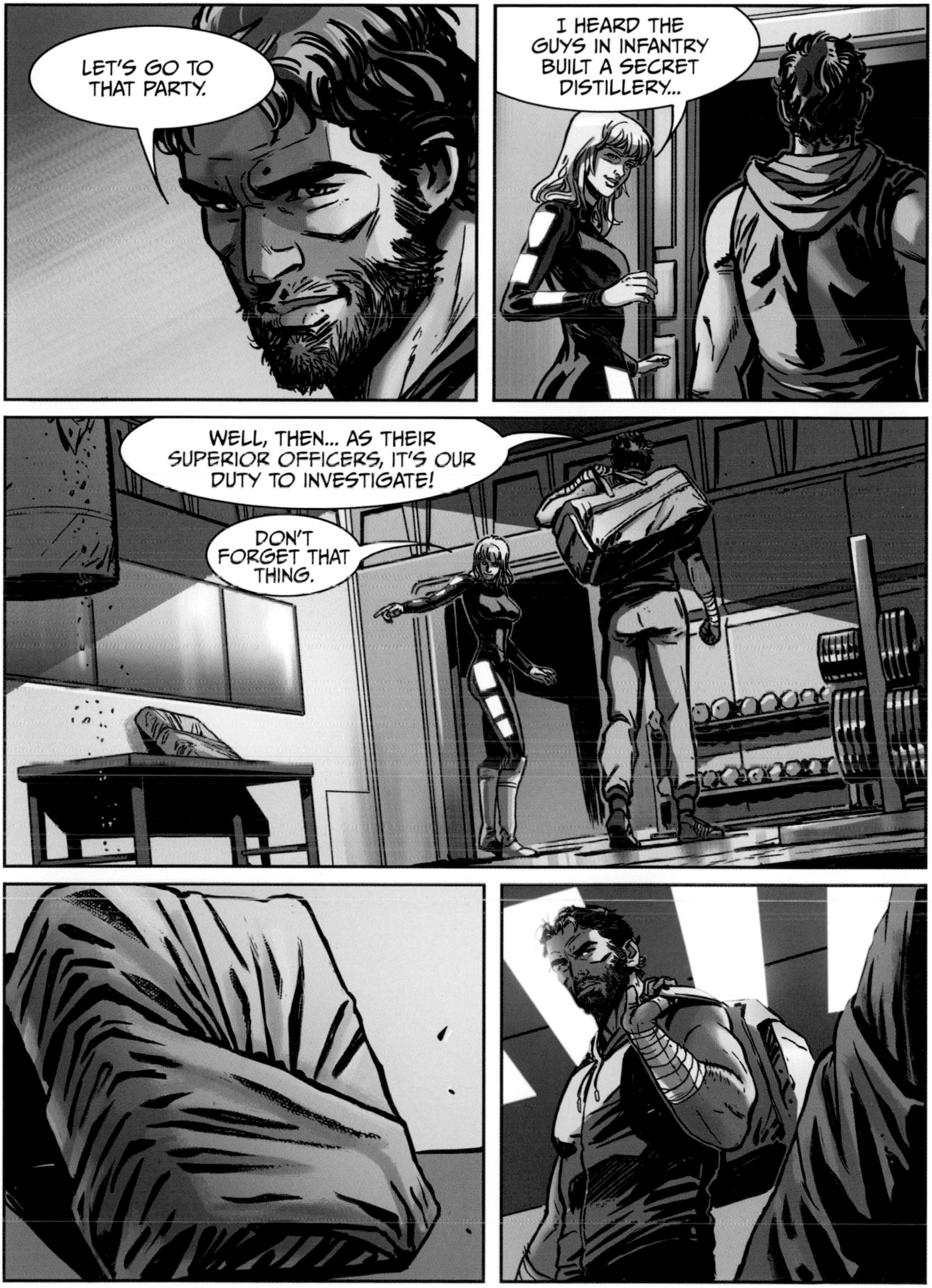
LET'S GO TO THAT PARTY.
I HEARD THE GUYS IN INFANTRY BUILT A SECRET DISTILLERY...
WELL, THEN... AS THEIR SUPERIOR OFFICERS, IT'S OUR DUTY TO INVESTIGATE!
DON'T FORGET THAT THING.

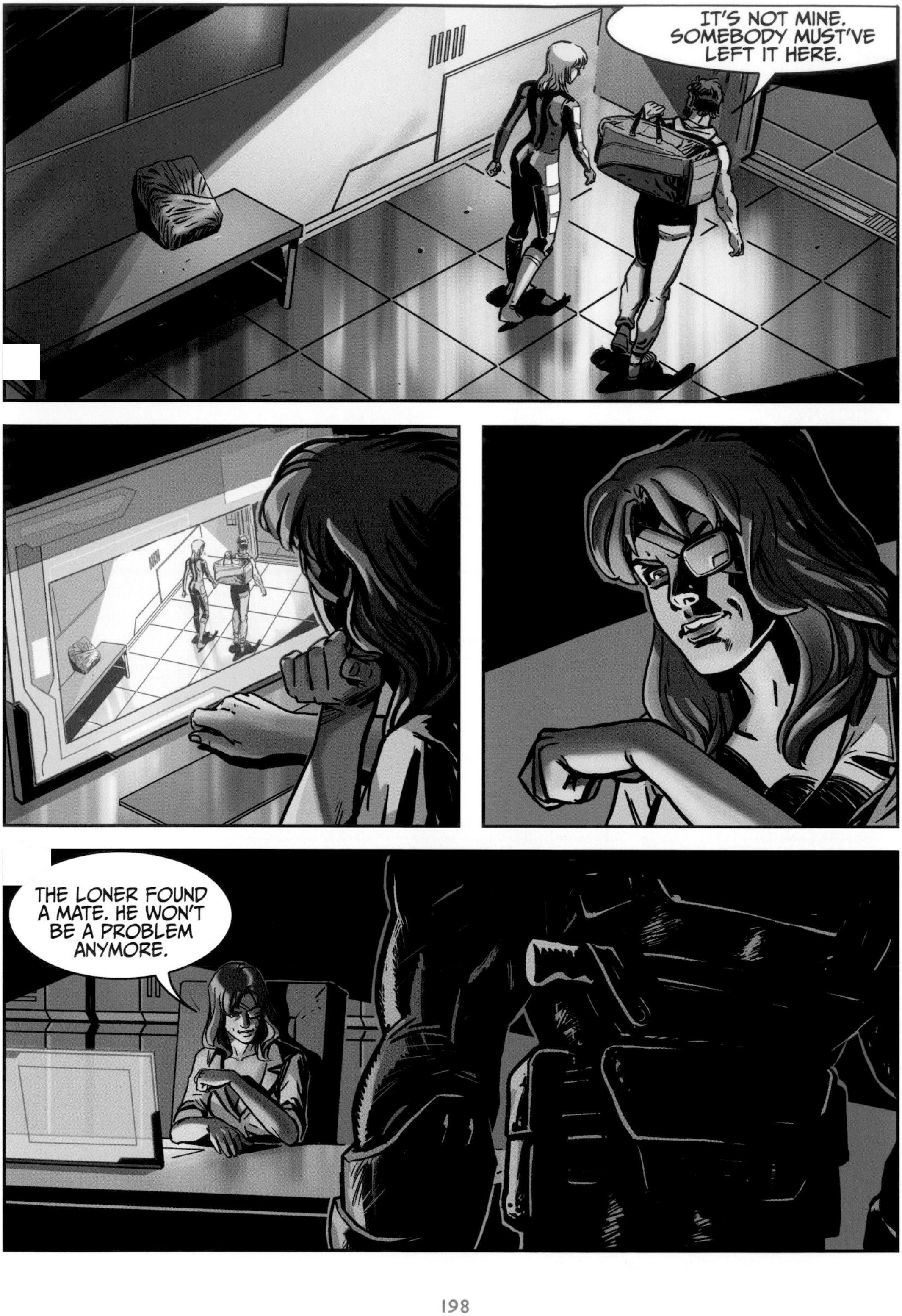
IT'S NOT MINE. SOMEBODY MUST'VE LEFT IT HERE.
THE LONER FOUND A MATE. HE WON'T BE A PROBLEM ANYMORE.

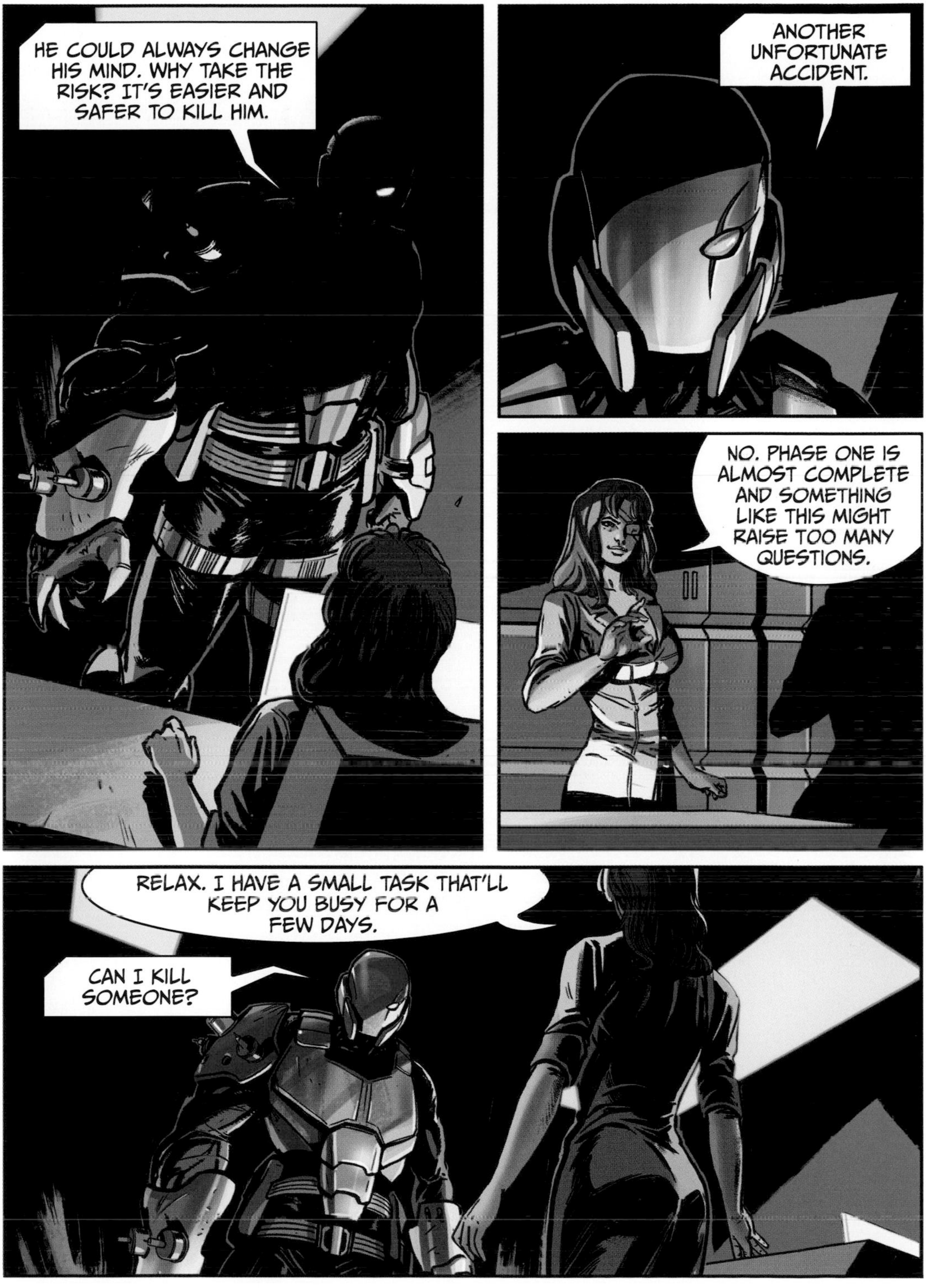
HE COULD ALWAYS CHANGE HIS MIND. WHY TAKE THE RISK? IT'S EASIER AND SAFER TO KILL HIM.
ANOTHER UNFORTUNATE ACCIDENT.
NO. PHASE ONE IS ALMOST COMPLETE AND SOMETHING LIKE THIS MIGHT RAISE TOO MANY QUESTIONS.
RELAX. I HAVE A SMALL TASK THAT'LL KEEP YOU BUSY FOR A FEW DAYS.
CAN I KILL SOMEONE?

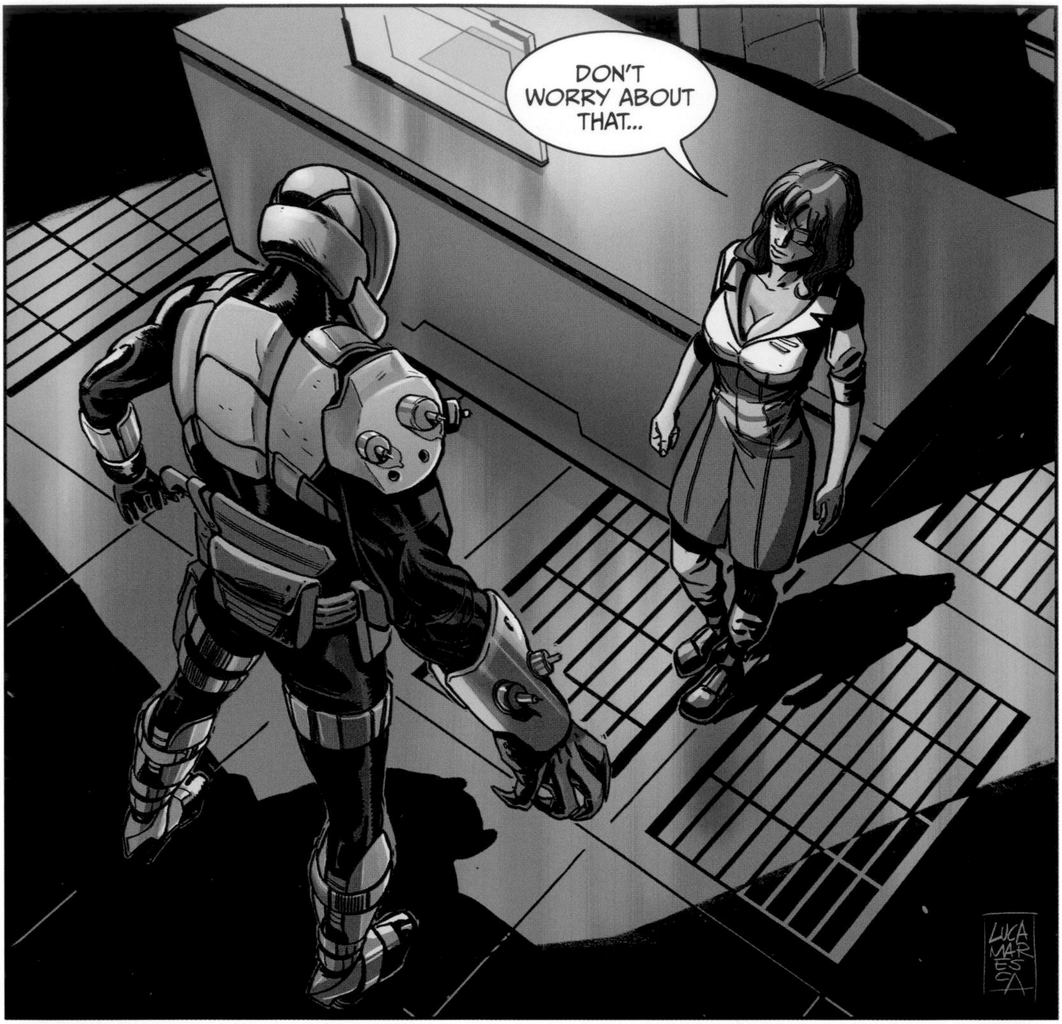
DON'T WORRY ABOUT THAT...
LUCA MARESCA

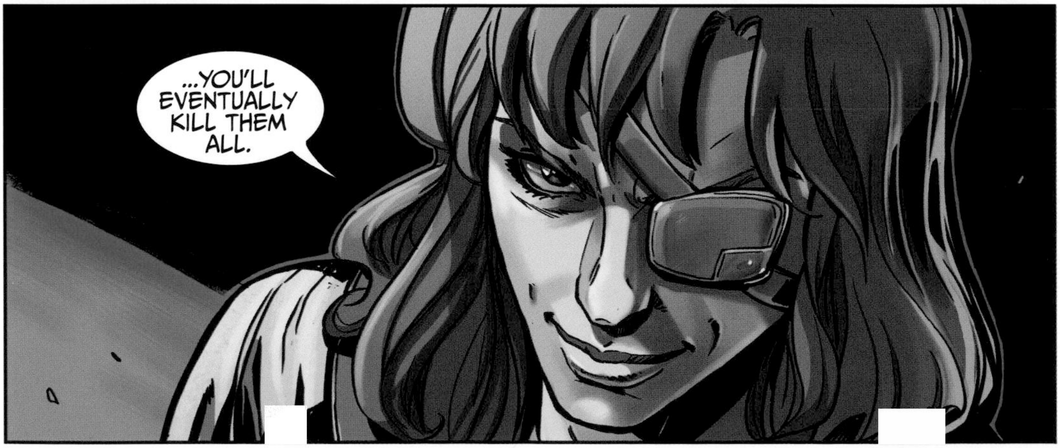
...YOU'LL EVENTUALLY KILL THEM ALL.

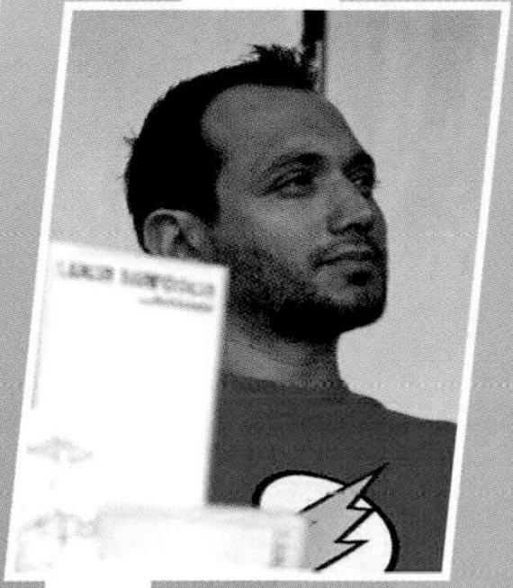

LUCA MARESCA

ARTIST

When and where were you born? Where do you live now?
I was born in Salerno, Italy, on August 21, 1983, and still live around here.

What sort of artistic education did you have?
My family has always been involved with art. My grandfather was a renowned painter and ceramist, and my parents are both painters whose works are on display both in Italy and abroad. I was raised surrounded by drawings, brushes, paintings, and art books. I attended the Art Institute and the Academy of Fine Arts (which I haven't finished yet), along with the Italian School of Comics in Naples. After spending a few years as a musician, I started working in the comic industry full time.

Tell us about your previous works, before *Orphans*.
I started with small gigs for minor publishers, then I made my official debut on *John Doe* for Eura/Aurea Editoriale, working on issues #69, #3, and #6. In the meantime, I illustrated *Dibbuk*, a splatter comic for Edizioni BD. It was while finishing *John Doe #6* that I got hired by Bonelli to work on *Orphans*.

When did you start working on *Orphans*, and when did you finish drawing your chapter?
I started in June 2011, and, due to my performance anxiety, I didn't finish until April 2013.

What tools did you use?
Pencils, brushes, and digital ink.

What was the most difficult scene and which one did you have to redraw more times?
I honestly don't remember. Nothing was easy. Sometimes the scenes I had to redraw the most were apparently the easiest ones. The one scene I had to redraw more times is the big panel on page 153... I can recall at least seven versions of that panel!

If you could go back in time, what would you change about this chapter?
The whole sequence in the forest with the four inmates; even though the pages work fine, I wish I had found a better way to render them visually in order to better study the characters' expressions and eliminate many of the little uncertainties that I can't help but notice now.

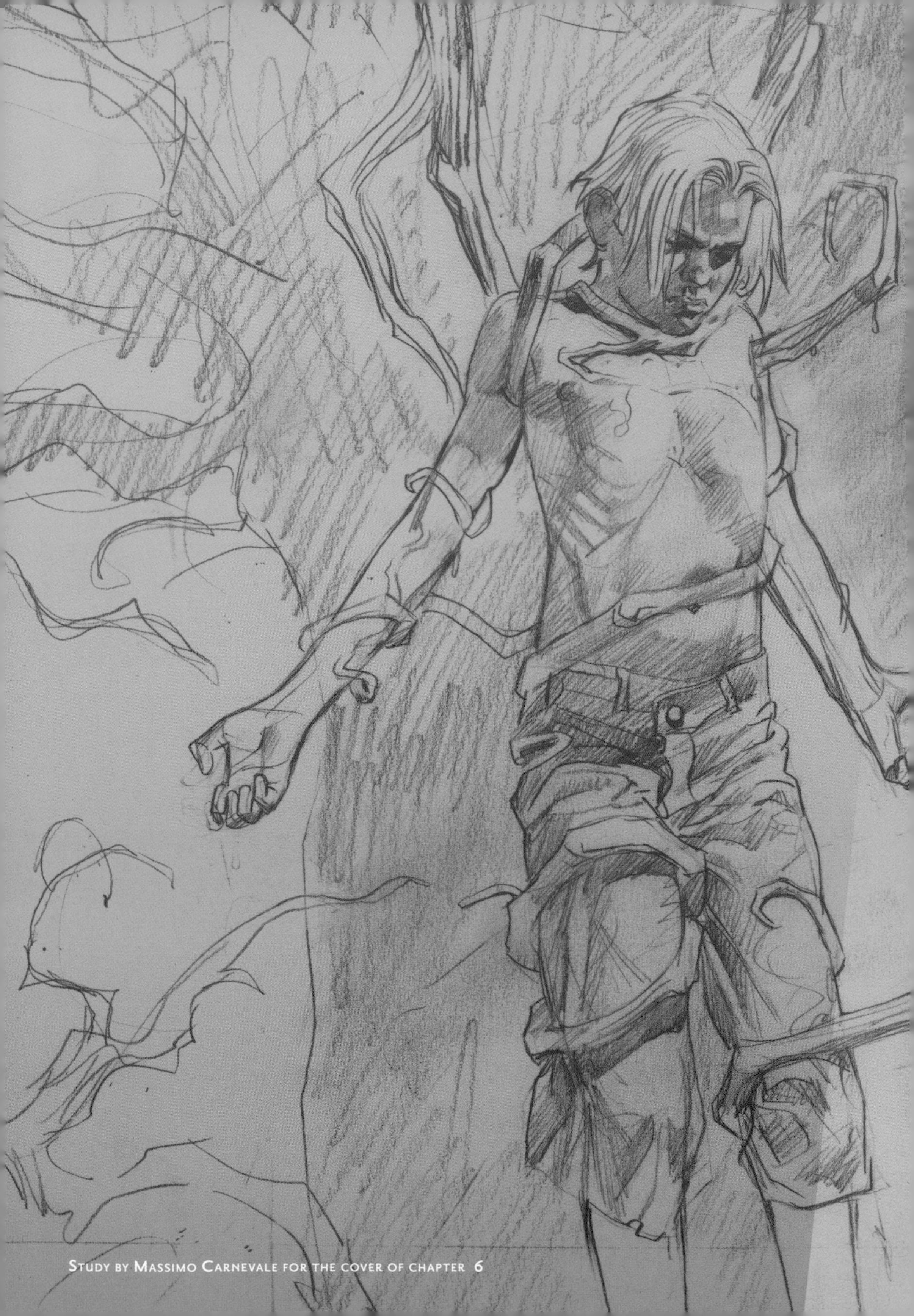

Study by Massimo Carnevale for the cover of chapter 6

...IN PAIN YOU WILL BE BORN AGAIN

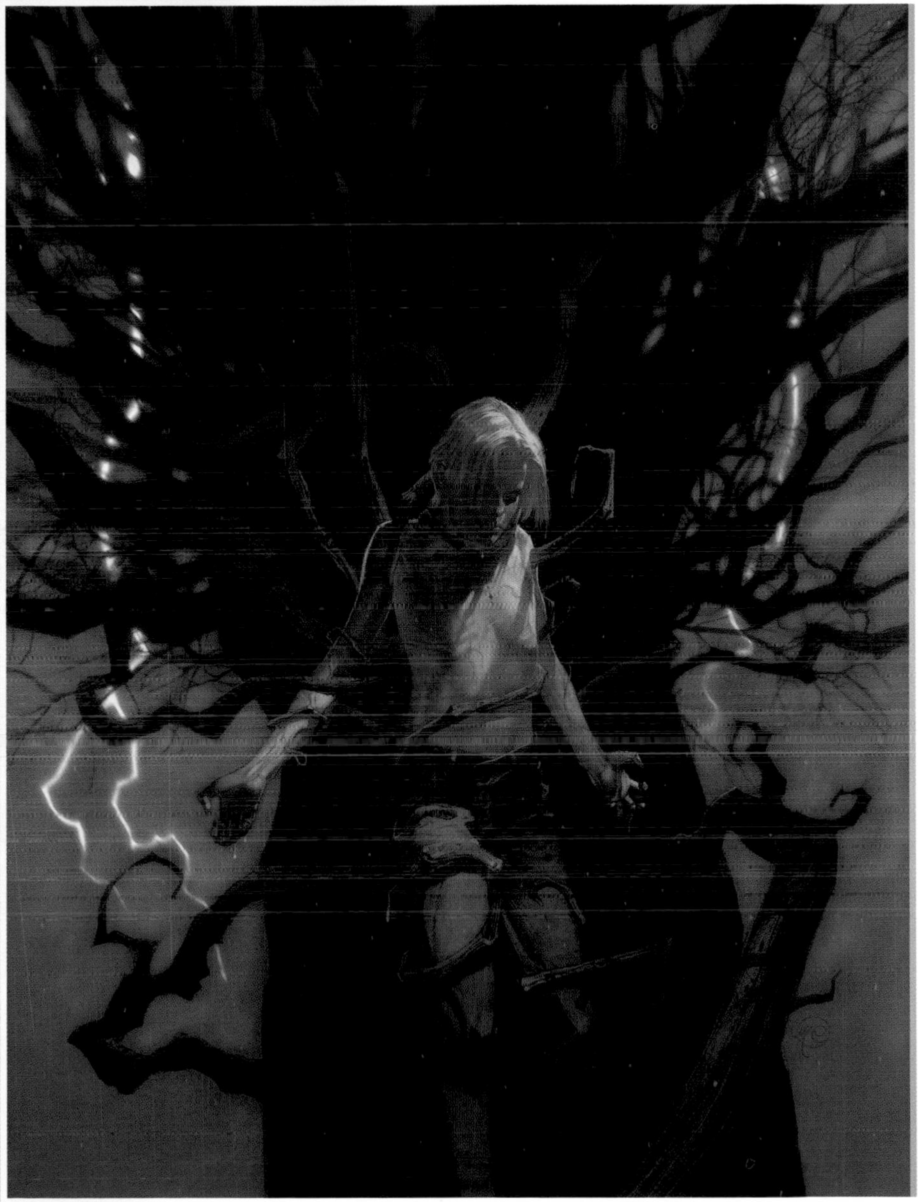

ORPHANS: CHAPTER 6

story: ROBERTO RECCHIONI
art: WERTHER DELL'EDERA
colors: GIOVANNA NIRO
cover: MASSIMO CARNEVALE

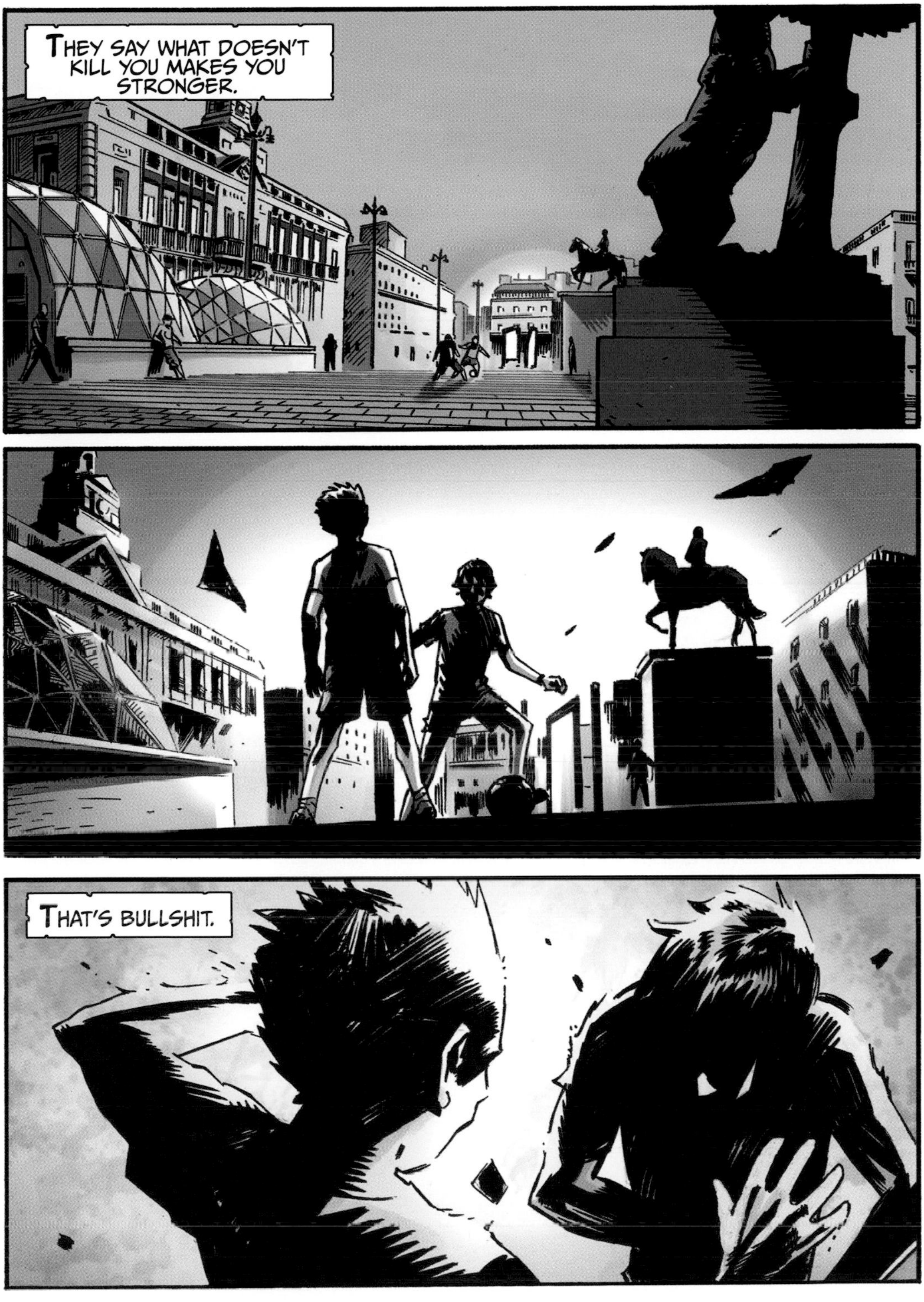
THEY SAY WHAT DOESN'T KILL YOU MAKES YOU STRONGER.
THAT'S BULLSHIT.

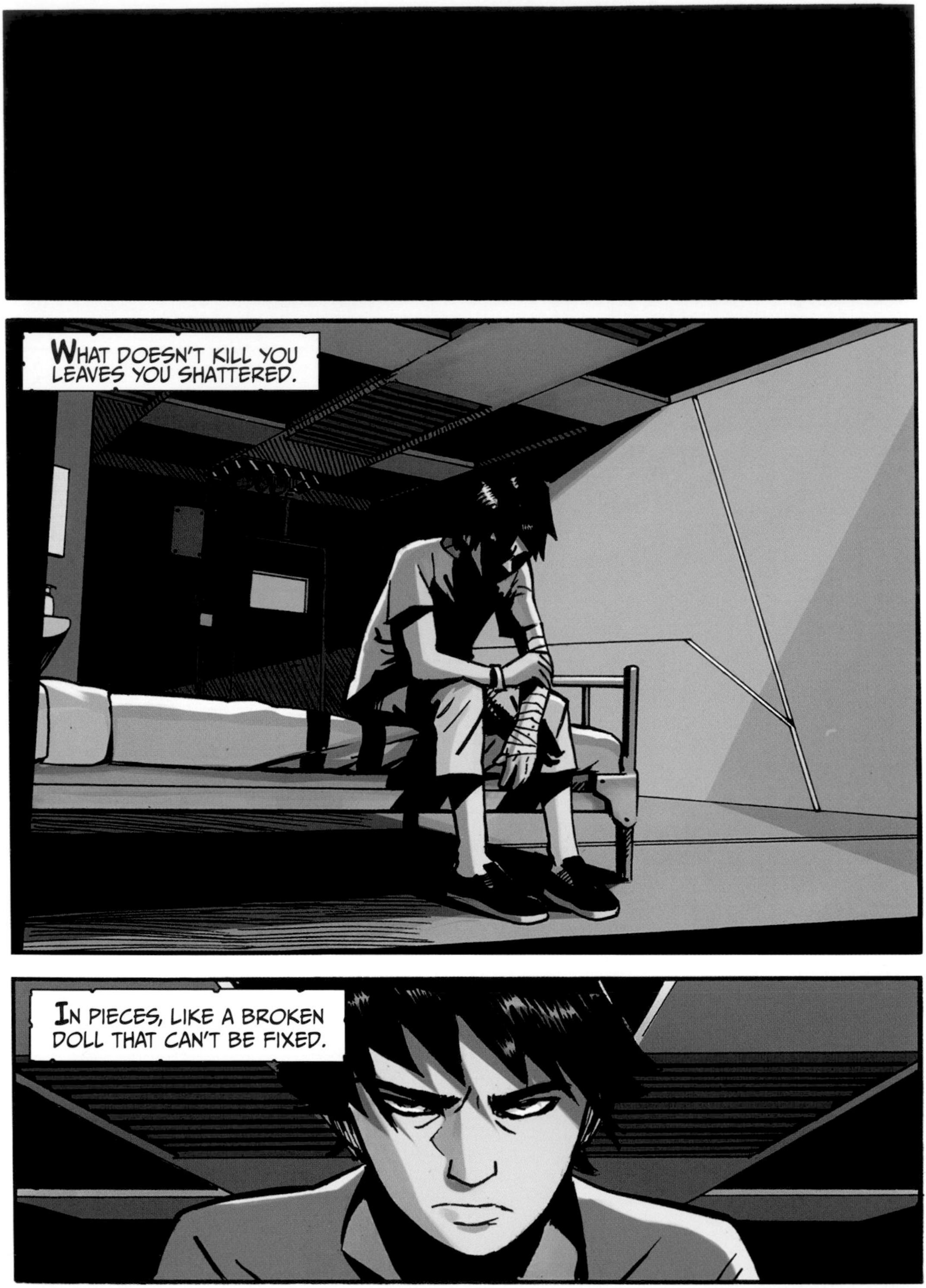
WHAT DOESN'T KILL YOU LEAVES YOU SHATTERED.
IN PIECES, LIKE A BROKEN DOLL THAT CAN'T BE FIXED.

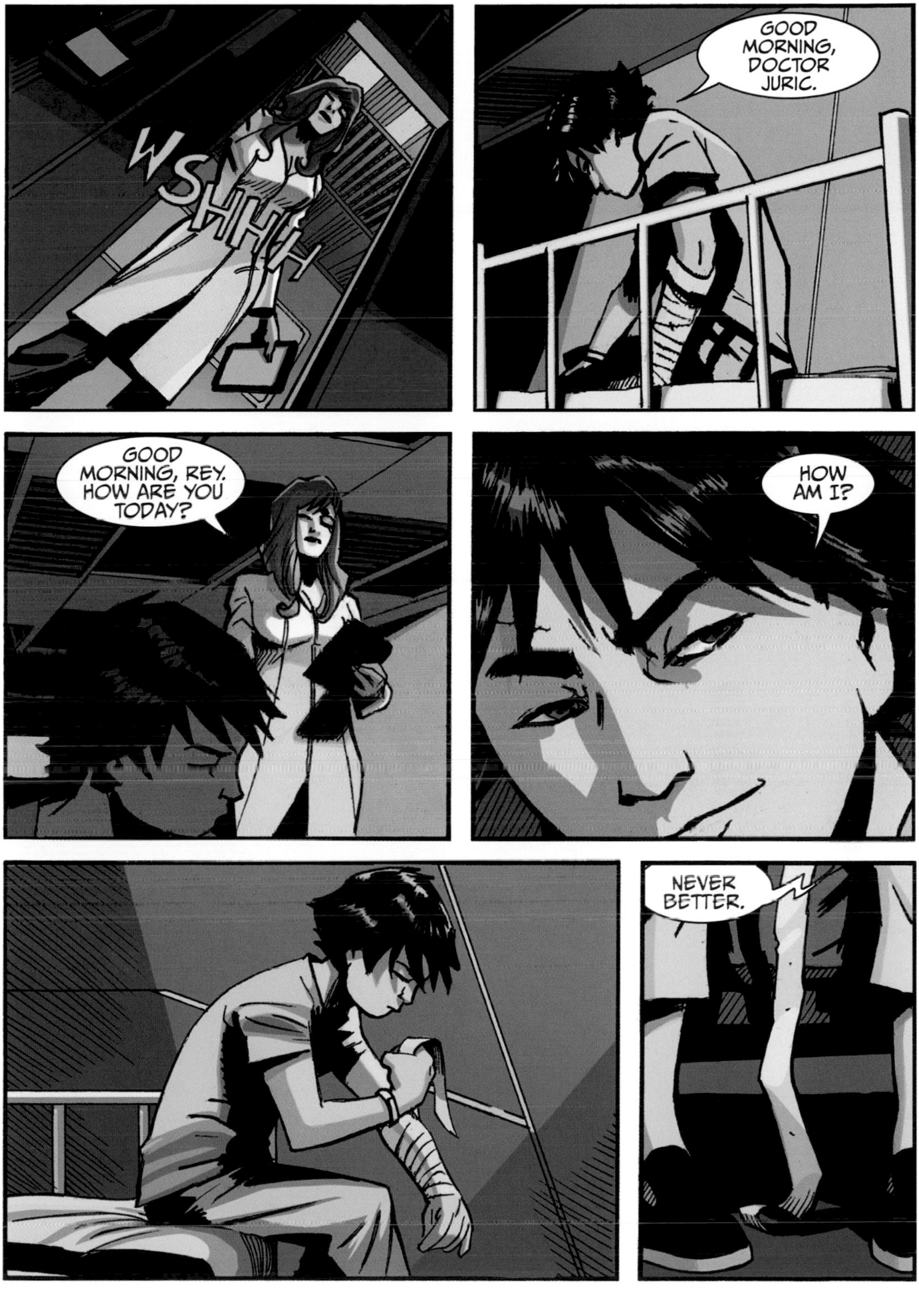
WSHHH
GOOD MORNING, DOCTOR JURIC.
GOOD MORNING, REY. HOW ARE YOU TODAY?
HOW AM I?
NEVER BETTER.

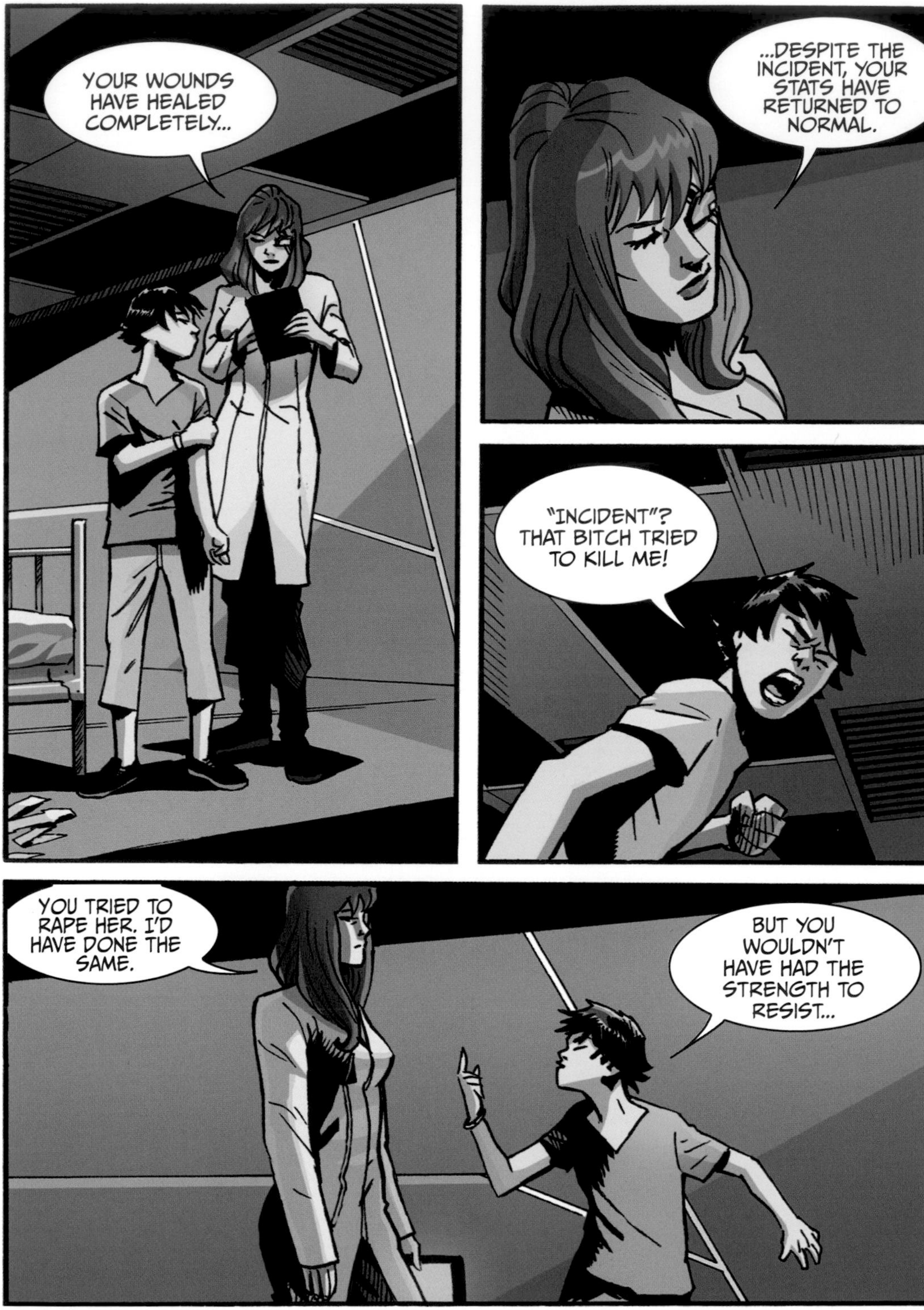
YOUR WOUNDS HAVE HEALED COMPLETELY...
...DESPITE THE INCIDENT, YOUR STATS HAVE RETURNED TO NORMAL.
"INCIDENT"? THAT BITCH TRIED TO KILL ME!
YOU TRIED TO RAPE HER. I'D HAVE DONE THE SAME.
BUT YOU WOULDN'T HAVE HAD THE STRENGTH TO RESIST...

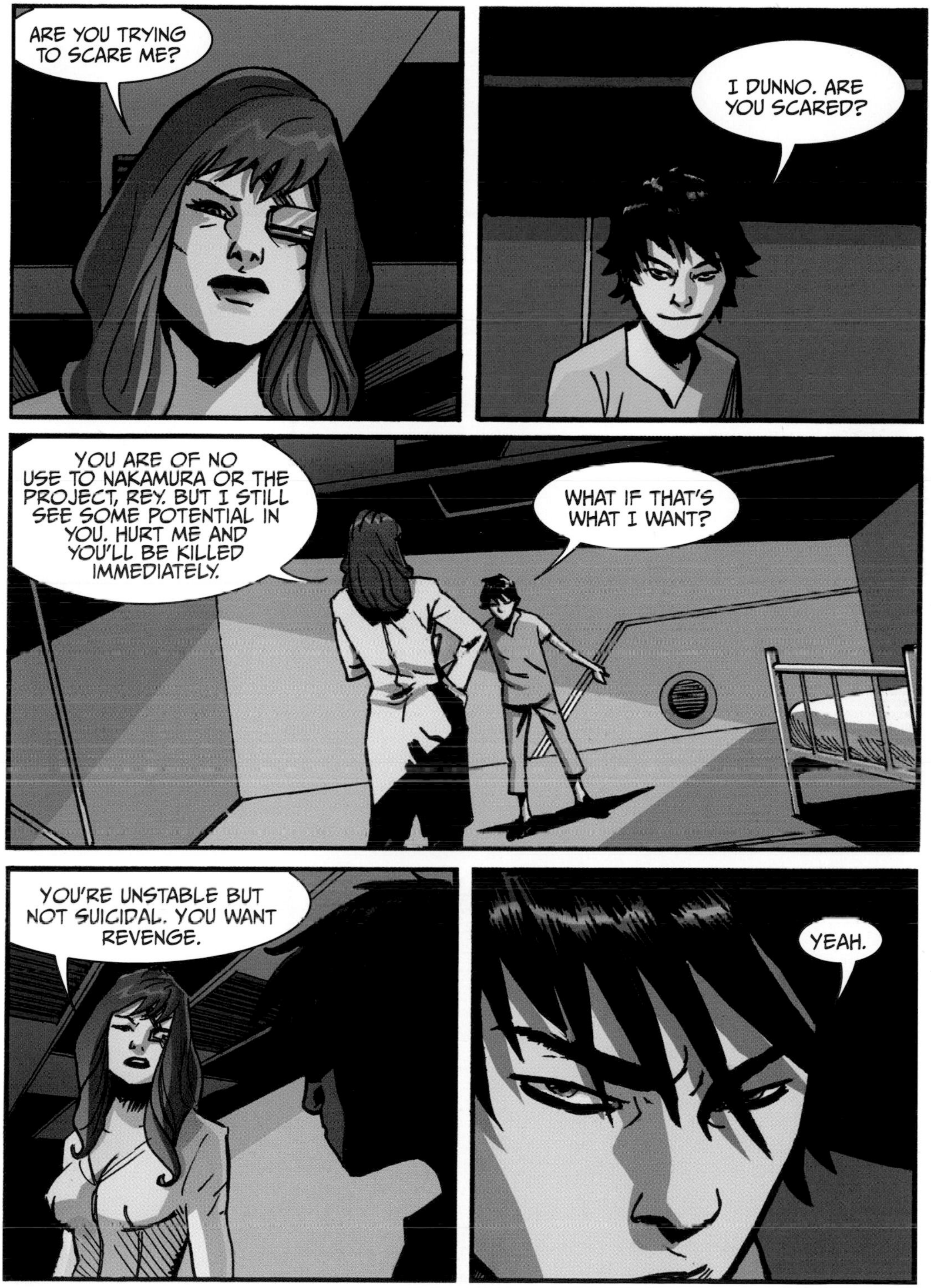
ARE YOU TRYING TO SCARE ME?
I DUNNO. ARE YOU SCARED?
YOU ARE OF NO USE TO NAKAMURA OR THE PROJECT, REY. BUT I STILL SEE SOME POTENTIAL IN YOU. HURT ME AND YOU'LL BE KILLED IMMEDIATELY.
WHAT IF THAT'S WHAT I WANT?
YOU'RE UNSTABLE BUT NOT SUICIDAL. YOU WANT REVENGE.
YEAH.

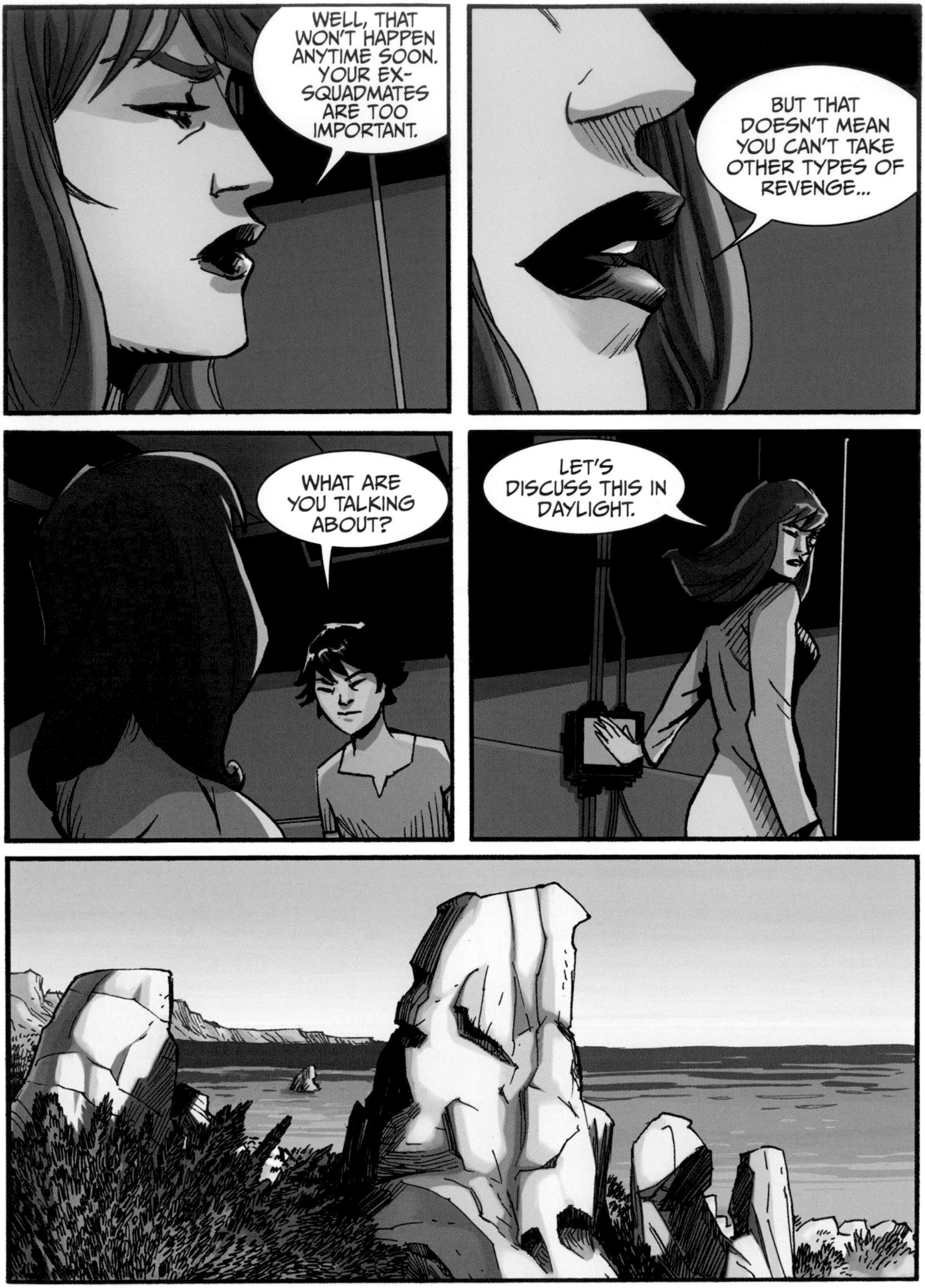
WELL, THAT WON'T HAPPEN ANYTIME SOON. YOUR EX-SQUADMATES ARE TOO IMPORTANT.
BUT THAT DOESN'T MEAN YOU CAN'T TAKE OTHER TYPES OF REVENGE...
WHAT ARE YOU TALKING ABOUT?
LET'S DISCUSS THIS IN DAYLIGHT.

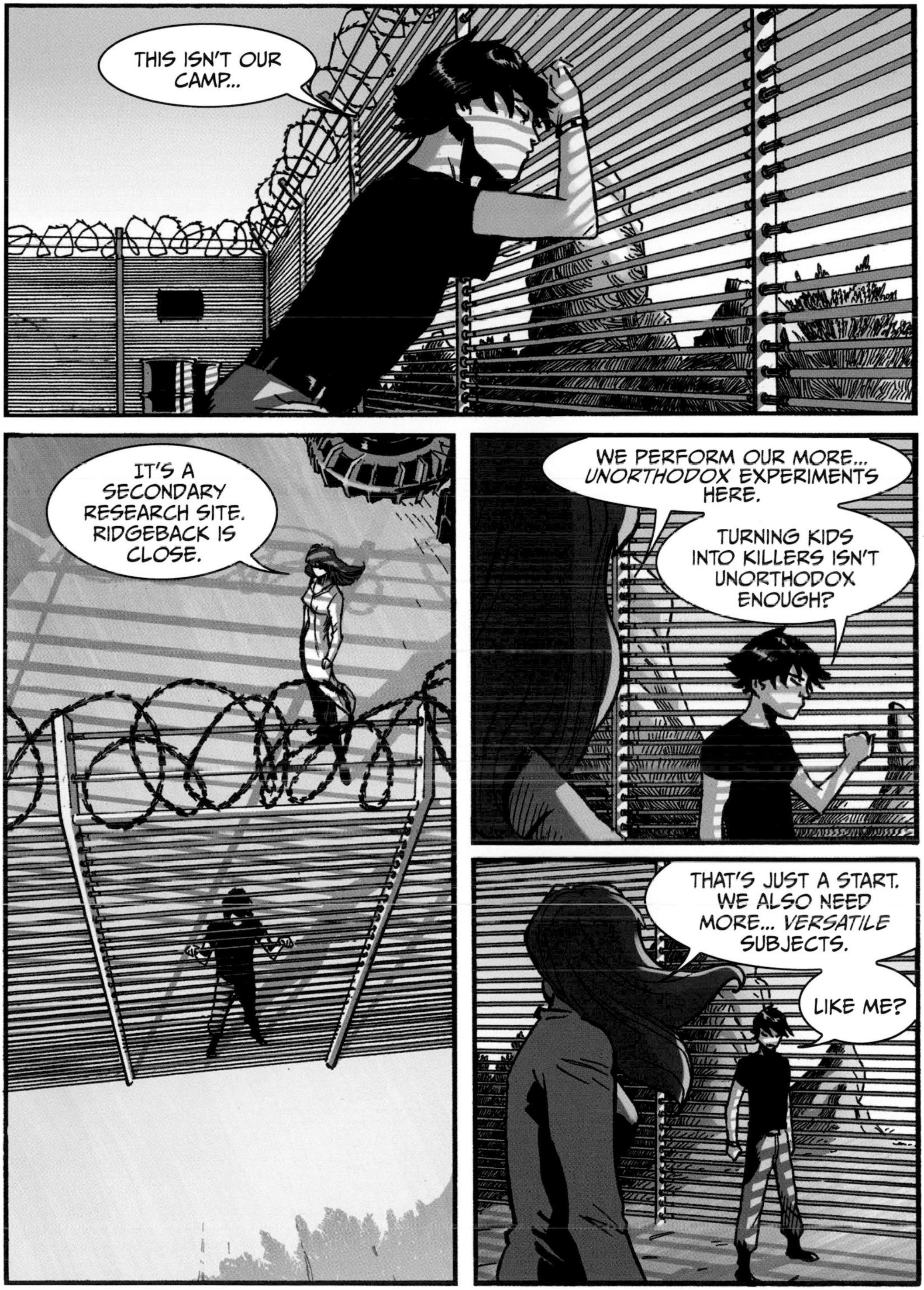
THIS ISN'T OUR CAMP...
IT'S A SECONDARY RESEARCH SITE. RIDGEBACK IS CLOSE.
WE PERFORM OUR MORE... *UNORTHODOX* EXPERIMENTS HERE.
TURNING KIDS INTO KILLERS ISN'T UNORTHODOX ENOUGH?
THAT'S JUST A START. WE ALSO NEED MORE... *VERSATILE* SUBJECTS.
LIKE ME?

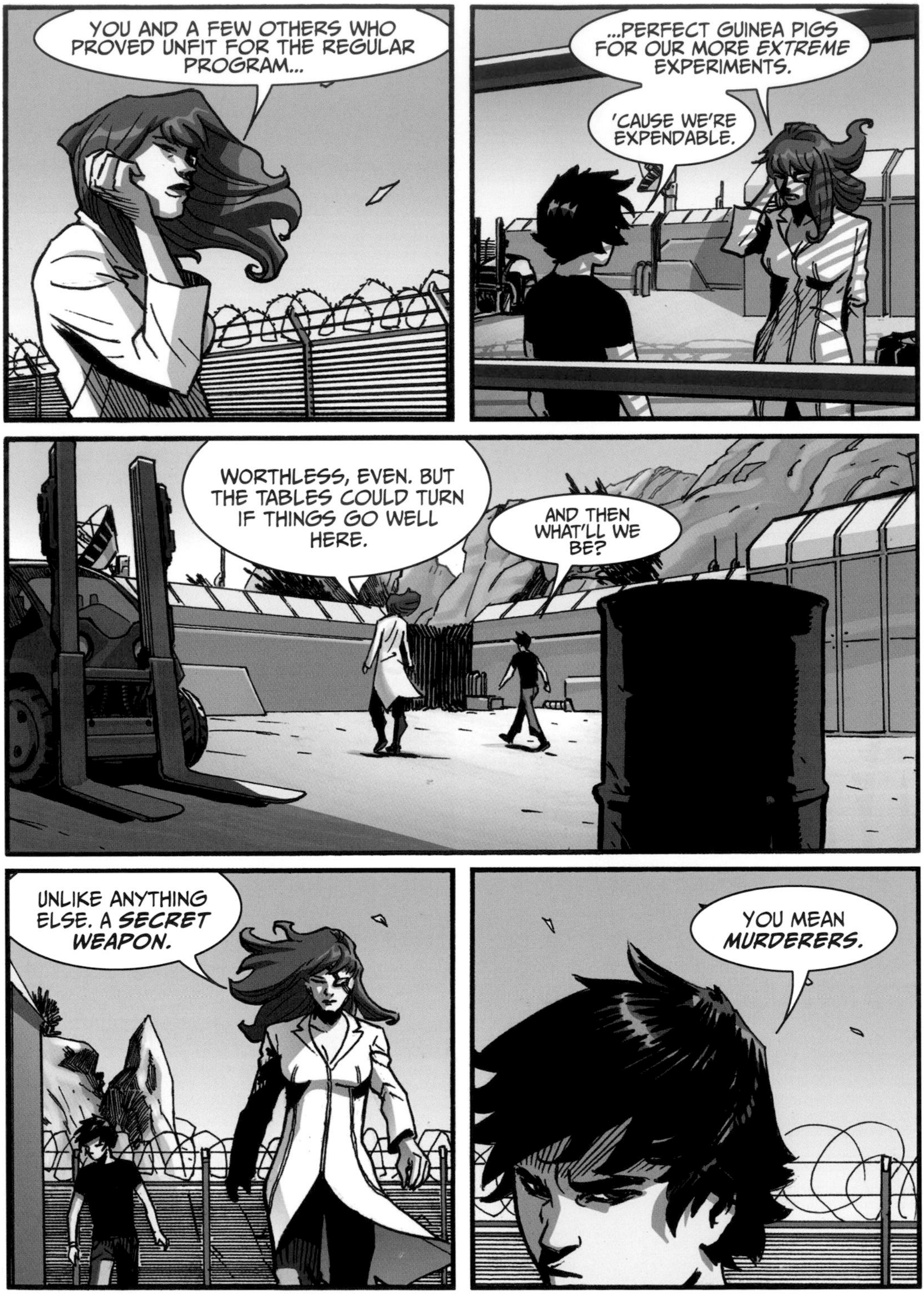
YOU AND A FEW OTHERS WHO PROVED UNFIT FOR THE REGULAR PROGRAM...
...PERFECT GUINEA PIGS FOR OUR MORE EXTREME EXPERIMENTS.
'CAUSE WE'RE EXPENDABLE.
WORTHLESS, EVEN. BUT THE TABLES COULD TURN IF THINGS GO WELL HERE.
AND THEN WHAT'LL WE BE?
UNLIKE ANYTHING ELSE. A SECRET WEAPON.
YOU MEAN MURDERERS.

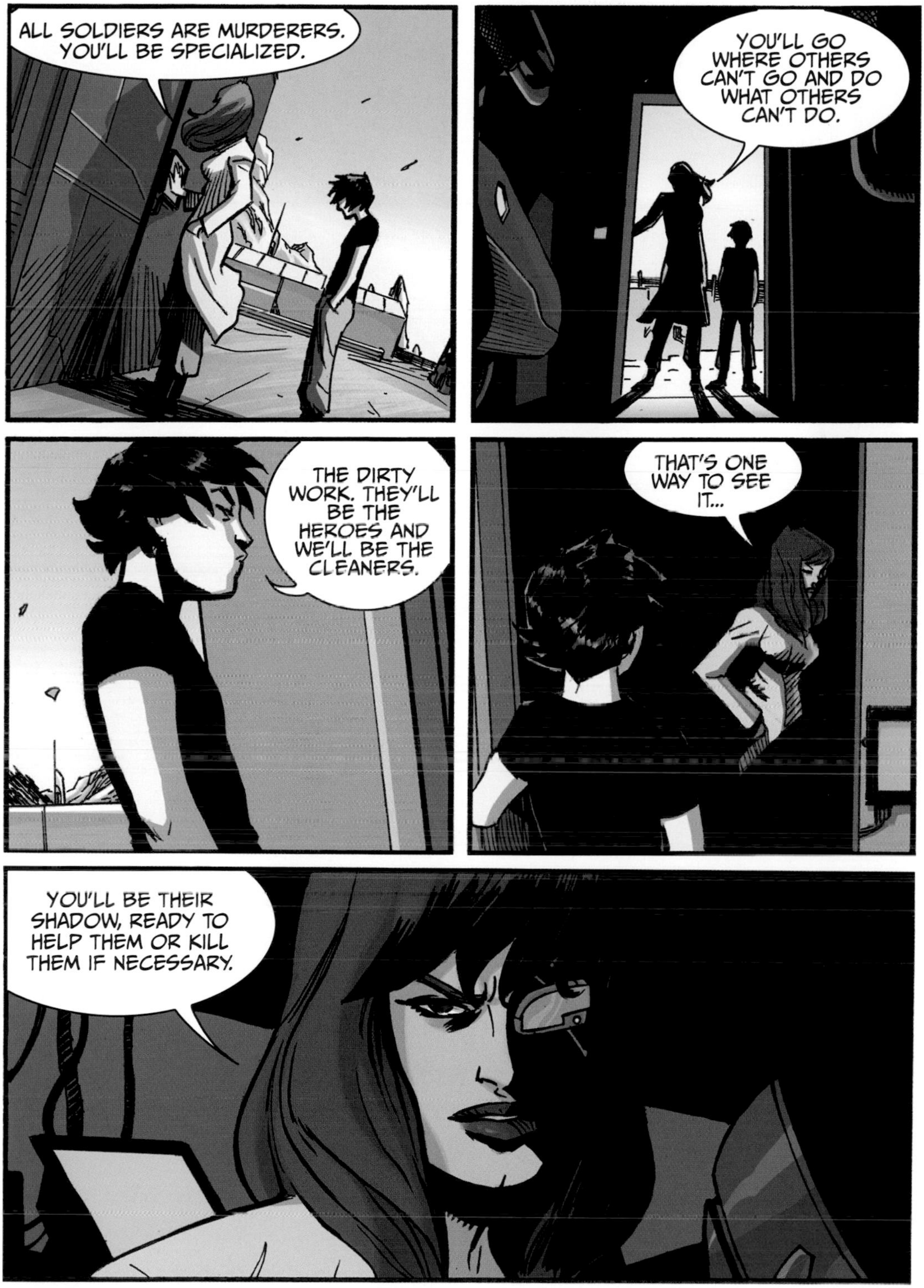
ALL SOLDIERS ARE MURDERERS. YOU'LL BE SPECIALIZED.
YOU'LL GO WHERE OTHERS CAN'T GO AND DO WHAT OTHERS CAN'T DO.
THE DIRTY WORK. THEY'LL BE THE HEROES AND WE'LL BE THE CLEANERS.
THAT'S ONE WAY TO SEE IT...
YOU'LL BE THEIR SHADOW, READY TO HELP THEM OR KILL THEM IF NECESSARY.

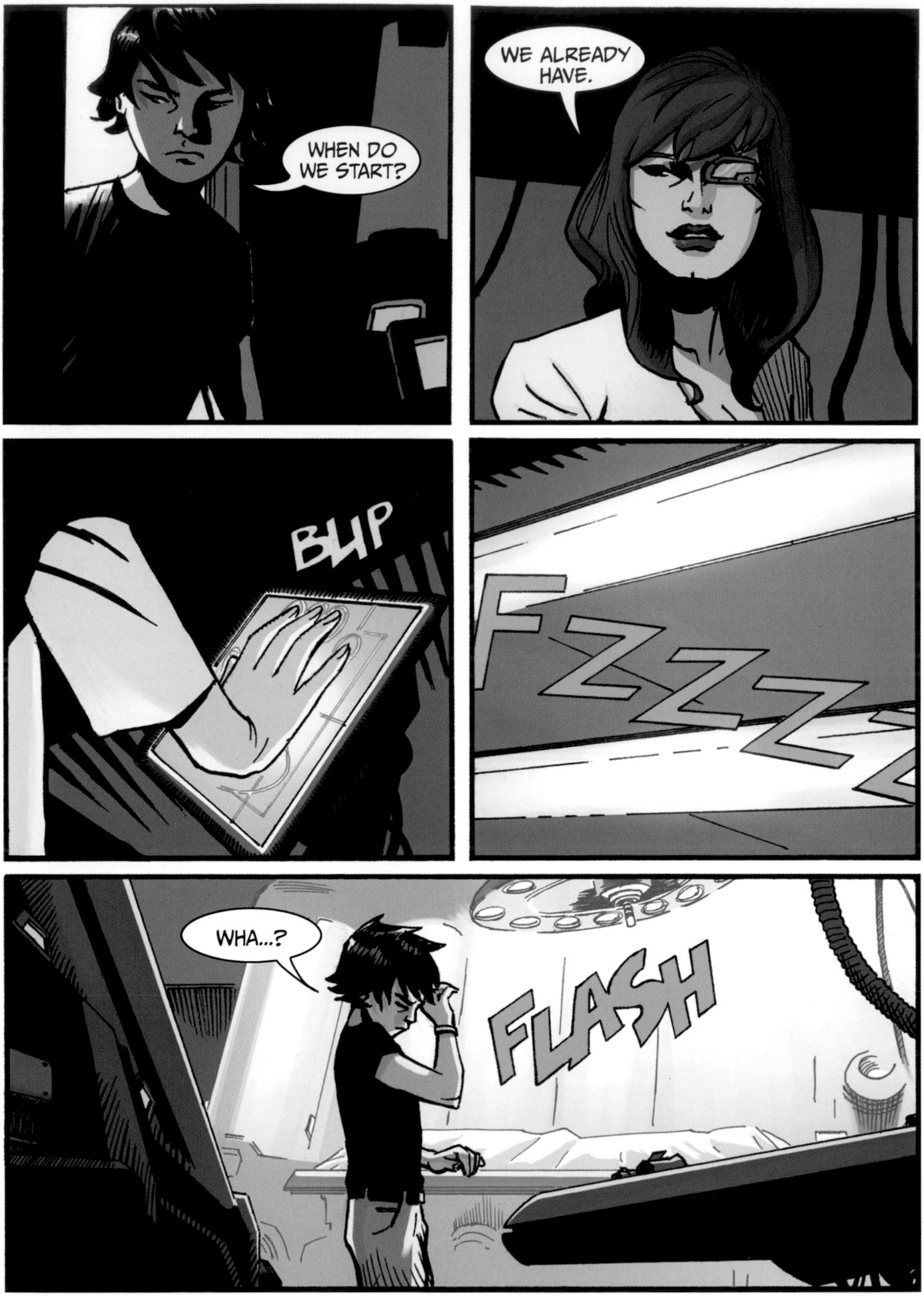
WHEN DO WE START?
WE ALREADY HAVE.
BLIP
FZZZZZ
WHA...?
FLASH

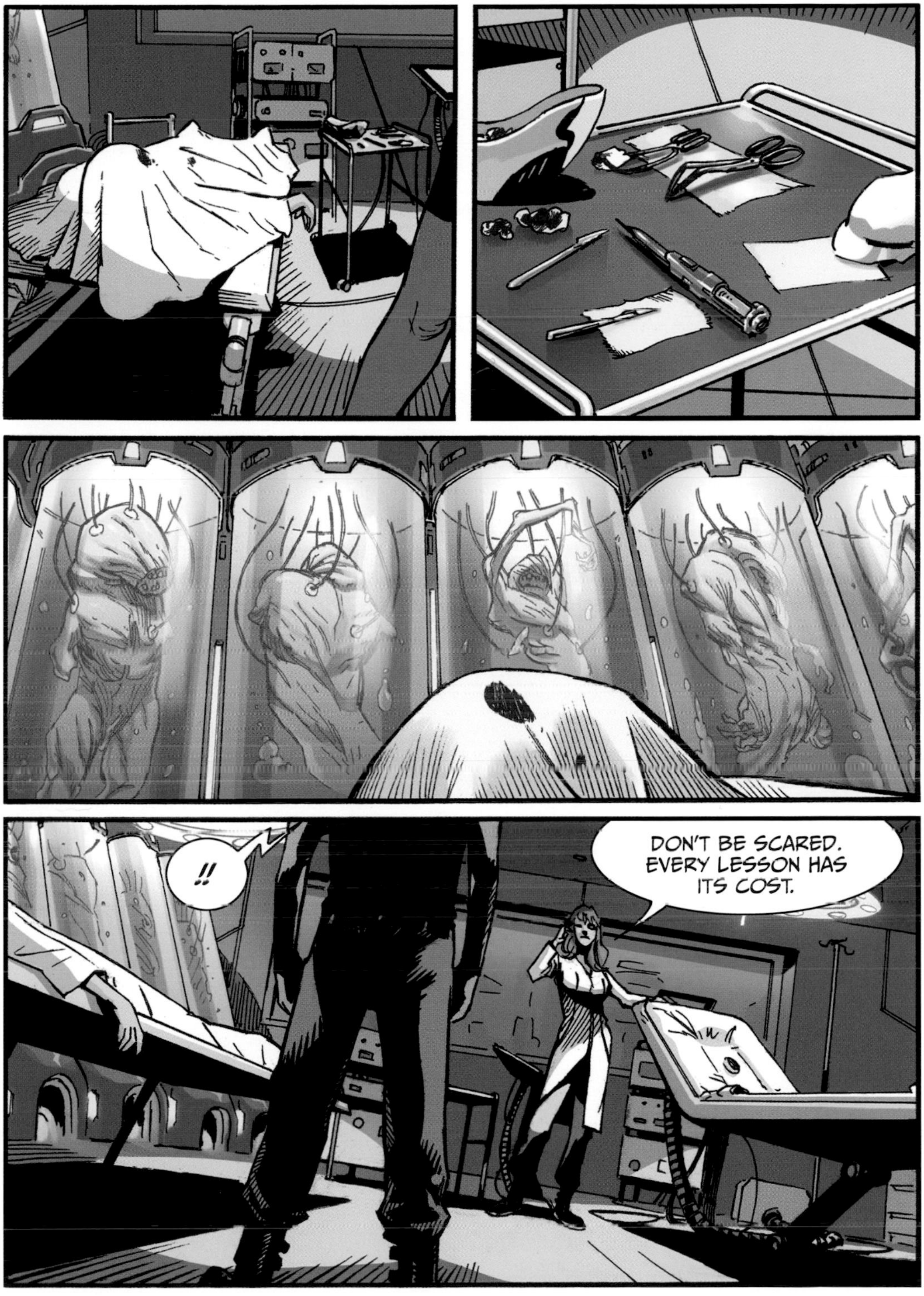
!!
DON'T BE SCARED. EVERY LESSON HAS ITS COST.

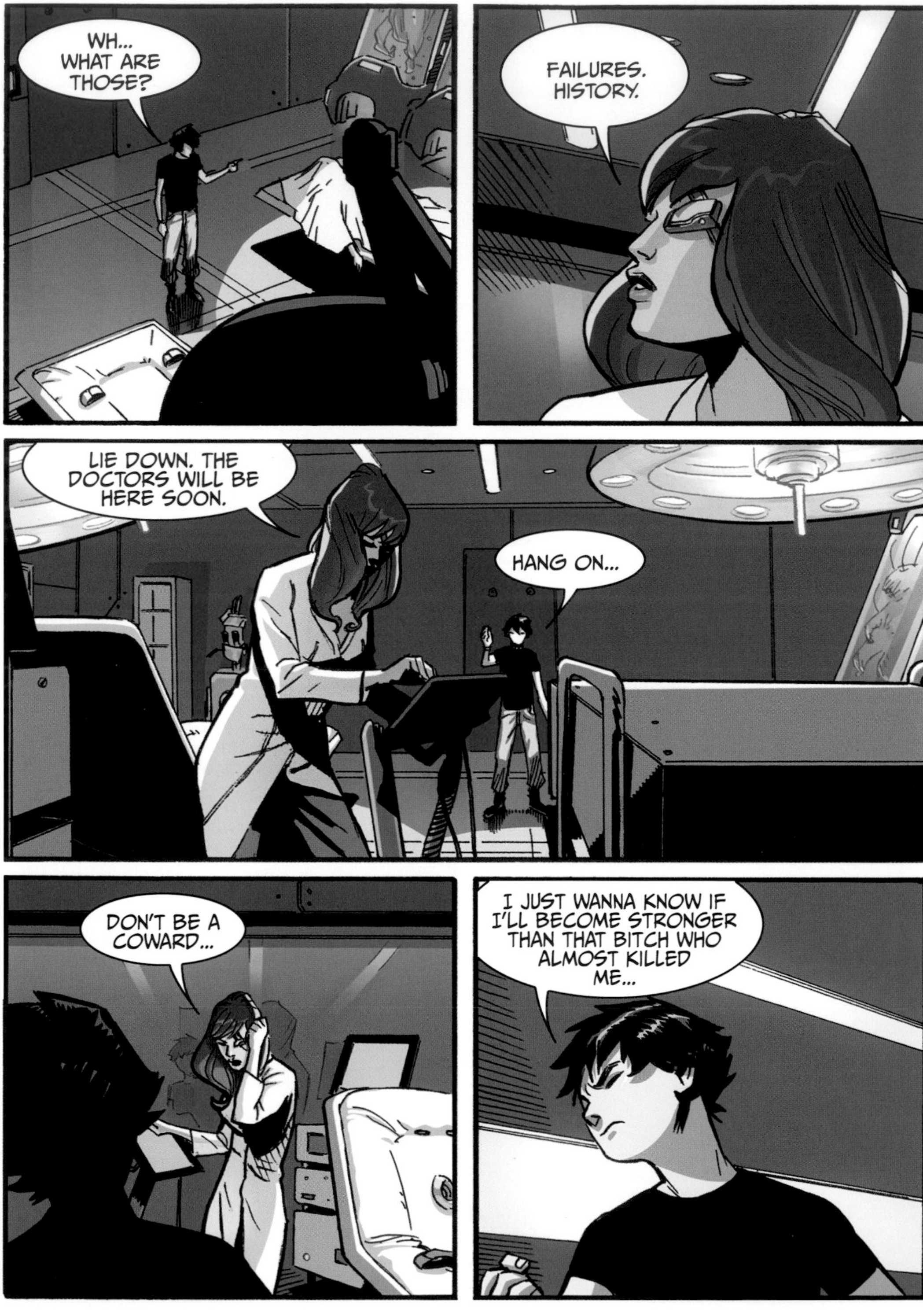
WH... WHAT ARE THOSE?
FAILURES. HISTORY.
LIE DOWN. THE DOCTORS WILL BE HERE SOON.
HANG ON...
DON'T BE A COWARD...
I JUST WANNA KNOW IF I'LL BECOME STRONGER THAN THAT BITCH WHO ALMOST KILLED ME...

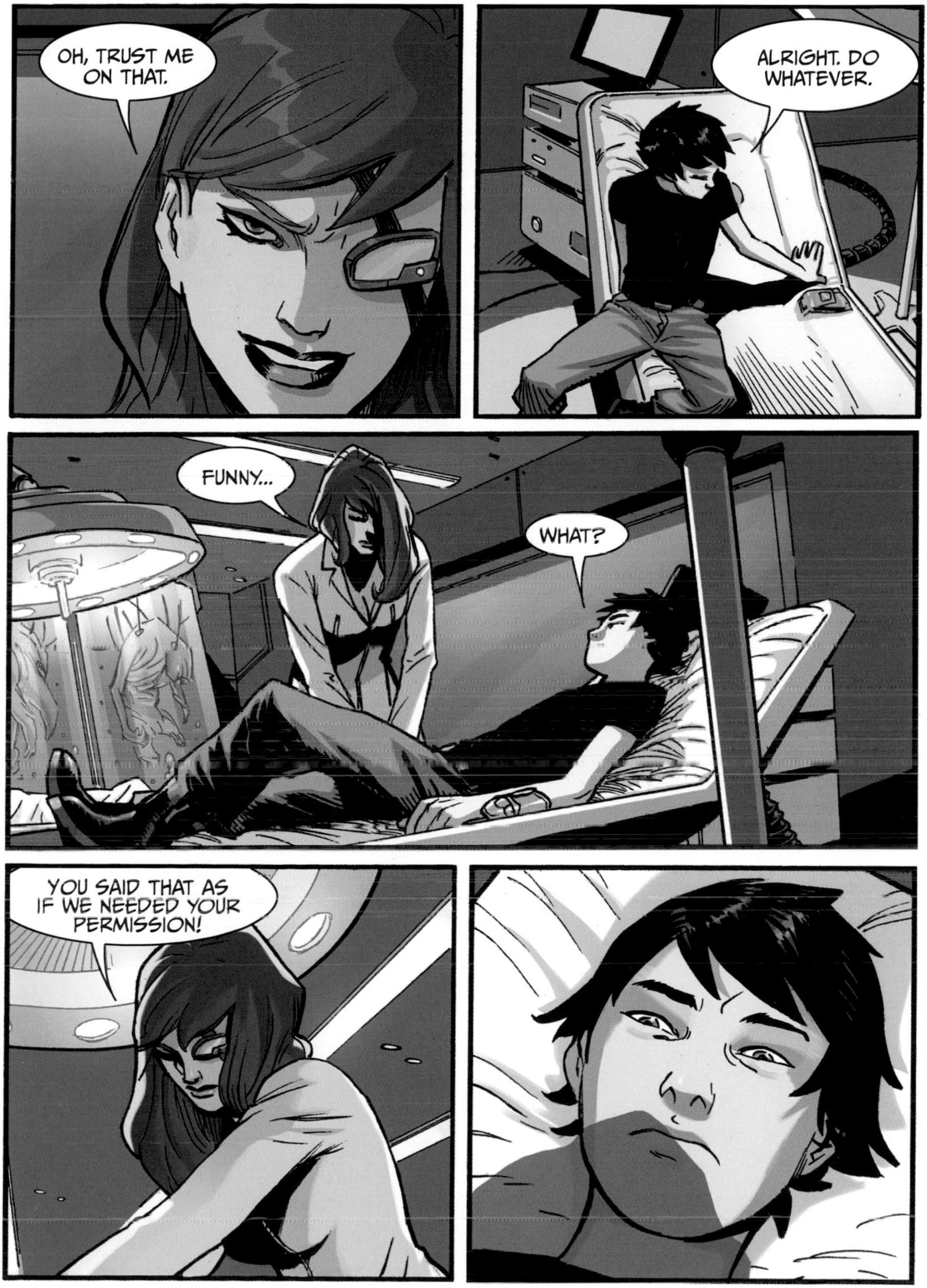
OH, TRUST ME ON THAT.
ALRIGHT. DO WHATEVER.
FUNNY...
WHAT?
YOU SAID THAT AS IF WE NEEDED YOUR PERMISSION!

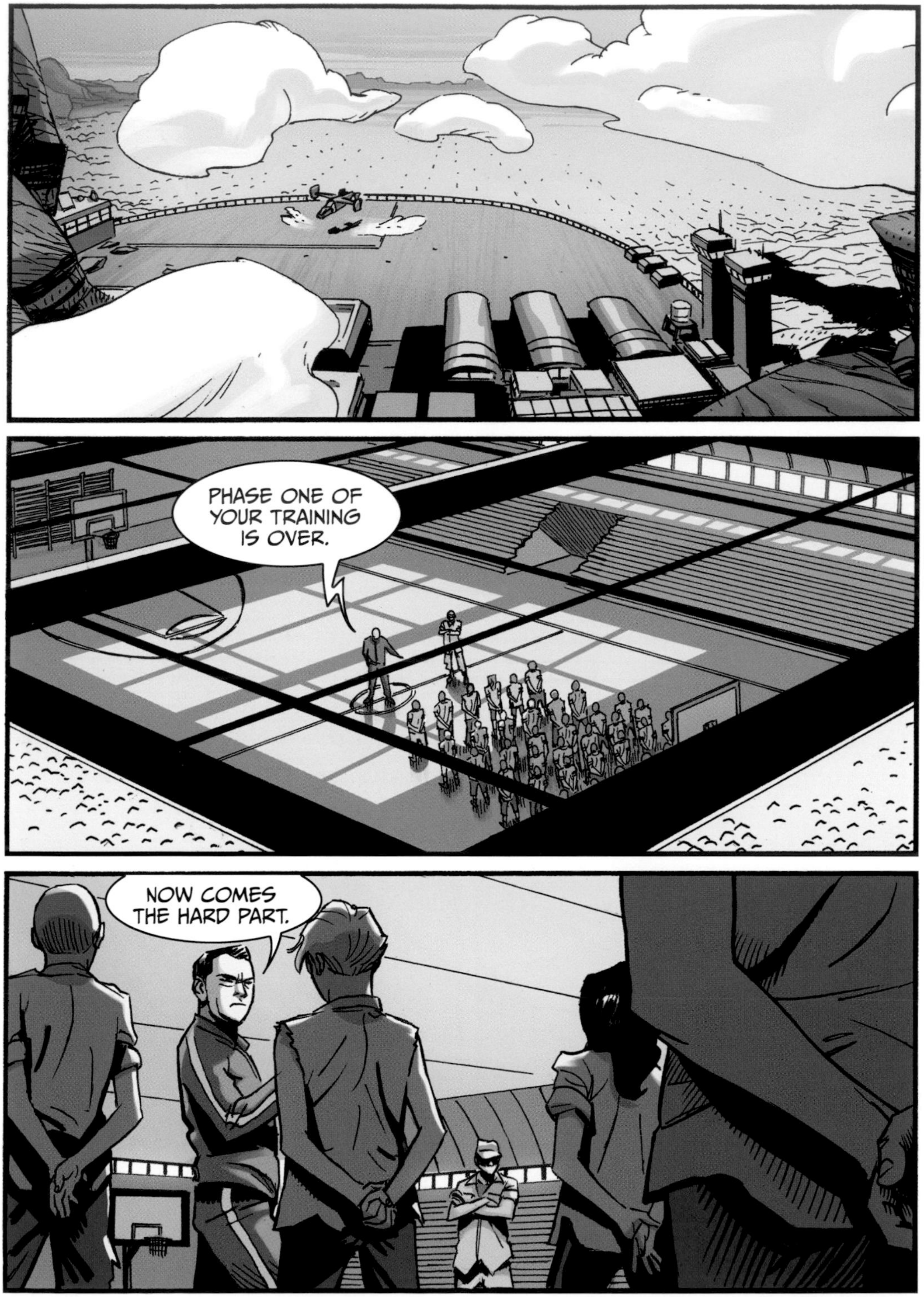
PHASE ONE OF YOUR TRAINING IS OVER.
NOW COMES THE HARD PART.

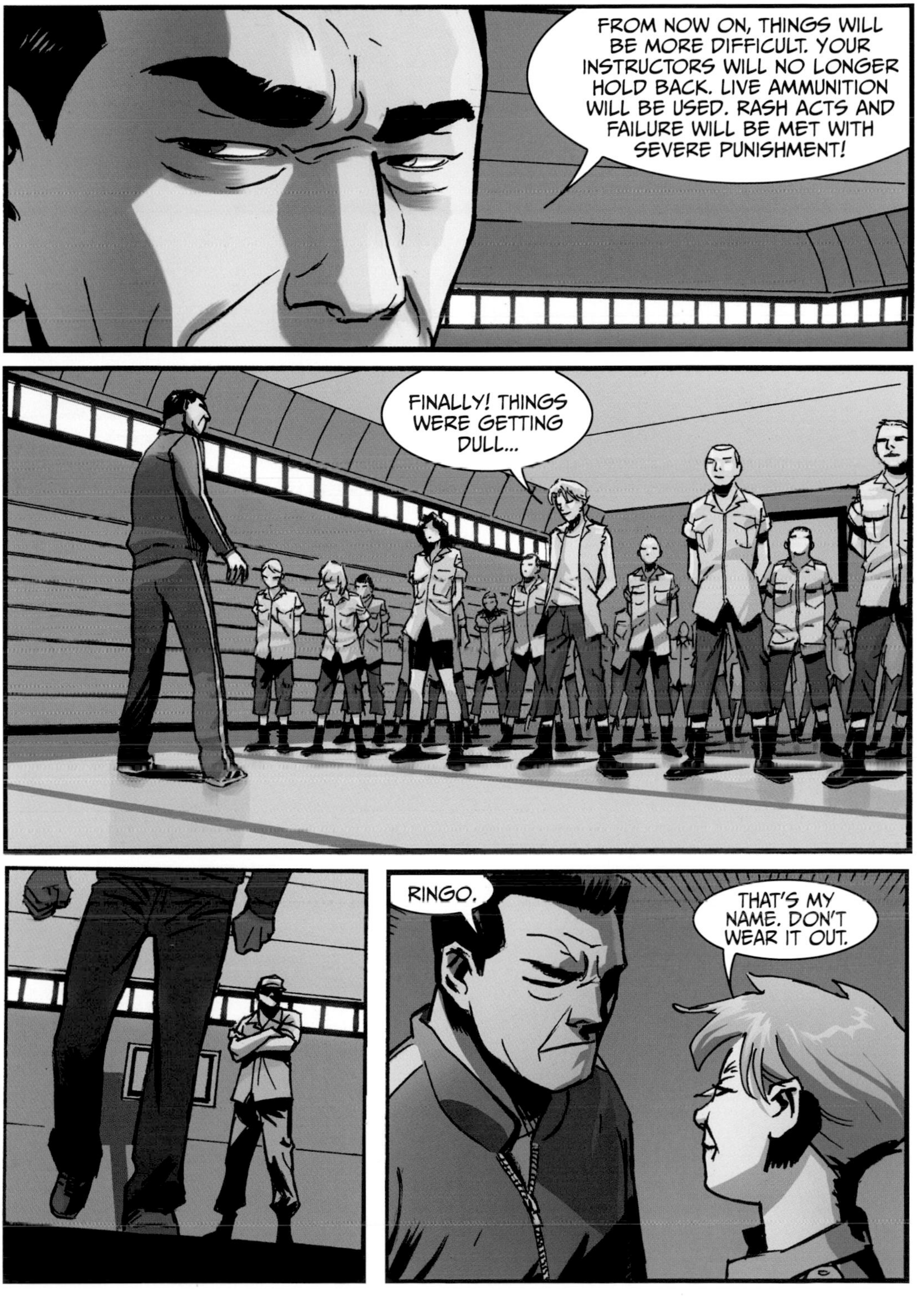
FROM NOW ON, THINGS WILL BE MORE DIFFICULT. YOUR INSTRUCTORS WILL NO LONGER HOLD BACK. LIVE AMMUNITION WILL BE USED. RASH ACTS AND FAILURE WILL BE MET WITH SEVERE PUNISHMENT!
FINALLY! THINGS WERE GETTING DULL...
RINGO.
THAT'S MY NAME. DON'T WEAR IT OUT.

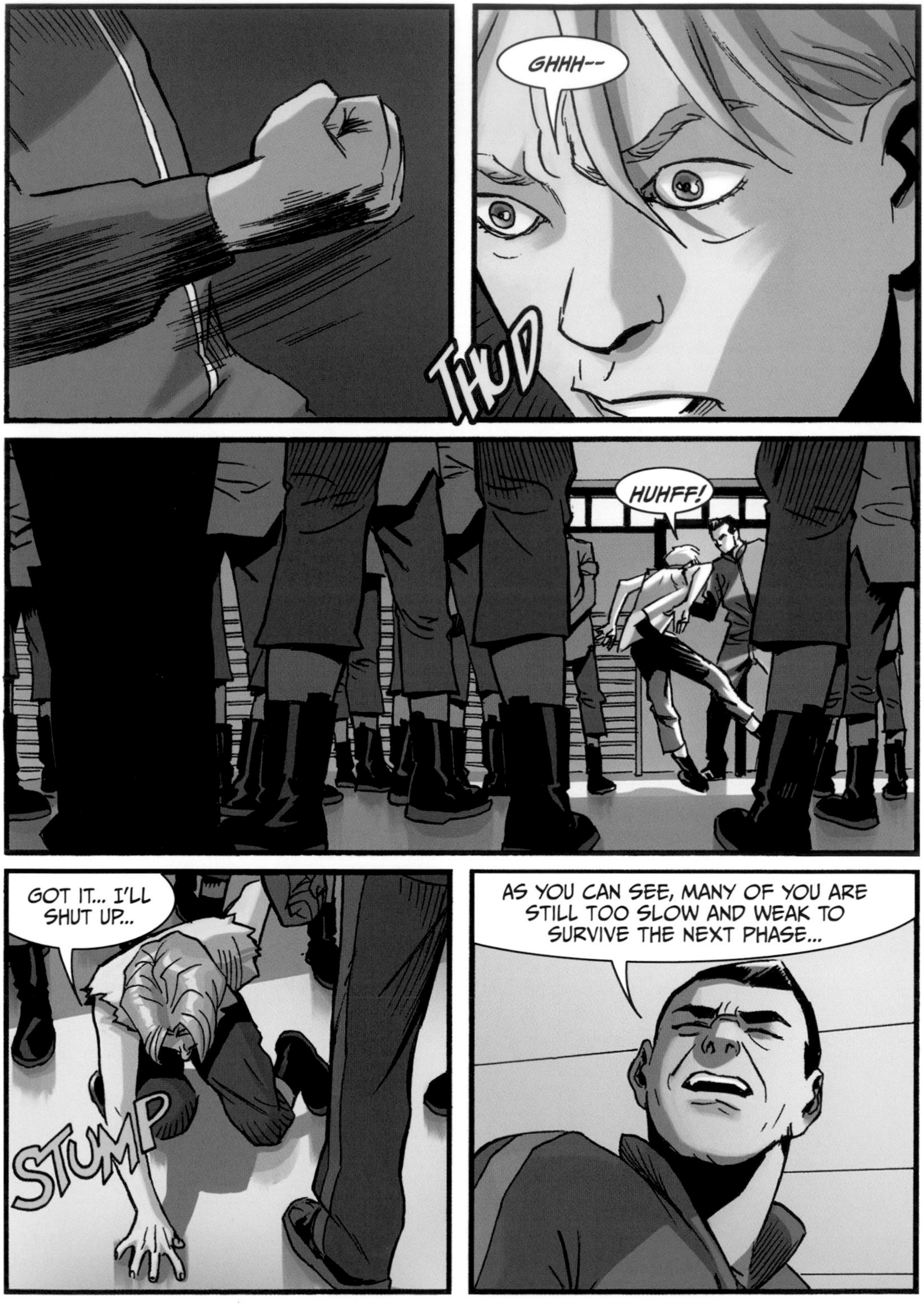
GHHH--
THUD
HUHFF!
GOT IT... I'LL SHUT UP...
STUMP
AS YOU CAN SEE, MANY OF YOU ARE STILL TOO SLOW AND WEAK TO SURVIVE THE NEXT PHASE...

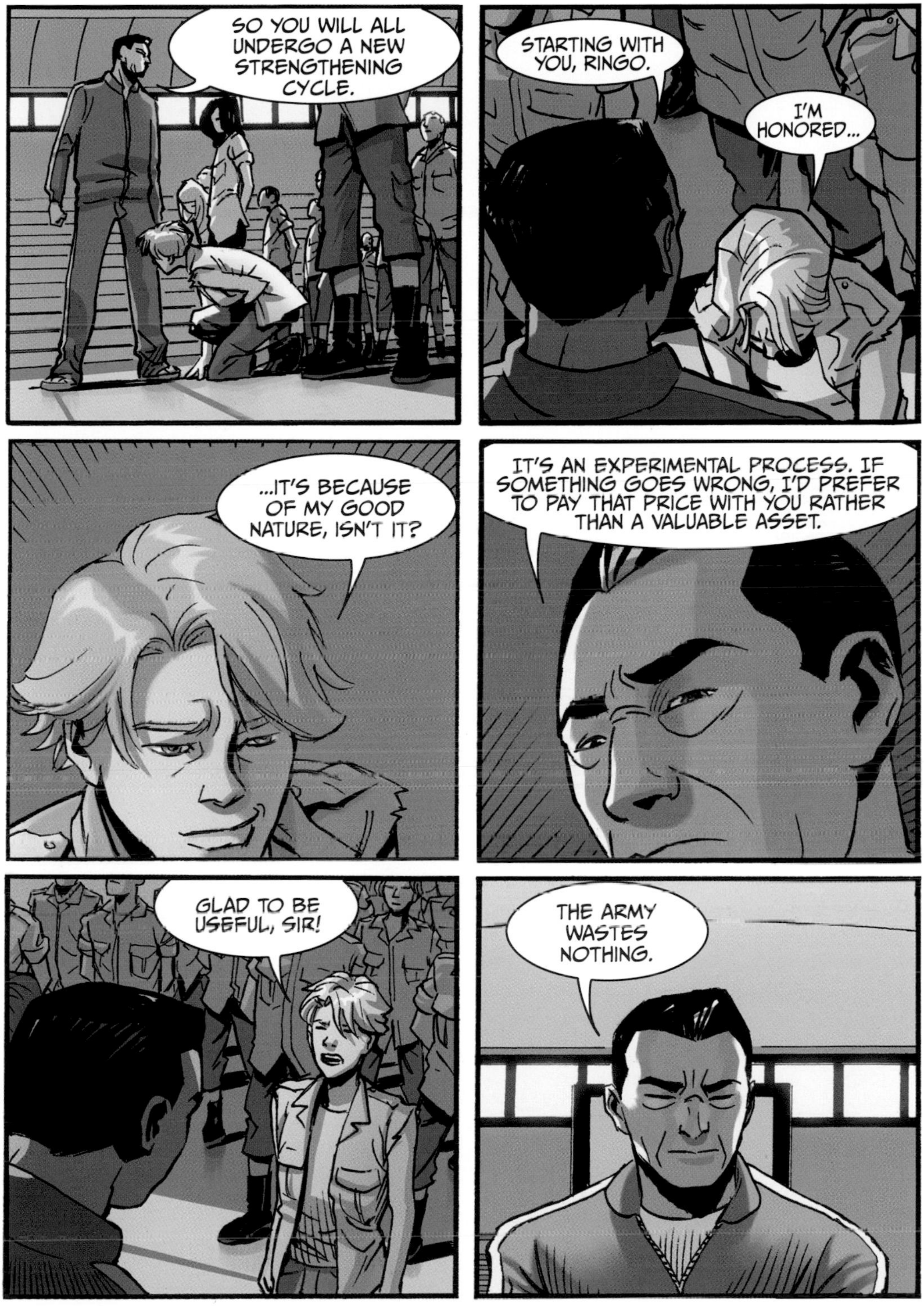
SO YOU WILL ALL UNDERGO A NEW STRENGTHENING CYCLE.
STARTING WITH YOU, RINGO.
I'M HONORED...
...IT'S BECAUSE OF MY GOOD NATURE, ISN'T IT?
IT'S AN EXPERIMENTAL PROCESS. IF SOMETHING GOES WRONG, I'D PREFER TO PAY THAT PRICE WITH YOU RATHER THAN A VALUABLE ASSET.
GLAD TO BE USEFUL, SIR!
THE ARMY WASTES NOTHING.

ECG

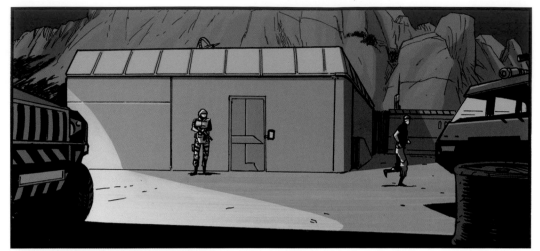

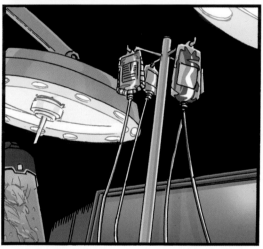

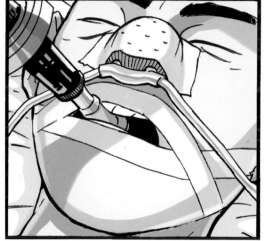

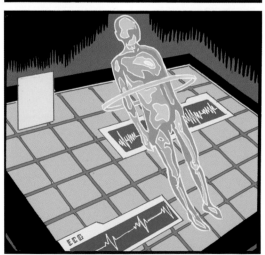

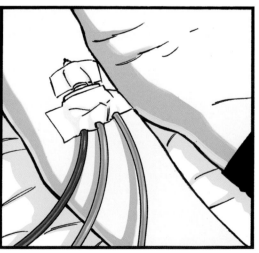

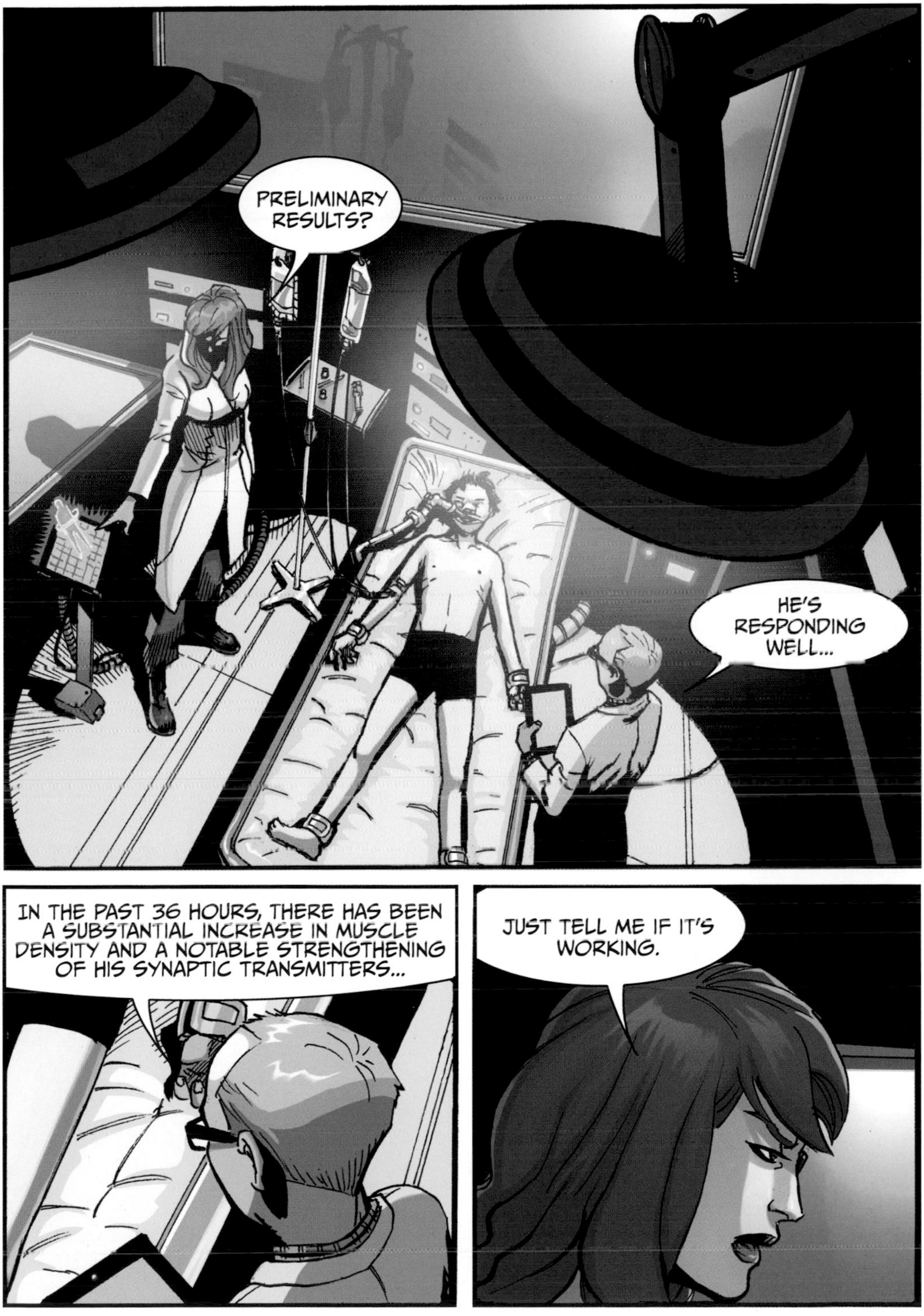
PRELIMINARY RESULTS?
HE'S RESPONDING WELL...
IN THE PAST 36 HOURS, THERE HAS BEEN A SUBSTANTIAL INCREASE IN MUSCLE DENSITY AND A NOTABLE STRENGTHENING OF HIS SYNAPTIC TRANSMITTERS...
JUST TELL ME IF IT'S WORKING.

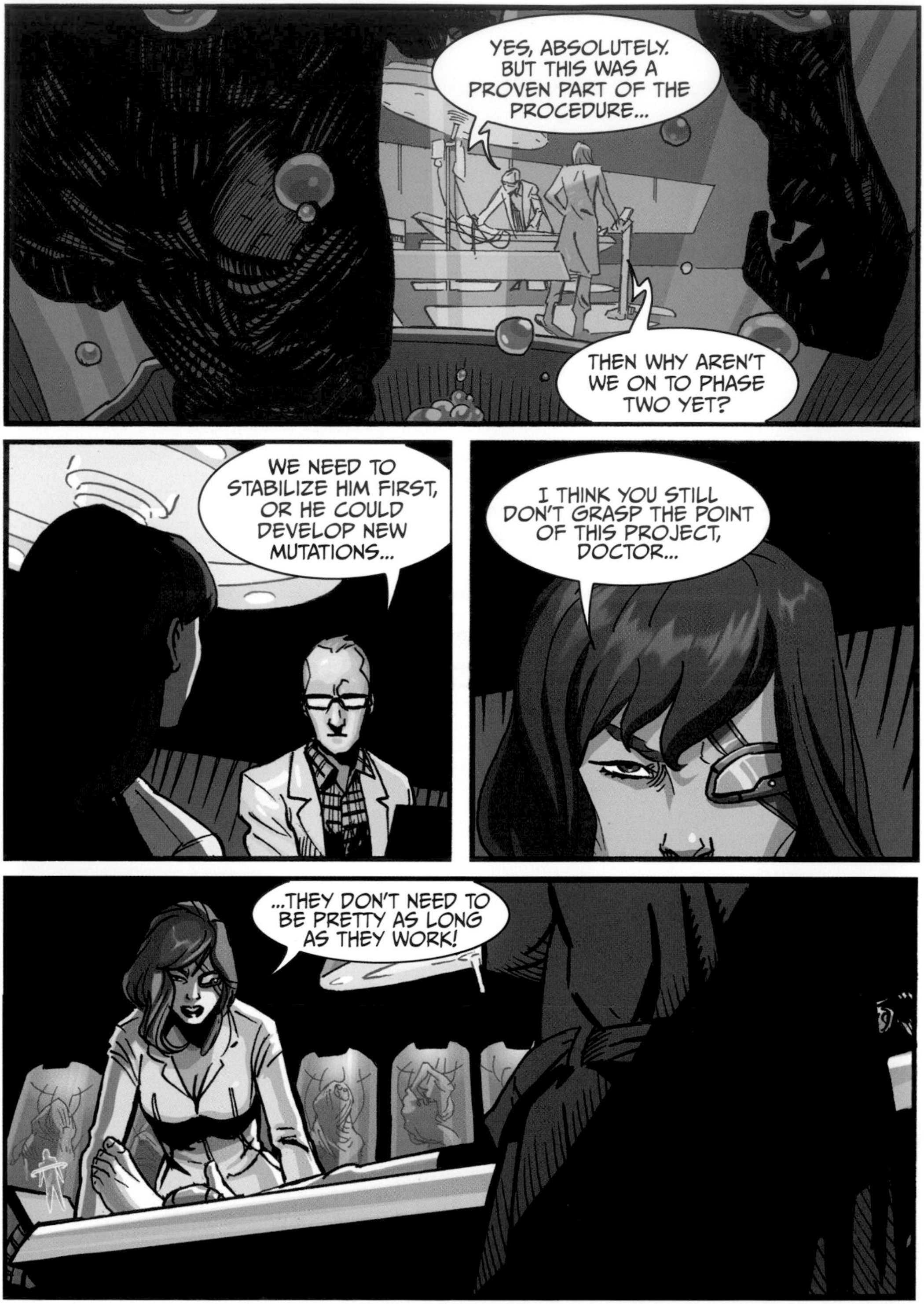
YES, ABSOLUTELY. BUT THIS WAS A PROVEN PART OF THE PROCEDURE...
THEN WHY AREN'T WE ON TO PHASE TWO YET?
WE NEED TO STABILIZE HIM FIRST, OR HE COULD DEVELOP NEW MUTATIONS...
I THINK YOU STILL DON'T GRASP THE POINT OF THIS PROJECT, DOCTOR...
...THEY DON'T NEED TO BE PRETTY AS LONG AS THEY WORK!

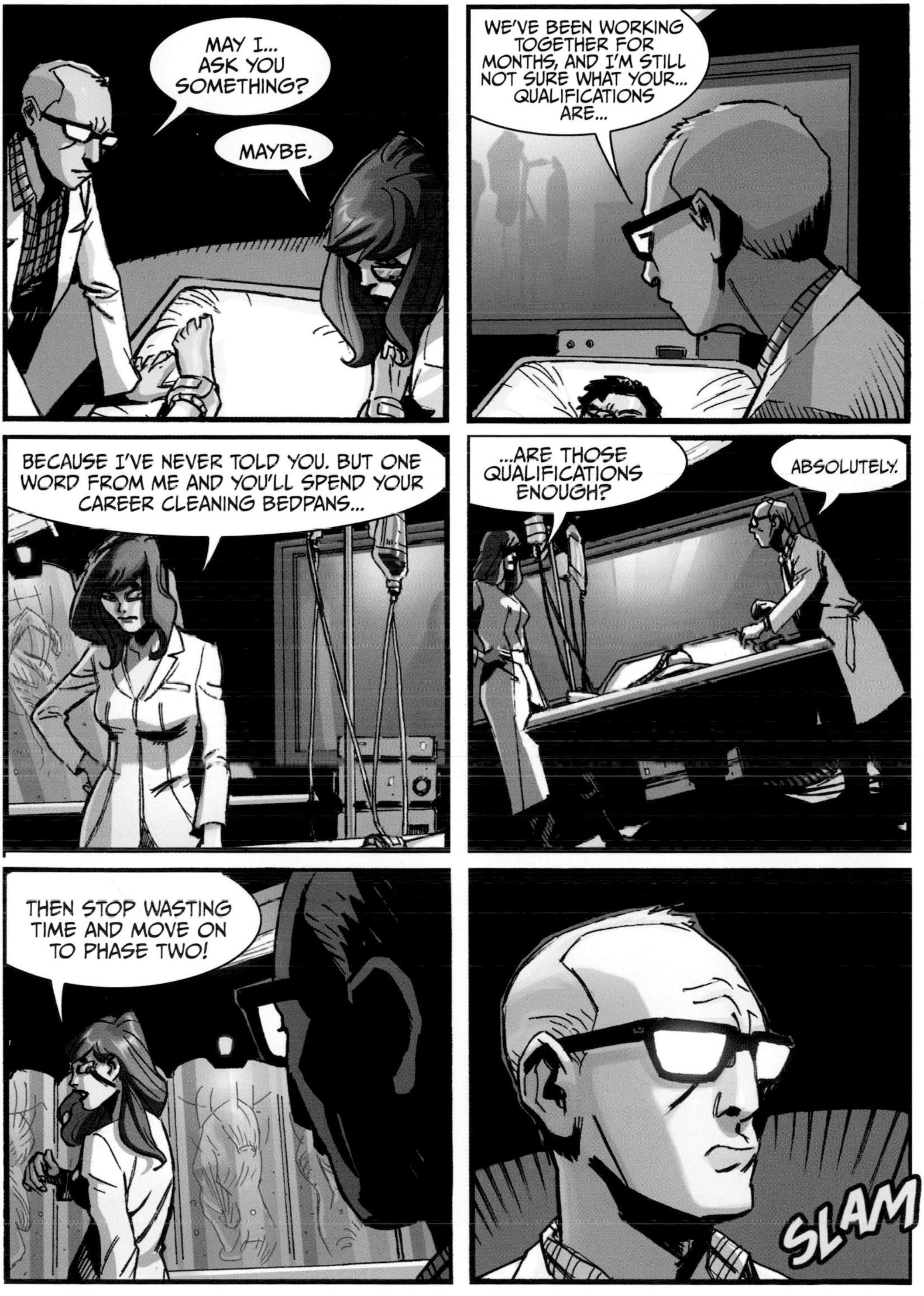
MAY I... ASK YOU SOMETHING?
MAYBE.
WE'VE BEEN WORKING TOGETHER FOR MONTHS, AND I'M STILL NOT SURE WHAT YOUR... QUALIFICATIONS ARE...
BECAUSE I'VE NEVER TOLD YOU. BUT ONE WORD FROM ME AND YOU'LL SPEND YOUR CAREER CLEANING BEDPANS...
...ARE THOSE QUALIFICATIONS ENOUGH?
ABSOLUTELY.
THEN STOP WASTING TIME AND MOVE ON TO PHASE TWO!
SLAM

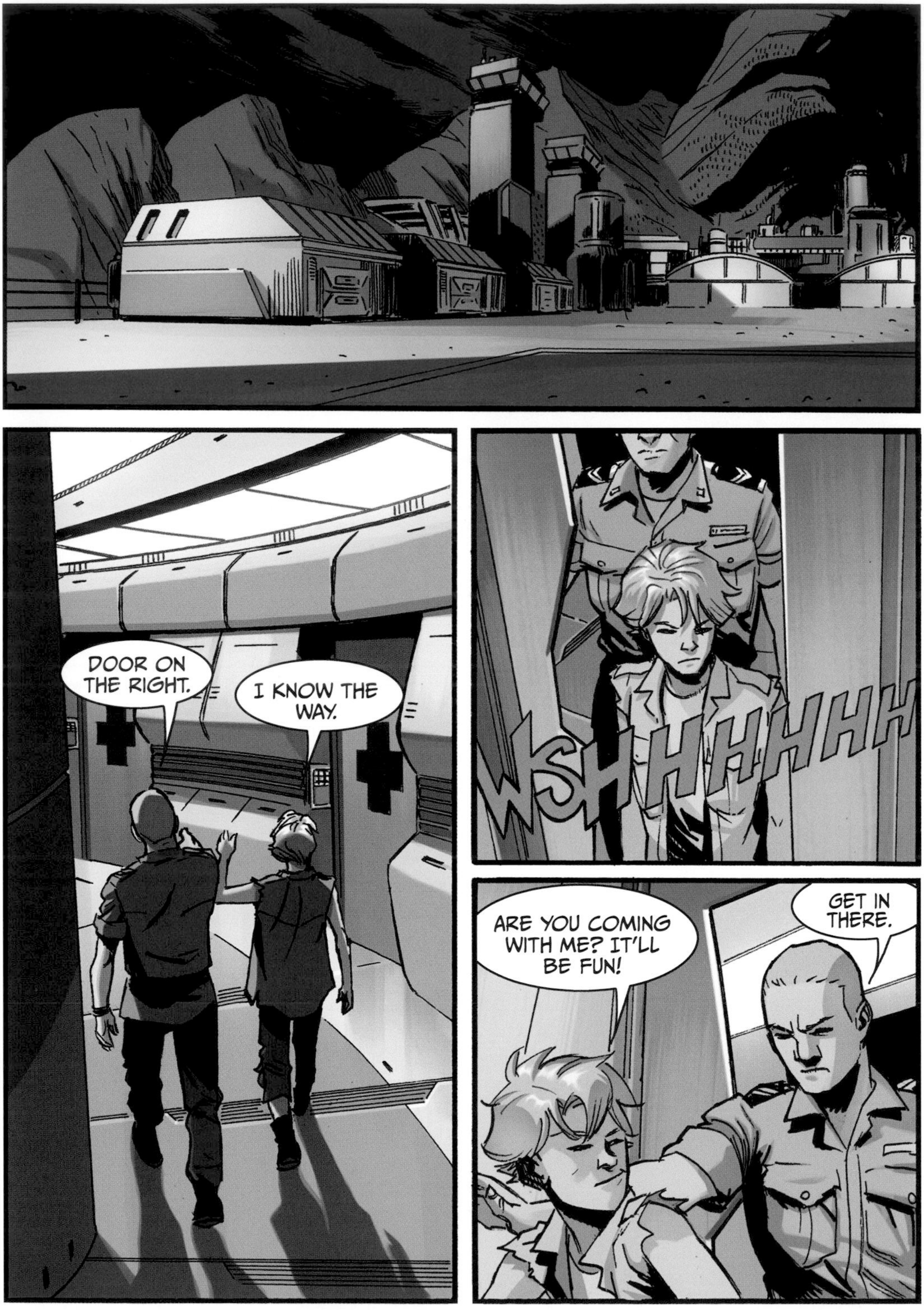
DOOR ON THE RIGHT.
I KNOW THE WAY.
WSHHHHHH
ARE YOU COMING WITH ME? IT'LL BE FUN!
GET IN THERE.

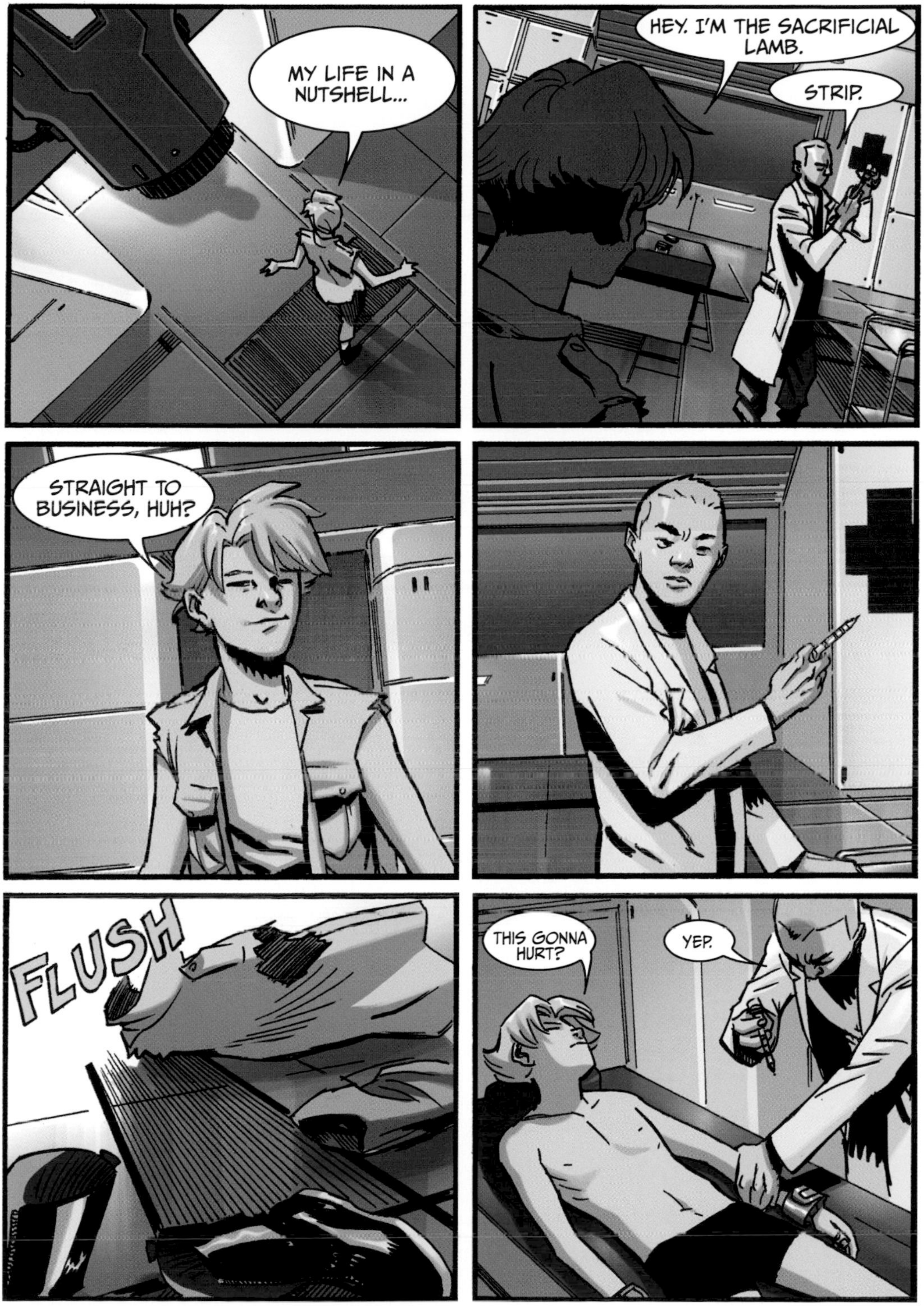
MY LIFE IN A NUTSHELL...
HEY. I'M THE SACRIFICIAL LAMB.
STRIP.
STRAIGHT TO BUSINESS, HUH?
FLUSH
THIS GONNA HURT?
YEP.

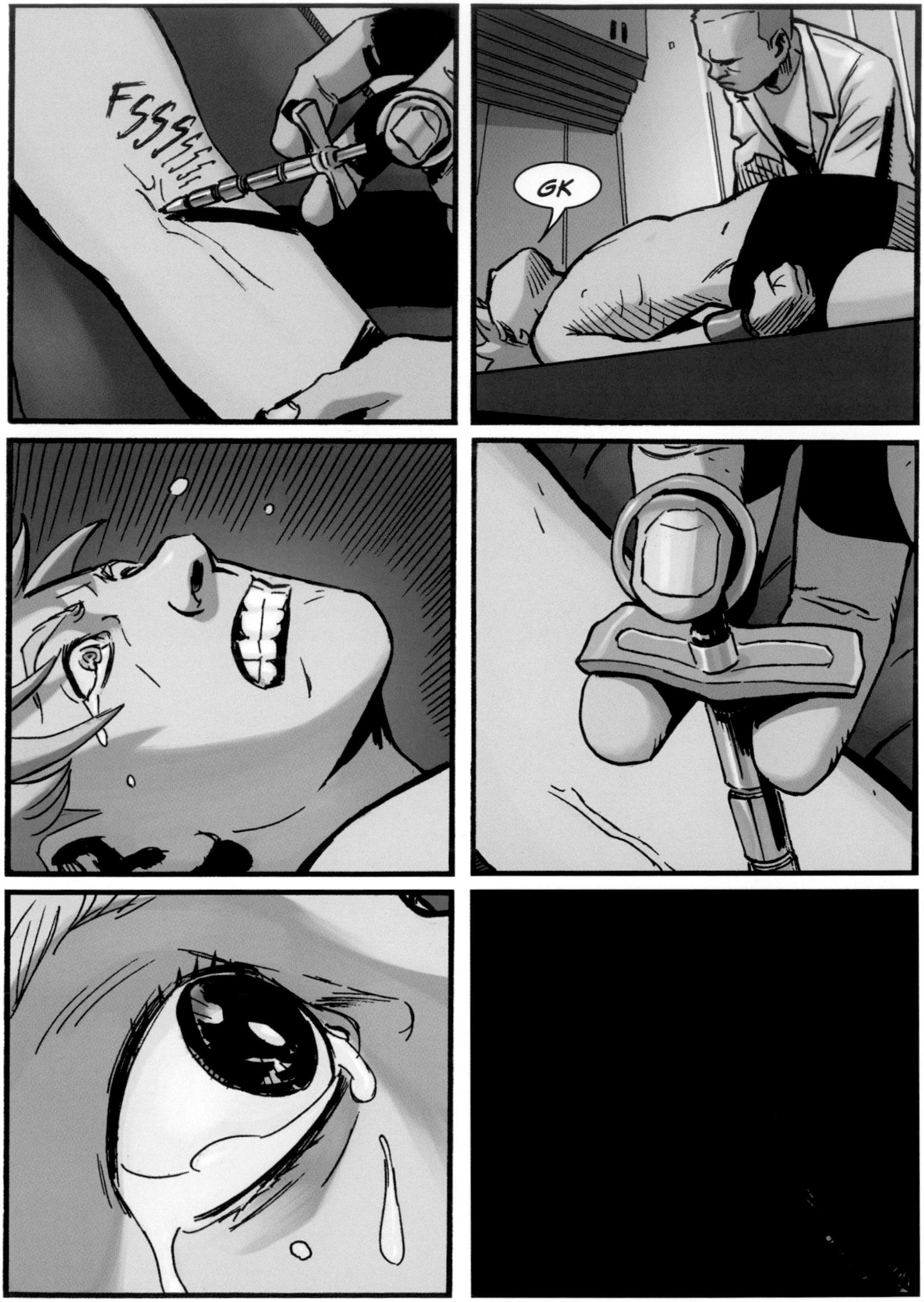
FSSSSSS
GK

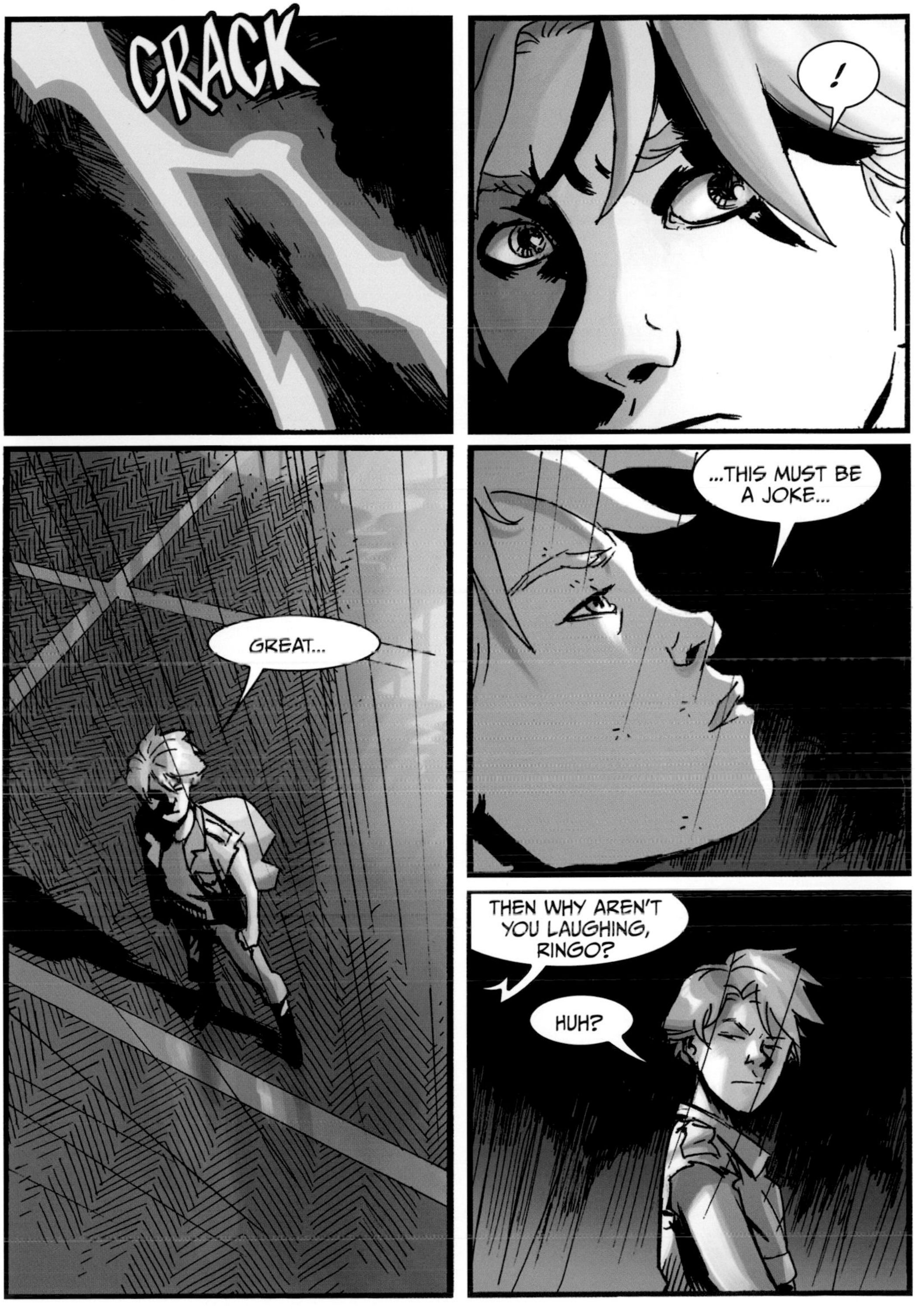
CRACK
!
GREAT...
...THIS MUST BE A JOKE...
THEN WHY AREN'T YOU LAUGHING, RINGO?
HUH?

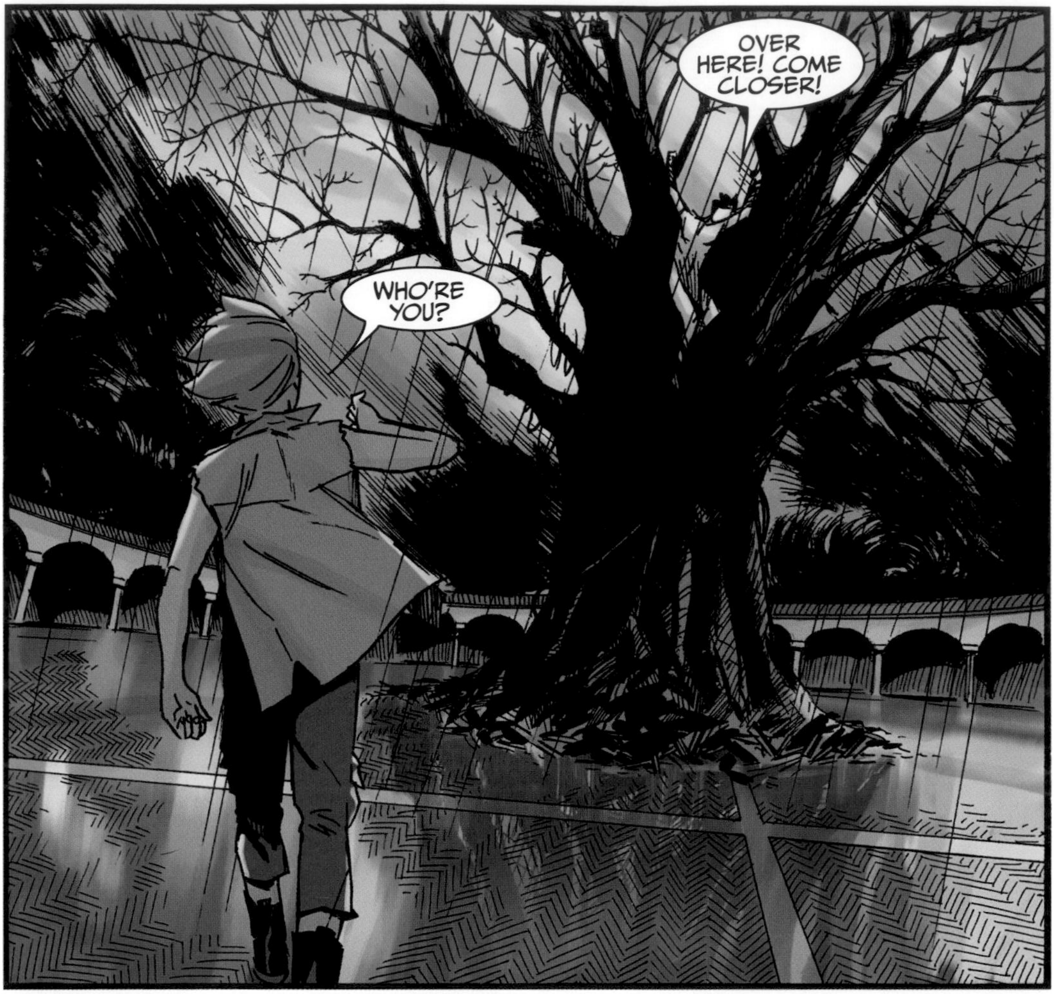
OVER HERE! COME CLOSER!
WHO'RE YOU?

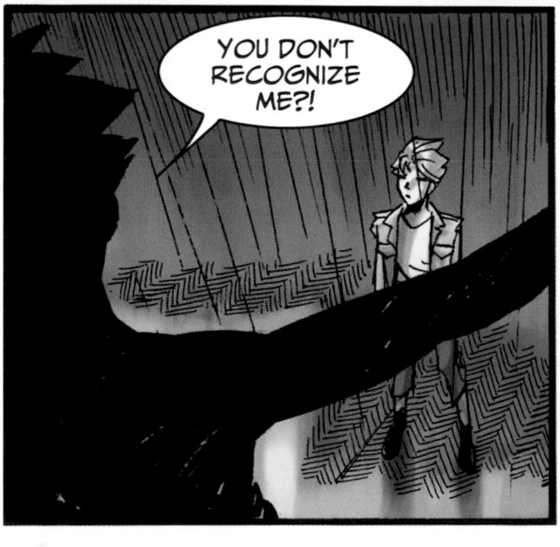
YOU DON'T RECOGNIZE ME?!

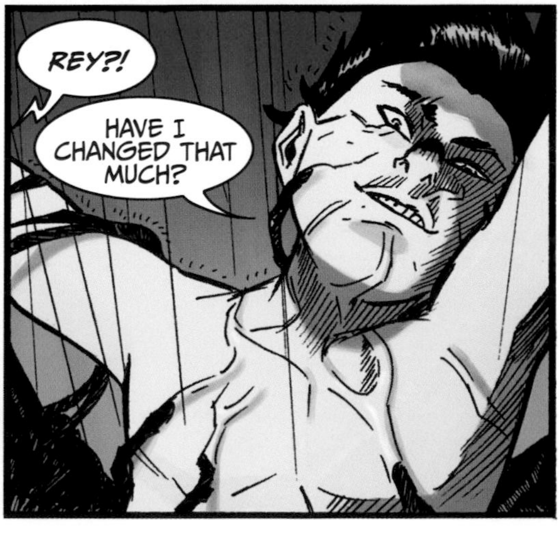
REY?!
HAVE I CHANGED THAT MUCH?

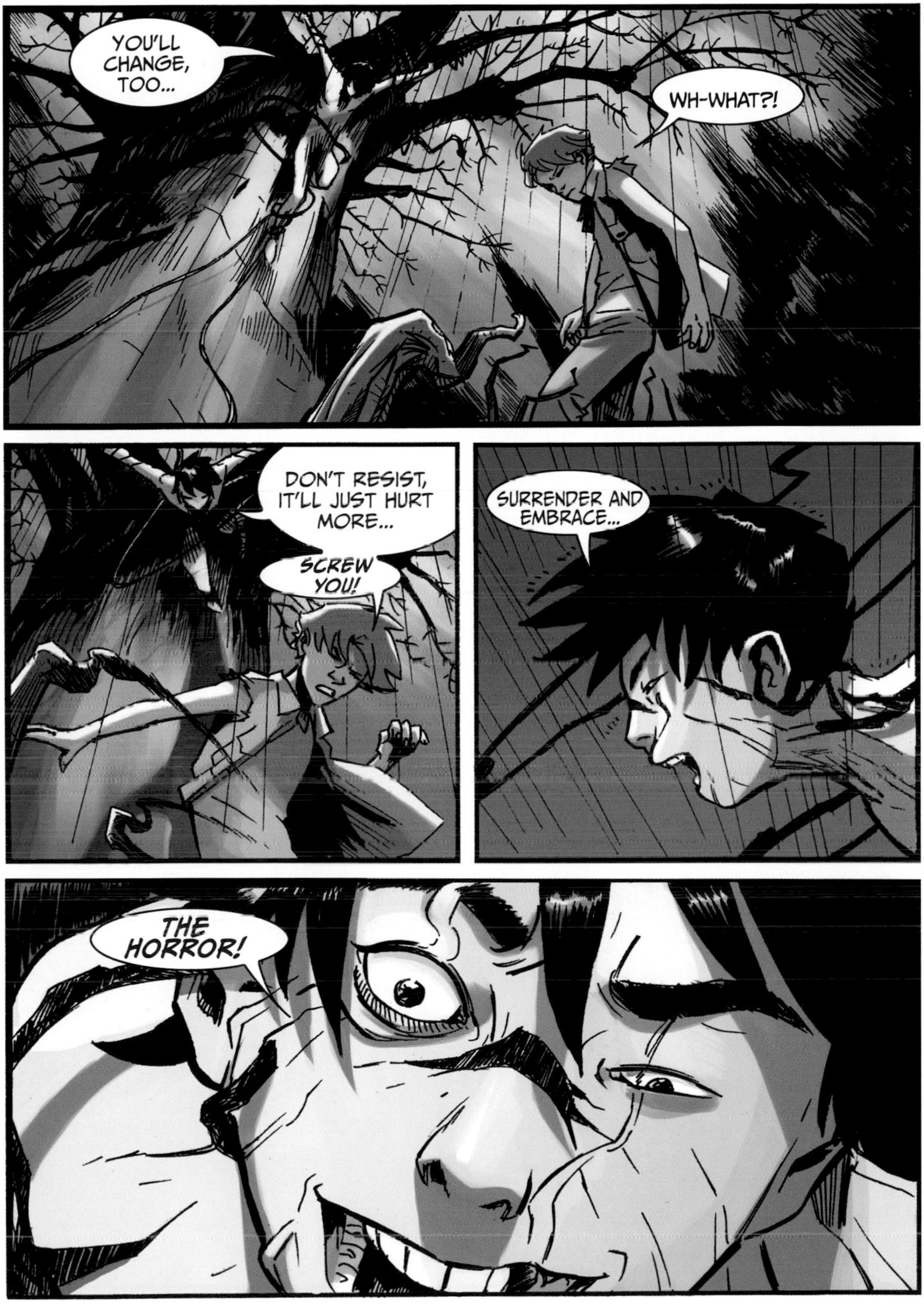
YOU'LL CHANGE, TOO...
WH-WHAT?!
DON'T RESIST, IT'LL JUST HURT MORE...
SCREW YOU!
SURRENDER AND EMBRACE...
THE HORROR!

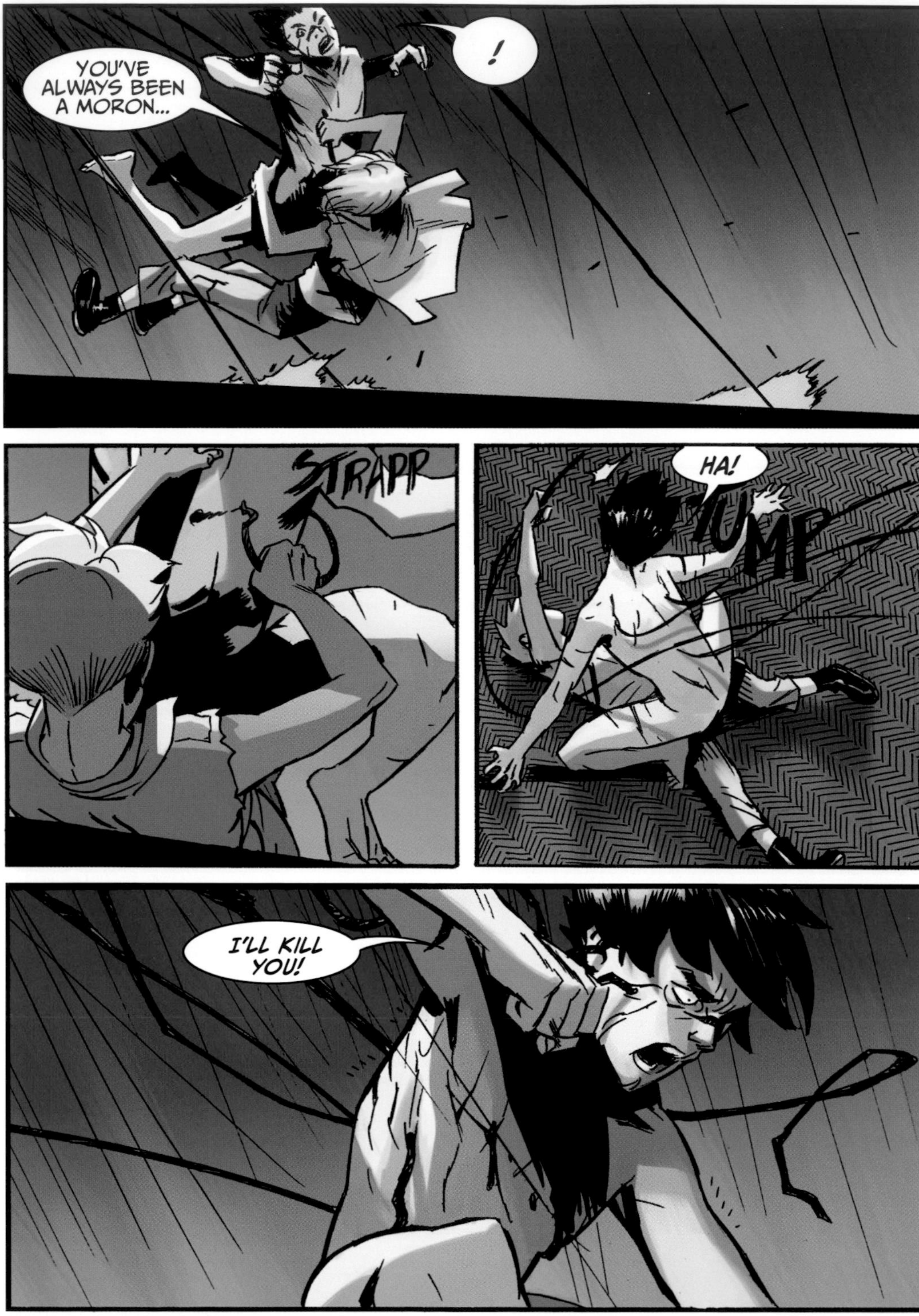
YOU'VE ALWAYS BEEN A MORON...
!
STRAPP
HA!
TUMP
I'LL KILL YOU!

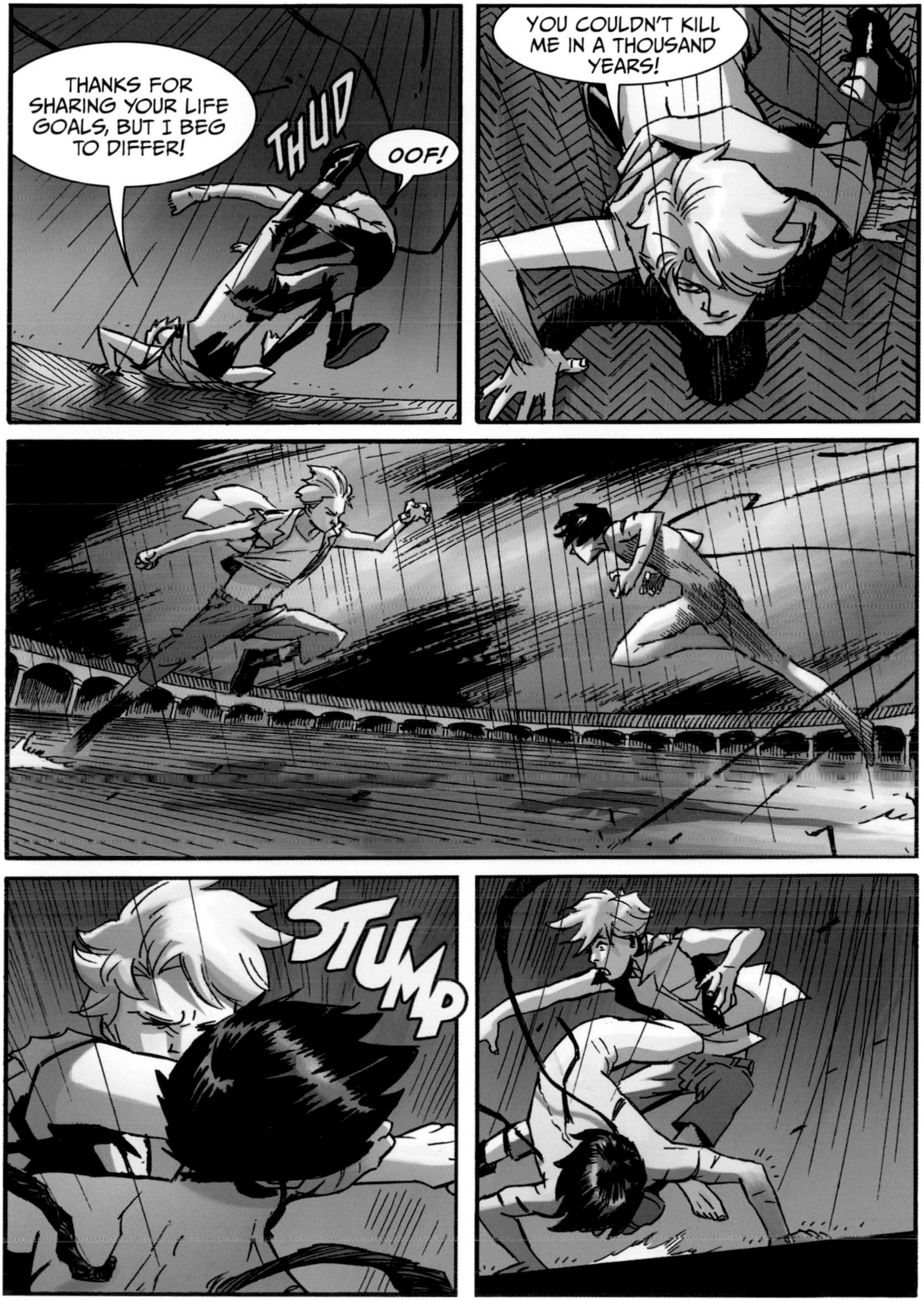
THANKS FOR SHARING YOUR LIFE GOALS, BUT I BEG TO DIFFER!
THUD
OOF!
YOU COULDN'T KILL ME IN A THOUSAND YEARS!
STUMP

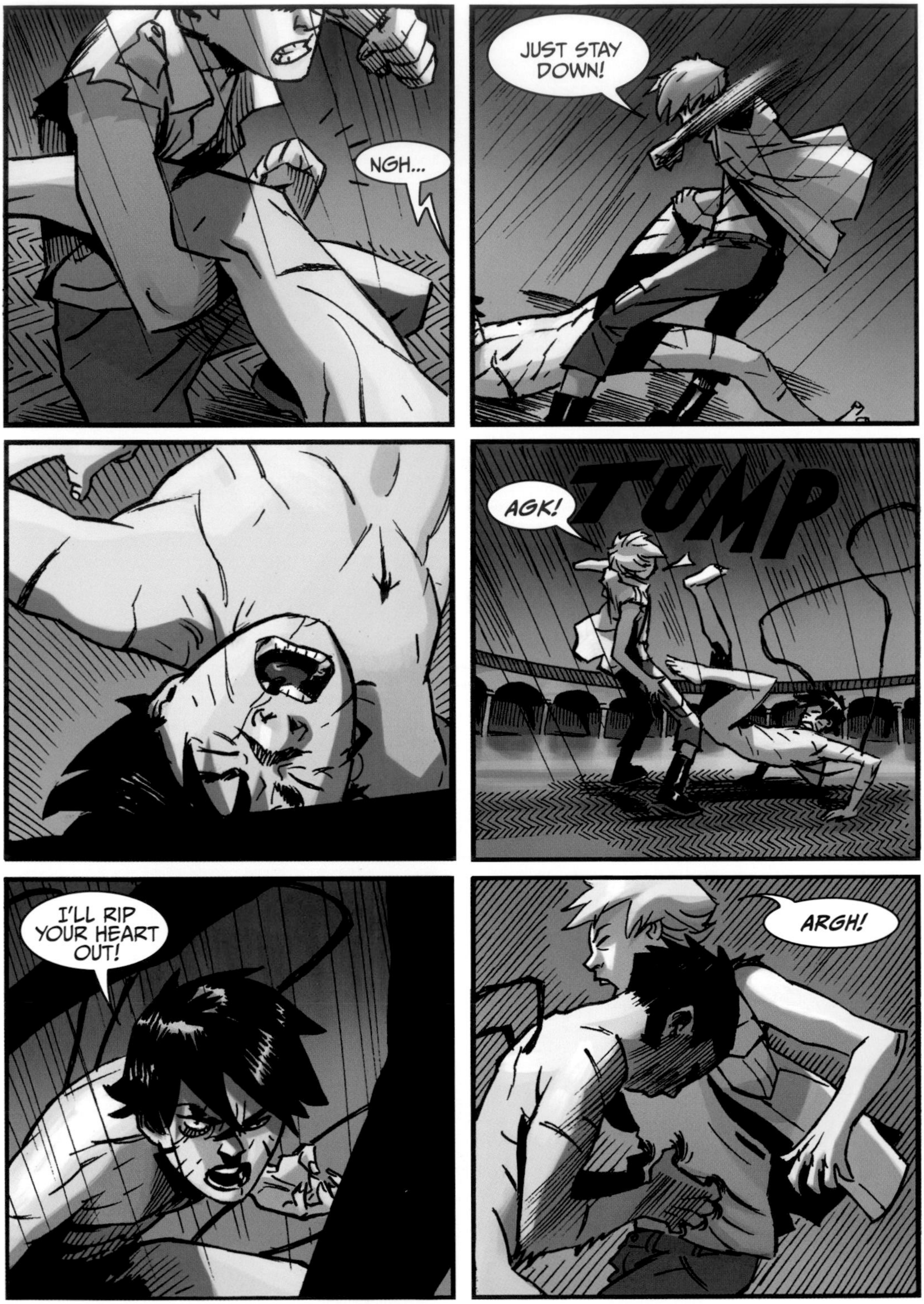
NGH...
JUST STAY DOWN!
AGK!
TUMP
I'LL RIP YOUR HEART OUT!
ARGH!

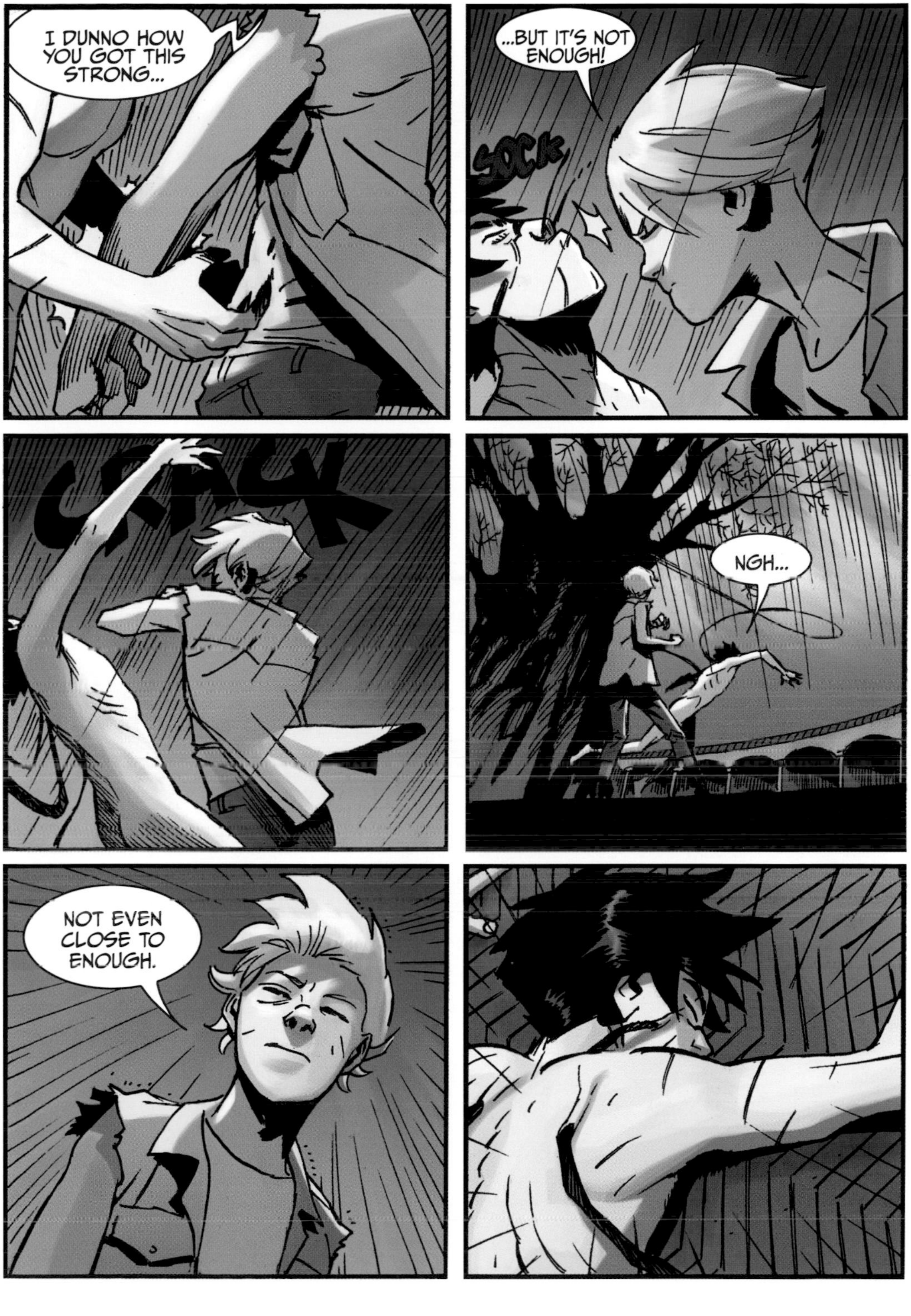
I DUNNO HOW YOU GOT THIS STRONG...
...BUT IT'S NOT ENOUGH!
SOCK
CRACK
NGH...
NOT EVEN CLOSE TO ENOUGH.

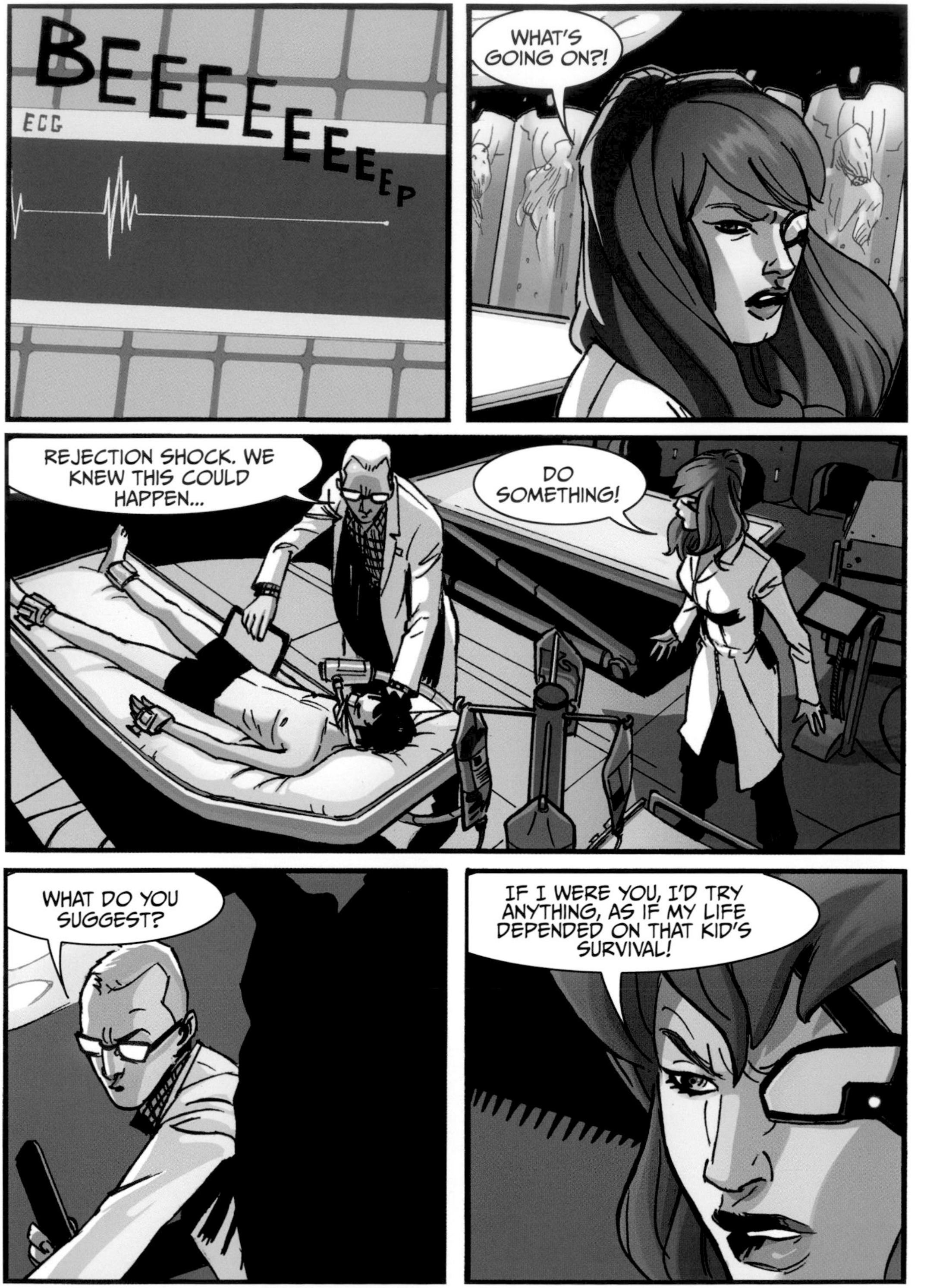
BEEEEEEEEEP
ECG
WHAT'S GOING ON?!
REJECTION SHOCK. WE KNEW THIS COULD HAPPEN...
DO SOMETHING!
WHAT DO YOU SUGGEST?
IF I WERE YOU, I'D TRY ANYTHING, AS IF MY LIFE DEPENDED ON THAT KID'S SURVIVAL!

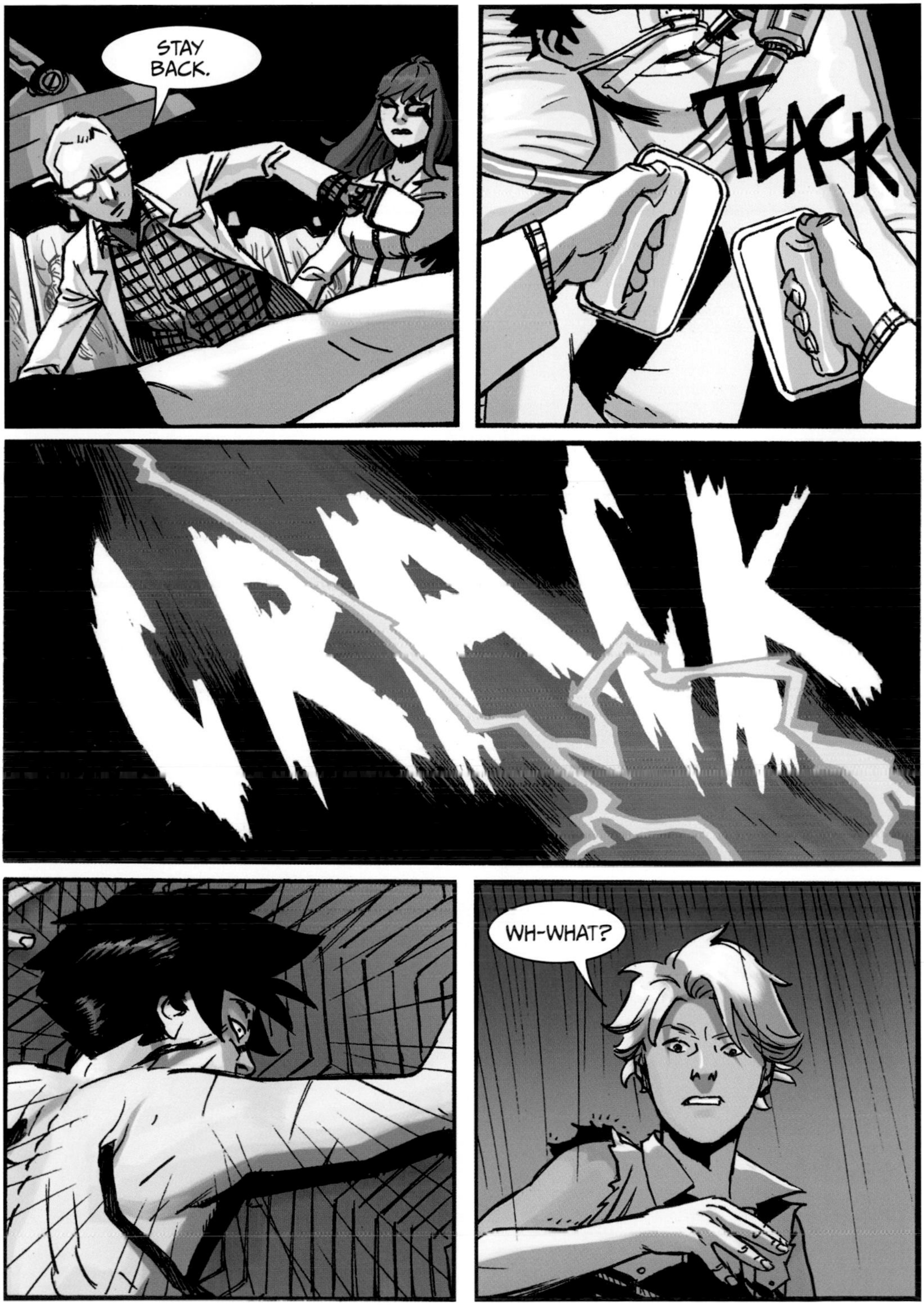
STAY BACK.
TLACK
CRAACK
WH-WHAT?

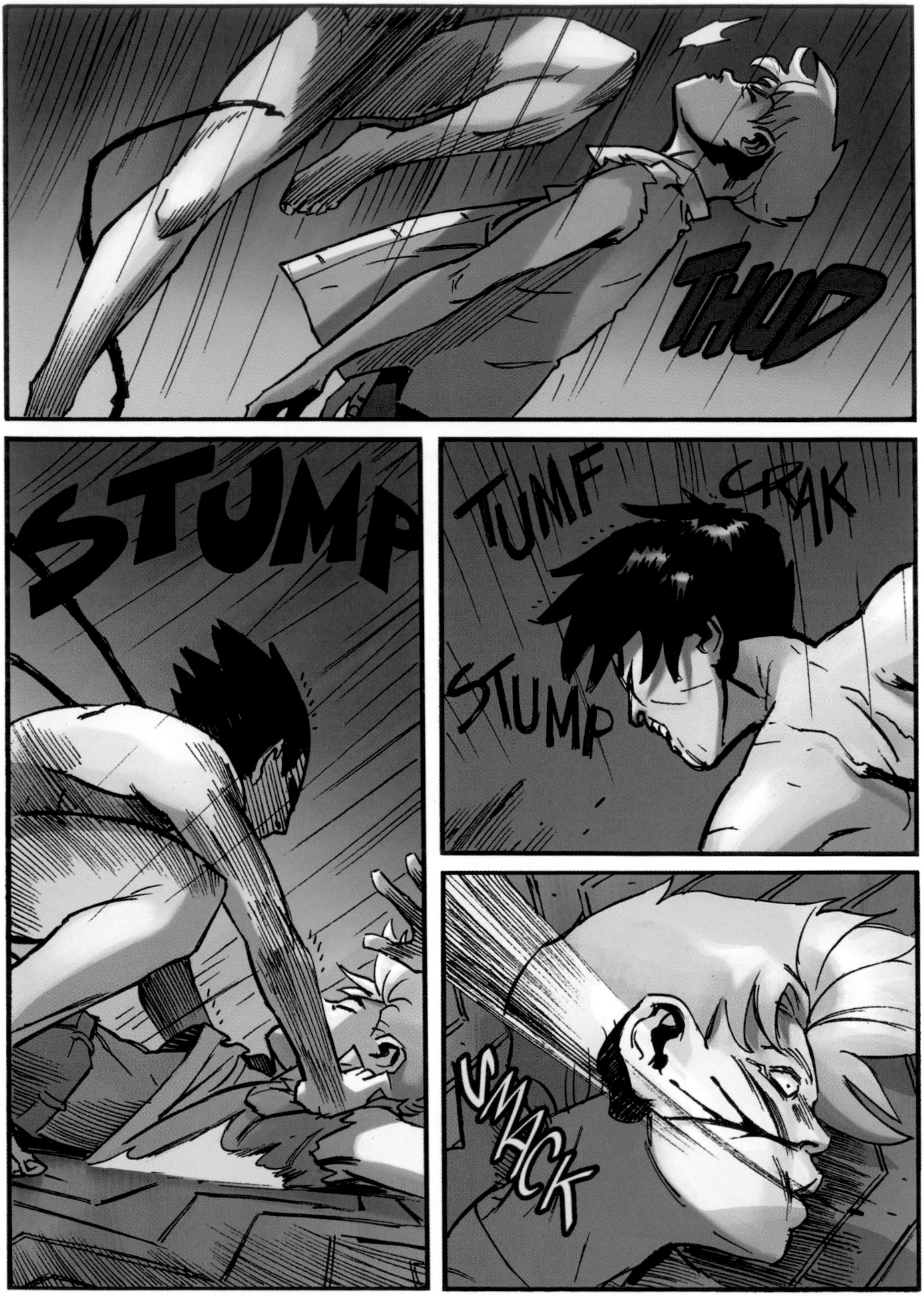
THUD
STUMP
TUMF
CRAK
STUMP
SMACK

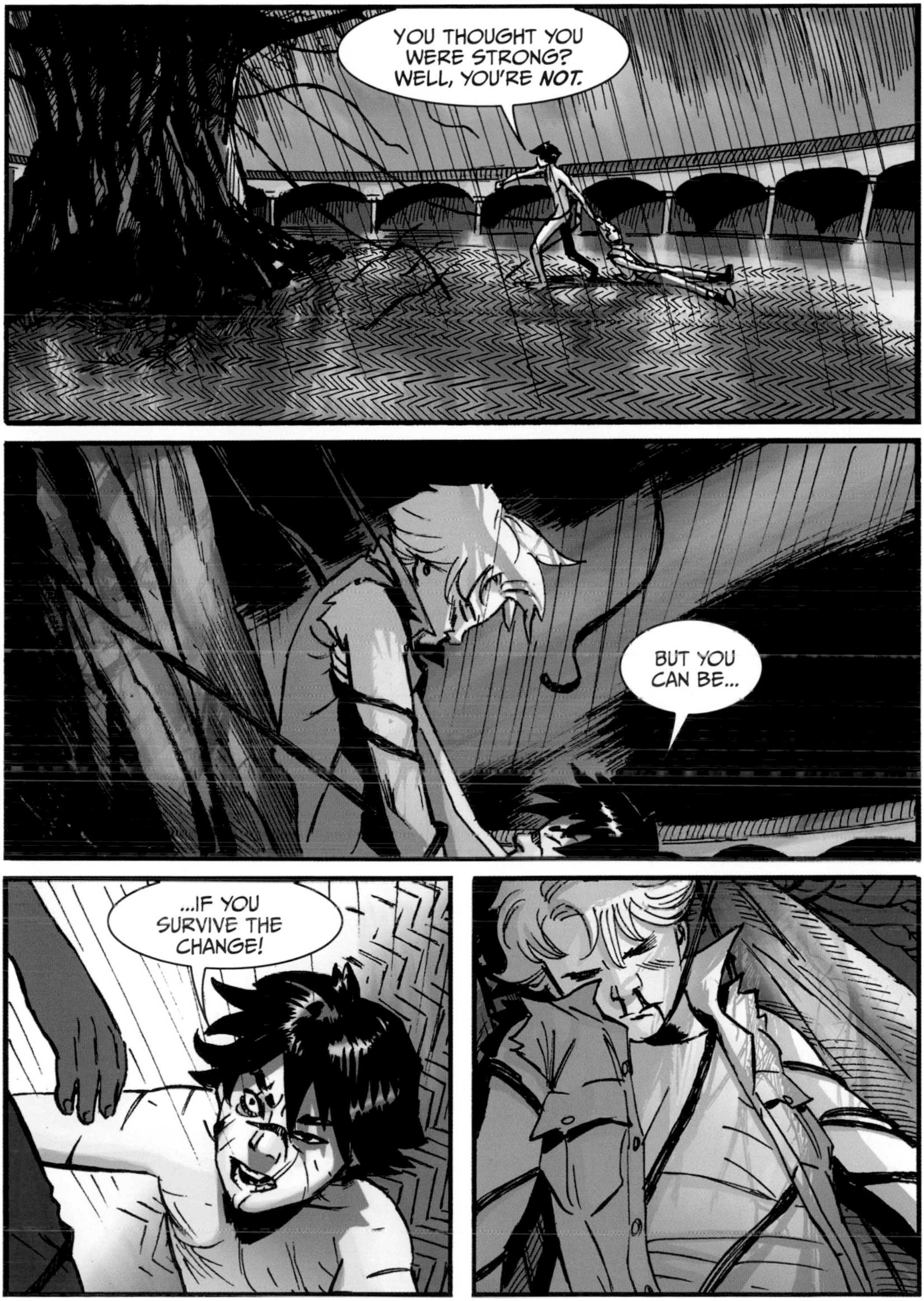
YOU THOUGHT YOU WERE STRONG? WELL, YOU'RE *NOT*.
BUT YOU CAN BE...
...IF YOU SURVIVE THE CHANGE!

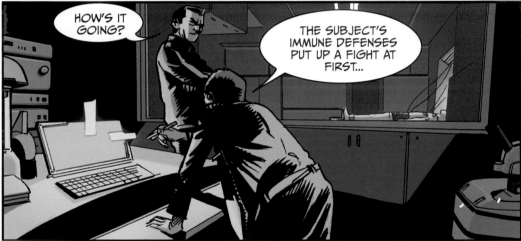

HOW'S IT GOING?

THE SUBJECT'S IMMUNE DEFENSES PUT UP A FIGHT AT FIRST...

...BUT THE TREATMENT SWEPT THEM AWAY, AS EXPECTED.

SO IS IT SAFE?

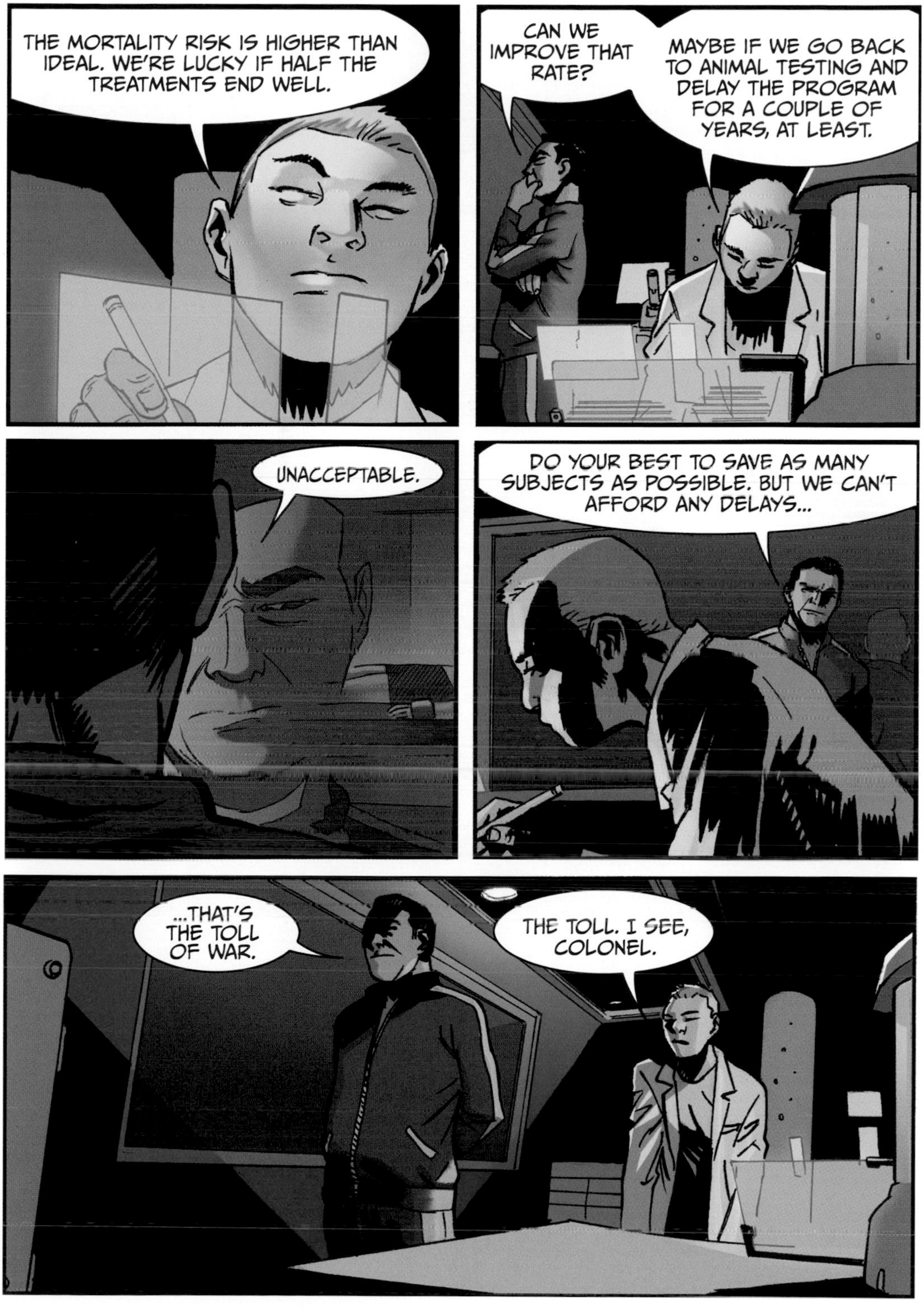
THE MORTALITY RISK IS HIGHER THAN IDEAL. WE'RE LUCKY IF HALF THE TREATMENTS END WELL.
CAN WE IMPROVE THAT RATE?
MAYBE IF WE GO BACK TO ANIMAL TESTING AND DELAY THE PROGRAM FOR A COUPLE OF YEARS, AT LEAST.
UNACCEPTABLE.
DO YOUR BEST TO SAVE AS MANY SUBJECTS AS POSSIBLE. BUT WE CAN'T AFFORD ANY DELAYS...
...THAT'S THE TOLL OF WAR.
THE TOLL. I SEE, COLONEL.

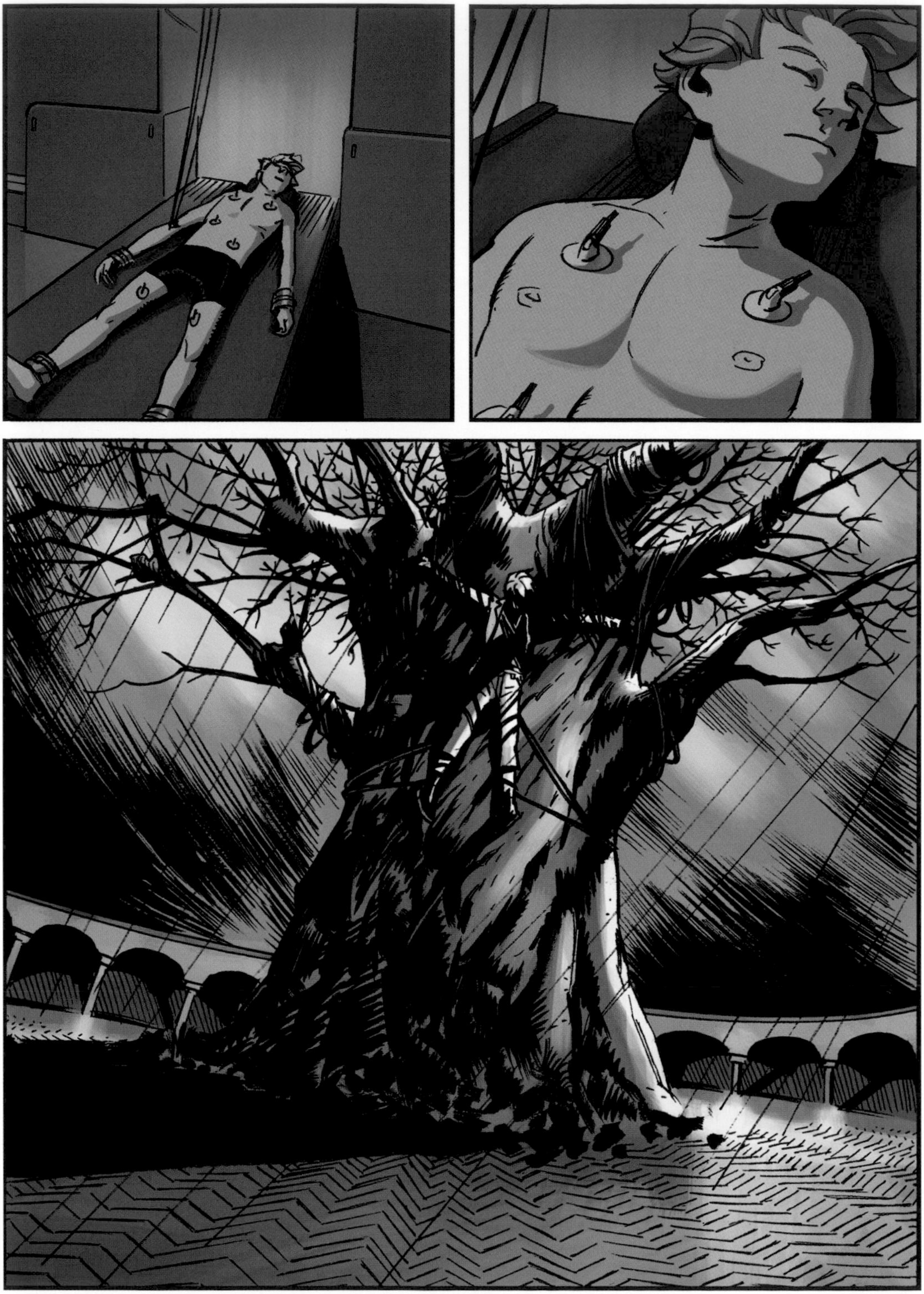

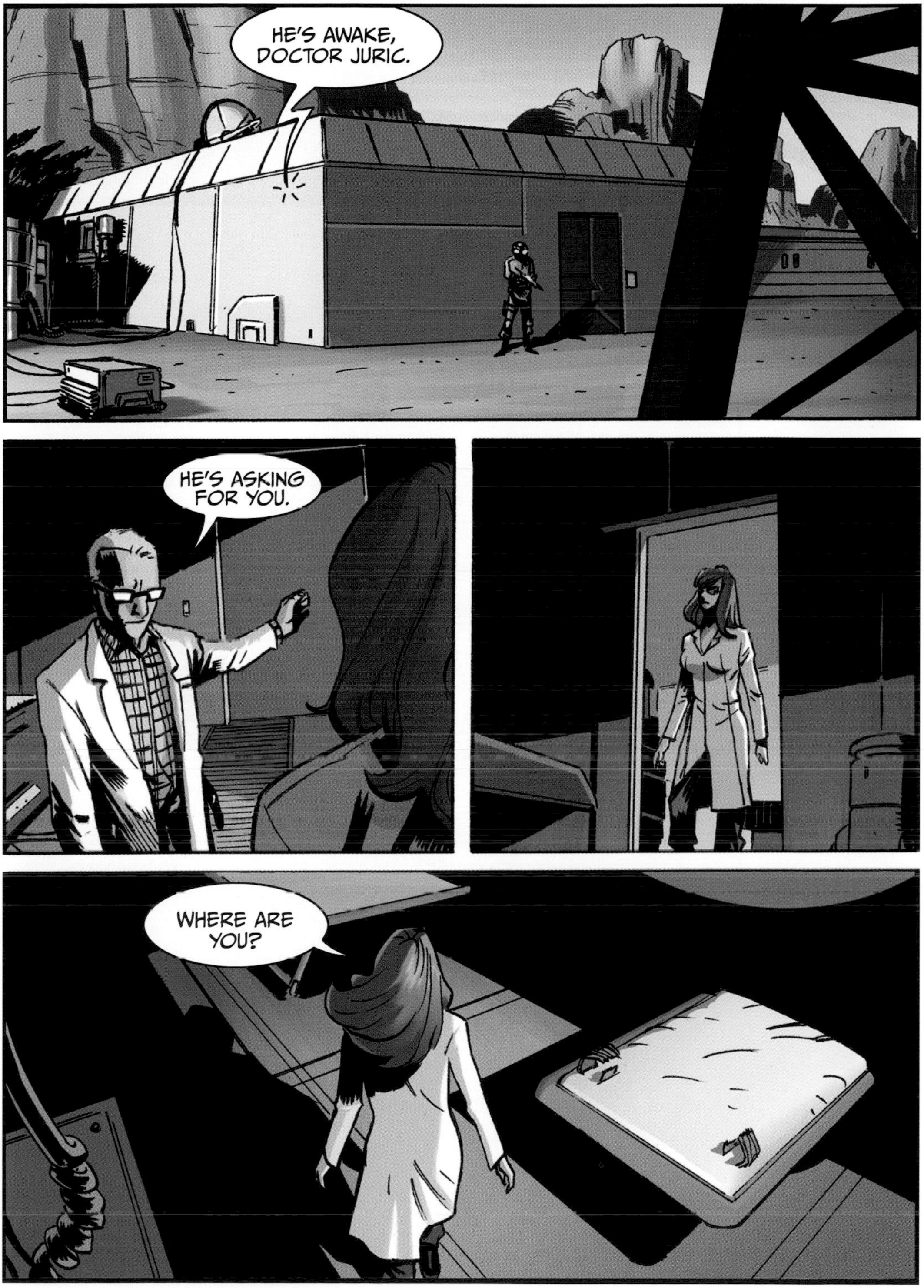
HE'S AWAKE, DOCTOR JURIC.
HE'S ASKING FOR YOU.
WHERE ARE YOU?

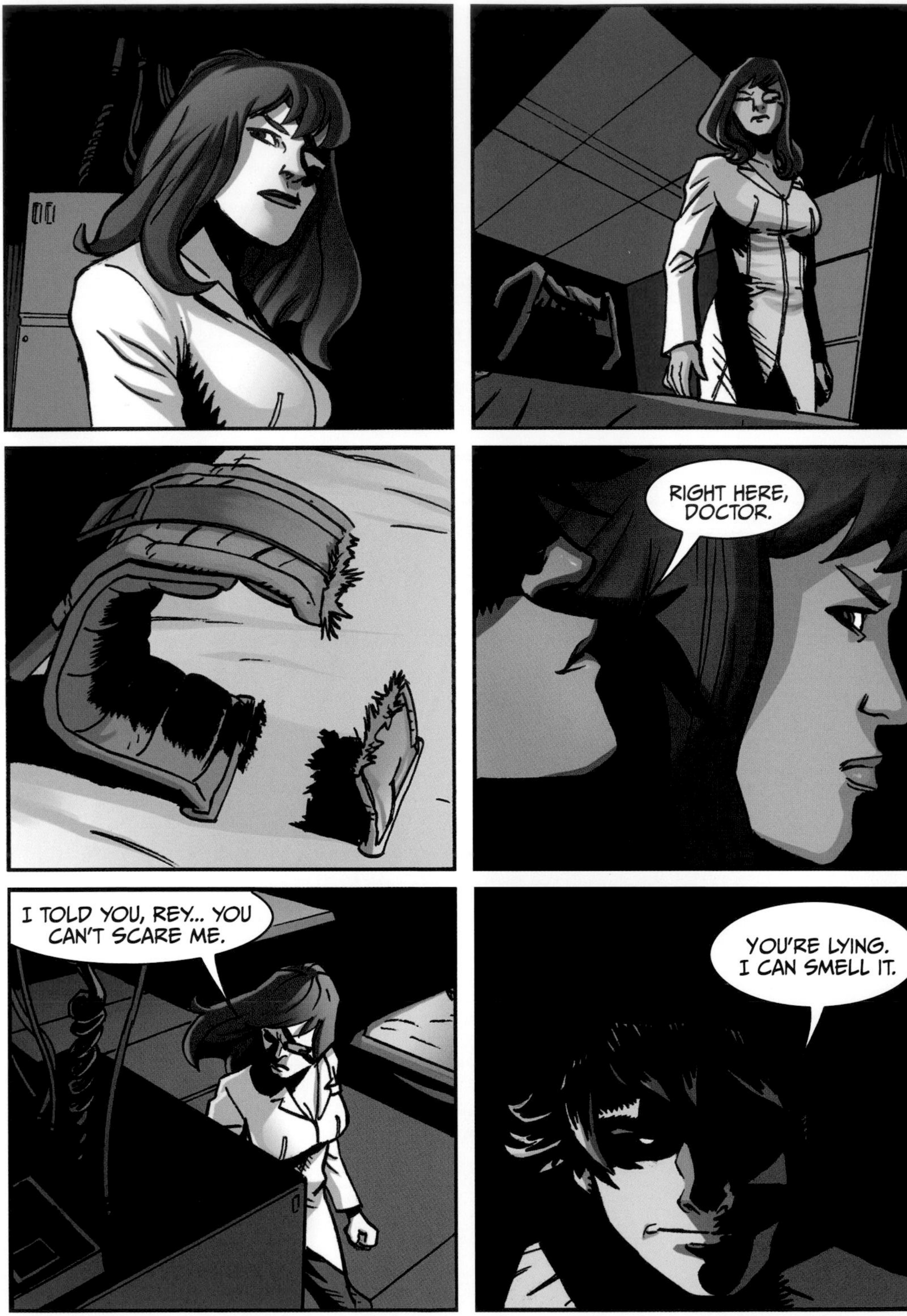
RIGHT HERE, DOCTOR.
I TOLD YOU, REY... YOU CAN'T SCARE ME.
YOU'RE LYING. I CAN SMELL IT.

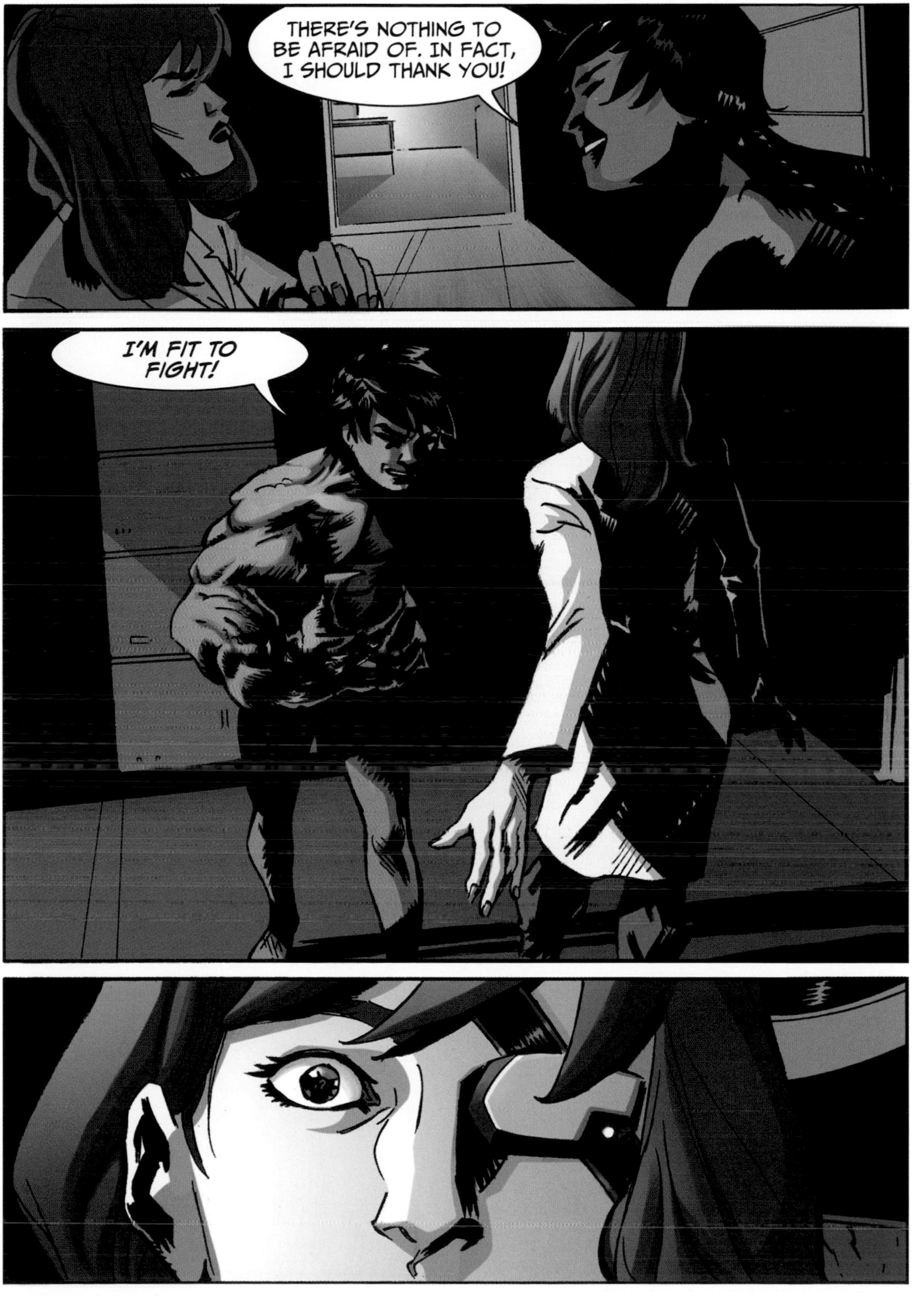
THERE'S NOTHING TO BE AFRAID OF. IN FACT, I SHOULD THANK YOU!
I'M FIT TO FIGHT!

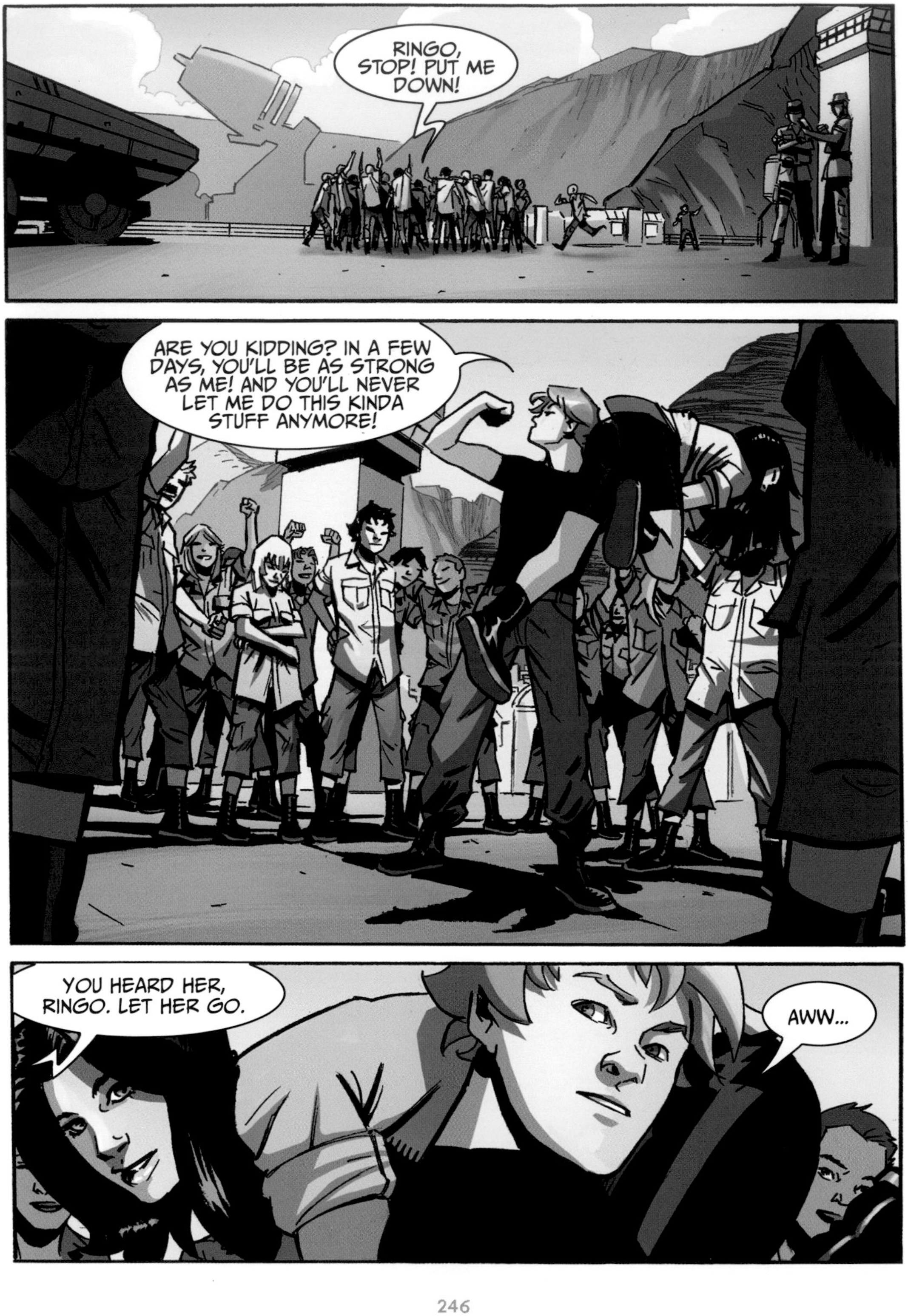
RINGO, STOP! PUT ME DOWN!
ARE YOU KIDDING? IN A FEW DAYS, YOU'LL BE AS STRONG AS ME! AND YOU'LL NEVER LET ME DO THIS KINDA STUFF ANYMORE!
YOU HEARD HER, RINGO. LET HER GO.
AWW...

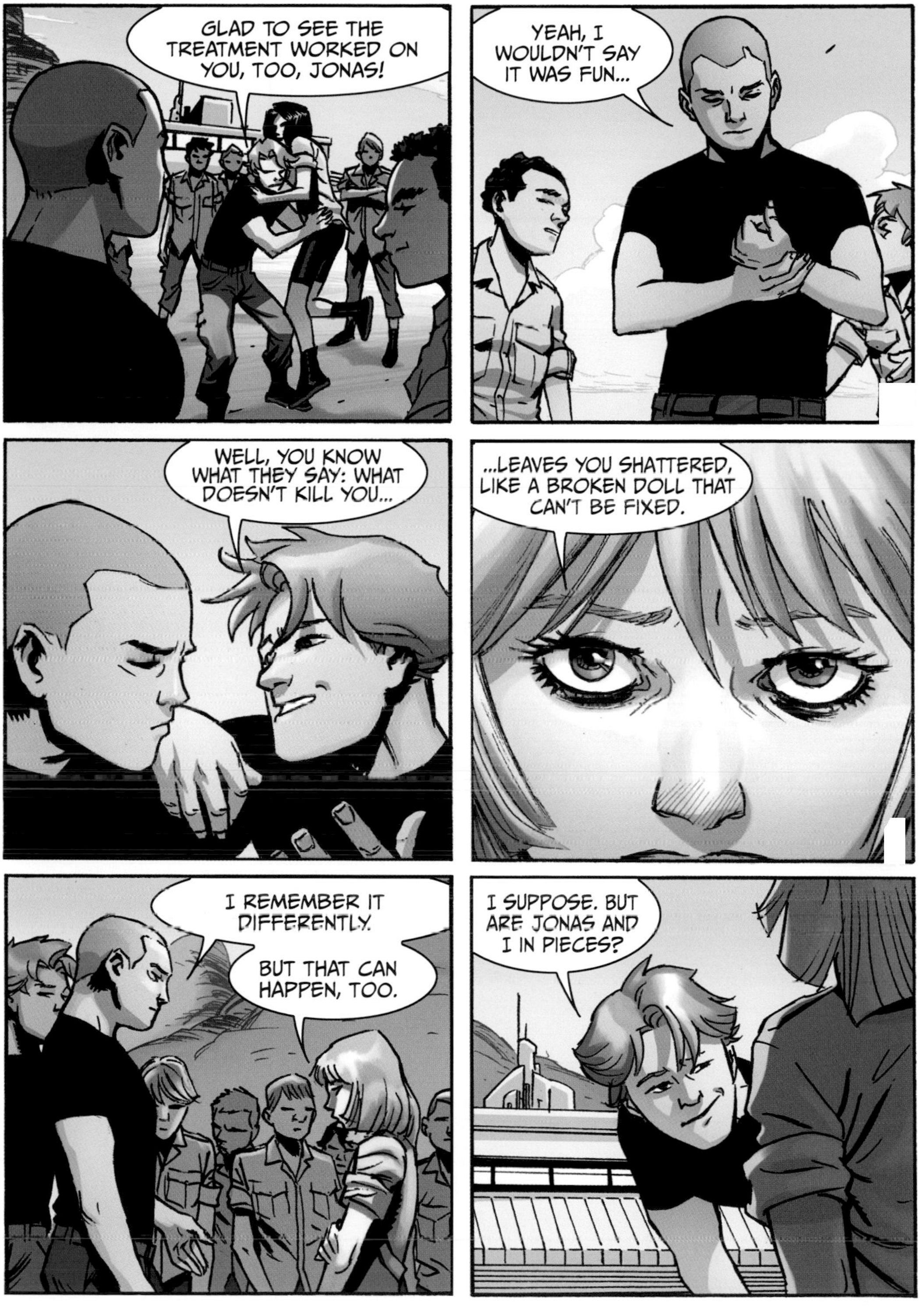
GLAD TO SEE THE TREATMENT WORKED ON YOU, TOO, JONAS!
YEAH, I WOULDN'T SAY IT WAS FUN...
WELL, YOU KNOW WHAT THEY SAY: WHAT DOESN'T KILL YOU...
...LEAVES YOU SHATTERED, LIKE A BROKEN DOLL THAT CAN'T BE FIXED.
I REMEMBER IT DIFFERENTLY.
BUT THAT CAN HAPPEN, TOO.
I SUPPOSE. BUT ARE JONAS AND I IN PIECES?

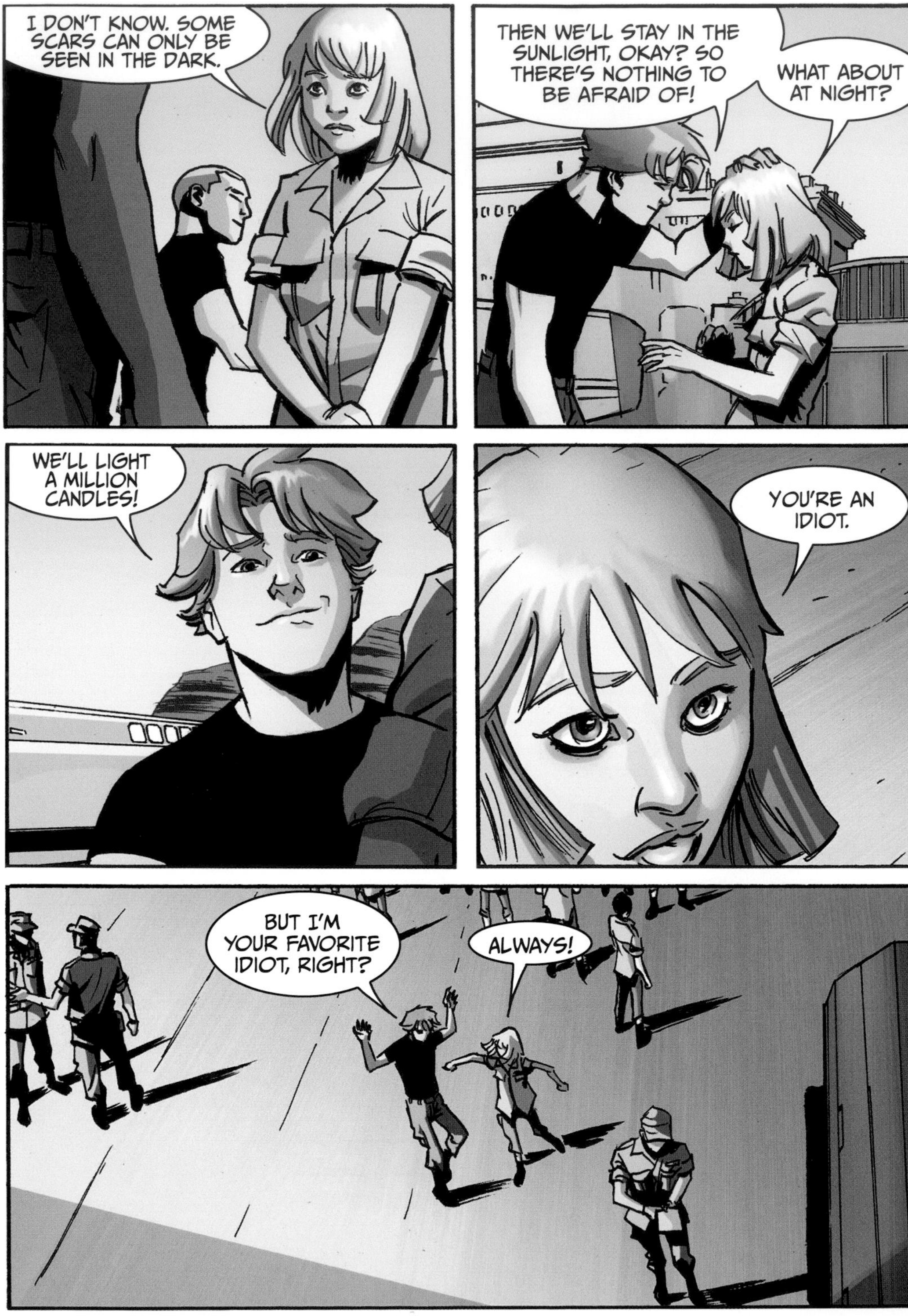
I DON'T KNOW. SOME SCARS CAN ONLY BE SEEN IN THE DARK.
THEN WE'LL STAY IN THE SUNLIGHT, OKAY? SO THERE'S NOTHING TO BE AFRAID OF!
WHAT ABOUT AT NIGHT?
WE'LL LIGHT A MILLION CANDLES!
YOU'RE AN IDIOT.
BUT I'M YOUR FAVORITE IDIOT, RIGHT?
ALWAYS!

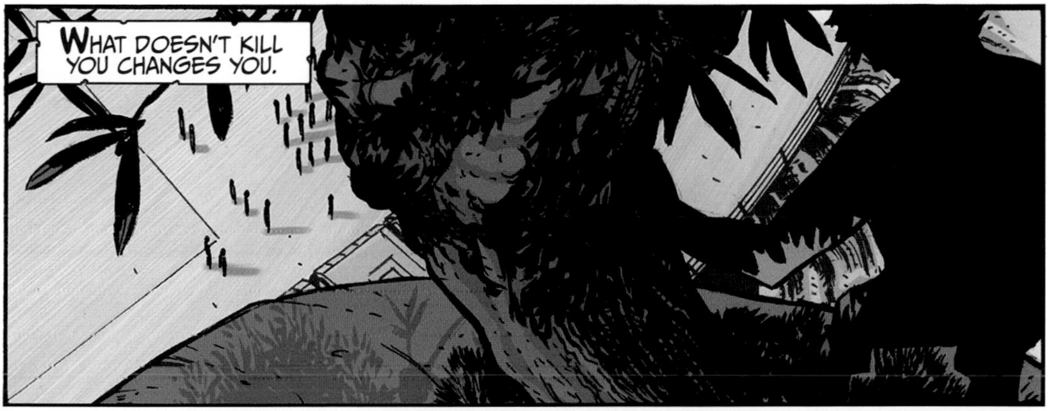
WHAT DOESN'T KILL YOU CHANGES YOU.

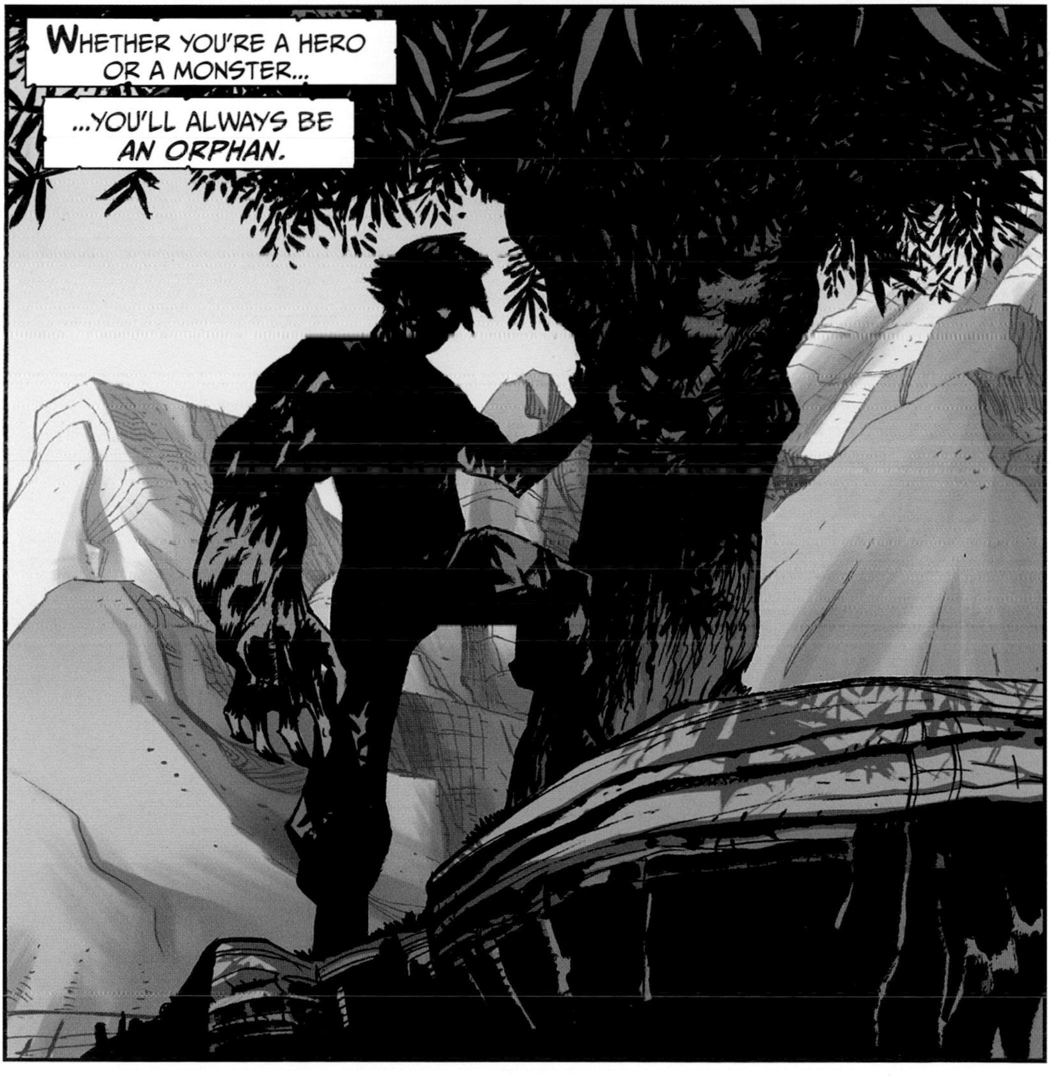
WHETHER YOU'RE A HERO OR A MONSTER...
...YOU'LL ALWAYS BE AN ORPHAN.

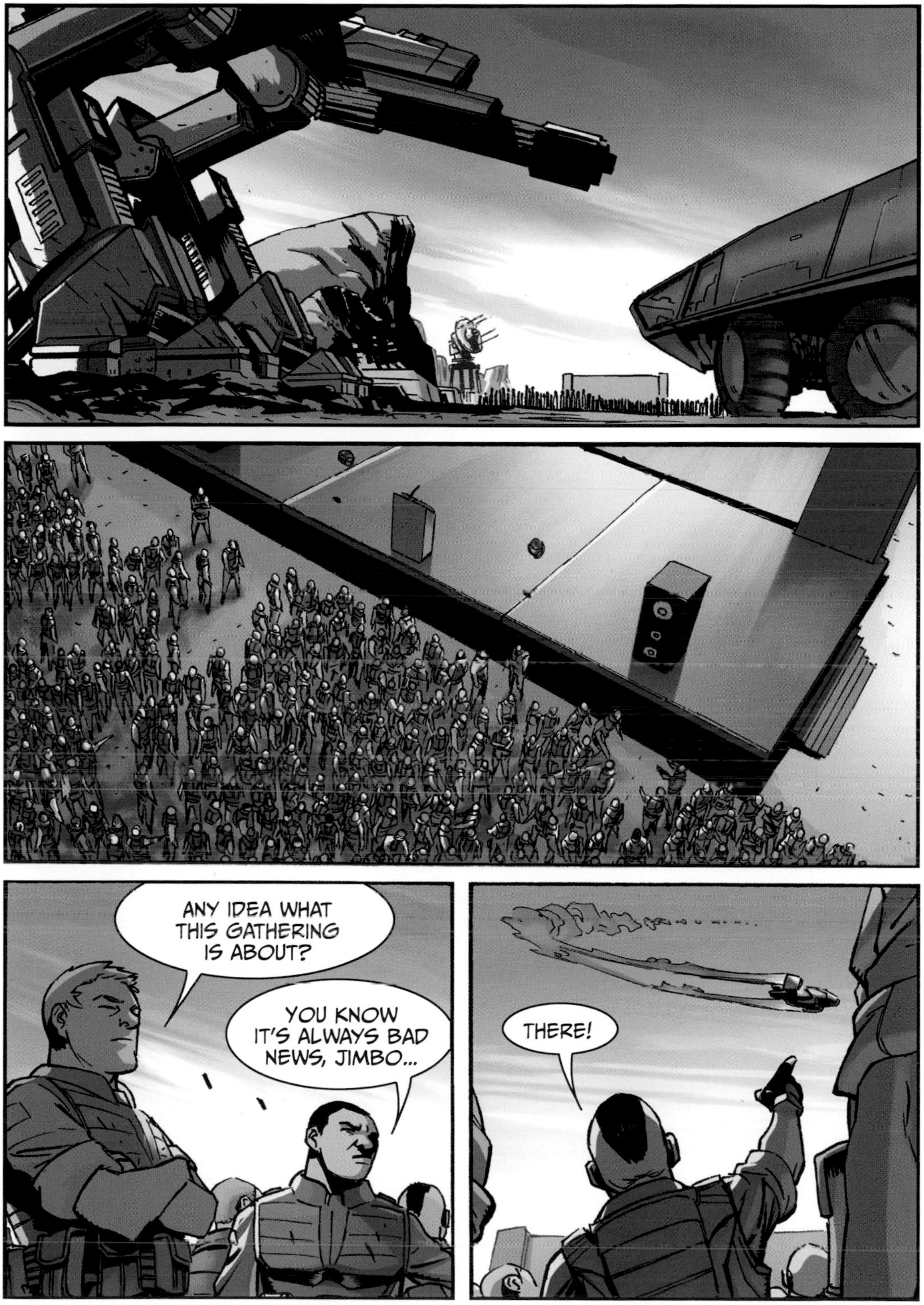
ANY IDEA WHAT THIS GATHERING IS ABOUT?
YOU KNOW IT'S ALWAYS BAD NEWS, JIMBO...
THERE!

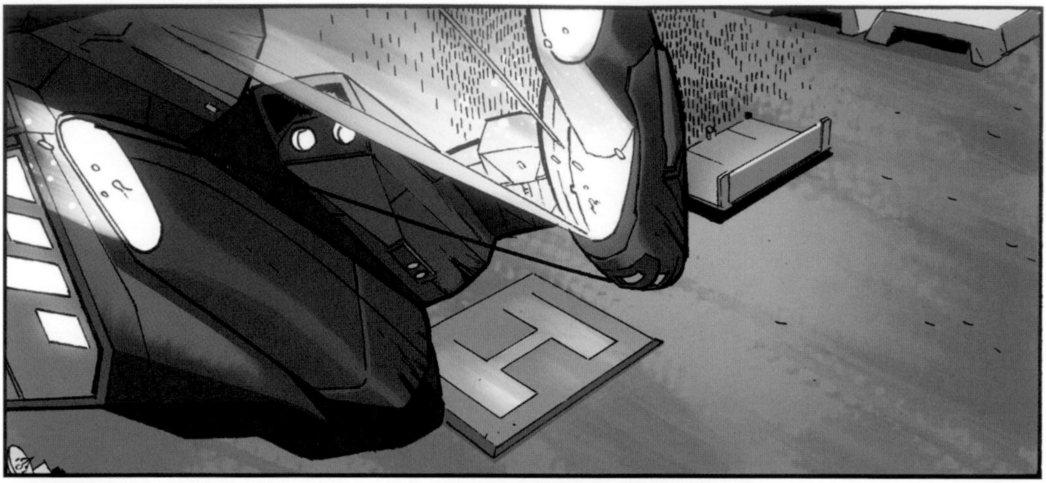

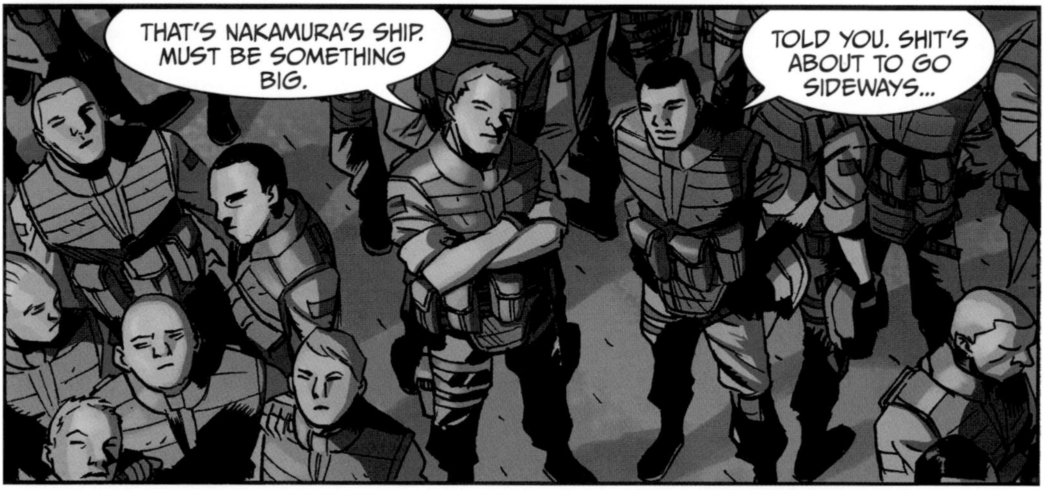
THAT'S NAKAMURA'S SHIP. MUST BE SOMETHING BIG.
TOLD YOU. SHIT'S ABOUT TO GO SIDEWAYS...

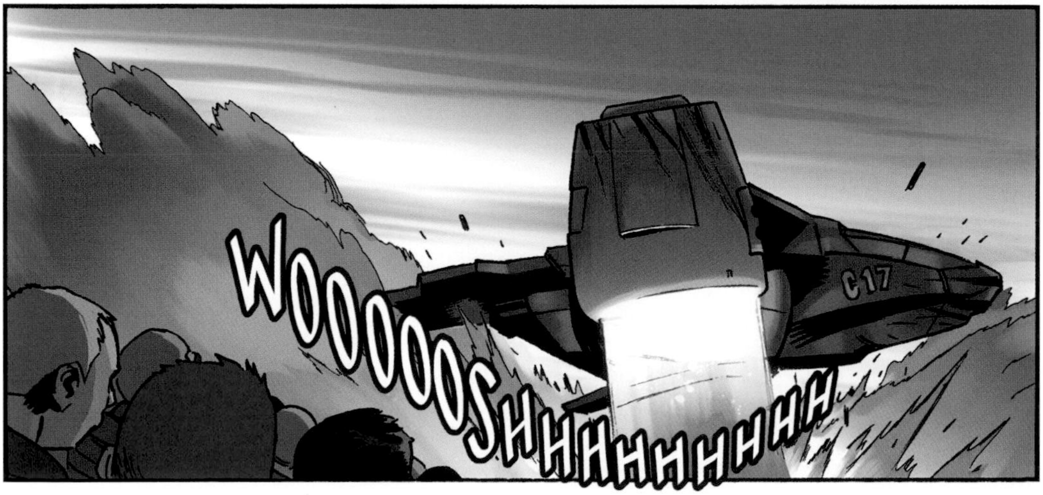
C17
WOOOOOSHHHHHHHHHH

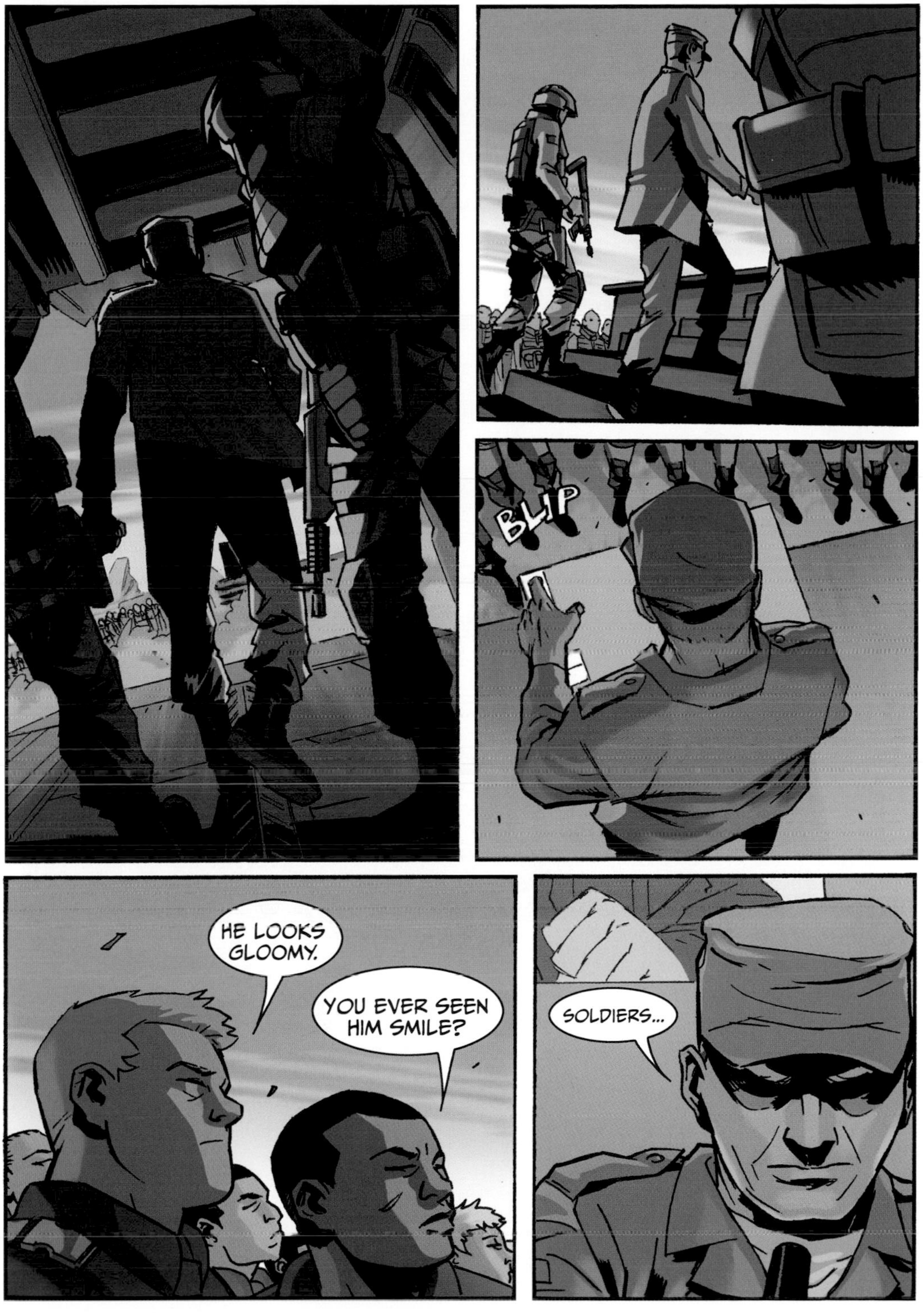
BLIP
HE LOOKS GLOOMY.
YOU EVER SEEN HIM SMILE?
SOLDIERS...

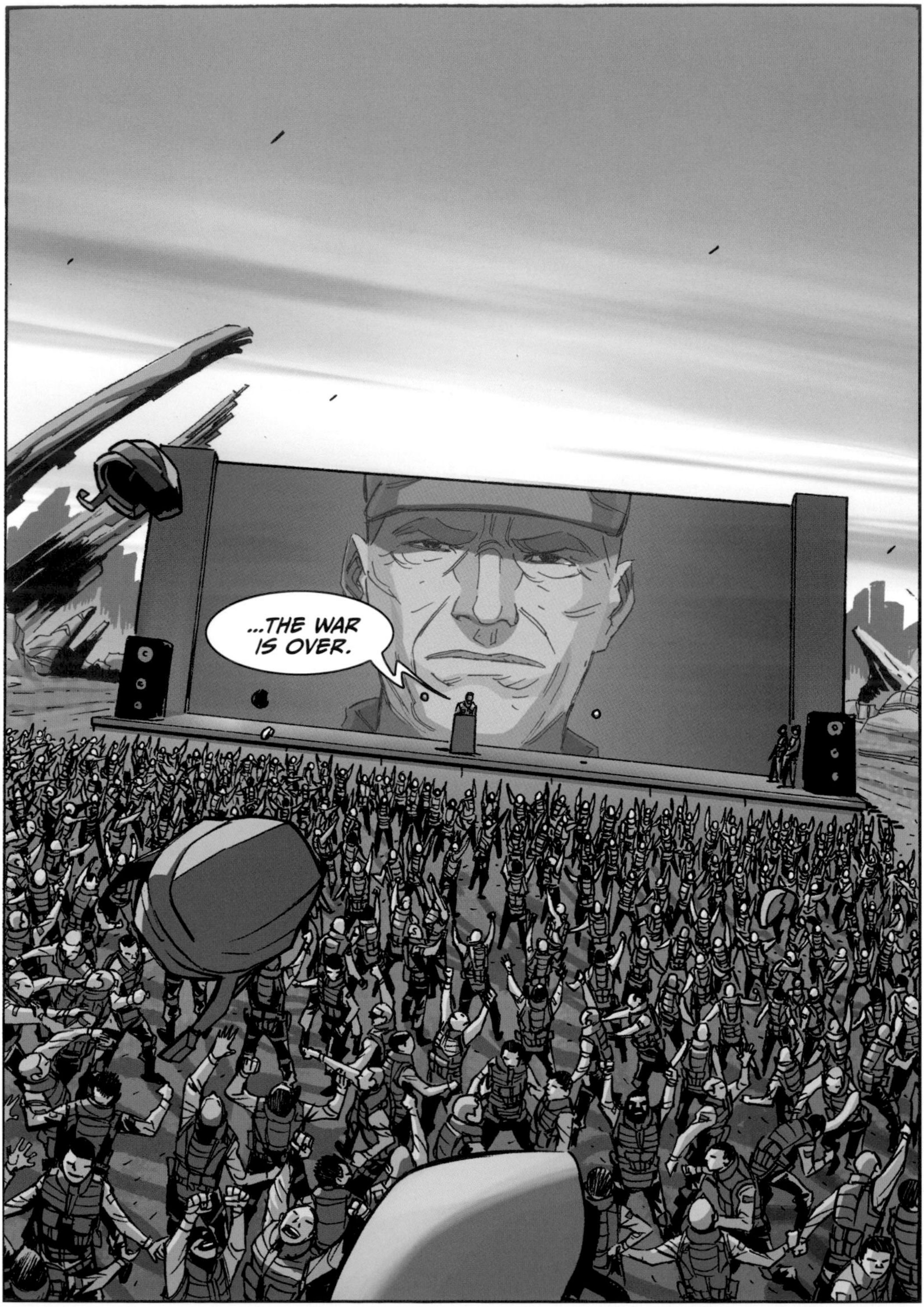
...THE WAR IS OVER.

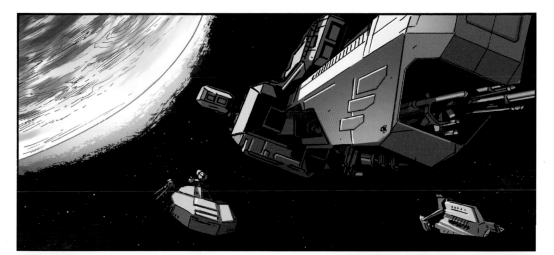

NAKAMURA MADE HIS ANNOUNCEMENT. THE SHOW'S OVER.

TIME FOR PHASE TWO?

NOT UNTIL WE SORT OUT THAT *LINGERING MATTER*...

THERE'S NOT MUCH CHANCE HE'S STILL ALIVE, DOC.

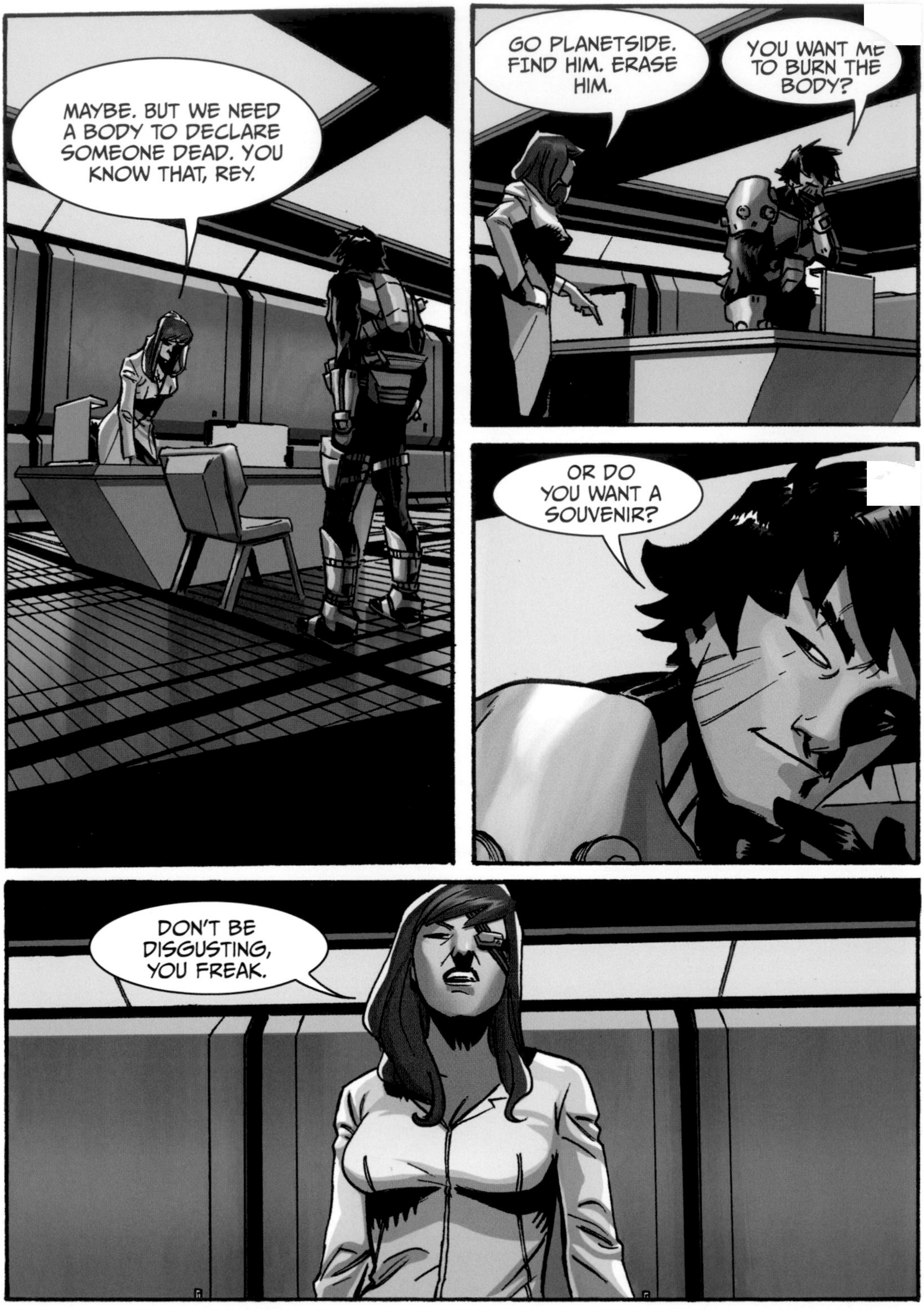
MAYBE. BUT WE NEED A BODY TO DECLARE SOMEONE DEAD. YOU KNOW THAT, REY.
GO PLANETSIDE. FIND HIM. ERASE HIM.
YOU WANT ME TO BURN THE BODY?
OR DO YOU WANT A SOUVENIR?
DON'T BE DISGUSTING, YOU FREAK.

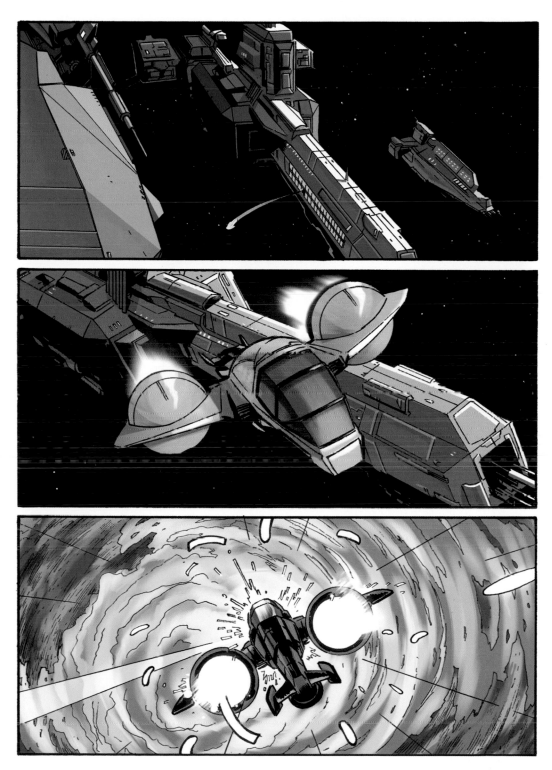

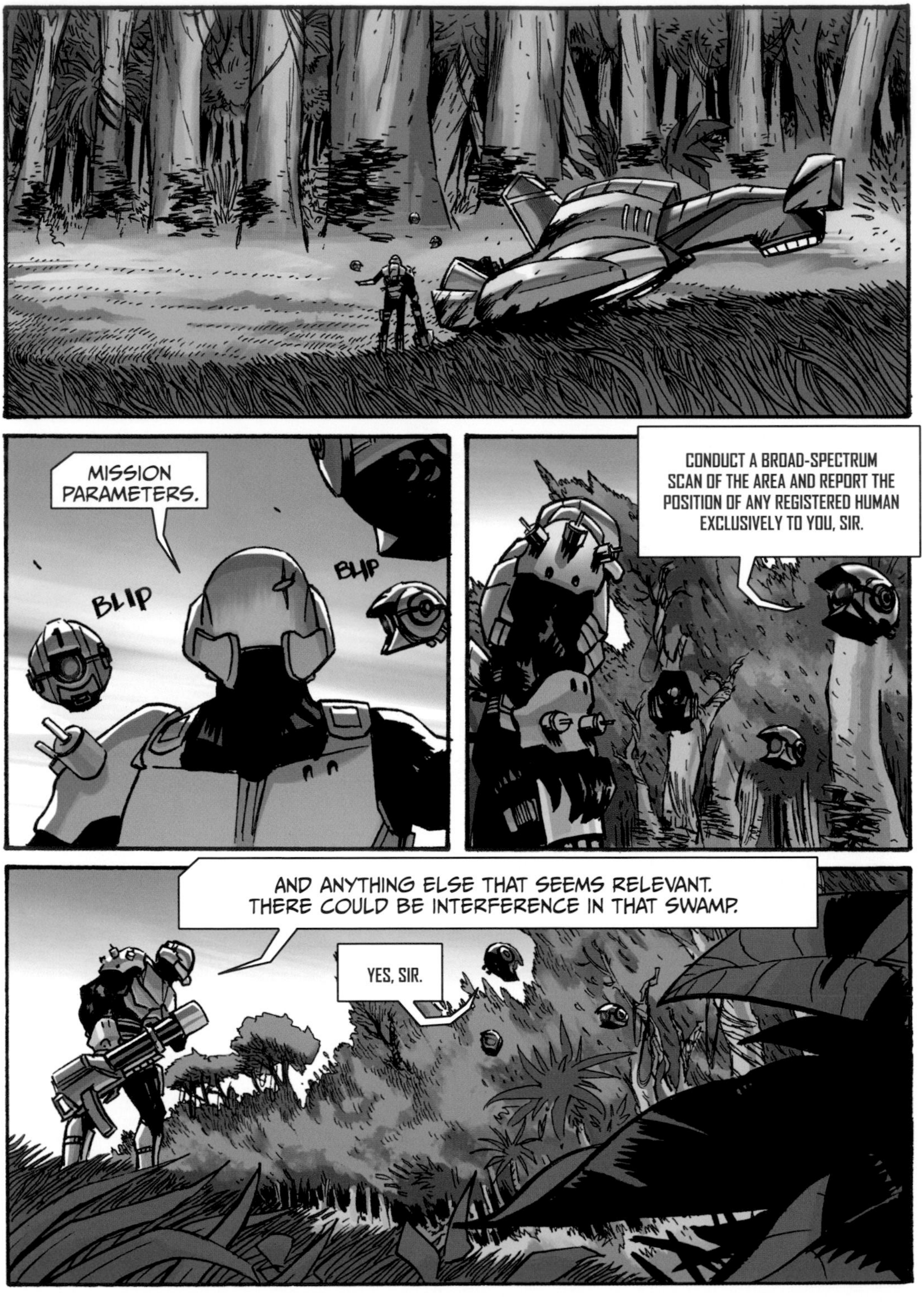
MISSION PARAMETERS.
BLIP
BLIP
CONDUCT A BROAD-SPECTRUM SCAN OF THE AREA AND REPORT THE POSITION OF ANY REGISTERED HUMAN EXCLUSIVELY TO YOU, SIR.
AND ANYTHING ELSE THAT SEEMS RELEVANT. THERE COULD BE INTERFERENCE IN THAT SWAMP.
YES, SIR.

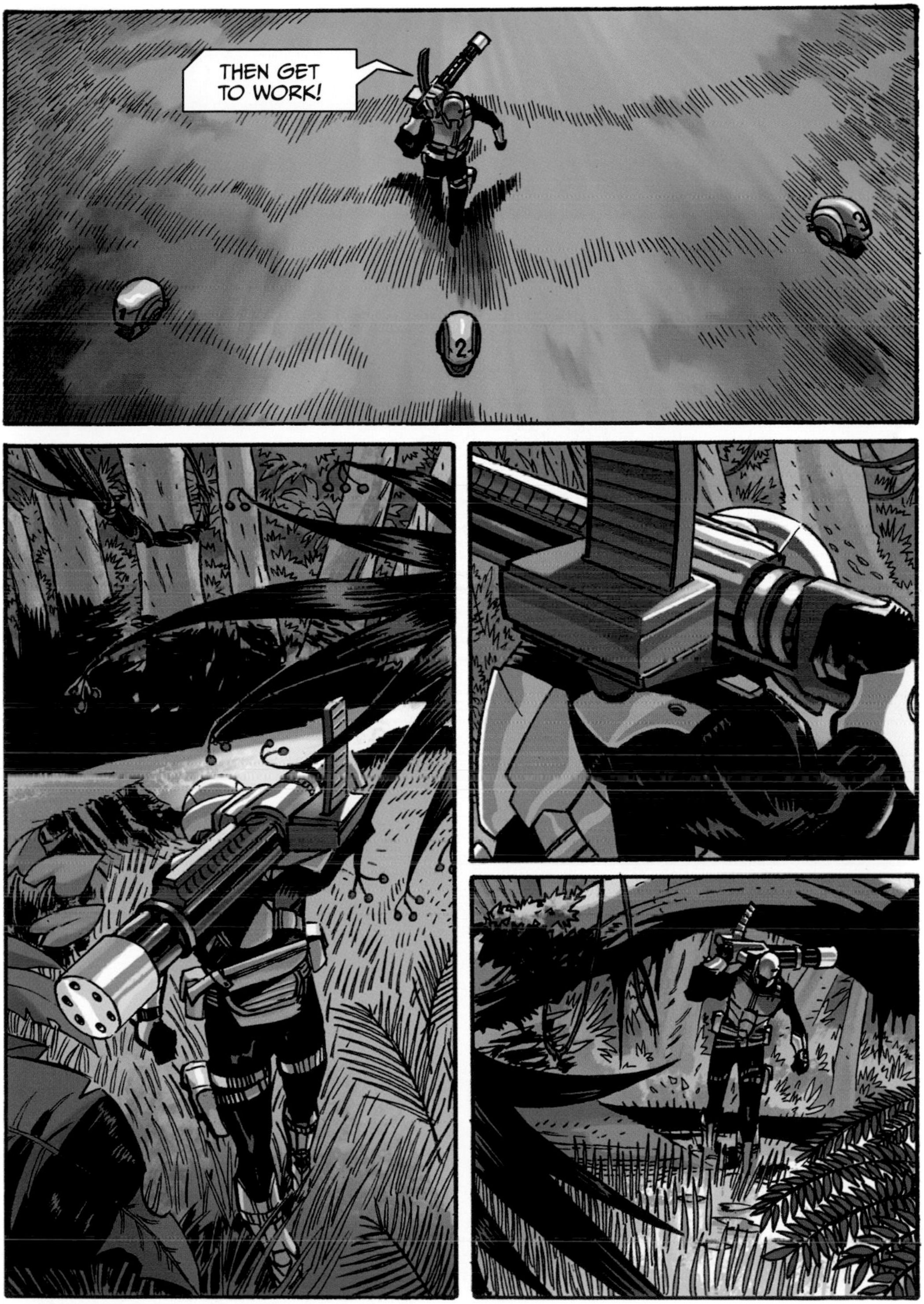
THEN GET TO WORK!
1
2

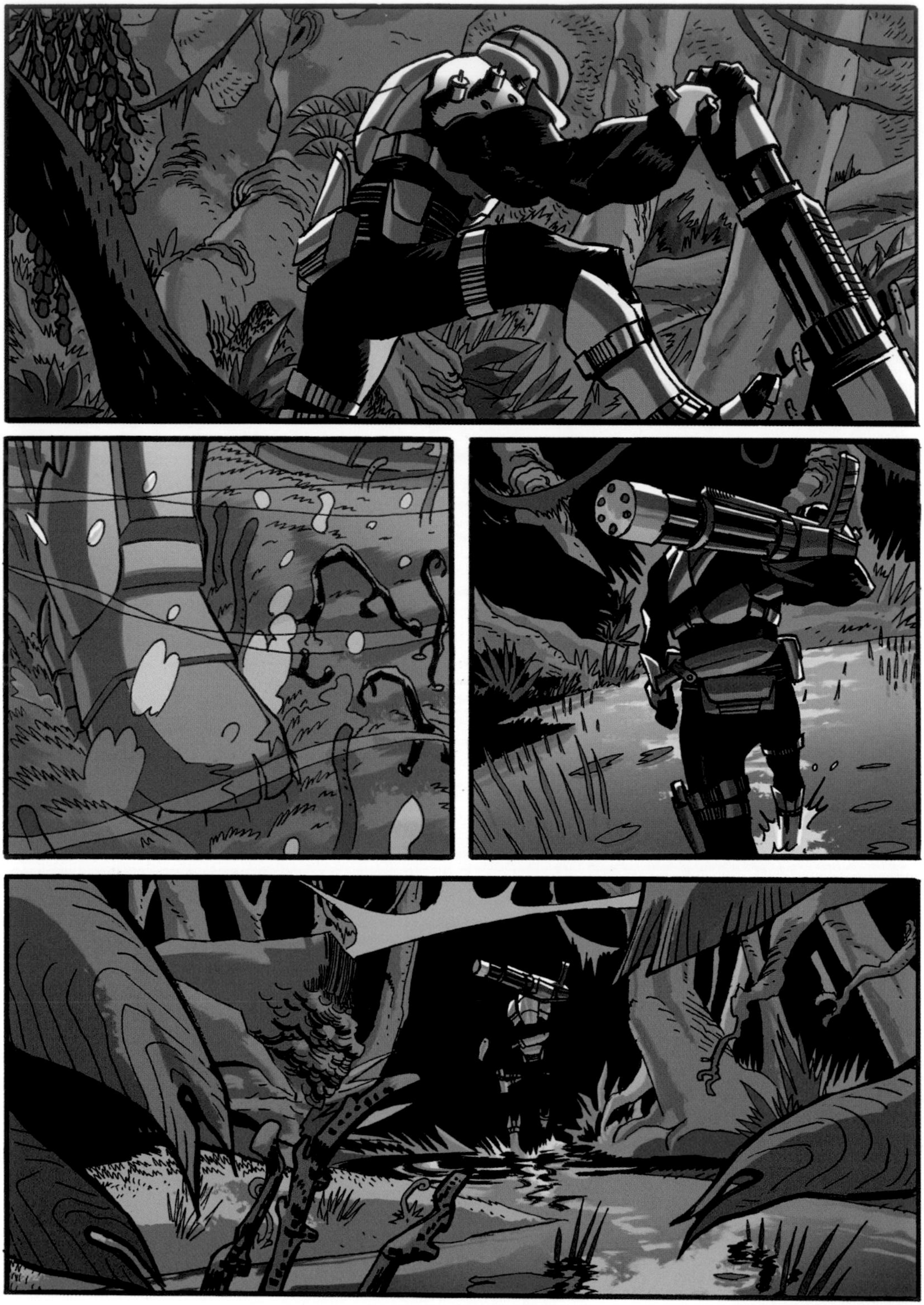

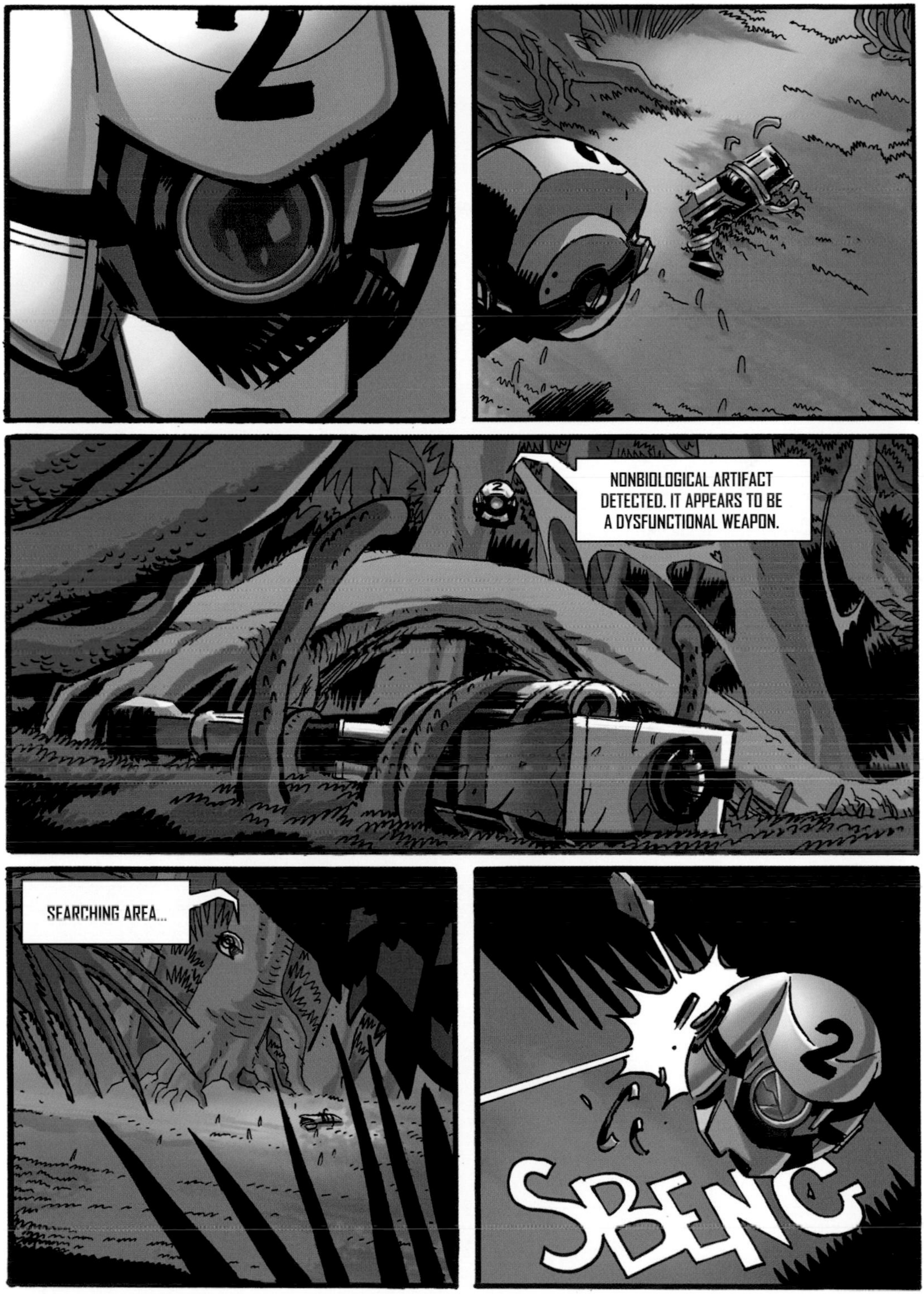

NONBIOLOGICAL ARTIFACT DETECTED. IT APPEARS TO BE A DYSFUNCTIONAL WEAPON.
SEARCHING AREA...
SBENG

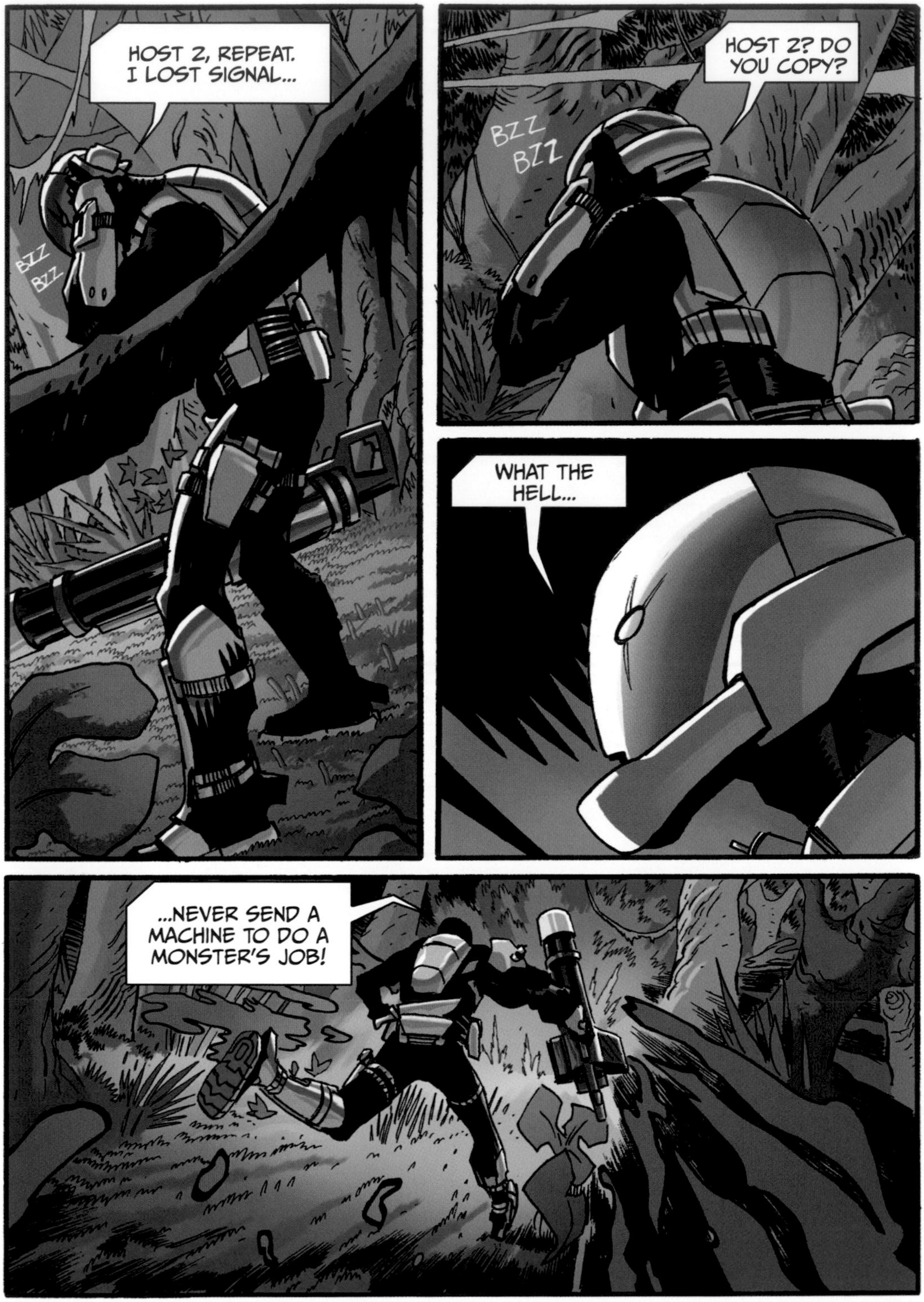
HOST 2, REPEAT. I LOST SIGNAL...
BZZ BZZ
HOST 2? DO YOU COPY?
BZZ BZZ
WHAT THE HELL...
...NEVER SEND A MACHINE TO DO A MONSTER'S JOB!

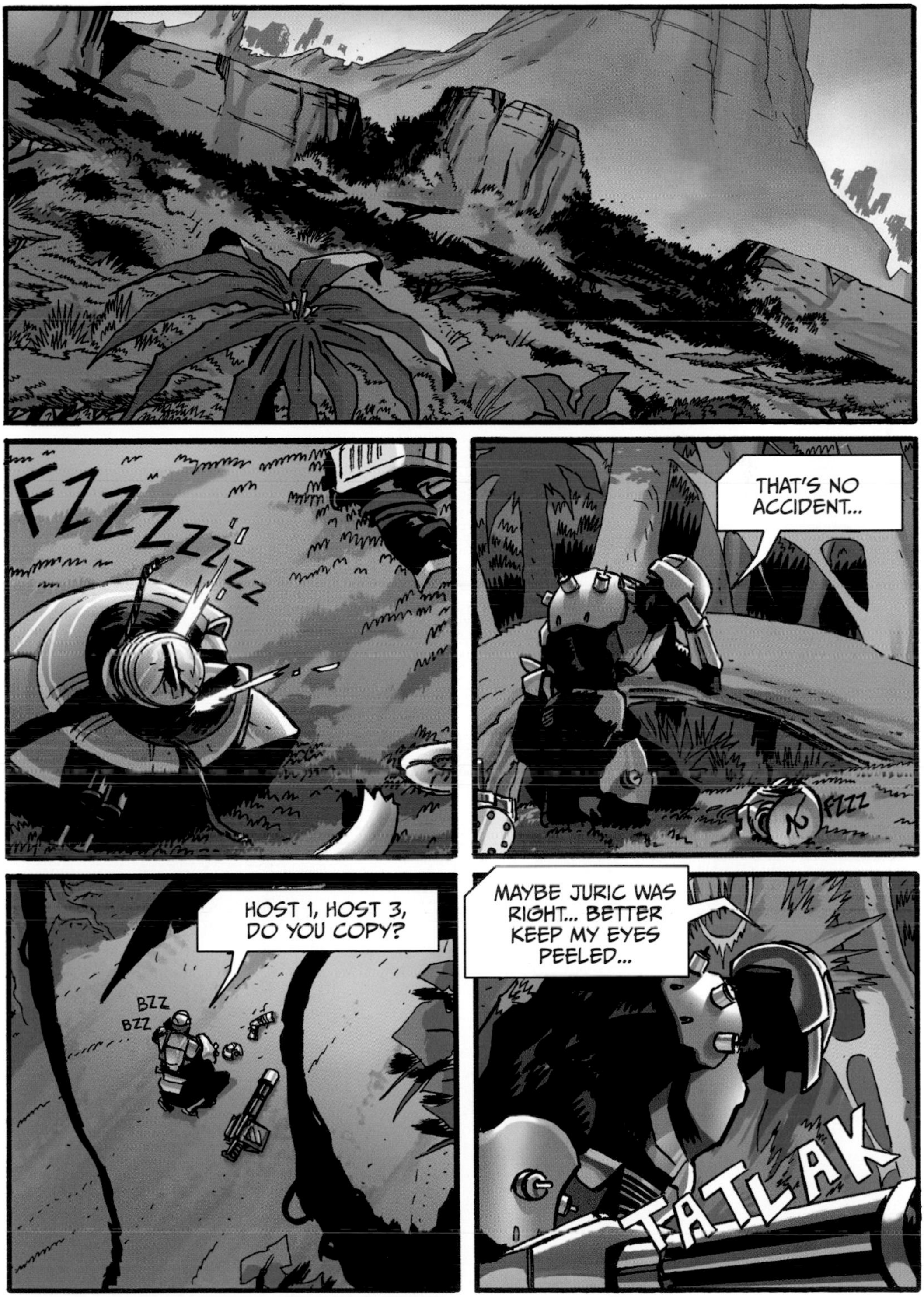

FZZZZZZZZ
THAT'S NO ACCIDENT...
FZZZ
HOST 1, HOST 3, DO YOU COPY?
BZZ
BZZ
MAYBE JURIC WAS RIGHT... BETTER KEEP MY EYES PEELED...
TATLAK

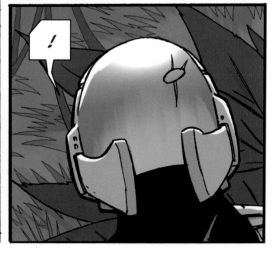

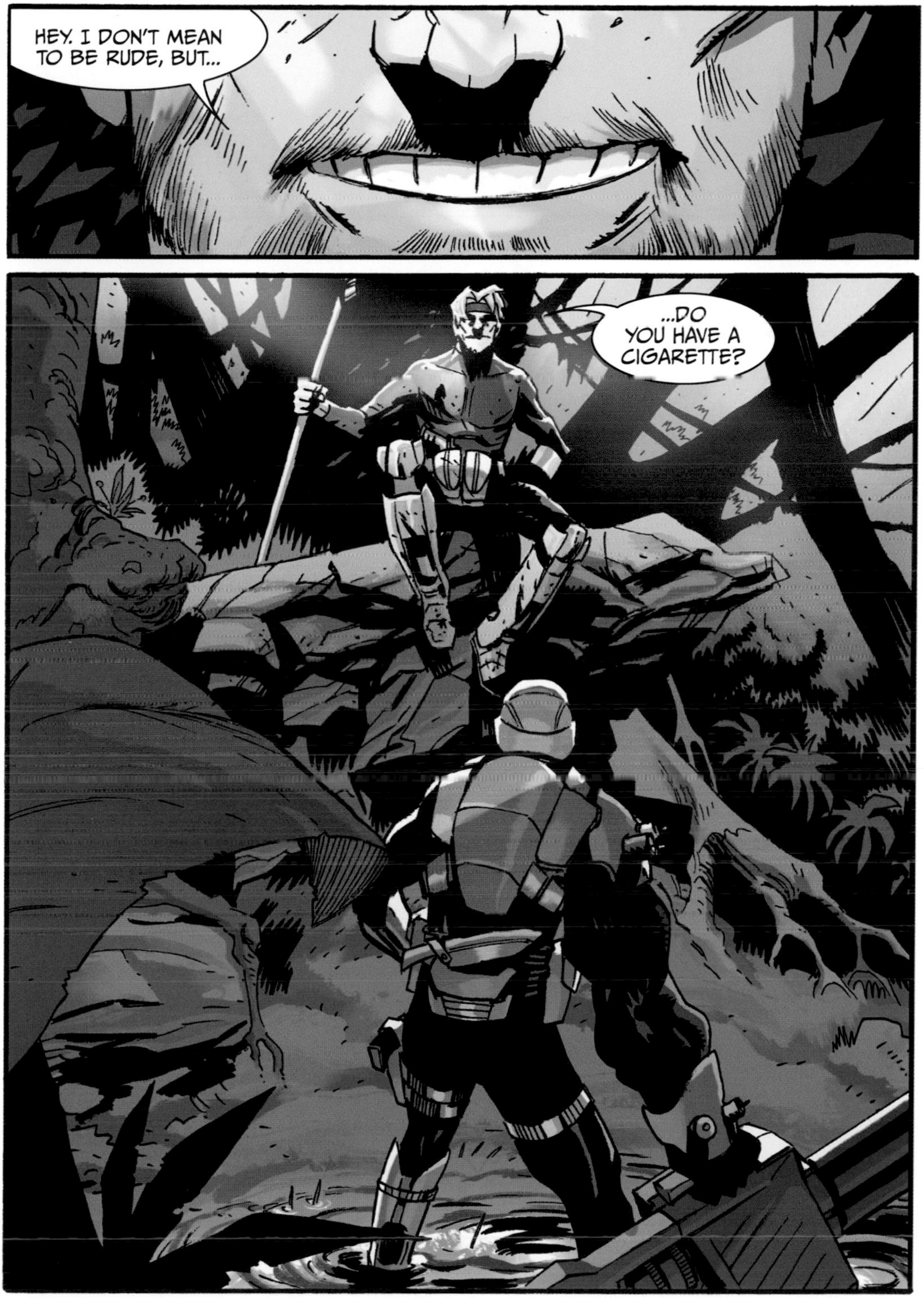
HEY. I DON'T MEAN TO BE RUDE, BUT...
...DO YOU HAVE A CIGARETTE?

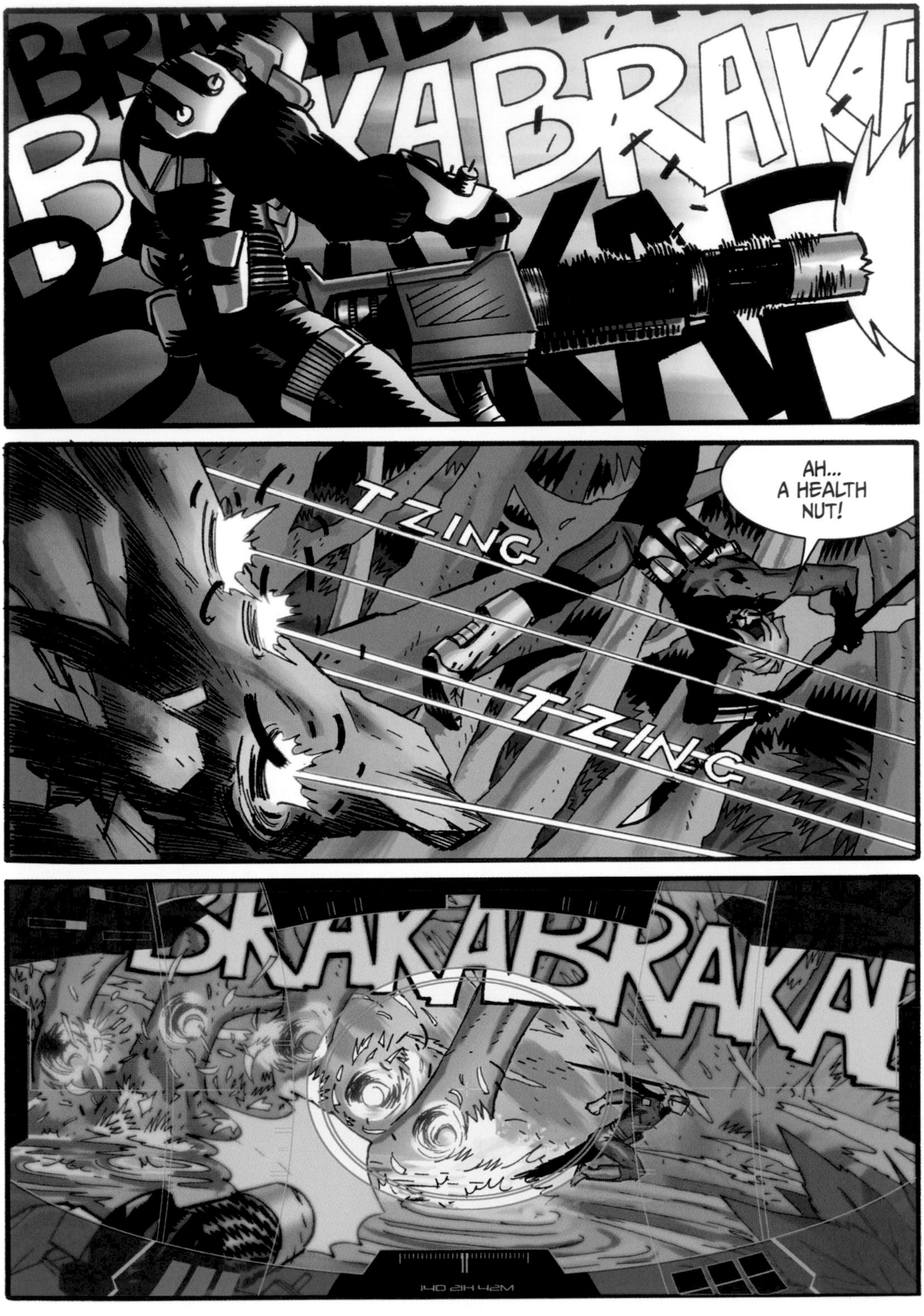
TZING
AH... A HEALTH NUT!
TZING

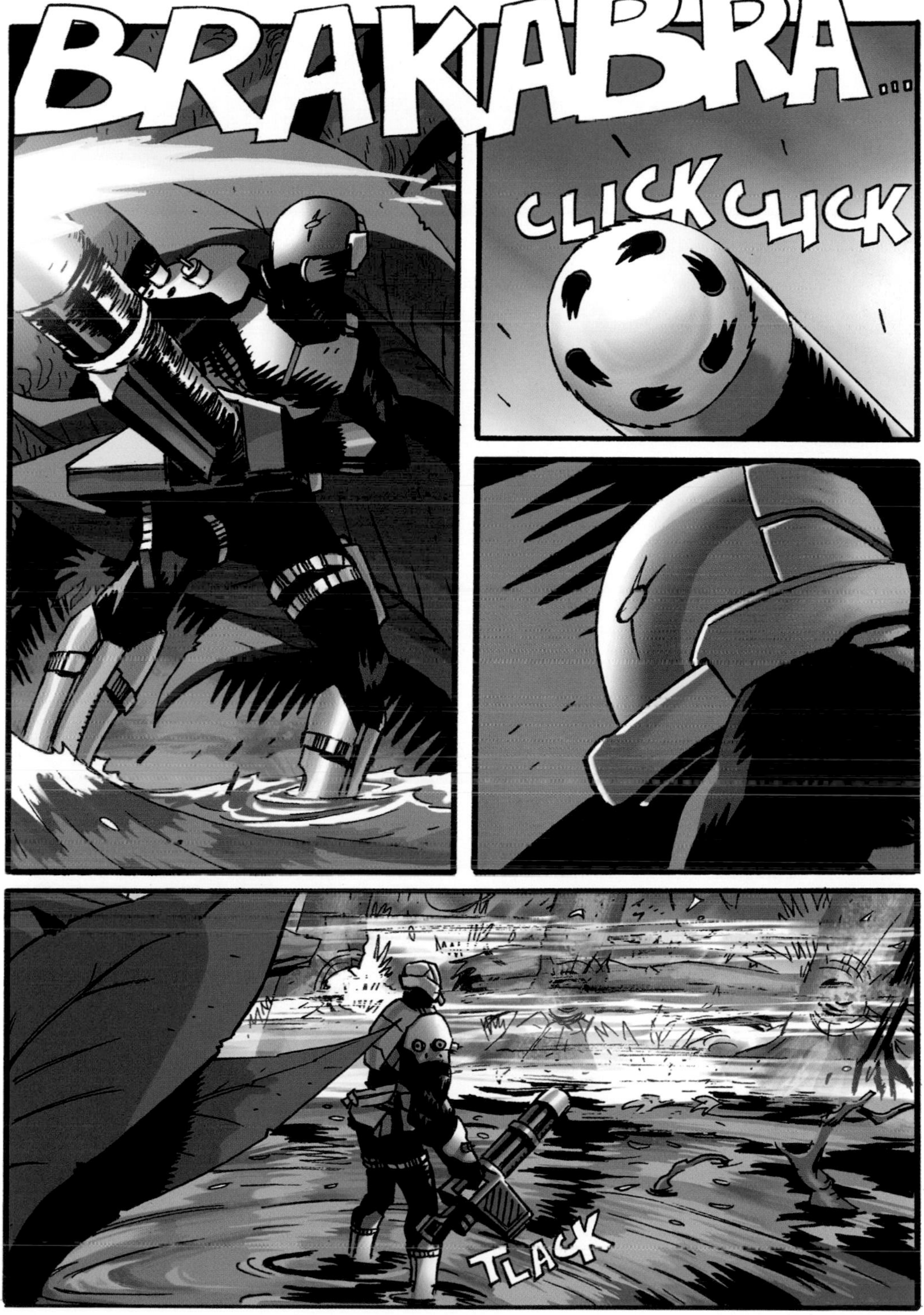
BRAKABRA...
CLICK CLICK
TLACK

PLUNF

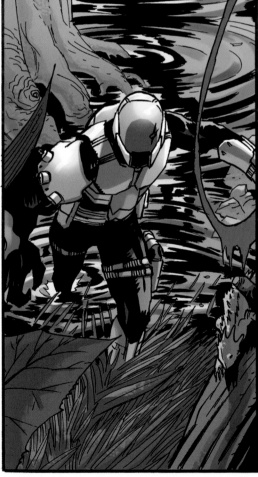

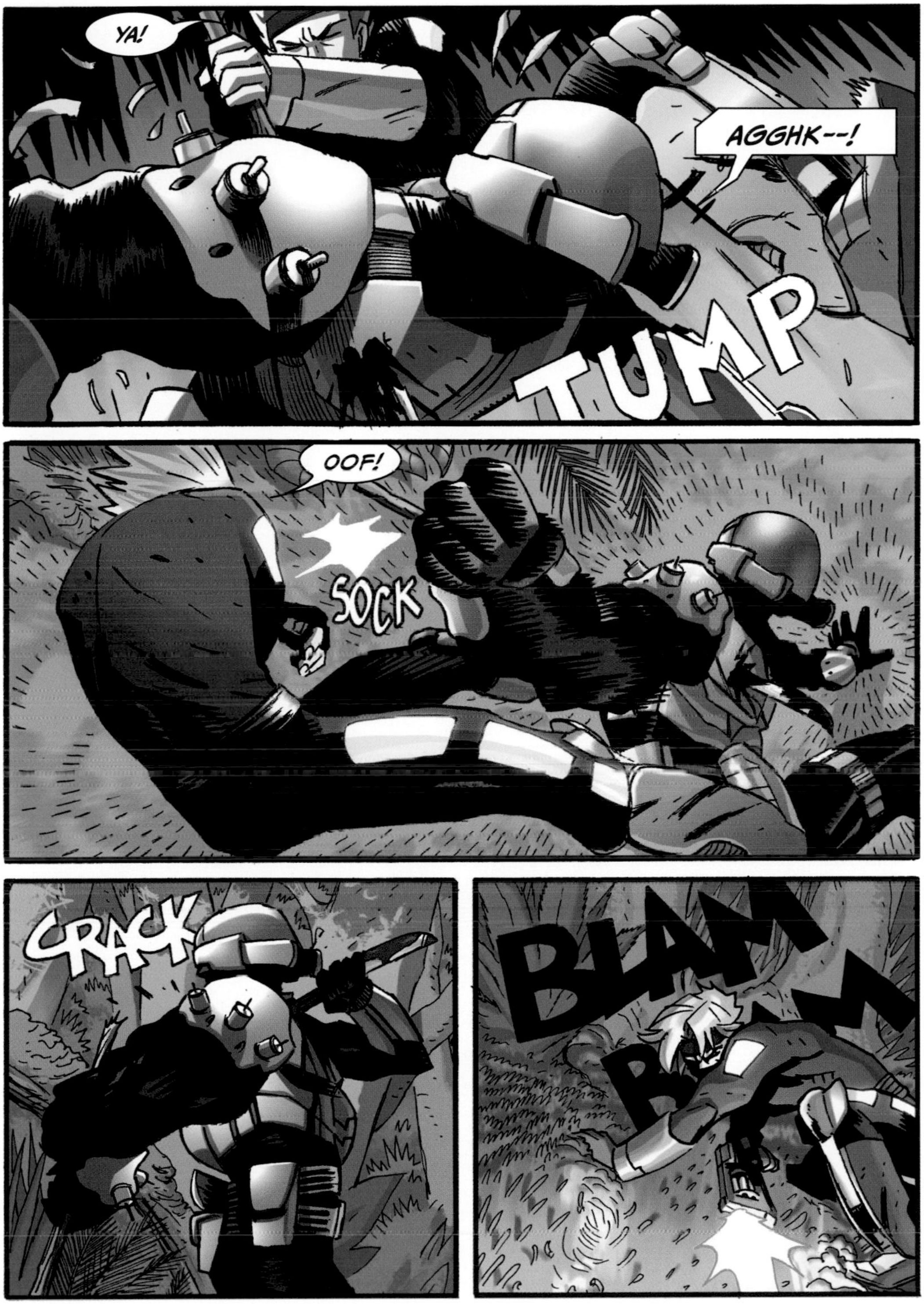
YA!
AGGHK--!
TUMP
OOF!
SOCK
CRACK
BLAM
BLAM

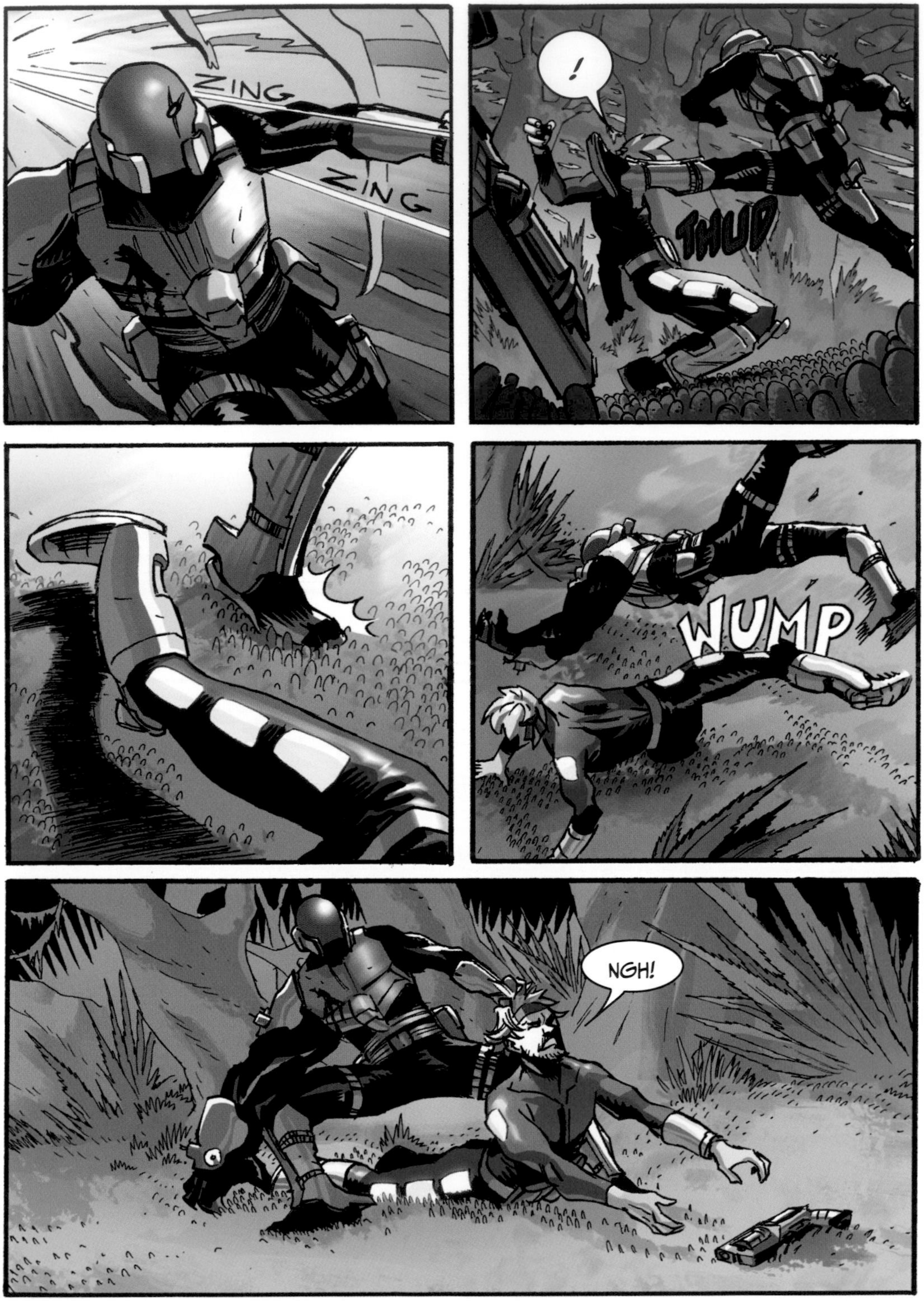
ZING
ZING
!
THUD
WUMP
NGH!

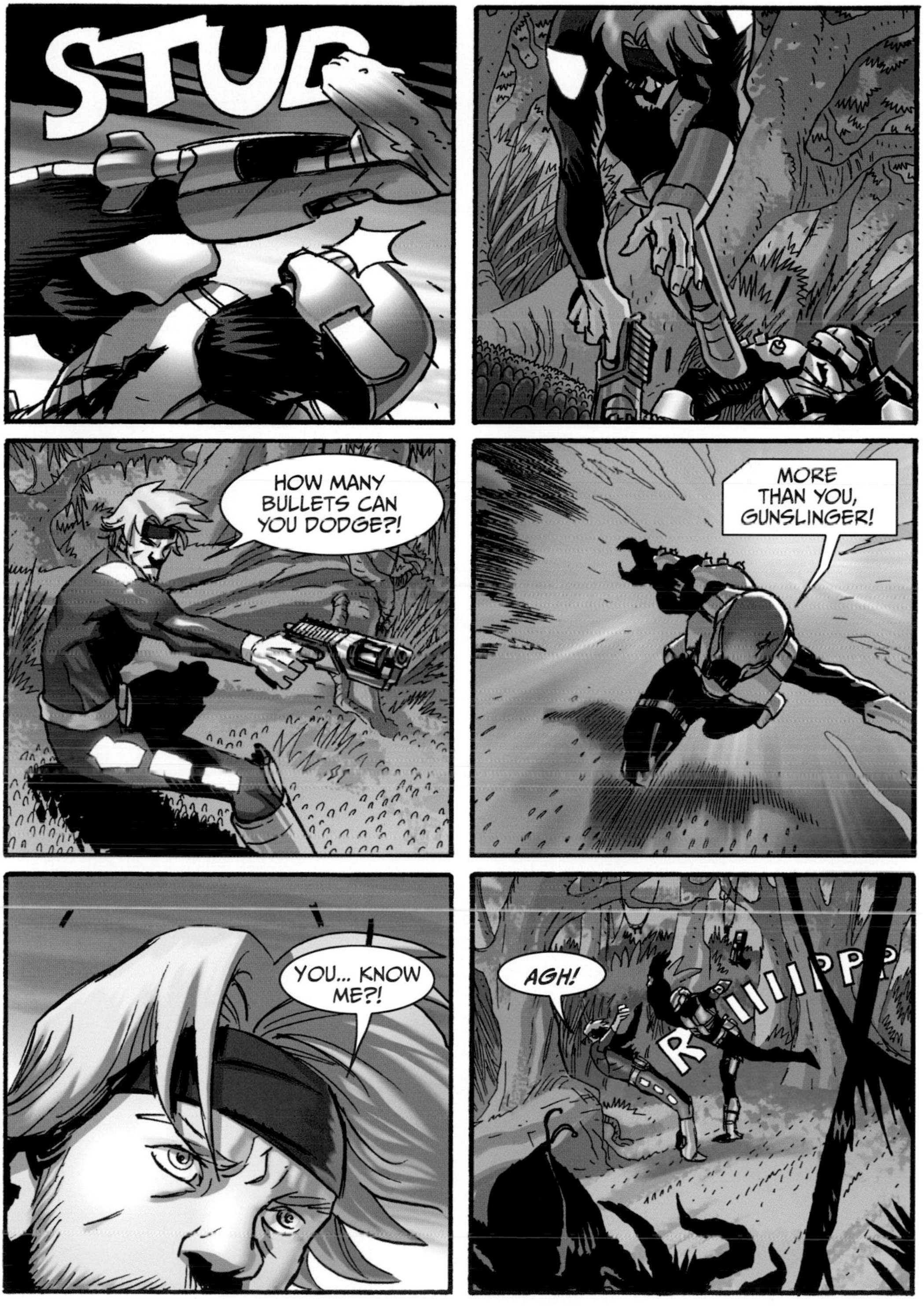
STUD
HOW MANY BULLETS CAN YOU DODGE?!
MORE THAN YOU, GUNSLINGER!
YOU... KNOW ME?!
AGH!
RIIIIPP

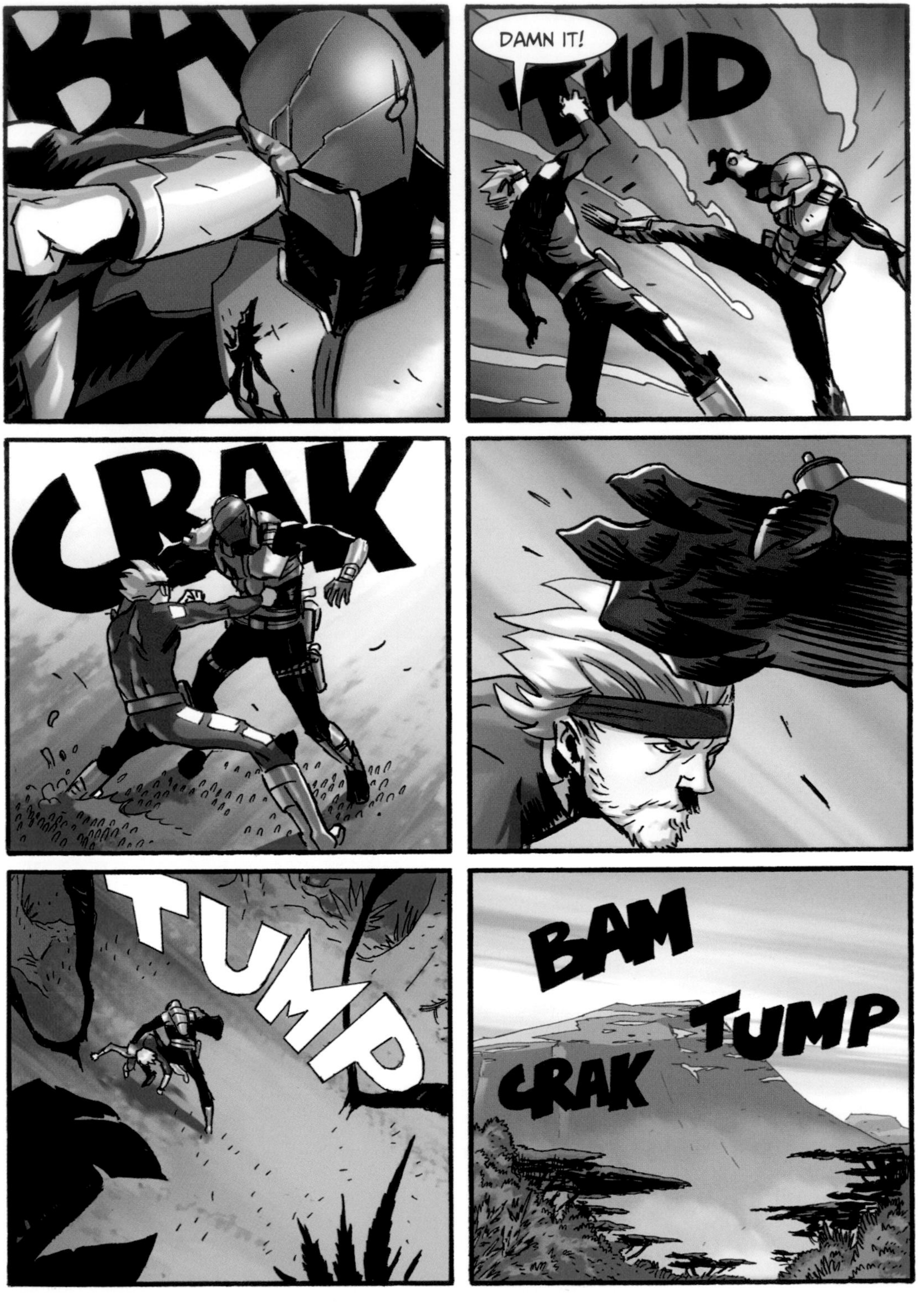
DAMN IT!
THUD
CRAK
TUMP
BAM
TUMP
CRAK

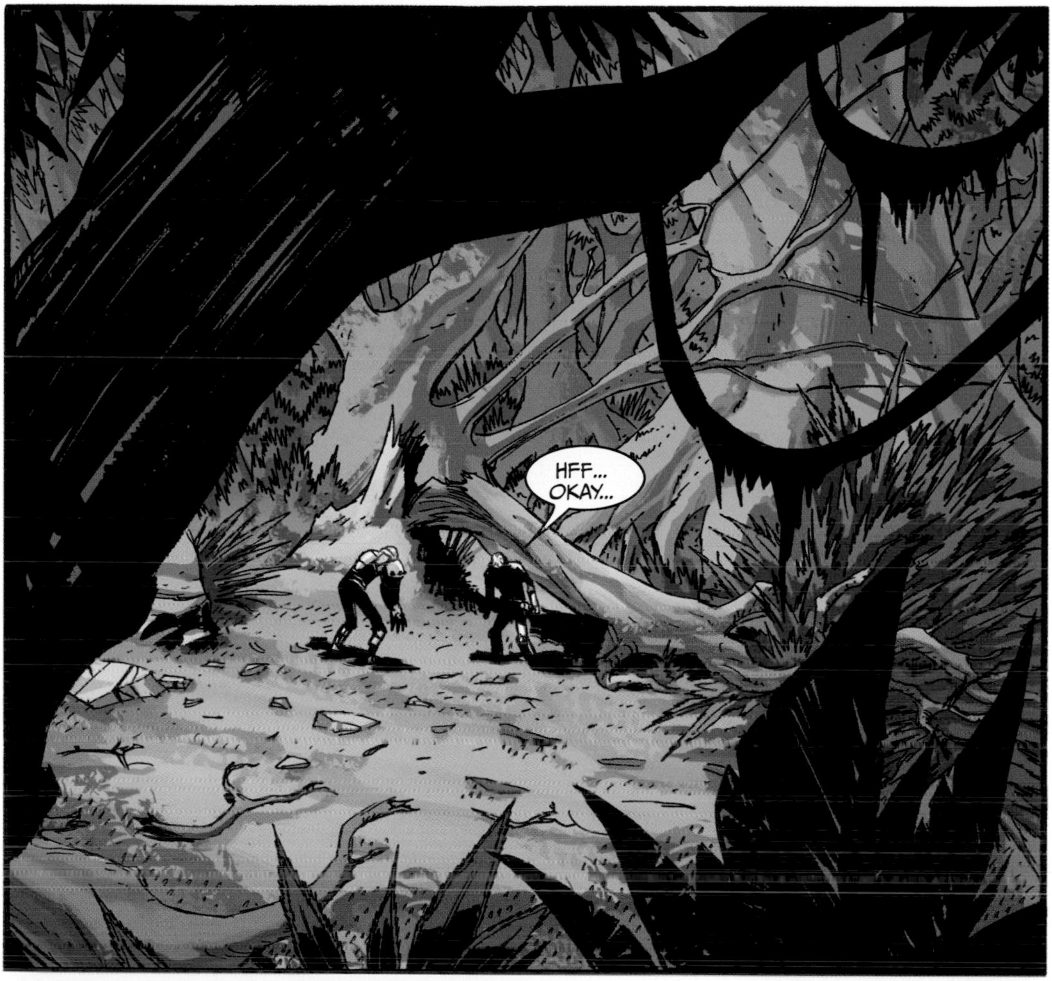
HFF... OKAY...

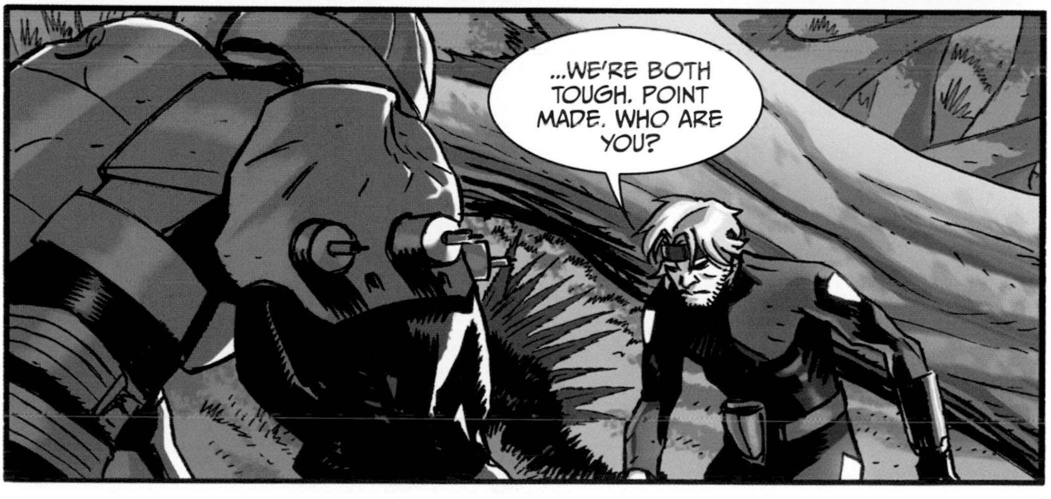
...WE'RE BOTH TOUGH. POINT MADE. WHO ARE YOU?

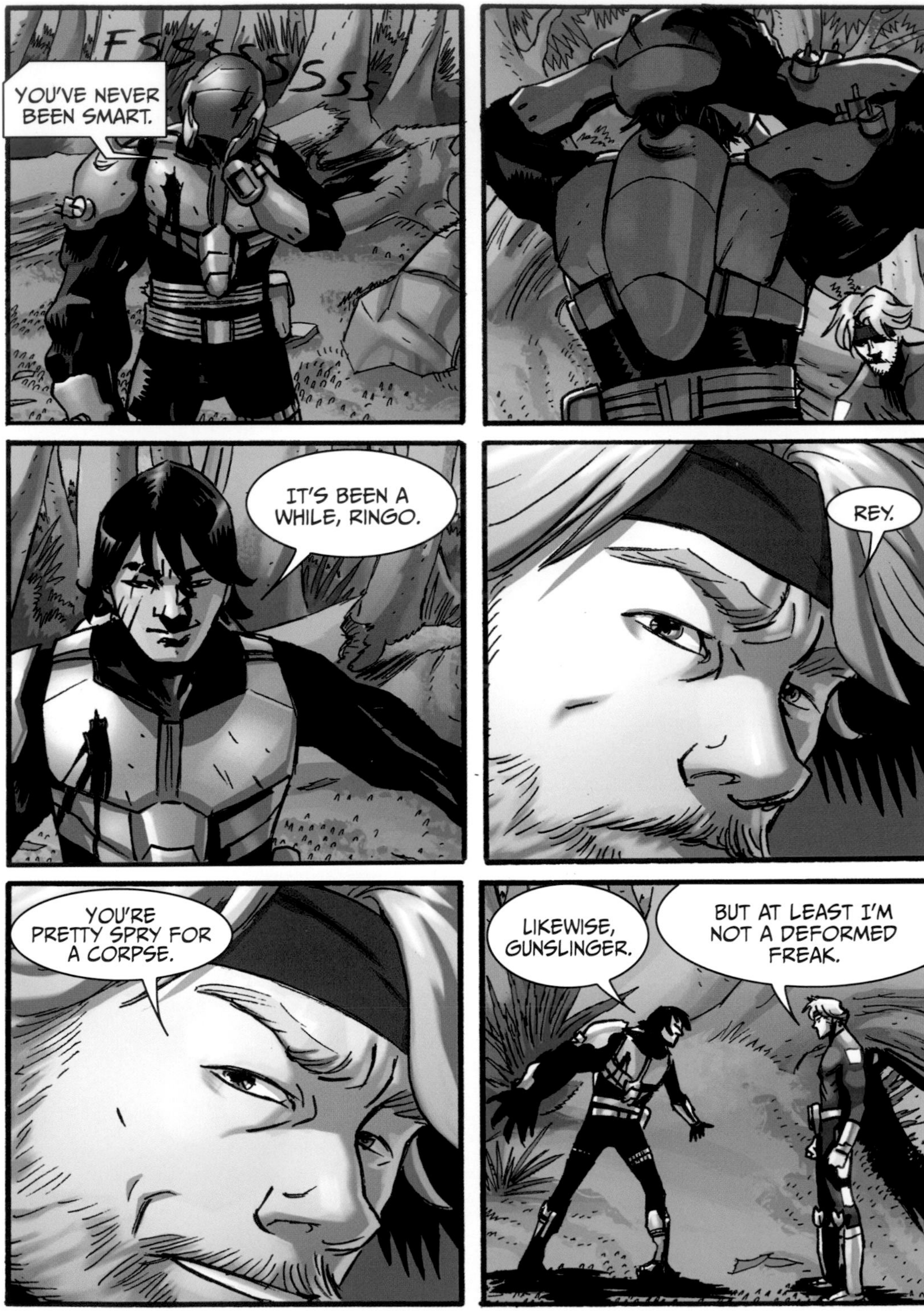
FSSSSSSSSS
YOU'VE NEVER BEEN SMART.
IT'S BEEN A WHILE, RINGO.
REY.
YOU'RE PRETTY SPRY FOR A CORPSE.
LIKEWISE, GUNSLINGER.
BUT AT LEAST I'M NOT A DEFORMED FREAK.

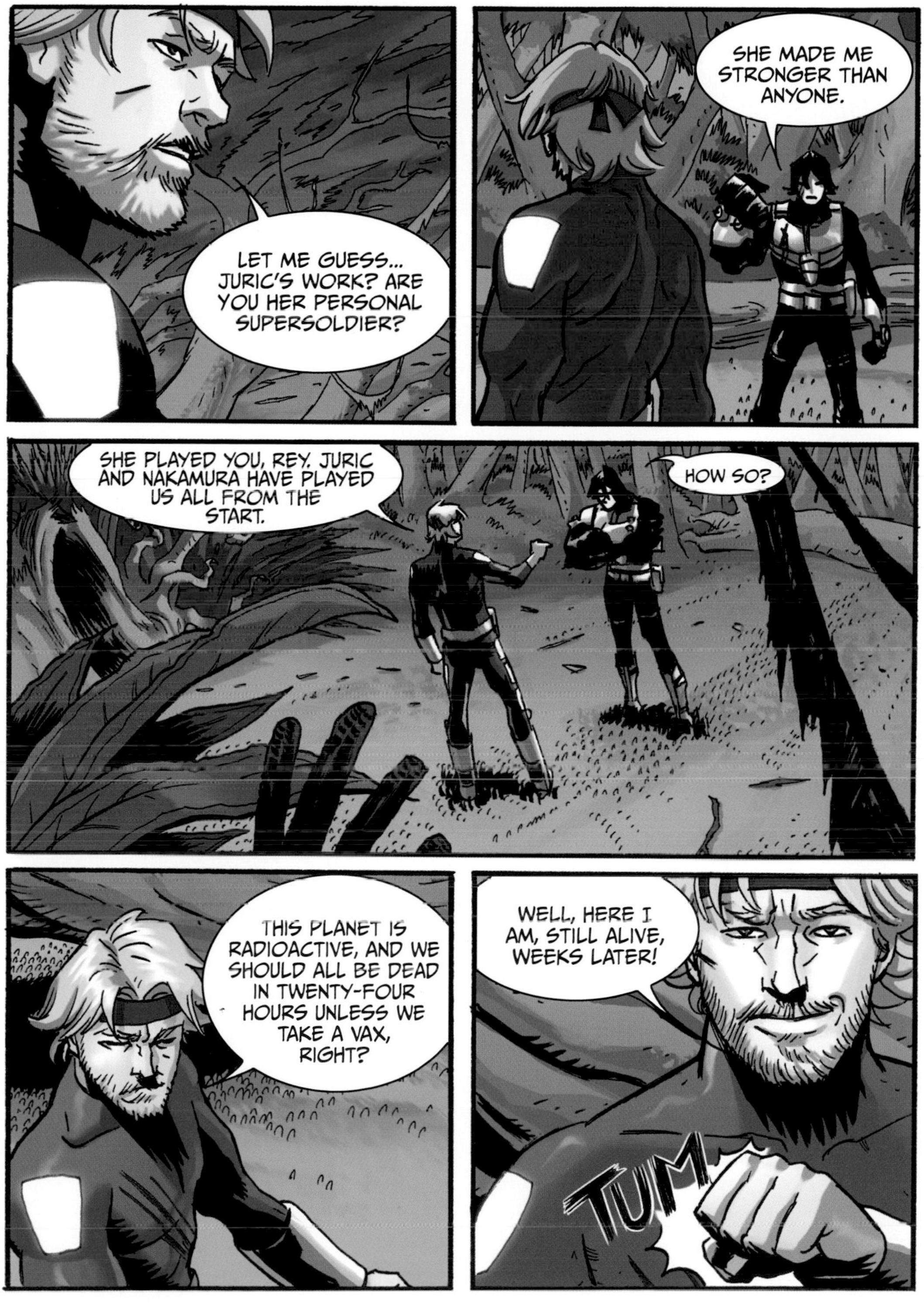
LET ME GUESS... JURIC'S WORK? ARE YOU HER PERSONAL SUPERSOLDIER?
SHE MADE ME STRONGER THAN ANYONE.
SHE PLAYED YOU, REY. JURIC AND NAKAMURA HAVE PLAYED US ALL FROM THE START.
HOW SO?
THIS PLANET IS RADIOACTIVE, AND WE SHOULD ALL BE DEAD IN TWENTY-FOUR HOURS UNLESS WE TAKE A VAX, RIGHT?
WELL, HERE I AM, STILL ALIVE, WEEKS LATER!
TUM

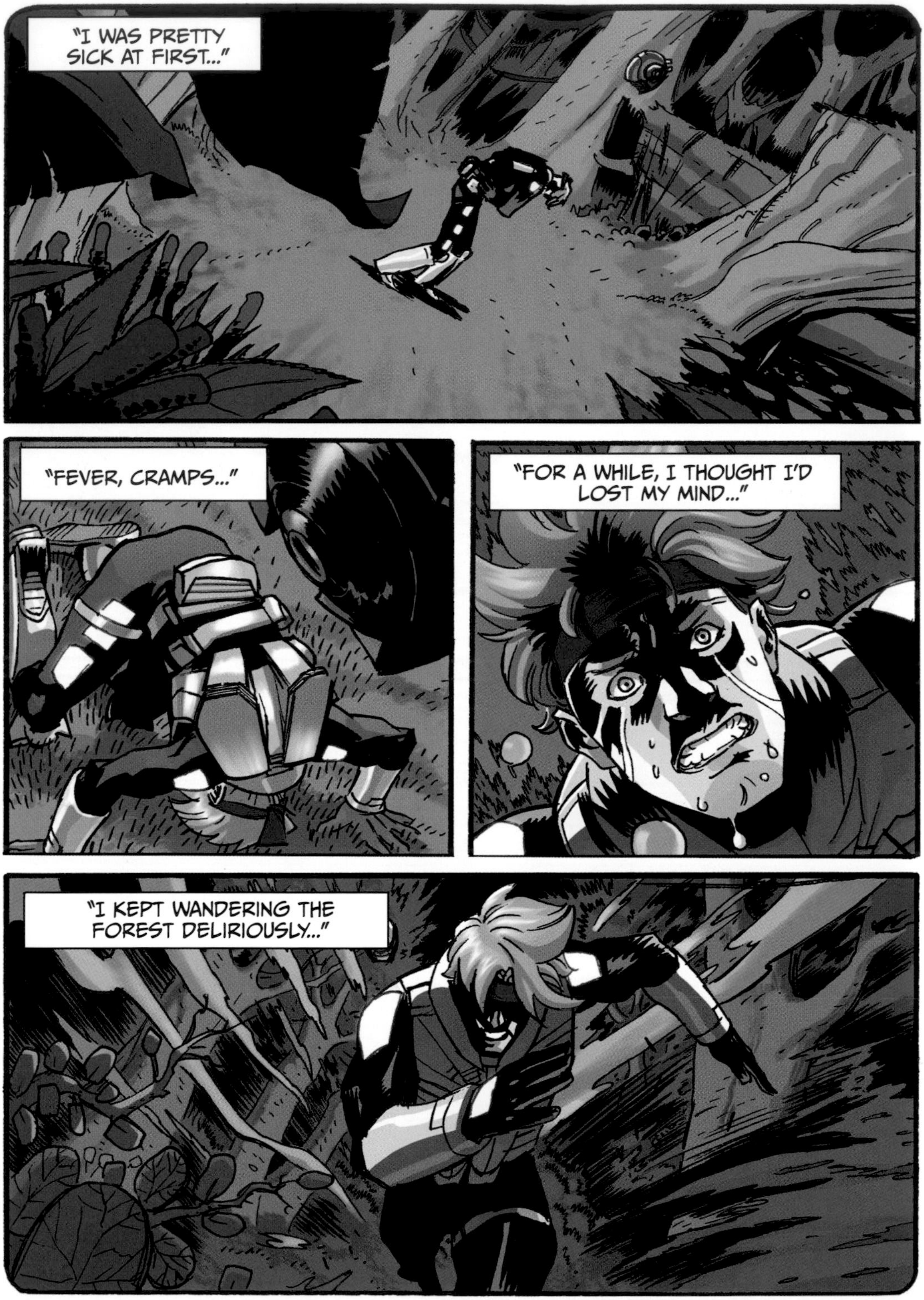
"I WAS PRETTY SICK AT FIRST..."
"FEVER, CRAMPS..."
"FOR A WHILE, I THOUGHT I'D LOST MY MIND..."
"I KEPT WANDERING THE FOREST DELIRIOUSLY..."

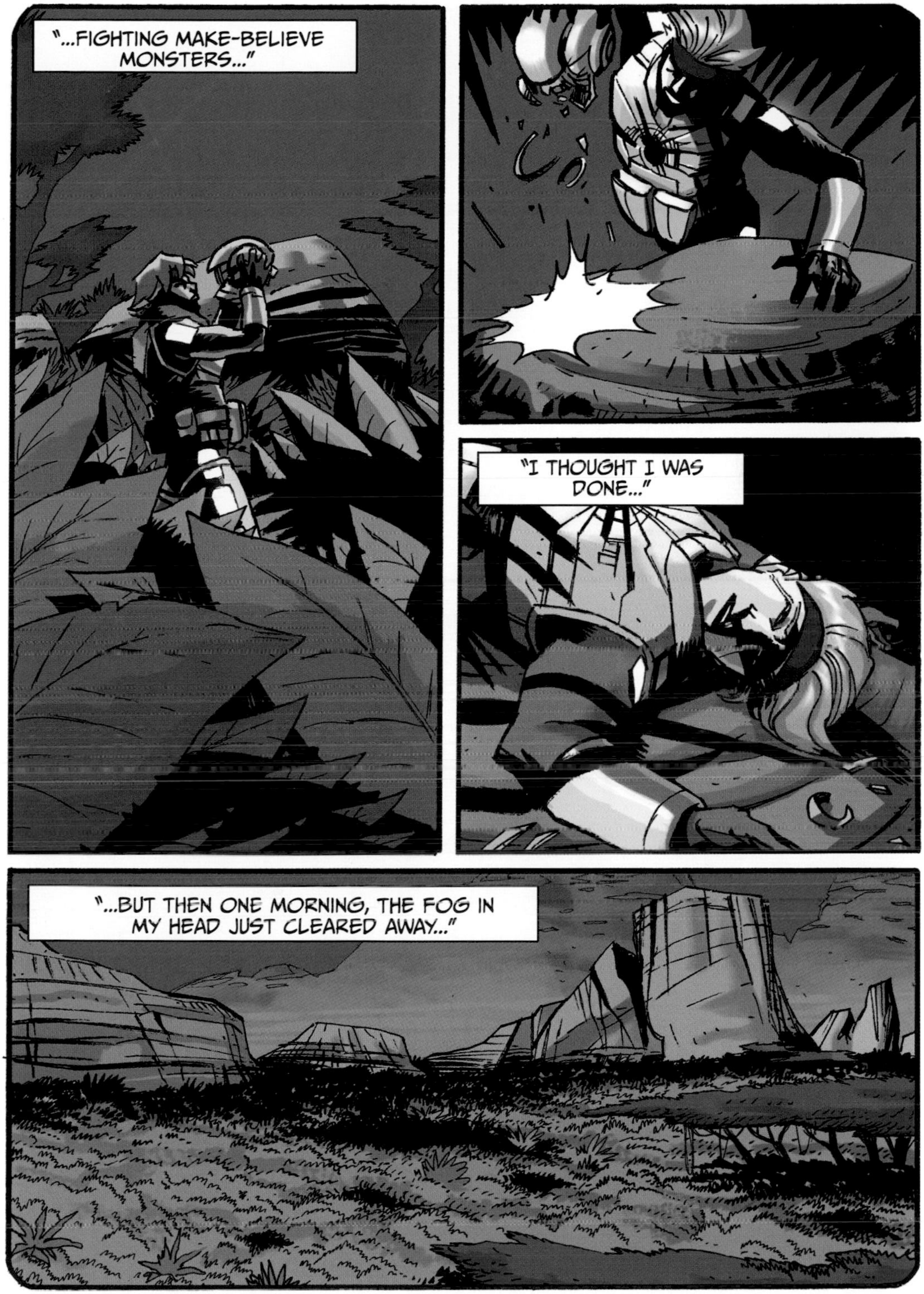
"...FIGHTING MAKE-BELIEVE MONSTERS..."
"I THOUGHT I WAS DONE..."
"...BUT THEN ONE MORNING, THE FOG IN MY HEAD JUST CLEARED AWAY..."

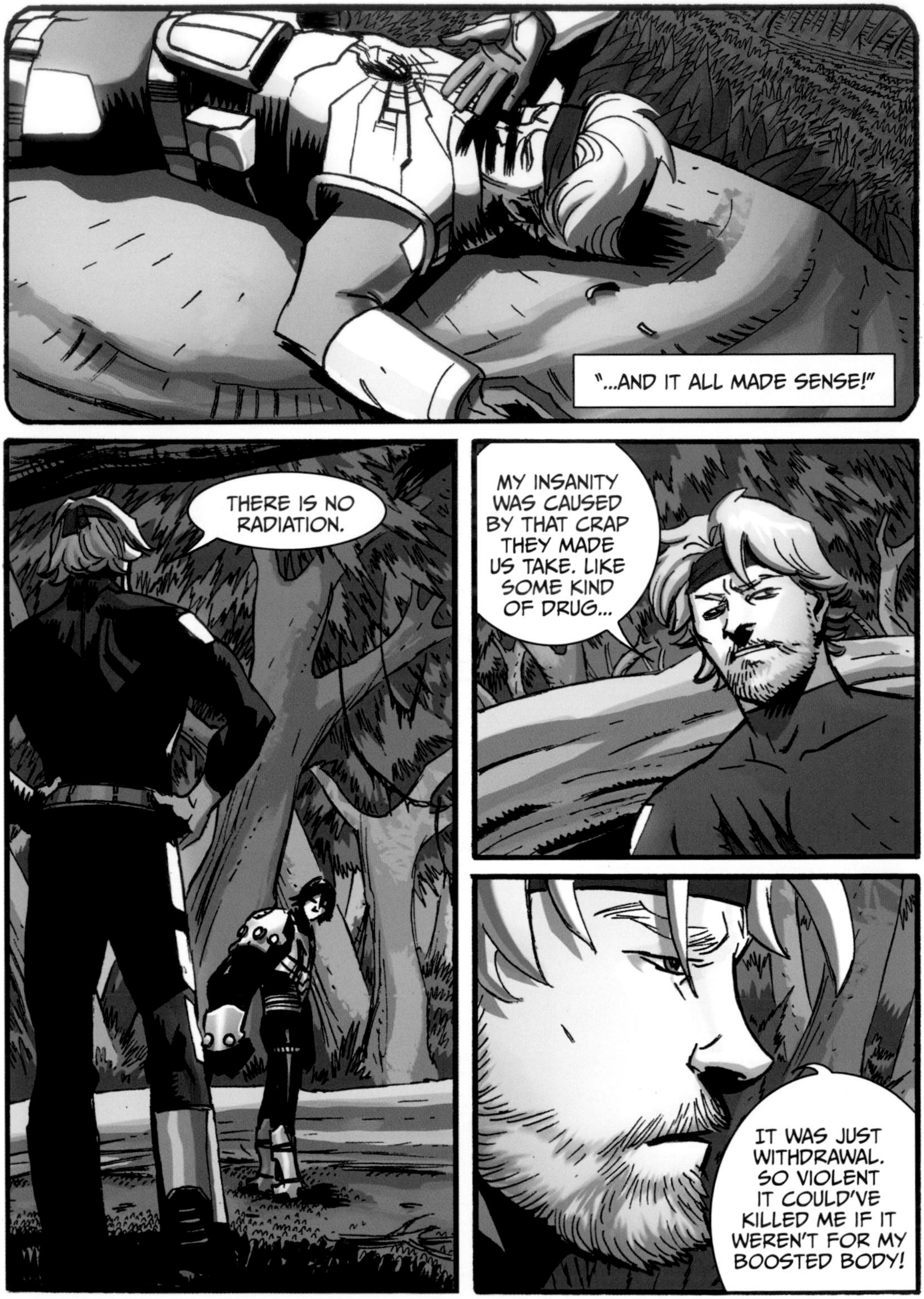
"...AND IT ALL MADE SENSE!"
THERE IS NO RADIATION.
MY INSANITY WAS CAUSED BY THAT CRAP THEY MADE US TAKE. LIKE SOME KIND OF DRUG...
IT WAS JUST WITHDRAWAL. SO VIOLENT IT COULD'VE KILLED ME IF IT WEREN'T FOR MY BOOSTED BODY!

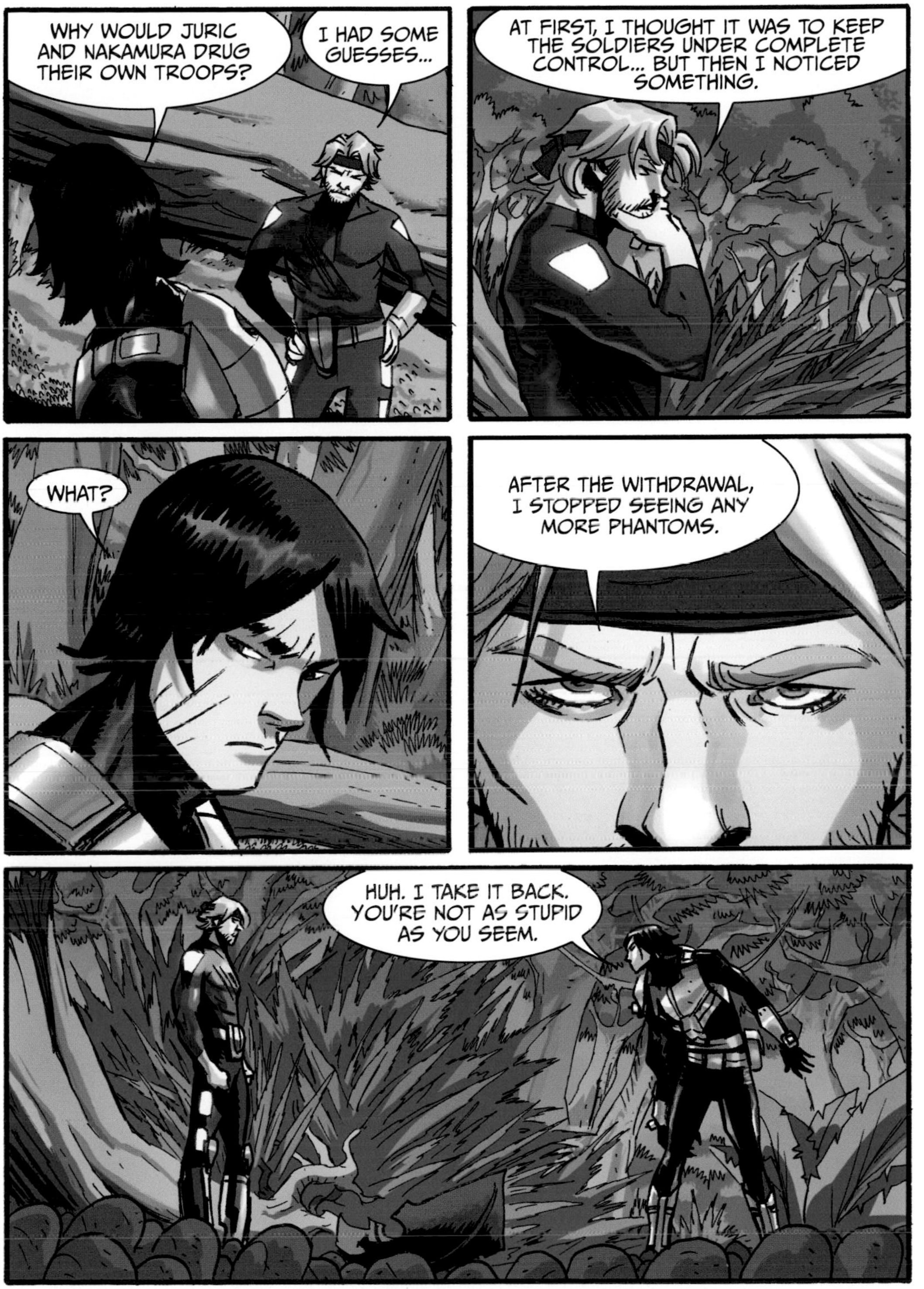
WHY WOULD JURIC AND NAKAMURA DRUG THEIR OWN TROOPS?
I HAD SOME GUESSES...
AT FIRST, I THOUGHT IT WAS TO KEEP THE SOLDIERS UNDER COMPLETE CONTROL... BUT THEN I NOTICED SOMETHING.
WHAT?
AFTER THE WITHDRAWAL, I STOPPED SEEING ANY MORE PHANTOMS.
HUH. I TAKE IT BACK. YOU'RE NOT AS STUPID AS YOU SEEM.

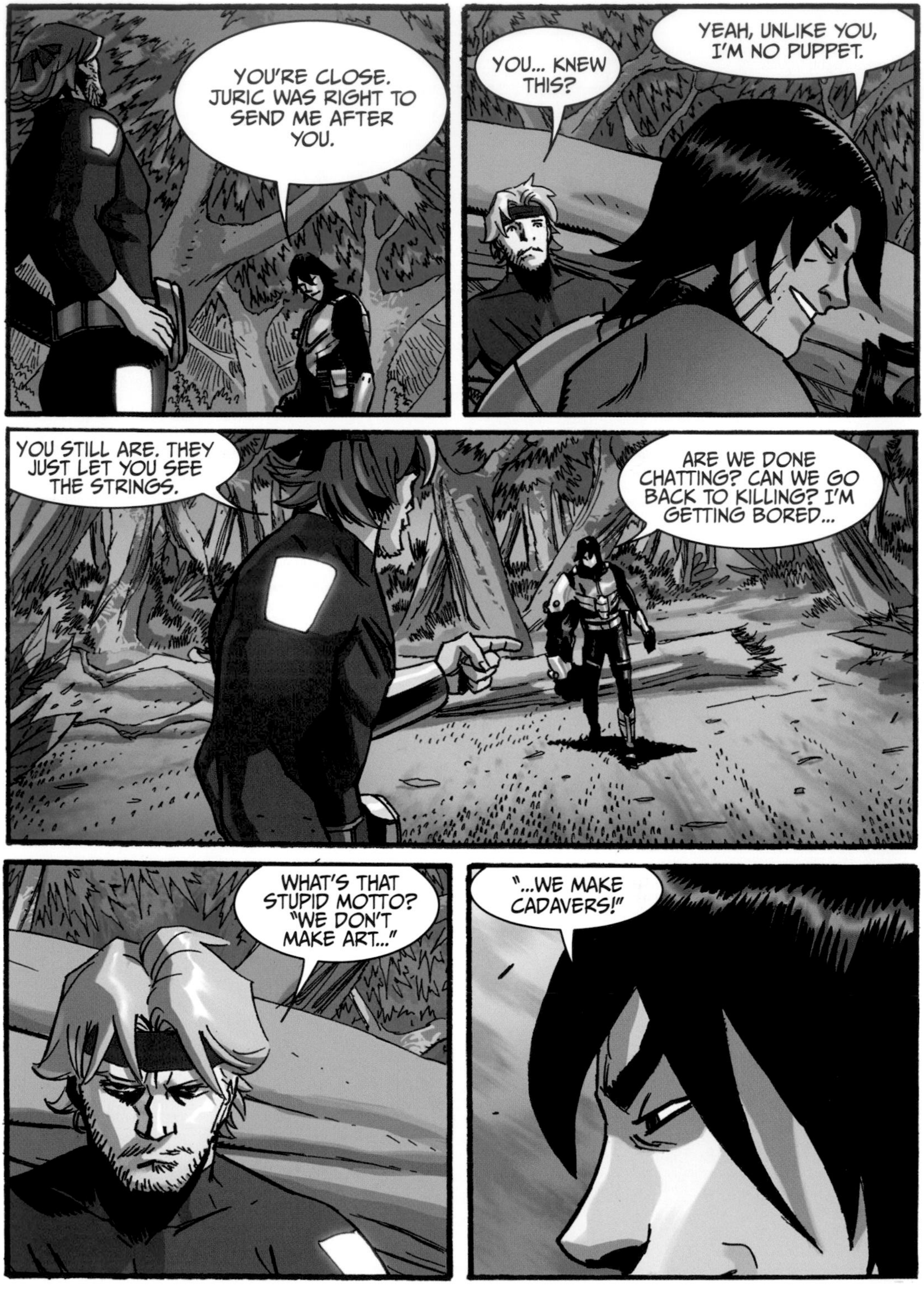
YOU'RE CLOSE. JURIC WAS RIGHT TO SEND ME AFTER YOU.
YOU... KNEW THIS?
YEAH, UNLIKE YOU, I'M NO PUPPET.
YOU STILL ARE. THEY JUST LET YOU SEE THE STRINGS.
ARE WE DONE CHATTING? CAN WE GO BACK TO KILLING? I'M GETTING BORED...
WHAT'S THAT STUPID MOTTO? "WE DON'T MAKE ART..."
"...WE MAKE CADAVERS!"

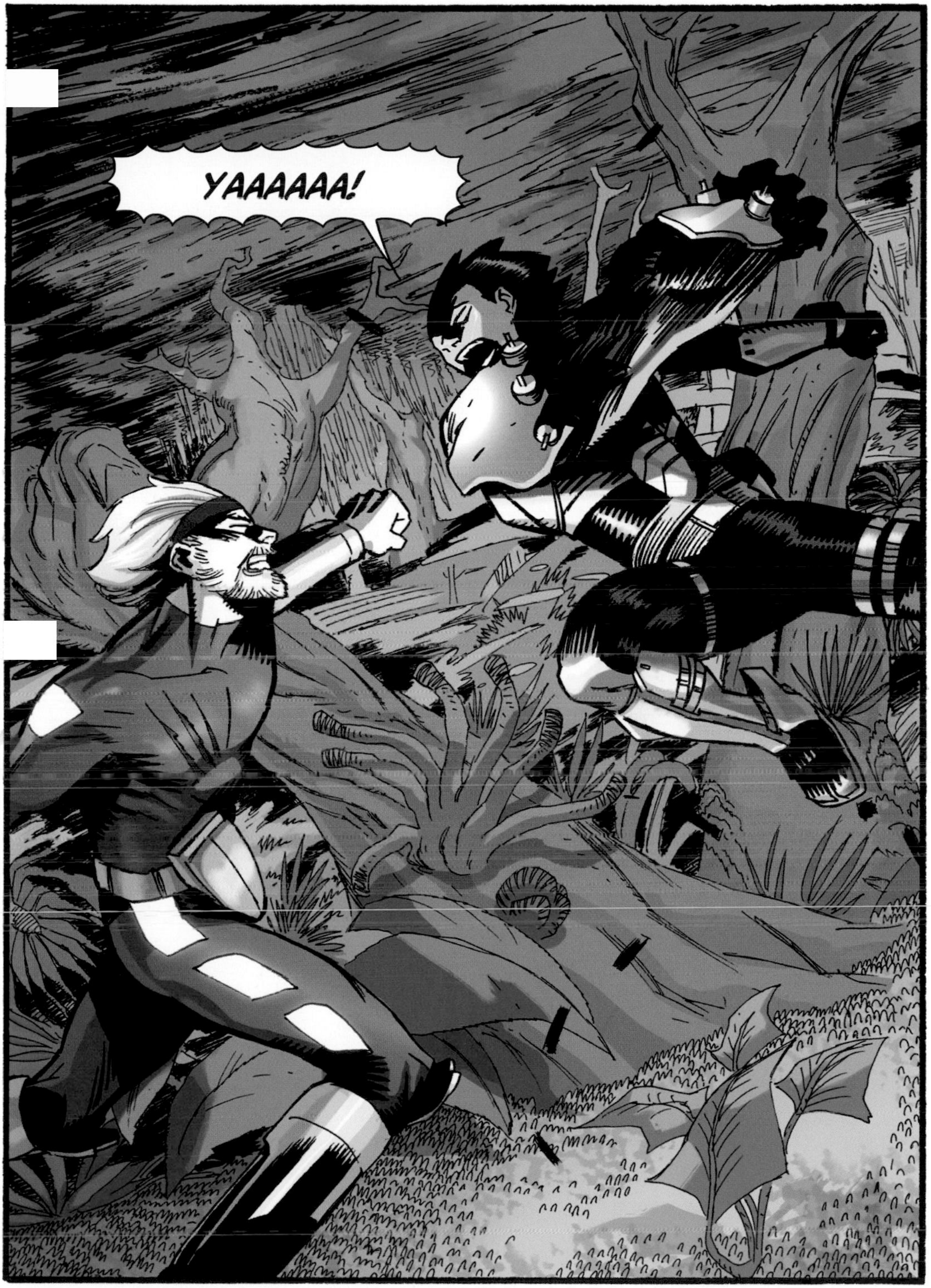
YAAAAAA!

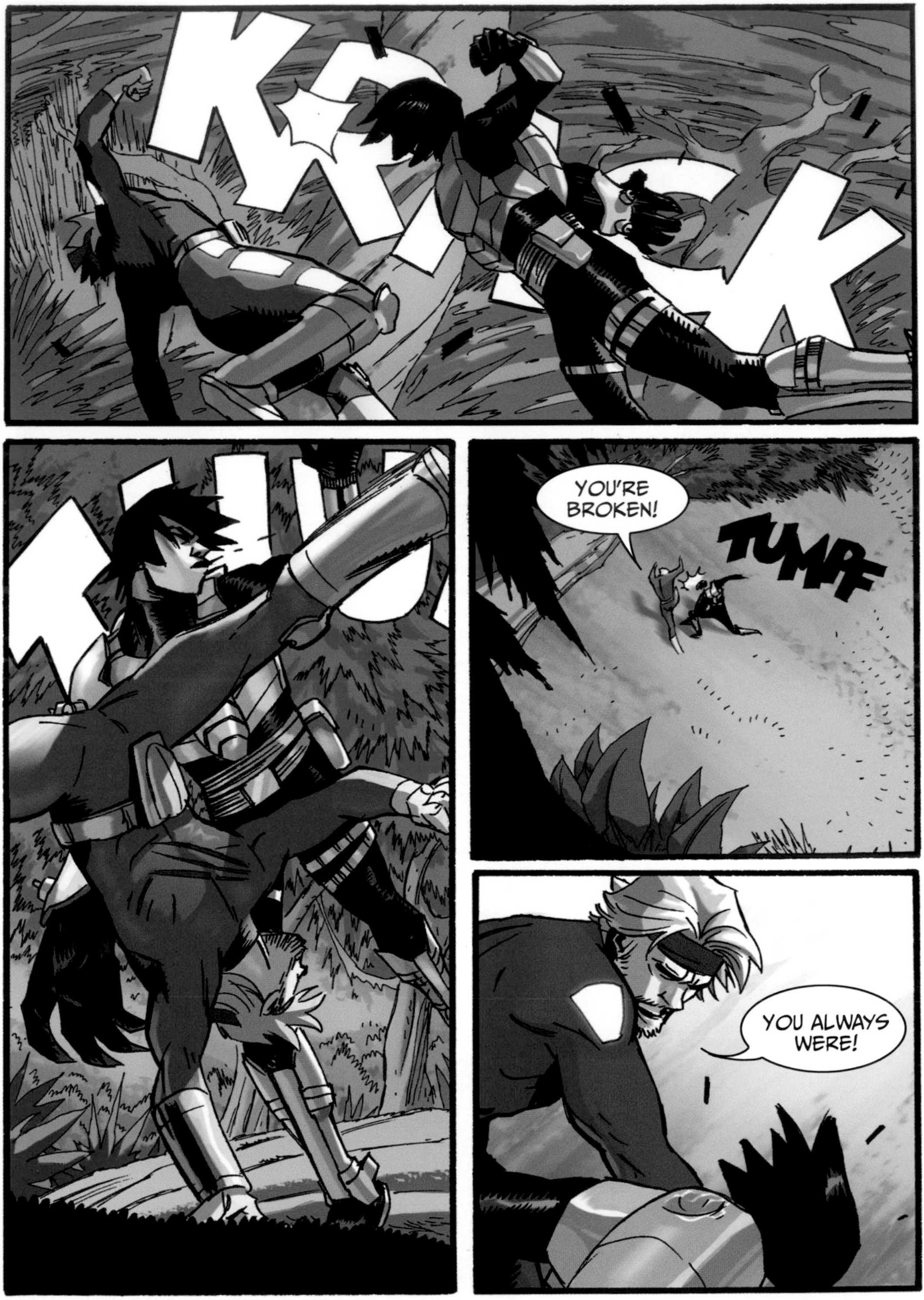
YOU'RE BROKEN!
TUMPF
YOU ALWAYS WERE!

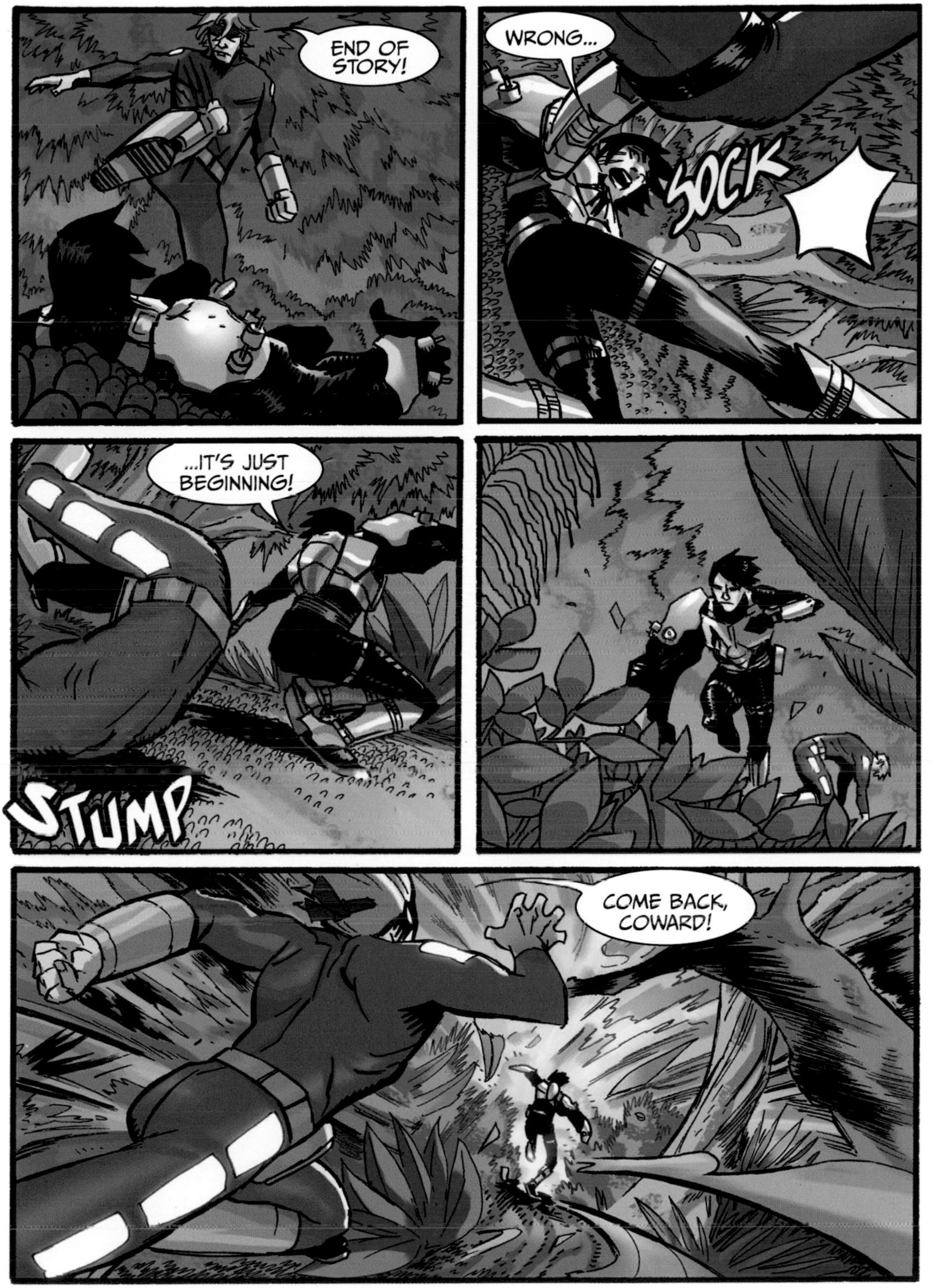
END OF STORY!
WRONG...
SOCK
...IT'S JUST BEGINNING!
STUMP
COME BACK, COWARD!

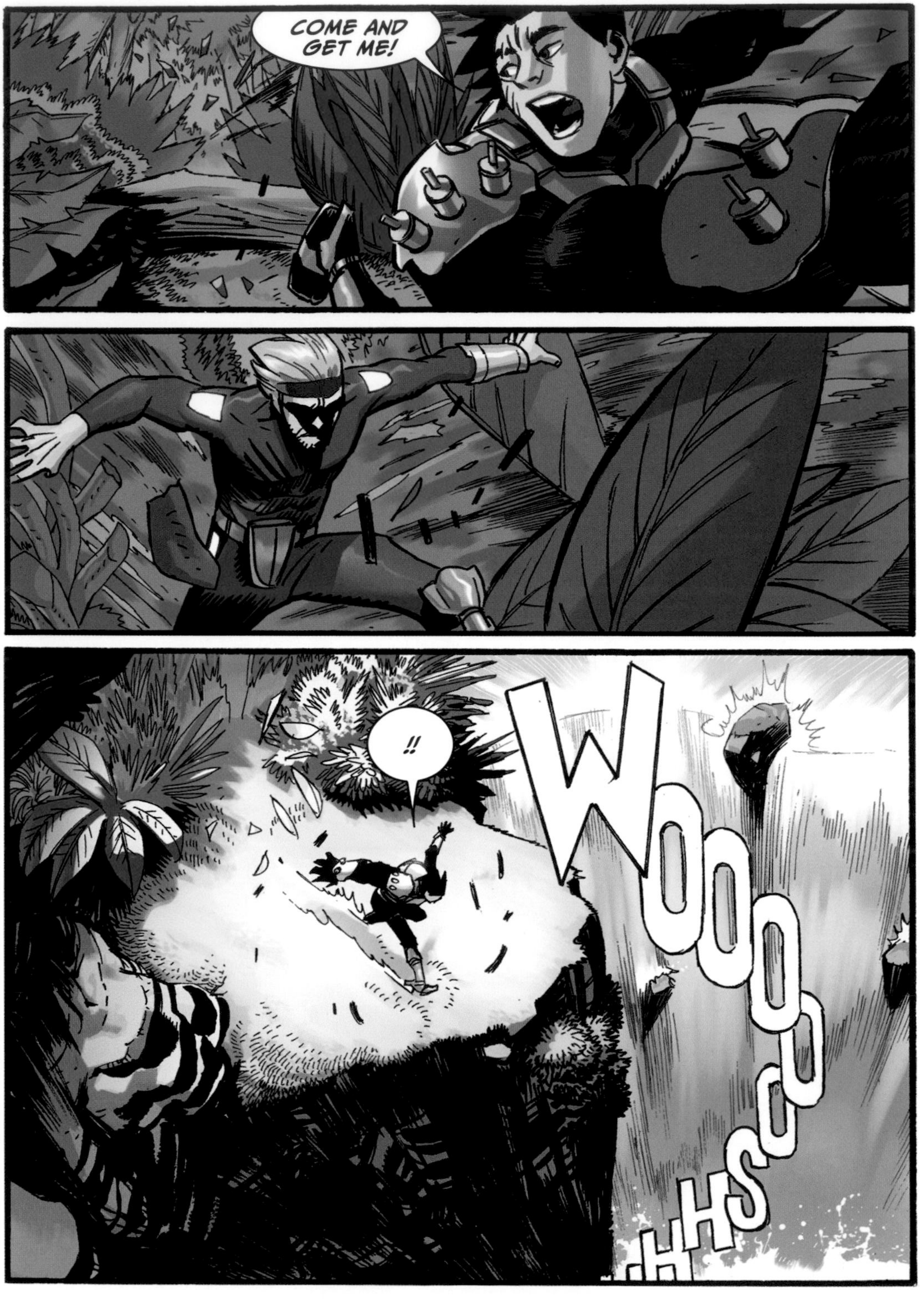
COME AND GET ME!
!!
WOOOOOOSHHH

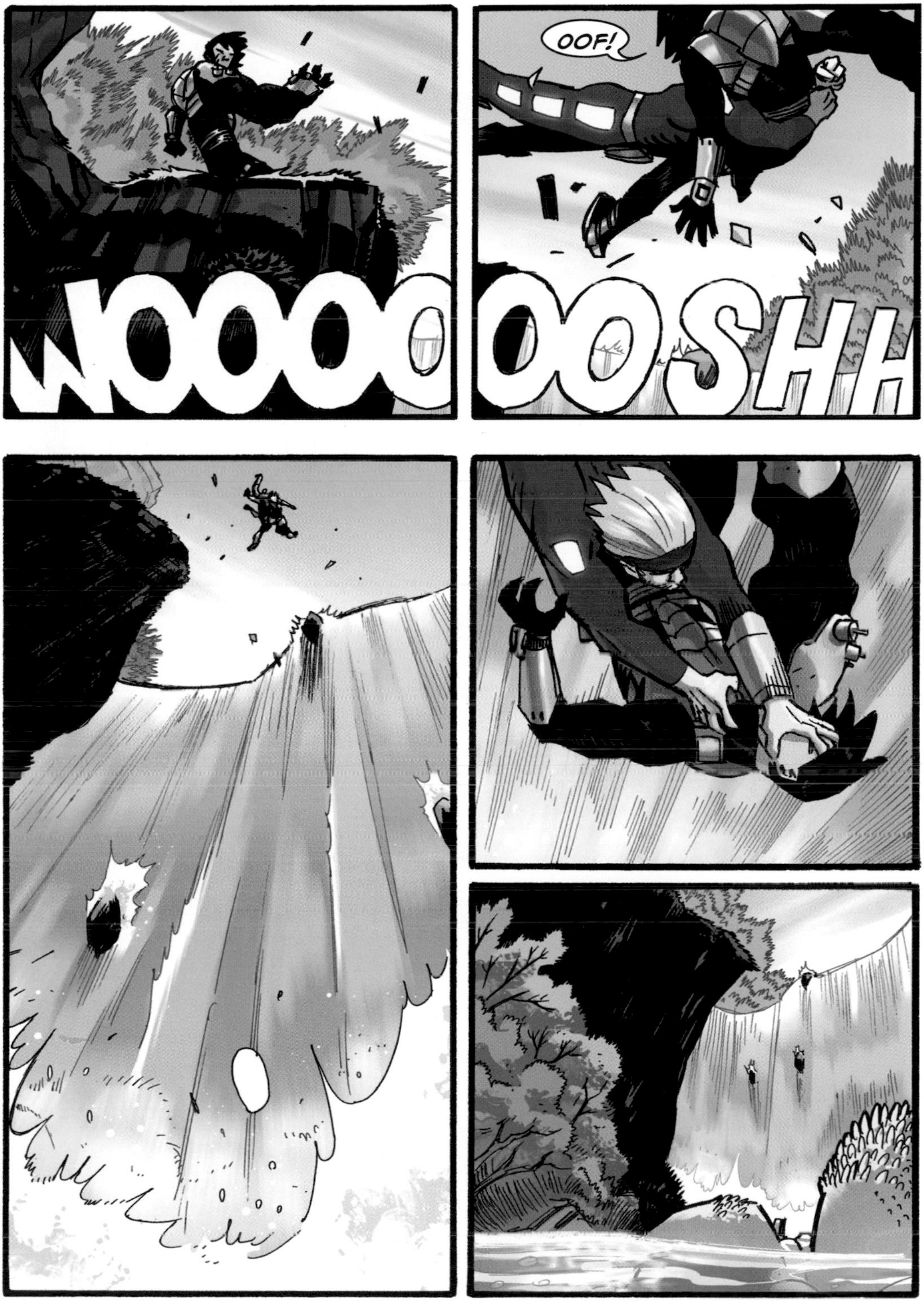
OOF!
WOOOOOOOSHH

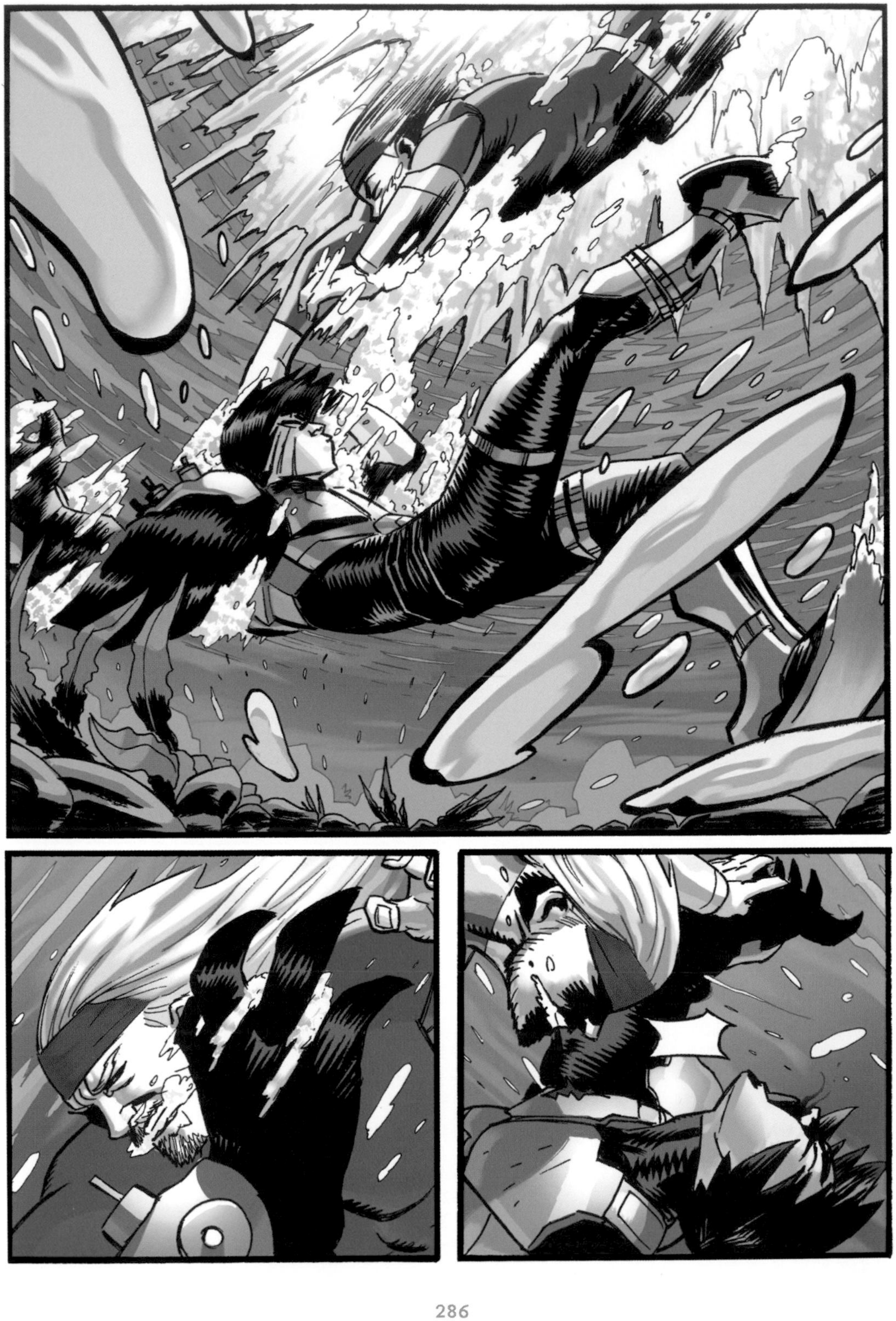

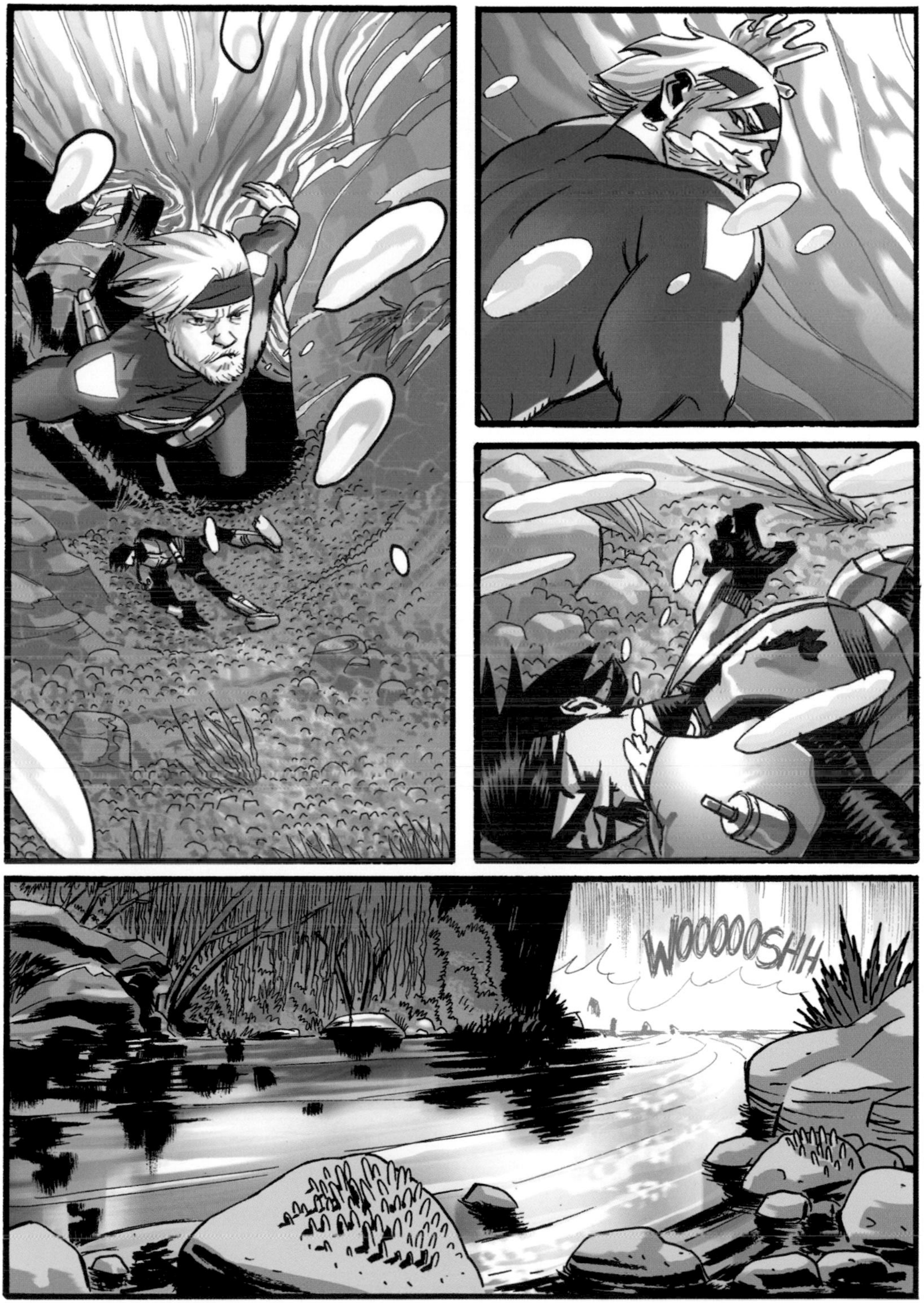
WOOOOOSHH

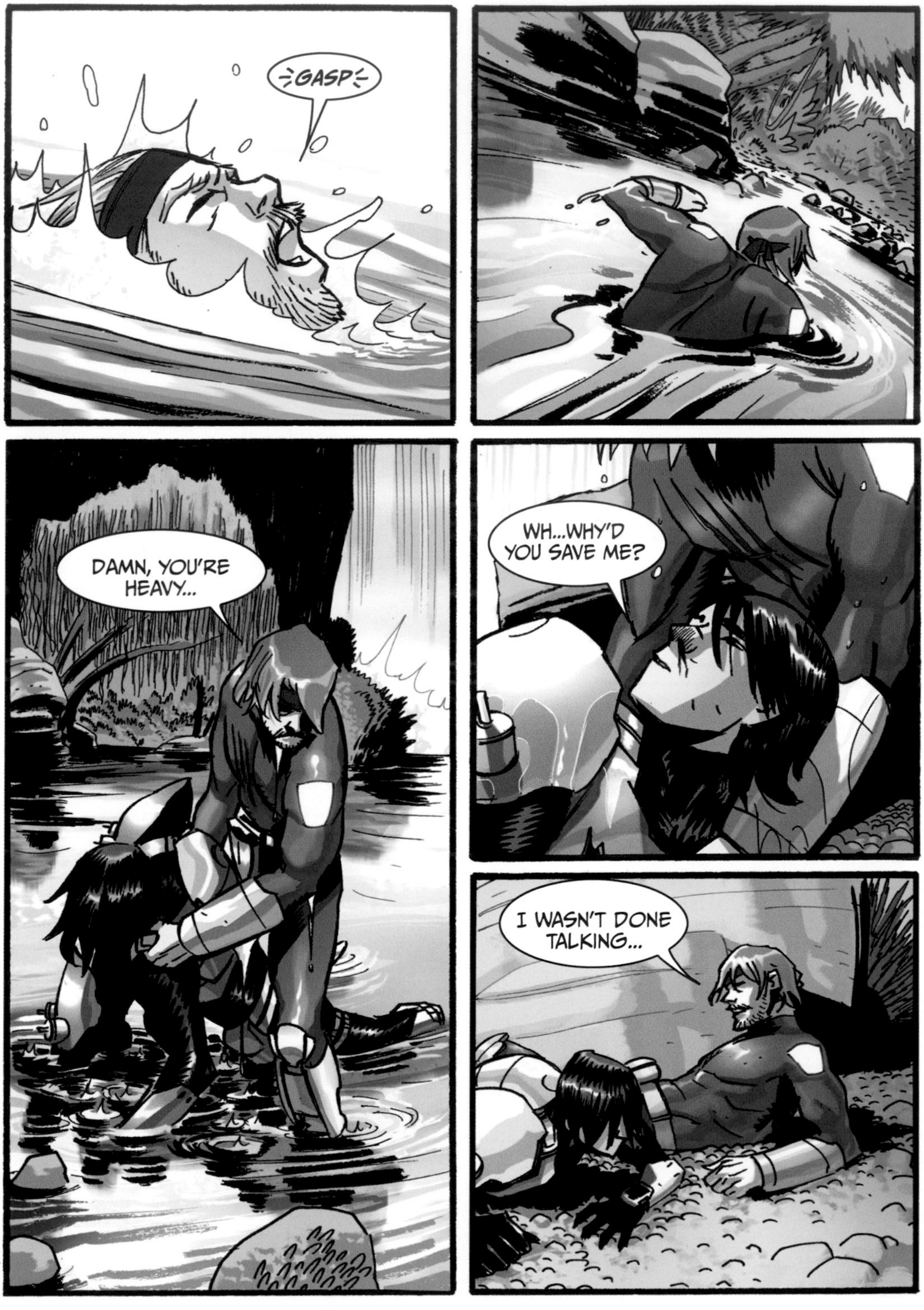
GASP
DAMN, YOU'RE HEAVY...
WH...WHY'D YOU SAVE ME?
I WASN'T DONE TALKING...

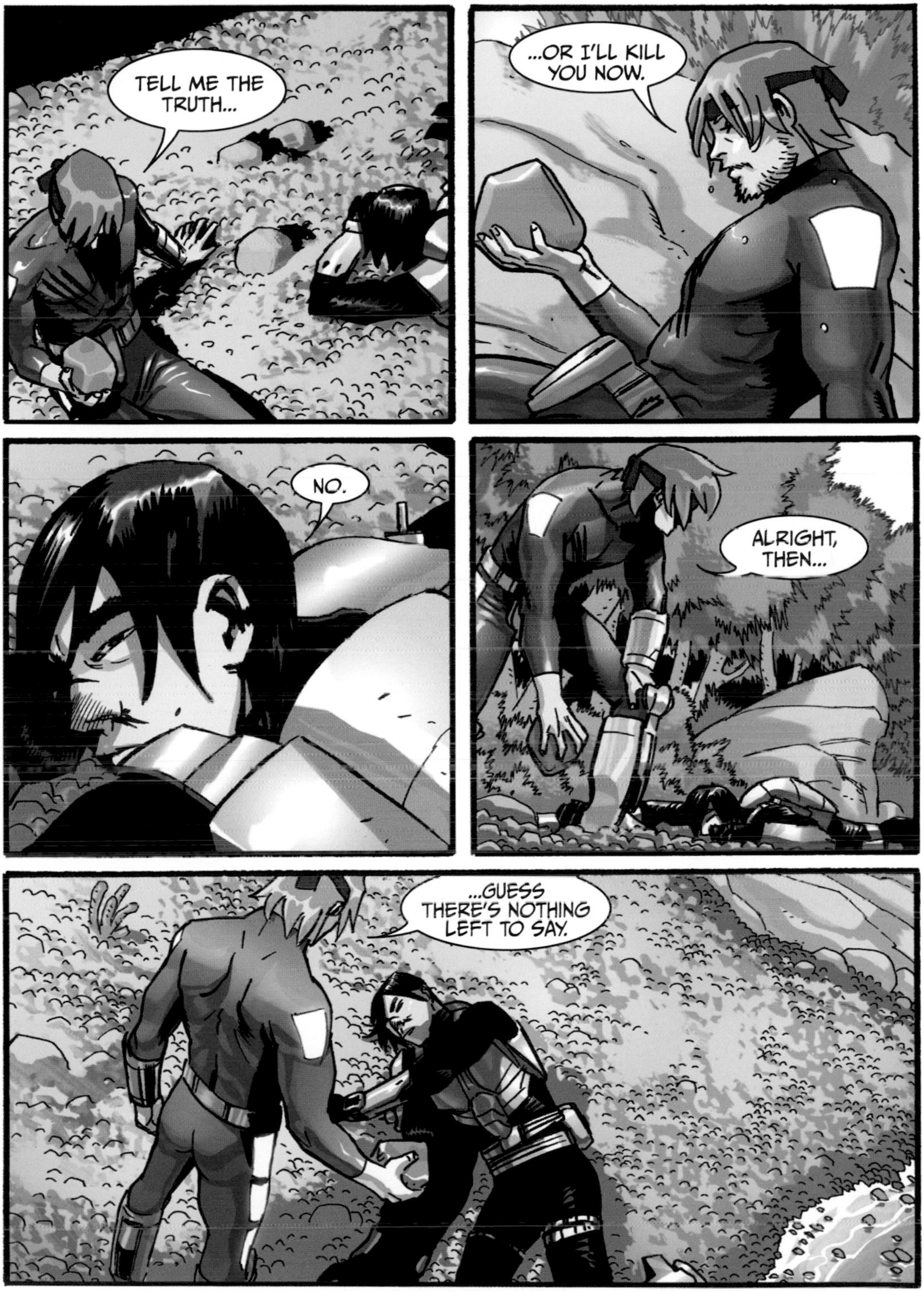
TELL ME THE TRUTH...
...OR I'LL KILL YOU NOW.
NO.
ALRIGHT, THEN...
...GUESS THERE'S NOTHING LEFT TO SAY.

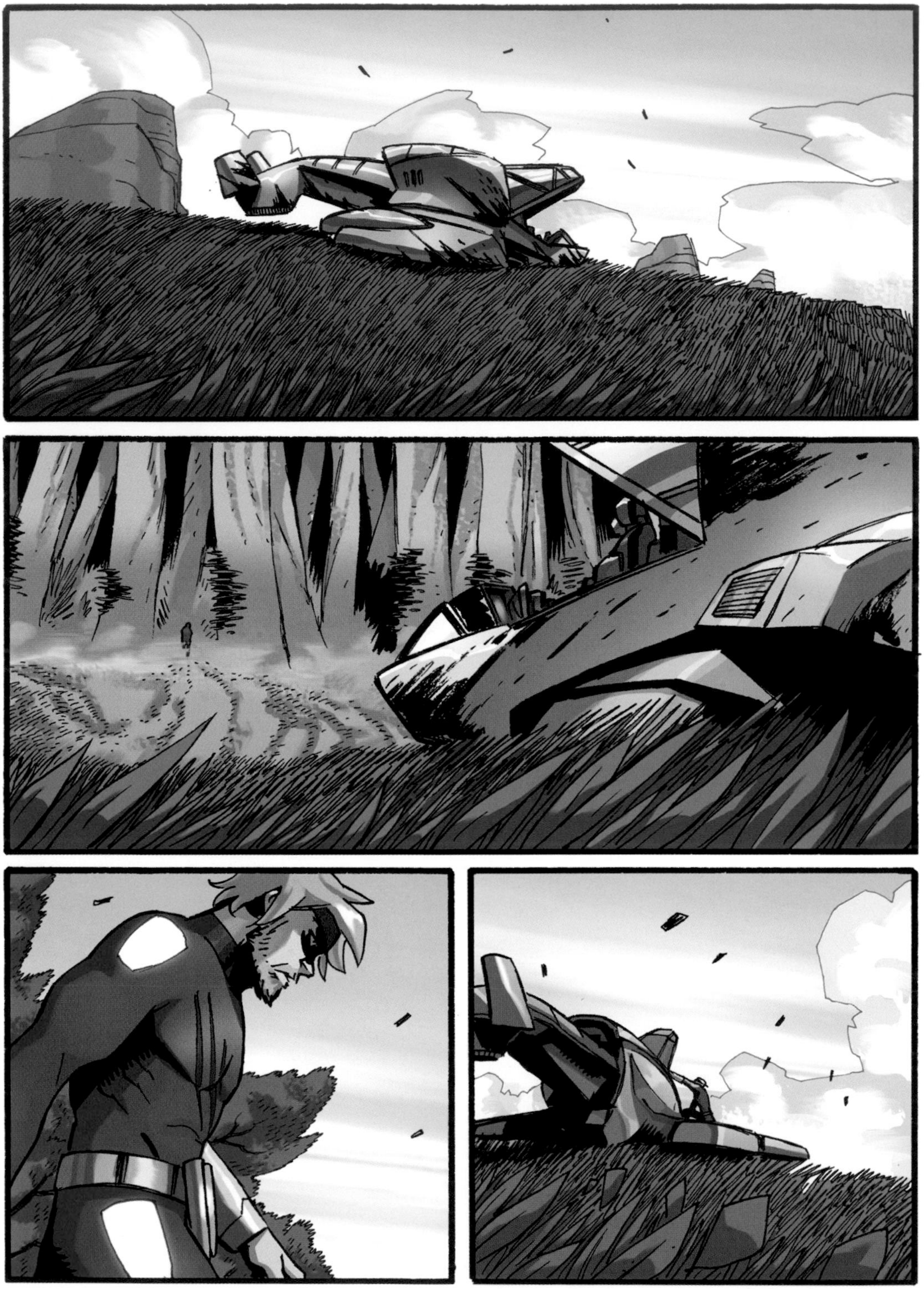

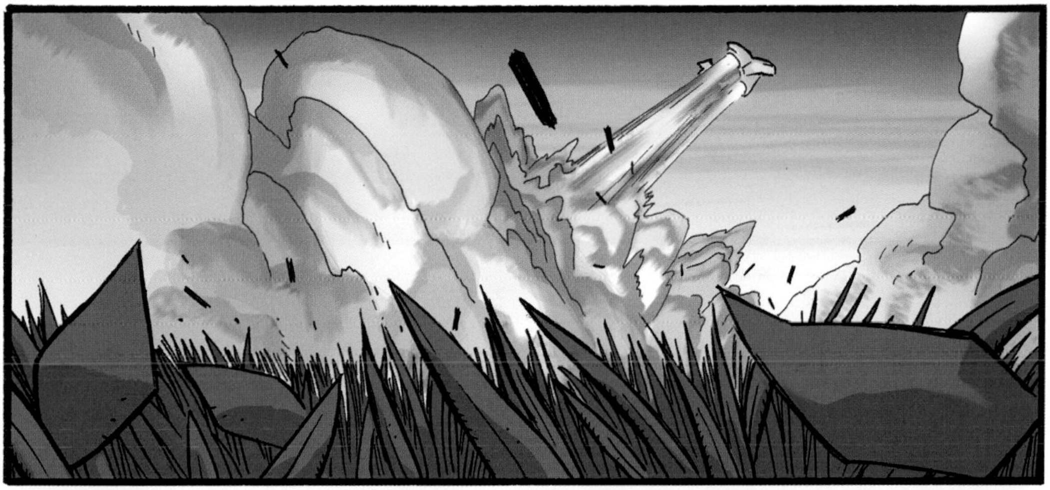

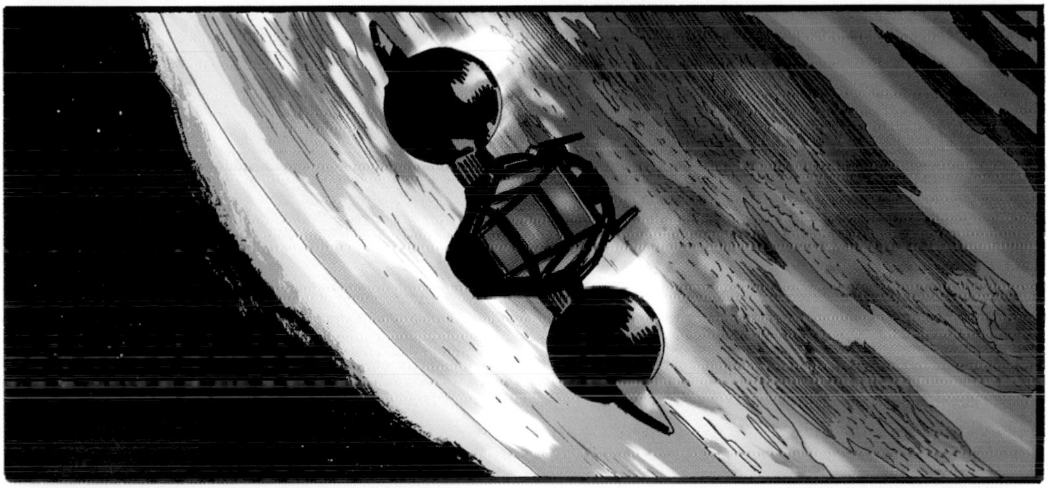

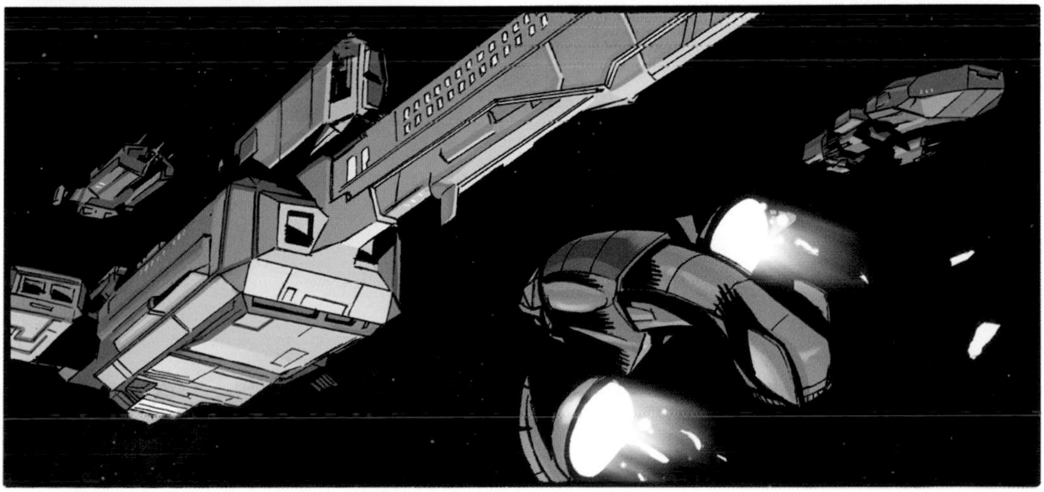

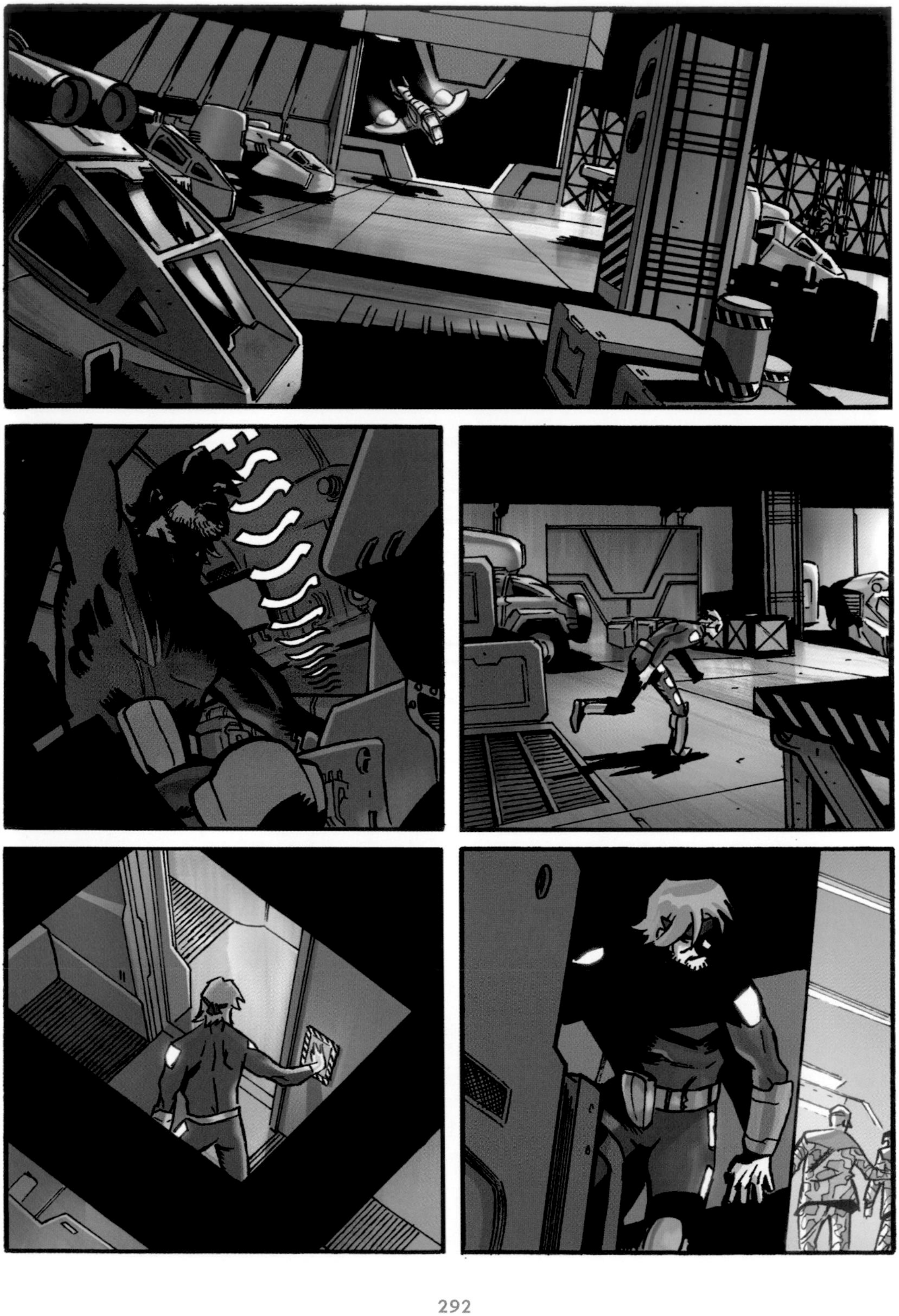

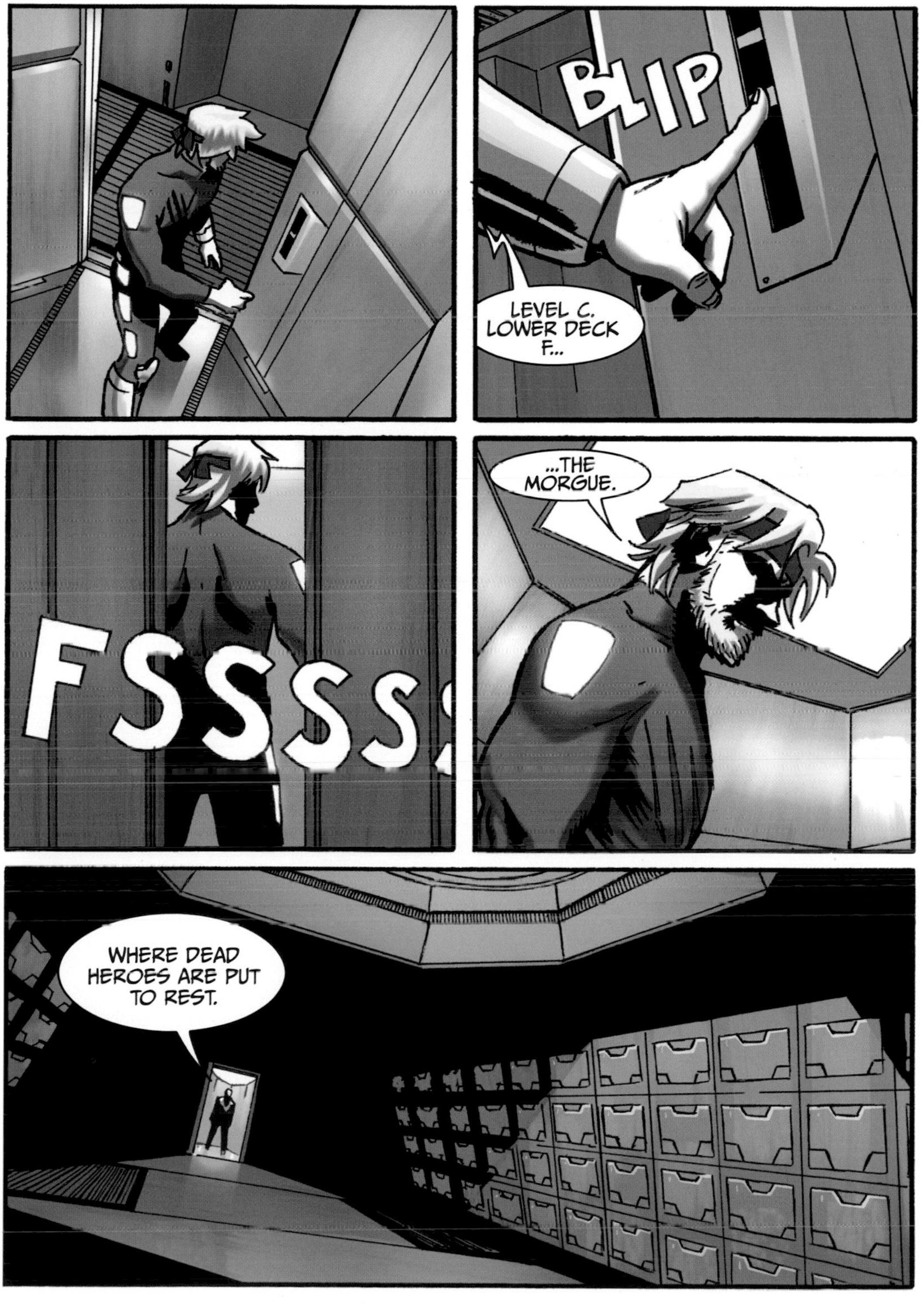
BLIP
LEVEL C. LOWER DECK F...
FSSSS
...THE MORGUE.
WHERE DEAD HEROES ARE PUT TO REST.

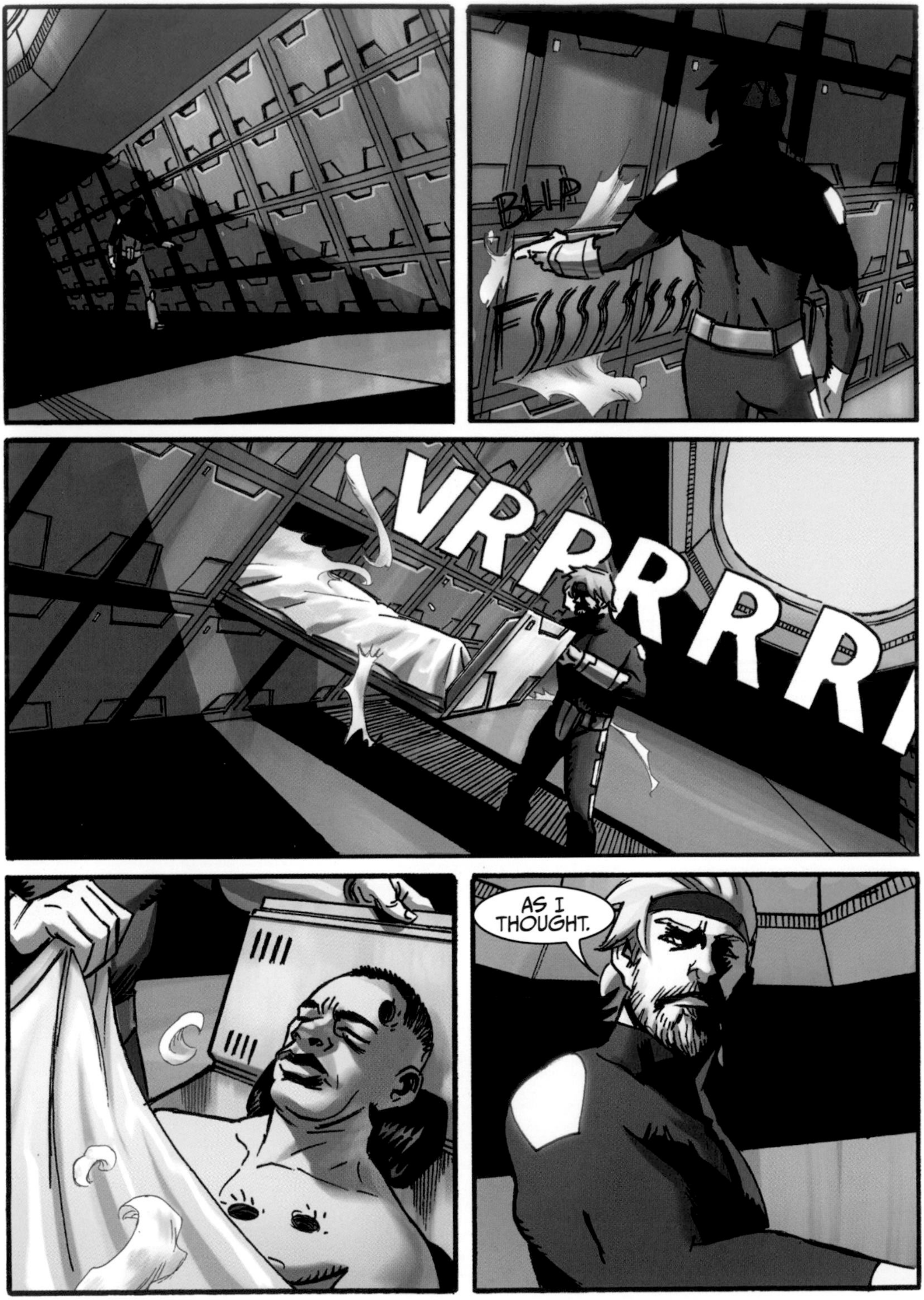
BLIP
FSSSSSSS
VRPRRRRR
AS I THOUGHT.

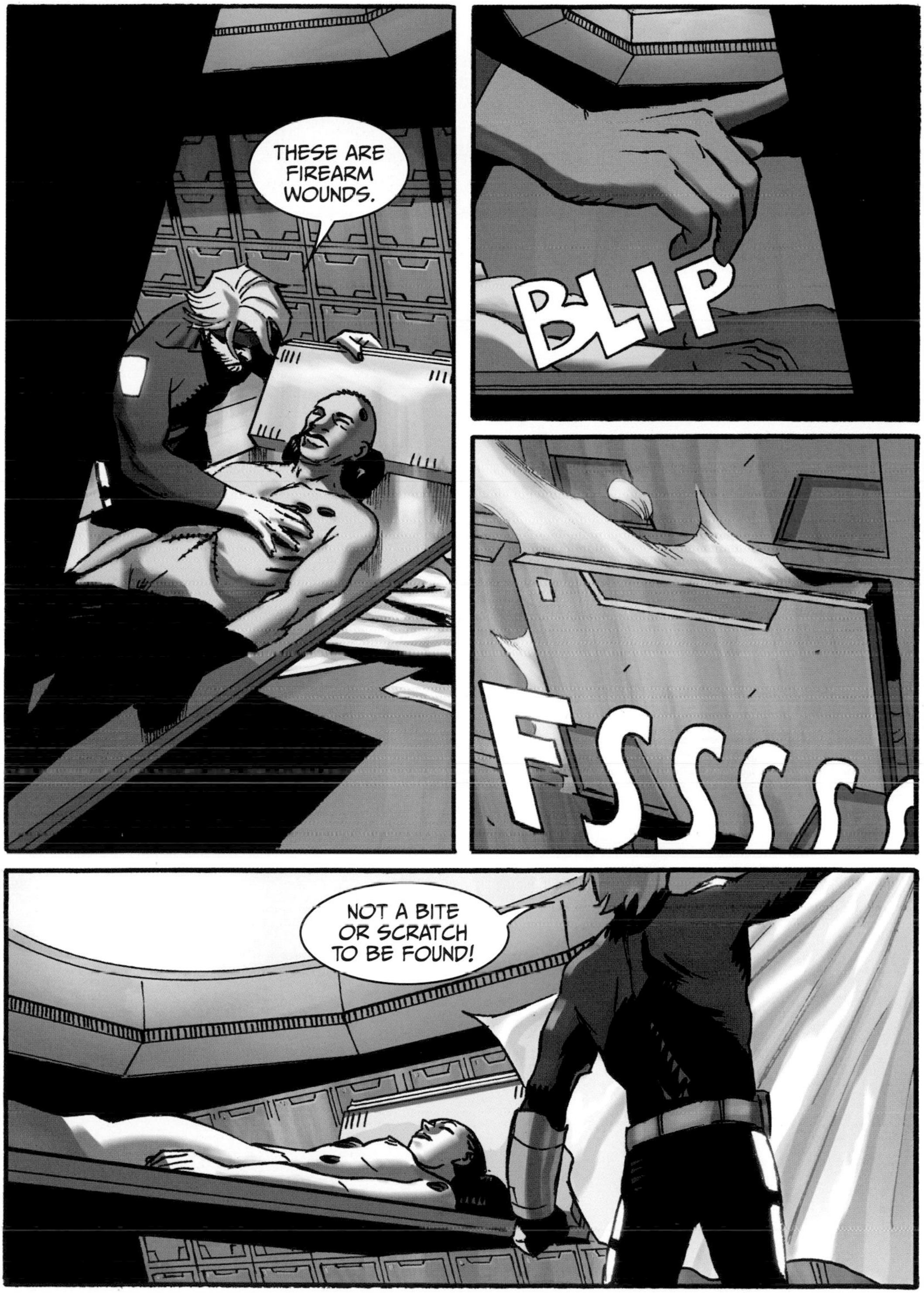
THESE ARE FIREARM WOUNDS.
BLIP
FSSSS
NOT A BITE OR SCRATCH TO BE FOUND!

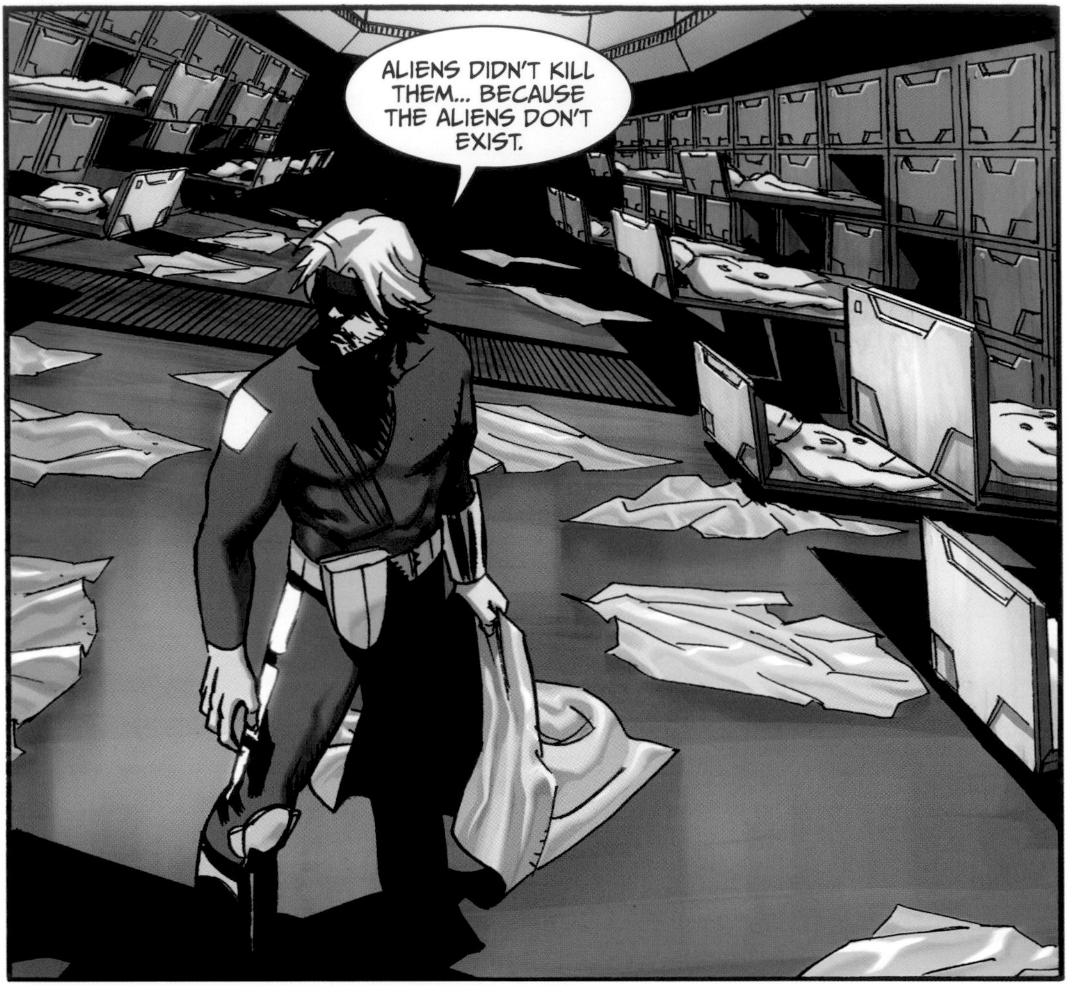
ALIENS DIDN'T KILL THEM... BECAUSE THE ALIENS DON'T EXIST.

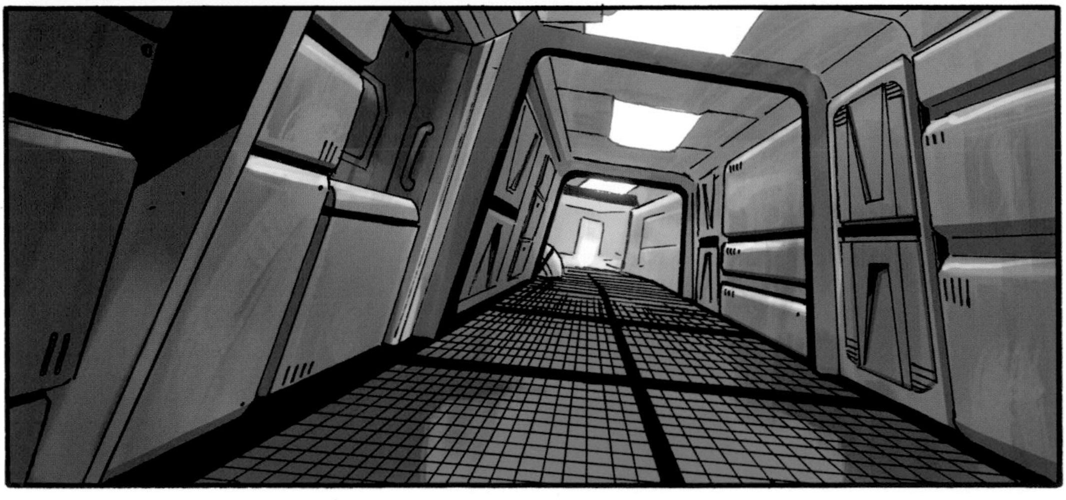

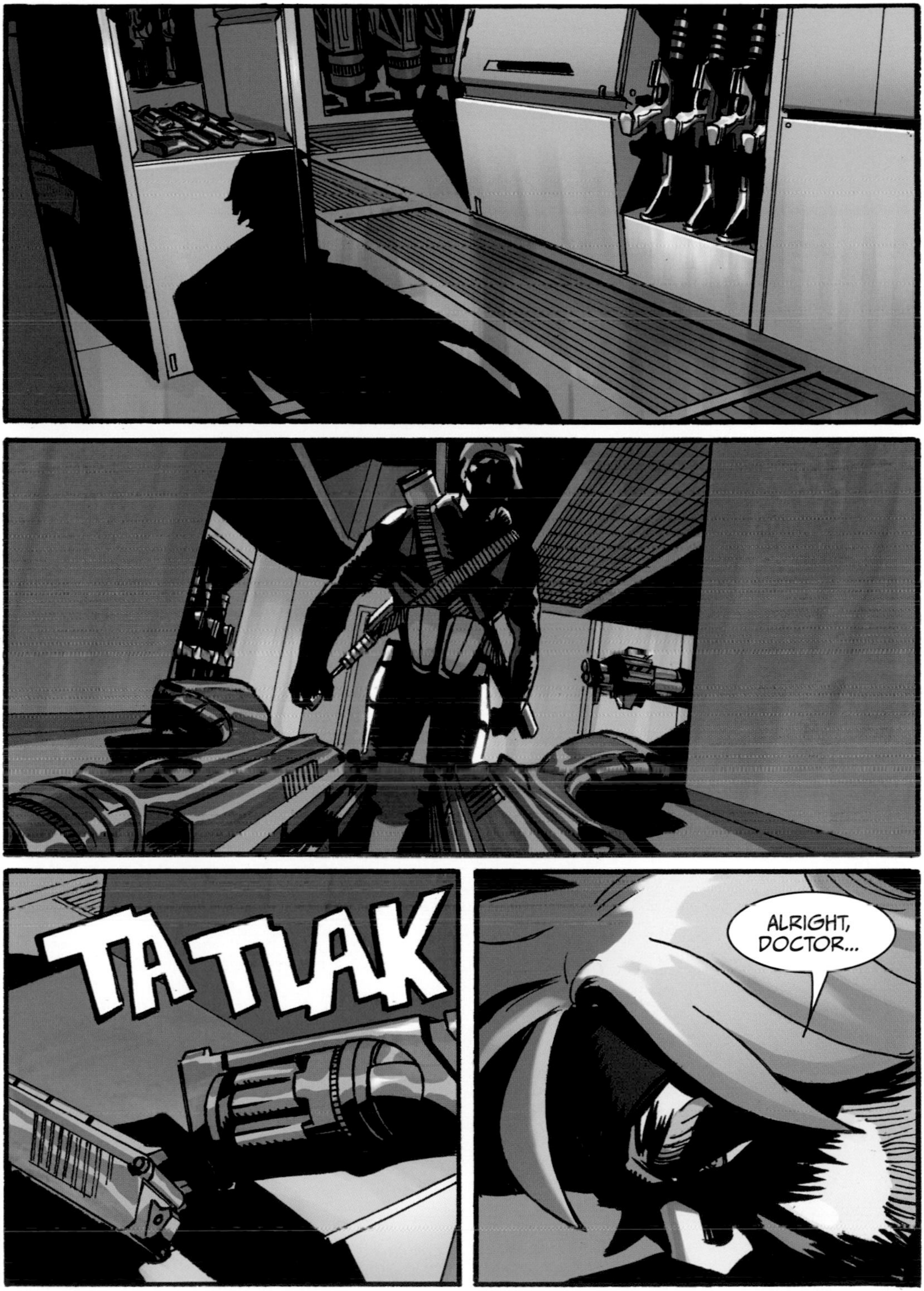
TA TLAK
ALRIGHT, DOCTOR...

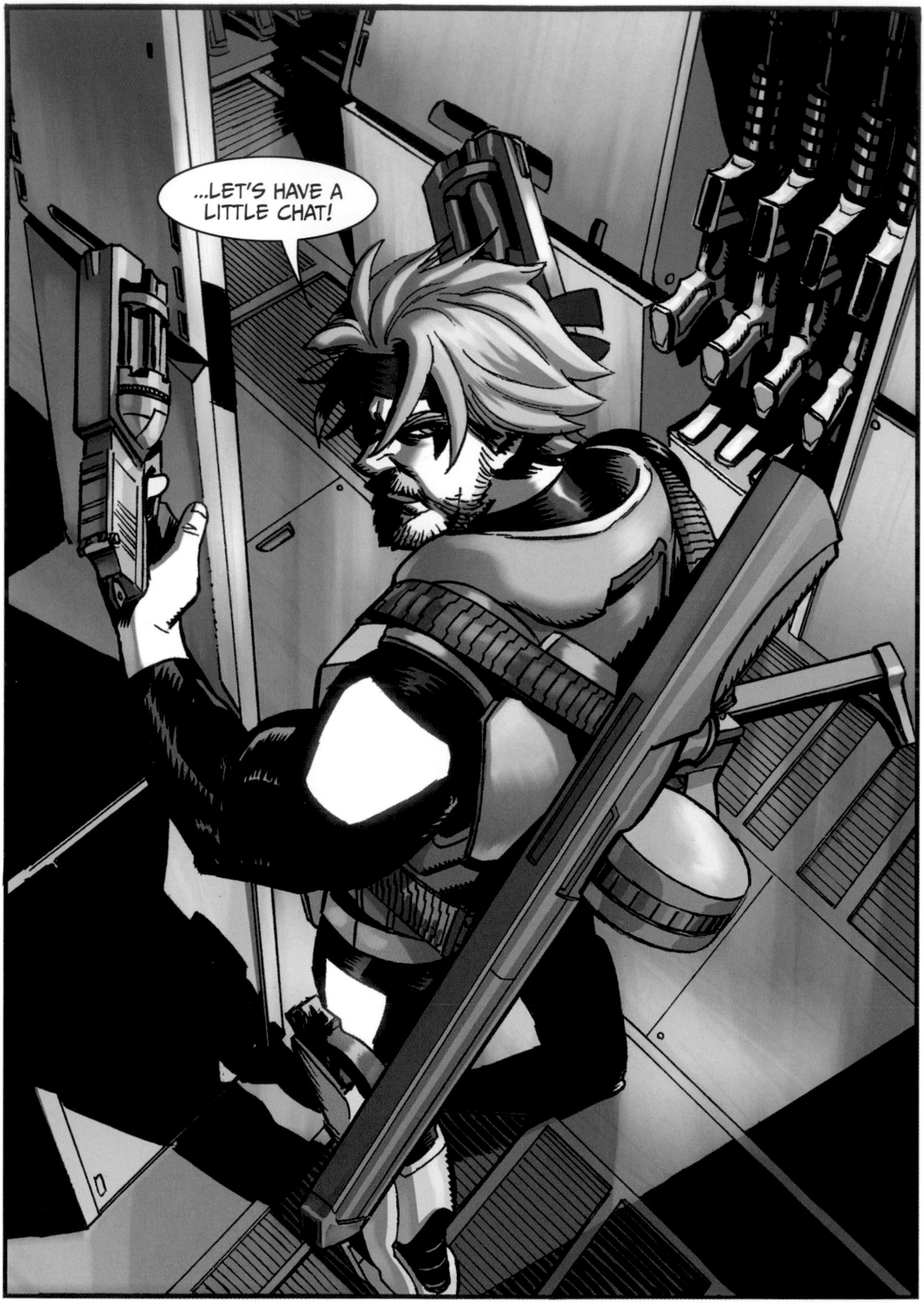
...LET'S HAVE A LITTLE CHAT!

WERTHER DELL'EDERA   **ARTIST**

When and where were you born? Where do you live now?

I was born in district 15 of Bari, Italy, in November 1975, and now I live in Rome.

What sort of artistic education did you have?

I started drawing as a child by copying *Spider-Man* covers, then went on to do the same with a lot of other stuff (including manga). After graduating high school, I attended the School of Comics in Rome.

Tell us about your previous works, before *Orphans*.

I've worked on *John Doe* by Recchioni and Bartoli for Eura, *Loveless* by Brian Azzarello, *Greek Street* by Peter Milligan, and *Dark Entries*, a story featuring Constantine written by the award-winning Scottish novelist Ian Rankin for Vertigo. I did the pencils for *Spider-Man Family Business* by Mark Waid and James Robinson for Marvel, which provided a base for Gabriele Dell'Otto's untouchable painting talent.

When did you start working on *Orphans*, and when did you finish drawing your chapter?

I started chapter 6 in 2011 and finished a year later, then I drew half of chapter 9 and half of chapter 11 (both other halves are completed by the extraordinary Gigi Cavenago).

What tools did you use?

Classic tools: Fabriano 4, 03 Faber-Castell copics, Davinci-Maestro series 6 brush, Pelikan ink.

What was the most difficult scene and which one did you have to redraw more times?

My entire first chapter was hard for me. I had to adapt to the Bonelli page style. Usually, apart from the editor's corrections, I might redraw a panel a few times over again until I get the result I had in mind. For example, I may keep erasing everything from a panel except maybe one shape that I like, but then I'll realize (or rather I'll surrender to the idea) that it's just that shape I have to erase, because even though I like it, it doesn't belong in the panel and therefore in the sequence that I'm working on.

If you could go back in time, what would you change about this chapter?

Everything I did wrong or not as nicely as the rest.

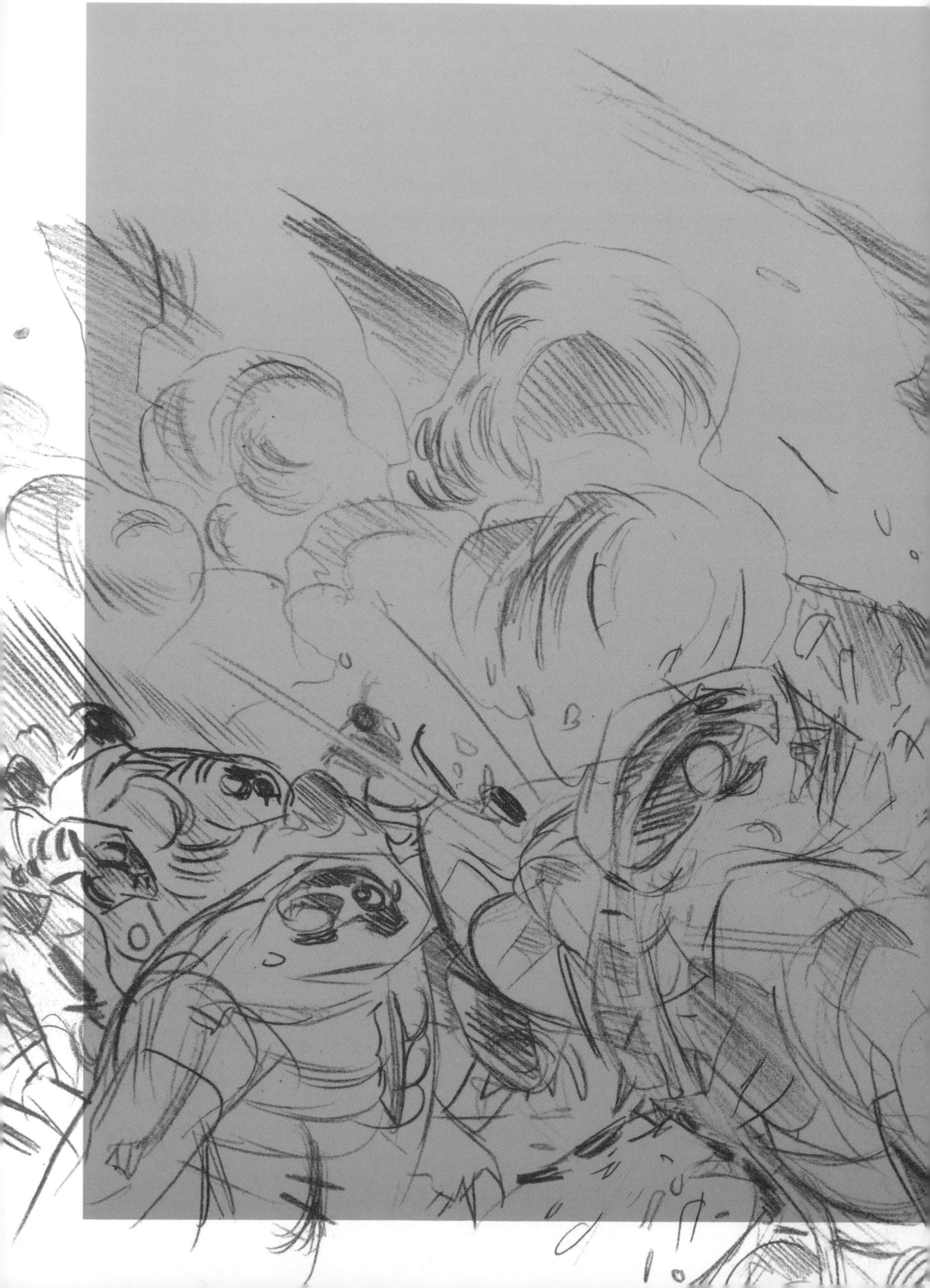

ORPHANS

EXTRAS

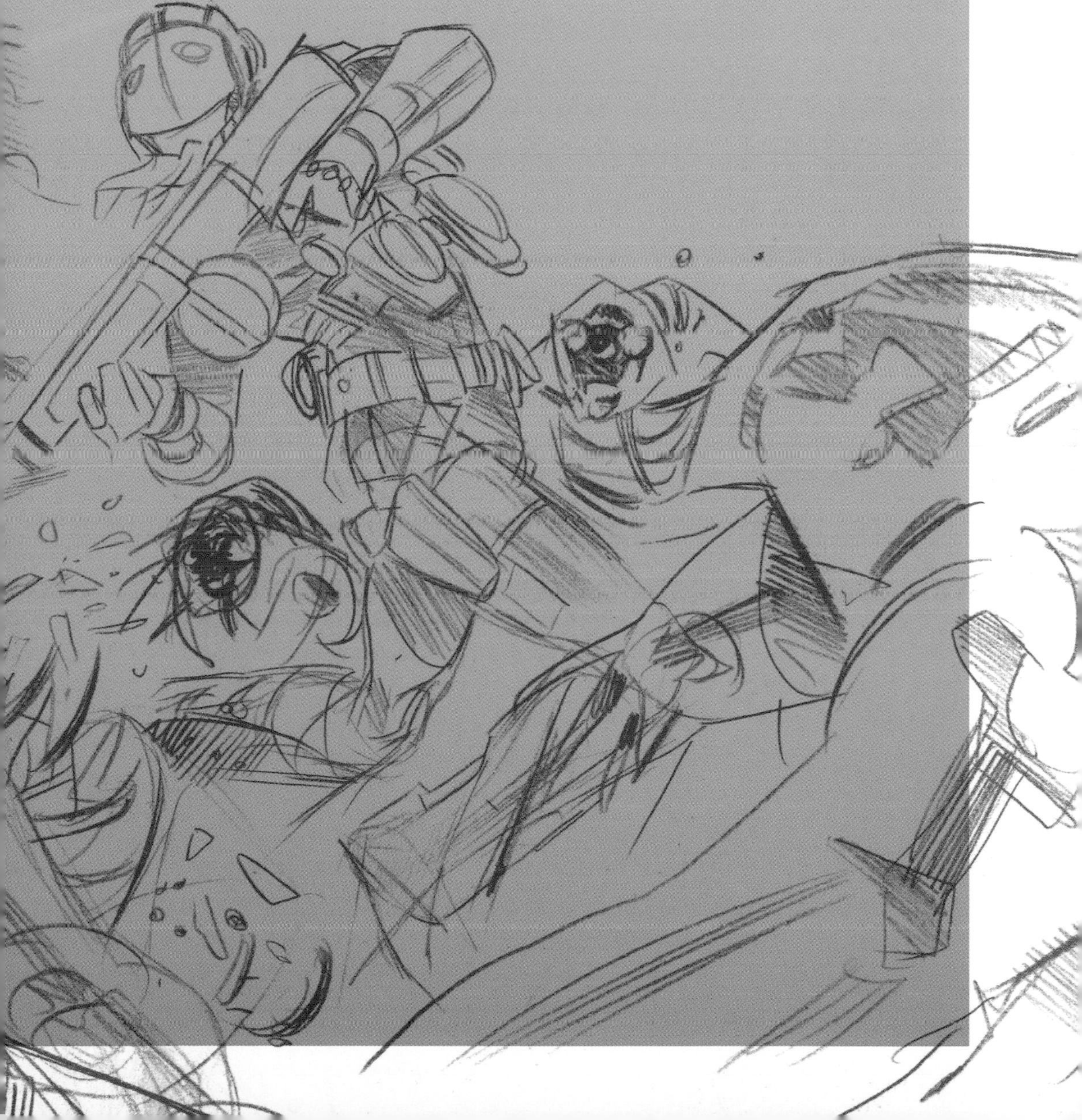

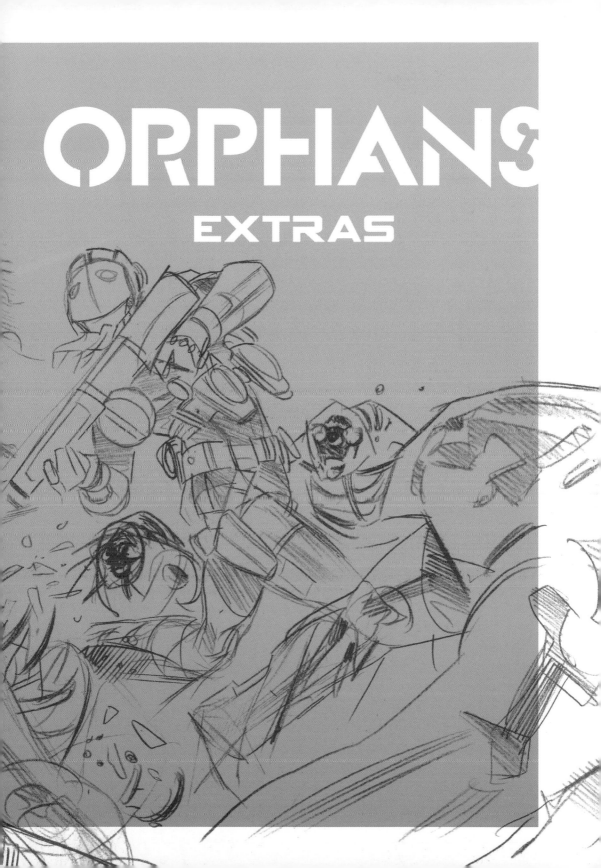

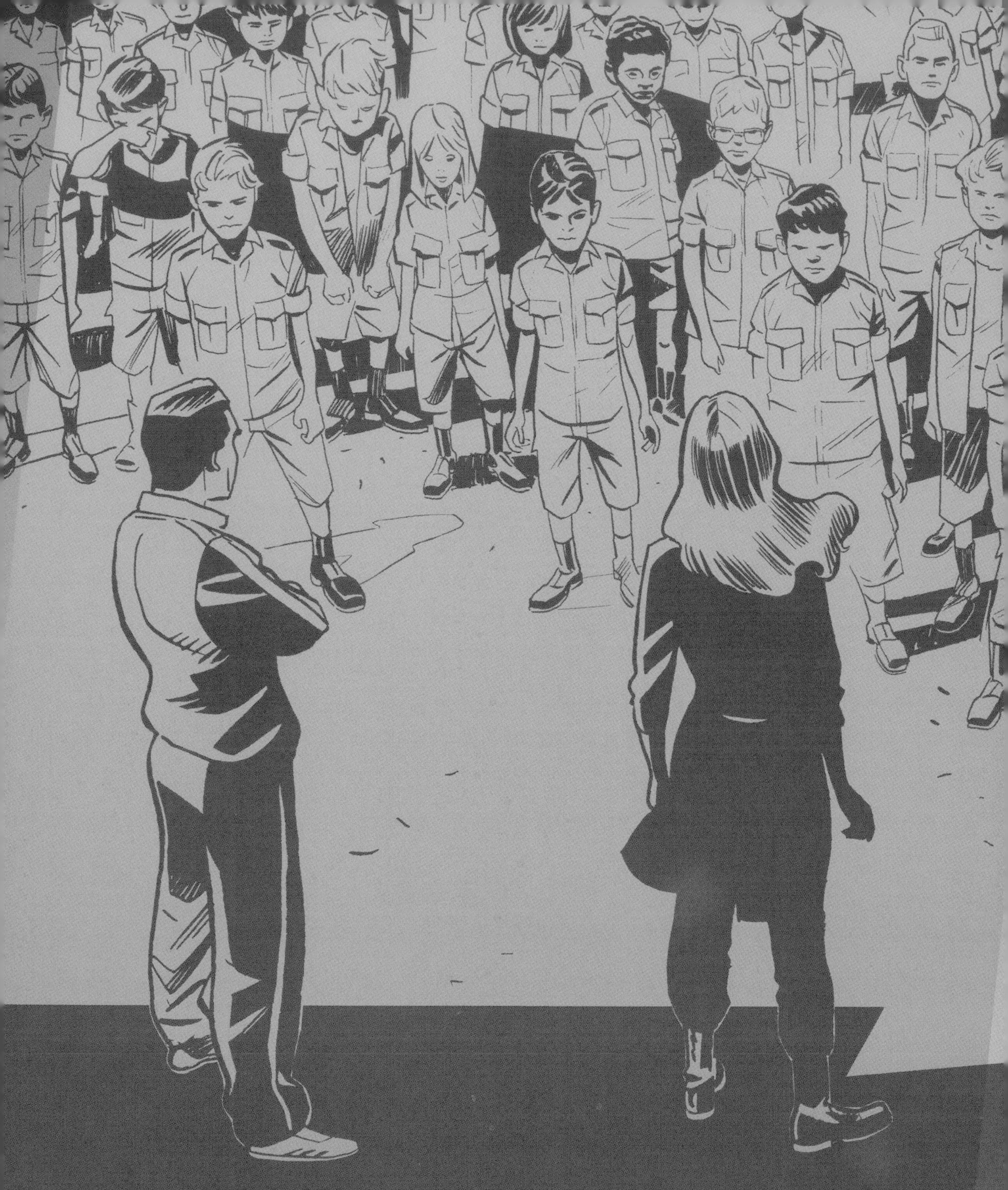

I'VE ALWAYS HAD A MORBID CURIOSITY ABOUT BODY LANGUAGE; I'M INTRIGUED BY THE IDEA OF MAKING THE CHARACTERS ACT WITH THEIR BODIES AS WELL AS THEIR FACES.

– EMILIANO MAMMUCARI

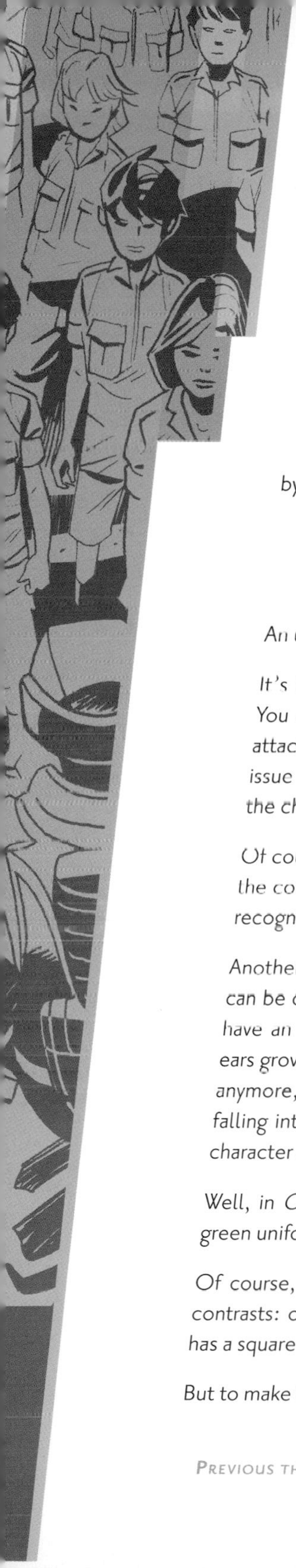

CHARACTERIZING THE ORPHANS

by **EMILIANO MAMMUCARI**

An unwritten rule about comics is that team stories don't often work.

It's hard to get into a story with more than a single leading actor. You don't understand who's who and the readers are slow to grow attached to the various characters. And when you change the artist issue after issue, there's a risk that the readers won't even recognize the characters.

Of course, we have the X-Men. And the Avengers. But in these cases, the costumes help, and we must admire that Kirby's design style is so recognizable that it easily survives, even with less astute artists.

Another thing you never think about is that characterizing a teenager can be complicated. At that age, you grow little by little: you already have an adult neck, even though your rib cage is still flat, and your ears grow faster than your nose. You're not an adult yet but not a child anymore, either. When drawing teenagers, you always run the risk of falling into a stereotype, and it's terrible when a reader recognizes a character only by his or her hairstyle.

Well, in *Orphans* we have seven characters. Kids. All with the same green uniform. And we see them grow issue after issue.

Of course, in the characterization of all these figures, I worked on contrasts: one character has brown hair, another one is blonde; one has a square jaw, the other one a sharp chin, and so on.

But to make things easier, I had to think about gestures.

PREVIOUS THREE PAGES: DRAWINGS BY EMILIANO MAMMUCARI

Allow me to digress for a moment—I've always had a morbid curiosity about body language; I'm intrigued by the idea of making the characters act with their bodies as well as their faces. Mind you, that's nothing new. Pratt used to do that back in the Sixties. When Corto Maltese enters the scene at the beginning of *The Ballad of the Salt Sea*, you can practically feel Rasputin's uneasiness. You understand that by the change in his gestures.

Another real master is Mazzucchelli. The scene in *Daredevil: Born Again* where Karen clutches Matt with all her strength, until she sinks her teeth into his shoulder... it gives me shivers every single time.

In cinema, there are actors capable of looking tall or short, fat or thin, depending on the character they're playing. Sometimes, rather than acting, they reinterpret themselves. In *Last Tango in Paris*, Marlon Brando doesn't give a damn about the screenplay and starts talking about himself, how his father used to beat him when he was a child. He has such an intense physicality you could almost hear his father thrashing him with his belt.

No need to bother studying Strasberg or Stanislavski: gestures have their own value, and you might as well use them.

In the first half of the century, there was a man called Reich who studied the relationship between traumas, psychological blocks, and muscular tensions. Never mind that he died in jail trying to invent a machine to measure orgasms and writing books about aliens. Reich was a psychologist and he discovered the connection between individuals and their body language.

In short, you can recognize different personalities by the way they move: one character who has schizophrenic tendencies will move in a certain way, a psychopath in a different way, a masochistic in another way, and so on.

Obviously, what follows is only for fun. There's no claim of truth in any of it, and frankly, I believe in psychoanalysis as much as astrology. But in developing a series with so many main characters, I tried to imagine a different physicality based on the most common personality types for each one.

PSYCHOPATHIC personality

...which is nothing like Hannibal Lecter at all. The classic psychopath had an absent father. Their mother told them, "We must do this on our own. You're a grown-up now." And they really did try to play that role. They tried but got trapped. A psycho always needs praise from others for their self-assertiveness. Usually, these subjects are manipulators and perfectionists. On the other hand, they're also great leaders because they're incapable of having intimate relationships. Their greatest fear is that someone might discover their inadequacy.

You can easily identify a psychopath: they only breathe with the upper part of their lungs, they have a protruding chest, as if they're supposed to. Their legs are usually thin and their ankles are delicate.

That's how I imagined Hector, Juno's brother, who in the first chapter carries the role of the leader on his back until making the ultimate sacrifice.

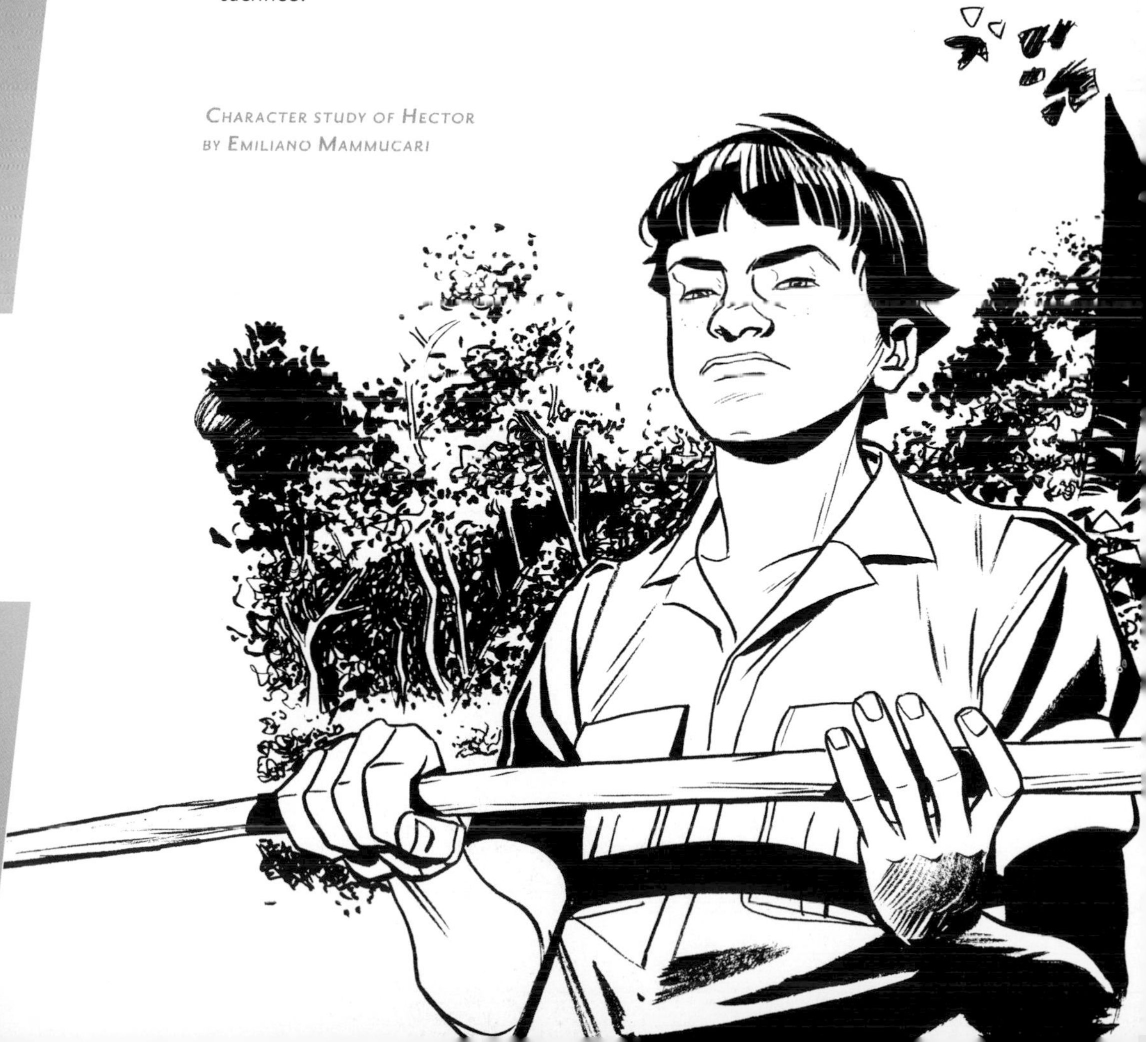

Character study of Hector by Emiliano Mammucari

SCHIZOID personality

That's the description of an unwanted child, perhaps put in an incubator or born by chance from a very young mother.

From the beginning, a schizoid understands that to survive, you must ignore negative input: smother your feelings and emotions. Controlling your breath, for example. These subjects never breathe out completely and use the lower part of their lungs. They have a separate emotional and psychological experience. For example, you can recognize them because they laugh only with the lower part of their face, while their eyes stay uninvolved. They can't stand someone else's glance; any emotional exchange is too much for them. Their outer world is deeply disconnected from their inner one; that's why they tend to be creative people. They can appear to be the sweetest person in the world, but inside they are hiding a huge, unexpected aggressiveness. Usually, to relate to the world they limit their gestures to the bare minimum because most of their energy is committed to filling the enormous void they feel under their diaphragm.

CHARACTER STUDY OF JUNO
BY EMILIANO MAMMUCARI

IN DEVELOPING A SERIES WITH SO MANY MAIN CHARACTERS, I TRIED TO IMAGINE A DIFFERENT PHYSICALITY BASED ON THE MOST COMMON PERSONALITY TYPES FOR EACH ONE.

– Emiliano Mammucari

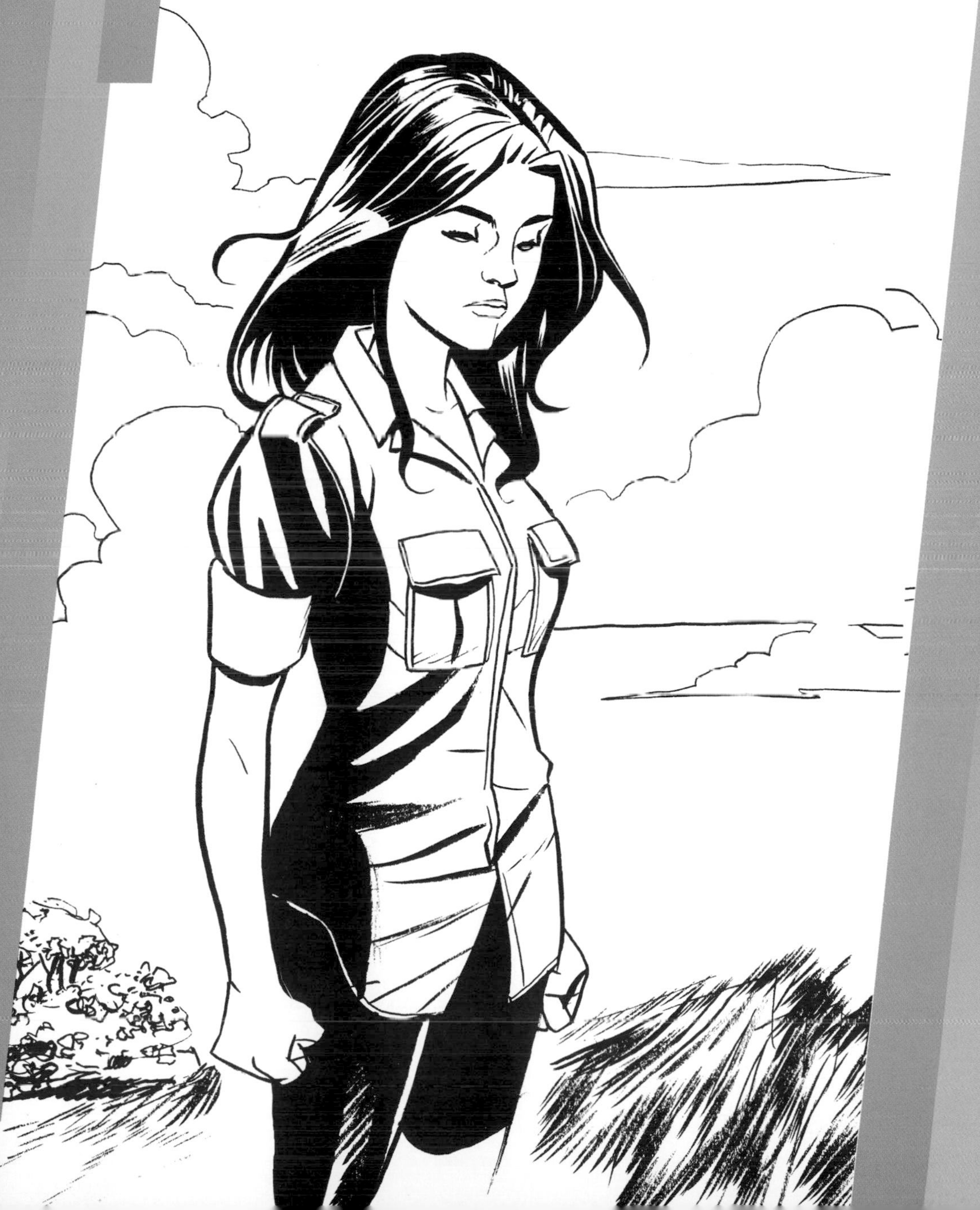

ORAL personality

A child who has been treated coldly. They cried in the cradle until they lost their voice, and their mother didn't come to hug them. They soon learned the only way to be noticed was to stop asking and become seductive. An oral individual will always look at you like you were the last person on Earth, even though they don't really think so.

This kind of person can only deal with the world by giving; they go out of their way to help others and prove they can survive alone. Physically, they're thin (or, if they gain some weight, it's to better stick to the ground) with weak arms and pale lips. They're used to clenching their jaws and almost all of them have a socket where the pit of their stomach is. You can see some of them wearing short sleeves even in winter because they are never cold.

Their biggest fear is to be abandoned, and they don't know that what they feel is in fact a strong, tremendous rage.

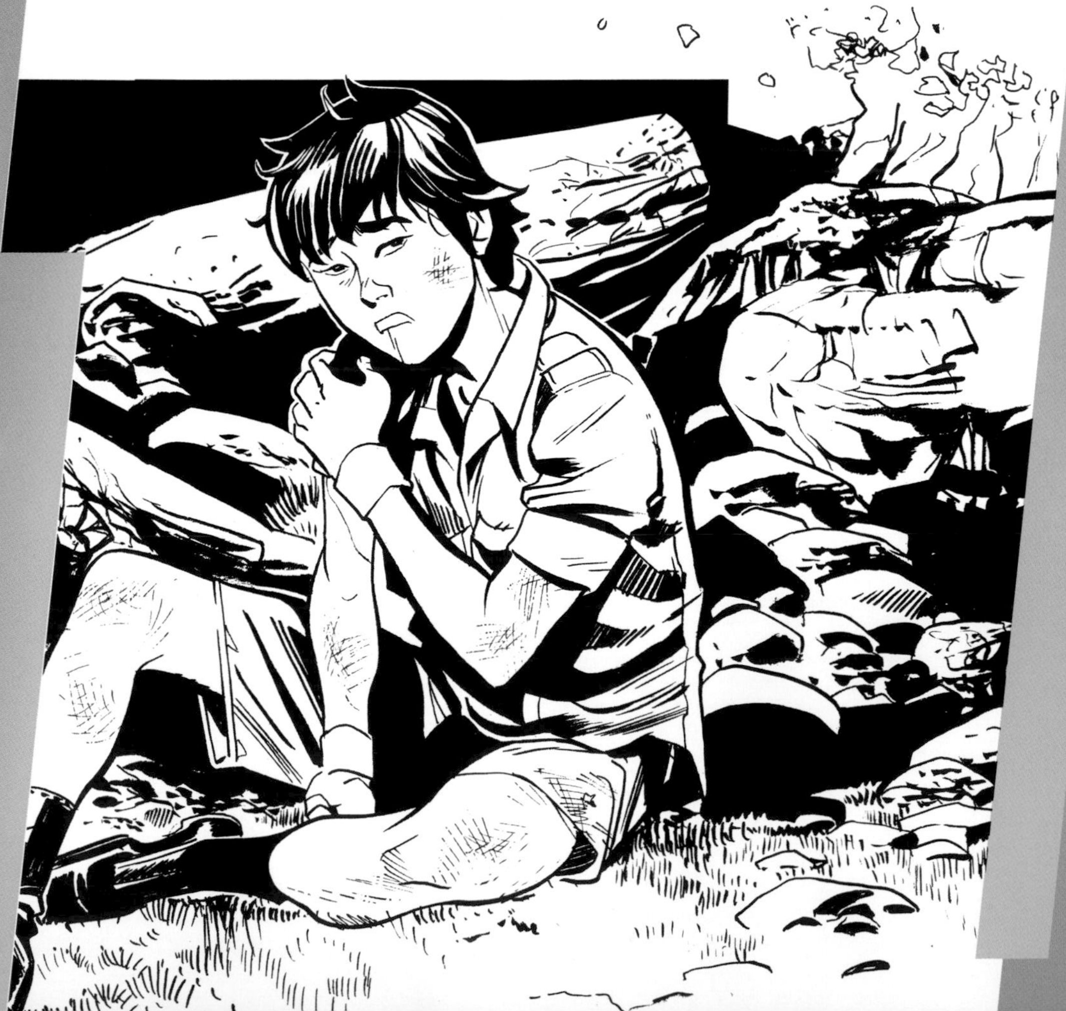

MASOCHISTIC personality

If you don't do as you're told, you're a bad person. Usually, masochistic individuals have an overdominant parent: for them, fulfilling their own needs and making their parent happy have always been incompatible options. So they've chosen to give themselves up in order to be loved.

Masochists are tireless workers, but they will tend to create situations about which they can complain, otherwise they'll feel uncomfortable. Succeeding in something doesn't cause them to release endorphins naturally, and they'll still feel unsatisfied and unacknowledged. Lonely. Never pay a compliment to a masochist: they'll feel mocked. Physically, they have a stocky torso, with the upper and lower part of the spine curved forward.

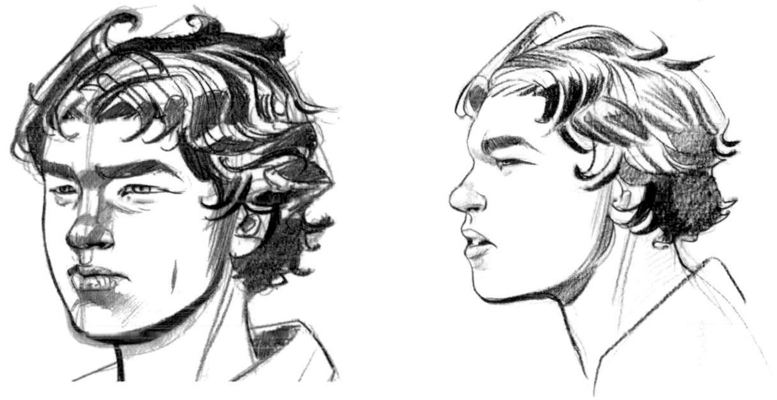

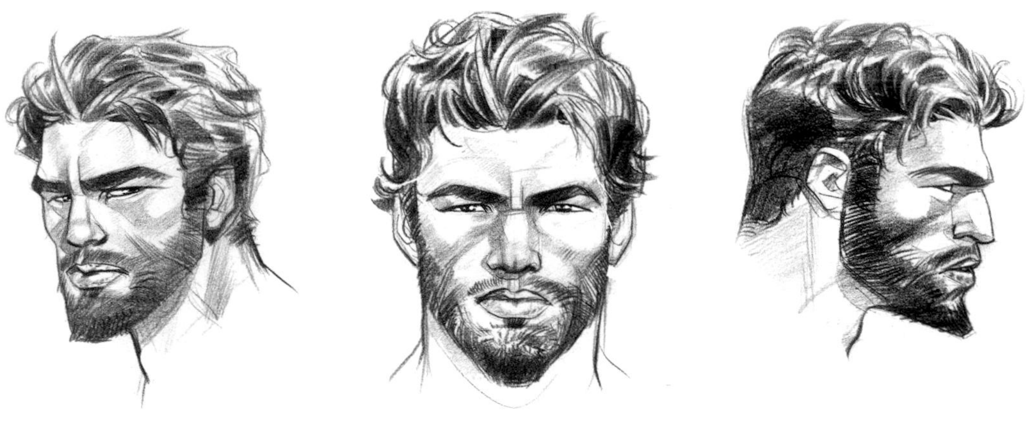

PREVIOUS PAGE: CHARACTER STUDY OF REY BY EMILIANO MAMMUCARI
ABOVE: CHARACTER STUDY OF RAUL BY EMILIANO MAMMUCARI

STERN personality

The classic time bomb. Their own existence was somehow perceived as a threat by one of their parents, and they're sure they deserve some kind of punishment. Many personalities fall under the "stern" category: from phallic-narcissists, to obsessive-compulsives, through hysterics.

Stern individuals tend to think in straight lines. They dread mistakes and therefore shy away from the idea of making decisions. They're afraid to give in and to be subdued, so they never truly relax. Their head is always up, their back always straight. The area between their chest and hips is curvaceous and it divides their body in half. Sterns build up their muscles even without practicing any sports because they're constantly tense, as terrified as they are by the idea of being overwhelmed by the hostility of the world.

CHARACTER STUDY OF SAM
BY EMILIANO MAMMUCARI

Then there's Jonas. Our most difficult character.

The others instinctively trust him because of his neutral, composed body language. He always leans on both his legs; he always looks you in the eye.

We haven't given Jonas a past. To me, it was the only way to imagine a natural-born leader.

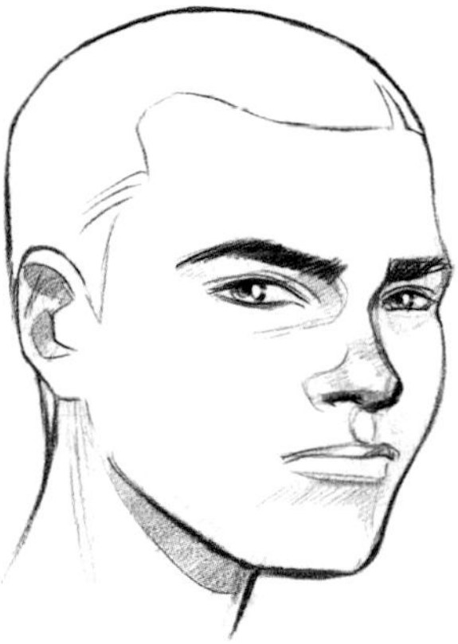

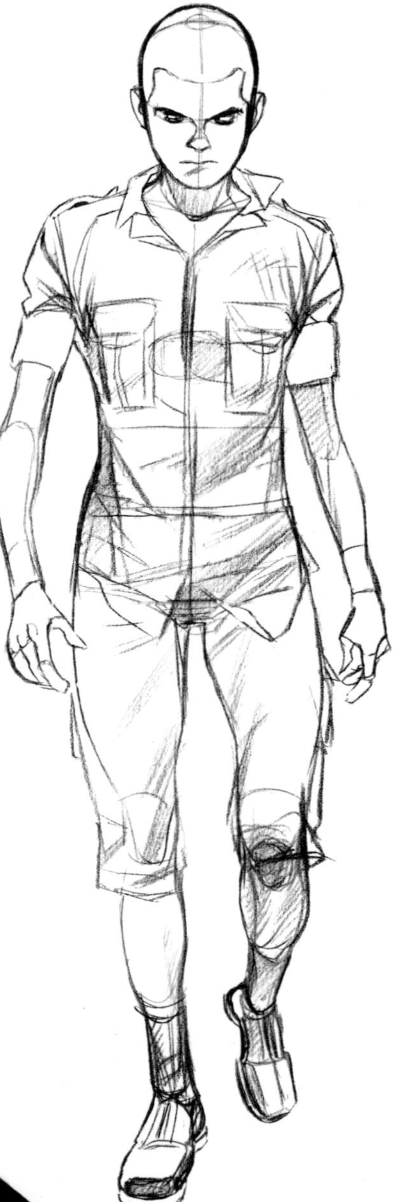

Character study of Jonas
by Emiliano Mammucari
colors by Massimo Carnevale

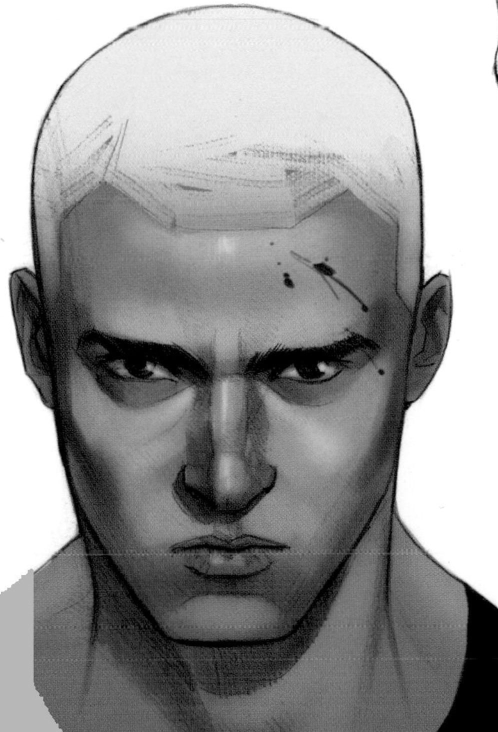

AS CHARACTERS ARE ALWAYS AT THE CENTER OF THE STORY, I HAD TO WORK ON CLEAR AND ESSENTIAL SHAPES.

– GIGI CAVENAGO

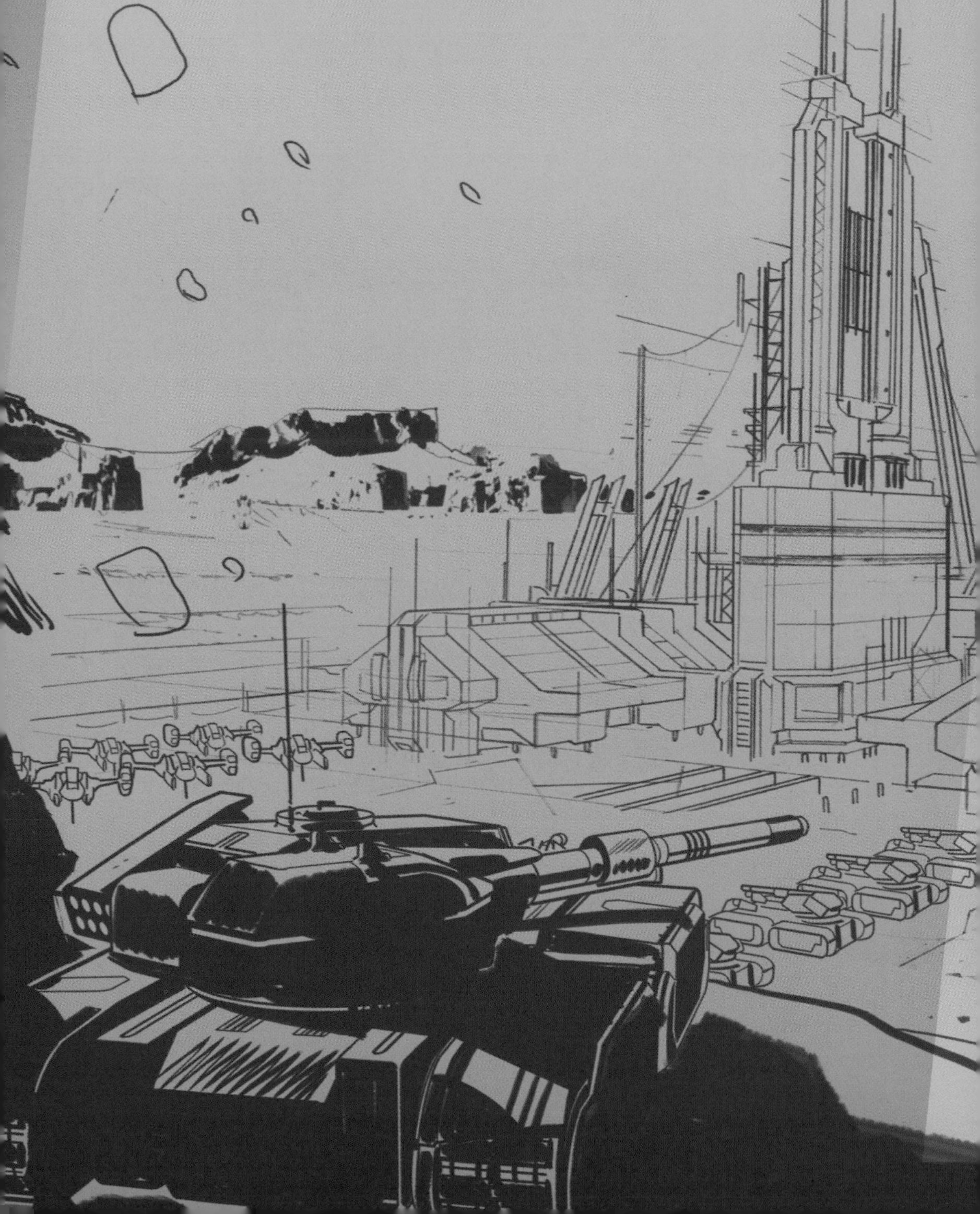

LEARNING CURVE

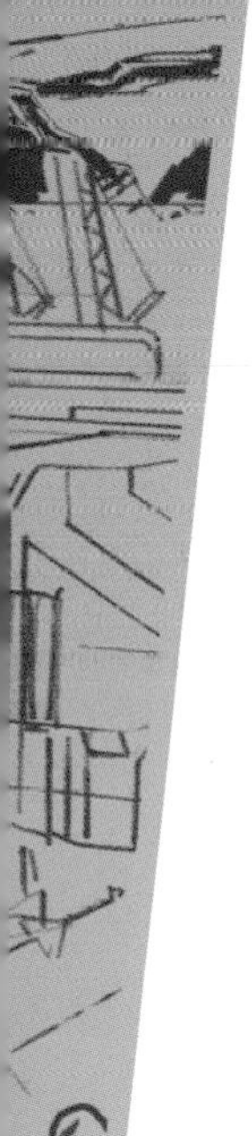

GIGI CAVENAGO: *At the end of chapter 3, I wasn't particularly satisfied with what I'd done so far, so before starting with the new script, I took a couple of weeks to think it over. I flicked through some nudes and anatomy manuals to strengthen my familiarity to make characters more realistic using "body language."*

To that end, the first pages of chapter 4, when Juno meets Sam in her quarters, were just what I needed.

The story then shifted to more animated scenarios, but I was able to maintain similar conditions.

But my real turning point came from a hint given to me by Roberto: he suggested that, to heighten the action scenes, I should continuously play with and emphasize the camera's perspective. From that moment on, it was just a ride to the finish line.

This wasn't an easy chapter because at least thirty pages out of fifty consisted of pure action.

For the crowded scenes, I drew inspiration from Emiliano's chapter I and tried to convey that same colossal, sci-fi style.

To cap it all off were Lorenzo De Felici's colors; he's a real ace. When I talk about him, I always say that "I'm honored to have 'outlined his colors.'" That may sound more flattery than a joke, but it's absolutely true.

As for technical elements, once again we had to create some things from practically nothing, such as the briefing room and the observatory where Nakamura and Juric conspire at the end of the chapter. But most of all, the construction site with the massive antenna.

PREVIOUS PAGE: LOCATION STUDY BY GIGI CAVENAGO

We already talked about how simple we must keep the technology in *Orphans*. As characters are always at the center of the story, I had to stick with clear and essential shapes: basically, the site of the antenna is a conglomerate of simple polygons; the only area inspired by something real is the portion with the cranes, like those seen at commercial harbors.

Once the settings were chosen, we just had to make all our characters move through them. Crowded scenes are always hard to draw, especially if you have to make them clear and understandable, and in that regard, the colors were a big help.

I've never drawn as many soldiers as I did in this chapter, and the most difficult ones weren't those running or shooting in the snow but the ones sitting on the pews in the briefing scene!

Briefing room study by Gigi Cavenago

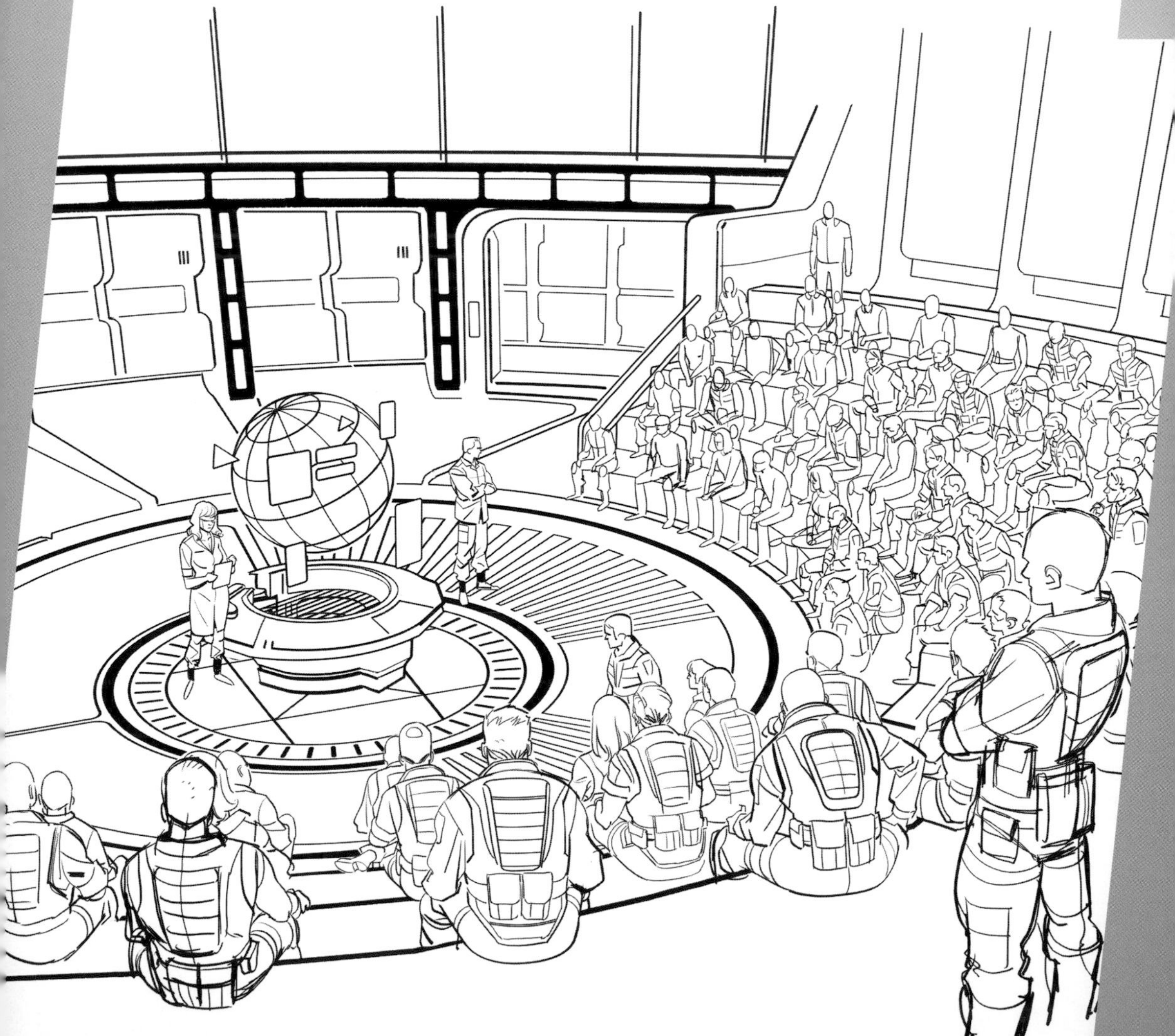

Character study by Emiliano Mammucari

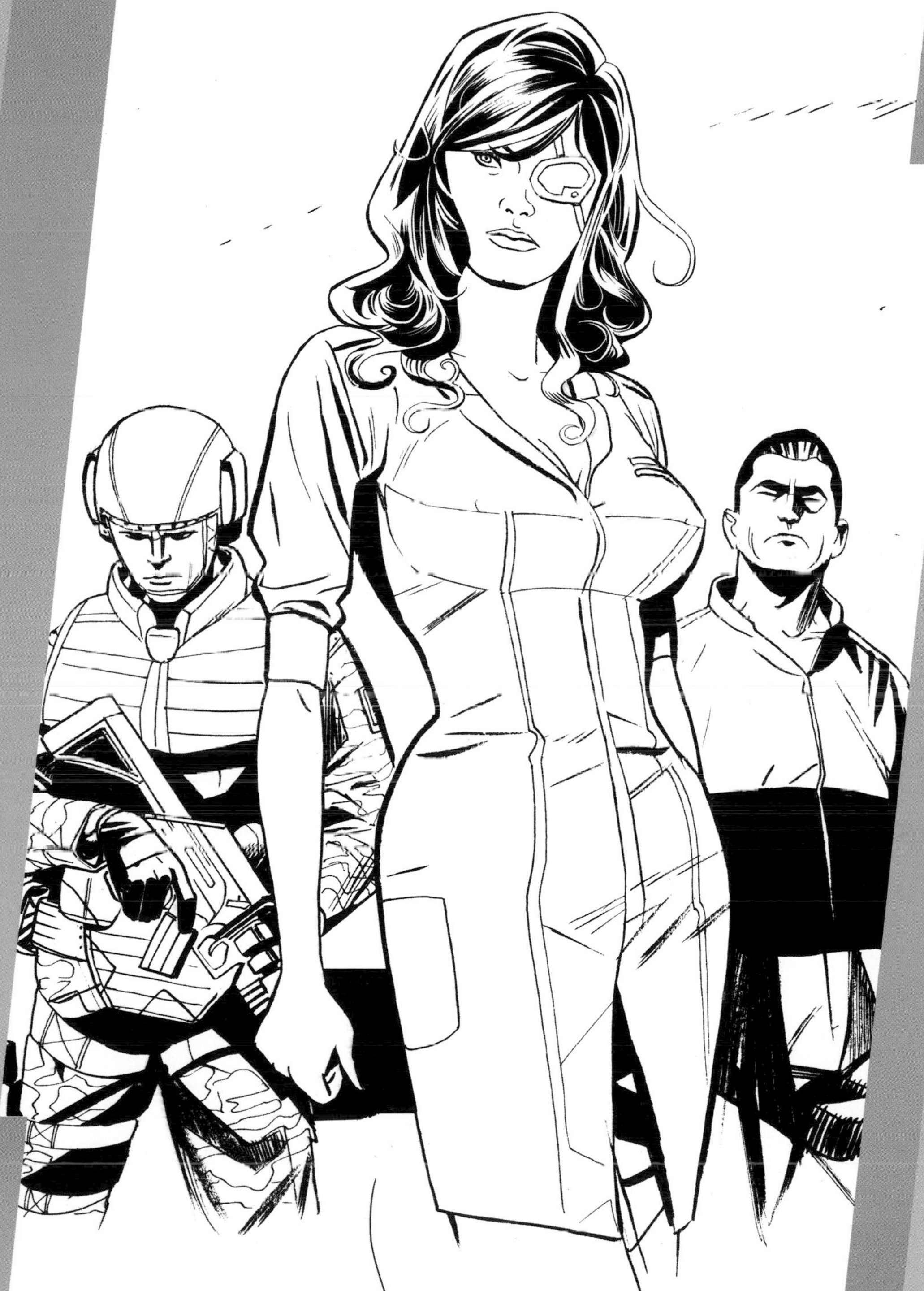

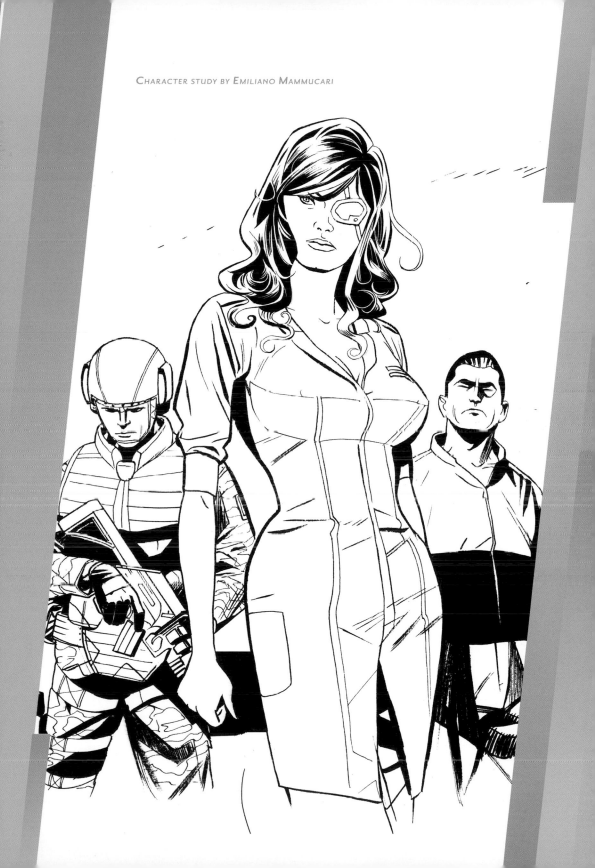

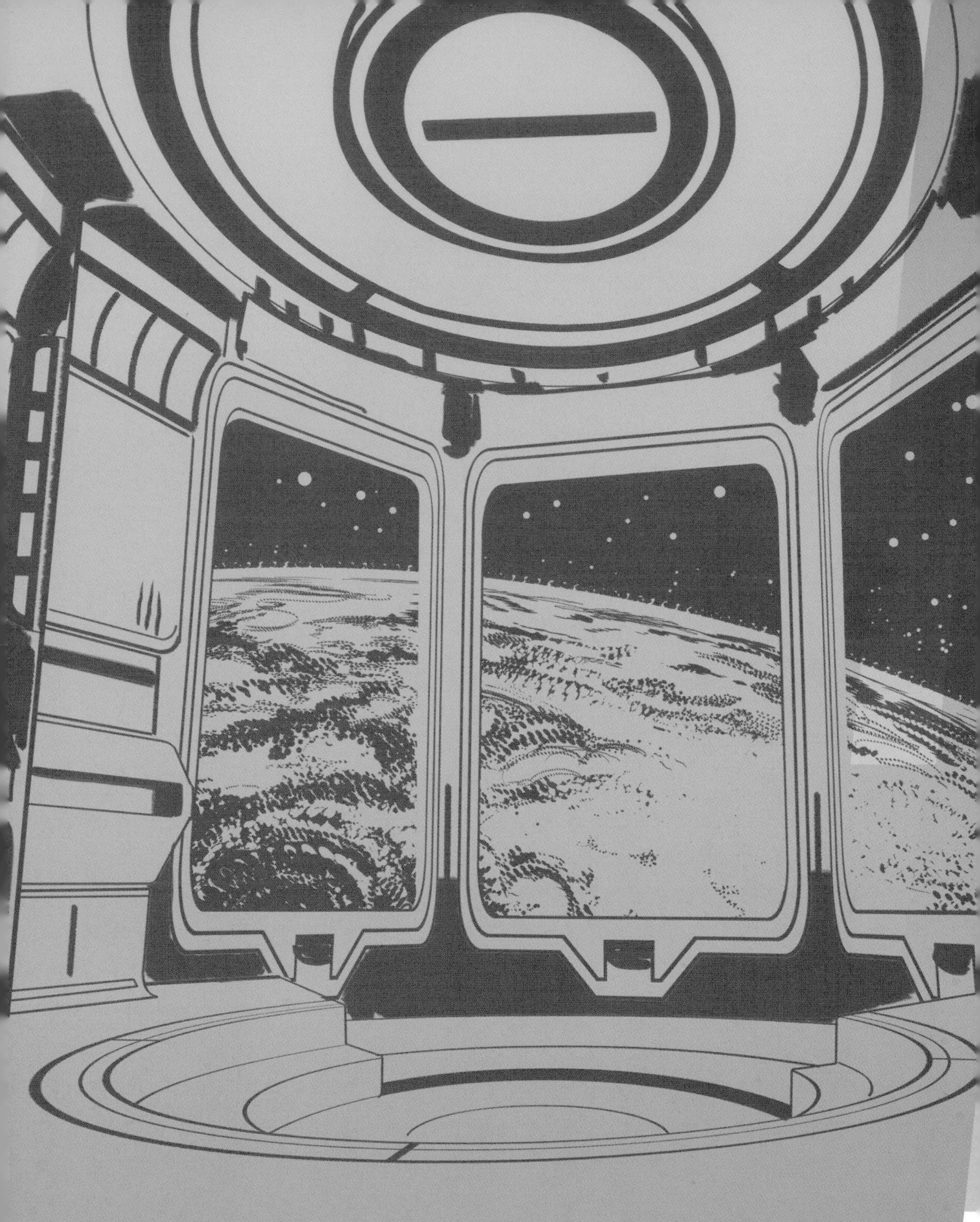

I'VE NEVER DRAWN AS MANY SOLDIERS AS I DID IN THIS CHAPTER.

– Gigi Cavenago

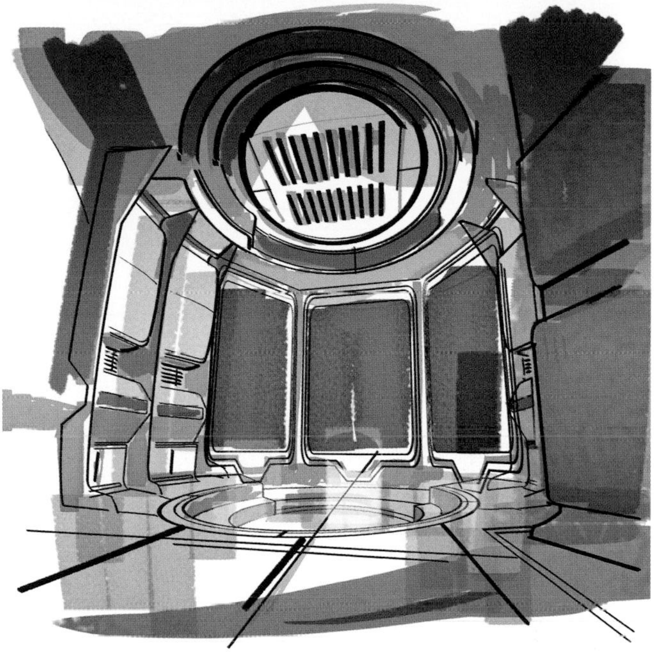

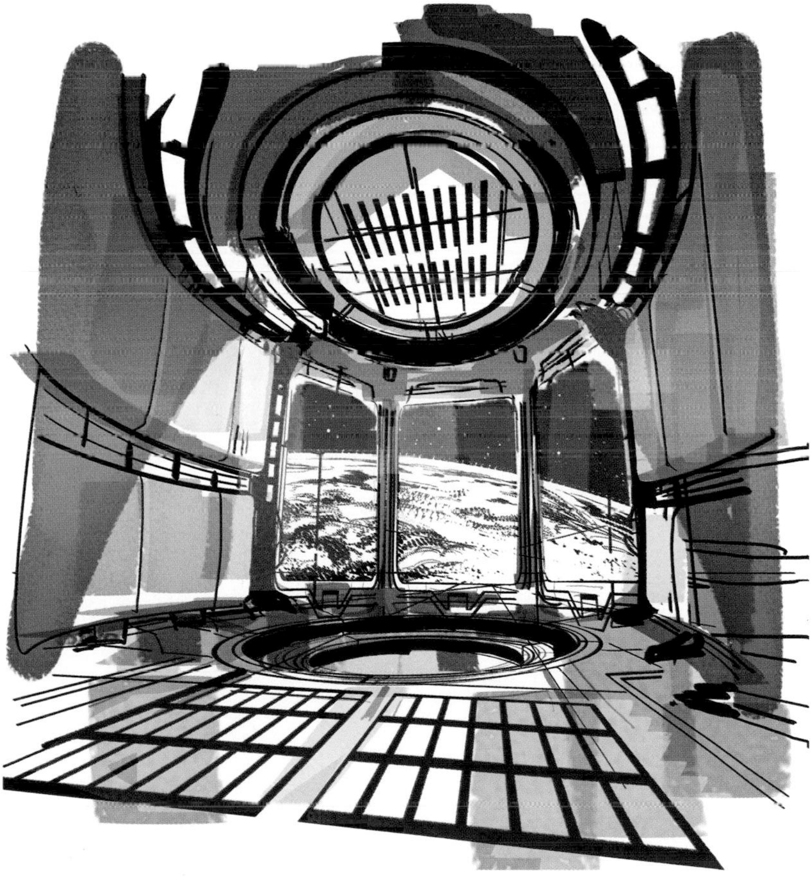

Set designs by Gigi Cavenago

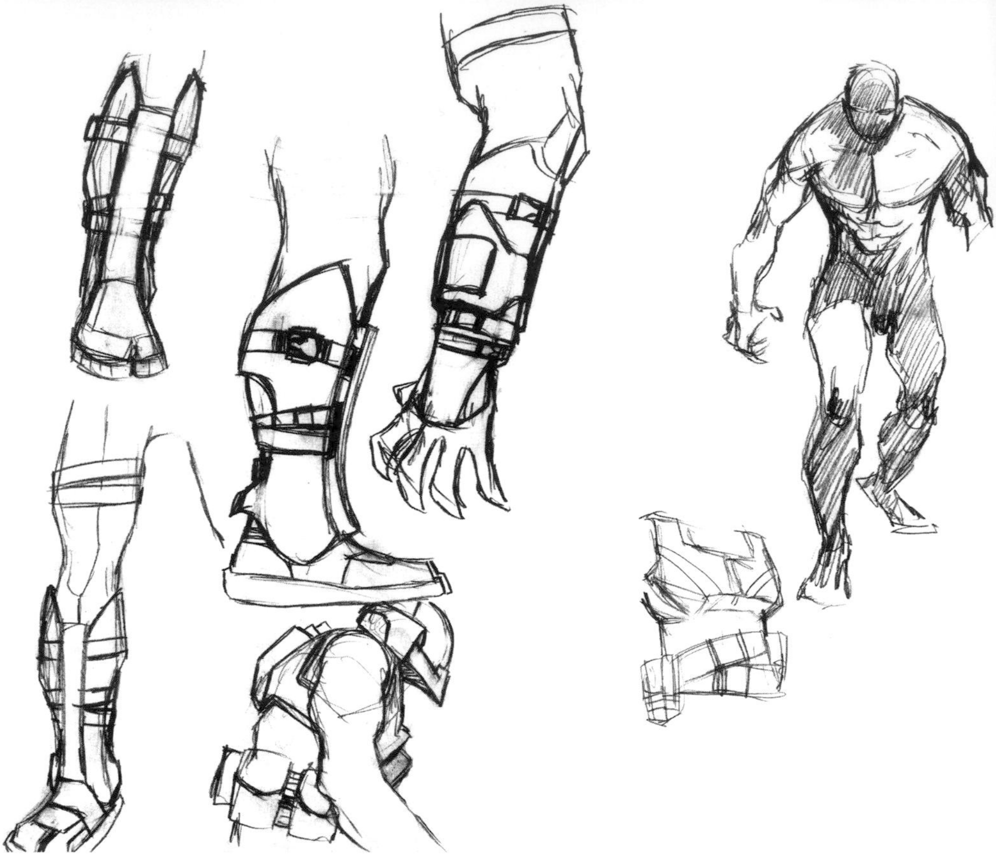

Above: dynamic studies by Werther Dell'Edera
Next page and below: dynamic studies by Gigi Cavenago

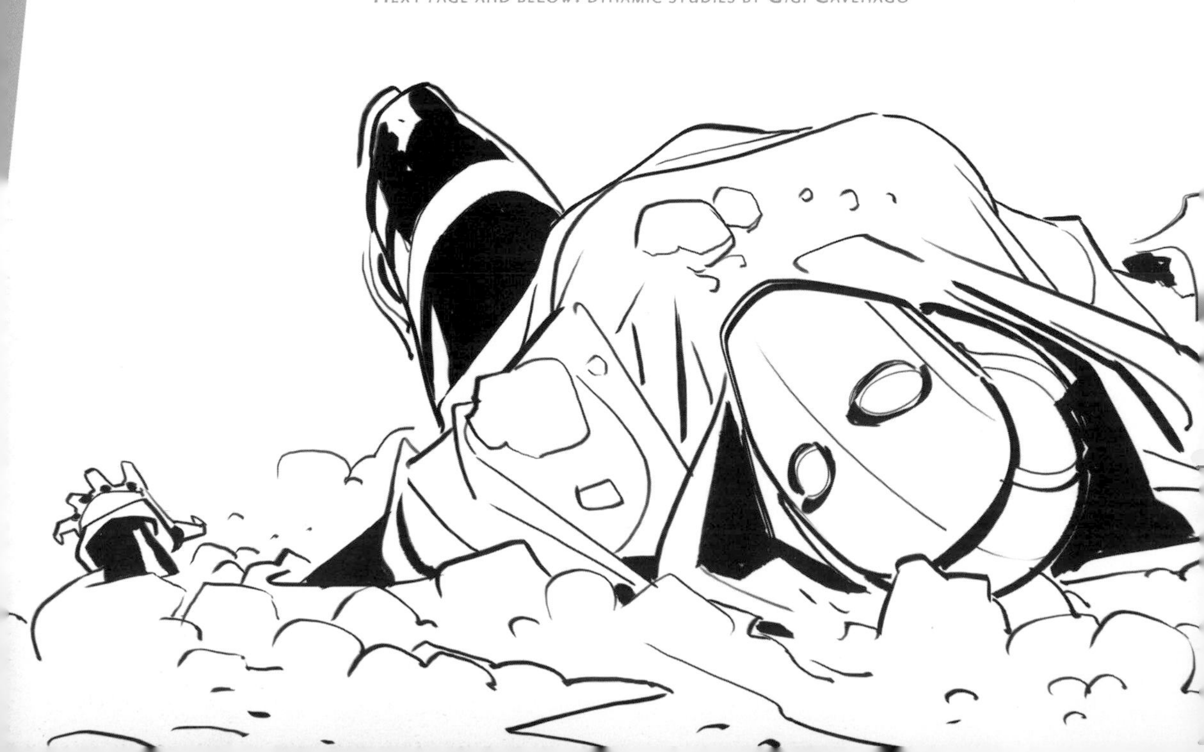

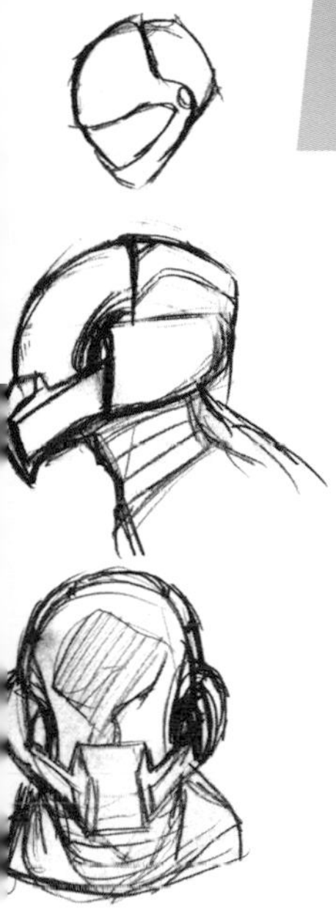
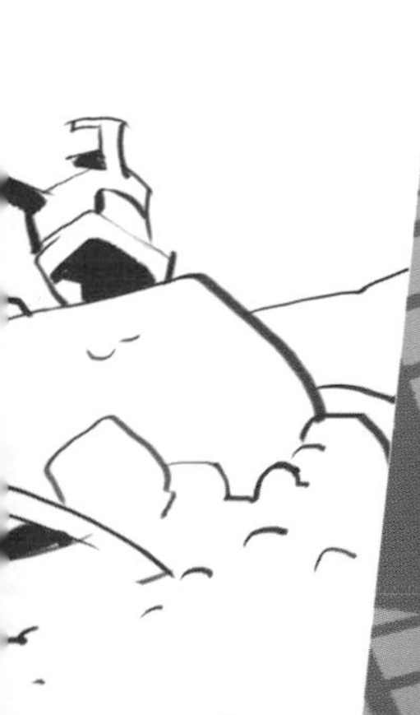
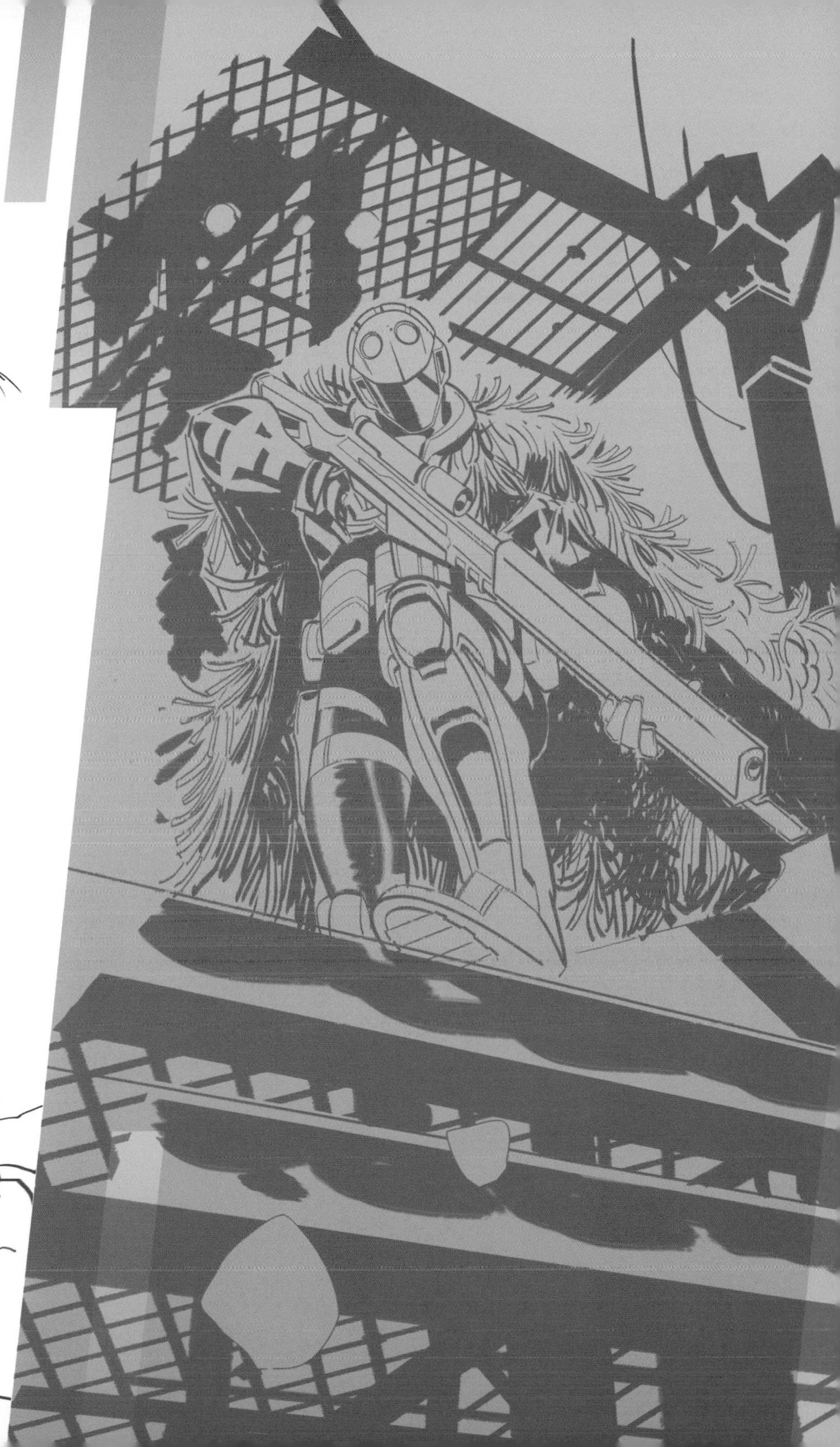

ROBERTO RECCHIONI: I knew the readers would start to feel really excited by this second batch of chapters. When I write a series, I always know that, no matter how explosive I try to make the first episode, things will move slowly until everything falls into its proper place. The way I orchestrate my stories depends on the characters and their relationships more than on the plot, so I need time to give those characters depth and clarify how the dynamics of their relationships work. Once the pieces are all in position, things come to a head and it all flows like the final part of a roller coaster. It happened for every season of *John Doe* and it's going be the same for *Orphans*.

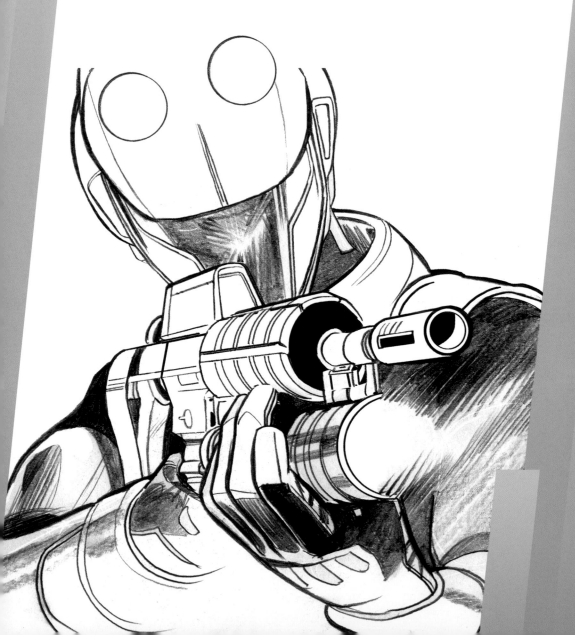

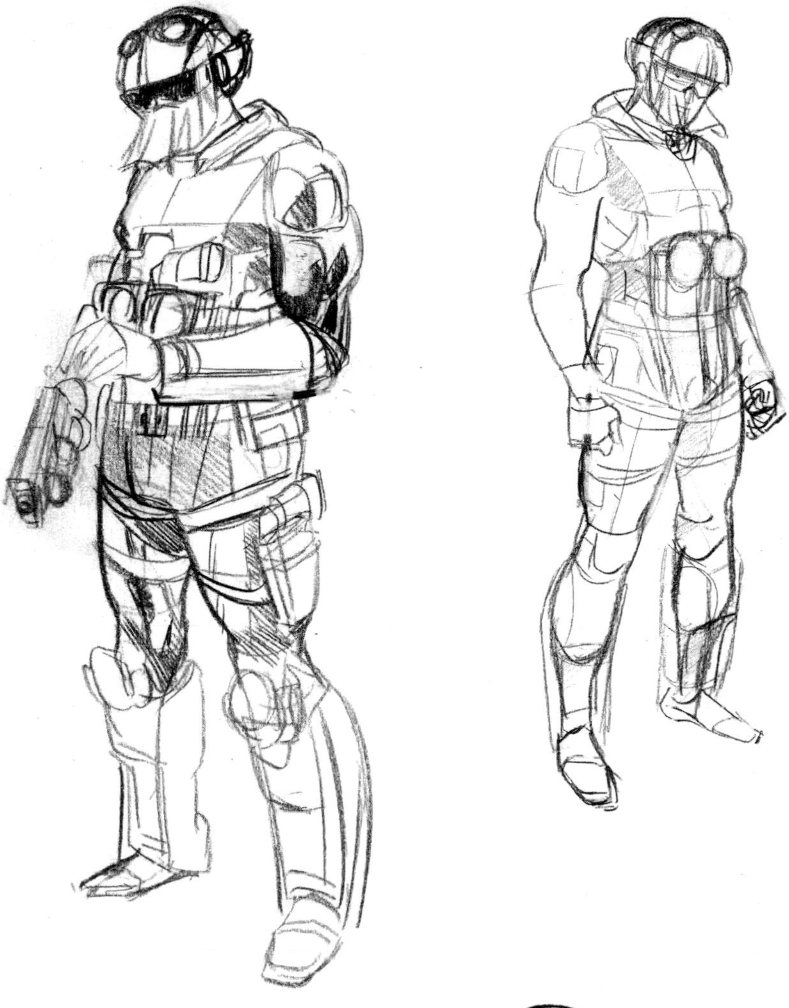

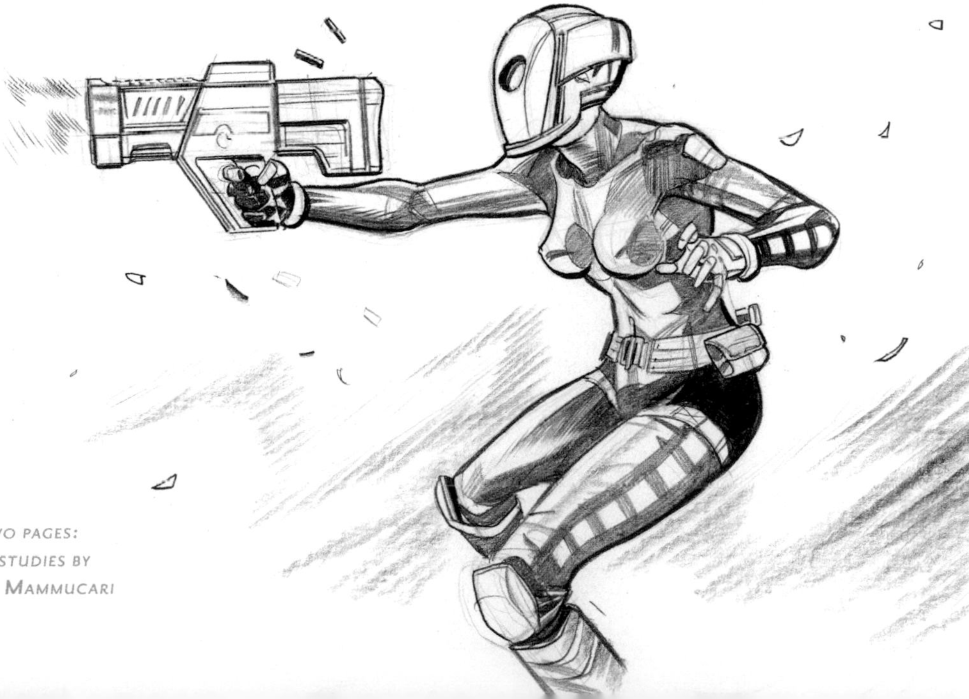

These two pages: dynamic studies by Emiliano Mammucari

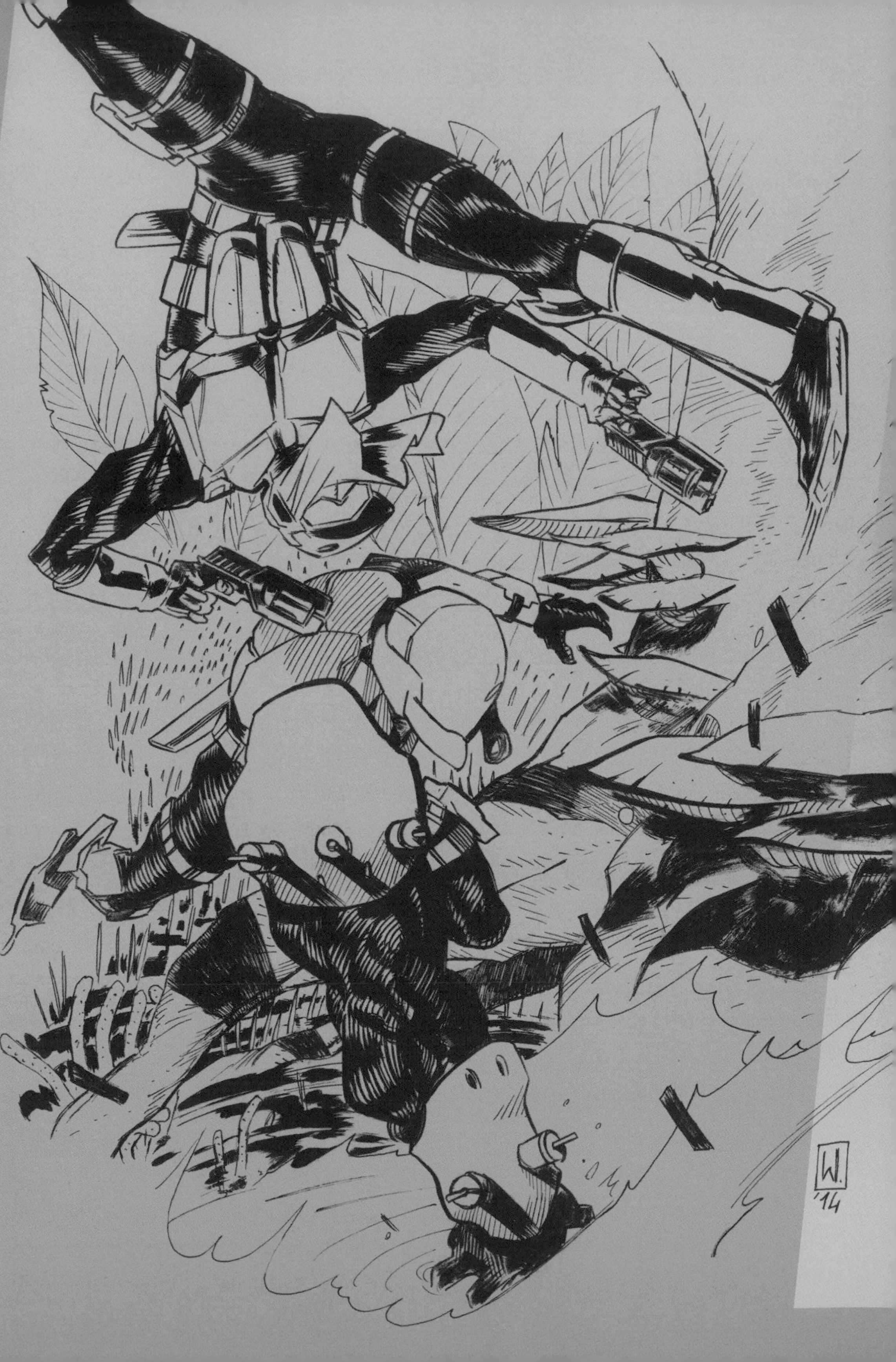
W.
'14

WERTHER DELL'EDERA: Rey is the one character who needed the most study. In the first chapters, he's given up for dead before coming back in the chapter that I drew, bigger and angrier than before. Roberto, Emiliano, and I worked hard on Rey to obtain the right appeal. As far as the rest is concerned, I didn't have to study much, as everything was already well established. Roberto and Emiliano did an incredibly detailed job laying out the series, perfectly defining the characters, the vehicles, the tools, the settings, the costumes, etc., so all I had to do was follow that guide.

THESE TWO PAGES:
CHARACTER STUDIES OF THE TRANSFORMED ADULT REY
BY WERTHER DELL'EDERA

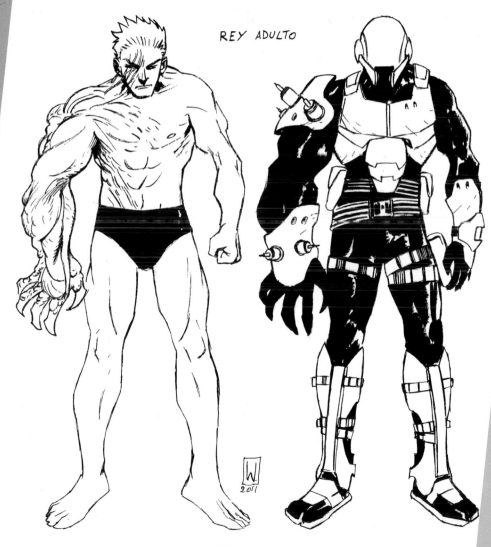

REY ADULTO

Clockwise from top left:
character studies of Doctor Juric
by Emiliano Mammucari,
Gigi Cavenago, and Werther Dell'Edera

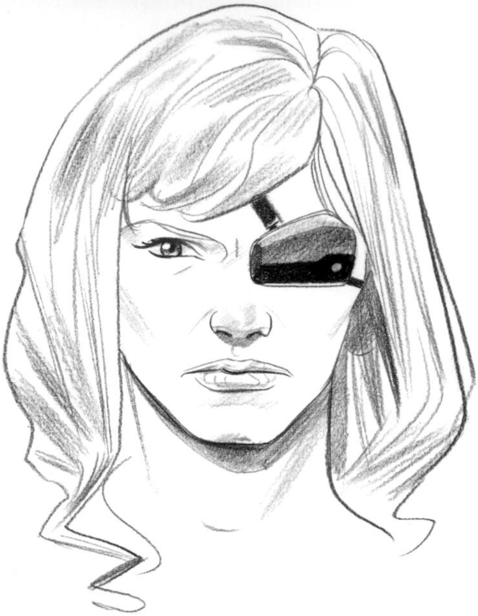

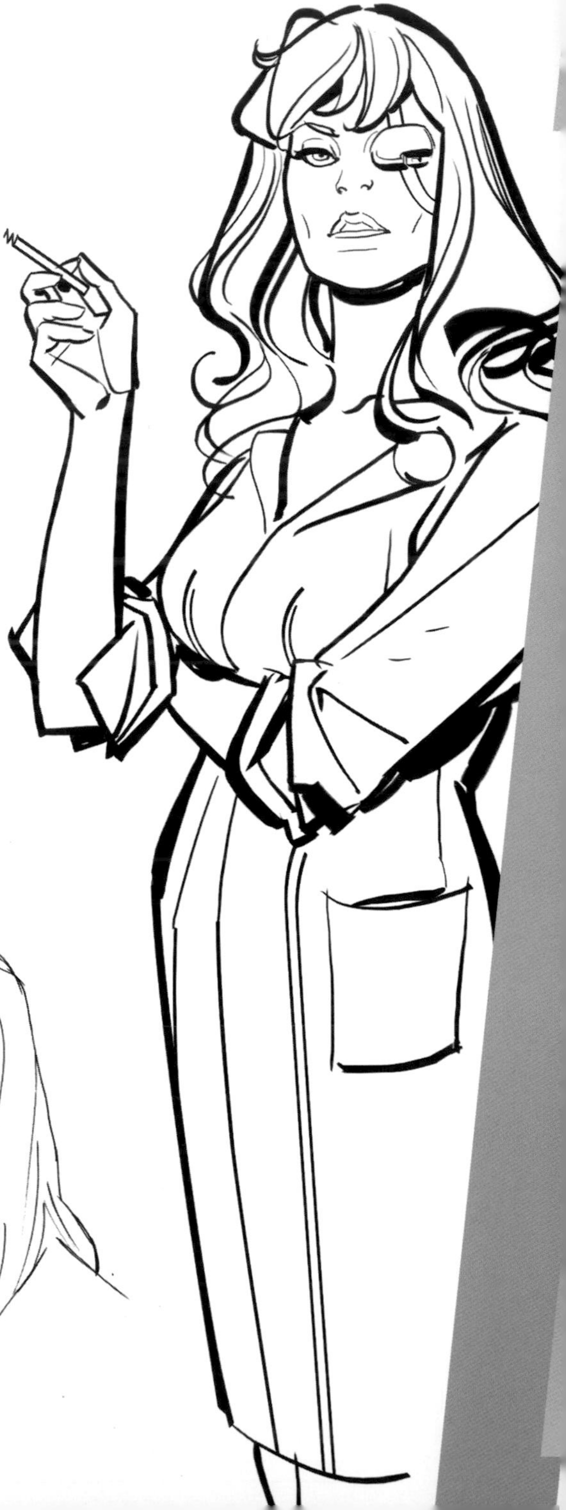

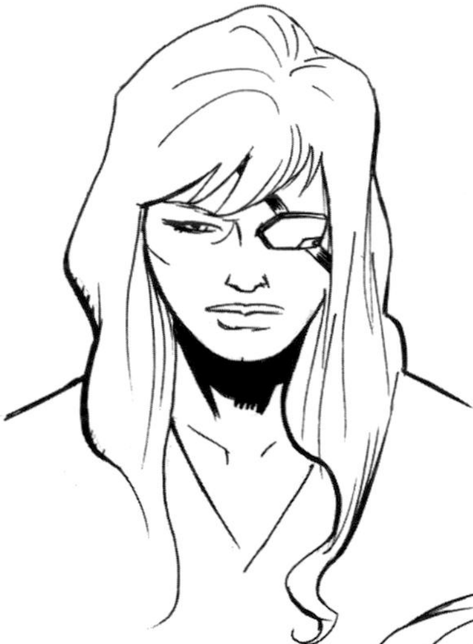

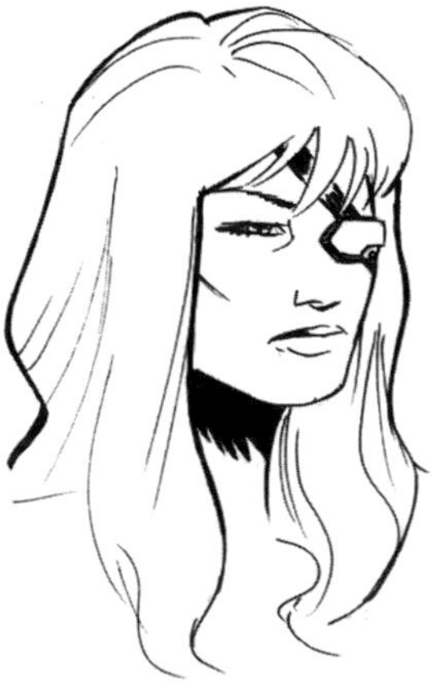

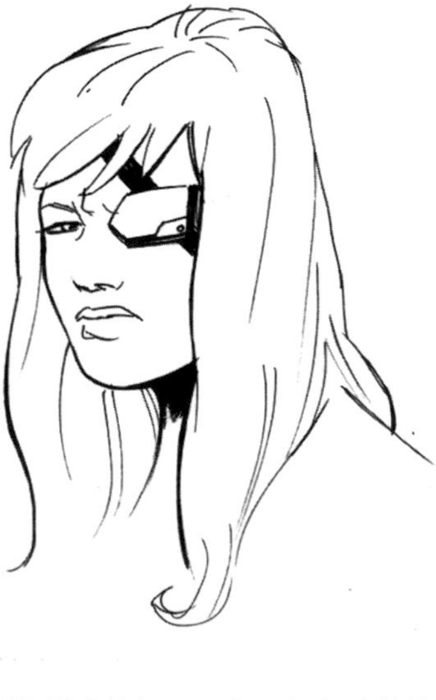

WERTHER DELL'EDERA: *Roberto and I worked on a bunch of pages together, and I hope we'll make more. He knows all my weaknesses and my strengths, so he knows perfectly well how to get the results he wants from me. I've always had a lot of fun working on his stories (I think he is a great writer), so all my efforts are focused on self-improvement. This was also the first time I've worked with Emiliano, and it was instructive. He truly helped me overcome some limitations I had in my style, providing me with a different yet useful point of view about pages in general and Bonelli page structure in particular.*

BELOW: INKING STUDY BY LUCA MARESCA

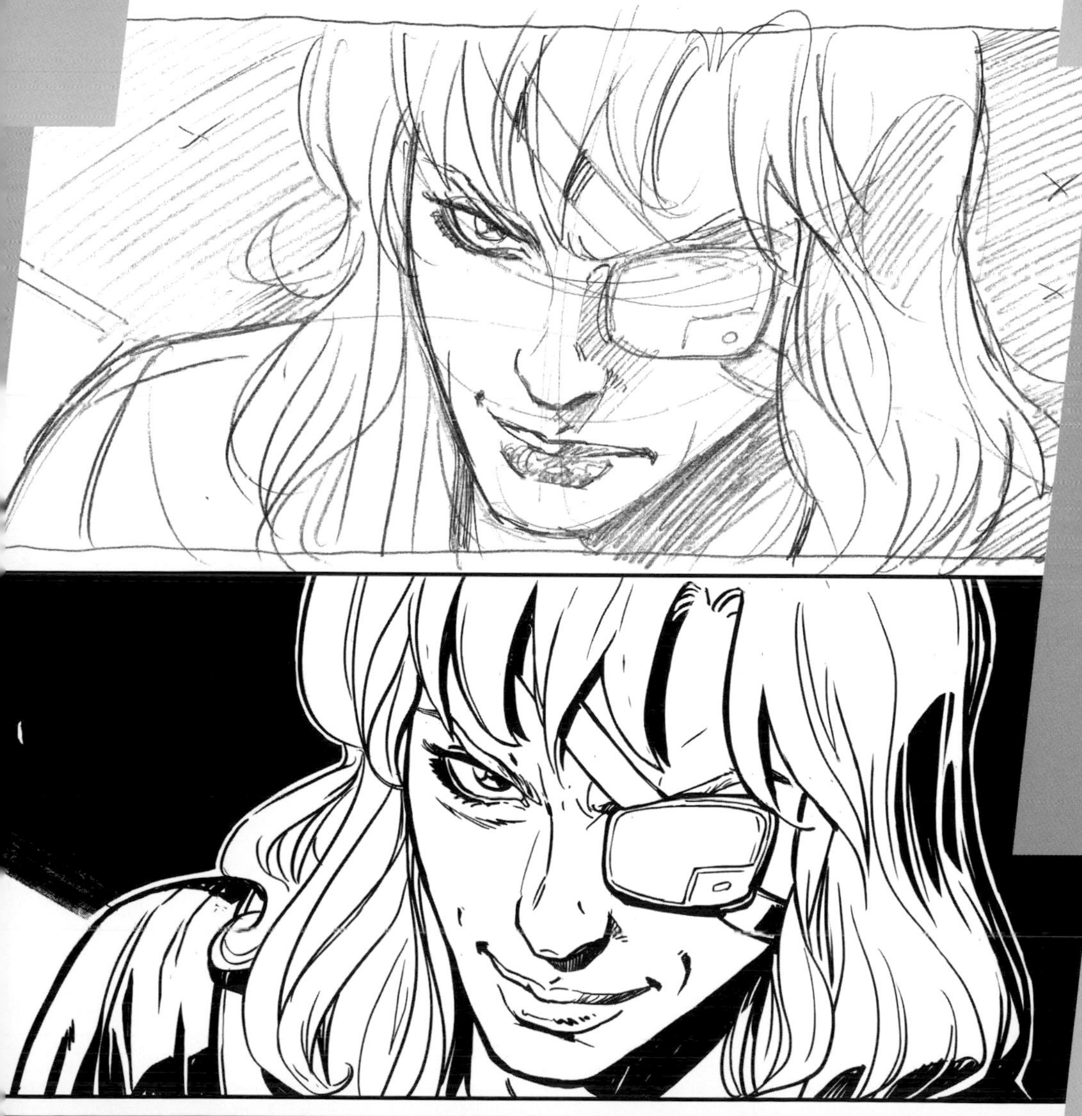

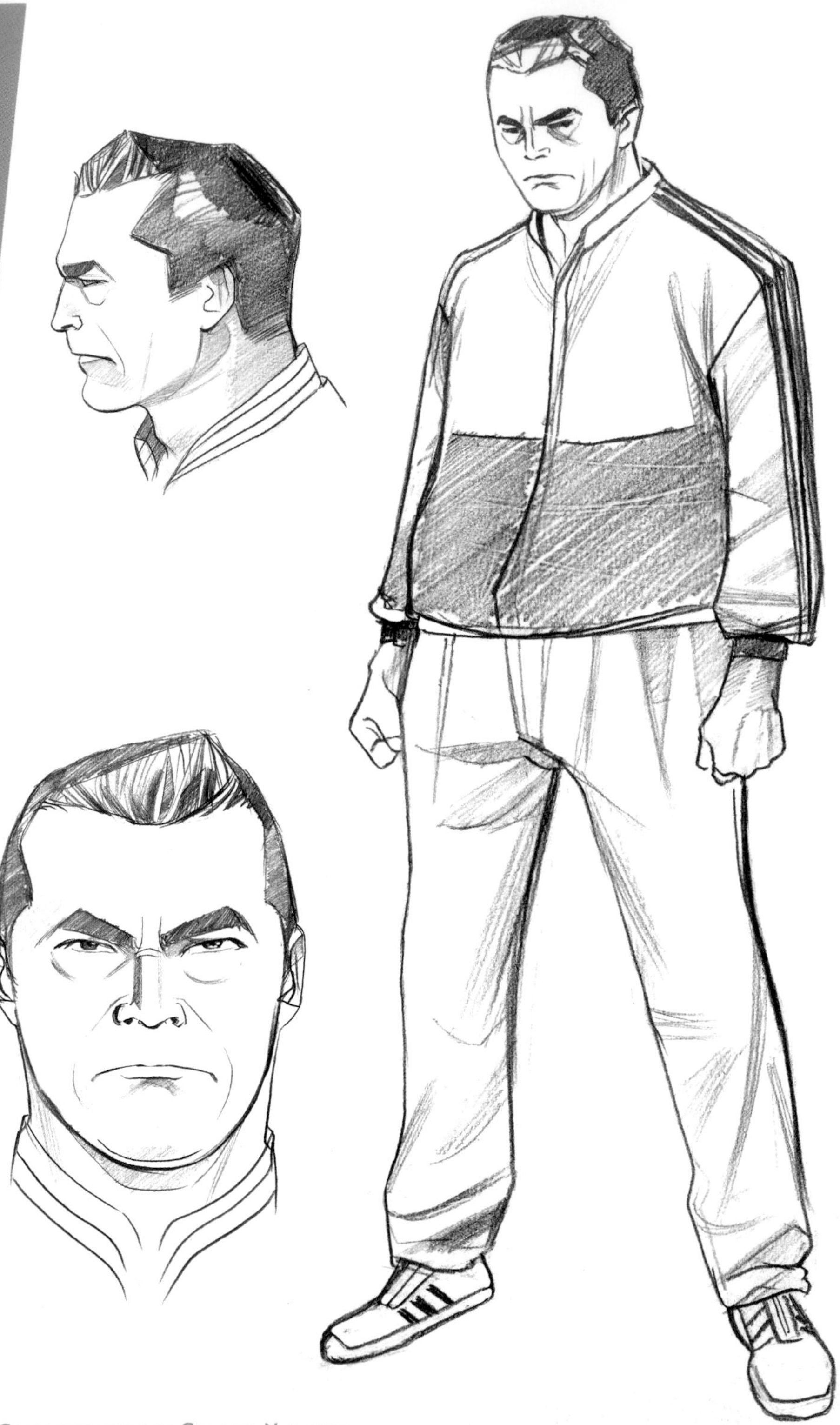

Character study of Colonel Nakamura
by Emiliano Mammucari

LUCA MARESCA: *Working on* Orphans, *I had to draw the three things I usually hate: weapons, spaceships, and kids. I have to say we artists had lots of reference material: a property bible full of every kind of character design and a lot of input to collect as much documentation as possible, so the rest came pretty naturally.*

BELOW: PANEL STUDY BY LUCA MARESCA

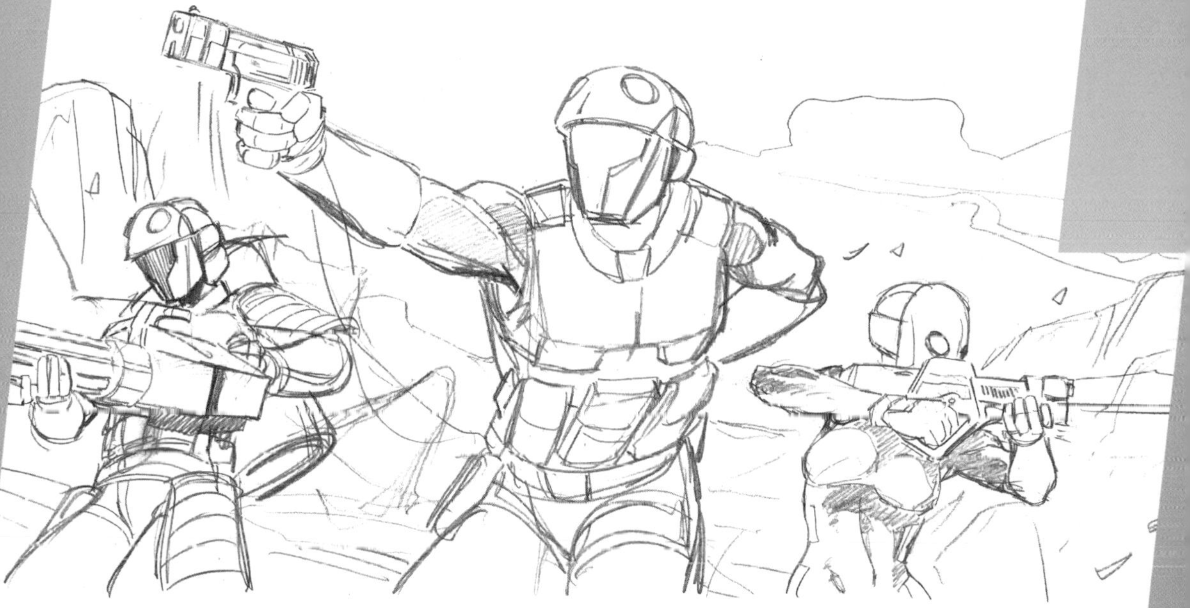

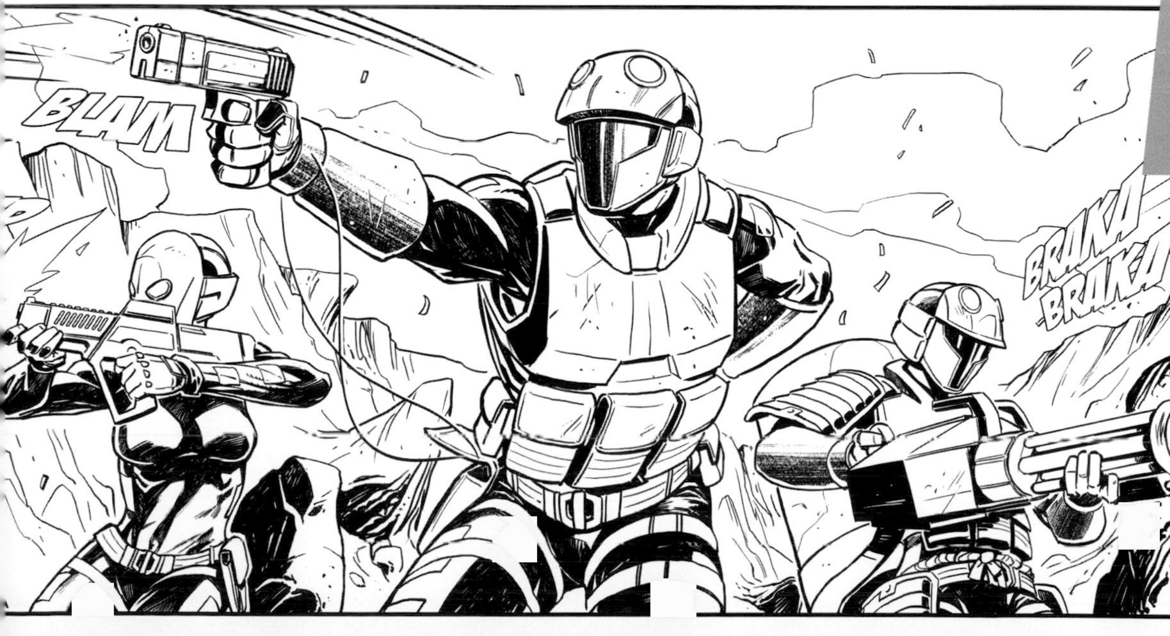
BLAM
BRAKA
BRAKA

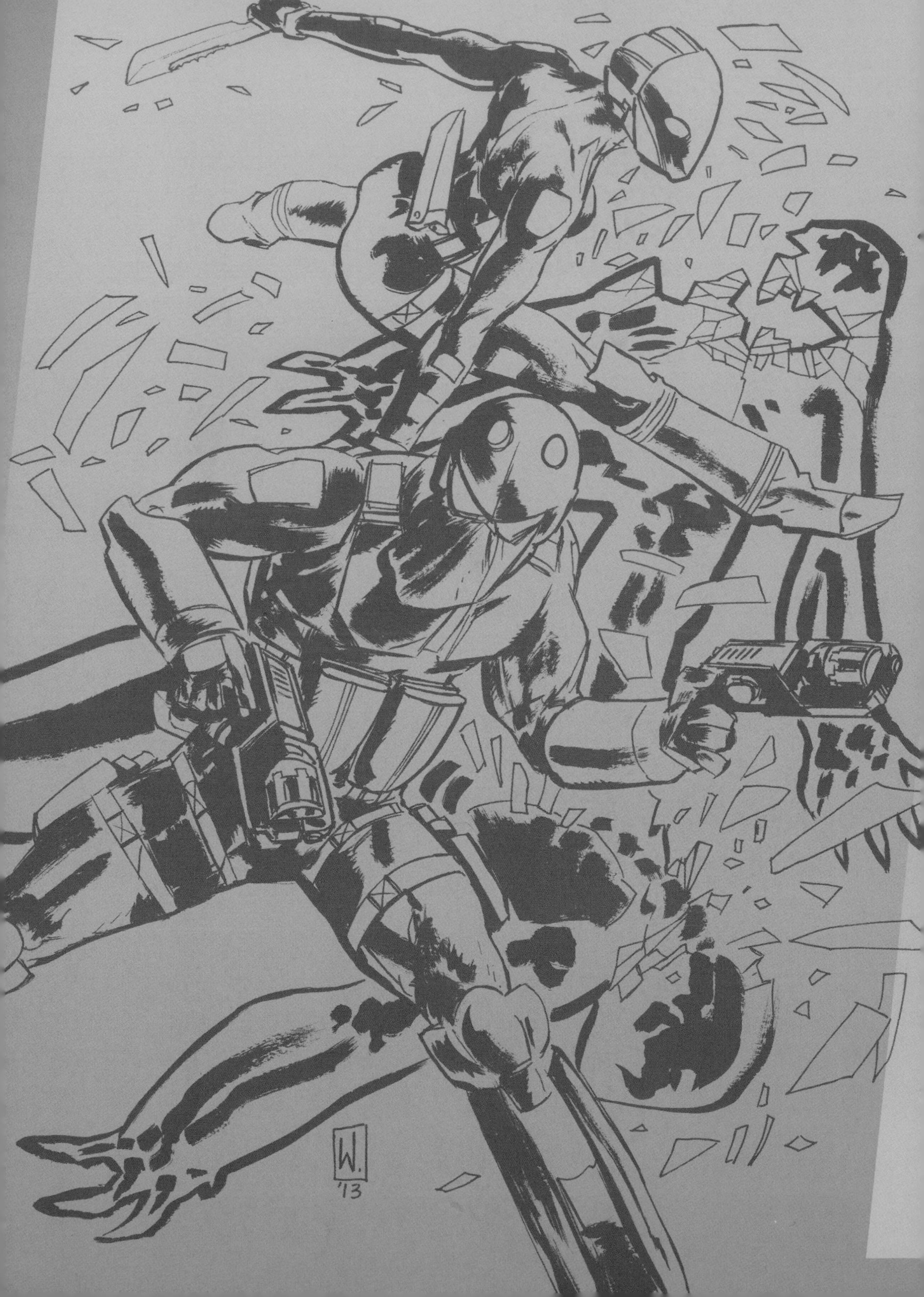
W.
'13

LUCA MARESCA: *Pencil studies are beautiful because most of the time they occur instantly. The greatest difficulty is in not losing that freshness in the inking process. In some ways, everything was easy for me because most settings had already been developed by the authors in the previous chapters, so I didn't have to reinvent anything... I was lucky!*

PREVIOUS PAGE: DYNAMIC STUDY BY WERTHER DELL'EDERA
BELOW: DYNAMIC STUDY BY GIGI CAVENAGO

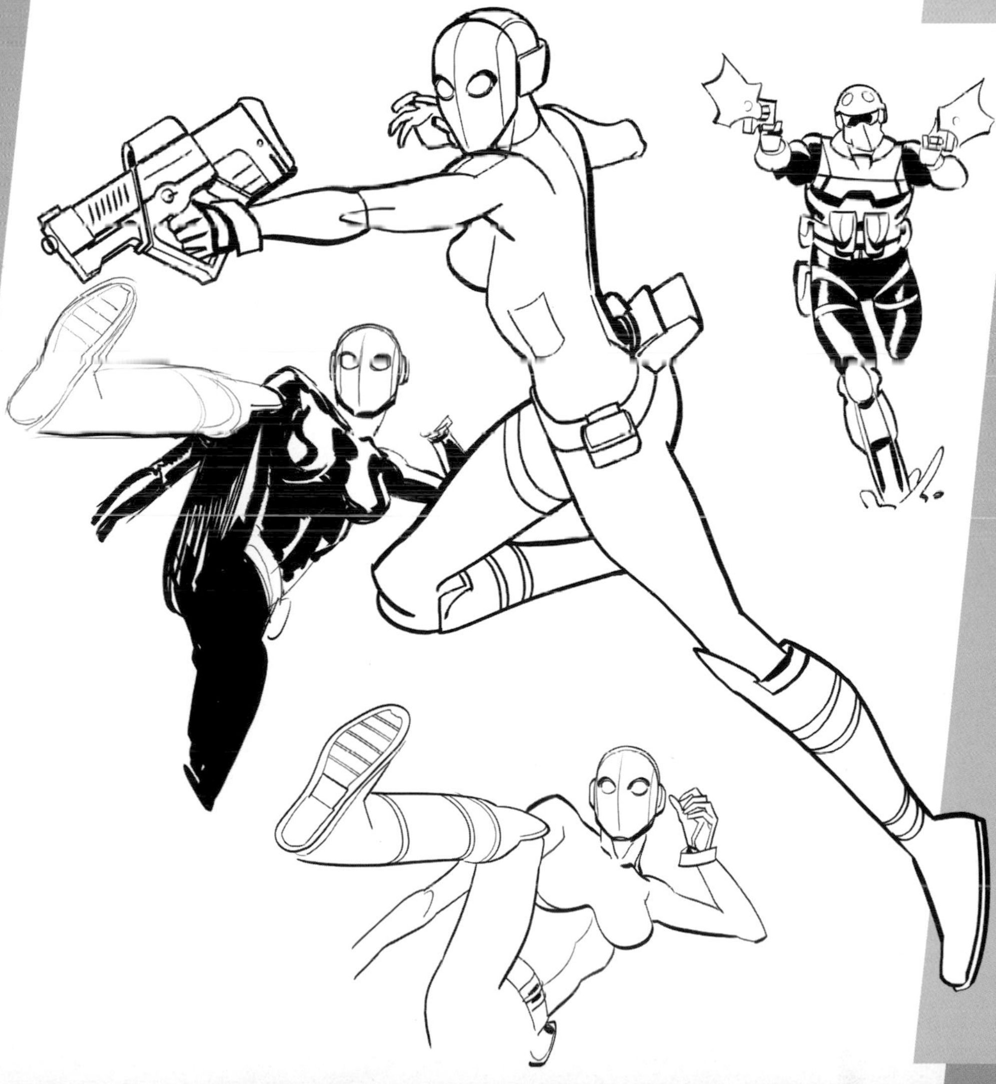

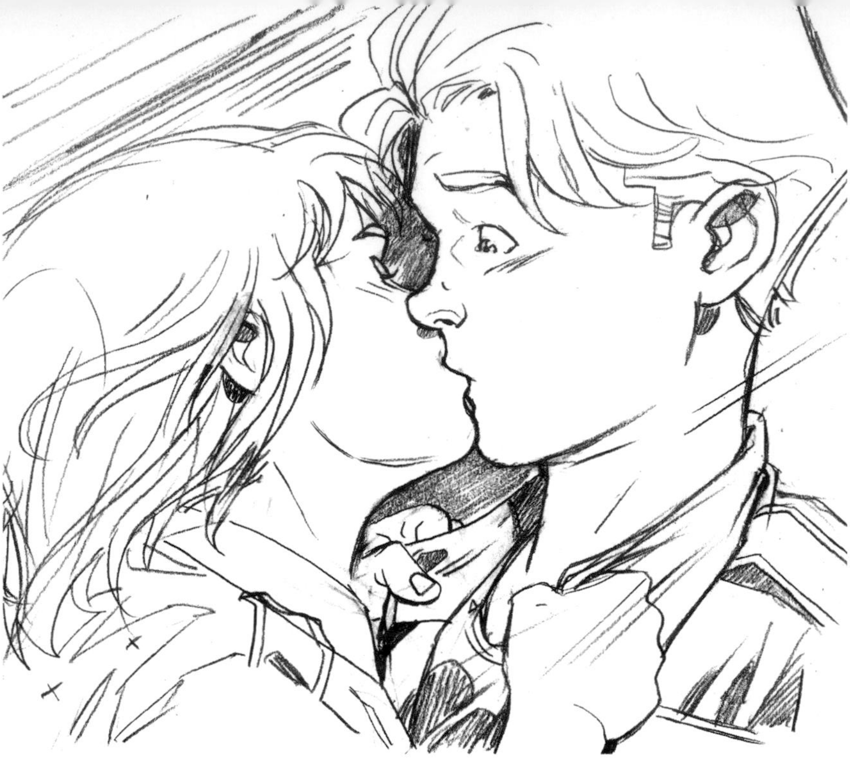

These two pages: panel studies by Luca Maresca

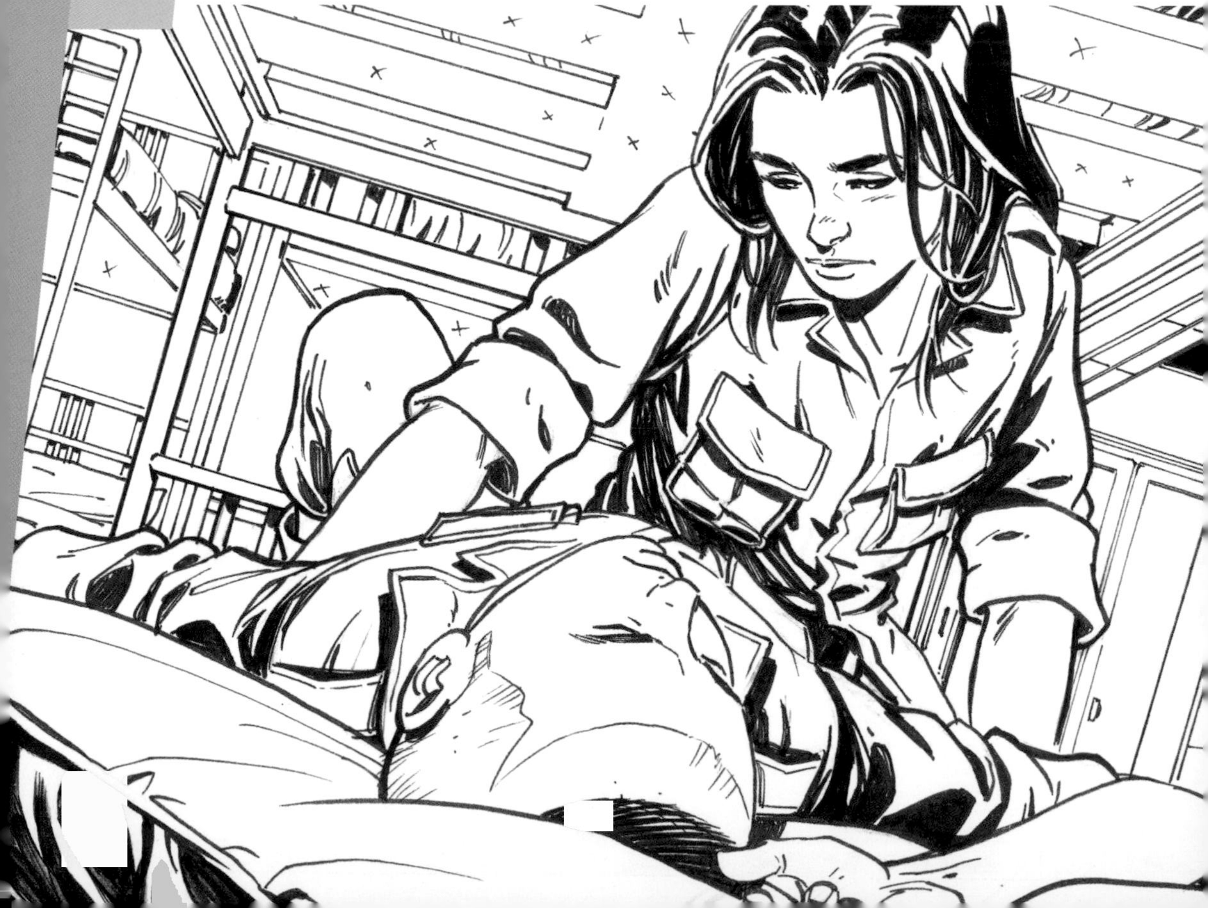

WHEN I WRITE A SERIES, I ALWAYS KNOW THAT, NO MATTER HOW EXPLOSIVE I TRY TO MAKE THE FIRST EPISODE, THINGS WILL MOVE SLOWLY UNTIL EVERYTHING FALLS INTO ITS PROPER PLACE.

– Roberto Recchioni

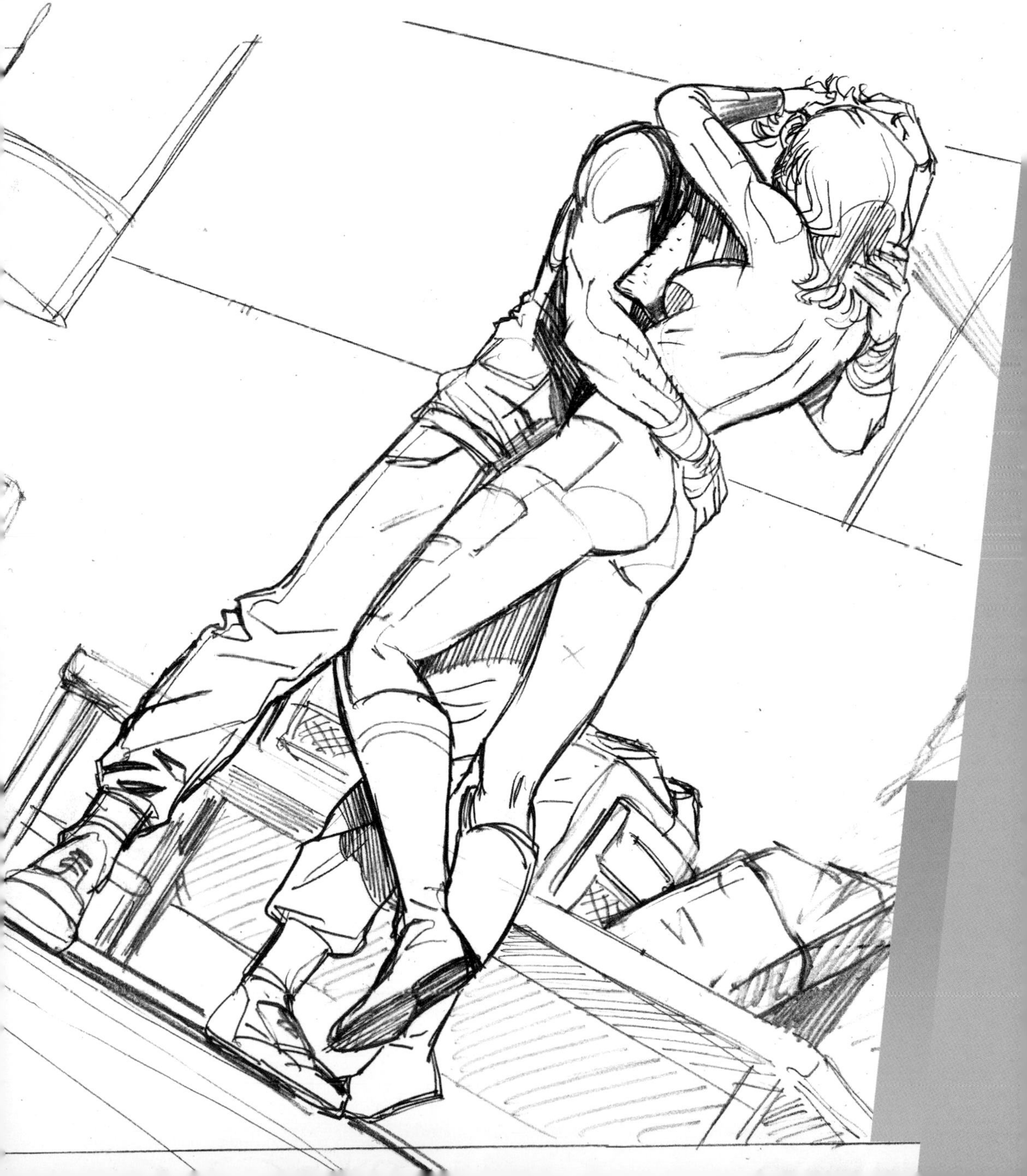

LUCA MARESCA: *It was great to work with the two creators of the series. I'd already worked with Roberto on John Doe and we always got along well, but it was my first time working shoulder to shoulder with Emiliano, and I have to say that I've learned a lot. Redrawing things, making corrections, fixing pages, and redrawing again… it was an exhausting and stressful job. There were entire weeks I didn't pick up the pencil because I was angry, but sometimes you need to face things honestly, and if I've improved, I have Roberto and Emiliano to thank.*

Illustration by Werther Dell'Edera

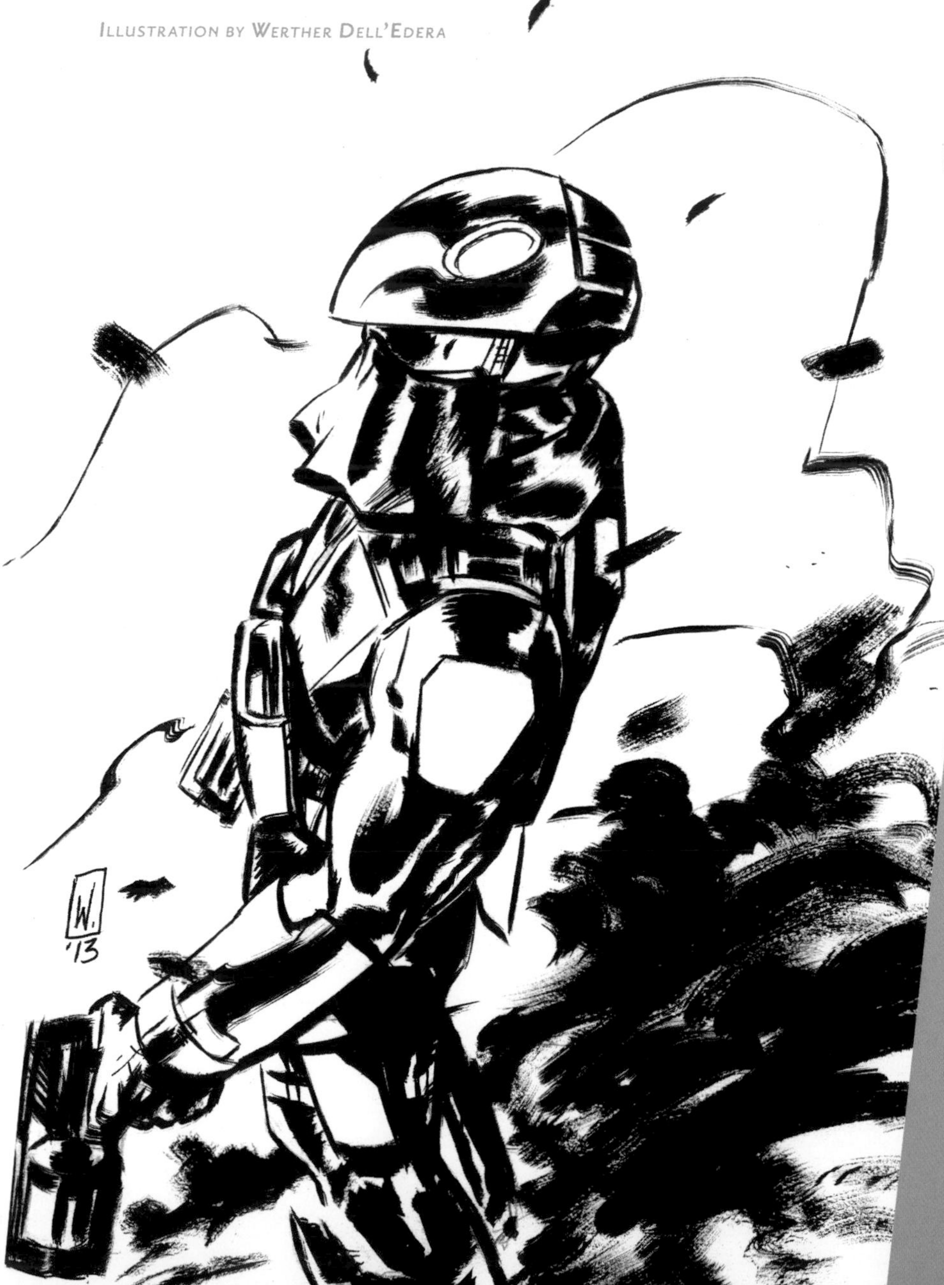
W. '13

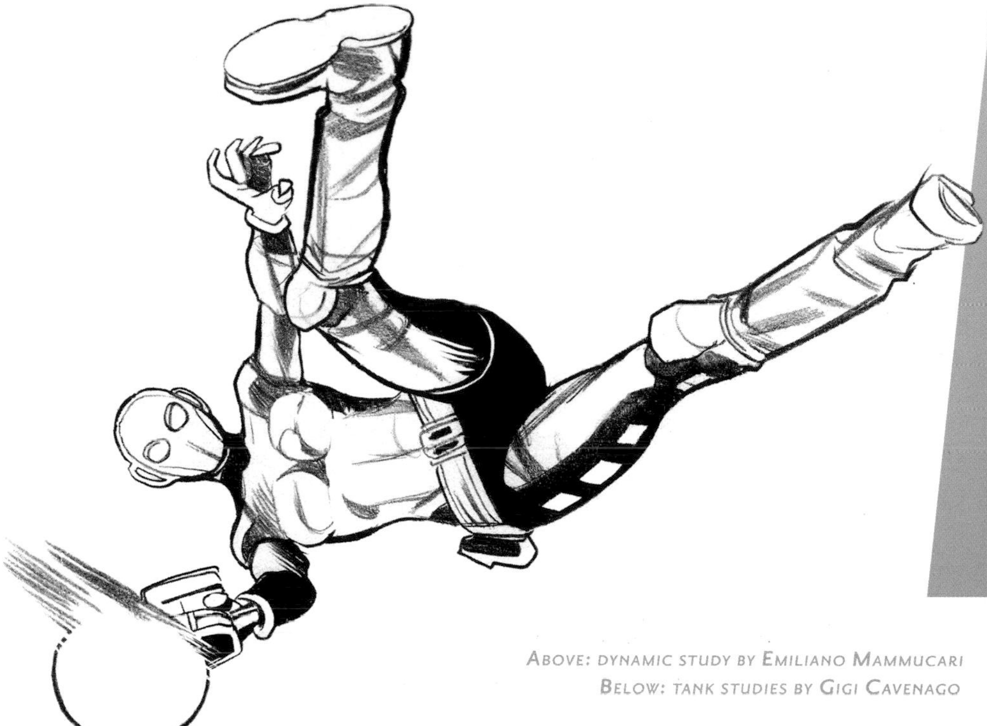

Above: dynamic study by Emiliano Mammucari
Below: tank studies by Gigi Cavenago

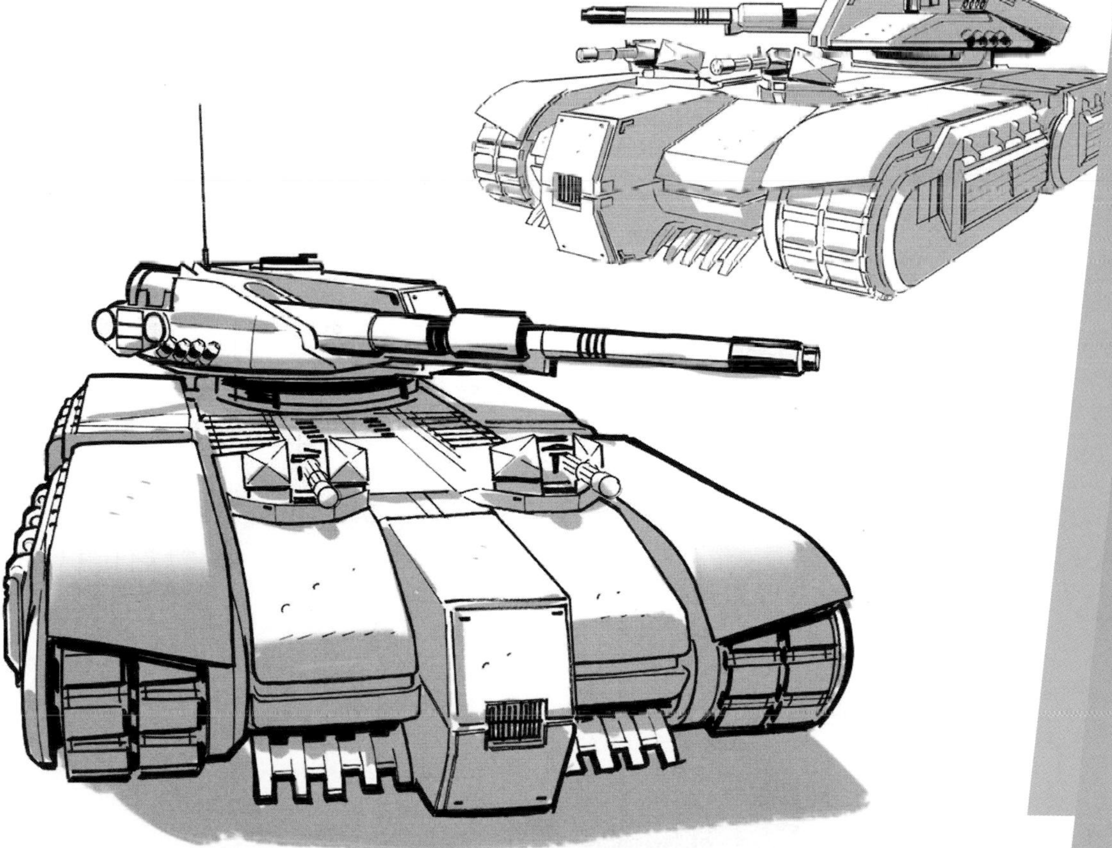

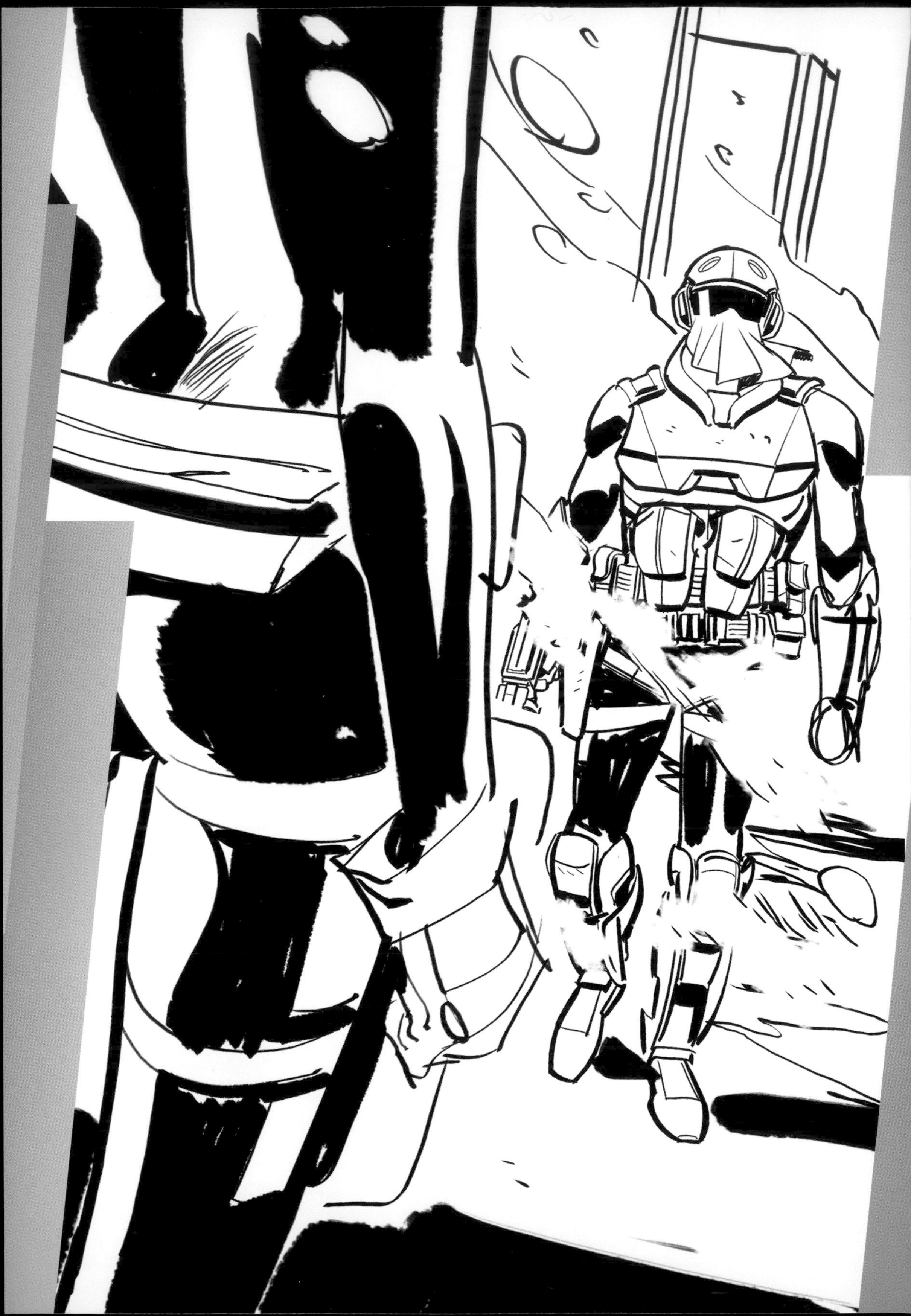

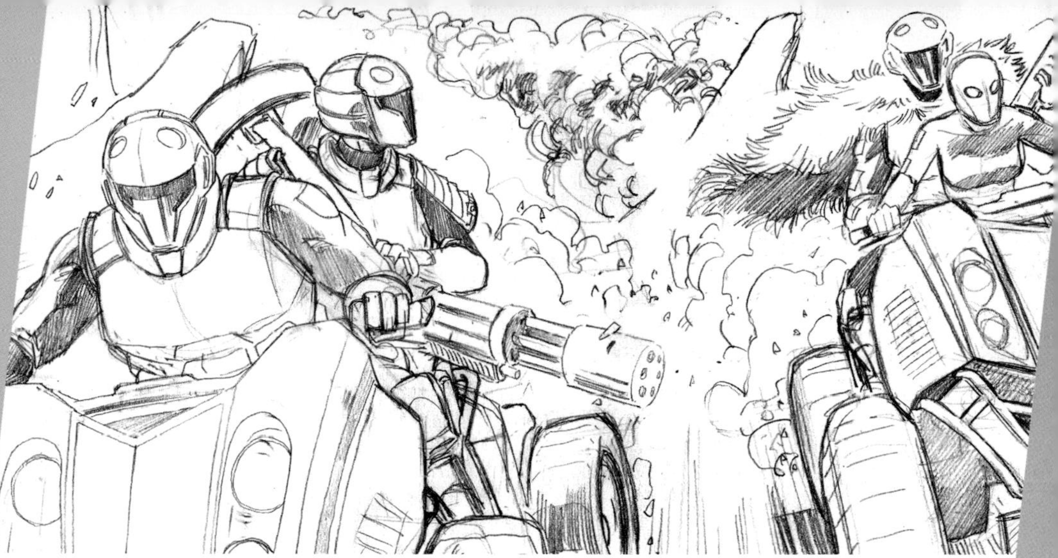

ROBERTO RECCHIONI: *As long as the story went on, I've been asked whether there was a character who surprised me for their emotional growth. Well, yes and no. Ringo is clearly my favorite character, and he really does practically write himself (also because he's very similar to the type of hero I usually write about). But that was something I knew from the beginning, so it was no surprise at all.*

Previous page: panel study by Gigi Cavenago
This page: panel studies by Luca Maresca

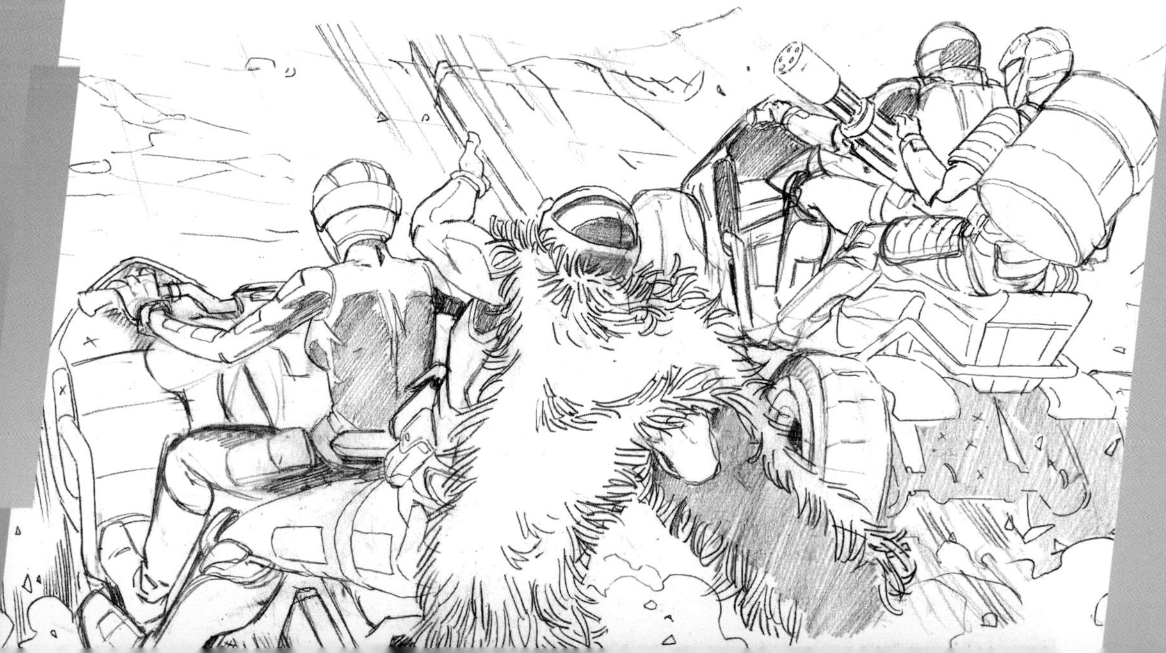

RINGO IS CLEARLY MY FAVORITE CHARACTER, AND HE REALLY DOES PRACTICALLY WRITE HIMSELF.

– ROBERTO RECCHIONI

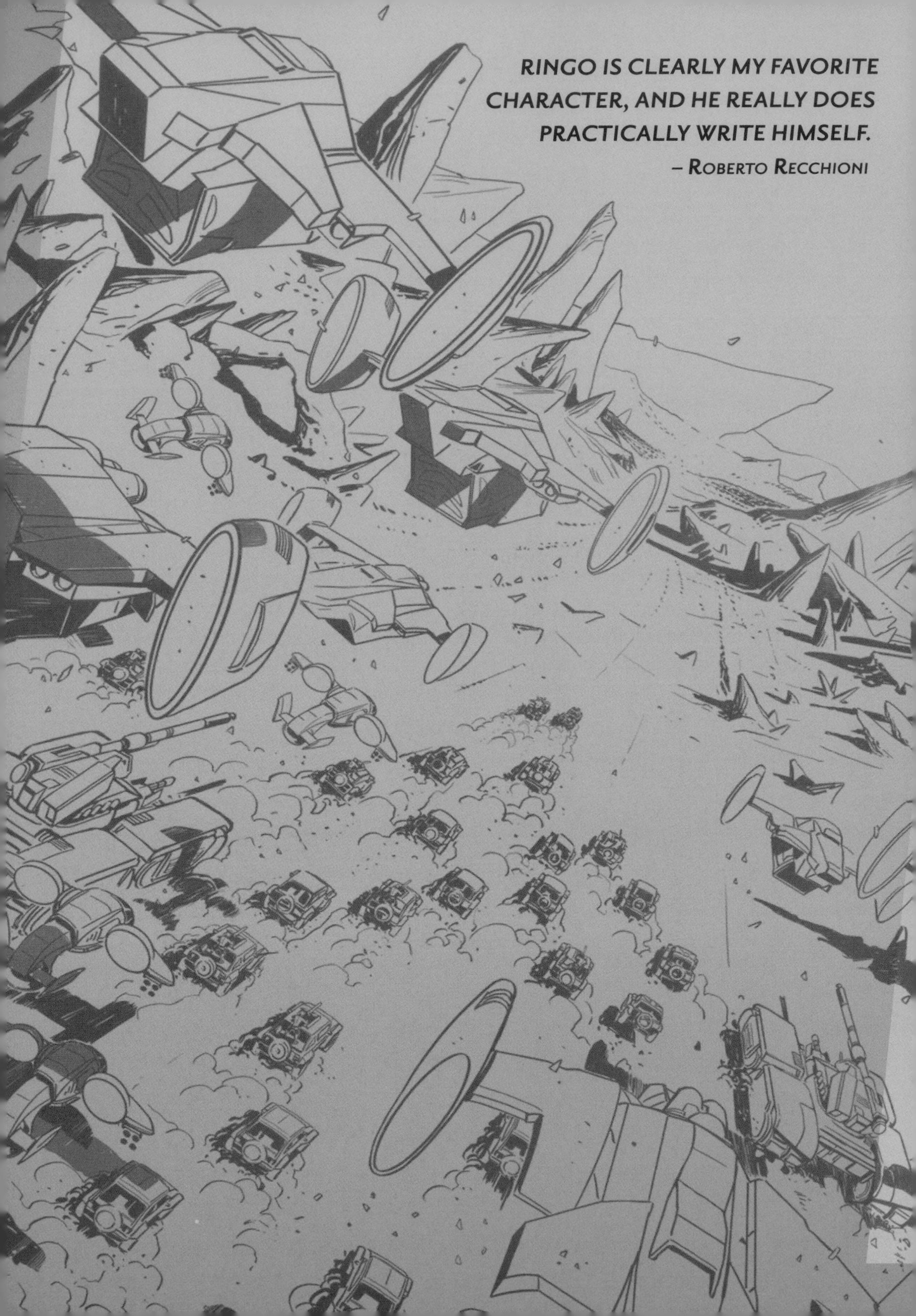

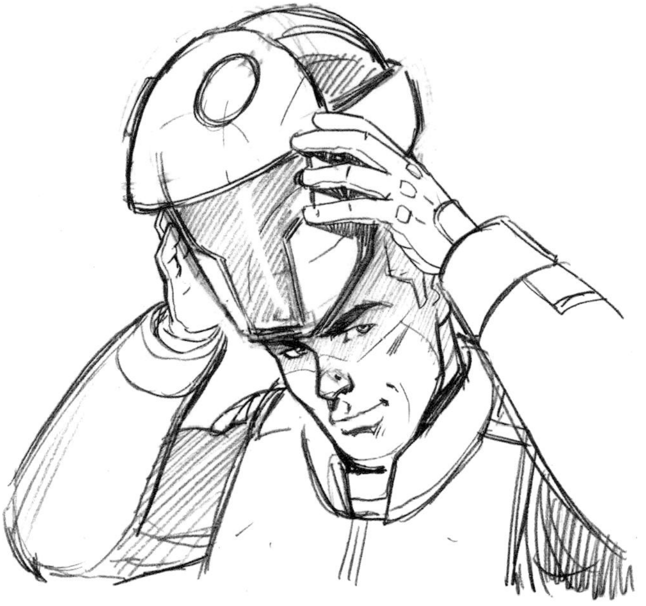

ROBERTO RECCHIONI: *As the story goes on, I don't know how the readers will react. As a writer, I really do love the third, sixth, ninth, and tenth episodes. As a reader, the ninth and tenth are what I call "a superhero comic, full of all the typical superheroes comic stuff."*

Panel studies by Luca Maresca

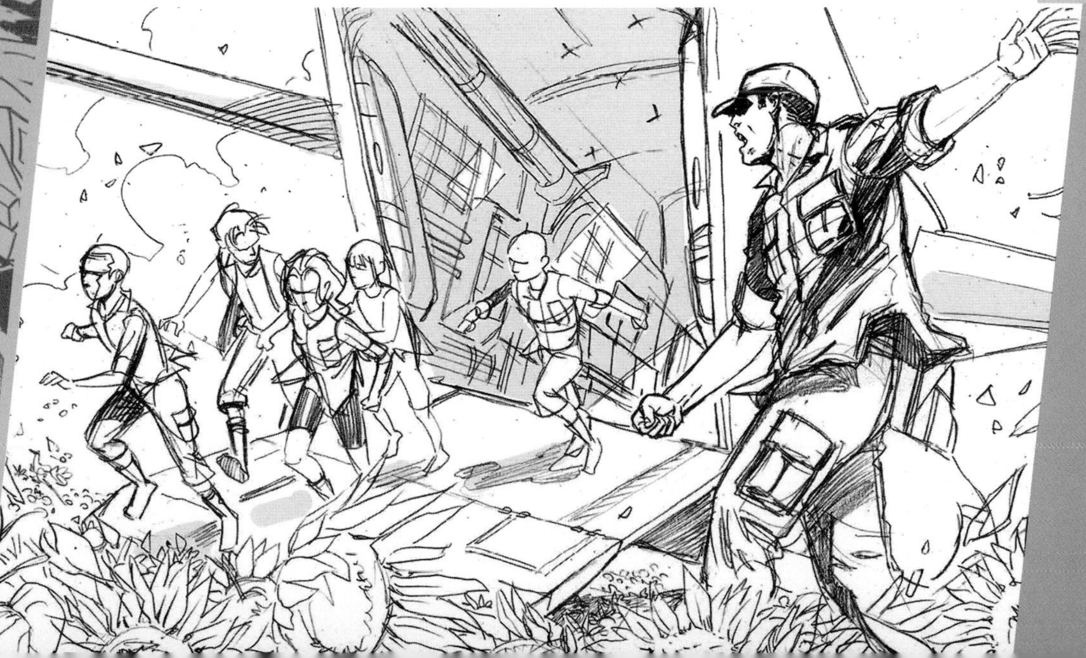

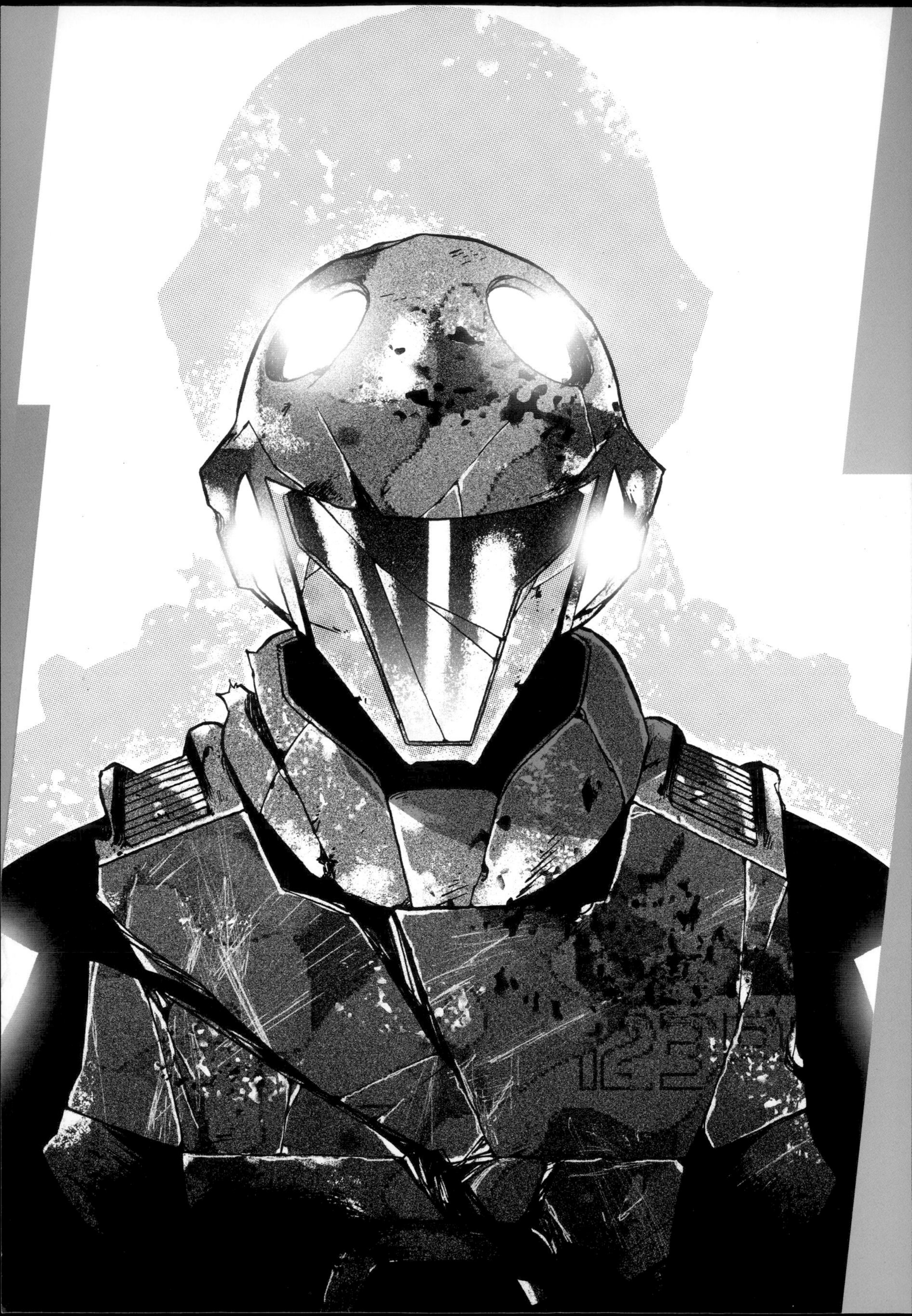

MASSIMO DALL'OGLIO: *The hardest part to draw was the initial explosion, the light bubble, and the following apocalyptic fallout. I had an extremely "eastern" insight of that scene, and it was pretty difficult to ignore that imagery.*

PREVIOUS PAGE: ILLUSTRATION BY MASSIMO DALL'OGLIO
BELOW: CHARACTER STUDIES BY GIGI CAVENAGO

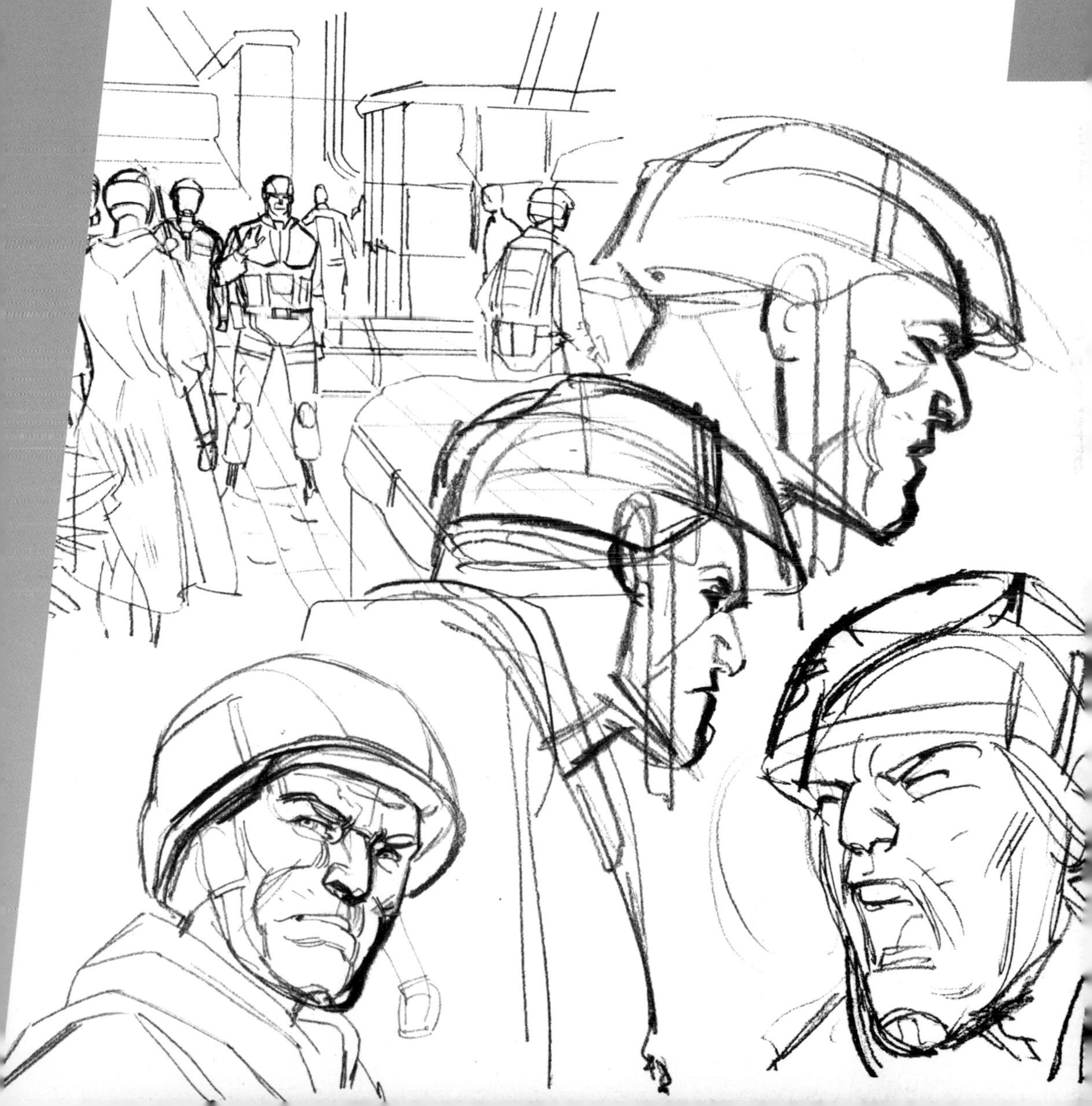

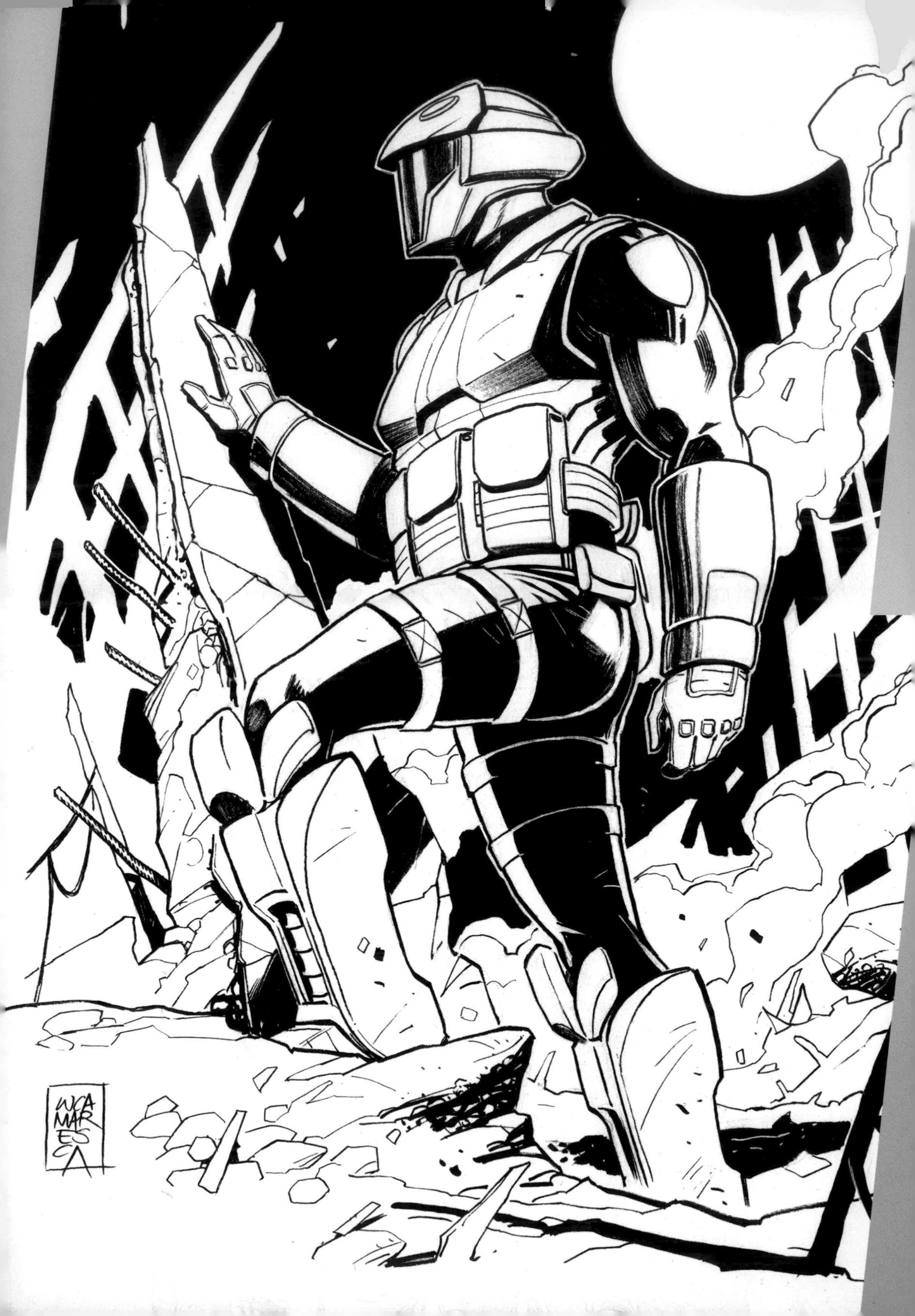

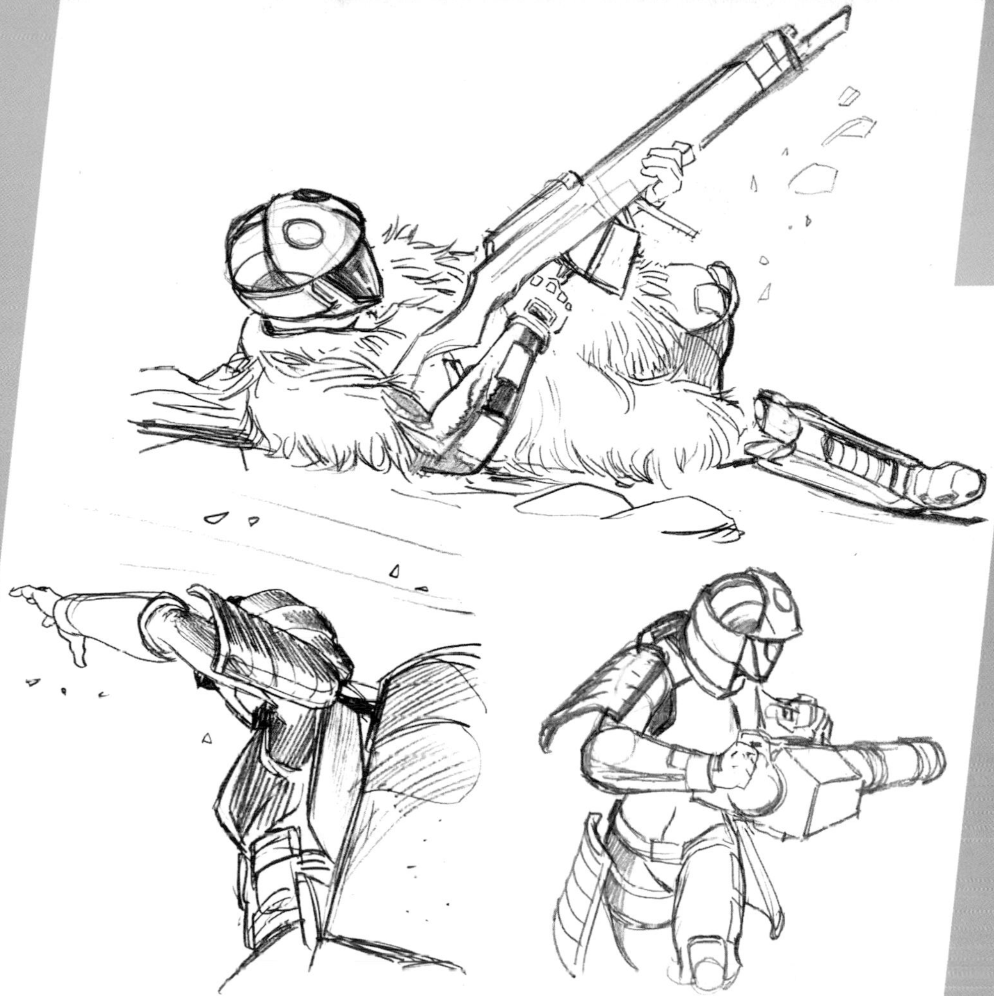

These two pages: dynamic studies by Luca Maresca

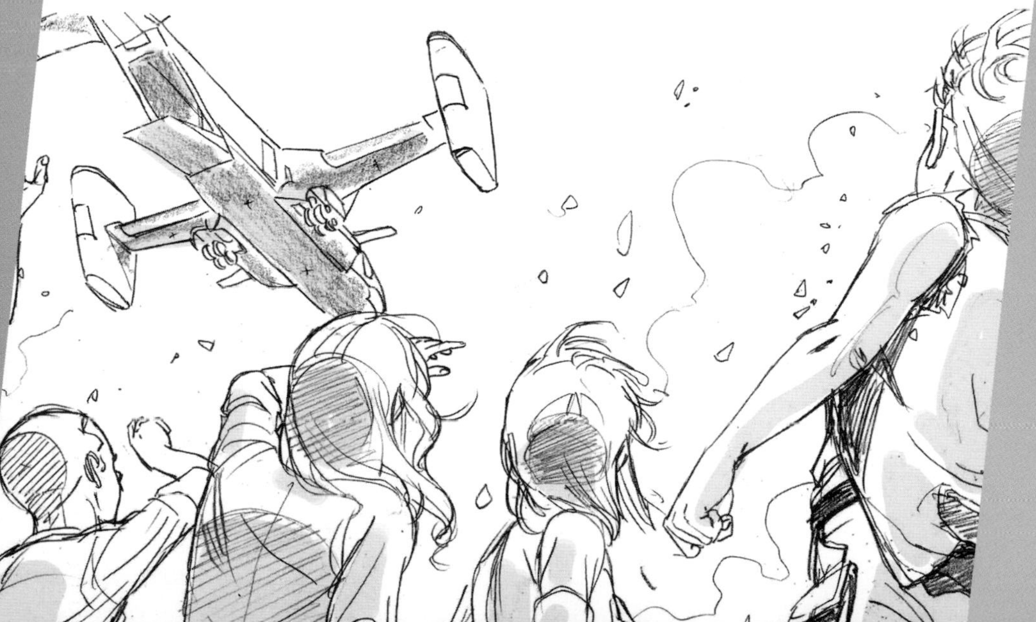

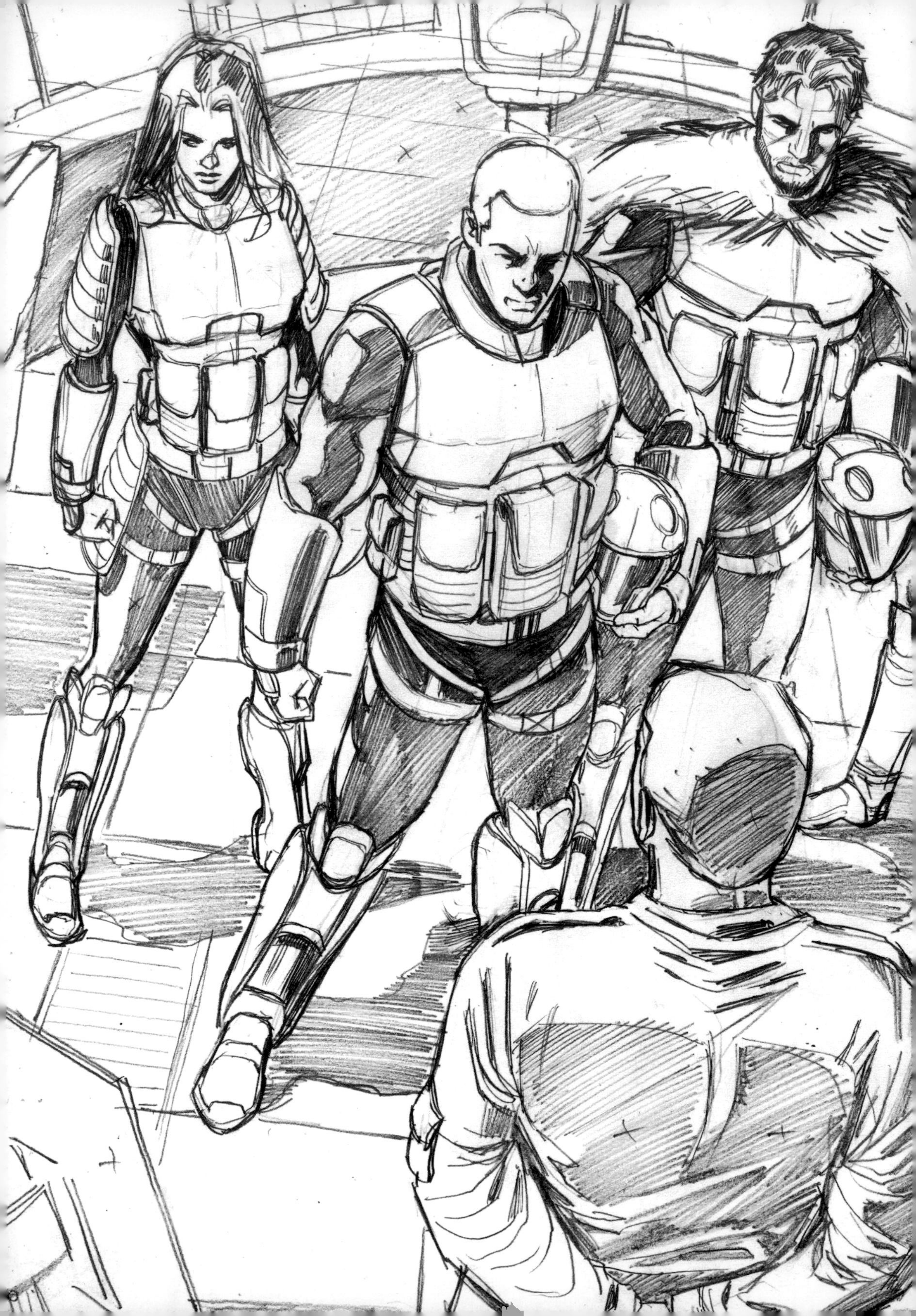

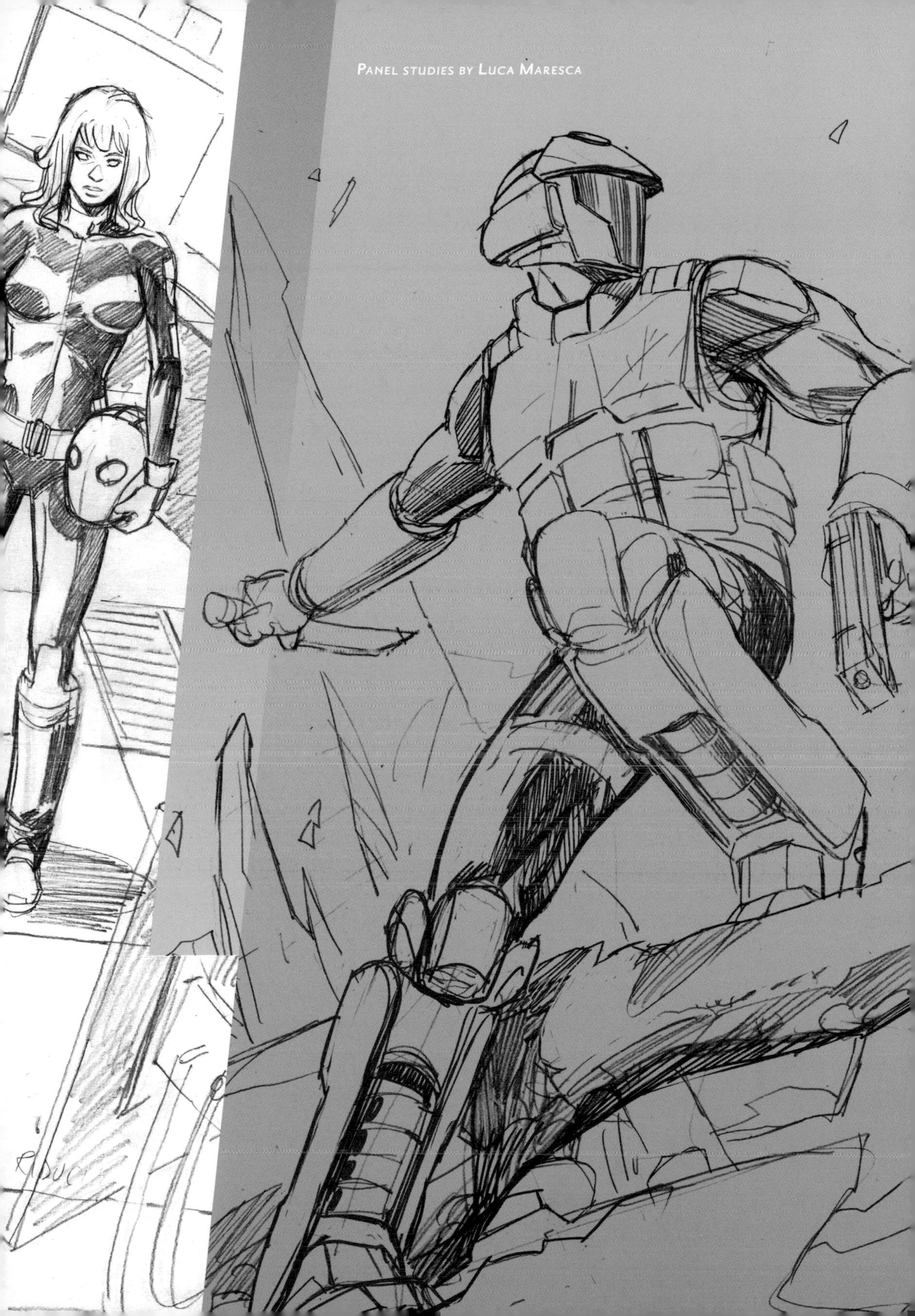

Panel studies by Luca Maresca

WHEN I DESIGN A COVER, MY FIRST IDEA IS ALWAYS TO HIGHLIGHT WHAT'S GOING ON INSIDE THE CHARACTERS' HEADS.

– Massimo Carnevale

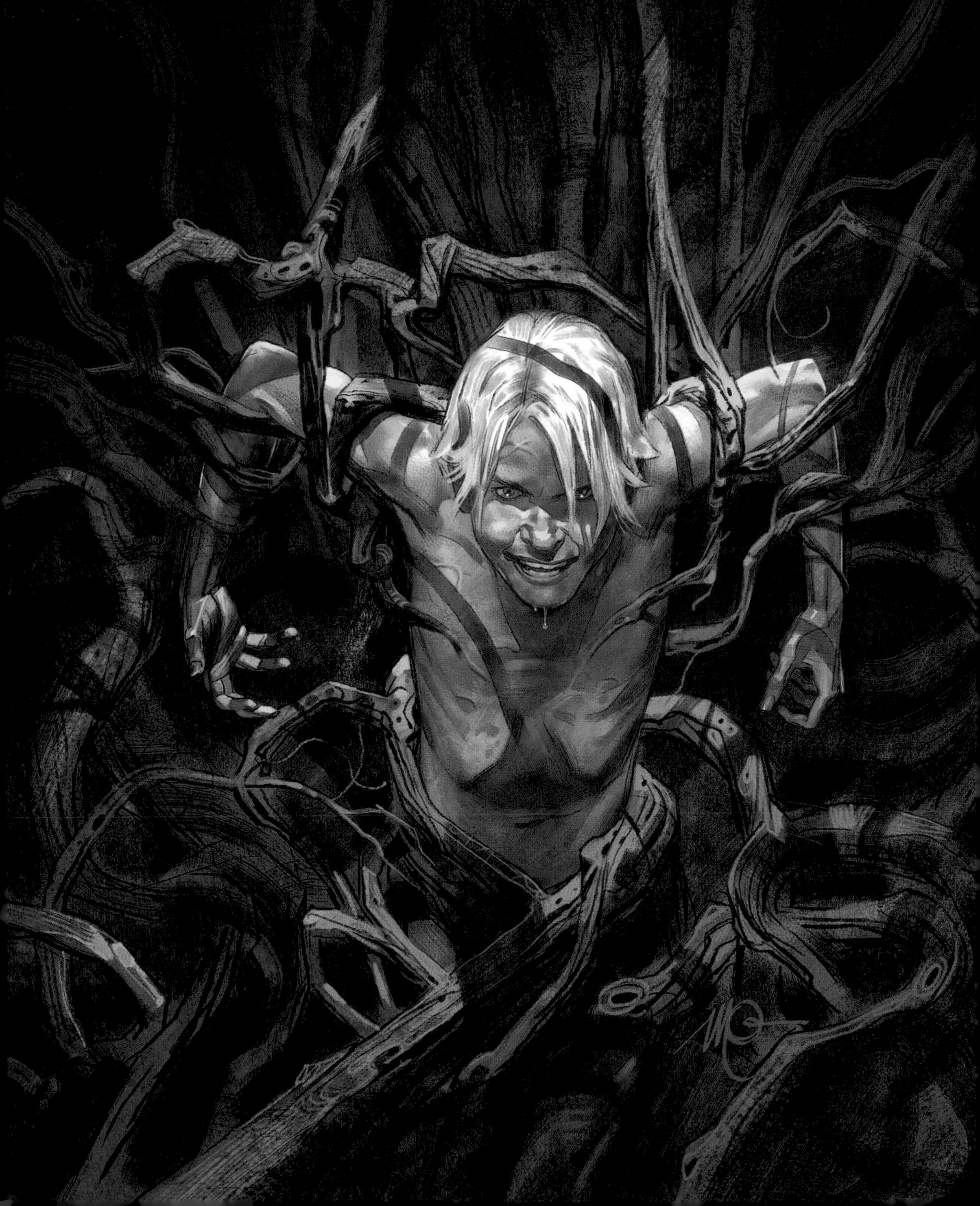

COVERS

MASSIMO CARNEVALE: For chapter 6, my first idea was to focus on the main character and on what he could represent in the story, but both Roberto and Emiliano had a different opinion. They wanted the cover to be more spacious, where the tree was the real protagonist and Ringo only a victim in a dramatic setting. Honestly, the final version feels more complete and I'm very happy with the result.

MASSIMO CARNEVALE: When I design a cover, I always try to be myself as much as I can, never stepping over the limitations of Bonelli standards. I often draw inspiration from my own interests and experiences, but also from cinema, whose ideas I often rework, even unwittingly.

My first idea is always to highlight what's going on inside the characters' heads, but it's not always easy. On the contrary, it proves to be a limit, because while on the one hand I make a cover that truly reflects me, on the other hand I run the risk of being repetitive. It happens very rarely, though, and considering all the covers I've produced along the years, this is a great result.

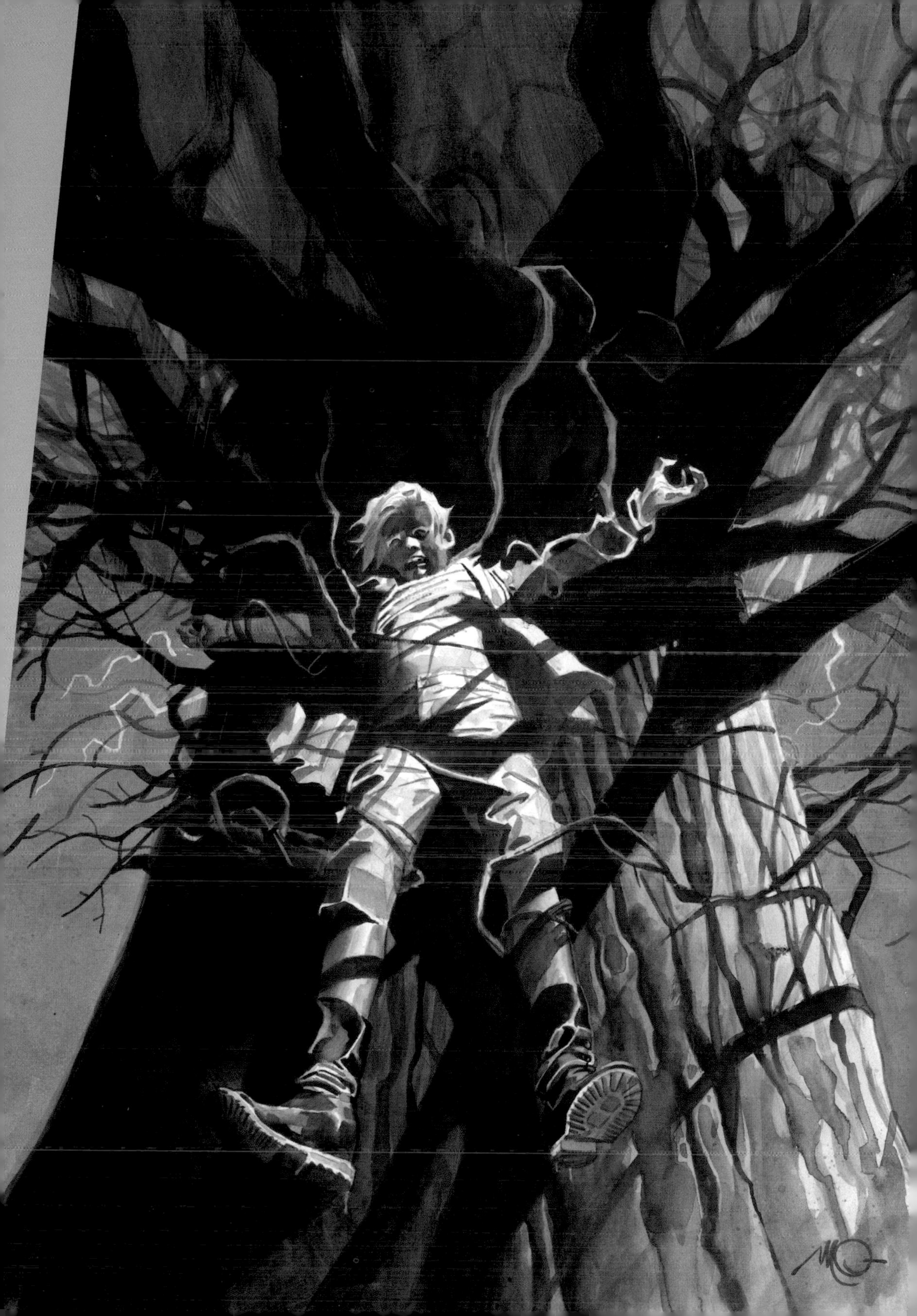

Rendering stages for the cover of Volume 2 by Massimo Carnevale

Next page: an early sketch for the cover of chapter 6

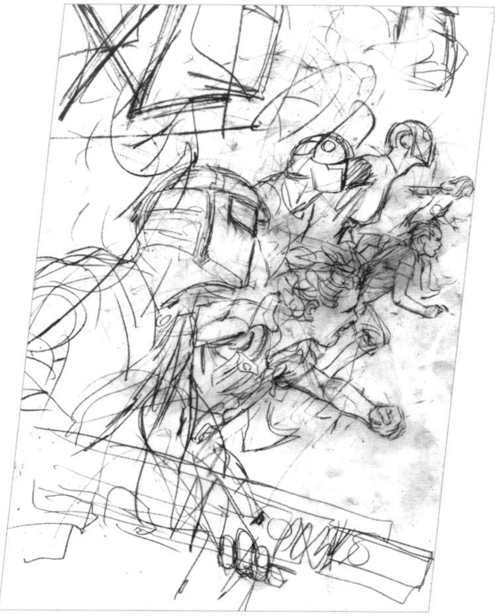

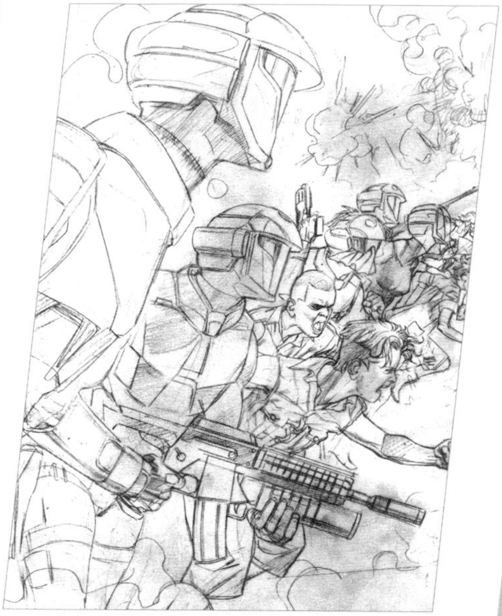

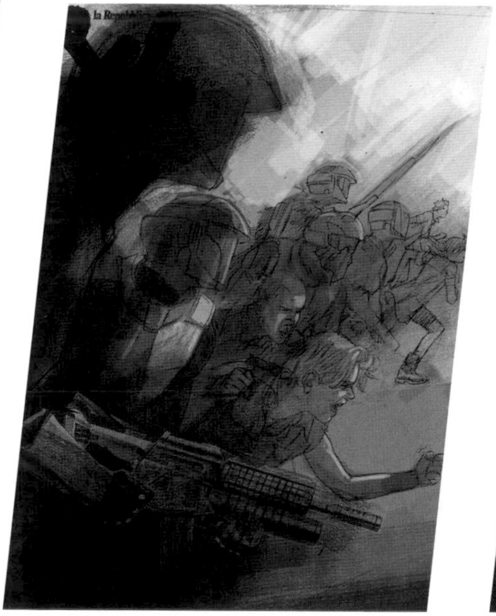

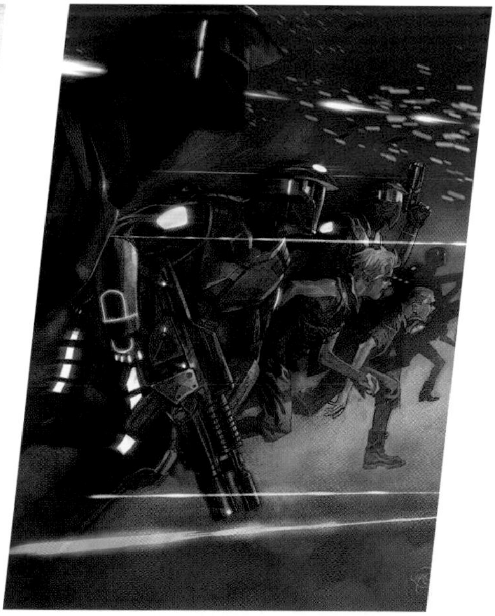

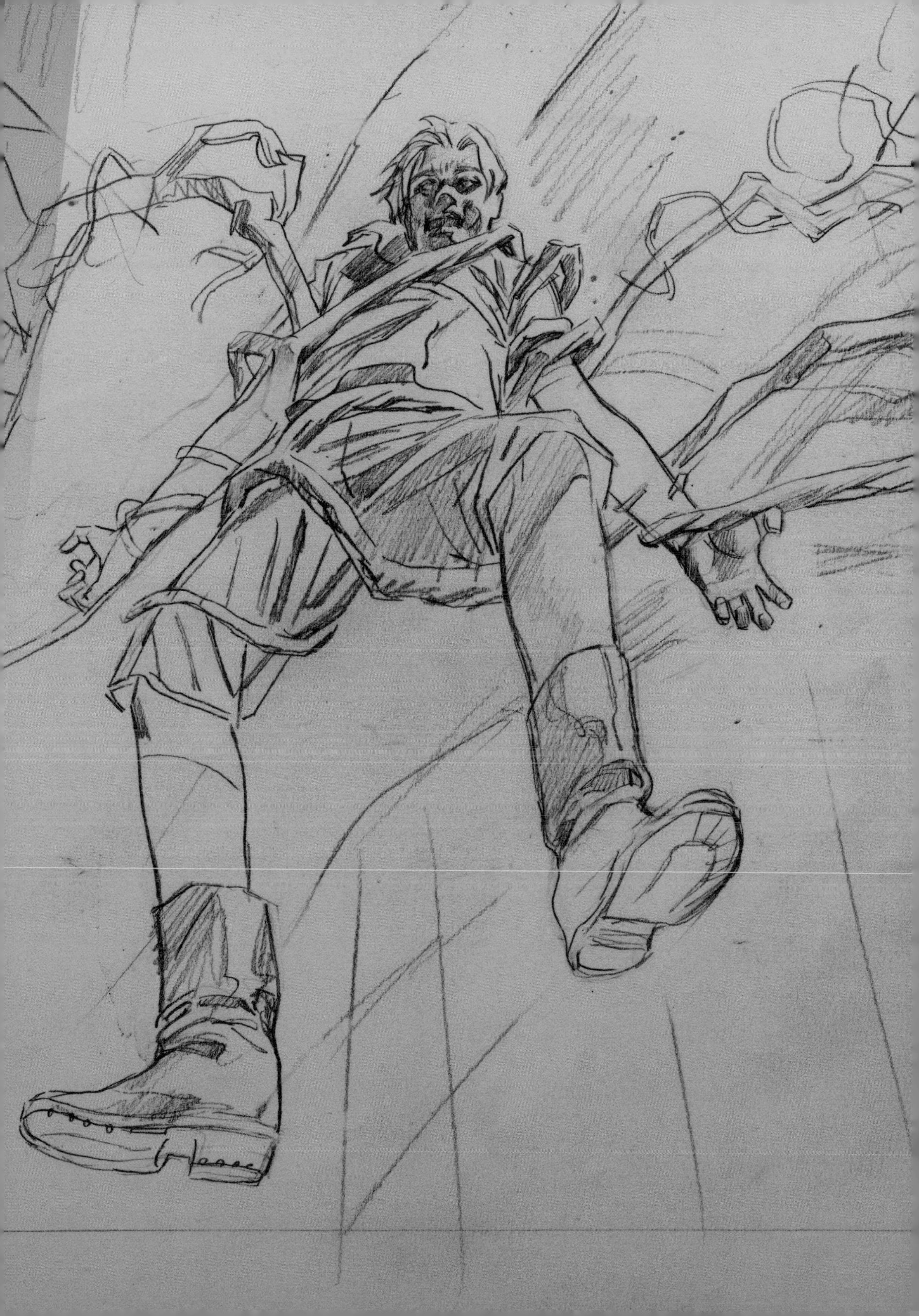

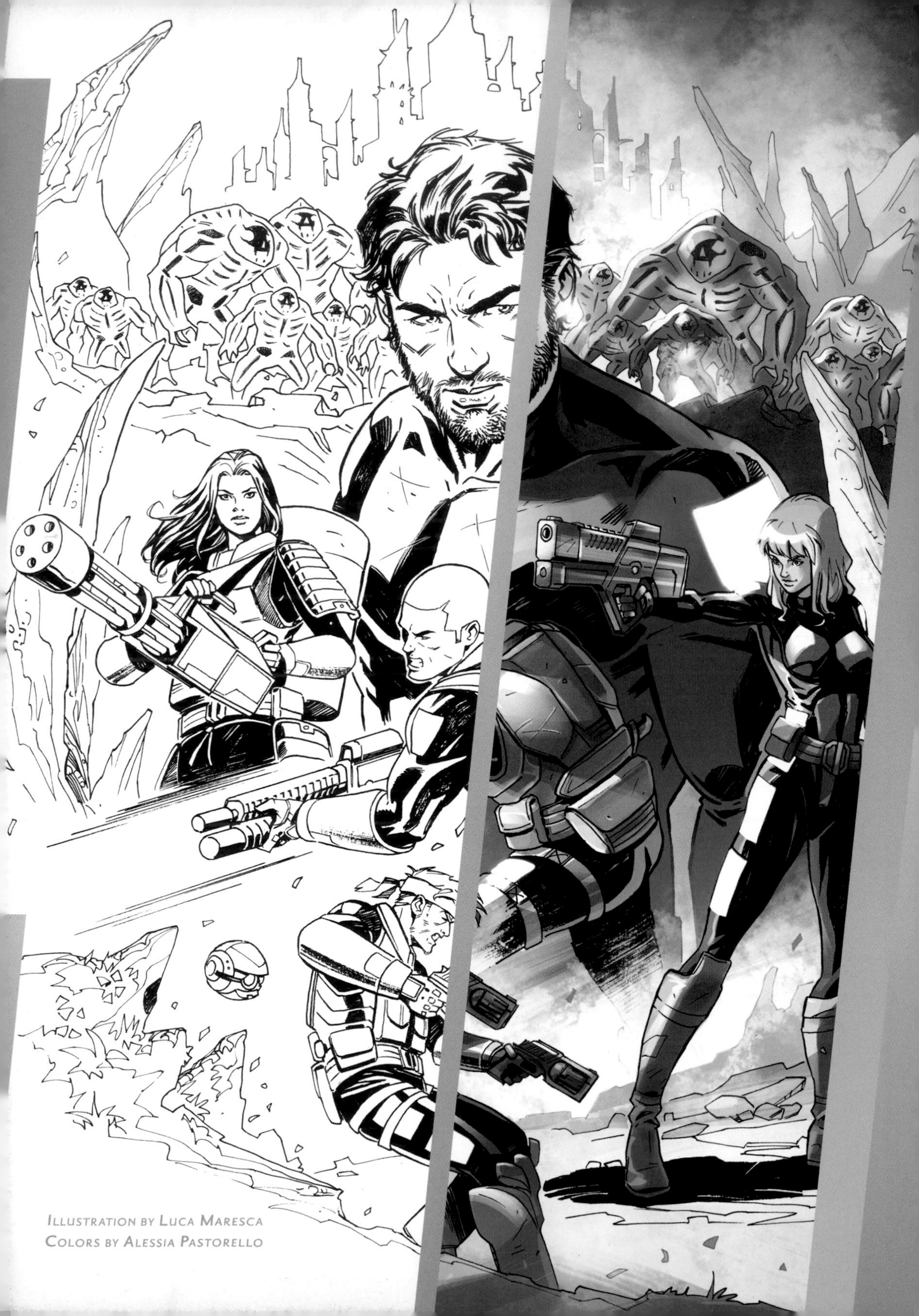

Illustration by Luca Maresca
Colors by Alessia Pastorello

IN THE NEXT VOLUME...

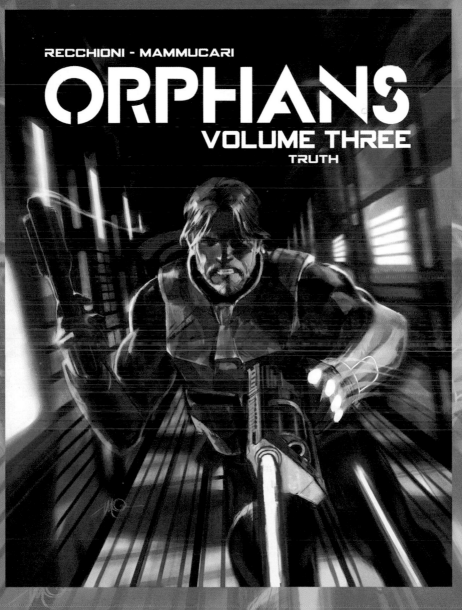

RECCHIONI - MAMMUCARI

ORPHANS
VOLUME THREE
TRUTH